London

timeout.com/london

Penguin Books

PENGUIN BOOKS

Published by the Penguin Group
Penguin Books Ltd, 80 Strand, London WC2R ORL, England
Penguin Books USA Inc., 375 Hudson Street, New York, New York 10014, USA
Penguin Books Australia Ltd, 250 Camberwell Road, Camberwell, Victoria 3124, Australia
Penguin Books Canada Ltd, 10 Alcorn Avenue, Toronto, Ontario, Canada M4V 3B2
Penguin Books (NZ) Ltd, cnr Rosedale and Airborne Roads, Albany, Auckland, New Zealand

Penguin Books Ltd, Registered Offices: Harmondsworth, Middlesex, England

First published 1989
First Penguin edition 1990
Second edition 1992
Third edition 1994
Fourth edition 1995
Fifth edition 1997
Sixth edition 1998
Seventh edition 1999
Eighth edition 2000
Ninth edition 2001
Tenth edition 2002
Eleventh edition 2003
Twelfth edition 2004

10 9 8 7 6 5 4 3 2 1

Copyright © Time Out Group Ltd 1989, 1990, 1992, 1994, 1995, 1996, 1997, 1998, 1999, 2000, 2001, 2002, 2003, 2004
All rights reserved

Colour reprographics by Icon, Crowne House, 56-58 Southwark Street, London SE1 1UN
Printed and bound by Cayfosa-Quebecor, Ctra. de Caldes, Km 3 08 130 Sta, Perpètua de Mogoda, Barcelona, Spain

Except in the United States of America, this book is sold subject to the condition that it shall not, by way of trade or otherwise, be lent, re-sold, hired out, or otherwise circulated without the publisher's prior consent in any form of binding or cover other than that in which it is published and without a similar condition including this condition being imposed on the subsequent purchaser.

Edited and designed by
Time Out Guides Limited
Universal House
251 Tottenham Court Road
London W1T 7AB
Tel + 44 (0)20 7813 3000
Fax + 44 (0)20 7813 6001
Email guides@timeout.com
www.timeout.com

Editorial
Editor Ronnie Haydon
Deputy Editor Christi Daugherty
Listings Editors Evelyn Crowley, Jill Emeny, Holly Furneaux, Andrew Williams
Proofreader Tamsin Shelton
Indexer Jackie Brind

Editorial/Managing Director Peter Fiennes
Series Editor Ruth Jarvis
Deputy Series Editor Lesley McCave
Guides Co-ordinator Anna Norman
Accountant Sarah Bostock

Design
Art Director Mandy Martin
Acting Art Director Scott Moore
Acting Art Editor Tracey Ridgewell
Senior Designer Averil Sinnott
Designers Astrid Kogler, Sam Lands
Digital Imaging Dan Conway
Ad Make-up Charlotte Blythe

Picture Desk
Picture Editor Jael Marschner
Acting Picture Editor Kit Burnet
Picture Researcher Alex Ortiz

Advertising
Sales Director/Sponsorship Mark Phillips
Sales Manager Alison Gray
Advertising Sales Simon Davies, Terina Rickit, Matthew Salandy, Jason Trotman
Advertising Assistant Sabrina Ancilleri
Copy Controller Oliver Guy

Marketing
Marketing Manager Mandy Martinez
US Publicity & Marketing Associate Rosella Albanese

Production
Guides Production Director Mark Lamond
Production Controller Samantha Furniss

Time Out Group
Chairman Tony Elliott
Managing Director Mike Hardwick
Group Financial Director Richard Waterlow
Group Commercial Director Lesley Gill
Group Marketing Director Christine Cort
Group General Manager Nichola Coulthard
Group Art Director John Oakey
Online Managing Director David Pepper

Contributors
Introduction Ronnie Haydon. **History** David Littlefield. **London Today** Ronnie Haydon. **Architecture** David Littlefield. **London in Verse** Rick Jones. **Where to Stay** Hugh Graham; *additional reviews* Sam Le Quesne, Lesley McCave. **Sightseeing: Introduction:** Ronnie Haydon. **South Bank & Bankside** Ronnie Haydon; *additional reviews* Stuart Weightman. **The City** Rick Jones, Will Fulford-Jones. **Holborn & Clerkenwell** Hugh Graham. **Bloomsbury & Fitzrovia** Hugh Graham. **Marylebone** Ronnie Haydon. **Mayfair & St James's** Christi Daugherty. **Soho** Hugh Graham. **Covent Garden & St Giles's** Cyrus Shahrad. **Westminster** Hugh Graham. **South Kensington & Knightsbridge** Cyrus Shahrad. **Chelsea** Ronnie Haydon. **North London** Fiona Hook (*Village green: Highgate* Laura Martz). **East London** Simon Coppock. **South-east London** Ronnie Haydon (*Pride of London: Trees* Paul Edwards). **South-west London** Ronnie Haydon (*additional reviews and Village green: Kew Green* Cyrus Shahrad). **West London** Sharon Lougher, Ronnie Haydon (*Tag along* Cyrus Shahrad). **Restaurants** Christi Daugherty (*Posh tea* Ronnie Haydon). **Pubs & Bars** Andrew Humphreys (*Pride of London: The two brewers* Rick Jones). **Shops & Services** Christi Daugherty (*Craft complexes* Laura Martz; *Smart tailoring* Jill Emeny). **Festivals & Events** Christi Daugherty (*Bankers' holidays* Chloë Lola Riess). **Children** Ronnie Haydon. **Comedy** Sharon Lougher. **Dance** Donald Hutera. **Film** Tom Morgan. **Galleries** Martin Coomer. **Gay & Lesbian** Dan Gould. **Music** Rick Jones (*Classical & Opera*); Will Fulford-Jones (*Rock, Roots & Jazz*). **Nightlife** Chloë Lola Riess. **Sport & Fitness** Cyrus Shahrad. **Theatre** Kieron Quirke. **Trips Out of Town** Ronnie Haydon (*Take to the hills* Cyrus Shahrad). **Directory** Ronnie Haydon.

Maps JS Graphics (john@jsgraphics.co.uk).

Photography pages iii, 1, 3, 5,24, 71, 75, 77, 78, 79, 81, 82, 85, 90, 93, 97, 98, 107, 108, 111, 112, 115, 117, 121, 123, 125, 128, 131, 135, 136, 137, 139, 141, 144, 147, 148, 154, 157, 158, 159, 161, 164, 165, 166, 169, 171, 172, 177, 182, 183, 186, 187, 325 Mockford & Bonetti; pages 7, 14, 17, 20, 21 AKG London; page 8 Francis G. Mayer/Corbis; page 11 Archivo Iconografico, S.A./Corbis; pages 22, 120 Amanda C.Edwards; pages 35, 36, 39, 43, 46, 47, 52, 59, 60, 63, 65, 118, 119, 178, 179, 189, 209, 218, 222, 226, 227, 238, 239, 250, 251, 253, 257, 262, 263, 350 Héloïse Bergman; pages 133, 230, 258 Hadley Kincade; pages 184, 202, 203, 249, 282, 283, 299, 303, 304, 306, 310, 311, 326 Andrew Brackenbury; pages 192, 274 Matt Carr; pages 191, 214, 337, 339, 342, 347 Alys Tomlinson; pages 197, 213, 242 Tricia de Courcy Ling; page 209 Tristan Newkey-Burden; pages 296, 297 Anthony Dickinson/Demon Imaging; pages 316, 317, 321 Sam Kesteven; page 352, 352 National Trust Photographic Library/David Sellman and Eric Crichton; pages 27, 30, 67, 88, 132, 267, 270, 272, 273, 294, 295, 319 Jonathan Perugia; page 301 Gaultier; page 355 Rob Greig. The following images were provided by the featured establishments/artist: pages 151, 231, 278, 290, 287, 329, 333, 334.

The Editor would like to thank: John, Bruce and Jane Jones, Teresa Trafford, Sarah Guy, Cath Phillips, Will Fulford-Jones and all contributors to previous editions of the *Time Out London Guide*.

© Copyright Time Out Group Ltd
All rights reserved

Contents

Introduction

Two thousand years in the making and still a work in progress, London's a dear old soul. Pretty in some lights, with a middle-aged suburban spread and a comfortable bosom for an annual 28 million or so guests, there's fine romance in the city's heart, and fun to be had in teasing it out.

You don't have to be far into your first visit to London to realise that for every iconic sight you whip out your camera to capture – the Tower of London, the Houses of Parliament, Buckingham Palace – there's much you just can't place and would rather keep out of the album. What's Elephant & Castle all about, for example? Why is Oxford Circus tube station such a hideous mess? What is that plasticky-looking white building by Cannon Street Station that resembles something out of a child's home-made Thunderbird Island?

London's rather sprawling habit, and the fact that generations of self-important aristocrats, city slickers and government fixers have, over the centuries, built, then ripped up, then replaced much of the city's fabric, make it a disparate, daunting – and always stimulating – entity to explore.

But don't believe for a moment that it's only the tourists who are bewildered by the sheer magnitude of this city. Most Londoners who stray from their own well-tramped manors are unlikely to do so without the comforting bulk of their *A-Z of London*. Someone who has lived all their life in Southwark may well be hazy as to the exact location of a certain Park Road, N15. (And it doesn't help that there are 42 other Park Roads, either). It would be impossible for any Londoner – born-and-bred Cockney sparra they may well be – to know all of the city's well-kept secrets.

But then it's unknowable, its grey suburban *longueurs* inscrutable, its benighted transport system unspeakable. It's also a bottomless repository of olde worlde quaintness, cutting-edge fashion, quiet courtesy and peerless culture.

Once you start to explore you'll find all this and more to be true. London's benign heart is uncovered as you wander from museum to gallery, down Victorian arcades and heaving streets, across vast expanses of parkland and cobbled Dickensian streets. Scruffy, tawdry, glitzy, bustling, regal, pastoral and workaday London all prop each other up. Hard by every ancient edifice steeped in history there's a boot-faced tower block gleaming with modern prosperity. Every time you emerge, replete, from one of London's world-famous restaurants, you know you'll never be far from the globally recognised illuminated logo of a certain burger chain. You can boggle at the chocolate-box Englishness of Fortnum & Mason, but know that the place is a bit of a parody – as much a tourist attraction as a purveyor of high-class comestibles.

The paradoxes are endless, discovering them is an addiction, which is why we love this city and delight in finding out more about it. For beneath the weight of history and all those world-capital responsibilities the game old bird is still as seductive and free-thinking as a model half her age.

ABOUT TIME OUT GUIDES

This is the 12th edition of the *Time Out London Guide*, one of the expanding series of *Time Out* guides produced by the people behind London and New York's successful listings magazines. Our guides are written and updated by resident experts who have striven to provide you with all the most up-to-date information you'll need to explore the city or read up on its background, whether you're a local or a first-time visitor.

THE LIE OF THE LAND

Thanks to the chaotic street plan – or, rather, the lack of one – London is one of the most complicated of all major world cities to find your way around. To make it a little easier, we've included an area designation for every venue in this guide (such as Soho, Covent Garden, et cetera), along with map references that point to our street maps at the back of the book (starting on page 394). However, for the sake of comprehensiveness, we recommend that you follow the example of the locals and invest in an *A-Z* map of the city the minute you arrive.

ESSENTIAL INFORMATION

For all the practical information you might need for visiting the area – including visa and customs information, details of local transport, a listing of emergency numbers and a directory of useful websites – turn to the Directory chapter at the back of this guide. It starts on page 356.

THE LOWDOWN ON THE LISTINGS

We have tried to make this book as easy to use and practically useful as possible. Addresses, phone numbers, transport information, opening times and admission prices are all included. However, owners and managers can change their arrangements at any time. Before you go out of your way, we'd advise you to phone ahead to check opening times and other particulars. While every effort and care has been made to ensure the accuracy of the information contained in this guide, the publishers cannot accept responsibility for any errors it may contain.

PRICES AND PAYMENT

In the listings, we have noted which of the following credit cards are accepted: American Express (AmEx), Diners Club (DC), MasterCard (MC) and Visa (V). Some venues will also accept other cards, such as Delta, Switch or JCB.

The prices we've listed in this guide should be treated as guidelines. If prices vary wildly from those we've quoted, ask whether there's a good reason. We aim to give the best and most up-to-date advice, so please let us know if you've been badly treated or overcharged.

Advertisers

We would like to stress that no establishment has been included in this guide because it has advertised in any of our publications and no payment of any kind has influenced any review. The opinions given in this book are those of *Time Out* writers and entirely independent.

TELEPHONE NUMBERS

The area code for London is 020. All telephone numbers given in this guide take this code unless otherwise stated: add 020 to the numbers listed throughout the book if calling from outside London; otherwise, simply dial the number as written. For more details of phone codes and charges, *see p371*. The international dialling code for the UK is 44.

MAPS

The map section at the back of this book includes a trips out of town map, orientation and neighbourhood maps of the London area, and street maps of most of central London, with a comprehensive street index. The maps start on page 389.

LET US KNOW WHAT YOU THINK

We hope you enjoy the *Time Out London Guide*, and we'd like to know what you think of it. We welcome your tips for places to include in future editions and take note of your criticism of our choices. There's a reader's reply card at the back of this book for your feedback, or you can email us at guides@timeout.com.

There is an online version of this guide, and guides to over 35 international cities, at **www.timeout.com**.

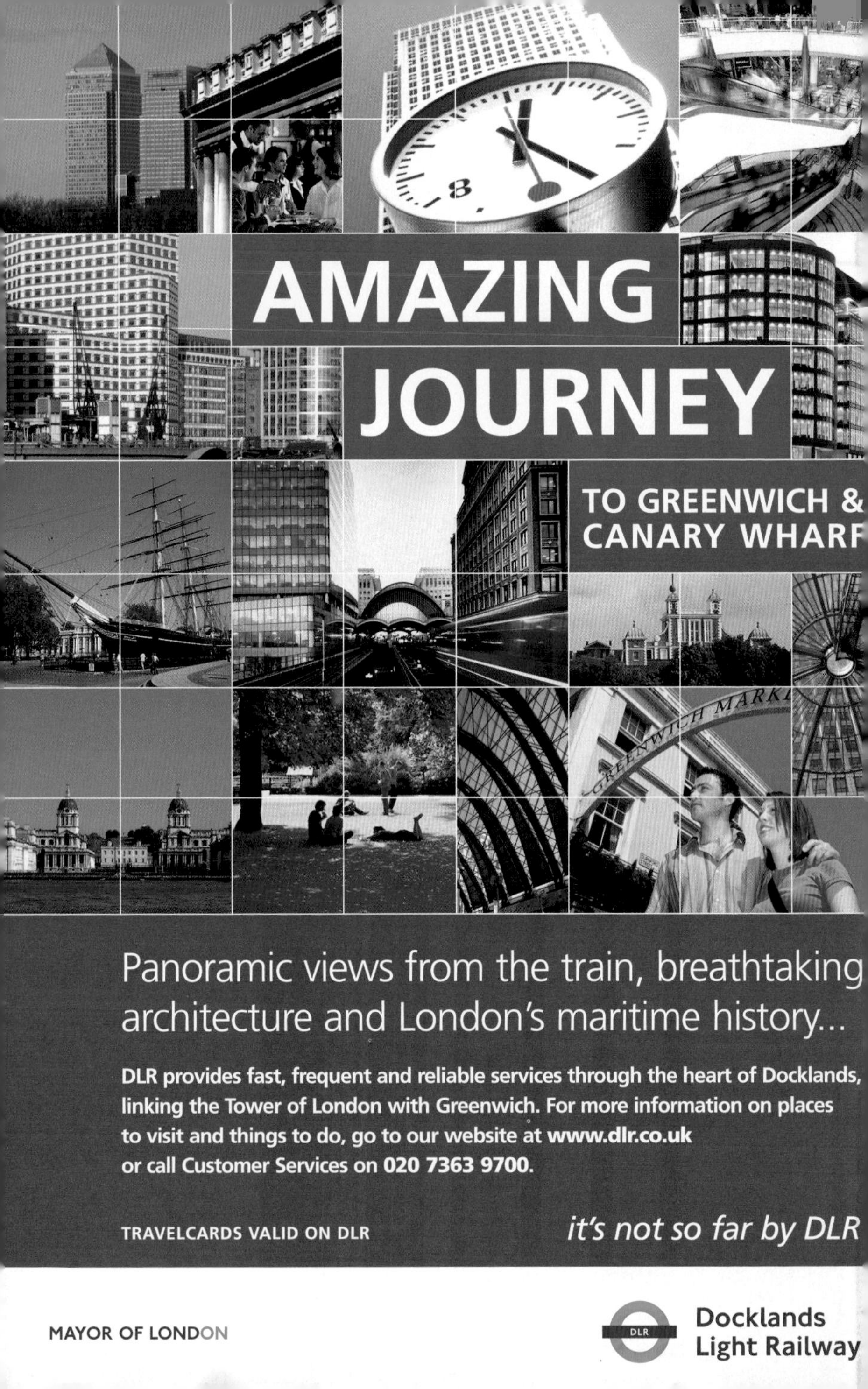

AMAZING JOURNEY

TO GREENWICH & CANARY WHARF

Panoramic views from the train, breathtaking architecture and London's maritime history...

DLR provides fast, frequent and reliable services through the heart of Docklands, linking the Tower of London with Greenwich. For more information on places to visit and things to do, go to our website at www.dlr.co.uk or call Customer Services on 020 7363 9700.

TRAVELCARDS VALID ON DLR

it's not so far by DLR

MAYOR OF LONDON

In Context

Features

MUSEUM OF LONDON

Put a smile on your face

The only museum that tells the story of London and its people from prehistoric to modern times

ADMISSION FREE Open 7 days Close to St Paul's www.museumoflondon.org.uk

Afbeelding van de
ADT LONDON.
Reprefentation curieufe de l'embrafement de la
VILLE de LONDRES,
Avec une Demonftration exacte de ce qui en eft demuré de refte.
Delineation of the
CITIE

History

Past times.

The 12th-century chronicler Geoffrey of Monmouth would have it that London was founded by the Trojan prince Brutus and run by a race of heroic giants descended from the Celtic King Lud. The truth is rather more prosaic. Though Celtic tribes lived in scattered communities along the banks of the Thames prior to the arrival of the Romans in Britain, there's no evidence to suggest that there was a settlement on the site of the future metropolis before the invasion of the Emperor Claudius' legions in AD 43. During the Romans' conquest of the country, they forded the Thames at its shallowest point and, later, built a timber bridge here (near the site of today's London Bridge). Over the following decade, a settlement developed on the north side of this crossing.

During the first two centuries AD, the Romans built roads, towns and forts in the area, and trade flourished. Progress was brought to a halt in AD 61 when Boudicca, the widow of an East Anglian chieftain, rebelled against the Imperial forces who had seized her land, flogged her and raped her daughters. She led the Iceni in a savage revolt, destroying the Roman colony at Colchester and then marching on London. The inhabitants were massacred and the settlement burned to the ground.

After order was restored, the town was rebuilt and, around AD 200, a two-mile (three-kilometre) long, 18-foot (six-metre) high defensive wall was constructed around it. Chunks of the wall survive today, and the names of the original gates – Ludgate, Newgate, Bishopsgate and Aldgate – are preserved on the map of the city. The street known as London Wall traces part of its original course.

By the fourth century, racked by barbarian invasions and internal strife, the Empire was in decline. In 410 the last troops were withdrawn and London became a ghost town. The Roman way of life vanished, their only enduring legacies being roads and early Christianity.

SAXON AND VIKING LONDON

During the fifth and sixth centuries, history gives way to legend. The Saxons crossed the North Sea and settled in eastern and southern England, apparently avoiding the ruins of London; they built farmsteads and trading posts outside the walls.

Pope Gregory sent Augustine to convert the English to Christianity in 596. Ethelbert, Saxon King of Kent, proved a willing convert, and consequently Augustine was appointed the first Archbishop of Canterbury. Since then, the Kentish city of Canterbury has remained the centre of the English Christian Church. London's first Bishop, though, was Mellitus: one of Augustine's missionaries, he converted the East Saxon King Sebert and, in 604, founded a wooden cathedral dedicated to St Paul inside

Henry VIII. The marrying kind. *See p10.*

the old city walls. On Sebert's death, his fickle followers gave up the faith and reverted to paganism, but later generations of Christians rebuilt what is now St Paul's Cathedral.

London, meanwhile, continued to expand. The Venerable Bede, writing in 731, described 'Lundenwic' as 'the mart of many nations resorting to it by land and sea'. This probably refers to a settlement west of the Roman city in the area of today's Aldwych (Old English for 'old settlement'). During the ninth century the city faced a new danger from across the North Sea: the Vikings. The city was sacked in 841 and, in 851, the Danish raiders returned with 350 ships, leaving London in ruins. It was not until 886 that King Alfred of Wessex – aka Alfred the Great – regained the city, soon re-establishing London as a major trading centre with a merchant navy and new wharfs at Billingsgate and Queenhithe.

Throughout the tenth century the Saxon city prospered. Churches were built, parishes established and markets set up. However, the 11th century brought more harassment from the warlike Vikings, and the English were even forced to accept a Danish king, Cnut (Canute, 1016-40), during whose reign London replaced Winchester as the capital of England.

In 1042 the throne reverted to an Englishman, Edward the Confessor, who devoted himself to building the grandest church in England two miles (three kilometres) west of the City at Thorney ('the isle of brambles'). He replaced the timber church of St Peter's with a huge abbey, 'the West Minster' (Westminster Abbey; consecrated in December 1065), and moved his court to the new Palace of Westminster. A week after the consecration, Edward died and was buried in his new church. London now grew around two hubs: Westminster, as the centre for the royal court, government and law, and the City of London, as the commercial centre.

THE NORMAN CONQUEST

On Edward's death, there was a succession dispute. William, Duke of Normandy, claimed that the Confessor, his cousin, had promised him the English Crown, but the English instead chose Edward's brother-in-law Harold. Piqued, William gathered an army and invaded; on 14 October 1066 he defeated Harold at the Battle of Hastings and marched on London. City elders had little option but to offer William the throne, and the conqueror was crowned in Westminster Abbey on Christmas Day, 1066.

'Rioting, persecution... lynching and pogrom were all commonplace'

Recognising the need to win over the prosperous City merchants by negotiation rather than force, William granted the Bishop and burgesses of London a charter – still kept at Guildhall – that acknowledged their rights and independence in return for taxes. But, 'against the fickleness of the vast and fierce population', he also ordered strongholds to be built alongside the city wall, including the White Tower (the tallest building in the Tower of London) and the now-lost Baynard's Castle at Blackfriars. The earliest surviving written account of contemporary London was written 40 years later by a monk, William Fitz Stephen, who conjured up the walled city and the pastures and woodland outside the perimeter.

MIDDLE AGED LONDON

In the growing city of London, much of the politics of the Middle Ages – the late 12th to the late 15th centuries – revolved around a constant three-way struggle for power between the king and the aristocracy, the Church, and the Lord Mayor and city guilds.

The king and his court frequently travelled to other parts of the kingdom and abroad in the early Middle Ages. However, during the 14th and 15th centuries, the Palace of Westminster became the seat of law and government. The noblemen and bishops who attended court built themselves palatial houses along the Strand from the City to Westminster, with gardens stretching to the river.

The Model Parliament, which agreed the principles of government, was held in Westminster Hall in 1295, presided over by Edward I and attended by barons, clergy and representatives of knights and burgesses. The first step towards establishing personal rights and political liberty – not to mention curbing the power of the king – had already been taken in 1215 with the signing of the Magna Carta by King John. Later, in the 14th century, subsequent assemblies gave rise to the House of Lords (which met at the Palace of Westminster) and the House of Commons (which met in the Chapter House at Westminster Abbey).

Relations between the monarch and the City were never easy. Londoners guarded their privileges with self-righteous intransigence, and resisted all attempts by successive kings to squeeze money out of them to finance wars and building projects. Subsequent kings were forced to turn to Jewish and Lombard moneylenders, but the City merchants were as intolerant of foreigners as of the royals. Rioting, persecution and the occasional lynching and pogrom were all commonplace in medieval London.

TAX AND SPEND

The privileges granted to the City merchants under Norman kings, allowing independence and self-regulation, were extended by the monarchs who followed, in return for financial favours. In 1191, during the reign of Richard I, the City of London was formally recognised as a commune – a self-governing community – and in 1197 it won control of the Thames, which included lucrative fishing rights that the City retained until 1857. In 1215 King John confirmed the city's right 'to elect every year a mayor', a position of great authority with power over the Sheriff and the Bishop of London. A month later, the Mayor had joined the rebel barons in signing the Magna Carta.

Over the next two centuries, the power and influence of the trade and craft guilds – later known as the City Livery Companies – increased as trade with Europe grew, and the wharfs by London Bridge were crowded with imports such as fine cloth, furs, wine, spices and precious metals. Port dues and taxes were paid to Customs officials such as part-time poet Geoffrey Chaucer, whose *Canterbury Tales* became the first published work of English literature.

The City's markets, already established, drew produce from miles around: livestock at Smithfield, fish at Billingsgate and poultry at Leadenhall. The street markets, or 'cheaps', around Westcheap (now Cheapside) and Eastcheap were crammed with a variety of goods. As commerce increased, foreign traders and craftsmen settled around the port; the population within the city wall grew from about 18,000 in 1100 to well over 50,000 in the 1340s.

UNHEALTHY UNREST

However, perhaps unsurprisingly, lack of hygiene became a serious problem in the City. Water was provided in cisterns at Cheapside and elsewhere, but the supply, which came more or less direct from the Thames, was limited and polluted. The street called Houndsditch was so named because Londoners threw their dead animals into the furrow that formed the City's eastern boundary. There was no proper sewerage system; in the streets around Smithfield (the Shambles), butchers dumped the entrails of slaughtered animals.

These appalling conditions provided the breeding ground for the greatest catastrophe of the Middle Ages: the Black Death of 1348 and 1349. The plague came to London from Europe, carried by rats on ships. During this period, about 30 per cent of England's population died of the disease. Although the epidemic abated, it was to recur in London on several occasions during the next three centuries, each time devastating the population.

The outbreaks of disease left the labour market short-handed, causing unrest among the overworked peasants. The imposition of a poll tax of a shilling a head proved the final straw, leading to the Peasants' Revolt of 1381. Thousands marched on London, led by Jack Straw from Essex and Wat Tyler from Kent. In the rioting and looting that followed, the Savoy Palace on the Strand was destroyed, the Archbishop of Canterbury was murdered and hundreds of prisoners were set free. When the 14-year-old Richard II rode out to Smithfield to face the rioters, Wat Tyler was fatally stabbed by Lord Mayor William Walworth. The other ringleaders were subsequently rounded up and hanged. But no more poll taxes were imposed.

THE TUDORS AND STUARTS

Under the Tudor monarchs (who reigned from 1485 until 1603) and spurred by the discovery of America and the ocean routes to Africa and the Orient, London became one of Europe's largest cities. Henry VII brought to an end the Wars of the Roses by defeating Richard III at the Battle of Bosworth and marrying Elizabeth of York. Henry VII's other great achievements included the building of a merchant navy, and the Henry VII Chapel in Westminster Abbey, the eventual resting place for him and his queen.

Henry VII was succeeded in 1509 by arch wife-collector (and dispatcher) Henry VIII. Henry's first marriage to Catherine of Aragon failed to produce an heir, so the King, in 1527, determined that the union should be annulled. As the Pope refused to co-operate, Henry defied the Catholic Church, demanding that he himself be recognised as Supreme Head of the Church in England and ordering the execution of anyone who refused to go along with the plan (including his chancellor Sir Thomas More). Thus England began the transition to Protestantism. The subsequent dissolution of the monasteries transformed the face of the medieval city with the confiscation and redevelopment of all property owned by the Catholic Church.

On a more positive note, Henry found time to develop a professional navy, founding the Royal Dockyards at Woolwich in 1512 and at Deptford the following year. He also established palaces at Hampton Court and Whitehall, and built a residence at St James's Palace. Much of the land he annexed for hunting became the Royal Parks, including Hyde, Regent's, Greenwich and Richmond parks.

Post-Henry, there was a brief Catholic revival under Queen Mary (1553-8), though her marriage to Philip II of Spain met with much opposition in London. She had 300 Protestants burned at the stake at Smithfield, earning her the nickname 'Bloody Mary'. However, this upturn in fortunes for Catholicism ended almost as soon as it had begun.

ELIZABETHAN LONDON

Elizabeth I's reign (1558-1603) saw a flowering of English commerce and arts. The founding of the Royal Exchange by Sir Thomas Gresham in 1566 gave London its first trading centre, allowing it to emerge as Europe's leading commercial centre. The merchant venturers and the first joint-stock companies (Russia Company and Levant Company) established new trading enterprises, and Drake, Raleigh and Hawkins sailed to the New World and beyond. In 1580 Elizabeth knighted Sir Francis Drake on his return from a three-year circumnavigation; eight years later, Drake and Howard defeated the Spanish Armada.

As trade grew, so did London. It was home to some 200,000 people in 1600, many living in dirty, overcrowded conditions; plague and fire were constant, day-to-day hazards. The most complete picture of Tudor London is given in John Stow's *Survey of London* (1598), a fascinating first-hand account by a diligent Londoner whose monument stands in the City church of St Andrew Undershaft.

The glory of the Elizabethan era was the development of English drama, popular with all social classes but treated with disdain by the Corporation of London, which went as far as to ban theatres from the City in 1575. Two theatres, the Rose (1587) and the Globe (1599), were erected on the south bank of the Thames at Bankside, and provided homes for the works of Marlowe and Shakespeare. Deemed 'a naughty place' by royal proclamation, Bankside was the Soho of its time: home not just to the theatre, but also to bear-baiting, cock-fighting, taverns and 'stewes' (brothels).

The Tudor dynasty ended with Elizabeth's death in 1603. Her successor, the Stuart King James I, narrowly escaped assassination on 5 November 1605, when Guy Fawkes and his gunpowder were discovered underneath the Palace of Westminster. The Gunpowder Plot had been hatched in protest at the failure to improve conditions for the persecuted Catholics, but only resulted in an intensification of anti-papist feelings in ever-intolerant London. To this day, 5 November is commemorated with fireworks as Bonfire Night.

But aside from his unwitting part in the Gunpowder Plot, James I merits remembering for other, more important reasons. For it was he who hired Inigo Jones to design court masques, and what ended up as the first – beautiful and hugely influential – examples of classical Renaissance style in London, the Queen's House in Greenwich, south-east London (1616) and the Banqueting House in Westminster (1619).

CIVIL WAR

Charles I succeeded his father in 1625, but gradually fell out with the City of London (from whose citizens he tried to extort taxes) and an increasingly independent-minded and antagonistic Parliament. The last straw finally came in 1642 when he intruded on the Houses of Parliament in an attempt to arrest five MPs. The country soon slid into a civil war (1642-9) between the supporters of Parliament (led by Puritan Oliver Cromwell) and those of the King.

Both sides knew that control of the country's major city and port was vital for victory. London's sympathies were firmly with the Parliamentarians and, in 1642, 24,000 citizens assembled at Turnham Green, west of the City, to face Charles's army. Fatally, the King lost his nerve and withdrew. He was never to seriously threaten the capital again; eventually, the Royalists were defeated. Charles was tried for treason and, though he denied the legitimacy of the court, he was declared guilty. He was then

Elizabeth I didn't take after her father.

taken to the Banqueting House in Whitehall on 30 January 1649, and, declaring himself to be a 'martyr of the people', beheaded.

For the next 11 years the country was ruled as a Commonwealth by Cromwell. However, the closing of the theatres and the banning of the supposedly Catholic superstition of Christmas, along with other Puritan strictures on the wickedness of any sort of fun, meant that the restoration of the exiled Charles II in 1660 was greeted with relief and rejoicing by the populace.

PLAGUE, FIRE AND REVOLUTION

However, two major catastrophes marred the first decade of Charles's reign in the capital. In 1665 the most serious outbreak of bubonic plague since the Black Death killed many of the capital's population. By the time the winter cold had put paid to the epidemic, nearly 100,000 Londoners had died. On 2 September 1666 a second disaster struck. The fire that spread from a carelessly tended oven in Farriner's Baking Shop on Pudding Lane was to rage for three days and consume four-fifths of the City, including 89 churches, 44 livery company halls and more than 13,000 houses.

The Great Fire at least allowed planners the chance to rebuild London as a rationally planned modern city. Many blueprints were considered, but, in the end, Londoners were so impatient to get on with business that the City was reconstructed largely on its medieval street plan, albeit in brick and stone rather than wood. The towering figure of the period turned out to be the prolific Sir Christopher Wren, who oversaw work on 51 of the 54 churches rebuilt. Among them was his masterpiece, the new St Paul's, completed in 1711 and, effectively, the world's first Protestant cathedral.

After the Great Fire, many well-to-do former City residents moved to new residential developments in the West End. In the City, the Royal Exchange was rebuilt, but merchants increasingly used the new coffee houses in which to exchange news. With the expansion of the joint-stock companies and the chance to invest capital, the City was emerging as a centre not of manufacturing, but of finance.

Anti-Catholic feeling still ran high. The accession of Catholic James II in 1685 aroused fears of a return to the Pope, and resulted in a Dutch Protestant, William of Orange, being

See London differently

BRITISH AIRWAYS
London eye

0870 5000 600 or ba-londoneye.com Nearest tubes Waterloo and Westminster

British Airways London Eye was conceived and designed by Marks Barfield Architects

Saints...

Monks, friars and priors in medieval London.

If sin and political power attract the attention of the Church, the cut and thrust of medieval London was an attractive proposition indeed. Around the 13th century the religious orders crossed the Channel and began a steady 300-year programme of education, healthcare provision, land acquisition, building development and, of course, worship.

Their presence has become part of the fabric of London's geography. The Dominicans, who wore black habits, were dubbed 'blackfriars' in 1221 when they settled in on Shoe Lane a stone's throw from where you'll now find the railway station of the same name. The Carmelites (in white), brought over by Crusaders in 1241, built a priory just around the corner in what are now Whitefriars and Carmelite Streets, while the Franciscans (sporting grey outfits) arrived in 1224, and are commemorated in Greyfriars Passage just up the road near St Paul's.

Along with these holy orders there were plenty of others: Augustinians, Benedictines, Bridgettines, Carthusians... In fact, the Church soon grew to be a major industry in its own right, and was an enormous employer. Records show that in the medieval era the City of London boasted more churches than any other city in Europe (at a time when Paris, Naples and Milan were considerably more populous). In fact, there were 126 parish churches, 13 conventual churches, seven friaries, five priories, five priests' colleges and four large nunneries. Plus hospitals, schools, private chapels and so on. All this for a population of around 50,000 people. It has been said that in those days you couldn't walk down a single London street without passing either a religious building or someone associated with one.

Many of the bigger building projects were located in the countryside just outside the city walls, such as Charterhouse, the Carthusian monastery in Clerkenwell, and St Bart's (founded by an Augustinian in 1123). Further afield, the church of St Laurence Pountney in Barking became a refuge for the insane (hence 'Barking mad').

The whole edifice came tumbling down in the 1530s with the Acts of Supremacy and Succession, which obliged the religious orders to swear an oath that a) Henry VIII was the legitimate head of the Church and b) that he could marry (and divorce) whomever he liked. Most agreed to these terms quietly. Others, like three priors from Charterhouse, begged to differ and were hung, drawn and quartered for merely wanting to discuss the issue. Two years later ten monks from the same monastery (brave souls indeed) further refused to sign the oath and were hung in chains at Newgate jail – nine died of starvation and the survivor was transferred to the Tower and executed in 1540.

Henry was also after the Church's wealth and property, and so began a systematic programme of destruction and confiscation. In just two years the sale of Church land bolstered the King's coffers by £330,000 – then a staggering sum. In a sense, worse than the wanton destruction wrought on the buildings was the less than holy use to which the surviving religious buildings were often put. Some parts of the black and white friars' monasteries became rowdy playhouses (a heinous act in an age when theatres were usually frowned upon by the righteous). The Greyfriars monastery fared little better; it was used for the rather ignoble purpose of storing quantities of herring and wine.

invited to take the throne with his wife, Mary Stuart (James's daughter). James fled to France in 1688 in what became known – by its beneficiaries – as the 'Glorious Revolution'. One development during William III's reign was the founding of the Bank of England in 1694, initially to finance the King's wars with France.

BY GEORGE

After the death of Queen Anne, according to the Act of Settlement (1701), the throne passed to George, great-grandson of James I, who had been born and raised in Hanover, Germany. Thus, a German-speaking king – who never learned English – became the first of four long-reigning Georges in the Hanoverian line.

During his reign (1714-27), and for several years afterwards, Sir Robert Walpole's Whig party monopolised Parliament. Their opponents, the Tories, supported the Stuarts and had opposed the exclusion of the Catholic James II. On the King's behalf, Walpole chaired a group of ministers (the forerunner of today's Cabinet), becoming, in effect, Britain's first prime minister.

Walpole was presented with 10 Downing Street (constructed by Sir George Downing) as a residence; it remains the official home of all serving prime ministers.

During the 18th century London grew with astonishing speed, in terms of both population and construction. New squares and many streets of terraced houses spread across Soho, Bloomsbury, Mayfair and Marylebone, as wealthy landowners and speculative developers who didn't mind taking a risk given the size of the potential rewards cashed in on the demand for leasehold properties. South London, too, became more accessible with the opening of the first new bridges for centuries, Westminster Bridge (1750) and Blackfriars Bridge (1763). Until then, London Bridge had been the only bridge over the Thames. The old city gates, most of the Roman Wall and the remaining houses on Old London Bridge were demolished, allowing access to the City for traffic.

THE RUINED POOR VS THE IDLE RICH

In the older districts, however, people were still living in terrible squalor and poverty, far worse than the infamous conditions of Victorian times.

Inebriated London by **Hogarth** (1751).

Some of the most notorious slums were located around Fleet Street and St Giles's (north of Covent Garden), only a short distance from streets of fashionable residences maintained by large numbers of servants. To make matters worse, gin ('mother's ruin') was readily available at very low prices, and many poor Londoners drank excessive amounts in an attempt to escape the horrors of daily life. The well-off seemed complacent, amusing themselves at the popular Ranelagh and Vauxhall Pleasure Gardens or with organised trips to Bedlam to mock the mental patients. On a similar level, public executions at Tyburn – near today's Marble Arch – were among the most popular events in the social calendar.

The outrageous imbalance in the distribution of wealth encouraged crime, and there were daring daytime robberies in the West End. Reformers were few, though there were exceptions. Henry Fielding, author of the picaresque novel *Tom Jones,* was also an enlightened magistrate at Bow Street Court. In 1751 he and his blind half-brother John set up a volunteer force of 'thief-takers' to back up the often ineffective efforts of the parish constables and watchmen who were the only law-keepers in the city. This crime-busting group of early cops, known as the Bow Street Runners, were the forerunners of today's Metropolitan Police (established in 1829).

Disaffection was also evident in the activities of the London mob during this period. Riots were a regular reaction to middlemen charging extortionate prices, or merchants adulterating their food. In June 1780 London was hit by the anti-Catholic Gordon Riots, named after ringleader George Gordon; the worst in the city's violent history, they left 300 people dead.

Some attempts were made to alleviate the grosser ills of poverty with the setting up of five major new hospitals by private philanthropists. St Thomas's and St Bartholomew's were already long established as monastic institutions for the care of the sick, but Westminster (1720), Guy's (1725), St George's (1734), London (1740) and the Middlesex (1745) went on to become world-famous teaching hospitals. Thomas Coram's Foundling Hospital for abandoned children was another remarkable achievement of the time.

THE VICTORIAN METROPOLIS

It wasn't just the indigenous population of London that was on the rise. Country people, who had lost their land because of enclosures and were faced with starvation wages or unemployment, drifted into the towns in large numbers. The East End became the focus for poor immigrant labourers with the building of the docks towards the end of the century.

...and sinners

Crime and punishment in the capital.

If you're one of those suffering from fear of crime, don't read on. In June 2003 the Met police were called to the scene of 17 murders, 466 cases of GBH and 244 rapes. Apart from those there were 8,809 burglaries, 2,405 people pickpocketed, 1,772 victims of fraud, 12,103 cases of criminal damage and 1,772 bikes nicked. There were even 14 cases of common assault at Heathrow airport. And that's just one month in the capital. (By the way, at the time of writing the police had apprehended 15 suspects for those murders and 53 for the rapes.)

Officials reckon that crime has dropped slightly over the last year or so, but looking back over decades the trend is moving only one way – upward. In 1938 95,000 crimes were reported (compare that with 90,000 for last June). Having said that, London has always been a violent and vulnerable place. In 1751 Henry Fielding wrote that London's network of alleyways, narrow lanes and courts appeared to be designed to facilitate crime. 'The whole appears as a vast Wood or Forest, in which a Thief may harbour with as great Security as wild Beasts do in the Desarts of Africa or Arabia.'

Statistics are almost non-existent, but you can be fairly sure that Fielding's London (and the London of any other time) was a place of murder, assault, robbery, kidnap and pickpockets (called Foysters and Nyppers). There was gun crime ('Stand and deliver!'), which culminated in the assassination of Prime Minister Spencer Perceval, gunned down in the house of Commons in 1812.

Then, as now, there were criminal gangs – like the Gregory gang of which highwayman Dick Turpin was a member. Jonathan Wild, who ruled the criminal underworld from 1712 to 1725, is said to have had 7,000 people working for him, including trained artisans who would alter the appearance of watches, jewellery and snuffboxes before shipping them off to Holland for disposal.

Then, as now, arguments raged over the cause of such uncivil behaviour. Many put it down to heavy gin-drinking, others on gambling. Henry Fielding's half-brother John was convinced that mass immigration was to blame. He asserted that the likelihood of robbery would drop if restrictions were placed on the number of foreigners (in his case, the Irish) entering the country. Sound familiar?

A century later medical journal the *Lancet* estimated there were 6,000 brothels in the capital, serviced by 80,000 prostitutes. Tragically, child prostitution was also common. This is partly explained by the curious and repugnant belief that the act of deflowering would cure venereal disease.

Considering the punishments meted out to many offenders, it is a wonder anyone broke the law at all. Conditions in London's filthy, infamous Newgate prison (on the site of today's Old Bailey) were appalling. Fielding called it the 'prototype of Hell'. Jailers made handsome profits from selling candles and even water, and they would even let you out of your shackles for a price.

Execution was one way out of this misery, and there was plenty of it. In fact, it was good old-fashioned public entertainment until 1868. Apprentices were encouraged to watch and execution days were given as holidays (probably as a disincentive to commit crime – apprentice boys were notorious rioters). Gibbets could be erected anywhere, often on the site of the crime itself, and thousands would gather to watch. Generally, though, executions were carried out at Tyburn (now Marble Arch), Smithfield, Newgate and Kennington Common. Tyburn was the site of London's first permanent gallows, and it was quite something: at 18 feet (5.5metres) high, it had three beams eight or nine feet (2.4 or 2.7 metres) across. Eight people could hang from each beam at once, affording more varied entertainment for a bloodthirsty crowd. Today, we get *Crimewatch*.

London's population had grown to almost a million by 1801, the largest of any city in Europe. And by 1837, when Queen Victoria came to the throne, five more bridges and the capital's first passenger railway (from Greenwich to London Bridge) gave hints that a major expansion might be around the corner.

As well as being the administrative and financial capital of the British Empire, which spanned a fifth of the globe, London was also its chief port and the world's largest manufacturing centre, with breweries, distilleries, tanneries, shipyards, engineering works and many other grimy industries lining the south bank of the

Thames. On the one hand, London boasted splendid buildings, fine shops, theatres and museums; on the other, it was a city of poverty, disease and prostitution. The residential areas were becoming polarised into districts with fine terraces maintained by squads of servants, and overcrowded, insanitary, disease-ridden slums.

The growth of the metropolis in the century before Victoria came to the throne had been spectacular enough, but during her reign, which lasted until 1901, thousands more acres were covered with housing, roads and railway lines. Today, if you pick any street within five miles (eight kilometres) of central London, chances are that its houses will be mostly Victorian. By the end of the 19th century, the city's population had swelled to in excess of six million.

Despite social problems – memorably depicted in the writings of Charles Dickens – major steps were being taken to improve conditions for the majority of Londoners by the turn of the century. The Metropolitan Board of Works installed an efficient sewerage system, street lighting and better roads. The worst slums were replaced by low-cost building schemes funded by philanthropists such as the American George Peabody, who established the Peabody Donation Fund, which continues to

Urban sprawl

The London we know today is essentially a Victorian city – what are now inner-city nodes within a larger whole were, before the 1830s, entirely separate villages and hamlets. Islington, Paddington, Bayswater, Lambeth, Peckham, Clapham, Ealing; these were once country escapes. Hyde and Regent's parks were originally constructed at the edge of the city, effectively fenced-off enclosures within open spaces. In the 16th century Moorfields was exactly that – fields.

Believe it or not, the Euston Road (called New Road when it was completed in 1756) was constructed along the edge of the capital as a way of bypassing busy Oxford Street.

By the 1870s people were becoming worried by the spread, and many mourned the loss of an older London. One newspaper reporter wrote, 'the London of our youth... is becoming obliterated by another city which seems to be rising up through it'. Disraeli complained of the number of 'flat, dull spiritless streets', while another disillusioned commentator described the capital as a 'monster'. In 1790 the number of baptisms exceeded the number of burials for the first time. One million people lived in London in 1800; a century later the population had grown to around five million. By 1911 it was up to a whopping seven million. People have to live somewhere.

The history of Clapham goes back to Saxon times, when it was known as Clopeham or Clappeham. It remained a small village until the plague and fire of 1665-6, when Londoners sought refuge from the capital, braving attacks from highwaymen hiding in the marshland that was later to become Clapham Common. It wasn't until the arrival of the railways in the late 19th century, which permitted people to live outside the noise and smoke of the capital, that rows of terrace houses caused the area to merge with its neighbours Battersea and Lambeth.

The railways also wrought fundamental change on Camden, which in the early 19th century was a countryside retreat. One writer at the time waxes lyrical about its 'rural lanes, hedgeside roads, lovely fields and fresh air', all of which apparently provided a rest cure for the busy Londoner.

In 1749 Camden was characterised by fields of cows, but 100 years later the district had been transformed by loading and shunting operations for the railways, and large portions of the population earned their income from the manufacture of scientific and musical instruments, and telescopes. By 1870, there was such a shortage of building land that most houses had lodgers.

Islington is no different. Listed in the *Domesday Book* (a census compiled in 1086) as Isendone and Iseldone, this borough was once a countryside stopping place for royalty leaving and approaching the capital. Like Clapham in the south, Islington became a refuge for people fleeing fire and plague, but it retained its rural character until the Victorian era. In the 18th century the area was known for its gardens and nurseries. By the early 19th century, however, many of its fields were being used for brick-making, and these inevitably were used to build houses.

The arrival of the Regent's Canal in 1820 brought more industry to the neighourhood and, consequently, many more people. Although remaining prosperous, Islington began to develop slum areas and wealthy homeowners moved out – a trend that only began to reverse in the 1960s.

Philanthropy (top) and travel, **Victorian** style.

this day to provide subsidised housing to the working classes. The London County Council (created in 1888), also helped to house the poor.

'A touch of Parisian chic came to London with the opening of the Ritz Hotel'

The Victorian expansion would not have been possible without an efficient public transport network with which to speed workers into and out of the city from the new suburbs. The horse-drawn bus appeared on London's streets in 1829, but it was the opening of the first passenger railway seven years later that heralded the commuters of the future. The first underground line, which ran between Paddington and Farringdon Road, opened in 1863 and proved an instant success, attracting more than 30,000 travellers on the first day. Soon after, the world's first electric track in a deep tunnel – the 'tube' – opened in 1890 between the City and Stockwell, later becoming part of the Northern line.

ALBERT'S PRIDE

The Great Exhibition of 1851 captured the zeitgeist: confidence and pride, discovery and invention. Prince Albert, the Queen's Consort, helped organise this triumphant event, for which the Crystal Palace, a giant building of iron and glass – designed not by a professional architect but by the Duke of Devonshire's gardener, Joseph Paxton – was erected in Hyde Park. During the five months it was open, the Exhibition drew six million visitors from Great Britain and abroad, and the profits inspired the Prince Consort to establish a permanent centre

SHAKESPEARE'S GLOBE
THEATRE TOUR AND EXHIBITION
Bankside - London
TEL +44 (0) 20 7902 1500   FAX +44 (0) 20 7902 1515
www.shakespeares-globe.org

for the study of the applied arts and sciences: the result is the South Kensington museums and Imperial College. After the Exhibition, the Palace was moved to Sydenham and used as an exhibition centre until it burned down in 1936.

When the Victorians were not colonising the world by force, they combined their conquests with scientific developments. The Royal Geographical Society sent navigators to chart unknown waters, botanists to bring back new species, and geologists to study the earth. Many of their specimens ended up at the Royal Botanic Gardens at Kew.

THE NOUGHTIES

During the brief reign of Edward VII (1901-10), London regained some of the gaiety and glamour it lacked in the dour last years of Victoria's reign. A touch of Parisian chic came to London with the opening of the Ritz Hotel in Piccadilly; the Café Royal hit the heights of its popularity as a meeting place for artists and writers; and 'luxury catering for the little man' was provided at the Lyons Tea Shops and new Lyons Corner Houses (the Coventry Street branch, which opened in 1907, could accommodate an incredible 4,500 people). Meanwhile, the first department store, Selfridges, opened on Oxford Street in 1909.

Road transport, too, was revolutionised. Motor cars put-putted around the city's streets, before the first motor bus was introduced in 1904. Double-decked electric trams had started running in 1901 (though not through the West End or the City), and continued doing so for 51 years. In fact, by 1911 the use of horse-drawn buses had been abandoned.

A few years later, London suffered its first devastating air raids in World War I. The first bomb over the city was dropped from a Zeppelin near Guildhall in September 1915, and was followed by many gruelling nightly raids on the capital; bomb attacks from planes began in July 1917. In all, around 650 people lost their lives as a result of Zeppelin raids.

ROARING BETWEEN THE WARS

Political change happened quickly after World War I. Lloyd George's government averted revolution in 1918-19 by promising (but not delivering) 'homes for heroes' for the embittered returning soldiers. But the Liberal Party's days in power were numbered, and by 1924 the Labour Party, led by Ramsay MacDonald, had enough MPs to form its first government.

After the trauma of World War I, a 'live for today' attitude prevailed in the Roaring '20s among the young upper classes, who flitted from parties in Mayfair to dances at the Ritz. But this meant little to the mass of Londoners, who were suffering greatly in the post-war slump. Civil disturbances, brought on by the high cost of living and rising unemployment, resulted in the nationwide General Strike of 1926, when the working classes downed tools in support of the striking miners. Prime Minister Baldwin encouraged volunteers to take over the public services and the streets teemed with army-escorted food convoys, aristocrats running soup kitchens and students driving buses. After nine days of chaos, the strike was called off by the Trades Union Congress (TUC).

The economic situation only worsened in the early 1930s following the New York Stock Exchange crash of 1929; by 1931 more than three million Britons were jobless. During these years, the London County Council began to have a greater impact on the city's life, undertaking programmes of slum clearance and new housing, creating more parks and taking under its wing education, transport, hospitals, libraries and the fire service.

London's population increased dramatically between the wars, too, peaking at nearly 8.7 million in 1939. To accommodate the influx, the suburbs expanded quickly, particularly to the north-west with the extension of the Metropolitan line to an area that became known as Metroland. Identical gabled, double-fronted houses sprang up in their hundreds of thousands, from Golders Green to Surbiton.

All these new Londoners were entertained by the new media of film, radio and TV. London's first radio broadcast was beamed from the roof of Marconi House in the Strand in 1922, and families were soon gathering around enormous Bakelite wireless sets to hear the British Broadcasting Company (the BBC; from 1927 called the British Broadcasting Corporation). Television broadcasts started on 26 August 1936, when the first telecast went out live from Alexandra Palace.

WORLD WAR II (1939-45)

Neville Chamberlain's policy of appeasement towards Hitler's increasingly aggressive Germany during the 1930s collapsed when the Germans invaded Poland, and on 3 September 1939 Britain declared war. The government implemented precautionary measures against the threat of air raids – including the digging of trench shelters in London parks, and the evacuation of 600,000 children and pregnant mothers – but the expected bombing raids did not happen during the autumn and winter of 1939-40, a period that became known as the Phoney War. In July 1940, though, Germany began preparations for an invasion of Britain with three months of aerial attack that came to be known as the Battle of Britain.

For Londoners, the Phoney War came to an abrupt end on 7 September 1940, when

Flattened by **The Blitz**...

hundreds of German bombers dumped their loads of high explosives on east London and the docks. Entire streets were destroyed; the dead and injured numbered more than 2,000. The Blitz had begun. The raids on London continued for 57 consecutive nights, then intermittently for a further six months. Londoners reacted with tremendous bravery and stoicism, a period still nostalgically referred to as 'Britain's finest hour'. After a final massive raid on 10 May 1941, the Germans focused their attention elsewhere, but by the end of the war, a third of the City and the East End was in ruins.

From 1942 onwards, the tide of the war began to turn, but Londoners still had a new terror to face: the V1, or 'doodlebug'. Dozens of these deadly, explosives-packed pilotless planes descended on the city in 1944, causing widespread destruction. Later in the year, the more powerful V2 rocket was launched and, over the winter, 500 of them dropped on London, mostly in the East End. The last fell on 27 March 1945 in Orpington, Kent, around six weeks before Victory in Europe (VE Day) was declared on 8 May 1945.

POST-WAR BLUES

World War II left Britain almost as shattered as Germany. Soon after VE Day, a general election was held and Churchill was heavily defeated by the Labour Party under Clement Attlee. The new government established the National Health Service in 1948, and began a massive nationalisation programme that included public transport, electricity, gas, postal and telephone services. But for all the plans, life in London for most people was regimented and austere.

In war-ravaged London, the most immediate problem faced by both residents and the local authorities was a critical shortage of housing. Prefabricated bungalows provided a temporary solution for some (though many of these buildings were still occupied 40 years later), but the huge new high-rise housing estates that the planners devised were often badly built and proved to be unpopular with their residents.

However, there were bright spots during this dreary time. London hosted the Olympics in 1948; three years later came the Festival of Britain (100 years after the Great Exhibition), a celebration of British technology and design. The exhibitions that took over land on the south bank of the Thames for the Festival provided the incentive to build the South Bank Centre.

HAVING IT GOOD THEN LOSING IT

As the 1950s progressed, life and prosperity gradually returned to London, leading Prime Minister Harold Macmillan in 1957 to famously proclaim that 'most of our people have never had it so good'. The coronation of Queen Elizabeth II in 1953 had been the biggest television broadcast in history, and there was the feeling of a new age dawning.

However, many Londoners were moving out of the city. The population dropped by half a million in the late 1950s, causing a labour shortage that prompted huge recruitment drives in Britain's former colonies. London Transport and the National Health Service were particularly active in encouraging West Indians to emigrate to Britain. Unfortunately, as the Notting Hill race riots of 1958 illustrated, the welcome these new emigrants received was

...so it's all down the tube in **World War II**.

rarely friendly. Yet there were several areas of tolerance: among them was Soho, which, during the 1950s, became famed for its smoky, seedy, bohemian pubs, clubs and jazz joints, such as the still-jumping Ronnie Scott's (*see p312*).

THE SWINGING '60S

By the mid '60s, London had started to swing. The innovative fashions of Mary Quant and others broke Paris's stranglehold on couture: boutiques blossomed along King's Road, while Biba set the pace in Kensington. Carnaby Street became a byword for hipness as the city basked in its new-found reputation as the music and fashion capital of the world. The year of student unrest in Europe, 1968, saw the first issue of *Time Out* (a fold-up sheet for 5p) hit the streets in August. The decade ended with the Beatles naming their final album *Abbey Road* after their studios in London, NW8, and the Rolling Stones playing a free gig in Hyde Park that drew around 500,000 people.

The bubble, though, had to burst – and burst it did. Many Londoners remember the 1970s as a decade of economic strife: inflation, the oil crisis and international debt caused chaos, and the IRA began its bombing campaign on mainland Britain. The explosion of punk in the second half of the decade, sartorially inspired by the idiosyncratic genius of Vivienne Westwood, provided some nihilistic colour.

LIFE UNDER MRS THATCHER

Historians will regard the 1980s as the decade of Thatcherism. When the Conservatives won the general election in 1979, Britain's first woman prime minister, the propagandist for 'market forces' and Little Englander morality, set out to expunge socialism and the influence of the '60s and '70s. A monetarist economic policy and cuts in public services widened the divide between rich and poor. While a new breed of professionals – known as 'yuppies' (Young Urban Professionals) – profited from tax cuts and easy credit, unemployment soared.

In London, riots in Brixton (1981) and Tottenham (1985) were linked to unemployment and heavy-handed policing. The Greater London Council (GLC), led by Ken Livingstone, mounted spirited opposition to the government with a series of populist measures, the most famous being a fare-cutting policy on public transport. So effective was the GLC, in fact, that Thatcher decided to abolish it in 1986.

The spectacular rise in house prices at the end of the 1980s was followed by an equally alarming slump and the onset of a severe recession that only started to lift in the mid 1990s. The Docklands development – one of the Thatcher enterprise schemes, set up in 1981 in order to create a new business centre in the Docklands to the east of the City – has faltered many times, although it can now be counted a qualified success in terms of attracting business and a rapidly increasing number of residents to the Isle of Dogs and surrounding areas.

RECENT PAST AND NEAR FUTURE

The replacement of the by-now hated Margaret Thatcher by John Major in October 1990 signalled a rather shortlived upsurge of hope among the people of London. A riot in Trafalgar Square had helped to see off both Maggie and her inequitable Poll Tax.

High rise made good, the **Trellick Tower** (1973).

Yet the early 1990s were scarred by continuing recession and the problem of homelessness in London. Shortly after the Conservatives were elected for another term in office in 1992, the IRA detonated a massive bomb in the City, killing three people. This was followed by a second bomb a year later, which shattered buildings around Bishopsgate, and by a Docklands bomb in February 1996 that broke a fragile 18-month ceasefire. The Good Friday agreement of 1998 raised hopes for peace in the province, although disagreements about the decommissioning of weapons remain.

In May 1997 the British people ousted the tired Tories and Tony Blair's Labour Party swept to victory. However, initial enthusiasm from a public delighted to see fresh faces in office didn't last. The government hoped the Millennium Dome, built on a patch of Greenwich wasteland, would be a 21st-century rival to the 1851 Great Exhibition. It wasn't. Badly mismanaged, the Dome eventually ate nearly £1 billion of public money and become something of a national joke along the way.

This was not the government's only problem. Some serious rail accidents (on a network already on its knees), worsening crime, an epidemic of foot and mouth disease among livestock in 2001 and dissatisfaction with the National Health Service all led to Blair and Labour's approval rating dropping, amid suspicion that the government was all style and no substance. Yet the lack of a credible opposition meant Labour was re-elected with ease in 2001. The government's plans for Iraq in 2003, however, generated the largest public demonstration in London's history; more than two million participated, but were powerless against Blair's decision to go to war.

This wasn't the first time the government had ignored the people's wishes. The new millennium saw Ken Livingstone, former leader of the GLC, become London's first directly elected mayor in circumstances embarrassing to Labour. Despite evidence that most London voters wanted to see Livingstone as the Labour candidate, Blair, despising Livingstone's lack of obeisance to the party line, all but imposed his own candidate on the party. Livingstone quit Labour in disgust and ran in the election as an independent, winning in a landslide to head the new Greater London Assembly (GLA).

Almost four years on, Ken's congestion charge, which forces drivers pay a fiver every to enter the capital's centre, has shown what the mayor can do. His Totally London Campaign in 2003, to get visitors back into the city following the tourist slump of 2001-2, was a success. Despite the mayor's efforts, though, the city is still beset by problems – insane property prices and appalling traffic and public transport chief among them. But while the city has its critics people are still moving here, and London is more crowded, chaotic and lovable than ever.

Key events

AD 43 The Romans invade; a bridge is built on the Thames; Londinium is founded.
61 Boudicca burns Londinium; the city is rebuilt and made the provincial capital.
122 Emperor Hadrian visits Londinium.
200 A city wall is built; Londinium becomes capital of Britannia Superior.
410 Roman troops evacuate Britain.
c600 Saxon London is built to the west.
604 St Paul's is built by King Ethelbert.
841 The Norse raid for the first time.
c871 The Danes occupy London.
886 King Alfred of Wessex takes London.
1013 The Danes take London back.
1042 Edward the Confessor builds a palace and 'West Minster' upstream.
1066 William I is crowned in Westminster Abbey; London is granted a charter.
1067 The Tower of London begun.
1123 St Bartholomew's Hospital founded.
1197 Henry Fitzalwin is the first mayor.
1213 St Thomas's Hospital is founded.
1215 The Mayor signs the Magna Carta.
1240 First Parliament sits at Westminster.
1290 Jews are expelled from London.
1348-9 The Black Death.
1381 The Peasants' Revolt.
1388 Tyburn becomes place of execution.
1397 Richard Whittington is Lord Mayor.
1476 William Caxton sets up the first ever printing press at Westminster.
1512-3 Royal Dockyards at Woolwich and Deptford founded by Henry VIII.
1534 Henry VIII cuts off Catholic Church.
1554 200 martyrs burned at Smithfield.
1566 Gresham opens the Royal Exchange.
1572 First known map of London printed.
1599 The Globe Theatre opens.
1605 Guy Fawkes fails to blow up James I.
1642 The start of the Civil War.
1649 Charles I is executed; Cromwell establishes Commonwealth.
1664-5 The Great Plague.
1666 The Great Fire.
1675 Building starts on the new St Paul's.
1686 The first May Fair takes place.
1694 The Bank of England is established.
1711 St Paul's is completed.
1750 Westminster Bridge is built.
1766 The city wall is demolished.
1769 Blackfriars Bridge opens.
1780 The Gordon Riots take place.
1784 The first balloon flight over London
1802 The Stock Exchange is founded.
1803 The first horse-drawn railway opens.
1812 Spencer Perceval PM assassinated.
1820 Regent's Canal opens.
1824 The National Gallery is founded.
1827 Regent's Park Zoo opens.
1829 London's first horse-drawn bus runs; the Metropolitan Police Act is established.
1833 The London Fire Brigade is set up.
1835 Madame Tussaud's opens.
1836 The first passenger railway opens.
1837 Parliament is rebuilt after a fire.
1843 Trafalgar Square is laid out.
1848-9 Cholera epidemic sweeps London.
1851 The Great Exhibition takes place.
1853 Harrods opens its doors.
1858 The Great Stink: pollution in the Thames reaches hideous levels.
1863 The Metropolitan line, the world's first underground railway, opens.
1864 The Peabody buildings, cheap housing for the poor, are built in Spitalfields.
1866 London's last major cholera outbreak; the Sanitation Act is passed.
1868 The last public execution is held at Newgate Prison.
1884 Greenwich Mean Time established.
1888 Jack the Ripper prowls the East End; a London County Council is created.
1890 The Housing Act enables the LCC to clear the slums; the first electric underground railway opens.
1897 Motorised buses introduced.
1915-8 Zeppelins bomb London.
1940-1 The Blitz devastates much of the city.
1948 The Olympic Games are held.
1951 The Festival of Britain takes place.
1952 The last London 'pea-souper' smog
1953 Queen Elizabeth II is crowned.
1966 England win World Cup at Wembley.
1975 Work begins on the Thames barrier
1982 The last of London's docks close.
1986 The GLC is abolished.
1990 Poll Tax protesters riot.
1991 Riots in Brixton.
1992 Canary Wharf opens; an IRA bomb hits the Baltic Exchange in the City.
1997 Diana, Princess of Wales dies.
2000 Ken Livingstone is elected mayor; Tate Modern and the London Eye open.
2001 The Labour government re-elected.
2002 Queen mother dies age 101.
2003 London's biggest ever public demonstration – against the war on Iraq.

London Today

The old city has a new heart, but the arteries are still unhealthily clogged.

There were a few cheerful London news stories in 2003. Precious few, admittedly, but they came as welcome relief, tucked in between shaming reports about this dirty old town being the grime capital of Europe with a spiralling cost of living, and dark predictions of total transport meltdown.

The first eye-catching headline? The one about London's business prowess. The city's centuries-old reputation as business capital, if no longer of the world, certainly of Europe, received a boost when the European Cities Monitor 2003 ranked London above Paris, Frankfurt and Brussels as a commercial centre. London came out on top because, according to '500 top executives' surveyed, it had 'the best qualified staff, best access to markets and best external transport links'. The key word here, of course, is 'external'. The internal transport links are another matter to be dealt with later.

Further cause for celebration came with the announcement that London was in the running to host the 2012 Olympics, and, moreover, that it was in with as good a chance as any of its rivals, including Madrid, New York and Paris.

Other scraps of cheer for optimists included the effectiveness of Mayor Ken Livingstone's much-vaunted Congestion Charge; the success of his 'Totally London' campaign to lure terrorism/SARS-shy tourists back into the city; and the regeneration of a famous city square – the pedestrianised Trafalgar Square. In 2003 its 'Summer in the Square' programme of al fresco events coincided with the sunniest summer for decades. We can't thank the mayoralty for the sunshine, but Mr Livingstone's stated aim to reduce car pollution in the city centre has, if nothing else, made sitting at pavement tables to enjoy the weather a rather less toxic experience.

GRIM READING

In the wake of each of these little victories, however, trail the qualifiers. First, that survey that found London so irresistible to business travellers judged it poorly on the 'quality of life index' for people who actually live here. Londoners, it appeared, considered themselves less happy than those in Rome, Munich and Dublin. The reason? Transport problems, traffic congestion, pollution and high prices.

These are the same negatives that come up whenever London is the subject of conversation. They're the reason the gloom merchants reckon the city hasn't a hope of being the Olympic venue in eight years' time. How, they say, can London be a serious contender for a prestigious world sporting event with its current transport system buckling, the potential for traffic gridlock, excessive levels of pollution and general air of chaos? Well, probably in much the same way as Athens can, but the bottom line is, of course, what in the name of Ken is to be done about London's appalling transport?

CHARGED UP

Ken Livingstone, who became Mayor of London in a landslide victory in May 2000, was voted in on the 'getting London moving' ticket. He was a comfortingly familiar face to many Londoners anyway, well known as a champion of public transport and enemy of the car from his days as leader of the defunct Greater London Council. Now the hottest favourite for another four years in office (the mayoral elections take place in June 2004), Mayor Ken is known as a tireless campaigner for improvements in every aspect of London life. Initiative after initiative has rolled out of City Hall since 2000, but the most significant achievement to date has been the Congestion Charge.

From 17 February 2003, anyone who wanted to drive their car into central London had to pay a £5 charge to do so. The idea was met with derision – for a year before the charge was levied the pundits were saying it would never work. A year on, the Congestion Charge has been hailed as a success – but rather too much of one. So many people have given up driving into London that there aren't enough £5 tolls going into the coffers to pay for the ambitious overhaul the public transport system needs. Nonetheless, walkers around the city centre now cannot fail to notice the drop in car numbers. Even if taxis and buses are still getting into a diesel-fumed ruck along the Strand, they're making better progress than they did in the days of free-for-all car travel.

'Improving this vast and in parts obsolete passenger transit system is going to take huge amounts of cash.'

The downside of the Congestion Charge is that many more people have turned to the Mayor's city transport provider, known as Transport for London, to get them moving. While their numbers have been mopped up with ease by the buses that are beautiful, fast, comfortable and new (*see p26* **Life in the bus lane**), too many travellers have hopped on to the tube. And the tube has gone into spasm.

2003 saw the Central line closed for months after an accident, the Piccadilly and Northern lines both briefly shut after derailments, and the whole system grind to a halt during a rush hour power cut. Improving this vast and in parts obsolete passenger transit system is going to take time and huge amounts of cash. The scene has been set, however, for improvements to the Underground. On 15 July London Underground Ltd was transferred from the government to the control of Transport for London in a deal known as the Public Private Partnership (PPP) . Under this banner, private money from business funds the tube's maintenance while public money through taxation pays for the management and operation of the system. Mayor Ken promises a 'safe, reliable and clean service' for the three million people who currently use it. It's early days for the new arrangements but already the number of stoppages and delays, along with the frequent strikes by tube workers, are testing the patience of the beleaguered tube traveller. Transport for London is up against it.

Commuters on overground rail are as familiar with hideous conditions as their companions-in-suffering below the surface. Overcrowded, expensive and fraught with delay, Network Rail has come in for an equally bad press from the disgruntled public. In a number of typically mischievous tabloid articles the inflated salaries commanded by various railway chiefs were set against the catalogue of disasters that users of their product had to face.

More positive was the long-awaited decision to go ahead with the new Crossrail transport link: a new £10 billion railway that will join Heathrow to the Isle of Dogs. It is hoped Crossrail will prove a selling point in the Olympic challenge. The leader of London's bid, Barbara Cassini, needs all the help she can get to convince sceptics that London can not only build world-class sporting venues but also provide an efficient transit system to ferry competitors and spectators between them. Opposition to the Olympic dream is mainly on the lines of 'and how much is all this going to cost?'. Both the Green and the Conservative opposition parties within the London Assembly have pointed out that overtaxed Londoners aren't going to love forking out the billions of pounds it will cost to host the Games, even if the potential earnings from the event are huge.

TOO TIGHT TO MENTION

Even without the onus of digging deep to pay for an Olympic building spree, many Londoners are finding it hard to make ends meet. As the city becomes more obviously divided between the extremes of wealth creation and success on the one hand, and deprivation and social exclusion on the other, many people on low-to-average incomes are choosing to give up on London. The cost of living in the city is beyond the £20,000 average salary of a teacher or nurse. Renting a flat is expensive, but buying one is out of reach – the grottiest little flat above a shop now costing upward of £100,000. At current rates, the buyer needs to earn at least £30,000 to afford a mortgage for it.

Affordable housing has therefore become a big issue for the Greater London Assembly and the Mayor. Although neither has the direct power to provide housing, they have a crucial role to play in dealing with London's accommodation problems. With a government

Life in the bus lane

He may not yet have managed to get the trains to run on time, but Mayor Ken Livingstone's increased bus budget has changed the face of bus travel in London. Quite literally in some cases. Some of the flashy new models that ply the bus lanes these days have enormous open-plan windscreens and what appears to be a smirk on their frontage. Look at the number 77A to Aldwych and you'll see what we mean.

The new models, and the elongated deck 'bendy buses' with their three-door system and concertina effect in the middle, are part of the Mayor's four-year campaign to get more people on the omnibus. Many London streets now have more tarmac devoted to bus lanes than to other traffic, and anyone caught driving their car in one of these dedicated thoroughfares can expect an £80 fine. Put these penalties together with the Congestion Charge, add in draconian parking restrictions and the speed cameras festooning any attractive stretch of highway and you get the picture: buses rule round here.

Nearly 80 per cent of Londoners now use buses regularly, and the new additions to the fleet and widespread use of pre-pay tickets means they travel much faster than they did four years ago. A new breed of bus driver, whose brief is apparently to keep their foot on the gas at all times, has the big red designer buses fairly hurtling down uncongested lanes. Hold very tight when negotiating the stairs to the top deck: violent braking occasioned by a devil-may-care taxi driver's foray into bus-only territory can send you catapulting down them before you've had a chance to grab the rail.

With all these new buses on the block – some have telly screens, others, such as the RV1 riverside bus, kitted out with sightseeing brochures for the tourists – the oldest model is struggling to maintain its dignity. We're talking about the Routemaster, the real icon in the bus lane. Routemasters are the buses with the open end which tempt a whole load of inter-bus-stop derring do, such as rakish pole-hanging and running leaps on to the footplate. All of which malarkey is going to have to stop. Routemasters, with their chuggy diesel engines, their conductors and their vertiginous stairs, some of which have been serving Londoners with nary a day off for 40 years, are slowly being phased out. They do not conform to rules about accessibility (they're useless to people in wheelchairs or travelling with babies in pushchairs) and must all be off the road by 2016. There are only 19 routes now served by Routmasters and there will even fewer by the end of 2004. The good news, however, is that some will be kept on the road for the benefit of tourists and romantic old fools like us who log on, misty eyed, to the website for Routemaster fans: www.routemaster.org.uk.

plan promising over £5 billion for housing investment in London and the South-east, including £1 billion for homes for key workers, it would seem that the situation can improve for the city's beleaguered would-be buyers. Once again, however, it is Livingstone's plans that really look most attractive to the low-paid house buyer, if they can be set in stone, or at least bricks and mortar. The Mayor supports the London Housing Strategy to provide at least 23,000 new homes in London per year. He has also pledged that of the 10,000 new homes planned for the Greenwich Peninsula (around the Millennium Dome site), 4,100 will be affordable or specialised low-cost homes.

► For more on **Trafalgar Square** *see p129.*
► For more on **public transport** *see p356.*
► For more on the **Congestion Charge** for car drivers *see p360.*

TOTALLY TURNED ON

To return to the bright side, London, with its cultural and artistic heritage, is an unrivalled place to visit for those who aren't looking for a three-bedroom semi in a desirable area, or rushing to a 9am meeting on the stopping service from Staines. The streets became safer in 2003 (crime was down 16 per cent), fewer cars choke them up and the Mayor's Totally London scheme made a range of attractions, restaurants and shows more affordable. The campaign was an effort to raise London's profile for guests and citizens. Rebranding the city's geographical heart as its cultural heart is the figurehead of the game plan. As the Mayor put it when Trafalgar Square and its patrolling 'heritage wardens' were unveiled, the square is now a 'high profile space representing the richness and diversity of culture in the capital'. And very lovely it is. But bear in mind, feeding the pigeons is forbidden and, if you plan to visit by train, you may experience some delays.

Deptford Pride – **Laban Centre**. *See p28.*

Architecture

From the sublime to the ridiculous – it's all here.

The government's decision to press ahead with a 2012 Olympic bid could be the biggest boost to the capital's architecture since the turn of the millennium. If London wins – and that's a big 'if' considering the competition from Paris, Madrid and New York – the city is going to have to pump vast sums of money into its decrepit East End (specifically, the Lower Lea Valley). This particular site has the twin benefit of being in serious need of urban regeneration and having land cheap and plentiful enough for the construction of the various stadia, Olympic villages and media centres.

Better still, the authorities might even be forced to add a sense of urgency to long-overdue plans to upgrade the capital's public transport infrastructure, which often seems to be held together by sticky tape and string. The capital breathed a collective sigh of relief in 2003 when it emerged that ministers had finally seen sense and agreed to give the green light to the long-awaited Crossrail scheme, an ambitious project that would permit mainline trains to run direct between Paddington and Liverpool Street, sparing commuters the agony of having to use the overcrowded tube lines between the two. Sadly, it is doubtful whether the scheme will be completely finished by 2012, so Crossrail is unlikely to feature as a part of London's Olympic bid.

Other schemes are also proceeding at a snail's pace, especially the oft-discussed redevelopment of the **South Bank Centre** arts complex. Pondering this thorny problem has become a common pastime and people have given up predicting an outcome. Essentially, the situation is this: that the complex, which takes up a good deal of Thames-side land to the north of Waterloo, has become a disjointed mess. People don't hate it, they just feel sorry for it. Meanwhile, the **Royal Festival Hall** (*see p73*) is in the throes of a £57 million refurbishment programme that will close the building for 15 months from the summer of 2005.

But the future of the concrete structures to the east is still unresolved. One idea was to construct a new complex of buildings, including an HQ for the British Film Institute underneath the nearby Jubilee Gardens. This caused a public outcry, however, and the scheme has been dropped. Instead, the park is to be landscaped into a 'world-class' public amenity. A coherent plan for the entire site, which includes the newly revamped **Hayward Gallery** (*see p73*), has been struggling to emerge for years. Grand designs have been biting the dust since the late 1980s.

All of which is terribly depressing. But it's not all bad. On the up side, the new, prizewinning **Laban Centre** in Deptford has had locals and architectural critics jumping for joy. Designed by Herzog & de Meuron (the Swiss design practice that masterminded the conversion of Bankside power station into Tate Modern), this multicoloured, iridescent object is the best thing to happen to south-east London for years. Quirky and well put-together, the building is sure to act as a spur for more urban regeneration, although Laban managers have not been best pleased with what is going before the planning officials. One developer proposed a block of flats that would both overshadow the Laban and spoil views of it. Pressure group the Creekside Forum told *Building Design* magazine the proposed flats were 'a great glass monster'.

Speaking of glass monsters, the result of the Heron Tower enquiry (which last year found in favour of the building on Bishopsgate) are almost certain to lead to a rash of applications to build tall buildings in the capital. Proposals are being published all the time, and a pair are almost certainly going to be built on the site of the present London Arena, whose sporting activities are likely to be moved to a freshly kitted-out **Dome**, on the Greenwich Peninsula (*see p167*). Another giant has been proposed to neighbour the original Canary Wharf tower.

At the same time, we await a decision on the future of the gigantic spike of **London Bridge Tower**, aka 'the Shard' (imagine Canary Wharf one third taller). English Heritage is dead against the scheme because, it says, it will ruin views of St Paul's, but other opponents have more sophisticated arguments – the main one being that, while the overall design of the building is good, the way it meets the ground is not. Architects speak of the building's 'footprint' and, in the Shard's case, critics argue that it is too big, lacks convincing public spaces and fails to integrate well enough with London Bridge railway station. Chances are, these problems will get resolved and the thing will be built. After all, Norman Foster's extraordinary **Swiss Re tower**, aka 'the Gherkin' (*see p83*), is already becoming a well-known and well-liked element of the London skyline.

Closer to the centre, the controversial **Paternoster Square** redevelopment was being unveiled as this guide went to press. Again, this has had a tortured history, largely because of its proximity to St Paul's and because of the unwanted attentions of Prince Charles. After more than ten years in the making, the result is a fairly restrained development that has tried hard to please everyone and delights almost no one. Architect Robert Adam calls it 'insipid classicism and dull modernist orthodoxy'.

Importantly (and thankfully), not all of London's new architecture is of the grand variety. There's plenty of smaller-scale stuff elbowing its way on to the capital's crowded streets. Take the **Cross**, for example, a small office development on King's Cross Road – an angular, metal-clad, four-storey scheme that gleams between its missable neighbours. Similarly, there's the steel and glass box that architect William Russell has built for himself a stone's throw from Brick Lane (he also designed the superb new Alexander McQueen store on Bond Street). And then there's the new ferry pier outside Tate Britain, an eye-catching, assymetrical steel and timber construction designed by the team behind the London Eye.

All good stuff, and these little gems are springing up all the time and will, eventually, begin to change the character of this elderly city. That is typical of this place. Unlike many other major cities, London has never been beautified or planned. It is a hotch potch, the product of a gradual accumulation of towns and villages, adapted, renewed and disfigured by the changing needs of its population. The tide of history has given London no distinctive architectural style, being at once imperial, industrial, medieval and experimental.

Too big for its brief

Built in three chunks that opened in 1922, 1933 and 1963, the neo-classical **County Hall** leapt into the public imagination in the early 1980s when Ken Livingstone made the building a political counterpoint to the Tory government over the river – a strategy that resulted in the abolition of the Greater London Council's in 1986. Since then, County Hall has only slowly re-entered the public consciousness, most recently as the venue for **Charles Saatchi**'s art collection (*see p73*).

Bought by the Osaka-based Shiriyama Corporation in 1991, Covent Garden-based architecture firm RHWL has been slowly waking this sleeping giant – resulting in a 200-bed Marriot, a 300-bed Travel Inn, a Namco gaming centre and the **London Aquarium** (*see p73*). Without anybody knowing it, smart new offices have been furnished for the Princess Diana Memorial Fund and the British Phonographic Institute, while pop impresario Pete Waterman has quietly put in a suite of four recording studios for musical wannabes – and a further five studios and a television project room are due to be added later this year.

Even with the addition of the 43,000-square-foot (4,000-square-metre) Saatchi Gallery, around one quarter of County Hall remains empty. Mr Shiriyama and co-director Mac Okamoto are in no hurry to occupy this most impressive and well-located space. There is no grand plan for County Hall, rather a general sense that it should become an all-purpose destination building.

'There is no brief, other than an aspiration to turn it into a family entertainment venue,' says RHWL partner Geoff Mann, adding that its owners are happy use it as a stick with which to poke the Establishment in the eye. 'Mac hates the British Establishment, he hates elitism, he hates the class system.'

He has good reason. After buying the building for £60 million, a rather snobbish and xenophobic campaign got underway to transfer ownership to the London School of Economics – a move which not only failed but bemused the new Japanese owners.

Most of the west wing, from the second floor upwards, lies empty and graffiti-strewn. These are spaces where anything could happen. Mann recalls that when he first toured the building, a man on a bike emerged out of the darkness, circumnavigated the room and disappeared again. 'I still don't know who he was,' he says.

Mann has been the inspiration behind many of the building's new uses. He was the one who first thought of building the London Aquarium here. Water has to be constantly pumped out of the basement because of WWII bomb damage, and a colleague joked about introducing fish.

The grand leather, oak and marble debating chamber – set squarely in the centre of this vast complex – is a conundrum. It's a peculiar place, unused since Red Ken vacated it. Nobody really knows what to do with it. This is the problem with a place like County Hall; its size defies the creation of an overall vision.

START WITH PUDDING LANE

The Great Fire of 1666 signalled the end of medieval London and the start of the city we know today. Commemorated by Christopher Wren's 202-foot (62-metre) high **Monument** (*see p92*), the fire destroyed five-sixths of the city, burning 13,200 houses and 89 churches.

But the city was asking for it. London was a densely populated city built of wood, where rubbish would go uncollected and fire control was primitive. It was only after a three-day inferno that the authorities felt they could insist on a few basic building regulations. From now on, brick and stone would be the construction materials of choice, and key streets would be widened to act as the fire breaks of the future. Most of what can now be seen is a testament to the talents of Wren and his successors.

In spite of grand proposals from architects hoping to remodel the city along Classical lines, London reshaped itself around its historic street pattern. And the buildings that had survived the fire stood as monuments to earlier ages. One building that managed to withstand the great heat, **St Ethelburga-the-Virgin** (*see p92*), is noteworthy as the city's smallest chapel as well as for its splendid name. Sadly, where the fire failed, the IRA succeeded, destroying two-thirds of this 13th-century building in a 1993 bomb attack. The church has now been reconstructed as a peace and reconciliation centre.

The Norman **Tower of London** (*see p94*), begun soon after William's 1066 conquest and extended over the next 300 years, remains the country's most perfect example of a medieval fortress. This is thanks to the Navy, which

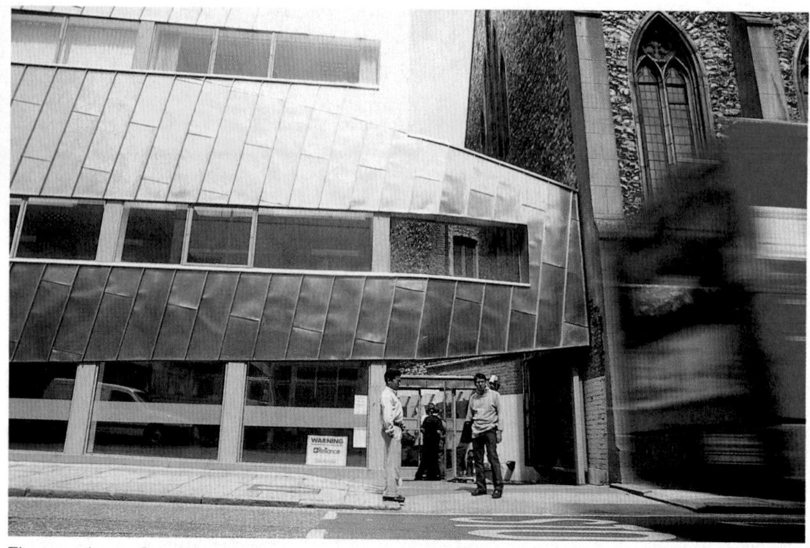

The wondrous **Cross** looks classy on King's Cross Road. *See p28.*

cheated the advancing flames of the Great Fire of London six centuries earlier by blowing up the houses surrounding the historic tower before the inferno could get to them.

And then there is **Westminster Abbey** (*see p133*), begun in 1245 when the site lay far outside London's walls and completed in 1745 when Nicholas Hawksmoor added the west towers. Cathedrals are never really finished, though: the statues set over the main entrance, with Martin Luther King taking centre stage, were added just a couple of years ago. Although the abbey is the most French of England's Gothic churches, deriving its geometry, flying buttresses and rose windows from across the Channel, the chapel, added by Henry VII and completed in 1512, is pure Tudor.

'Inigo Jones changed British architecture forever.'

The Renaissance made its laggardly London debut with Inigo Jones's 1622 **Banqueting House** (*see p131*). The addition of a gorgeously decorated ceiling by Rubens in 1635, celebrating the benefits of wise rule, made the building a must-see for the public who could watch from the balconies as Charles I dined. As it turned out, the King's wisdom was a trifle lacking: 14 years later, he provided the public with an even greater spectacle as he was led from the building and beheaded.

Tourists have Jones to thank for **Covent Garden** (*see p121*) and the **Queen's House** at Greenwich (*see p168*), but these are not his only legacies. By the 1600s Italian architecture, rooted in the forms and geometries of the Roman era, was all the rage. So, as a dedicated follower of fashion, Inigo Jones became proficient in the art of piazzas, porticos and pillasters, changing British architecture forever. His work not only influenced the careers of succeeding generations of architects, but introduced an unhealthy habit of venerating the past that would take 300 years to kick. Even today, London has a knack for glueing fake classical extras over the doors of cheap buildings in the hope it will lend a little dignity.

GOD IS IN THE DETAIL

Taking their cue from Jones, Christopher Wren and his contemporaries brandished classicism like a new broom: the pointed arches of English Gothic were rounded off, Corinthian columns appeared and church spires became as multi-layered as a baroque wedding cake. Indeed, the spire of Wren's **St Bride**, Fleet Street, is said to have inspired the wedding cake.

Wren blazed the trail with daring plans for **St Paul's Cathedral** (*see p87*), spending an astonishing £500 on the oak model of his proposal. But the scheme, incorporating a Catholic dome rather than Protestant steeple, was too Roman for the reformist tastes of the Establishment and the design was rejected. To his credit, the undaunted architect did what any wounded ego would do. He quickly produced a redesign and gained planning permission by incorporating the much-loved spire, only to set about a series of mischievous U-turns once work had commenced, giving us the building – domed and heavily suggestive of an ancient temple – that has survived to this day.

So prolific was the building of churches that Londoners turned a blind eye to the odd synagogue. Allowed back into England by Oliver Cromwell in 1657, the city's Sephardic community from Spain and Portugal later commissioned a Quaker to build them a simple and elegant home in a quiet enclave. **Bevis Marks Synagogue** (2 Heneage Lane, The City, EC3), the UK's oldest, was completed in 1701 and gives little of its semitic purpose away from the outside… and very little internally. It is a tribute to the pride lavished on the building that the extraordinary chandeliers that festoon the interior have yet to be electrified, leaving the staff to spend hours lighting and extinguishing hundreds of candles for each service.

After Wren, Nicholas Hawksmoor and James Gibbs benefited from an anxiety that London's population was becoming ungodly. The 1711 initiative to construct an extra 50 churches was, therefore, a career opportunity. Gibbs became busy in and around Trafalgar Square, building the steepled Roman temple that is **St Martin-in-the-Fields** (*see p128*), the baroque **St Mary-le-Strand** (Strand, WC2; now set against the monstrous lump of King's College) and the tower of **St Clement Danes** (*see p96*).

Gibbs's work was well received, but the more prolific and experimental Hawksmoor had a rougher ride (*see p155*). His imposing **St Anne's** (Commercial Road, Limehouse, E14) proved so costly that the parish was left with insufficient funds to pay for a vicar, and **St George** in Bloomsbury (Bloomsbury Way, WC1) also broke the bank. Hawksmoor spent three times its £10,000 budget and took 15 years to build it, although the cracks in the interior suggest the renovation programme the church is currently undergoing (it will be closed until after Christmas 2004) is long overdue.

St George's tries to evoke the spirit of the ancients. Rather than a spire, there is a pyramid topped by a statue of George I decked out in a toga, while the interior boasts all the Corinthian columns, round arches and gilding you'd expect from a man steeped in Antiquity. Many of these features are repeated in Hawksmoor's rocket-like **Christ Church Spitalfields** (*see p155*), currently undergoing much-needed restoration. Strangely, this dedication to his subject never extended to seeing the ancient sights at first hand, and Hawksmoor never left the country.

ADAM AND SOANE

Robert Adam was a considerable traveller. One of a large family of Scottish architects, Adam was at the forefront of a movement that came to see Italian baroque as a corruption of the real thing. Such architectural exuberance was eventually dropped in favour of a much simpler interpretation of the ancient forms.

The best surviving work of Adam and his brothers James, John and William can be found in London's great suburban houses **Osterley Park**, **Syon House** (*see p188* for both) and **Kenwood House** (*see p150* **The crown of Iveagh**), but the project for which they are most famous no longer stands. In 1768 they embarked on the cripplingly expensive Adelphi housing estate (after the Greek for 'brothers') off the Strand. Built over vaults used to store goods offloaded from river barges, most of the complex was pulled down in the 1930s, but part of the original development survives in what is now the **Royal Society for the Arts** (8 John Adam Street, Covent Garden, WC2), a good example of how the family relieved the simplicity of brick with elegant plasterwork.

'Regent Street began as a device to separate the toffs and the riff-raff.'

Just as the first residents were moving into the Adelphi, a young unknown called John Soane was embarking on a tour of his own. In Rome, Soane met the wealthy Bishop of Derry who persuaded the 25-year-old to abandon his travels and accompany him to Ireland in order to build a house. In the end, though, the project came to nothing. Soane dealt with the setback by working hard and marrying into money.

His loss is our gain, however, as he went on to build the Bank of England and the recently remodelled **Dulwich Picture Gallery** (*see p170*). Sadly, the Bank was demolished between the wars, leaving nothing but the perimeter walls and depriving London of what is said to have been Soane's masterpiece. But a hint of what these ignorant bankers might have enjoyed can be gleaned from a visit to Soane's house, now the **Sir John Soane's Museum** (*see p97*), a collection of exquisite architectural experiments with mirrors, coloured glass and folding walls. During museum tours, the architectural inventiveness of Soane's work makes visitors gasp out loud.

A committed Mason, Soane shared the fascination with death that seems to characterise the fraternity. The Dulwich Picture Gallery incorporates a dimly lit mausoleum containing the earthly remains of the building's

Pretty old

Apart from the obvious picture postcard images, St Pancras Station is arguably one of London's most recognisable buildings. So, too, is Battersea power station, that neglected, iconic shell that looks like a giant upturned table. And then there's St Martin-in-the-Fields, the 18th-century church overlooking Trafalgar Square.

London is full of buildings like this – elderly, under-used and crumbling. Bankside power station was just one more of these until Lottery cash funded its reincarnation into **Tate Modern** a couple of years back.

But things are about to change.

Planning permission has been granted to turn **St Pancras Chambers** (the building that fronts the railway station) back into what it was designed for – a hotel. The edifice – like something out of a particularly dark fairy tale – is London's best example of High Victorian Gothic. It ceased to be used as the Grand Midland Hotel in 1935 when it became too expensive to run. Since then it's been semi-derelict as BR offices or just ignored completely. The plan is now to turn it into a five-star, 300-bed Marriott, with upmarket apartments built by the Manhattan Loft Company slotted into its huge attic spaces. Scheduled for completion in 2008, this development will make it the ideal sleepover for people newly-arrived on the Eurostar, which will be running into a vastly expanded St Pancras Station from 2007.

St Martin-in-the-Fields (*see p128*), too, is to undergo a renaissance. This is hardly a derelict building, of course, but a cash injection is long overdue. Now £34 million will pay for restoration, build a new public space on the site of the existing market and renew and expand the crypt spaces below ground. Drawings from designer Eric Parry (one of London's more intelligent and sensitive architects) show that you will be able to stand in the crypt, look up through a lightwell and see the steeple of the church framed above.

Not all elderly buildings have been so lucky. Grandiose plans for **Battersea power station** have gone quiet. Although all the planning permissions are now in place, many worry that nothing is going to happen to it for some time. This may not be such a bad thing – the developers have been planning a 'mixed-use' scheme of shops, flats, cinemas, and just about everything else you can think of. Mixed-use is all right, but it's also the last resort for people who can't think of a better idea.

Part of Smithfield meat market is also up for regeneration, so is an ex-wallpaper factory in Islington, a clutch of Victorian schools and the buildings currently inhabited by **Chelsea Art School** (which is moving into an old army hospital). Lack of space drives us to reinvent and reclaim these old buildings, but whether they'll end up any good (and whether future generations will have to undo the damage done by ours), is yet to be seen.

benefactors, a rehearsal for the design of his own resting place. This is worth the walk north to the churchyard of **St Pancras Old Church**: just look for the square tomb with the curving roof – one of only two Grade I-listed tombs in the country, the other being that of Karl Marx.

A near-contemporary of Soane, John Nash was arguably a less talented architect, but his contributions to the fabric of London have proved greater. Among his buildings are **Buckingham Palace** (*see p113*), the **Haymarket Theatre** (Haymarket, St James's, W1) and **Regent Street** (W1). The latter began as a proposal to link the West End to the planned park further north, as well as a device to effect, in Nash's words, 'a complete separation between the Streets occupied by the Nobility and Gentry, and the narrow Streets and meaner houses occupied by mechanics and the trading part of the community'.

THE NEW ROMANTICS

By the 1830s the classical form had been established for 200 years, and a handful of upstarts began pressing for change. In 1834, the **Houses of Parliament** burned down, leading to the construction of Charles Barry's Gothic masterpiece (*see p132*). This was the beginning of the Gothic Revival, a move to replace foreign and pagan styles with one that was not only native but Christian. The architectural profession was divided, but the argument was never resolved, merely made irrelevant by the advent of modernism a century later.

Barry would have preferred a classical design, but the brief was unambiguous and Gothic was to prevail. He needed help, and sought out designer Augustus Welby Northmore Pugin. The result of Pugin's labours was a Victorian fantasy that, while a fine example of the perpendicular form, shows how the Middle Ages had become distorted in the minds of 19th-century architects. New buildings were constructed as a riot of turrets, towers and winding staircases that would today be condemned as the Disney-fication of history.

Even in renovating ancient buildings, architects would often decide that they weren't Gothic enough; as with the 15th-century **Guildhall** (*see p89*), which gained its corner turrets and central spire in 1862. Bombed by the Luftwaffe, the Guildhall was rebuilt much as the Victorians had left it, apart from the statues of Gog and Magog, protagonists in a legendary battle between ancient Britain and Troy.

The argument between the classicists and Goths erupted in 1857, when the government commissioned Sir George Gilbert Scott, a leading light of the Gothic movement, to design a new HQ for the Foreign Office. Scott's design incensed anti-Goth Lord Palmerstone, then prime minister, whose diktats prevailed. But Scott exacted his revenge by building an office in which everyone hated working, and by going on to construct Gothic edifices all over the capital, among them the **Albert Memorial** (*see p139*) and **St Pancras Station** (*see p103*).

St Pancras was completed in 1873, after the Midland Railway commissioned Scott to build a London terminus that would dwarf that of their rivals next door at King's Cross. Using the project as an opportunity to show his mastery of the Gothic form, Scott built an asymmetrical castle that obliterated views of the train shed behind, itself an engineering marvel completed earlier by William Barlow. This 'incongruous medievalism' did not go unnoticed by contemporary critics, prompting one to write that company directors should go the whole hog and dress their staff in period costume.

Still, the Gothic style was to dominate until the 20th century, leaving London littered with imposing buildings such as the **Royal Courts of Justice** (*see p96*), the **Natural History Museum** (*see p135*), **Liberty** (*see p233*) and **Tower Bridge** (*see p94*). World War I and the coming of modernism led to a spirit of renewal, resulting in the handsome **Royal Institute of British Architects** (aka RIBA; *see p106*), **Freemason's Hall** (Great Queen Street, WC2) and the **BBC's Broadcasting House** (Portland Place, Marylebone, W1), all examples of the pared-down style of the '20s and '30s.

MODERN TASTES

Perhaps the finest example of between-the-wars Modernism can be found at **London Zoo** (*see p108*). Built by Russian émigré Bethold Lubetkin and the Tecton group, the spiral ramps of the Penguin Pool were a showcase for the possibilities of concrete, which was also put to good use on the Underground: it enabled the quick and cheap building of large, cavernous spaces with the sleek lines and curves associated with speed. The Piccadilly line was a particular beneficiary: its 1930s expansion yielded the likes of Charles Holden's **Arnos Grove Station**, the first of many circular station buildings and the model for the new Canada Water Station on the Jubilee line.

There was nothing quick or cheap about the art deco **Daily Express building** (Fleet Street, The City, EC4). A black glass and chrome structure built in 1931, it is an early example of 'curtain wall' construction where the façade is literally hung on to an internal frame. Recently refurbished and extended for a new occupant, the developers have, happily, not compromised the deco detailing of the original building, leaving the crazy flooring, snake handrails and funky lighting. Being a corporate HQ, public access is not guaranteed, but it's worth sticking your head around the door of what the *Architects' Journal* has called a 'defining monument of 1930s London'.

POST-WAR DRAB

Lamentably, the city was little improved by the rebuild following destruction wrought by World War II, and, in many cases, was left worse off. The capital's dire housing shortage gave architects a chance to demonstrate the speed and efficiency with which they could house large numbers of families in tower blocks. Many were not a success, partly because of poor build quality, partly because of lack of maintenance. Many have now been pulled down, but others – such as Sir Denys Lasdun's fabulous 'cluster block' **Keeling House** in Bethnal Green – have been reclaimed and offered up to wealthy private tenants.

The legacy of post-war architecture is viewed with anything from suspicion to horror by most Londoners, an experience that has both tempered the arrogance of the architectural profession and created a planning process that places so many hurdles in the way of developers that it's a wonder anything gets built at all. There are notable exceptions, however, including the **Royal Festival Hall** on the South Bank (*see p73*). The sole survivor of the 1951 Festival of Britain, the RFH was built to celebrate the war's end and the centenary of the Great Exhibition (the event that gave us Joseph Paxton's Crystal Palace, which burnt down in 1936). In spite of its size, the Festival Hall can be a crowded and awkward space, but refurbishment work is restoring what little grandeur the builders of post-war Britain managed to impart. It's now a much-loved piece of London's fabric – unlike the neighbouring **Hayward Gallery** (*see p73*) and **Queen Elizabeth Hall** (*see p302*), concrete, windowless structures and exemplars of the '60s vogue for brutalist experimentation.

But brutalism (a term of dubious origin; some say it reflects the brutal lives of the British working class, others that it derives from the French for rough concrete – *beton brut*) couldn't last forever. The '70s and '80s offered up a pair of architectural replacements: postmodernism and high tech. The former is represented by Cesar Pelli's **Canary Wharf** tower (Isle of Dogs, E14) an oversized obelisk that has become the archetypal expression of 1980s architecture and holds an ambiguous place in the city's affections. Its splendid isolation lent it an element of star quality, but the building boom has provided this beacon with equally large neighbours, opening up another part of the city's low-rise skyline to high-rise clutter.

Richard Rogers' **Lloyd's Building** (Lime Street, The City, EC3) is London's best-known example of high tech, where commercial and industrial aesthetics combine to produce one of the most significant British buildings since the war. Mocked upon completion in 1986, the building still outclasses more recent projects, a fact not lost on Channel 4 when it commissioned Rogers to design its new HQ in Horseferry Road, SW1, in the early 1990s.

Such projects are rapidly making London a showcase for brave and innovative buildings. Future Systems' NatWest Media Centre at **Lord's Cricket Ground** (*see p144*), built from aluminium in a boatyard and perched high above the pitch, is a daring construction, especially given its traditional, old-world setting. Will Alsop's **Peckham Library** (171 Peckham Hill Street, Peckham, SE15) redefined community architecture so comprehensively that it walked away with the £20,000 Stirling Prize in 2000. The annual award, bestowed by the Royal Institute of British Architects, fielded a particularly strong shortlist in the millennium year, including the **British Airways London Eye** (*see p70*), a 450ft (137metre)-high global icon, and Norman Foster's **Canary Wharf Station** on the Jubilee line, a poem in concrete.

The problem with being innovative, though, is that things can go wrong. And there's no better example of this than the daring **Millennium Bridge**, which links St Paul's with Tate Modern, created by Foster and engineers Arup. Designed as an elegantly thin suspension structure, the bridge's opening descended into farce when it began to sway noticeably. This steel and aluminium structure now offers a wobble-free crossing to pedestrians and skateboarders. There's even talk of slinging a similar bridge between Chelsea and Battersea.

OLD BUILDINGS, NEW TRICKS

In consort with a small but vocal army of conservationists, an architectural 'green belt' forces architects to work with old buildings rather than pull them down. Done well, the new is grafted on to the old in a way that is often invisible from street level; visitors will be surprised by the way contemporary interiors have been inserted into elderly buildings.

Fortunately, the best examples of this can be found in the public museums and art galleries, many of which have undergone millennium makeovers and expansion programmes. The **National Portrait Gallery** (*see p128*) and the **Royal Opera House** (*see p122*) both show how architects have successfully added modern signatures to old buildings. The **British Museum** (*see p101*), the **National Maritime Museum** (*see p168*) and the **Wallace Collection** (*see p107*) have gone one better. With the help of large Lottery grants and glass roofs, these last have considerably added to their facilities by invading what were once external courtyards. Foster's exercise in complexity at the British Museum, where the spectacular £100 million Great Court has created the largest covered square in Europe, is most impressive – every one of its 3,300 triangular glass panels is unique.

The National Gallery is also next in line for this treatment, with Dixon.Jones, the architects responsible for redeveloping the NPG and the opera house, planning to slot new galleries and public spaces into what are presently hidden courtyards of little practical value.

It's this mentality that made possible the conversion of Sir Giles Gilbert Scott's power station into a premier league art venue, **Tate Modern** (*see p78*), making a mockery of the architectural mantra 'form follows function'. This imposing edifice was dragged from obscurity and thrust before an adoring public by Swiss architects Herzog & de Meuron, who preserved much of the original building while installing seven new floors of exhibition space.

None of these architectural gems counts for much if London's visitors can't get to them – or if they choke on vehicle emissions on the way. Richard Rogers' ambitious plans for a **Terminal 5** at Heathrow have finally been given the green light, and it looks like the East London line is to be extended into Hackney. And then there are plans to lengthen the Docklands Light Railway as far as City Airport. One architectural practice has even suggested constructing a monorail along Euston Road. As they say, desperate problems require radical solutions, and no problem is more desperate than this city's collapsing transport infrastructure.

Westminster Bridge, immortalised by William Wordsworth.

London in Verse

This lyric city both inspires and repels the poetic soul.

In London the streets are not paved with gold but etched with poems. Literally – you can see them in the pavement slabs along the South Bank. Even the tube trains have sonnets pasted up among the ads for exotic holidays, exciting new computer software and pregnancy tests. Love of the lyric arts has even provided the city with a dedicated Poetry Library of 80,000 books. For the versifiers, the city can provide any number of official positions to be resident in, garrets to starve in and suburbs to despair in. Modern poets, like the oral poet Benjamin Zephaniah, perform and attend the dozens of poetry events listed weekly in the press. The great poets of the past are commemorated with plaques and statues. Such is the respect afforded John Keats that the London house in which he languished for two years is a shrine with its own poetry reading room (*see p148*). Keats is one of many poets with a memorial in the stone heart of Westminster Abbey.

In fact, the British, who have given nothing more lasting to the world than their language, treat their poets, the custodians of the tongue, with the reverence others pay to saints.

DEAD POETS SOCIETY

Poets' Corner, the usual name for the south transept of **Westminster Abbey** (*see p133*), has been the burial place of writers ever since Geoffrey Chaucer was laid to rest there in 1400. Their memorials blend with the stonework, unnoticeable at first. Then the visitor spots Tennyson under a long black marble slab and, next to him, the World War I poets Brooke, Owen, Sassoon and a dozen others bundled together as if in a mass grave. Suddenly, you notice every stone and window panel bears an inscription. More than 100 poets are commemorated here. There are Keats and Shelley on teardrop tablets linked by a wreath about the head of Shakespeare, and Dylan Thomas's plaque is flat on the floor, just as they used to find him lying in New York gutters.

Thomas Hardy was buried here without his heart – which was removed for a separate ceremony in Dorset and then supposedly eaten by his dog as it lay on a sideboard. Poets' bones are kept in London, but their hearts are all too often elsewhere.

Poetic licence...

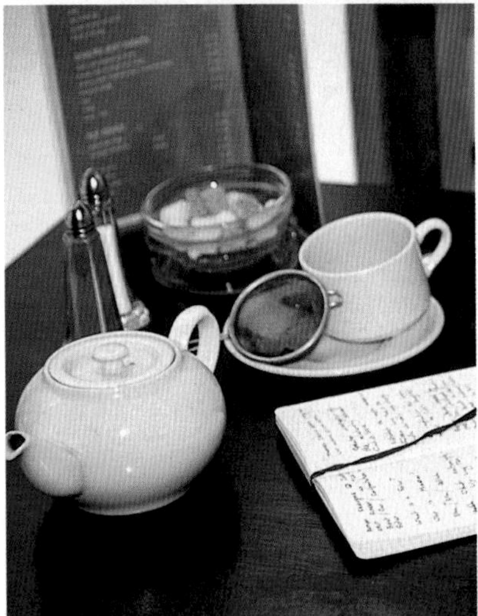

plus tea and inspiration, at the **Poetry Café**.

CAPITAL INSPIRATIONS

It was with the enthusiasm of an excited and impressed visitor that William Wordsworth wrote of the views of London from his vantage point on Westminster Bridge. But his heart, of course, was in the wilds of the picturesque Lake District. Indeed, his trips to London were occasional and his view of the city may possibly have been idealistic.

Another rather wide-eyed visitor was the 15th-century Scottish diplomat and sometime Franciscan friar William Dunbar. He visited London as Ambassador for James IV, and his lines on the visit suggest he had a high old time in the Tudor city among 'lords, barons, many goodly knights… and delectable lusty ladies bright'. Dunbar chooses not to expand, in this poem, on the jolly times he may or may not have enjoyed in the 'flower of cities all'. He was not above the bawdy, though. Some historians credit Dunbar as having been responsible for the first printed use of the word 'fuck' (1508).

Not so John Wilmot, Earl of Rochester, writing in the 17th century, who delights lewdly in the nightly 'rapes, buggeries and incests' made among the glades of St James's Park. An attractive man and a war hero, he was everyone's favourite libertine-about-town and a frequent visitor in the Restoration court of Charles II, although he was as often banished for bad behaviour as he was welcomed for his wit. His poems are full of the filthiest words imaginable. If there had been a censor around then, we probably wouldn't have a stanza to remember him by.

A less effusive view of London life is given by poets who had to earn a crust here. A blue plaque at 3 Kensington Court Gardens, W8, announces that the poet Thomas Stearns Eliot lived and died in the Royal Borough of Kensington and Chelsea. A brief stint working as a bank clerk prior to the publication of his first volume of poetry gave him personal experience of the existential angst for which he pities the poor souls trudging over London Bridge in *The Waste Land*, a lament for the civilisation of the 20th century contrasted with earlier and finer ages. His inspiration in this poem was the dead-eyed commuters he saw travelling to work every morning. Of course, some would have said those were the lucky ones. The poet and comedian Spike Milligan recalled the hideous sense of disillusionment in the grey of south-east London's mean suburbs after an idyllic early childhood in India. Holed up in cramped quarters in Lewisham, his father decommissioned from the army and looking for work, Milligan recalled the horror of those dark days in the poverty-stricken London of the 1930s in his poem *Catford*, written in 1979. London writers are always there when you need them to deliver unpalatable truths.

SONNET BOOM

Unpalatable truths of the late 20th century were, and continue to be, given voice by a new generation of poets who aim less for publication and more for presenting their poetry as performance art. The growth of the number of performing poets in the capital over the last two decades has been phenomenal. Black writers such as Benjamin Zephaniah, Lemn Sissay and Grace Nichols have fuelled the upsurge of interest with their own style of vibrant and witty verse. Their work lacks the obscurities of poetry forged in ivory towers, and addresses life from an angle that many people recognise.

The fact that live performance is now the preferred medium for such poetry rather than publication makes it similar, but for length, to the ancient Greek conception of poetry. In those days, aged longbeards would relate the history of a people or a war to the descriptive accompaniment of a lyre, and now London has returned to the Homerian ideal, albeit in abbreviated form. The whoops of large audiences at poetry events held in venues around the capital (and listed weekly in *Time Out* magazine) indicate that the city offers a welcoming reception to this art form.

Poetry Central in London is the **Poetry Place**, in Covent Garden (22 Betterton Street). This is the headquarters of the **Poetry Society** (7420 9880), a sort of industry HQ, which now also include a licensed café (**The Poetry Café**, 7420 9888). Twenty years ago the society occupied a building full of desks and paper and so many marble busts that many of them were used as door-stops. Now, along with booze, there is a performance space in the basement that draws large enthusiastic crowds for poetry evenings (and on Saturdays, poetry and jazz together). What used to be considered a dry and dusty art form now has a measure of excitement in its image.

The same could be said of the bohemian west London old timer, the **Troubadour Café** (265 Old Brompton Road, SW5, 7370 1434), although the versification occurs somewhat less frequently (every other Monday from 8pm). Likewise the **Pentameters Theatre** in Hampstead (in the Three Horseshoes, 28 Heath Street, NW3, 7435 3648), where weekly poetry events take place in the pub's upper room. Anyone may contribute after the invited guest writers have performed, so bring your own elegies, sonnets and villanelles.

Poetry in motion

Poems on the Underground – the pasting on tube trains of selected poems as if they were ads – have been part of the transport scenery for the last 17 years. A welcome and widely emulated feature of city life, the verses enable Londoners to educate themselves, even when they're in the most tedious of circumstances.

The idea first came to the poet Judith Chernaik after she saw the poems carved in flagstones along the South Bank. The scheme was such a success that it has now been copied by more than 100 cities around the world.

It all began in 1986, when Chernaik raised money for 500 advertising spaces on tube trains and persuaded London Underground to match it. Impressed by the response, the agency eventually decided to give Chernaik 2,000 spaces on its 4,000 tube carriages free of charge for two out of every four months. (No poems go on the Piccadilly line, because advertising on the Heathrow service is just too valuable.)

The new owner of the tube, Transport for London, has agreed to continue the arrangement. Poems are selected three times a year, and while many are by new, young writers, the old and historic are not ignored. After they've appeared on the tube, the poems are gathered in anthologies. The tenth edition was published in 2002, and celebrated with an above-ground concert and celebrity reading at Conway Hall in Holborn (*see p97*).

Capital lines

London has been immortalised in the work of great poets across the centuries. Not all of them were as complimentary as the happy tourist Wordsworth, moved to rapturous verse by his bridgetop sojourn.

'Earth hath not anything to show more fair:
Dull would he be of soul who could pass by
A sight so touching in its majesty:'
Upon Westminster Bridge, **William Wordsworth** (1770-1850)

'Hell is a city much like London –
A populous and smoky city.'
Peter Bell the Third, **Percy Bysshe Shelly** (1792-1822)

'O London's a fine town and London sights are rare
And London ale is right ale, and brisk's the London air,
And busily goes the world there but crafty grows the mind
And London Town of all towns I'm glad to leave behind.'
London Town, **John Masefield** (1878-1967)

'The coconuts are getting paid.
Men, women and Brixton are being betrayed.'
The Race Industry, **Benjamin Zephaniah** (born 1958)

'Unreal city,
Under the brown fog of a winter dawn,
A crowd flowed over London Bridge, so many,
I had not thought death had undone so many.'
The Waste Land, **TS Eliot** (1888-1965)

WHERE THE POETS ARE

In the wonderful 50-year-old **Poetry Library** (7921 0943/www.poetrylibrary.org.uk) noticeboards flap with listings for readings, groups, conferences, courses and workshops all over the city and beyond. The 80,000 volumes of poetry contained here include poetry for children and teachers, poetry on tape, record and video and a huge collection of literary magazines. The library is on the fifth floor (west side) of the **Royal Festival Hall** (*see p73*), and has a window on to the Thames. The entrance to the collection is marked by the renowned 'Lost Quotations' board into which the librarians slot half-remembered lines of poetry handed in by members of the public. Some, alas, never find owners. 'Youth had left me long abandoned' has been on the board since 1963. Half the library's collection is for hire. The 40,000 reference only-books sit on large movable shelves that readers can operate themselves (once they've checked that no one is standing between them – there have been nasty incidences of poet-crushing).

Next door to the library is the Festival Hall's dedicated poetry performance space, known as the **Voice Box** (bookings on 7921 3906). It opens at least once a week for events and hosts readings by visiting poets from all over the world, both established and unknown.

Venture outside the Festival Hall to walk along the **Jubilee Walkway** – created during the 25th year of the Queen's reign in 1977 – and once again you find words underfoot. Lines from TS Eliot's *The Waste Land*, Sheridan's *The Woman of Fashion*, Wordsworth's *In Remembrance of Collins*, Luttrell's *A London Fog 1822*, and Spenser's *Prothalamion* are etched into the slabs along a pleasant riverside mile. The poetry shares the paving with pieces of sculpture such as Sir Frank Dobson's *London Pride* (two women and a bowl), which was commissioned for the Festival of Britain in 1951. To have one's work carved into the concrete is an honour for a poet: Sue Hubbard, a former *Time Out* journalist, must have swelled with London pride to see her lovelorn lyric adorning the walls of the tunnel from Waterloo Station to the IMAX Cinema (*see p284*).

The greatest honour of all, though, is to have your poetic bones laid to rest, or at least to earn an engraving to your memory, in Westminster Abbey. As might be expected, it can take the abbey a while to come around to more controversial writers – it was a century before the great playwright and general wit Oscar Wilde was granted a window pane, in 1999. Indeed, the latest to receive a memorial in Westminster Abbey is Christopher Marlowe, the master of blank verse, who lived so disreputable a life that he had to wait 400 years for access. Not for no reason, of course. Marlowe died in 1593, after a drunken pub brawl in Deptford, south-east London, just before he was scheduled to go on trial for atheism, then a capital offence. He said, 'I count religion but a childish toy, and hold there is no sin but ignorance'. Today, the line that outraged God-fearing folk is quoted in stone (with 'darkness' instead of 'sin') on a statue (apparently of Shakespeare) in the middle of Leicester Square.

Where to Stay

Features

Half price London hotels.
Every day.

You can now book your hotel by phone on 0207 437 4370
International: +44 207 437 4370

Where to Stay

Desire the luxury. Check the rates. Have a lie down.

For London hoteliers, the last year has been an *annus horribilis*. During the first half of 2003, occupancy rates dropped to an average of 69 per cent – the worst since 1996. This trend was attributed to a general reluctance to travel, particularly during the war on Iraq, when rates dipped to a measly 67.1 per cent. The panic over the SARS virus just rubbed salt into the wound.

Luck favours the brave, however: those travellers who made the trip were offered bargains galore. Herein lies the paradox: while a fear of terrorism is bad for business, it might finally give London hoteliers a badly needed kick up the backside. Because, let's face it, terrorism isn't the only thing scaring off visitors. London, it seems, has the priciest hotel rooms in the world. A survey by property company Jones Lang LaSalle in 2003 found a night's stay in London cost more than twice the price of a night in Sydney, Toronto, Edinburgh or San Francisco, and 25 times the room rate in Mexico City. A night in some of London's luxury hotels costs more than a month's rent for many Londoners.

The special packages and extras London hoteliers are offering while feeling the pinch should be permanent fixtures, not just the response to a crisis. Ian Schrager is learning the hard way: the king of the boutique hotel – his London properties include the **Sanderson** and **St Martin's Lane** (*see p46* and *p53*) – was reported to have financial problems in 2003. Le Meridien luxury hotel chain, was also having money problems. In the midst of all this strife, the opening within months of each other of **City Inn Westminster** (30 John Islip Street, SW1P 4DD, 7630 1000) – a 460-room luxury extravaganza, the largest new-build hotel in London for 30 years – and International Luxury Hotels' splendid 64-room **Bentley** (27-33 Harrington Gardens, SW7 4JK, 7370 6486) – with Turkish bath and spa – seem audacious. Just what London needs: more expensive luxury hotels. Especially when its cheap hotels are, generally speaking, so poor: poky rooms and shared bathrooms are the norm. For that reason, many visitors prefer to stick to bland but reliable chains (*see p56*).

Many of London's swankier hotels are in **Mayfair**. **Bloomsbury** is good for mid-priced hotels. For cheap ones, try Ebury Street near **Victoria** (SW1), Gower Street in **Bloomsbury** (WC1) and **Earl's Court** (SW5). Other areas worth exploring for budget hotels include **Bayswater**, **Paddington** (W2) and **South Kensington** (SW7).

INFORMATION AND BOOKING

If you haven't booked ahead, the obliging staff at **Visit London** will look for a place within your selected area and price range for a £5 fee. You can also check availability and reserve rooms on its website.

Visit London Booking Line
7932 2020/www.visitlondon.com. **Open** 9am-6pm Mon-Fri; 10am-2pm Sat.

PRICES AND CLASSIFICATION

Though British hotels are classified according to a star system agreed by the English Tourism Council, the AA and the RAC, we don't list star ratings, which tend to reflect facilities rather than quality; instead, we've classified hotels,

The best Hotels

For your wallet
Chic comes cheap at the **Rushmore Hotel** in Earl's Court. *See p63*.

For your ego
'Nuff respect at the **Dorchester**. *See p49*.

For your image
Hob nob with the stars at the **Covent Garden Hotel**. *See p52*.

For your chi
Let it flow freely in sleek **myhotel bloomsbury**. *See p45*.

For your physique
Hit the gym at the **Sanderson**. *See p46*.

For your lungs
No cigs at the **Jenkins Hotel**. *See p46*.

For your stomach
Book well ahead for a meal to remember at Gordon Ramsay, **Claridge's**. *See p49*.

For your sanity
Float away at **One Aldwych**. *See p52*.

within their area headings, according to the price of the cheapest double room per night.

Despite the fact that VAT is included in the quoted price of almost everything in the UK, many high-end hotels sneakily quote room prices exclusive of the tax. Always ask whether the price you're being quoted includes tax or not. We've included the 17.5 per cent VAT (sales tax) in prices listed here; however, room prices change frequently, so do call and verify prices before you book.

Many hotels that attract business travellers offer discounted rates on weekends: deals are often available throughout the year via hotels' websites. Check online for special offers.

FACILITIES AND ACCESSIBILITY

We've listed the main services offered by each hotel, but always check before booking if you require a particular service, such as babysitting, which many of the high-end hotels can arrange for young guests. Rooms in hotels listed as Deluxe, Expensive or Moderate will include a TV and a telephone. Some hotels in the Cheap bracket have shared bathrooms.

We've tried to indicate which hotels offer rooms adapted for the needs of disabled guests, but check when booking. **Holiday Care** (0845 124 9971/www.holidaycare.org.uk) has details of places accessible for the disabled and elderly.

EMERGENCY ACCOMMODATION

Shelter is a national charity that provides advice on housing and homelessness. If you get stranded in London without anywhere to stay, call its 24-hour helpline on 0808 800 4444.

The South Bank & Bankside

Cheap

London County Hall Travel Inn Capital

County Hall, Belvedere Road, SE1 7PB (0870 238 3300/fax 7902 1619/www.travelinn.co.uk). Waterloo tube/rail. **Rates** £79.95-£82.95 double. **Credit** AmEx, DC, MC, V. **Map** p401 M9.

This branch of the Travel Inn chain has a perfect location: it's across the river from the Houses of Parliament, and the London Eye and Eurostar and Tate Modern are walkable. The lobby looks rather like a hospital waiting room, the restaurant is less than fashionable and the rooms are ordinary, but it's tourist-friendly and good value. Other locations include Tower Bridge (Tower Bridge Road, SE1; 0870 238 3303), Euston (1 Dukes Road, WC1; 0870 238 3301) and Kensington (11 Knaresborough Place, SW5; 0870 238 3304).

Hotel services *Bar. Disabled: adapted rooms. No-smoking rooms. Payphones. Restaurant.* **Room services** *Dataport. Telephone. TV.*

Mad Hatter

3-7 Stamford Street, SE1 9NY (7401 9222/fax 7401 7111/www.fullershotels.com). Southwark tube/ Waterloo tube/rail. **Rates** £85-£105 double. **Credit** AmEx, DC, MC, V. **Map** p404 N8.

The bargain-priced Mad Hatter is owned by the Fuller pub chain, so it's got a bit of theme parkery Englishness about it, glossed over by a corporate sheen. However, it's a serviceable and well-run place. The friendly staff are efficient, the rooms are large and comfortable and there are disabled-adapted rooms (which you definitely wouldn't find in an authentic English inn). The South Bank is a short walk away, and the attached Fuller's pub offers a decent selection of English ales.

Hotel services *Bar. Concierge. Disabled: adapted. No-smoking floor. Payphone. Restaurant.* **Room services** *Dataport. Telephone. TV: cable/satellite.*

The City

Deluxe

Great Eastern Hotel

40 Liverpool Street, EC2M 7QN (7618 5000/fax 7618 5011/www.great-eastern-hotel.co.uk). Liverpool Street tube/rail. **Rates** (breakfast not incl) £264 single; £311-£370 double; £393-£581 suite. **Credit** AmEx, DC, MC, V. **Map** p405 Q6.

Three years after its £70-million overhaul, Sir Terence Conran's flagship hotel shows no sign of resting on its laurels. On the contrary: it recently added a residents' bar to its already-impressive portfolio of eating and drinking options (and these are not your average stuffy hotel eateries). For a hotel of its size (267 guest rooms), it manages to have some personality, and the overall feel is modern, despite the fact that some parts of the huge building date from the late 19th century. Indeed, along with modern flourishes such as the gorgeous white rotunda you'll see original fittings like the beautiful glass dome in Aurora (the posh Modern European restaurant). The combination might seem slightly jarring, but at least the place has character. Rooms are well sized and the beds are kitted out in luxurious Frette linen. They're well appointed, too – for business: ergonomic desks (sorry, 'workstations') with broadband net access; for pleasure: DVD and CD players, power showers and REN toiletries. The minibar selection could be better, and the muted tones of fabrics within the room may be too dull for some, but if this was our home from home while working in London, you wouldn't hear us complaining.

Hotel services *Air-conditioning. Babysitting. Bars. Beauty salon. Business services. Concierge. Disabled: adapted rooms. Gym. Laundry (self-service). Limousine service. No-smoking floors. Parking (valet). Restaurants.* **Room services** *Dataport. Minibar. Room service (24hrs). Turndown. TV: cable/pay movies/satellite/VCR/DVD.*

Covent Garden Hotel. *See p52.*

Holborn & Clerkenwell

Expensive

Rookery

12 Peter's Lane, Cowcross Street, EC1M 6DS (7336 0931/fax 7336 0932/www.rookeryhotel.com). Farringdon tube/rail. **Rates** £252 single; £288 double; £323-£581 suite. **Credit** AmEx, DC, MC, V. **Map** p402 O5.

Hidden down a Dickensian lane in Clerkenwell, right near Smithfield market, the Rookery oozes authentic historical charm. Discreet yet raffish, the hotel boasts 33 unique rooms in a row of converted 18th-century houses. It has the sedate air of a gentleman's club, with plenty of dark panelling and Gothic furniture. You could film a period drama in the rooms, with their elaborate 18th-century beds, plaster busts, and clawfoot bathtubs, copper pipes and cast-iron toilets in the Victorian bathrooms. Don't worry, the place has all the modern luxuries – the sheets are of crisp Egyptian cotton, soft towels are draped generously over heated towel racks – and technology: the antique desks conceal those essential fax and modem lines. It's also cosy: during the winter, order a whisky and curl up on a sofa before the fire in the sitting room. If you can afford it, the best berth here is the Rook's Nest, a two-floor suite with a retractable roof and views towards St Paul's.

Hotel services *Bar. Concierge. Garden. Limousine service. No-smoking floors.* **Room services** *Dataport. Minibar. Room service (7am-10.30pm). TV: cable/satellite.*

Dolphin Square Hotel

living, eating, relaxing

Situated in 3½ acres of landscaped gardens in Westminster, central London, the hotel's position and facilities make it ideal for both business and pleasure.

• 4 star rating • English Tourism silver award for quality
• 145 one, two and three bedroom suites • brasserie • bar
• conference suites • Zest! Health & Fitness Spa • swimming pool
• squash and tennis courts • shopping mall • car parking

Our restaurant, Allium, features contemporary European cooking with depth of flavours and simplicity, from the kitchen of Chef Patron Anton Edelmann. Enjoy lunch or dinner in the relaxed but sophisticated atmosphere of the restaurant's elegant art-deco dining room.

Weekend breaks and special rates available.

Call the reservations team on:
Telephone +44 (0)20 7798 8890 **Freephone** 0800 616 607
E-mail reservations@dolphinsquarehotel.co.uk
Website www.dolphinsquarehotel.co.uk

Dolphin Square, Chichester Street, London SW1V 3LX

Bloomsbury & Fitzrovia

Expensive

Academy Hotel

21 Gower Street, WC1E 6HG (7631 4115/fax 7636 3442/www.theetoncollection.com).Goodge Street tube. **Rates** £164 single; £192-£222 double; £252-£265 suite. **Credit** AmEx, DC, MC, V. **Map** p399 K5.

London is full of period townhouse hotels, but the Academy is more refreshing than most. Housed in five connected Georgian townhouses, its traditional decor is elegant, combining a summery garden feel with a sense of modernity and comfort. The pretty rooms are done up in pastels with luxurious upholstery and plush carpets. The two libraries are pure English country house, with their views of the walled garden. By contrast, the basement Alchemy Bar tries too hard to be hip: lurid purple walls, funky mirrors etc. Have your breakfast here, but in the evening, try one of Bloomsbury's atmospheric pubs.

Hotel services *Air-conditioning. Bar. Business services. Disabled: adapted rooms. Gardens. Limousine service. No-smoking rooms.* **Room services** *Dataport. Minibar. Room service (24hrs). Turndown. TV.*

Blooms Townhouse

7 Montague Street, WC1B 5BP (7323 1717/fax 7636 6498/www.grangehotels.com). Holborn or Russell Square tube. **Rates** (breakfast not incl) £125 single; £155-£165 double; £220 suite. **Credit** AmEx, DC, MC, V. **Map** p399 L5.

This discreet townhouse hotel attracts a mature and well-heeled business clientele, who appreciate the clubby library bar with its 35-strong selection of malt whiskies. Other highlights include an elegant sitting room with pinstripe sofas and oil paintings, and an ivy-covered walled garden. The bedrooms are quite tasteful – pastel coloured walls, chintz curtains and bedspreads – and cooled by ceiling fans in the summer. Themed rooms include the Dickens, with memorabilia loaned from the nearby Dickens Museum, the Theatre Royal, a shrine to the London stage, and, for cricket lovers, the Lords.

Hotel services *Babysitting. Bar. Business services. Concierge. Disabled: adapted rooms. Garden. Limousine service. No-smoking floors. Restaurant.* **Room services** *Dataport. Minibar. Room service (24hrs). Turndown. TV.*

Charlotte Street Hotel

15-17 Charlotte Street, W1T 1RJ (7806 2000/ fax 7806 2002/www.firmdale.com). Tottenham Court Road tube. **Rates** (breakfast not incl) £230 single; £259-£323 double; £400-£764 suite. **Credit** AmEx, MC, V. **Map** p399 J5.

This gorgeous boutique hotel – one of five in the Firmdale mini-chain – is the apotheosis of the 'modern English' style taking the hotel world by storm. Designed by Kit Kemp, the hotel is a textbook example of how to fuse traditional with avant-garde. The public rooms have Bloomsbury paintings, including works by Duncan Grant and Vanessa Bell, mixed with quirky abstract art. The twist continues in the bedrooms, where English country house meets quirky touches and transatlantic treats: shiny granite bathrooms, bulging mini-bars and technological conveniences. Other highlights include a screening room for movie classics on Sundays, and the chi-chi Oscar restaurant and bar.

Hotel services *Air-conditioning. Bar. Concierge. Disabled: adapted room. Gym. No-smoking rooms. Restaurant.* **Room services** *Dataport. Hi-fi. Minibar. Room service (24hrs). Turndown. TV:* cable/DVD/VCR.

Montague on the Gardens

15 Montague Street, WC1B 5BJ (7637 1001/fax 7637 2516/www.redcarnationhotels.com). Holborn or Russell Square tube. **Rates** (breakfast not incl) £211 single; £240 double; £411-£511 suite. **Credit** AmEx, DC, MC, V. **Map** p399 L5.

There's something delightfully gaudy about the Montague. The entrance is flanked by riotous floral displays and doormen in top hats and tails. The sitting room is pure Victorian glitz: sparkling chandeliers, elaborate moulded ceilings, velvet drapes, crimson walls and flowers everywhere – great for glamorous grannies. The conservatory bar is all flamboyant flora, and so are the curtains, bedspreads and wallpaper in the handsome and luxurious bedrooms. The nostalgic appeal is tempered by essential modernity: excellent business and entertainment technology and a damn good gym. The formal restaurant, the Chef's Table, does a roaring trade, and is notable for its panoramic frieze of 18th-century London. In short, if you can't afford the Ritz, but are looking for opulence, the Montague's for you.

Hotel services *Air-conditioning. Babysitting. Bar. Business services. Concierge. Disabled: adapted room. Gym. Limousine service. No-smoking floors. Parking (valet). Restaurant.* **Room services** *Dataport. Minibar (only in suites). Room service (24hrs). Turndown (on request). TV: cable/pay movies.*

myhotel bloomsbury

11-13 Bayley Street, WC1B 3HD (7667 6000/ fax 7667 6001/www.myhotels.co.uk). Tottenham Court Road tube. **Rates** £117-£146 single; £162-£217 double; £256-£293 studio. **Credit** AmEx, DC, MC, V. **Map** p399 K5.

A sleek Conran-designed hotel teeming with young movers and shakers who lap up its Asian fusion decor and feng shui principles. The lobby sets the tone: a minimalist space highlighted by a beautiful aquarium, scented candles and abstract art. The bedrooms are clean and uncluttered. The modern bathrooms are stocked with Aveda toiletries. Everything is arranged for the smooth flow of chi: no mirrors opposite the bed, crystals to give you energy etc. Downstairs, the library has couches and alcoves with free internet terminals. Nearby are the gym and de rigueur treatment rooms. On the main floor, the adjoining Yo! Sushi restaurant fits with the

The awesome **One Aldwych**. *See p52.*

hotel's smooth East-meets-West philosophy effortlessly. One of the best features is the hip, buzzing bar, where you can linger over a pot of tea, enjoy cocktails or chow down on a light buffet, depending on the time of day.
Hotel services *Air-conditioning. Bar. Beauty salon. Business services. Concierge. Gym. No-smoking floors. Restaurant.* **Room services** *Dataport. Hi-fi. Room service (24hrs). TV: cable/pay movies/VCR.*

Sanderson

50 Berners Street, W1T 3NG (7300 1400/fax 7300 1401/www.ianschragerhotels.com). Oxford Circus tube. **Rates** £252-£393 single; £258-£423 double; £417-£763 suite. **Credit** AmEx, DC, MC, V. **Map** p398 J5.
This Schrager and Starck creation is a dreamier version of its predecessor, the St Martin's Lane Hotel (*see p53*). A former wallpaper factory, the exterior is 1950s ugly office-block chic. But the male-model doormen hint at beauty within. The lobby is fantasyland, all diaphanous curtains and avant-garde furniture. The dream extends into the silvery Long Bar, for immaculate, expensive cocktails. The glam Purple Bar – open to residents only – is dark and discreet. Upstairs, the minimalist bedrooms are clean and serene, with crisp white bedding, lots of mirrors and glass-walled bathrooms. The spa has more sheer flowing curtains, great lighting and beautiful creatures enjoying decadent treatments. There's a good gym too.
Hotel services *Air-conditioning. Babysitting. Bars. Beauty salon. Business services. Concierge. Disabled: adapted rooms. Garden. Gym. Limousine service. No-smoking floors. Restaurant.* **Room services** *Dataport. Minibar. Room service (24hrs). Turndown. TV: cable/DVD/satellite.*

Moderate

Harlingford Hotel

61-3 Cartwright Gardens, WC1H 9EL (7387 1551/ fax 7387 4616/www.harlingfordhotel.com). Russell Square tube/Euston tube/rail. **Rates** £75 single; £95 double; £105 triple; £110 quad. **Credit** AmEx, MC, V. **Map** p399 L3.
The Harlingford has undergone a radical facelift, replacing flock wallpaper with plain white walls and modern art and chintz with bright contemporary fabrics. In the modish purple lounge, meanwhile, design mags are scattered just so. To complement the snazziness, the hotel is updating the bathrooms. Not exactly cutting edge cool, but for style on a budget, a formidable effort. The hotel has a great location on a Georgian crescent, with gardens and a tennis court, to which the guests have access.
Hotel services *Restaurant.* **Room services** *Dataport. TV.*

Jenkins Hotel

45 Cartwright Gardens, WC1H 9EH (7387 2067/fax 7383 3139/www.jenkinshotel.demon.co.uk). Russell Square tube/Euston tube/rail. **Rates** £72 single; £85 double; £105 triple. **Credit** MC, V. **Map** p399 L3.
Handsomely situated on a lovely sweeping crescent, the Jenkins is homelier than neighbouring budget hotels. It's relaxed: the check-in desk is in the owners' kitchen, and there's a bookshelf crammed with London guides for guests to use. The rooms are decorated in a traditional English style, and painted in yellows and creams. Guests have access to the garden and tennis court out front, another plus.
Hotel services *No-smoking throughout.* **Room services** *TV.*

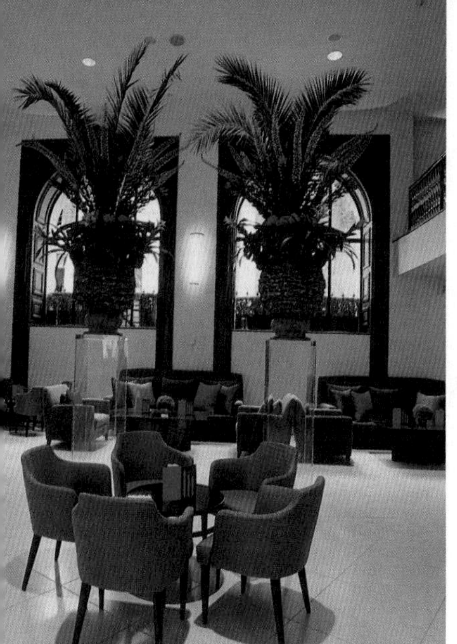

Morgan Hotel

24 Bloomsbury Street, WC1B 3QJ (7636 3735/fax 7636 3045). Tottenham Court Road tube. **Rates** £68-£80 single; £98 double; £180 triple. *Flat* £98 1 person; £130 2 people. **Credit** MC, V. **Map** p399 K5.

This cheerful, family-run hotel is a little slice of *EastEnders* transplanted into Bloomsbury: chirpy down-to-earth staff, chintz upholstery and a cosy panelled breakfast room stuffed full of London memorabilia. The hotel was renovated room by room in 2003. There are new beds, air-conditioning in each room and more modern bathrooms. For one of the best deals in London, check out the hotel's separate annexe of spacious flats.

Hotel services *Air-conditioning. No-smoking floors.* **Room services** *Dataport. Kitchenette (flats). TV.*

Cheap

Arosfa

83 Gower Street, WC1E 6HJ (tel/fax 7636 2115). Euston Square or Goodge Street tube. **Rates** £45 single; £66 double; £79 triple. **Credit** MC, V. **Map** p399 K4.

Arosfa means 'place to stay' in Welsh, and, in past years, it was an apt summary of the hotel: it was a roof over your head, and, well… not much more to be honest. But things have changed for the better: this terraced townhouse has been extensively refurbished. The rooms have been given fresh paint jobs, new furniture and carpets, and, most importantly, their own bathrooms. It's always had a great location – in the heart of Bloomsbury, opposite the best Waterstone's in London – friendly owners, clean rooms and a sweet walled garden. Luckily, the hotel's prime attraction hasn't changed: it's still one of the best bargains in town.

Hotel services *Garden. No-smoking throughout. Payphone.* **Room service** *Telephone. TV.*

Ashlee House

261-5 Gray's Inn Road, WC1X 8QT (7833 9400/ fax 7833 9677/www.ashleehouse.co.uk). King's Cross tube/rail. **Rates** (per person) £36 single; £24 twin; £22 triple; £13-£19 dorm. **Credit** MC, V. **Map** p399 M3.

Ashlee House isn't your typical youth hostel – and thank goodness for that. For one thing, you don't have to be a young party animal to stay here: the oldest guest when we visited was an 86-year-old Japanese man. If you are a party animal, you don't have to worry about that ridiculous curfew business: unlike other hostels, there's a 24-hour reception here. The rooms aren't bad: they're clean and decorated in cheery yellows and shocking pinks. Other attractions: free luggage storage, a London walk included in the price, and a common room with footie table, stereo and internet station. The hostel's best asset, however, is its friendly, chatty staff.

Hotel services *Business services. Cooking facilities. Garden. Laundry (self-service). No-smoking throughout. Payphone.*

Generator

37 Tavistock Place, WC1H 9SD (7388 7666/fax 7388 7644/www.generatorhostels.com). Russell Square tube. **Rates** (per person) £36 single; £26.50 twin/double; £22.50 multi; £15-£17 dormitory. **Credit** MC, V. **Map** p399 K4.

London's version of a Club 18-30 holiday, the Generator is party central for the backpackers' brigade. It's got a cool industrial look: steel, chrome, exposed pipes, all mixed with that MTV aesthetic: neon signs, coloured lights, video games. There's a massive bar, with karaoke nights and happy hours, a 24-hour games room with pool tables, and a movie lounge. It's not all about partying, though: there's practical stuff like an internet room, a restaurant and a travel agent. There are 837 beds, should you ever want a rest. Quiet rooms are available on request.

Hotel services *Bar. No-smoking throughout. Payphone. Restaurant.*

St Margaret's Hotel

26 Bedford Place, WC1B 5JL (7636 4277/fax 7323 3066). Holborn or Russell Square tube. **Rates** £50.50 single; £62.50-£97 double; £90.50-£105.50 triple. **Credit** MC, V. **Map** p399 L5.

This bustling townhouse hotel is enormous, but retains a homely atmosphere. It's been run by the same warm Italian family for yonks. The rooms are spotless, the beds are comfortable and all have reading lights. If space is an issue, ask for a triple room: they're huge. Bedrooms at the back overlook gardens: one is the Duke of Bedford's, the other belongs to the hotel. Guess which one you can go in.

Hotel services. *Garden. No-smoking throughout. Payphones.* **Room services** *Telephone. TV: cable.*

Our Warm Family Welcome...

The Lancaster Court Hotel is an imposing, Victorian listed building situated on a tree-lined street. It is easily accessible by Heathrow Express, Eurostar, tube and rail.

Centrally located for sightseeing, shopping restaurants, theatre and recommended by all established guides.

Prices start at just £25 per night.

202/204 Sussex Gardens
Hyde Park London W2 3UA

For more information call us on
020 7402 8438

email us on lancohot@aol.com

or visit our website
www.lancaster-court-hotel.co.uk

LANCASTER COURT HOTEL

THE ABBEY COURT

20 Pembridge Gardens • Kensington
London W2 4DU • England
Telephone 020 7221 7518 • Fax 020 7792 0858
www.abbeycourthotel.co.uk

This multi award winning elegant 4 star townhouse hotel dating back to 1830 has been newly renovated and sympathetically restored to provide a haven of tranquillity for today's discerning business & leisure visitors. The comfortable beds range from brass to traditional four posters. Our en-suite Italian marble bathrooms feature relaxing Jacuzzi baths to pamper you in luxury! All the amenities you can expect from a hotel with luxury service are here, now with high speed broadband internet access for your laptops, direct dial modem phones and personal digital safes.
Please visit our website for "Best Rates & Secure Online Reservations". Special packages online are also tailored to your requirements.

The Gallery
(South Kensington)
A haven of quiet elegance and also a living tribute to the art and artists of Victorian times. 'The Victorian Artist At Home' - a vision beautifully realised in the character and charm of The Gallery.

The Gainsborough
(South Kensington)
The feel of an English country home; the pleasure of being close to London's finest museums, shopping, dining, living. Relax and enjoy yourself in a setting of timeless elegance.

The Willett
(Sloane Square)
Your home from home in London's charming Sloane Gardens. A quiet retreat of terracotta terraces, seemingly far from the workaday world yet close to everything that makes this part of Chelsea renowned.

Rates from £80 to £250
Reservations:
Freephone: (USA) 1-800 270 9206 (UK) 0-500 826 187
Tel: 44 (0)20 7970 1802 E-mail: reservations@eeh.co.uk
www.eeh.co.uk

GARDEN COURT HOTEL

1954 - 2004
50th Anniversary

30-31 Kensington Gardens Square
London W2 4BG

Tel: 020 7229 2553
Fax: 020 7727 2749

Email: info@gardencourthotel.co.uk
Website: www.gardencourthotel.co.uk

Marylebone

Moderate

Dorset Square Hotel

39 Dorset Square, NW1 6QN (7723 7874/fax 7724 3328/www.dorsetsquare.co.uk). Baker Street tube/ Marylebone tube/rail. **Rates** (breakfast not incl) £147 single; £188-£230 double; £282 suite. **Credit** AmEx, MC, V. **Map** p384 F4.

Once a Firmdale hotel, now under new ownership, this Regency house is situated opposite the original Lord's cricket ground, which explains the odd cricket-related decorative touch. There's not much to do around here at night, but the sitting room is a particularly cosy spot for a drink, with its grandfather clock, bookshelves and roaring fire.

Hotel services *Air-conditioning. Bar. Business services. Garden. No-smoking rooms. Restaurant.* **Room services** *Dataport. Minibar. Room service (24hrs). Turndown. TV: cable.*

Sherlock Holmes Hotel

108 Baker Street, W1U 6LJ (7486 6161/fax 7958 5211/www.sherlockholmeshotel.com). Baker Street tube. **Rates** (breakfast not incl weekdays) £128-£145 double; £186 suites. **Credit** AmEx, DC, MC, V. **Map** p398 G5.

Watson would be baffled: the Sherlock Holmes Hotel, until recently a chintz-filled Hilton, has been reborn. Gone is the twee tourist tat, replaced by a chilled boutique hotel. The lobby is a casual, New York-style cocktail bar, with wood floors, cream walls and brown leather furniture. The rooms are like hip bachelor pads: beige, brown and wood, leather headboards, pinstripe sheets and swanky bathrooms. There's a gym, sauna and steamroom, and an award-winning restaurant, Sherlock's Grill. True, Marylebone isn't exactly the hub of London nightlife, but with a bar this pleasant, who cares?

Hotel services *Air-conditioning. Babysitting. Bar. Business services. Concierge. Disabled: adapted rooms. Gym. No-smoking rooms. Restaurant.* **Room services** *Dataport. Minibar. Room service (24hrs). Turndown. TV: cable/pay movies/satellite.*

Mayfair & St James's

Deluxe

Claridge's

55 Brook Street, W1A 2JQ (7629 8860/fax 7950 5481/www.claridges.co.uk). Bond Street tube. **Rates** (breakfast not incl) £315-£345 single; £395-£450 double; £565-£3,850 suite. **Credit** AmEx, DC, MC, V. **Map** p400 H6.

It may not be as famous as the Ritz or the Savoy, but Claridge's is the most exclusive of London's Grand Old Dames. Its most striking feature is its art deco interior: the 1930s decor is so convincing you could skip the Victoria & Albert museum. The rooms are cool and elegant, rather than flashy: soft mauves and olive greens, lovely cherrywood furniture and pretty glass lamps. There are exceptions: some of the rooms really go to town, with dramatic Chinese flourishes, bold colour schemes and jazzy mirrors. All have up-to-date business/entertainment technology, and luxurious marble bathrooms. The rooftop gym is well equipped – and almost too beautiful to get sweaty in – and the spa is so elegant you almost expect to bump into Audrey Hepburn. Then there's Gordon Ramsay's famous restaurant: the crème de la crème of gourmet dining, it gets booked up several months in advance.

Hotel services *Air-conditioning. Babysitting. Bar. Beauty salon. Business services. Concierge. Gym. Limousine service. No-smoking rooms. Restaurant.* **Room services** *Dataport. Hi-fi. Minibar. Room service (24hrs). Turndown. TV: cable/pay movies/VCR.*

Dorchester

Park Lane, W1A 2HJ (7629 8888/fax 7409 0114/ www.dorchesterhotel.com). Hyde Park Corner tube. **Rates** £270-£370 single; £387-£452 double; £587-£2,496 suite. **Credit** AmEx, DC, MC, V. **Map** p400 G7.

The Dorchester is the epitome of old-fashioned glamour: it's got the most opulent lobby in London, Elizabeth Taylor and Richard Burton had a honeymoon here, and Liberace's piano is in the bar. If that sounds intimidating, don't worry: it may not be the People's Palace, but it feels less snooty than the Ritz. A multimillion pound refurb has left the bedrooms luxurious, with floral upholstery and mountains of plump cushions on four-poster beds. The suites remain hilariously ostentatious: the Oliver Meissel suite, for instance, has gold-leaf toilet seats and a fake bookcase that hides a bar. But the biggest revolution at the Dorchester has been technological: the plasma screen TVs double as personal PCs with high-speed internet access and thousands of movies and CDs. Should it all prove too daunting, the hotel's much-vaunted and very pleasant E-butlers – computer geeks in tails – are at your beck and call.

Hotel services *Air-conditioning. Babysitting. Bar. Beauty salon. Business services. Concierge. Disabled: adapted rooms. Garden. Gym. No-smoking floors. Parking. Restaurant.* **Room services** *Dataport. Hi-fi. Minibar. Room service (24hrs). Turndown. TV: cable/DVD/pay movies/VCR.*

Metropolitan

19 Old Park Lane, W1K 4LB (7447 1000/fax 7447 1100/www.metropolitan.co.uk). Green Park or Hyde Park Corner tube. **Rates** from £250-£365 double; £300-£2,300 suite. **Credit** AmEx, DC, MC, V. **Map** p400 G8.

The Metropolitan is famous for two reasons: it's home to the Met Bar, London's hottest celeb hangout during the late 1990s, and Nobu, the trendy Japanese restaurant, where, in a moment of lust, Boris Becker sired a child in a broom cupboard. Given its shallow reputation, it would be easy to dismiss the place as a style-over-substance

LINCOLN HOUSE HOTEL

This friendly, family run bed & breakfast hotel with Georgian charm, modern comforts and en-suite rooms is ideally located in the heart of London. Close to Oxford Street and Marble Arch. Public Transport from here is easy, with connections to all tourist attractions of the capital and its famous shops.

SINGLE £59 - £69 DOUBLE £69 - £89
INC ENGLISH BREAKFAST & TAX

33 Gloucester Place, Marble Arch, London W1 U 8HY

Telephone: +44 (0) 20 7486 7630
Fax: +44 (0) 20 7486 0166
Email: reservations@lincoln-house-hotel.co.uk

Special offers at www.lincoln-house-hotel.co.uk

One of London's Best Bed & Breakfast Hotel

Hart House Hotel

★Clean & Comfortable Fully Refurbished Bedrooms★

★Centrally located in the heart of London's West End★

★Reasonable Rates★

Awarded 4 Diamonds by the AA & London Tourist Board

OUR AIM IS SIMPLE

We wish to provide a warm welcome in a friendly, clean, cosy atmosphere that is good value for money.

51 GLOUCESTER PLACE, LONDON W1U 8JF
TEL: 020 7935 2288 FAX: 020 7935 8516
E-mail: reservations@harthouse.co.uk
Website: www.harthouse.co.uk

City University
London

SUMMER & THE CITY

TOTALLY LONDON
www.visitlondon.com

Explore London's Attractions from our centrally located Residences

Situated in Central London Zone 1, close to all forms of public transport, our Residences provide easy access to London's famous tourist attractions, shopping and nightlife.

- Accommodation offered in single rooms with either shared or private facilities
- Rooms serviced daily and include bed linen/towels
- Rates start from £19.00 per night for groups of 10 or more

AVAILABLE 7 JUNE–12 SEPTEMBER 2004

Event Management Service
City University London
Northampton Square
London EC1V 0HB

For more information:
+44 (0)20 7040 8037
events@city.ac.uk
or visit www.city.ac.uk/ems

ASTONS
APARTMENTS

"...best value in London"
says 'Frommers International Travel Guide'

Self-catering designer or standard apartments with satellite television, direct dial facilities and daily maid service.

Occupying three lovingly restored Victorian townhouses, in fashionable South Kensington, central to London's finest attractions.

At a fraction of the cost of comparable hotel accomodation, from £41 per night per person (weekly and exhibition discounts on enquiry).

Suitable for one to four persons and within a close proximity to museums and transportation

31 Rosary Gardens
London SW7 4NH
Fax: 020 7590 6060
Email: info@astons-apartments.com
www.astons-apartments.com

+44 (0) 20 7590 6000
US Toll Free 1 800 525 2810

operation. But the Metropolitan is a thoroughly classy joint. In decorative terms, it's not as flashy as St Martin's Lane, and has aged much better. The rooms have pleasing splashes of colour and, in some cases, gorgeous views of Hyde Park. The staff are as beautiful as you'd expect, but quite unpretentious. The Met Bar has lost some of its cachet – these days, it's more Eurotrash than A-list – but it's still got a buzz to it, and there's always the hope that Liam Gallagher will show up and start a brawl.
Hotel services *Air-conditioning. Babysitting. Bar. Business services. Concierge. Gym. No-smoking floors. Parking. Restaurant.* **Room services** *Dataport. Hi-fi. Minibar. Room service (24hrs). Turndown. TV: cable/DVD/pay movies/VCR.*

Ritz

150 Piccadilly, W1J 9BR (7493 8181/fax 7493 2687/www.theritzlondon.com). Green Park tube. **Rates** (breakfast not incl) £352 single; £429-£505 double; £587-£2,291 suite. **Credit** AmEx, DC, MC, V. **Map** p400 J8.

Not surprisingly, this grand hotel has the poshest doormen in London. The public rooms are deliciously ostentatious (*see p62*) and the bedrooms are equally opulent, decorated in a Louis XVI style, with baroque mirrors, exquisite damask upholstery, and heavy drapes. It's not too overbearing – the colour schemes are kept to soft pastels and creams. And the Bulgari toiletries are a bonus. The downside: it falls behind the Dorchester in terms of multimedia technology, and the gym is puny. But you don't come to the Ritz to use a Stairmaster. You're better off having a cocktail in the Rivoli Bar, an exquisite new spot with art deco touches that should give the Savoy's American Bar (*see p52*) a run for its money.
Hotel services *Air-conditioning. Babysitting. Bar. Beauty salon. Business services. Concierge. Disabled: adapted rooms. Garden. Gym. Limousine service. No-smoking floors. Restaurant.* **Room services** *Dataport. Hi-fi. Minibar. Room service (24hrs). Turndown. TV: cable/satellite/VCR.*

Expensive

No.5 Maddox Street

5 Maddox Street, W1S 2QD (7647 0200/fax 7647 0300/www.living-rooms.co.uk). Oxford Circus tube. **Rates** (breakfast not incl) £270-£381 double suite; £500 2-bedroom suite; £675 3-bedroom suite. **Credit** AmEx, DC, MC, V. **Map** p398 J6.

Fancy a hip pad in the heart of swinging London? This suites-only boutique hotel is just the ticket. Blink and you'll miss the entrance: a meek door flanked by a couple of bamboo trees. The lobby, with its aquarium, is like a chic bank. Inside the suites, the theme is East meets West: black lacquered furniture and the odd Far Eastern piece, coupled with blonde wood floors, arty photographs, brown suede cushions, fake fur throws and, of course, the obligatory crisp white sheets. The kitchens are filled with organic food and other treats, and room service will do the shopping should you want to cook. There's no hotel bar, but Soho is steps away. In any case, you get the feeling that plenty of good parties happen right here in these suites.
Hotel services *Air-conditioning. Babysitting. Business services. Concierge. Gym. Limousine service. No-smoking rooms.* **Room services** *Dataport. Minibar. Room service (24hrs). TV: cable/satellite/VCR.*

Trafalgar

2 Spring Gardens, SW1A 2TS (7870 2900/fax 7870 2911/www.hilton.co.uk/trafalgar). Charing Cross tube/rail. **Rates** (breakfast not incl) £158-£292 double; £380-£450 suite. **Credit** AmEx, DC, MC, V. **Map** p401 K7.

London's latest boutique hotel is a Hilton and a very good hotel it is too. For one thing, it's got the best location in London: many of its rooms overlook Trafalgar Square, and its rooftop bar has breathtaking views of the capital. Its airy lobby bar, Rockwell, is modish, buzzing and unpretentious. More importantly, it's open 24 hours for hotel guests and until 2am for the public: a rare and beautiful thing in London. The cocktails are ridiculously expensive, but they are immaculately made – the Rockwell won *Time Out*'s Best Bar Award in 2002. The bedrooms are comfortable, cool and modern, with crisp white sheets (there's a surprise), colourful pop art, streamlined walnut furniture and sleek marble bathrooms. Add thoroughly professional staff and you've got a rare breed: a hip hotel where the style matches the substance.
Hotel services *Air-conditioning. Bar. Business services. Concierge. Disabled: adapted rooms. Garden (rooftop). Limousine service. No-smoking floors. Parking. Restaurant.* **Room services** *Dataport. Hi-fi. Minibar. Room service (24hrs). TV: cable/pay movies/web TV.*

Soho & Chinatown

Expensive

Hazlitt's

6 Frith Street, W1D 3JA (7434 1771/fax 74391524/ www.hazlittshotel.com). Tottenham Court Road tube. **Rates** £205 single; £240 double; £352 suite. **Credit** AmEx, DC, MC, V. **Map** p399 K6.

Named after William Hazlitt, the 18th century essayist who lived and died here, this creaky Georgian townhouse has an immaculate literary pedigree: some rooms are named after some of the better known writers who have stayed under its roof (Jonathan Swift, for instance); in the library there are signed first editions by modern authors who have been enchanted by the place (Ted Hughes, JK Rowling). Bill Bryson immortalised Hazlitt's in *Notes from a Small Island.* Non-writers stay here, too, lured by the hotel's excellent location, friendly staff and enormous historical charm. The floors are lopsided, the walls are warped, and the rooms are full of antiques: gigantic oak beds, clawfoot bathtubs, worn Persian rugs. Hazlitt's is joining the

The Gore. Blimey. *See p53.*

21st century: an ambitious technology programme has brought high-speed internet access and interactive entertainment systems to every room.
Hotel services *Business services. Concierge. No-smoking floors.* **Room services** *Dataport. Minibar. Room service (7.30am-10.30pm). TV: cable/VCR.*

Covent Garden & St Giles's

Deluxe

One Aldwych

1 Aldwych, WC2B 4RH (7300 1000/fax 7300 1001/www.onealdwych.com). Covent Garden or Temple tube/Charing Cross tube/rail. **Rates** (breakfast not incl) £210-£440 single; £210-£464 double; £405-£1,133 suite. **Credit** AmEx, DC, MC, V. **Map** p401 M7.

An alluring hybrid of traditional and trendy, One Aldwych has the great service of the Ritz, but without the pomp; its decor is as modern as the Sanderson, but without the flashiness; it's housed in a restored Edwardian bank building – but is resolutely forward-looking. The Lobby Bar boasts limestone floors, full-length arched windows and floral sculptures. The bedrooms have a streamlined, minimalist appeal with splashes of colour and lots of gadgetry. There are a couple of stylish restaurants, a gym and a plush private cinema. But the jewel in this hotel's crown is its underground swimming pool, which pipes classical music underwater.
Hotel services *Air-conditioning. Babysitting. Bars. Beauty salon. Concierge. Disabled: adapted rooms. Gym. Limousine service. No-smoking floors. Parking (valet). Restaurants. Swimming pool (indoor).* **Room services** *Dataport. Hi-fi. Minibar. Room service (24hrs). Turndown. TV: cable/pay movies/satellite.*

Savoy

Strand, WC2R 0EU (7836 4343/fax 7240 6040/ www.savoygroup.com). Covent Garden or Embankment tube/Charing Cross tube/rail.
Rates (breakfast not incl) £341-£376 single; £405-£441 double; £582-£1,469 suite. **Credit** AmEx, DC, MC, V. **Map** p401 L7.

A rethink of the hotel's restaurants were major changes in 2003. The redesigned Grill Room restaurant gained a new executive chef in Marcus Wareing. Plans have also been drawn up for a second, less formal restaurant, as well as a new lobby bar. Otherwise, the Savoy continues much as it has for the last 115 years – the service is flawless, the public spaces are effortlessly grand and the rooms (particularly the newer ones with their vast bathrooms) are comfortable. River-facing rooms justify their prices with what must surely be the most impressive views in London. There's live music in the River Restaurant every night and the American Bar attracts the capital's cocktail set.
Hotel services *Air-conditioning. Babysitting. Bar. Business services. Concierge. Gym. No-smoking rooms. Parking. Restaurants. Swimming pool (indoor).* **Room services** *Dataport. Hi-fi. Minibar. Turndown. TV: cable/pay movies/satellite.*

Expensive

Covent Garden Hotel

10 Monmouth Street, WC2H 9HB (7806 1000/fax 7806 1100/www.firmdalehotels.com). Covent Garden or Leicester Square tube. **Rates** (breakfast not incl) £246 single; £287 double; £412-£935 suite. **Credit** AmEx, MC, V. **Map** p399 L6.

The smartest link in Tim and Kit Kemp's mini-chain of stylish boutique hotels is certainly the most showbiz in feel. Film stars stay here, and Hollywood execs

attend screenings in the basement cinema (which shows classics every Sunday night). Kit Kemp's modern English style is bold. There's the traditional stuff – pinstriped wallpaper, floral upholstery, plaid curtains, but it all has a modern twist: flamboyant colour schemes, avant-garde art, quirky sculptures. The granite-and-oak bathrooms complement the luxurious rooms, which have all the required gadgetry (DVDs, CD players, modem points etc). The loveliest spot is the clubby library, theatrical with its pink plaid couches and glamorous curtains. Snuggle up by the fire with a drink and hope that a Hollywood heartthrob walks in.
Hotel services *Air-conditioning. Babysitting. Bar. Beauty salon. Business services. Concierge. Gym. Limousine service. No-smoking rooms. Parking (valet). Restaurant.* **Room services** *Dataport. Minibar. Room service (24hrs). Turndown. TV: DVD/satellite/VCR.*

St Martin's Lane Hotel

45 St Martin's Lane, WC2N 4HX (reservations 0800 634 5500/7300 5500/fax 7300 5501/ www.ianschragerhotels.com). Covent Garden or Leicester Square tube. **Rates** (breakfast not incl) £247 single; £270-£329 double; £493-£1,645 penthouse. **Credit** AmEx, DC, MC, V. **Map** p401 L7.
Once the most fashionable hotel in London, this Schrager and Starck creation seems less than cutting edge these days. The 'theatrical minimalist' decor is striking, but the flashier gimmicks are starting to feel old: the headache-inducing purple lighting in the lifts, for instance, is annoying and the Starck gold-tooth stools in the lobby can now be found in trendy home decor shops. The rooms, white minimalist affairs, are definitely good-looking, but the standard doubles are tiny. We like the Asia de Cuba restaurant; after all these years, the food here is still imaginative and delicious. And the Light Bar – open to residents only – is still a smart and starry place for a cocktail, although guest-list-only places really are a bit naff.
Hotel services *Air-conditioning. Babysitting. Bar. Business services. Concierge. Disabled: adapted rooms. Gym. Limousine service. No-smoking rooms. Restaurant.* **Room services** *Hi-fi. Minibar. Room service (24hrs). Turndown. TV: cable/DVD.*

South Kensington & Knightsbridge

Deluxe

Blakes

33 Roland Gardens, SW7 3PF (7370 6701/fax 7373 0442/www.blakeshotels.com). Gloucester Road or South Kensington tube. **Rates** (breakfast not incl) £200 single; £299-£393 double; £640-£1,051 suite. **Credit** AmEx, DC, MC, V. **Map** p397 D11.
Opened in 1983, this exotic Anouska Hempel creation was London's first boutique hotel. In a welcome respite from the ubiquitous white minimalist look, the bedrooms here are done up in richer colours: blacks, golds and crimsons. The rooms evoke the romance of colonial travel, with influences from India, Turkey, Russia and China. Antique treasures are everywhere: there are exquisite black lacquered cabinets, Chinese birdcages, bamboo chairs. Canopy beds and heavy silk drapes add luxury. Downstairs, there's a chic Thai restaurant, once described as resembling 'an opium den run by Coco Chanel' and a discreet Chinese-themed bar, favoured by celebs.
Hotel services *Air-conditioning. Babysitting. Bar. Beauty salon. Business services. Concierge. Garden. Gym. Limousine service. No-smoking rooms. Parking (valet). Restaurant.* **Room services** *Dataport. Minibar. Room service (24hrs). Turndown. TV: cable/pay movies/satellite/VCR.*

Expensive

The Gore

189 Queen's Gate, SW7 3EX (7584 6601/fax 7589 8127/www.gorehotel.com). Gloucester Road tube. **Rates** (breakfast not incl) £182-£199 single; £223-£335 double; £346 suite. **Credit** AmEx, DC, MC, V. **Map** p397 D9.
Like its sister hotels Hazlitt's (*see p51*) and the Rookery (*see p43*), the Gore oozes character. Situated in a couple of Victorian townhouses, it's crammed with period paintings – 4,500 to be precise. The bedrooms have massively appealing 18th-century oak beds, Persian rugs and any number of handsome antiques; the bathrooms feature Victorian clawfoot tubs and brass taps. There are some utterly bewitching suites: the Dame Nellie is a madly theatrical affair, with leopard-print chairs and bronze nudes surrounding the bathtub; the Miss Ada suite comes with an original ornate china Thomas Crapper toilet; and the Tudor Room has a 15th-century bed, a minstrel's gallery and atmospheric beamed ceilings. The whole place has a delightful air of shabby chic, from the worn leather sofas to the casual, wood-panelled bar.
Hotel services *Bar. Business services. Concierge. No-smoking floor. Restaurant.* **Room services** *Dataport. Minibar. Room service (7am-11pm). TV: cable.*

Knightsbridge Hotel

12 Beaufort Gardens, SW3 1PT (7584 6300/fax 7584 6355/www.firmdalehotels.com). Knightsbridge tube. **Rates** (breakfast not incl) £170-£182 single; £205-£300 double; £393-£464 suite. **Credit** AmEx, MC, V. **Map** p397 F9.
The latest in Tim and Kit Kemp's mini-empire of boutique hotels, the Knightsbridge is on a quiet, tree-lined street a hop and a skip away from shopping central: namely, Harrods. It's just as chic as any of the other Firmdale hotels, but because there's no smart restaurant or flashy bar, it's more affordable. Kit has done her usual modern English schtick with the decor, but she's getting quirkier with each hotel. This one's lobby is full of strange and

Our Warm Family Welcome... and a lot, lot more

There are so many good reasons to stay at The Lancaster Court Hotel:

- **Central Location** near Paddington and Lancaster Gate ⊖
- **Convenient** for all major sights, museums, shops, restaurants and theatres
- **Easy to reach.** Just 3 minutes from mainline rail, buses, taxis and Heathrow Express (Heathrow 15 mins). The Eurostar and Waterloo is just 20 minutes by tube.
- All rooms with colour TV; luggage room facility; car parking by arrangement

Unbeatable prices: singles from £25, doubles from £45. Special reduced rates for longer stays

LANCASTER COURT HOTEL

202/204 Sussex Gardens
Hyde Park London W2 3UA

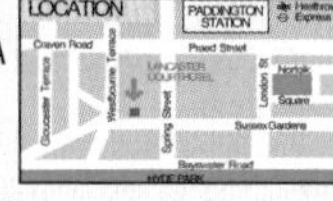

Tel: 020 7402 8438
Fax: 020 7706 3794
E-mail: lancohot@aol.com
www.lancaster-court-hotel.co.uk

RAMSEES HOTEL

32/36 Hogarth Road, Earls Court,
London SW5 0PU
Tel: 020 7370 1445 Fax: 020 7244 6835
Email: ramsees@rasool.demon.co.uk
Web: www.ramseeshotel.com

• Single from £33, Double from £45 •
• Triple from £70, Family from £79 •
• For the best rates and location. •
• Open 24 hours, most rooms with private showers. •
• All rooms with colour TV, Sky Movies & Sport Channels and telephone. •

CARDIFF HOTEL

IDEAL CENTRAL LOCATION

Run by the Davies Family for 40 years, the Cardiff Hotel overlooks a quiet tree-lined square. Enjoy our friendly service and become one of our regular visitors. 60+ rooms.

Singles: **£49 - £55** Doubles **£65 - £85**

DELICIOUS ENGLISH BREAKFAST INCLUDED

150 metres to Heathrow Express & Paddington Station

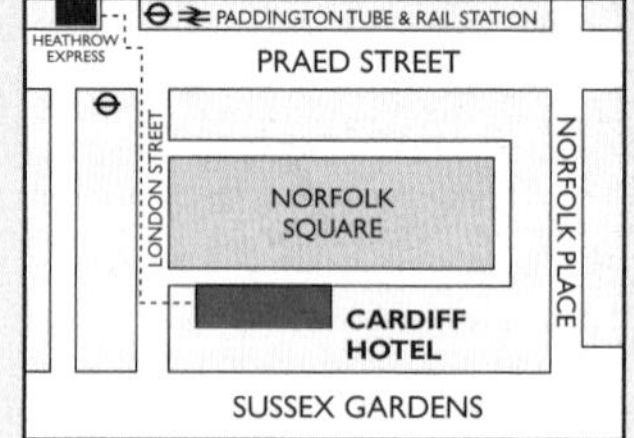

5, 7, 9 Norfolk Square London W2 1RU
Tel: (020) 7723 9068 / 7723 3513
Fax: (020) 7402 2342
email: stay@cardiff-hotel.com
www.cardiff-hotel.com

Int'l Tel: + 44 20 7723 9068
Int'l Fax: + 44 20 7402 2342

fascinating sculptures and weird modern art, and the drawing room is a brilliant African pastiche. The bedrooms, meanwhile, are fresh and summery: creams, soft greens and purples, a bit of chintz, some bold checks, the odd work of abstract art and a few antiques. As usual, there are all the modern creature comforts in terms of bathrooms and gadgetry, and minibars filled with posh snacks.
Hotel services *Air-conditioning. Babysitting. Business services. Concierge. No-smoking rooms.* **Room services** *Dataport. Hi-fi. Minibar. Room service (24hrs). Turndown. TV: satellite/DVD.*

The Milestone Hotel & Apartments

1 Kensington Court, W8 5DL (7917 1000/fax 7917 1010/www.milestonehotel.com). High Street Kensington tube/9 10, 52 bus. **Rates** (breakfast not incl) £305-£340 queen; £370-£395 deluxe, queen, twin; £635-£950 suite; £2,760-£3,231 apartments/wk. **Credit** AmEx, DC, MC, V. **Map** p395 B9.
Now that this small Victorian hotel overlooking Kensington Palace and Gardens has won a slew of industry awards, its 'best-kept secret' status has been blown. It's a lovely place to stay: discreet, romantic and luxurious. The rooms are exquisitely decorated in a range of themes: English rose, Venetian, Ascot and, most amazingly, Africa: the Safari suite is adorned with ostrich eggs, leopard-print upholstery and lion-shaped soaps. The sumptuous bedrooms have the requisite technology (broadband internet, DVD player) and the public rooms are as swish as the suites, with a jazzy conservatory and the cosy Stable Bar. The hotel's impeccable decor is the work of South African owner Beatrice Tillman, who could soon give Kit Kemp a run for her money. Speaking of money, you'll need vast quantities of it to stay here, but the Milestone's quiet charm is a pleasing alternative to the pomposity of London's more famous luxury hotels.
Hotel services *Air-conditioning. Babysitting. Bar. Business services. Concierge. Gym. Laundry (self-service apts only). No-smoking rooms. Parking (valet). Restaurant.* **Room services** *Dataport. Minibar. Room service (24hrs). Turndown. TV: pay movies/satellite.*

myhotel chelsea

35 Ixworth Place, SW3 3QX (7225 7500/fax 7225 7555/www.myhotels.com). South Kensington tube. **Rates** (breakfast not incl) £223 single; £258 double; £423 suite. **Credit** AmEx, DC, MC, V. **Map** p397 E11.
This trendy new boutique hotel is a softer, gentler version of its flashier alter ego, myhotel bloomsbury. It was created by the same design team, which explains all the feng shui touches: an aquarium in the lobby, crystals and candles scattered just so, mirrors in all the right places. But they've toned down the oriental look – so late 1990s – and concocted a new fusion: what they call 'traditional English meets *Sex and the City*'. Presumably, this is due to the Chelsea location: female shopaholics will appreciate the feminine colours – dusty pinks and purples – and lush fabrics: cashmere throws, satin curtains and velvet cushions. All rooms come with myhotel's New Agey accessories: Aveda toiletries and herbal wellness/hangover kits. There are also treatment rooms where you can have everything from a facial to a full wax. Chillout places include the Cape Cod-influence bar and conservatory-style lounge.
Hotel services *Air-conditioning. Babysitting. Bar. Beauty salon. Concierge. Gym. Limousine service. No-smoking rooms. Restaurant.* **Room services** *Dataport. Hi-fi. Minibar. Room service (24hrs). Turndown. TV: DVD/Pay movies/satellite.*

Number Sixteen

16 Sumner Place, SW7 3EG (7589 5232/fax 7584 8615/www.firmdalehotels.com). South Kensington tube. **Rates** £111-£152 single; £194-£264 double. **Credit** AmEx, MC, V. **Map** p397 D11
Tim and Kit Kemp's luxurious modern English hotels are an interior decorator's dream: trouble is, they're too expensive for ordinary mortals. But not any more: this gorgeous B&B has all the decorative genius of the Firmdale chain, but at a greatly reduced price. More than any of the Kemps' hotels, this one has a garden-fresh appeal: the drawing room has paintings of butterflies and birds, not to mention fresh sunflowers, and the bedrooms have a summery look, with subtle floral patterns and tasteful colour combinations: cream, olive greens, purples. There's no restaurant or bar – which probably explains the lower room rates – but there's a gourmet, 24-hour room service menu. And you can have your breakfast in the idyllic conservatory, which overlooks a garden complete with gurgling fountain and carp pond.
Hotel services *Air-conditioning. Babysitting. Concierge. Garden. Limousine service. No-smoking rooms. Parking (valet).* **Room services** *Dataport. Minibar. Room service (24hrs). Turndown. TV: satellite.*

Pelham

15 Cromwell Place, SW7 2LA (7589 8288/fax 7584 8444/www.firmdalehotels.com). South Kensington tube. **Rates** (breakfast not incl) £176 single; £211-£294 double; £323-£811 suite. **Credit** AmEx, MC, V. **Map** p397 D10.
Handily placed for the three big South Kensington museums (*see p135*), the Pelham is one of London's most sophisticated townhouse hotels. It's certainly the most traditional of the Firmdale boutique chain, although it's not staid by any means: in fact its fresh, modern approach to the country house look has made it a favourite with fashion editors. In the library, for instance, an old-fashioned oil painting has a frame made from dried flowers. In the bedrooms, meanwhile, you might get pinstriped wallpaper in bold red, or the floral bedspreads might be juxtaposed with vibrant plaid upholstery. Each room is different, veering from the subtle to the playful, but Kit Kemp has decorated every one with panache, without scrimping on luxuries. In the basement, the cheery yellow restaurant, Kemp's, offers good value. It's open from breakfast onwards and is

Hotel chains

Many global chains have branches in London. Don't, as a rule, expect a great deal of individual character, but do rest assured that you'll get the standard of service and comfort you last found at the same chain's outlets in New York, Sydney, Kuala Lumpur, wherever, really. At the top end, there are the **Four Seasons** at Canary Wharf (46 Westferry Circus, E14 8RS; 7510 1999) and Mayfair (Hamilton Place, Park Lane, W1A 1AZ; 7499 0888). **Sheraton** hotels sit in Mayfair (Piccadilly, W1J 7BX; 7499 6321), Belgravia (20 Chesham Place, SW1X 8HQ; 7235 6040) and Heathrow (Colnbrook and Bath Road, UB7 0HJ; 8759 2424), with the more luxurious Sheraton Park Tower on Knightsbridge (No.101, SW1X 7RN; 7235 8050). For full details, see www.starwood.com/sheraton. Among the innumerable London **Marriott** hotels (see www.marriott.com for a full list) are the branches in Belgravia (10 Grosvenor Square, W1K 6JP ; 7493 1232) and Mayfair (140 Park Lane, W1K 7AA; 7493 7000), as well as at County Hall (Westminster Bridge Road, SE1 7PB; 7928 5200). See www.hilton.com for the full story on the range of **Hilton** hotels in London, or just go directly to Islington (53 Upper Street, N1 0UY; 7354 7700), Mayfair (22 Park Lane, W1K 1BE; 7493 8000) or Paddington (225 Edgware Road, W2 1JU; 7402 4141).

On a budget? You could do worse than **Holiday Inn**. The global chain has many hotels scattered around London, from fashionable Hoxton (275 Old Street, EC1V 9LN; 7300 4300) to rarefied Hampstead (215 Haverstock Hill, NW3 4RB; 0870 400 9037) via bustling Oxford Circus (57-9 Welbeck Street, W1G 9BL; 7935 4442). You can consult www.holiday-inn.com for a full list.

perfect for well-proportioned light lunches and hearty suppers. Take afternoon tea and scones in the lovely drawing room after a museum-filled day.
Hotel services *Air-conditioning. Babysitting. Bar. Concierge. Limousine service. Parking (valet). No-smoking rooms. Restaurant.* **Room services** *Dataport. Minibar. Room service (24hrs). Turndown. TV: cable/pay movies/VCR.*

Moderate

Aster House

3 Sumner Place, SW7 3EE (7581 5888/fax 7584 4925/www.asterhouse.com). South Kensington tube. **Rates** £90 single; £140 double. **Credit** MC, V. **Map** p397 D11.

Sumner Place is one of London's most elegant addresses, and Aster House bravely attempts to live up to its upscale location. In reality, the lobby – with its pink faux marble and gold chandeliers – is more kitsch than glam, but the effect is still charming. So is the lush garden, with its pond and wandering ducks. Even lovelier is the palm-filled conservatory, where guests eat breakfast and read the papers. The bedrooms are comfortable, with traditional floral upholstery, and swish marble bathrooms – ask for one with a power shower. The hotel, two-time winner of London Tourism's Best B&B award, now lends its guests mobile phones during their stay, and the rooms all have modem points. If all that isn't enough, it's just a damn good location: the museums and big-name shops are all close at hand.
Hotel services *Air-conditioning. Babysitting. Business services. Garden. No-smoking throughout.* **Room services** *Dataport. TV: cable/satellite.*

Cranley Gardens Hotel

8 Cranley Gardens, SW7 3DB (7373 3232/fax 7373 7944/www.cranleygardenshotel.com). Gloucester Road tube. **Rates** £79-£89 single; £109-£115 double; £135 triple. **Credit** AmEx, DC, MC, V. **Map** p397 D11.

Formerly a Hilton, this Victorian townhouse hotel still has a whiff of an American chain hotel about it. But it's also got some of the charming touches of a small English hotel, such as in the faux gentleman's club lobby, with its plush sofas and piped-in classical music, and in the traditional bar. The rooms are less trad English than Holiday Inn, but, for some people, this may not be such a bad thing. The hotel has been run by the same family for aeons, which keeps it from feeling too corporate. Then there's the superb location: walking distance to museums, and shopping in Knightsbridge and Chelsea.
Hotel services *Babysitting. Bar. Business services. No-smoking rooms. Coffee shop.* **Room services** *Dataport. Room service (8am-midnight). TV: cable/satellite.*

Five Sumner Place

5 Sumner Place, SW7 3EE (7584 7586/fax 7823 9962/www.sumnerplace.com). South Kensington tube. **Rates** £100 single; £153 double. **Credit** AmEx, MC, V. **Map** p397 D11.

Situated in a row of white Victorian townhouses, Five Sumner Place has a picturesque location, and a convenient one, too: it's near the museums, and handy for shopping in Knightsbridge and Chelsea. The decor is pleasant, but nothing special: think faux period English. But the rooms are clean and comfortable, and very technologically advanced for a small hotel: all rooms now have free broadband

wireless access and voicemail. There's also a lovely conservatory, where breakfast is served, and heaven's above, there's a lift – always a godsend in townhouse hotels. In the past, this place has won a slew of tourism awards, and it's easy to see why: Tom Tyranowicz, the longtime manager, has a friendly and gentle manner.
Hotel services *Garden. No-smoking floors.* **Room services** *Dataport. Minibar. Room service (8am-10pm). TV.*

Gainsborough Hotel

7-11 Queensberry Place, SW7 2DL (7957 0000/fax 7957 0001/www.eeh.co.uk). South Kensington tube. **Rates** £88 single; £141 double; £223-£258 suite. **Credit** AmEx, DC, MC, V. **Map** p397 D10.
Part of the Elegant English Hotels mini-chain, the Gainsborough does its best to live up to the role. Full marks for the Gainsborough original that hangs in the traditional English lobby. For the price, the rooms are classy affairs: the odd piece of Louis XVI-style furniture, damask upholstery and oriental porcelain lamps. Downstairs, the Picasso Bar is almost chic, with its black and gold tasselled drapes. The Ritz it ain't, but it does a pretty good imitation – and it won't break the bank either.
Hotel services *Bar. Business services. Concierge. No-smoking rooms.* **Room services** *Room service (24hrs). TV: cable.*

Gallery Hotel

8-10 Queensberry Place, SW7 2DL (7915 0000/fax 7915 4400/www.eeh.co.uk). South Kensington tube. **Rates** £141-£170 double; £188 triple; £258 suite. **Credit** AmEx, DC, MC, V. **Map** p397 D10.
Like the Gainsborough, this is also part of the Elegant English Hotels mini-chain – and it, too, does a good pastiche of a grand London hotel. It's actually a cut above its sister hotel: the plush bedrooms bravely combine classical English chintz with abstract art, and the granite bathrooms are smart. The main rooms are classy, too: the stately lobby bar is pure gentleman's club (rich mahogany panelling, leather armchairs, Jacobean-style fireplace), and the basement Morris lounge is a delightful Arts and Crafts-style space.
Hotel services *Air-conditioning. Bar. Concierge. Gym. Limousine service.* **Room services** *Dataport. Minibar. Room service (24hrs). Turndown. TV: cable/VCR.*

Hotel 167

167 Old Brompton Road, SW5 0AN (7373 0672/fax 7373 3360/www.hotel167.com). Gloucester Road tube. **Rates** £72-£86 single; £90-£99 double. **Credit** AmEx, DC, MC, V. **Map** p397 D11.
It may be located in a Victorian townhouse, but this funky little hotel is no period clone. On the contrary, its decor is positively quirky. The lobby makes a bold statement, with its black and white tiled floor and striking abstract art. Upstairs, the bedrooms are an eclectic mix of traditional and bohemian: the odd antique piece or Victorian painting, with contemporary touches (Mexican bedspreads, Klee prints). The whole place has a whiff of bohemia (not to mention pot pourri), and its shambolic charm has inspired artists: it's been the subject of a song (an unreleased track by the Manic Street Preachers) and a novel (*Hotel 167* by Jane Solomons).
Room services *TV: satellite.*

Swiss House Hotel

171 Old Brompton Road, SW5 0AN (7373 2769/fax 7373 4983/www.swiss-hh.demon.co.uk). Gloucester Road tube. **Rates** £51-£71 single; £89-£104 double; £120 triple; £134 quad. **Credit** AmEx, DC, MC, V. **Map** p397 D11.
Don't expect an Alpine-themed hotel: this Victorian townhouse used to be a private residence for Swiss Air crews, hence the name. Still, the whole place has a country fresh appeal, an d quite tasteful decor from the attractive pine furniture to the dark wooden beams in the breakfast room. The bedrooms have a crisp, clean aesthetic, with white walls and classic navy bed linens making a welcome change from the chintz nightmare that is most budget hotels. Pretty good value, for the location.
Hotel services *No-smoking rooms.* **Room services** *TV.*

Cheap

Abbey House

11 Vicarage Gate, W8 4AG (7727 2594/fax 7727 1873/www.abbeyhousekensington.com). High Street Kensington or Notting Hill Gate tube. **Rates** £45 single; £74 double; £90 triple; £100 quad. **No credit cards. Map** p394 B8.
Located in a quiet Victorian square, this elegant townhouse hotel offers affordable access to the swanky shops and restaurants of Kensington Church Street. The lobby is in keeping with the upmarket location: glittering chandeliers, black and white tiled marble floor and attractive greenery. The rooms very simply decorated – but they're clean and comfortable, and many come with orthopaedic mattresses. Bathrooms must be shared, but they're spotless and not unattractive.
Hotel services *No-smoking throughout. Payphone.* **Room servic**e *TV.*

Vicarage Hotel

10 Vicarage Gate, W8 4AG (7229 4030/fax 7792 5989/www.londonvicaragehotel.com). High Street Kensington or Notting Hill Gate tube. **Rates** £46-£72 single; £78-£102 double; £95 triple; £102 quad. **No credit cards. Map** p394 B8.
This well-kept Victorian townhouse hotel has a split personality: the lobby is glitzy, with red and gold wallpaper and ornate mirrors. The rooms, however, are tasteful: they're painted in pastels and furnished with antiques, comfortable beds and subtle floral fabrics. The summery TV lounge is fresh and inviting. Another bonus: nine of the 17 rooms now have bathrooms, with more conversions on the way.
Hotel services *Payphone. TV room.*

Belgravia & Pimlico

Deluxe

Lanesborough

Hyde Park Corner, SW1X 7TA (7259 5599/fax 7259 5606/www.lanesborough.com). Hyde Park Corner tube. **Rates** (breakfast not incl) £335-£393 single; £464 double; £699-£5,875 suite. **Credit** AmEx, DC, MC, V. **Map** p400 G8.

Formerly a hospital, the Lanesborough has been reborn as one of London's most opulent hotels: it only opened in 1991, but it's already achieved that legendary status normally associated with the Ritz and the Savoy. The lobby has a luxurious, Italianate feel: cream-coloured marble, Ionic columns and elegant urns. The Conservatory restaurant is resplendent with Chinoiserie and lush greenery. The bedrooms are sheer luxury, with masculine oak panelling and four-poster beds. Each guest has a personal butler, who guides them through the multimedia system available on the TVs. If you've got a generous expense account, and feel like being pampered, the Lanesborough will spoil you rotten.

Hotel services *Air-conditioning. Babysitting. Bar. Business services. Concierge. Disabled: adapted rooms. Gym. Laundry. Limousine service. No-smoking rooms. Parking. Restaurant.* **Room services** *Dataport. Hi-fi. Minibar. Room service (24hrs). Turndown. TV: cable/DVD/satellite/web TV.*

The Halkin

5 Halkin Street, SW1X 7DJ (7333 1000/fax 7333 1100/www.halkin.co.uk). Hyde Park Corner tube. **Rates** (breakfast not incl) £364-£464 double; £582-£1,293 suite. **Credit** AmEx, DC, MC, V. **Map** p400 G9.

The Halkin is a suave and discreet designer hotel. It's gimmick free, with subtle design and attentive service, so it could outlast its trendier rivals. Decorated by chic Italian designers, the modern bedrooms are simply luxurious, with rich cherrywood walls and marble bathrooms – and those Bulgari toiletries are always the sign of a classy hotel. Cool bedside gadgetry controls the lighting and temperature. The hotel's other selling point is Nahm, an excellent Michelin-starred Thai restaurant (*see p211*).

Hotel services *Air-conditioning. Babysitting. Bar. Business services. Concierge. No-smoking rooms. Parking (valet). Restaurant.* **Room services** *Dataport. Hi-fi. Minibar. Room service (24hr). Turndown. TV: cable/satellite/VCR.*

Moderate

Dolphin Square Hotel

Dolphin Square, Chichester Street, SW1V 3LX (7798 8890/fax 7798 8896/www.dolphinsquarehotel.co.uk). Pimlico tube. **Rates** (breakfast not incl) £175 studio; £225 1 bedroom; £260-£330 2 bedrooms; £450 3 bedrooms. **Credit** AmEx, DC, MC, V. **Map** p401 M8.

Dolphin Square is a London legend. Not the hotel, but the flats: this massive 1930s mansion block is built like a fortress and survived bombing during the Second World War. Its posh flats are also home to politicians, barristers and civil servants. One wing of the building is devoted to a hotel, which is popular – and deservedly so. Its restaurant, formerly run by Gary Rhodes and recently taken over by the Savoy's Anton Edelmann, is fabulous. The rest of the hotel is casual, done up in a nautical theme – the lobby feels a bit like a cruise ship – mixed with art deco touches. The rooms are large, comfortable and contemporary, with stereos and kitchenettes. Then there's the indoor swimming pool, excellent health club and beautiful landscaped gardens, and a great old-fashioned shopping arcade. Best of all, it's very reasonably priced.

Hotel services *Bar. Beauty salon. Business services. Concierge. Disabled: adapted rooms. Garden. Gym. Laundry (self-service). No-smoking floors. Restaurant. Swimming pool (indoor).* **Room services** *Dataport. Kitchenettes. Room service (24hrs). TV: cable/pay movies/satellite.*

Tophams

28 Ebury Street, SW1W 0LU (7730 8147/fax 7823 5966/www.tophams.co.uk). Victoria tube/rail. **Rates** £115 single; £140 double; £170 triple; £260 family. **Credit** AmEx, DC, MC, V. **Map** p400 H10.

This cosy Georgian hotel is a little charmer. An atmospheric rabbit warren of a place, with narrow, meandering corridors, creaking floors and nooks and crannies, it's been run by the same family for more than 60 years. It has grandmotherly appeal: china cabinets, candlewick bedspreads, white wicker furniture. It's a pleasure to dine in the fab crimson restaurant, which has an adjoining bar. Service is personalised: one visitor returned so often the hotel's owners had a room decorated to his taste. Rooms at the back have a view of Margaret Thatcher's house, if that floats your boat.

Hotel services *Babysitting. Bar. Concierge. Limousine service. No-smoking rooms. Parking. Restaurant.* **Room services** *Dataport. Room service (24hrs). TV: cable/satellite.*

Cheap

Windermere Hotel

142-4 Warwick Way, SW1V 4JE (7834 5163/fax 7630 8831/www.windermere-hotel.co.uk). Victoria tube/rail. **Rates** £64-£96 single; £89-£139 double; £139-£149 family. **Credit** AmEx, MC, V. **Map** p400 H11.

Finalist in the 2003 London Tourism Awards' Best B&B category, the Windermere is a super small hotel. London's first-ever B&B opened on this site in 1881, and the current owners continue its proud legacy. The rooms are neat and comfortable and done up in reasonably tasteful English chintz. There are some classy touches to give them character, such as mother-of-pearl tea trays, chrome fans and the odd coronet bed. The bathrooms are clean and

Lanesborough does grand style. *See p58.*

modern, with power showers. It's unusual to find in a B&B such well-conceived extras as room service, modem points and satellite TV. Another rarity for a budget hotel is the basement restaurant, which has pleasant faux rustic decor and a sophisticated, decently priced menu.
Hotel services *Bar. Business services. No smoking floors. Restaurant.* **Room services** *Dataport. Room service (24hrs). Telephone. TV: cable.*

Woodville House & Morgan House

107 Ebury Street, SW1W 9QU (7730 1048/fax 7730 2574/www.woodvillehouse.co.uk) & 120 Ebury Street, SW1W 9QQ (7730 2384/fax 7730 8442/ www.morganhouse.co.uk). Victoria tube/rail. **Rates** £46-£74 single; £66-£86 double; £86-£110 triple; £122 quad. **Credit** MC, V. **Map** p400H10.
These sister hotels represent excellent value (for London), and are sweet and comfortable. They're owned by the husband-and-wife team of Rachel Joplin and Ian Berry, a friendly presence at both establishments. It's definitely a small-scale place (the entrance halls in both hotels are narrow, and some of the rooms are quite dinky), but run with great efficiency and concern for guests. Other characteristics shared by both hotels is a well-presented, but tiny, walled garden and prettily decorated breakfast rooms you cannot help but linger in. The bedrooms are cosy, and some of the beds have orthopaedic mattresses. The Woodville is decorated in a more traditional English style, the Morgan has a lighter, contemporary feel. Both have pleasant family rooms, with bunk beds and teddy bears for more diminutive guests.
Hotel services *Garden. No-smoking rooms. Payphone.* **Room services** *Telephone (incoming calls only). TV.*

North London

Cheap

Hampstead Village Guesthouse

2 Kemplay Road, NW3 1SY (7435 8679/fax 7794 0254/www.hampsteadguesthouse.com). Hampstead tube/Hampstead Heath rail. **Rates** (breakfast not incl) £48-£66 single; £72-£84 double; £90-£150 studio. **Credit** AmEx, MC, V.
Many Londoners would love to live in Hampstead; this comfy B&B, in a characterful Victorian pile, makes the fantasy an affordable reality. It's a short walk away from both Hampstead Heath and the quaint village, but the decor is more bohemian than *Country Life*: it's filled with an eccentric mix of books, rag dolls, Delft earthenware, and other curios. Some might find the rooms cluttered, but others think it's charming. It definitely feels like a home – owner Annemarie van der Meer lives on site. Breakfast is served in the garden, weather permitting; there's also a cottage, which sleeps five. There's a 5% surcharge if you pay by credit card.
Hotel services *Garden. No-smoking throughout. Parking.* **Room services** *Telephone. TV.*

South-west London

Moderate

Riverside Hotel

23 Petersham Road, Richmond-upon-Thames, Surrey TW10 6UH (tel/fax 8940 1339/ www.riversiderichmond.co.uk). Richmond tube/rail. **Rates** £65 single; £85-£90 double; £125 suite. **Credit** AmEx, DC, MC, V.

Comfortably affordable. The **Mayflower Hotel**. *See p63.*

Perched on the edge of the Thames, the Riverside Hotel is a rural retreat from the urban hurly burly. A 20-minute train journey from Waterloo Station, it's near Richmond Park, Kew Gardens and a few stately homes, including Marble Hill House and Ham House. The pleasing rooms are decorated in a traditional English style: some have views of the Thames, and all now have wireless broadband internet access. The spacious suites offer good value. But the best thing about the hotel is its proximity to the tranquil Thames footpath, on which you can follow the meandering river for miles.
Hotel services *No-smoking rooms. Parking.*
Room services *Dataport. Room service (10am-11.30pm). TV: satellite.*

The Victoria Pub

10 West Temple Sheen, SW14 7RT (8876 4238/ fax 8878 3464/www.thevictoria.net). Richmond tube/ Mortlake rail. **Rate** £82-£92 double. **Credit** AmEx, MC, V.

This classy gastropub has a delightful little bed & breakfast operation. Its seven en suite double bedrooms are a far cry from your typical room above a pub: they are decorated in tasteful neutral colour schemes, with beech beds and Egyptian cotton linen. This is obviously the option for those who want to stay away from the hurly burly – for central London sightseeing, it's a bit out of the way, but glorious Richmond Park, with its nearby swimming pools, riding schools and bike hire, is on your doorstep, and Heathrow Airport is easily accessible from here. If you fancy a quiet holiday with delicious food guaranteed (the menu in the restaurant is wonderful) this could be what you're looking for.
Hotel services *Bar. Business services. Garden. No-smoking throughout. Parking. Restaurant.*
Room services *Dataport. Room service (drinks only, noon-midnight). TV.*

West London

Deluxe

The Hempel

31-35 Craven Hill Gardens, W2 3EA (7298 9000/ fax 7402 4666/www.the-hempel.co.uk). Lancaster Gate or Queensway tube/Paddington tube/rail. **Rates** (breakfast not incl) £323 single; £346 double; £517-£1,527 suite. **Credit** AmEx, DC, MC, V.
Map p394 C6.

The Hempel is London's most breathtakingly minimalist hotel. It divides the critics: there are those who favour the feng shui/fashionista glamour look; others say it's cold, clinical and past its sell-by date. Either way, you can't fail to be impressed by its jaw dropping white lobby, where light spills down from a six-storey atrium. The rooms have a modern Japanese feel, all pristine whiteness with orchids. One of the suites even has a bed that hangs from the ceiling. Downstairs, a translucent staircase leads to the pricey and rather chi-chi I-Thai restaurant, which fuses Italian and Thai cuisines.
Hotel services *Air-conditioning. Babysitting. Bar. Business services. Concierge. Disabled: adapted rooms. Garden. Limousine service. No-smoking rooms. Parking (valet). Restaurant.* **Room services** *Dataport. Hi-fi. Minibar. Room service (24hrs). Turndown. TV: cable/pay movies/satellite.*

Moderate

Amsterdam Hotel

7 Trebovir Road, SW5 9LS (0800 279 9132/fax 7244 7608/www.amsterdam-hotel.com). Earl's Court tube. **Rates** £78-£86 single; £88-£100 double; £112-£135 triple. **Credit** AmEx, DC, MC, V.
Map p396 B11.

We don't know why it's called the Amsterdam, since the whole place feels like a Florida condo, with a palm-filled lobby, tropical upholstery and Caribbean prints. The rooms are done up in Key West pastels, and are comfortable and modern. (There are no modem points, but you can check your email in the basement internet room.) The breakfast room, too, feels more Gulf of Mexico than Earl's Court, with its white wicker and bamboo furniture. All the cheery decor is great on a grey London day. For longer stays, ask about the wing of private apartments.
Hotel services *Business services. Garden. No-smoking throughout. TV room.* **Room services** *Dataport. Room service (7.30am-9.30pm). TV.*

Colonnade Town House

2 Warrington Crescent, W9 1ER (7286 1052/fax 7286 1057/www.etontownhouse.com). Warwick Avenue tube. **Rates** (breakfast not incl) £148 single; £173-£211 double; £270-£288 suite. **Credit** AmEx, DC, MC, V.

This luxurious Victorian townhouse hotel is more reasonably priced than others of its ilk. The catch? Its off-the-beaten track location. But this is also an advantage: Little Venice is one of London's most picturesque neighbourhoods, and it's close to Paddington and the Heathrow Express. The rooms are plush: beds are draped in Egyptian cotton sheets and crushed velvet bedspreads. The hotel also has a historical legacy: the JFK suite has an enormous four-poster bed built for the president's 1962 state visit; there's a magnificent suite named after Sigmund Freud, a former guest; and Alan Turing, who cracked the Enigma code, was born here. Downstairs, the contemporary Enigma bar and restaurant serves up Mediterranean cuisine.
Hotel services *Air-conditioning. Bar. Concierge. Limousine service. No-smoking rooms. Parking. Restaurant.* **Room services** *Dataport. Hi-fi. Minibar. Room service (24hrs). Turndown. TV: cable/satellite.*

London Elizabeth Hotel

4 Lancaster Terrace, W2 3PF (7402 6641/fax 7224 8900/www.londonelizabethhotel.co.uk). Lancaster Gate tube. **Rates** £100 single; £115-£140 double; £180-£250 suite. **Credit** AmEx, DC, MC, V. **Map** p395 D6.

This glitzy old hotel has seen better days – it was probably a glamorous address in the 1960s – but faded grandeur is part of its charm. The lobby has gaudy chandeliers and worn damask, and the pink Rose Garden restaurant (only open for breakfast) gives kitsch a good name. The bar is theatrical, and opens on to a terrace garden. The standard rooms are a bit dowdy, but the suites are treats. The Conservatory Suite has stained-glass windows and old-fashioned features; the Hyde Park Suite, with ornate furniture and mirrors, is straight out of Dynasty. Both are, by London standards, a bargain.
Hotel services *Air-conditioning (deluxe rooms & suites). Bar. Business services. Garden. Parking.* **Room services** *Dataport. Room service (24hrs). TV.*

Mornington Lancaster Hotel

12 Lancaster Gate, W2 3LG (7262 7361/fax 7706 1028/www.mornington.com). Lancaster Gate tube. **Rates** £125 single; £140 double; £165 triple; £175 suite. **Credit** AmEx, DC, MC, V. **Map** p395 D7.

This hotel, recently taken over by Best Western, used to be owned and run by Swedes, who built up a loyal following among Scandinavian businessmen. They'd certainly feel at home in the rooms, with their clean, contemporary wooden floors and IKEA-style furniture. In keeping with the Nordic heritage, there's a smörgåsbord-style breakfast alongside the traditional English variety. If you're here on business, as many of the guests are, there's a guest office with PC, internet connection and printer.
Hotel services *Bar. Concierge. No-smoking floors.* **Room services** *Dataport. Room service (24hrs). TV: cable/pay movies.*

Pembridge Court

34 Pembridge Gardens, W2 4DX (7229 9977/fax 7727 4982/www.pemct.co.uk). Notting Hill Gate tube. **Rates** £125-£165 single; £160-£195 double. **Credit** AmEx, DC, MC, V. **Map** p394 A7.

This restored townhouse hotel has a friendly atmosphere and a theatrical feel. Rooms are done up in floral upholstery with heavy drapes; marble bathrooms have brass taps and huge showerheads. Downstairs, the sitting room is homely: there are squashy sofas, shelves lined with paperback novels, and Churchill, the hotel's resident ginger cat. There's also an internet station so you can check your email; on the coffee table copies of *Billboard* magazine reflect the hotel's status among music biz types, who can reach trendy Portobello Road through the back door.
Hotel services *Air-conditioning. Babysitting. Bar. Breakfast room. Business services. TV room.* **Room services** *Dataport. Room service (24hrs). TV: satellite/VCR.*

Portobello Hotel

22 Stanley Gardens, W11 2NG (7727 2777/fax 7792 9641/www.portobello-hotel.co.uk). Notting Hill Gate tube. **Rates** £120 single; £160-£275 double. **Credit** AmEx, MC, V. **Map** p394 A6.

There's a whiff of bohemian chic about the Portobello, a towering townhouse hotel. The rooms have a colonial feel: potted palms, ceiling fans, wooden shutters and riental antique furniture. Some are pokey, some are spectacular: Room 16, for instance, has a clawfoot bathtub in the middle of the room and a circular bed – and is a favourite with wealthy actors. Indeed, hip stars flock to the place, drawn by its eccentric charm: past guests include Reese Witherspoon, Kylie Minogue and Julianne Moore. To keep the celebs happy, there's organic food and 24-hour room service. There are modern comforts: jacuzzi tubs in many rooms and state-of-the-art technology, including internet access and electronic film libraries in each room.
Hotel services *Air-conditioning. Babysitting. Bar. Business services. No-smoking rooms. Restaurant.* **Room services** *Dataport. Minibar. Room service (24hrs). TV: cable/VCR.*

Where to Stay

Grand entrances

Even if you can't afford to stay in London's more luxurious hotels, you can still soak up the glamour in their substantial lobbies. For glitz, you can't beat the **Dorchester** (*see p49*), a breathtaking fantasy of marble and gilt. Elegant women take afternoon tea in the luxurious adjacent foyer, surrounded by crystal vases with fresh lilies, ornate statues and glittering mirrors. Elizabeth Taylor and Richard Burton spent their honeymoon here, which says it all: the Dorchester recalls a gorgeous pre-Met Bar age when the celebrities really were stars.

The lobby at the **Ritz** (*see p51*) is another baroque extravaganza, topped by a two-storey rotunda of iron-railed galleries with a stained-glass roof; in the centre of the room is a spectacular floral display. The cream marble walls are adorned with elaborate gilt mouldings, wall sconces and bronze statues. To the right of the entrance, dazzling gems from the Ritz jewellery shop up the glitter quotient. Straight ahead is a magnificent gallery, filled with Louis XVI furniture, sparkling chandeliers and sumptuous carpets. The hilariously pompous doormen will accost you the minute you walk in, but stand your ground and tell them you're there to have a look around.

For a serious helping of art deco glam, **Claridge's** (*see p49*) is your best bet. In the front hall, the black and white checked marble floor is jazzy, as are the blue glass mirrors and silver Ionic columns. Framed vintage photographs of Winston Churchill and a young Queen Elizabeth add to the retro feel. The avant-garde chandelier in the foyer, made from 800 different pieces of glass, is extraordinary.

At the other end of the style scale, nobody does minimalism quite like the **Hempel** (*see p60*). Its clinical style even affects the flora: on a table as you enter, 200 fresh white orchids stand at attention. This is a trance-inducing, white-on-white space, more chic gallery than hotel: it's an odd mixture of feng shui and glamour – at times you feel like you're cluttering up the place. And you are, really: luggage is an eyesore in these pristine surroundings, and the only furniture are four antique Burmese ox carts – if you want to sit down, try the floor. To add to the Zen mystique, fire leaps out of the Japanese stone gardens: suppress the urge to chant and walk barefoot over the flames.

The **St Martin's Lane Hotel** and the **Sanderson** both take the minimalist schtick and give it a theatrical spin (*see p53 and*

Twenty Nevern Square

20 Nevern Square, SW5 9PD (7565 9555/fax 7565 9444/www.twentynevernsquare.co.uk). Earl's Court tube. **Rates** £110-£175 double; £250 suite. **Credit** AmEx, DC, MC, V. **Map** p396 A11.

We didn't know Earl's Court could be so stylish. Like its sister hotel, the Mayflower (*see below*), 27 has just been refurbished in exotic style. Most impressive are the carved oriental headboards and wardrobes, and the silk curtains. The sleek marble bathrooms, too, imitate those found in designer hotels. The Far Eastern feel extends to the lounge and the light, airy conservatory breakfast room, done up in wicker furniture and greenery. The hotel overlooks an elegant square, which seems worlds away from the stamping grounds of the backpacker brigade normally associated with Earl's Court.

Hotel services *Bar. No-smoking floors. Parking. Restaurant.* **Room services** *Dataport. Room service (24hr). TV: cable.*

Vancouver Studios

30 Prince's Square, W2 4NJ (7243 1270/fax 7221 8678/www.vancouverstudios.co.uk). Bayswater or Queensway tube. **Rates** (breakfast not incl) £77 single; £97-£112 double; £132 triple. **Credit** AmEx, DC, MC, V. **Map** p394 B6.

This is a homely place with a cosy lounge, a fireplace and a wandering cat. The lush walled garden is lovely in the right weather. Each bedroom has a kitchenette, meaning you can save a bundle on eating out. They're bright and funky, too, with Kandinsky prints on the walls and contemporary bedspreads. All rooms have power showers. Throw in friendly staff, reasonable prices and a central location, and you've got one of London's best deals.

Hotel services *Business services. Garden. Internet room. Laundry (self-service).* **Room services** *Dataport. Kitchenette. Room service (9am-3pm). TV.*

Cheap

Garden Court Hotel

30-31 Kensington Gardens Square, W2 4BG (7229 2553/fax 7727 2749/www.gardencourthotel.co.uk). Bayswater or Queensway tube. **Rates** £39-£58 single; £58-£88 double; £72-£99 triple; £82-£120 quad. **Credit** MC, V. **Map** p394 B6.

Garden Court is another small townhouse hotel, but, unlike so many in London, it has a bit of panache: that becomes clear as soon as you enter the lobby, with its giant Beefeater statue, marble busts and bonsai trees. It's been run by the same family for 50

p46). At the former, luminescent yellow glass doors and designer-clad doormen give way to a tongue-in-chic space with oversized columns and quirky Starck creations: oversized chess pieces and gold-tooth stools are juxtaposed with Versailles-style furniture. It's not as cool as it once was, but there's still a showbiz buzz to the place. The Sanderson's lobby is more ethereal: flowing diaphanous curtains and surreal touches, red lip sofas, framed oil portraits of chihuahuas and, in the Long Bar, stools with eyes on the back.

The lobby at one of the smartest deluxe hotels, **One Aldwych** (*see p52*), is a pleasing fusion of traditional and modern. The hotel is housed in an old Edwardian bank building, but its imposing grey exterior gives way to an elegant, airy white-tiled lobby. Light pours in through the grand arched windows, but the even more striking is the avant-garde sculpture, bold, abstract art and the impossibly extravagant floral displays. Best of all, this place is remarkably unpretentious. Perhaps that's because it doubles as a cocktail bar, so you can linger to admire your elegant surroundings as long as you like – without a stuffy uniformed doorman to chase you away.

years. The rooms are cheery, with wooden furniture and comfy beds, and there's an attractive lounge. Guests have access to the square's pretty garden.
Hotel services *Business services. Garden. No-smoking throughout.* **Room services** *Telephone. TV: cable.*

Kensington Gardens Hotel

9 Kensington Gardens Square, W2 4BH (7221 7790/fax 7792 8612/www.kensingtongardenshotel.co.uk). Bayswater or Queensway tube.
Rates £45-£55 single; £75 double; £95 triple.
Credit AmEx, DC, MC, V. **Map** p394 B6.
Another pretty Victorian square, another small townhouse hotel. This one, however, is cheap, with an elegant lobby staffed 24 hours a day, and just a walk from Hyde Park and fashionable Westbourne Grove and Notting Hill. The rooms are clean and comfortable, if unspectacular, but the location's fab.
Room services *Minibar. TV.*

Mayflower Hotel

26-8 Trebovir Road, SW5 9NJ (7370 0991/fax 7370 0994/www.mayflowerhotel.co.uk). Earl's Court tube.
Rates £69-£79 single; £79-£109 double; £99-£129 triple; £110-£150 quad. **Credit** AmEx, MC, V. **Map** p396 B11.
The Mayflower is a cheap hotel and, following a major refurbishment, quite stylish too. Decorated in a minimalist theme, the rooms have wooden floors and hand-carved beds from the Far East. Ceiling fans add a tropical feel, and the marble bathrooms, CD players and dataports lend an air of modern luxury. Downstairs, the lobby has an impressive teak arch from Jaipur and a trendy juice bar.
Hotel services *Business services. No-smoking rooms.* **Room services** *Dataport. Hi-fi. Telephone. TV: satellite.*

Rushmore Hotel

11 Trebovir Road, SW5 9LS (7370 3839/fax 7370 0274/www.rushmorehotel.co.uk). Earl's Court tube.
Rates from £55 single; from £65 double; from £85 quad. **Credit** AmEx, DC, MC, V. **Map** p396 B11.
The Rushmore is a rare breed: a budget hotel with a bit of flair. The hotel's biggest talking point is the *trompe l'oeil* paintings which adorn the walls, depicting everything from pastoral Tuscany to tranquil ocean scenes. The Italianate breakfast room, with its granite surfaces and glass tables, is extremely stylish for such a low-cost hotel.
Hotel services *Business services. No-smoking rooms. TV room.* **Room services** *Dataport. Telephone. TV: cable.*

In the swim

With a few exceptions, London hotels that have swimming pools tend to be bland chains. In the interest of a good swim, however, we've put aside our prejudice against the chains – to hell with character when all you want to do is the breast stroke – and included them in our list of the best hotel swimming pools. With the exception of the Sheraton Skyline, the places listed below let non-residents use their pools, although most ask you to join the hotel health club before you can dive in.

One Aldwych (*see p52*) is a favourite of ours, not least because it has a stunning pool. Situated in the hotel's basement, it's a mellow spot: a circular staircase from the health spa leads down to the long pool, where dim lighting and classical music piped underwater create a romantic mood. The water is a surreal shade of blue, and the modern design is lovely.

The rooftop swimming pool at the **Savoy** (pictured; *see p52*) evokes the old-school glamour of an ocean liner – which is a polite way of saying it's tiny. Here's a tip: don't push off too hard, or you'll hurt yourself hitting the other side. But the Savoy has found a novel solution to the potentially embarrassing size issue. The installation of a jet stream system – a water version of a treadmill – now makes it possible to swim on the same spot for hours on end. It sounds like our idea of hell, but it's exercise: to find a pool of any size in one of London's grand old hotels is a bonus.

The **Berkeley Hotel** (Wilton Place, Knightsbridge, SW1; 7235 6000), on the other hand, combines the elegance of a grand hotel with a gem of a swimming pool. Surrounded by marble arches, this rooftop pool is pure neo-classical grace. It's outdoors, sort of – there's a retractable roof – and the walled terrace has sunbeds from which you can order a light lunch. Bliss. Through glass windows there are panoramic views of Hyde Park.

You won't get fantastic views from the pool at the **Dolphin Square Hotel** (*see p58*). In fact, you're more likely to get a glimpse of a Tory politician in his swimming trunks, as this all-suite hotel is part of a Thames-side complex of luxury flats favoured by politicians. Don't let that put you off: the 59-foot (18-metre) indoor pool is lovely, with a frosted glass roof and art deco flourishes for which the hotel is famous.

The **Carlton Tower Hotel** (2 Cadogan Place, SW3; 7235 1234), part of the Jumeirah group, has a 65-foot (20-metre) indoor pool resembles one you might find in a Caribbean resort. It is surrounded by palm trees and lush foliage; sunshine pours through the glass roof.

Youth hostels

Hostel beds are either in twin rooms or dorms. If you're not a member of the International Youth Hostel Federation (IYHF), you'll pay an extra £2 a night (after six nights you automatically become a member). Alternatively, join the IYHF for £13 (£6.50 for under-18s) at any hostel, or through www.yha.org.uk, which also allows you to book rooms. Always phone ahead for availability. The London hostels listed below take MasterCard and Visa; prices include breakfast.

City of London *36-8 Carter Lane, EC4V 5AB (7236 4965/fax 7236 7681). St Paul's tube/Blackfriars tube/rail.* **Reception open** 7am-11pm daily; 24hr access. **Rates** £15-£30; £15-£24 under-18s. **Map** p404 O6.

Earl's Court *38 Bolton Gardens, SW5 0AQ (7373 7083/fax 7835 2034). Earl's Court tube.* **Reception open** 7am-11pm daily; 24hr access. **Rates** £22.50; £20.25 under-18s. **Map** p396 B11.

Hampstead Heath *4 Wellgarth Road, NW11 7HR (8458 9054/fax 8209 0546). Golders Green tube.*
Reception open 7am-11pm daily; 24hr access. **Rates** £20.40; £18 under-18s.

Holland House *Holland Walk, W8 7QU (7937 0748/fax 7376 0667). High Street Kensington tube.* **Reception open** 7am-11pm daily; 24hr access. **Rates** £21; £18.75 under-18s. **Map** p394 A8.

Oxford Street *14 Noel Street, W1F 8GJ (7734 1618/fax 7734 1657). Oxford Circus tube.* **Reception open** 7am-11pm daily; 24hr access. **Rates** £25.40-£27.40; £20.75 under-18s. **Map** p398 J6.

Rotherhithe *Island Yard, 20 Salter Road, Rotherhithe, SE16 5PR (7232 2114/fax 7237 2919). Rotherhithe or Canada Water tube.* **Reception open** 7am-11pm; 24hr access. **Rates** £24; £20 under-18s.

St Pancras *79-81 Euston Road, NW1 2QS (7388 9998/fax 7388 6766). King's Cross tube/rail.* **Reception open** 7am-11pm daily; 24hr access. **Rates** £24; £20 under-18s. **Map** p399 L3.

The Grange chain (7233 7888) also has a couple of superb pools. The **Grange Holborn**, a mammoth five-star hotel favoured by business travellers, has a 49-foot (15-metre), indoor pool done up in a luxurious Roman spa style – think marble columns and exotic tiles. Health nuts can complement their training with a nutritious concoction from the juice bar. The **Grange City**, meanwhile, has a similarly opulent pool, surrounded by marble and palm trees, but it's even bigger: at 82 feet by 26 feet (25 metres by 8 metres) it's one of London's largest hotel pools.

The 49-foot (15-metre) indoor pool at the **Landmark Hotel** (222 Marylebone Road, W1; 7631 8000) is one of a new wave of pools that use ozone, an eco-friendly alternative to chlorine, to keep its water clean.

Other chain hotels with decent pools include the **May Fair Intercontinental** (Stratton Street, SW1; 7629 7777), which has a 32-foot (10-metre) indoor pool with sauna and solarium and **Le Meridien Grosvenor House** (86-90 Park Lane, W1; 7499 6363), which has a 72-foot (22-metre) pool (the largest underground pool in town).

Scoff if you will at airport hotels, but the **Sheraton Skyline Hotel** (8759 2535) has a huge, Miami-style pool with poolside bar, to get you in a Club Tropicana frame of mind.

YMCAs

You may need to book months ahead to stay at a YMCA, this Christian organisation is primarily concerned with providing housing for homeless young people across the world, so many of their hostels specialise in long-term accommodation for the needy. A few of the larger London hostels open to all are listed below (all are unisex), but you can get a full list from the National Council for YMCAs (8520 5599/www.ymca.org.uk). Prices are around £25-£30 per night for a single room and £40-£45 for a double.

Barbican YMCA *2 Fann Street, EC2Y 8BR (7628 0697/fax 7638 2420). Barbican tube.* **Map** p402 P5.

London City YMCA *8 Errol Street, EC1Y 8SE (7628 8832/fax 7628 4080). Barbican tube/Old Street tube/rail.* **Map** p402 F4.

Wimbledon YMCA *200 The Broadway, SW19 1RY (8542 9055/fax 8540 2526). South Wimbledon tube/Wimbledon tube/rail.*

Staying with the locals

These organisations can arrange accommodation in a Londoner's home (often more fun than an impersonal hotel); rates include breakfast.

At Home in London *70 Black Lion Lane, Hammersmith, W6 9BE (8748 1943/fax 8748 2701/www.athomeinlondon.co.uk).* **Open** 9.30am-5.30pm Mon-Fri. **Rates** £30-£65 single; £55-£90 double. Min stay 2 nights. **Credit** MC, V.

Bulldog Club *14 Dewhurst Road, Kensington, W14 0ET (7371 3202/fax 7371 2015/ www.bulldogclub.com).* **Open** *Phone enquiries* 10am-6pm Mon-Fri. **Rates** £85 single; £105 double. **Membership** £25/3yrs. **Credit** AmEx, MC, V.

Host & Guest Service *103 Dawes Road, Fulham, SW6 7DU (7385 9922/fax 7386 7575/ www.host-guest.co.uk). Fulham Broadway tube.* **Open** 9am-5.30pm Mon-Fri. **Rates** from £20/person. Min stay 2 nights. **Credit** MC, V.

London Bed & Breakfast Agency *71 Fellows Road, Swiss Cottage, NW3 3JY (7586 2768/fax*

7586 6567/www.londonbb.com). **Open** 9am-6pm Mon-Fri; 10am-1pm Sat. **Rates** £25-£60 single; £22-£44 (per person) double. Min stay 2 nights. **Credit** MC, V.

London Homestead Services *182 Lauderdale Road, W9 1NG (tel/fax 7286 5115/ www.lhslondon.com).* **Open** 9am-7pm daily. **Rates** (booking fee of £5) £20-£40 per person. Min stay 3 nights. **Credit** MC, V.

Self-catering apartments

It's expensive to rent in London, but if you're in a group, you may save money by renting from one of the following. All specialise in holiday lets; some have minimum stay requirements.

Accommodation Outlet *32 Old Compton Street, Soho, W1D 4TP (7287 4244/fax 7734 7217/ www.outlet.co.uk). Leicester Square tube.* **Open** 10am-6pm Mon-Fri; noon-5pm Sat. **Map** p399 K6. This service for lesbian and gay flat-seekers and landlords can find short-term accommodation and West End rooms from £50 per night.

Apartment Service *1st floor, 5-6 Francis Grove, Wimbledon, SW19 4DT (8944 1444/fax 8944 6744). Wimbledon tube/rail.* **Open** 9am-5.30pm Mon-Fri. **Rates** from £90 double studio. **Credit** AmEx, DC, MC, V.

Astons Apartments *31 Rosary Gardens, South Kensington, SW7 4NH (7590 6000/fax 7590 6060/ www.astons-apartments.com). Gloucester Road tube.* **Open** 8am-9pm daily. **Rates** £76.40 single studio; £105.75 double studio. **Credit** AmEx, MC, V. **Map** p396 C11.

Holiday Serviced Apartments *PO Box 226, Northwood, Middlx HA6 2DN (0845 060 4477/ fax 0845 060 4282/www.holidayapartments.co.uk). Northwood tube.* **Open** 9.30am-5.30pm Mon-Fri. **Rates** from £80 single/double studio. **Credit** AmEx, MC, V. **Map** p396 C11.

Independent Traveller *Thorverton, Exeter, Devon EX5 5NT (01392 860807/fax 01392 860552/www.gowithit.co.uk).* **Open** 9am-5pm Mon-Fri. **Rates** £270-£2,000/wk apartment. **Credit** MC, V.

Palace Court Holiday Apartments *1 Palace Court, Bayswater Road, Bayswater, W2 4LP (7727 3467/fax 7221 7824/www.palacecourt.co.uk). Notting Hill Gate or Queensway tube.* **Open** 8.30am-11pm daily. **Rates** (plus 10% service) £65 single studio; £79 double studio; £86 triple studio. **Credit** MC, V. **Map** p394 7B.

Perfect Places *53 Margravine Gardens, Hammersmith, W6 8RN (tel/fax 8748 6095/ www.perfectplaceslondon.co.uk).* **Open** 9am-7pm daily. **Rates** from £550/wk. **Credit** AmEx, MC, V.

University residences

During university vacations much of London's dedicated student accommodation is open to visitors, providing an obviously basic but cheap place to stay.

Arcade Halls *The Arcade, 385-401 Holloway Road, Holloway, N7 0RN (7607 5415/fax 7609 0052/www.unl.ac.uk/accommodation). Holloway Road tube.* **Rates** £78/wk. **Available** 30 June-1 Sept 2004.

Goldsmid House *36 North Row, Mayfair, W1R 5GB (01273 207481/fax 01273 322351). Bond Street or Marble Arch tube.* **Rates** from £25 single; £15 (per person) twin. **Available** 13 June-19 Sept 2004. **Map** p398 G6.

High Holborn Residence *178 High Holborn, Holborn, WC1V 7AA (7379 5589/fax 7379 5640/ www.lse.ac.uk/vacations). Holborn tube.* **Rates** £35 single; £57 twin; £67 triple. **Available** 17 Aug-29 Sept 2004. **Map** p399 M5.

International Students House *229 Great Portland Street, Marylebone, W1W 5PN (7631 8300/fax 7631 8315/www.ish.org.uk). Great Portland Street tube.* **Rates** *(per person)* £12-£18 dormitory; £33.50 single; £25.50 twin. **Available** all year. **Map** p398 H5.

King's College Conference & Vacation Bureau *Strand Bridge House, 138-142 Strand, Covent Garden, WC2R 1HH (7848 1700/fax 7848 1717/www.kcl.ac.uk/kcvb). Temple tube.* **Rates** £17-£34 single; £39.50-£49 twin. **Available** 18 June-9 Sept 2004. **Map** p404 N8.

Passfield Hall *1-7 Endsleigh Place, Bloomsbury, WC1H 0PW (7387 3584/fax 7387 0419/ www.lse.ac.uk/vacations). Euston tube/rail.* **Rates** £27 single; £48 twin; £62 triple. **Available** 20 Mar-26 Apr 2004. **Map** p399 K4.

Walter Sickert Hall *29 Graham Street, Islington, N1 8LA (7040 8822/fax 7040 8825/ www.city.ac.uk/ems). Angel tube.* **Rates** £30-£40 single; £50-£60 twin. **Available** mid June-mid Sept 2004. **Map** p402 P3.

Camping & caravanning

If the thought of going putting yourself at the mercy of the English weather in some far-flung suburban field doesn't put you off, the transport links into central London just might. Nevertheless, these campsites will undoubtedly offer a singular view of the city, and they are all conveniently cheap.

Crystal Palace Caravan Club *Crystal Palace Parade, SE19 1UF (8778 7155/fax 8676 0980). Crystal Palace rail/3 bus.* **Open** *Mar-Oct* 8.30am-8pm daily. *Nov-Feb* 9am-8pm daily. **Rates** £16.75-£19 caravan pitch. **Credit** MC, V.

Lee Valley Campsite *Sewardstone Road, Chingford, E4 7RA (8529 5689/fax 8559 4070/ www.leevalleypark.com). Walthamstow Central tube/rail then 215 bus.* **Open** *Apr-Oct* 8am-10pm daily. Closed Nov-Mar. **Rates** £5.75; £2.55 under-16s. **Credit** Am Ex, MC, V.

Lee Valley Leisure Centre Camping & Caravan Park *Meridian Way, Edmonton, N9 0AS (8803 6900/fax 8884 4975/www.leevalleypark.com). Edmonton Green rail/W8 bus.* **Open** 8am-10pm daily. **Rates** £5.95; £2.50 5-16s; free under-5s. **Credit** MC, V.

Sightseeing

Features

Introduction

How long have you got?

You're spoiled for choice of sights to see in London. Indoors, outdoors, underground, overground, traditional English heritage pomp and exotic cosmopolitan melting pot circumstance. Pace yourself, though. Some of the places we list in the following pages – the British Museum (*see p101*) springs immediately to mind – take days to fully appreciate.

It's gratifying that so many attractions are free to enter. If you're on a budget and time is on your side, you can tick off large numbers of places on your 'must see' list for the price of a bus pass (from £2.50 a day).

If you want to extend your sightseeing options to more expensive places, such as London Zoo (*see p108*) and the Tower of London (*see p94*), a **London Pass** (0870 242 9988, www.londonpass.com) may be of interest. This gives you pre-paid access to more than 50 sights and attractions and costs from £27 daily per adult, or £32 with a travelcard thrown in.

If we have included the initials '**LP**' before the admission price of a certain place, it means your London Pass will allow free admission, tours or free entry to exhibitions. The initials '**EH**' mean the sight is an **English Heritage** property, so members of that organisation can get in free. '**NT**' means that **National Trust** members can expect free admission.

See the sights

By balloon

Adventure Balloons *Winchfield Park, London Road, Hartley Wintney, Hampshire RG27 8HY (01252 844 222/www.adventureballoons.co.uk).* **Flights** *London* May-Aug 5am Tue, Wed, Thur. **Fares** *London* £165 per person. **Credit** MC, V.
Balloon flights over London leave from either Vauxhall Bridge or Tower Hill, very early in the morning (this is the only time when the air space is clear). Flights must be booked well ahead and are dependent on the weather. There's champagne or juice all round on landing.

By boat

City Cruises (*7740 0400/www.citycruises.com*).
The river's biggest pleasure cruise operator, whose fleet includes showboats, restaurant boats, sightseeing tours and rover tickets. The Rail and River Rover (£8.80 adults; £4.50 children), a collaboration with Docklands Light Railway, lets you combine a cruise with unlimited DLR travel, a pleasant way to explore the river's eastern reaches (*see p359*).

By bus

Big Bus Company *48 Buckingham Palace Road, Westminster, SW1W 0RN (0800 169 1365/7233 9533/www.bigbus.co.uk).* **Open-top bus tours** 3 routes, 2hrs; with commentary (recorded on Blue route, live on Red and Green). Tickets include river cruise and walking tours. **Departures** every 15mins from Green Park, Victoria & Marble Arch. *Summer* 8.30am-7pm daily. *Winter* 8.30am-4.30pm daily. **Pick-up** Green Park (near the Ritz); Marble Arch (Speakers' Corner); Victoria (outside Thistle Victoria Hotel, 48 Buckingham Palace Road). **Fares** £17 (£15 if booked online); £8 5-15s; free under-5s. Tickets valid for 24hrs, interchangeable between routes. **Credit** AmEx, DC, MC, V.

Original London Sightseeing Tour *8877 1722/ www.theoriginaltour.com.* **Departures** *Summer* 9am-7pm daily. *Winter* 9am-5.30pm daily. **Pick-up** Grosvenor Gardens; Marble Arch (Speakers' Corner); Baker Street tube (forecourt); Coventry Street; Embankment station; Trafalgar Square. **Fares** £15; £7.50 5-15s; free under-5s (£1 discount if booked online). **Credit** MC, V.

By duck

London Duck Tours 7928 3132/www.londonducktours.com. **Tours** *Feb-Dec* daily (ring for departure times). **Fares** £16.50; £11 under-12s; £49 family ticket.
City of Westminster tours in a DUKW (amphibious vehicle developed during World War II) comprise a 75-minute road and river trip starting at the London Eye and going in the Thames at Vauxhall.

By helicopter

Cabair Helicopters *Elstree Aerodrome, Borehamwood, Hertfordshire WD6 3AW (8953 4411/www.cabair.com). Edgware tube/Elstree rail.* **Flights** from 9.45am Sun. **Fares** £129 (age 7s and above only). **Credit** MC, V.

By pedal power

London Pedicabs
07866 628462/www.londonpedicabs.com. **Fares** £4-£10/mile/person.
Pedicabs (where someone cycles you to your destination in a rickshaw-style bike) are based around Covent Garden, Soho and Leicester Square.

London Bicycle Tour Company
7928 6838/www.londonbicycle.com/rickshaws.html or call 7928 6838. **Fares** £40/ hr, £70 2 hrs.
If you choose, you can 'drive' yourself for £12 per hour, £6 for half an hour.

Metrobike
08450801952/www.promobikes.co.uk/services/ metro.html. **Fares** from £2-£5 for a short trip; £40/hr private hire.

The best Sights

In the heart of the city
Sir John Soane's Museum (*see p97*); **St Paul's Cathedral** (*see p87*); **Somerset House** (*see p96*).

Worth the suburban jaunt
Red House, **Eltham Palace** (for both *see p170*); **Royal Air Force Museum Hendon** (*see p152*); **Osterley House** and **Syon House** (for both *see 188*); **Royal Botanic Gardens** (*see p175*).

For getting high
British Airways London Eye (*see p70*); **Monument** (*see p92*); **Tower Bridge Exhibition** (*see p93*); **Alexandra Park and Palace** (*see p152*).

For going underground
Cabinet War Rooms (*see p131*); the tube simulator at **London's Transport Museum** (*see p122*); **Chislehurst Caves** (*see p170*).

For blood and gore
London Dungeon (*see p79*); the Chamber of Horrors in **Madame Tussaud's** (*see p107*); **Old Operating Theatre, Museum & Herb Garret** (*see p80*).

For dem dry bones
The mummies in the **British Museum** (*see p101*); Spitalfields woman in the Roman Gallery at the **Museum of London** (*see p92*); Jeremy Bentham's Auto-Icon in **University College** (*see p100*).

For old soldiers
They also serve at the **National Army Museum** (*see p142*); and the **Imperial War Museum** (*see p168*); Beefeaters at the **Tower of London** (*see p94*).

For young artists
Saatchi Gallery (*see p73*); **Tate Modern** (*see p78*); **Whitechapel Art Gallery** (*see p153*); **Camden Arts Centre** (*see p147*).

For palatial splendour
Buckingham Palace (*see p112*); **Kensington Palace** (*see p138*); **Hampton Court Palace** (*see p178*).

For homely pleasures
Geffrye Museum (*see p156*); the Secret Life of the Home in the **Science Museum,** (*see p136*); **Dennis Severs' House** (*see p154*).

For sporting heroes
Lord's Tour & MCC Museum (*see p144*); **Wimbledon Lawn Tennis Museum** (*see p175*); **Rugby Museum/Twickenham Stadium** (*see p179*).

For bookish types
Dickens' House (*see p101*); **Dr Johnson's House** (*see p84*); **Keats House** (*see p148*).

For drama kings and queens
Shakespeare's Globe (*see p77*); **Theatre Museum** and **St Paul's Covent Garden** (for both *see p122*).

These futuristic bike taxis, which originated in Germany, can take two people on short trips around town, or longer sightseeing tours. Metrobikes are based around Regent Street.

By taxi
Black Taxi Tours of London *7935 9363/ www.blacktaxitours.co.uk.* **Cost** £75.
A tailored two-hour tour for up to five people.

On foot
Arguably the best company organising walks around London is **Original London Walks** (*7624 3978, www.walks.com*), which encompasses sorties on everything from the shadowy London of fictional 'tec Sherlock Holmes to picturesque riverside pubs. There are walks to 'Jack the Ripper Haunts' at 7.30pm daily, and 'Jack the Ripper's London' is at 3pm Saturdays. Both depart from Tower Hill tube exit; young children are discouraged on all. All tours cost £5 adults, £4 concessions.

Other walks companies worth noting include **Citisights** (8806 4325/www.chr.org.uk/cswalks), **Historical Tours** (86684019/www.historicalwalksoflondon.com) and **Stepping Out** (7435 4782). Good self-guided walks are listed in *Time Out London Walks* volumes 1 and 2 (£9.99 and £11.99).

With the specialists
Open House Architecture *Unit C1, 39-51 Highgate Road, NW5 1RS (7267 7644/ www.londonopenhouse.org).* Call for tour details. **Departures** 10.15am Sat. **Meeting point** in front of Royal Academy of Arts, Piccadilly (Piccadilly Circus tube). **Duration** 3hrs (& occasional 1-day tours). **Tickets** £18.50; £13 students; advance booking advisable. **Credit** MC, V.
Tour Guides *7495 5504/www.tourguides.co.uk.* Tailor-made tours with Blue Badge guides for individuals or groups, on foot, by car, coach or boat.
Premium Tours *www.premiumtours.co.uk* Private tours of specific sites and attractions in London and the south of England.

The South Bank & Bankside

Once a 'naughty place', this side of the Thames is really quite nice now.

Maps p403, p406 & p407

When Londoners want to show off their city to visitors, they take them to the river. On the south side, from Lambeth Bridge to Tower Bridge, the attractions line up proudly. It was much the same story half a millennium ago, as the marshy southern bank of the river was where Londoners went for pleasure during the reign of Henry VIII – bear-baiting, sex for sale, rowdy inns and theatres were the order of the day. Our fun may be more sanitised now, but witness Tracey Emin's seedy bed in the **Saatchi Gallery** (*see p73*) and you're reminded of the bawdier side of life once again.

The transformation of this stretch of river over the last 50 years or so has been steady but laborious. The Festival of Britain in 1951 opened the way for the building of the blockish South Bank Centre, whose brutalist exterior design is now considered the epitome of ugliness (*see p28*). The biggest and most expensive party, however, was the one to celebrate the turn of the century. Eight years earlier, Marks Barfield architects had taken part in a competition to come up with a structure to celebrate the millennium. Their amazing big wheel, the **British Airways London Eye** (*see p70*), came second. No one can remember what won. The 'blade of light' shooting across the river to St Paul's Cathedral is the **Millennium Bridge**, which has done wonders for visitor numbers, and the equally lovely **Hungerford** footbridges, linking the South Bank to Embankment on the north side, are yet another reason to start a walking tour of London here.

Finding your way around the area shouldn't be a problem as the museums and arts centres along the riverside stock any number of free brochures with maps and visitor information about this stretch of the Thames. The South Bank Marketing Group has a 24-hour leaflet ordering line (7202 6900) for its free *Walk This Way* guide series, which cover Riverside London, the South Bank and Bermondsey. Another good way to gauge the lie of the land is to hop on the wonderful RV1 bus, which links all the riverside attractions between Covent Garden and Tower Gateway.

The South Bank

Lambeth Bridge to Hungerford Bridge

Embankment or Westminster tube/Waterloo tube/rail.

The Lambeth Bridge is adorned by carved pineapples as a tribute to the father of British gardening (John Tradescant, whose plant-hunting habit brought the exotic fruit here in the 16th century). On its southern side **Lambeth Palace**, official residence of the Archbishops of Canterbury since the 12th century, opens to the public on high days and holidays, notably during London Open House (*see p264*). The church next door, St Mary-at-Lambeth, was deconsecrated in 1972 to become the **Museum of Garden History** (*see p74* **Pride of London**).

Walking west along the Albert Embankment and under **Westminster Bridge** you come to London's major tourist zone. The London Eye packs in the crowds waiting for a chance to experience its soaring views, while the various establishments inside the grand **County Hall** (once the residence of the London government) get them as they come off the wheel: the **Aquarium** (*see p73*) bags the family market and the surreal works of Salvador Dalí (**Dalí Universe**, *see p71*) vie for the arts crowd with Damien Hirst's pickled sharks in the new **Saatchi Gallery** (*see p73*), which specialises in modern British art, and has a propensity for making headlines and raising eyebrows.

British Airways London Eye

Riverside Building, next to County Hall, Westminster Bridge Road, SE1 7PB (0870 500 0600/customer services 0870 990 8883/www.ba-londoneye.com). Westminster tube/Waterloo tube/rail. **Open** *Oct-Apr* 9.30am-8pm daily. May-Sept 9.30am-8pm Mon-Thur; 9.30am-9pm Fri-Sun. **Admission** £11; £10 concessions; £5 5-15s; free under-5s. **Credit** AmEx, MC, V. **Map** p401 M8.

Such is its impact on the London skyline, it's hard to believe that this giant wheel was originally intended to turn majestically over the Thames for only five years. It's proved so popular that no one wants it to come down, so its life has been extended and it's now scheduled to keep spinning for another 20 years. The 450ft (137m) monster wheel, whose 32 glass capsules each hold 25 people, commands the best views over London. It attracts long queues in the summer, but it's worth the wait. A 'flight' (as a turn is called) takes half an hour, which gives you plenty of time to have an argument about which hill is which in south London, ogle at the Queen's back garden and follow the silver snake of the Thames. You can buy a guide to the landmarks for £2. Most people book in advance (although you take a gamble with the weather) but it is possible to turn up and queue for a ticket on the day. Night flights offer a more twinkly experience, with the bridges all lit up and lovely.

Dalí Universe

County Hall Gallery, County Hall Riverside Building, Queen's Walk, SE1 7PB (7620 2720/ www.daliuniverse.com). Waterloo tube/rail. **Open** 10am-5.30pm daily. **Admission** £8.50; £7.50 concessions; £4.95 10-16s; £1 2-10s; free under-2s. **Credit** AmEx, DC, MC, V. **Map** p401 M8.

2004 is the centenary of the Great Masturbator's birth, so the curators at the County Hall Gallery have planned special events to mark it. They'll include a big bash in May, an exhibit of Dalí-inspired designer fashion and a summer programme. Much of the art will be rehung, some taken away and replaced by other pieces (although the trademark attractions, such as the 'Mae West Lips' sofa and the *Spellbound* painting will remain). The main exhibition, curated by long-term Dalí friend Benjamin Levi, leaves you in no doubt as to the Spanish artist's eccentricity. The wall-mounted quotes by, and (silent) videos and photographs of, Dalí give an insight into his life. There are sculptures, watercolours (including his flamboyant tarot cards), rare etchings and lithographs. The work is arranged in three categories: the hyper-surreal 'Dreams and Fantasy'; the exotic and indulgent 'Femininity and Sensuality'; and 'Religion and Mythology', including an interesting series of Bible scenes by the Catholic-turned-atheist-turned-Catholic again.

Florence Nightingale Museum

St Thomas's Hospital, 2 Lambeth Palace Road, SE1 7EW (7620 0374/www.florence-nightingale.co.uk). Westminster tube/Waterloo tube/rail. **Open** 10am-5pm Mon-Fri (last entry 4pm); 11.30am-4.30pm Sat, Sun (last entry 3.30pm). **Admission** £4.80; £3.80 5-18s concessions; £12 family; free under-5s. **Credit** AmEx, MC, V. **Map** p401 M9.

A new permanent exhibition in this little museum dedicated to the Lady of the Lamp marks the 150th anniversary of Florence Nightingale's entry into the Crimea. The nursing skills and campaigning zeal that made her war work the stuff of legend are honoured with a chronological tour through a remarkable life illustrated along the way by her pronouncements. Upon returning from the battlefields of Scutari she opened the Nightingale Nursing School here in St Thomas's Hospital. The rest of the space in the museum is given over to displays of mementoes, clothing, furniture, books, letters and portraits dating from that period, as well as an audio-visual tribute to Nightingale. Free children's activities, such as art workshops, take place every other weekend; see the website or call for details.

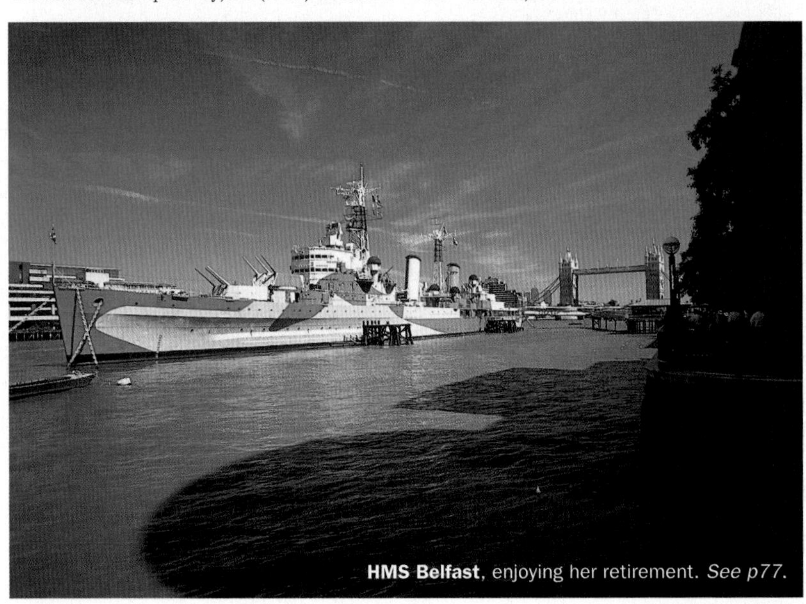

HMS Belfast, enjoying her retirement. *See p77.*

From sharks, stingrays and clownfish to moray eels, lionfish and sideways walking crabs, the London Aquarium is full of surprises with 350 different species to discover.

Located in County Hall, right next to the London Eye, the London Aquarium is just a short walk from Waterloo station.

So, don't plan a day out without visiting London's only Aquarium!

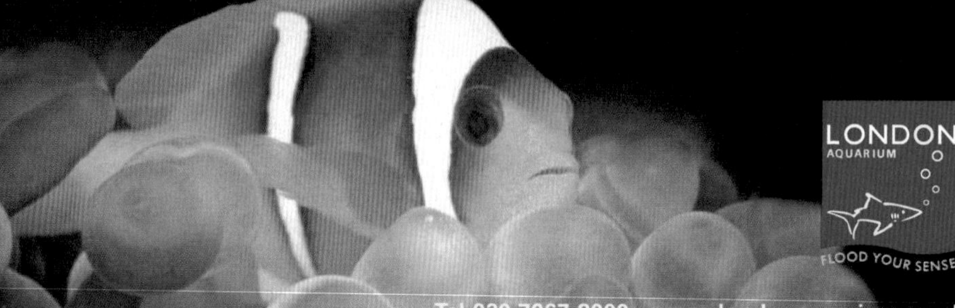

London Aquarium

County Hall, Riverside Building, Westminster Bridge Road, SE1 7PB (7967 8000/tours 7967 8007/www.londonaquarium.co.uk). Westminster tube/Waterloo tube/rail. **Open** 10am-6pm daily (last entry 5pm). **Admission** (LP) £8.75; £6.50 concessions; £5.25 3-14s; £3.50 disabled; free under-3s; £25 family. **Credit** AmEx, MC, V. **Map** p401 M9.

The exhibits here swim forgetfully around in 2.5 million litres of water. Occasionally, they notice the many children pressing their noses up against the glass of the tanks. The aquarium, one of Europe's largest exhibitions of global aquatic life, displays its livestock according to geographical origin, so there are tanks of bright fish from the coral reefs and the Indian Ocean, temperate freshwater fish from the rivers of Europe and North America, and crustaceans and rockpool plants from shorelines. Rays glide swiftly around touch pools, coming up to the surface frequently. There are tanks devoted to jellyfish, sharks and piranhas. Information is liberally posted around. The shop is a vast and garish provider of cuddly crabs and plastic sharks.

Saatchi Gallery

County Hall, Riverside Building, Westminster Bridge Road, SE1 7PB (7823 2363/www.saatchi-gallery.co.uk). Westminster tube/Waterloo tube/rail. **Open** 10am-8pm Mon-Thur, Sun; 10am-10pm Fri, Sat. **Admission** £8.50; £6.50 concessions. **Credit** AmEx, MC, V. **Map** p401 M9.

The work of YBAs (that's Young British Artists) is provocative, brazen and defiant. Many also say it's rubbish. Advertising impresario Charles Saatchi thinks otherwise, and has made it his business to discover emerging talent and back it. That's what he did with a young Damien Hirst, Tracey Emin and Marc Quinn, whose most famous pieces, 'The Physical Impossibility of Death in the Mind of Someone Living'; 'My Bed' and 'Self', respectively, are central to the permanent collection in the rotunda meeting room here. The Saatchi Collection moved to County Hall in 2003, and it's a bizarre setting for such diverse and challenging work, but the Edwardian splendour, the huge wood-panelled rooms provide a spacious backdrop. The advent of Saatchi in this central space has given the public a chance not only to judge for themselves the value of these pieces, but to marvel at the architecture. Upcoming exhibitions include a Chapman brothers retrospective running until 14 March 2004.

Hungerford Bridge to Blackfriars Bridge

Embankment or Temple tube/Blackfriars or Waterloo tube/rail.

When the riverside warehouses were cleared to make way for the **South Bank Centre** (*see p302*) in the 1960s, the big concrete complex, containing the Royal Festival Hall, Purcell Room and Queen Elizabeth Hall, was hailed as a daring testament to modern architecture. Sir Leslie Martin's **Royal Festival Hall** – built for the Festival of Britain – was given the title of the 'people's palace'. A Grade I-listed building, it's certainly the most accessible of the three performance spaces, even more so given the ongoing improvements; a new stairway links the Belvedere Road entrance to the Hungerford Bridge one, and an outdoor café has opened. Further internal improvements to the Royal Festival Hall, and a promised new Poetry Library (*see p38*) are liable to take some time to appear, although 2005 is the proposed completion date for these projects.

The **Hayward Gallery** (*see p73*), next door to the Festival Hall, is also part of the big renovation masterplan. Its new pavilion was designed in collaboration with light artist Dan Graham. The gallery's trademark neonlit rooftop tower, designed in 1970 by Phillip Vaughan and Roger Dainton, is an arrangement of yellow, red, green and blue tubes controlled by the direction and speed of the wind.

Another player, supposedly, in the proposed masterplan is the useful **National Film Theatre** (*see p284*), which squats sulkily underneath Waterloo Bridge. No one yet knows whether a proposed five-screen film centre will finally materialise, but we can all hope.

The **Royal National Theatre** (*see p331*) has emerged from its own renovation scheme with a restyled Lyttelton Theatre and praise heaped upon its new 100-seat Loft space.

Once you've emerged from the gloomy concrete of the South Bank Centre, the mellow red bricks of **Oxo Tower Wharf** come as light relief. The building's art deco tower incorporates advertising for the cooking stock cube company that bought it. It was actually earmarked for demolition in the 1970s, but the Coin Street Community Builders (*see p80* **Not for profit**) bought it and saved it, and it is now home to an excellent restaurant, bar and bistro with wonderful views (*see p191*). The bustling cafés and shops of pleasant **Gabriel's Wharf** nearby are another Coin Street enterprise.

Hayward Gallery

Belvedere Road, SE1 8XZ (box office 7960 4242/ www.hayward.org.uk). Embankment tube/Charing Cross or Waterloo tube/rail. **Open** *During exhibitions* 10am-6pm Mon, Thur-Sun; 10am-8pm Tue, Wed. **Admission** varies. **Credit** AmEx, MC, V. **Map** p401 M8.

A new foyer extension and mirrored, elliptical glass pavilion (*Waterloo Sunset at the Hayward Gallery*) was completed in October 2003. Casual visitors can watch cartoons on touch screens or wipe froth off their lips in the new Starbucks. Art lovers dismayed by the latter nonetheless enjoy the pavilion and the excellent exhibition programme. The new look

Hayward opened with a blockbuster celebration of the centenary of the National Art Collections Fund, and continues with the first major showing of the work of Pop artist Roy Lichtenstein (1923-97). This runs 26 February to 16 May 2004.

Around Waterloo

Waterloo tube/rail.

The South Bank redevelopment on the Belvedere Road side should improve access to busy **Waterloo Station**, where Nicholas Grimshaw's glass-roofed terminus for Eurostar trains provides an elegant departure point for travellers bound for Paris and Brussels. Outside, the vast space beneath the roundabout used to be 'cardboard city', where London's homeless built their shelters from boxes. These humble citizens were cleared away from the site when the stonking great £20-million BFI IMAX cinema (*see p284*) was built here in 1999.

Another place of interest around the station is the funny little market off **Lower Marsh** (the name originates from the rural village known as Lambeth Marsh until the 18th century). Across Waterloo Road at the southern end on the street known as the Cut, is the restored Victorian façade of the **Old Vic Theatre** on the corner opposite Waterloo Millennium Green, a public park in an area that hitherto lacked greenery. Further down The Cut is the functional exterior of a hotbed of youthful theatrical talent, the **Young Vic** (*see p336*).

Walking down Lower Marsh in the other direction takes you to Westminster Bridge Road, where at No.121 is what's left of a creepy old terminal – the **London Necropolis Station**, founded in 1854 and used purely for train transport of the city's dead to an overflow cemetery in Surrey. The ground floor was redeveloped after bombing in 1941, but much of the original façade remains.

Bankside

Borough or Southwark tube/London Bridge tube/rail.

The area around the river by London Bridge known as **Bankside** was the epicentre of bawdy Southwark in Shakespeare's day. As well as playhouses such as the Globe and the Rose stirring up all sorts of trouble among the groundlings, there were the famous 'stewes' (brothels), seedy inns and other dens of iniquity where decent folk could be led astray. Presiding over all this depravity were the Bishops of Winchester, who made a tidy income from the fines they levied on prostitutes (or 'Winchester Geese' as they were known at the height of the Bishops' power) and other lost souls. All that's

Pride of London Urban gardeners

Rosebay willowherb, a prolifically flowering native plant, endeared itself to the populace in the Second World War by covering much of the rubble on bombsites. That's how it earned the unofficial title, 'Pride of London'.

Creating splashes of colour and green oases amid the city grey is what urban gardening is all about. A stroll down any residential streets with their window boxes and flowery front plots or a suburban train ride past garden allotments and the diverse backyards of railside houses will reveal that the English passion for gardening is strong here too. Nowhere is this more evident than in the **Museum of Garden History**.

A little green gem, the world's first museum of horticulture opened in 1972. It is a fitting place to devote to horticulture, given that intrepid plant hunter and gardener to Charles I, John Tradescant is buried here. A replica of a 17th-century knot garden has been created in his honour. The garden uses geometric shapes based on squares and circles that incorporate the letter 'T' (for Tradescant). Topiary and box hedging, old roses, herbaceous perennials and bulbs give it all-year interest. A sarcophagus in the graveyard garden contains the remains of Captain Bligh, the breadfruit transplanter more famous for being abandoned in the Pacific by the mutinous crew of HMS *Bounty*.

Inside the museum are displays of ancient working tools, exhibitions about horticulture through the ages, a shop and a café.

While they're there, garden lovers should pick up a copy of the National Gardens Scheme yellow book. The slim volume lists all the plots, public and private, open to the public in London. For more information check the website www.ngs.org.uk.

Museum of Garden History

Lambeth Palace Road, SE1 7LB (7401 8865/www.museumgardenhistory.org). Waterloo tube/rail/C10, 507 bus. **Open** *Feb-mid Dec* 10.30am-5pm daily. **Admission** free. Suggested donation £3; £2.50 concessions. **Credit** AmEx, MC, V. **Map** p401 L10.

Shakespeare's Globe. *See p77.*

left of the grand Palace of Winchester, home of successive bishops, is the rose window of the Great Hall on Clink Street, a short walk from the river, next to the site of the Clink prison (now the **Clink Prison Museum**; *see p77*).

The parish church at this time was St Saviour's, formerly the monastic church of St Mary Overie and now (since 1905) the Anglican **Southwark Cathedral**. Shakespeare's brother Edmund was buried in the graveyard here and there's a monument to the playwright inside. You have to walk back down Clink Street, past **Vinopolis**, the wine experience (*see p79*), to reach **Shakespeare's Globe** (*see p77*). Built on the site of the original playhouse, this reproduction in wattle and daub is separated from its neighbour, **Tate Modern** (*see p78*), by a wonky terrace of houses, where Sir Christopher Wren stayed when building St Paul's across the water. The Tate's repository of modern art was a power station designed by Sir Giles Gilbert Scott. The crowds that pass daily through its massive portals prove it's culture vultures, rather than Winchester Geese, that seek their pleasures in Bankside now.

Bankside Gallery

48 Hopton Street, SE1 8JH (7928 7521/ www.banksidegallery.com). Blackfriars or Southwark tube. **Open** 10am-5pm Tue-Fri; 11am-5pm Sat, Sun. **Admission** £3.50; £2 concessions. **Credit** DC, MC, V.

Crouching behind the Tate, this little gallery is the home of the Royal Watercolour Society and the Royal Society of Painter-Printmakers. Its changing exhibitions reflect established and experimental practices. The RWS also runs courses in painting and drawing throughout the year. The shop has books and art materials, alongside prints and watercolours by members of both societies.

Bramah Museum of Tea & Coffee

40 Southwark Street, SE1 1UN (7403 5650/ www.bramahmuseum.co.uk). London Bridge tube/rail. **Open** 10am-6pm daily. **Admission** £4; £3.50 concessions. **Credit** AmEx, DC, MC, V. **Map** p405 S9.

As a nation we get through 100,000 tons of teabags a year, a fact that no doubt appals tea purist Edward Bramah, a former tea taster who set up this museum in the early 1990s. Bramah's collection displays pots, maps, caddies and ancient coffee makers. They work as visual aids to the history of the beverages and the role they have had to play in the refreshing (and near destruction) of nations. The exhibition, which moved to this street near Borough Market in 2001, doesn't take long to work round, but it's tempting to linger in the café (*see p192*).

Clink Prison Museum

1 Clink Street, SE1 9DG (7403 0900/ www.clink.co.uk). London Bridge tube/rail. **Open** 10am-9pm daily. **Admission** £4; £3 concessions, 5-15s; £9 family. **Credit** MC, V. **Map** p404 P8.

A new lease signed in 2003 meant the Clink can continue to hang its caged rotting corpse effigy outside for the next 15 years. No doubt the wolfish property developers looking to yuppify the building howled with indignation. The exhibition looks behind the bars of the hellish prison 'The Clink' owned by the Bishops of Winchester from the 12th

THE NATIONAL TRUST

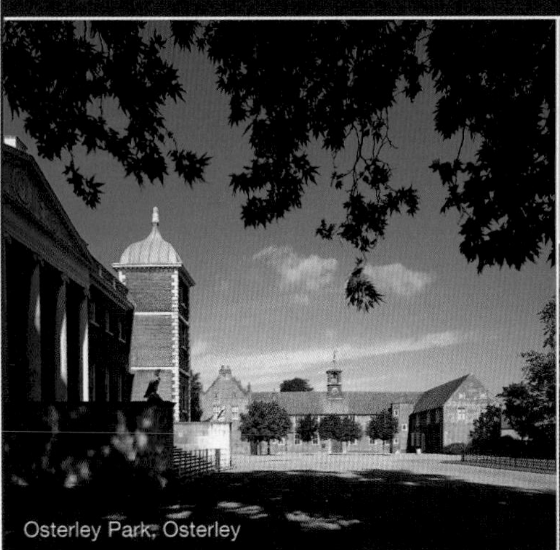
Osterley Park, Osterley

A **warm welcome** awaits you in London...

Fenton House, Hampstead

Telephone **01494 755500** for more information or visit www.nationaltrust.org.uk

breathtaking views of London, fine dining and world class entertainment from the best seat on the River Thames.

Try our Thames Circular Cruise or Point-to-Point service and discover London in style.

FOR FURTHER INFORMATION:

Restaurant Cruises
Tel: 020 7925 2215
www.bateauxlondon.com

Sightseeing Cruises
Tel: 020 7987 1185
www.catamarancruisers.co.uk

CATAMARAN CRUISERS

...Unique

to the 18th centuries. Thieves, prostitutes and debtors served their sentences within its walls during an era when boiling in oil was legal. On display for the 'hands-on' experience are torture devices and the iron fetters whose clanking gave the prison its name. The museum does not take long to walk through, but several audio stories from inmates make you linger by the waxworks.

Golden Hinde

St Mary Overie Dock, Cathedral Street, SE1 9DE (0870 011 8700/www.goldenhinde.co.uk). Monument tube/London Bridge tube/rail. **Open** daily, times vary. **Admission** £2.75; £2.35 concessions; £2 4-13s; £8 family; free under-4s. **Credit** MC, V. **Map** p404 P8.

Weekends see this reconstruction of Sir Francis Drake's 16th-century flagship swarming with children dressed up as pirates, as its birthday party service is as popular as ever. When it hasn't been taken over by cutlass-wielding youths, the five levels, recreated in minute detail, are fascinating to explore, although there can be no doubt that most of its income comes from the child-friendliness of its charms. 'Living History Experiences' (some overnight), in which participants dress in period clothes, eat Tudor fare and learn the skills of the Elizabethan seafarer, are a huge hit with the young.

HMS Belfast

Morgan's Lane, Tooley Street, SE1 2JH (7940 6300/www.iwm.org.uk). London Bridge tube/rail. **Open** *Mar-Oct* 10am-6pm daily (last entry 5.15pm). *Nov-Feb* 10am-5pm daily (last entry 4.15pm). **Admission** £6; £4.40 concessions; free under-16s (must be accompanied by an adult). **Credit** MC, V. **Map** p405 R8.

This 11,500-ton battlecruiser is a floating museum and an unlikely playground for children, who tear around its nine decks, boiler and engine rooms and gun turrets. *Belfast* was built in 1938 and played a leading role in the Normandy Landings. She supported UN forces in Korea before being decommissioned in 1965. Guided tours take in living quarters and explain what life was like on board. The Walrus Café is on the ship, the souvenir shop is on dry land.

Rose Theatre

56 Park Street, SE1 9AR (79021500/ www.rosetheatre.org.uk/www.shakespeares-globe.org). London Bridge tube/rail. **Open** by appointment for groups of 15+; phone for details. **Admission** only as part of summer tour with Shakespeare's Globe. **Credit** AmEx, MC, V. **Map** p404 P8.

The Rose – built by Philip Henslowe and operational from 1587 until 1606 – was the first playhouse to be built at Bankside. It's currently being looked after by the folks at Shakespeare's Globe (*see below*). Only groups of 15 or more can book guided tours, though it's possible that regular weekend opening hours may be in the offing. In the meantime, funds are sought for new excavation work in search of as yet uncovered portions of the old theatre that could completely restore its original ground plan.

Southwark Cathedral. *See p78.*

Shakespeare's Globe

21 New Globe Walk, Bankside, SE1 9DT (7902 1500/www.shakespeares-globe.org). Mansion House or Southwark tube/London Bridge tube/rail. **Open** *Tours & exhibitions* Oct-Apr 10am-5pm daily. May-Sept 9am-5pm daily. **Admission** (LP) £8; £6.50 concessions; £5.50 5-15s. **Credit** MC, V. **Map** p404 O7.

The original Globe Theatre, where many of William Shakespeare's plays were first staged and which he co-owned, burned down in 1613 during a performance of *Henry VIII*. Nearly 400 years later, it was rebuilt not far from its original site under the auspices of actor Sam Wanamaker (who, sadly, didn't live to see it up and running), using construction methods and materials as close to the originals as possible. The centrepiece is a guided tour of the theatre itself; note that there are none in the afternoon from May to September, when historically authentic (and frequently very good) performances are staged (*see p333*). However, during this period, visitors still have access to a fine exhibition based on famous productions of Shakespeare's plays.

Southwark Cathedral

London Bridge, SE1 9DA (7367 6700/tours 7367 6734/www.dswark.org/cathedral). London Bridge tube/rail. **Open** 8am-6pm daily (closing times vary on religious holidays). *Services* 8am, 8.15am, 12.30pm, 12.45pm, 5.30pm Mon-Fri; 9am, 9.15am, 4pm Sat; 8.45am, 9am, 11am, 3pm, 6.30pm Sun. *Choral Evensong* 5.30pm Tue, Fri; 3.30pm Sun (boys); 5.30pm Mon, Thur (girls). **Admission** *Exhibition* £3; £2.50 concessions; £1.50 5-16s; £12.50 family; free under-5s. **Credit** AmEx, MC, V. **Map** p404 P8.

The oldest bits of this partly ancient building are more than 800 years old. The Retro-Choir was where the trials of several Protestant martyrs took place during the reign of Mary Tudor. After the Reformation, the church fell into disrepair and parts of it became a bakery and a pigsty. In 1905 it became a cathedral and in 2000 it was given a facelift. The architects worked hard to make the recent additions sympathetic to the medieval and Victorian structure and it's a blend that works. An interactive museum, called the Long View of London, and a lovely garden are some of the millennial improvements that make Southwark look so ship-shape these days (*see p84* **A tale of two cathedrals**). There are memorials to Shakespeare, John Harvard (benefactor of the US university), Sam Wanamaker (the force behind **Shakespeare's Globe**, *see p77*) and stained-glass windows with images of Chaucer and John Bunyan.

Tate Modern

Bankside, SE1 9TJ (7887 8000/www.tate.org.uk). Blackfriars tube. **Open** 10am-6pm Mon-Thur, Sun; 10am-10pm Fri, Sat. *Tours* 11am, noon, 2pm, 3pm daily. **Admission** free. *Temporary exhibitions* prices vary. **Map** p401 O7.

A powerhouse of modern art, Tate Modern's enormous scale is awe inspiring even before you embark on a tour of the collection, moved here in 2000 from the orginal Tate, now called Tate Britain (*see p134*). Also impressive is the sheer number of visitors tramping through the vast Turbine Hall, wandering through galleries with titles like History/Memory/Society and Still Life/Object/Real Life. Arranging the works according to themes like this was considered by some critics to be a touch obtuse, but the innovation has gone down well with most visitors. The artists are listed on the doorway of each gallery, so it's pretty easy to find the one you want. If you don't know where to start in all the hugeness, take a guided tour (ask at the information desk). Leave time for the cafés and the shop.

The partnership between Unilever and Tate continues, allowing the commission of large-scale works for the Turbine Hall space. This year's piece, until March 2004, is by Olafur Eliasson, the Icelandic/Danish installation artist. Dates for the art lover's 2004 diary include a retrospective of the work of Edward Hopper (27 May-5 Sept) and an exhibition by painter Luc Tuymans (24 June-26 Sept).

The **Tate to Tate** boat service links Tates Britain and Modern and runs every 20 minutes, stopping along the way at the London Eye. Tickets are available from ticket desks at the Tates, on board the boat, online or by phone (7887 8888). Prices are £4.50 for an adult (£3 if you have a travelcard) and £2.30 for children.

Vinopolis, City of Wine

1 Bank End, SE1 9BU (0870 241 4040/ www.vinopolis.co.uk). London Bridge tube/rail. **Open** noon-9pm Mon, Fri, Sat; noon-6pm Tue-Thur, Sun (last entry 2hrs before closing). **Admission** £12.50; £11.50 concessions. **Credit** AmEx, MC, V. **Map** p404 P8.

This is more for wine amateurs than for oenophiles, but it helps to have a healthy interest in the fruit of the vine to get a kick out of this glossy experience. Participants are furnished with a wine glass and an audio guide. Exhibits are set out by country, with five opportunities to taste wine or champagne from

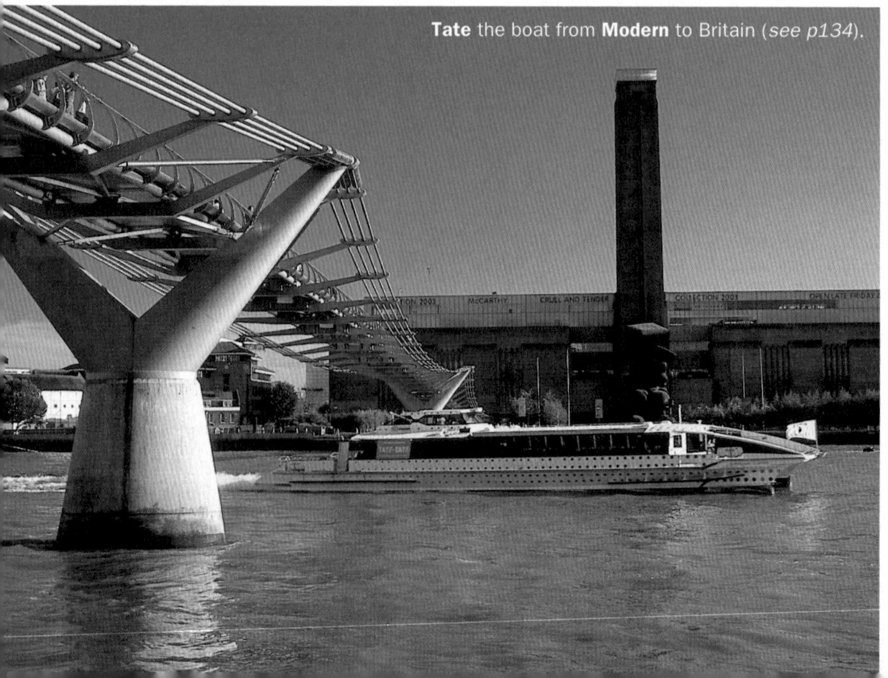

Tate the boat from **Modern** to Britain (*see p134*).

Scrummy. **Borough Market.**

different regions. Gin crashes the party courtesy of Bombay Sapphire (you get to sample a Bombay Sapphire cocktail – Ginopolis?). Highlights include a virtual voyage through Chianti on a Vespa and a virtual flight to the wine-producing regions of Australia. The wine shop has some interesting offers for dedicated tipplers and the restaurant Cantina Vinopolis is very smart.

Borough

Borough or Southwark tube/London Bridge tube/rail.

Hard by Southwark Cathedral is **Borough Market**, a bustling food market that dates back to the 13th century. It's a popular spot for film directors, as the appearance of a triple-deckered purple bus for *Harry Potter and the Prisoner of Azkaban* proved in 2003. For years this historic area has been under threat by the Thameslink rail extension, but campaigners are relatively confident that the market, now being renovated, will be safe for another 250 years.

The area rings literary bells, especially where Charles Dickens is concerned. Few of the landmarks he wrote about survive today. Marshalsea Prison, where Dickens's father was imprisoned for debt, which once stood just north of **St George-the-Martyr church** (on the corner of Borough High Street and Long Lane) and is long gone, but the George pub (77 Borough High Street), London's only surviving galleried inn, remains.

The area around **Borough High Street** was lively, especially until 1750, because nearby London Bridge was the only dry crossing point on the river. Nowadays bridges are plentiful on this stretch of the river, but that hasn't stopped the powers that be from planning yet another crossing, about two minutes away from London Bridge. It'll be called Jubilee Bridge and will be the only covered bridge across the Thames. There's no completion date set at present.

Around London Bridge Station tourist attractions clamour for attention. The one that attracts the biggest queues at weekends is the **London Dungeon** (*see p80*). Blood curdling shrieks emanate from the entrance, while next door the dulcet tones of Vera Lynn attempt to lure travellers to **Winston Churchill's Britain at War Experience** (*see p81*). Across Tooley Street from these pleasures stands a spookily empty mall called **Hay's Galleria**, once an enclosed dock, now dominated by a peculiar sculpture called *The Navigators* (by David Kemp). Here the twinkling Christmas Shop (7378 1998) remains doggedly festive, and half-hearted craft stalls await custom. Exiting on the river side, past the great grey hulk of **HMS Belfast**, you can walk east toward Tower Bridge and City Hall (*see p81*).

London Dungeon

28-34 Tooley Street, SE1 2SZ (7403 7221/ www.thedungeons.com). London Bridge tube/rail. **Open** *Sept-Nov* 10am-5.30pm daily. *Nov-Apr* 10.30am-5pm daily. *Apr-July* 10am-5.30pm daily. *July-Aug* 10am-7.30pm daily. **Admission** £12.50; £11.25 concessions; £8.25 5-14s. **Credit** AmEx, MC, V. **Map** p405 Q8.

Join the queue for this disturbing world of torture, death and disease under the Victorian railway arches of London Bridge and you file through a dry-ice fog past gravestones and hideously rotting corpses. Screeches and horror-movie soundtracks add to the experience. Don't inflict it on young children or anyone liable to be offended by fibreglass stonework, squeaking rats, skeletons that come to life and spilled guts.

There is plenty to offend. White-faced visitors experience nasty symptoms from the Great Plague exhibition: an actor-led medley of corpses, boils, projectile vomiting, worm-filled skulls and scuttling rats. Then there are the Wicked Women, the big, bad, brutal lady leaders such as Boudicca, Anne Boleyn, Queen Elizabeth I. A television presenter called Anne Robinson also gets a mention. Other hysterical revisions of horrible London history include the Great Fire and the Judgement Day Barge, in which visitors play the part of condemned prisoners (death sentence guaranteed). A 'seriously, folks' type notice on the wall at the exit remarks that torture is still widespread in many parts of the world. As well as Tooley Street. More horrors await in the shop (severed fingers, bulgy eyeballs, fake blood). The café has burger and chips for £3.50.

London Fire Brigade

94A Southwark Bridge Road, SE1 0EG (7587 2894/ www.london-fire.gov.uk). Borough tube. **Open** *Shop* 9am -5pm Mon-Fri. *Tours* 10.30am, 2pm Mon-Fri by appointment only. **Admission** £3; £2 7-14s, concessions; free under-7s. **Credit** MC, V. **Map** p404 O9.

Visitors must book in advance to explore this small eight-room museum, which traces the history of firefighting from the Great Fire of London in 1666 to the present. Tours last roughly an hour and take in the appliance bay, where pumps dating back to 1708 stand it tribute to conflagrations of the past. Exhibits include uniforms, medals, equipment and paintings executed by firemen-artists recording their Blitz experiences.

Old Operating Theatre, Museum & Herb Garret

9A St Thomas's Street, SE1 9RY (7955 4791/ www.thegarret.org.uk). London Bridge tube/rail. **Open** 10.30am-5pm daily (last entry 4.45pm). **Admission** £4.25; £3.25 concessions; £2.50 6-16s; £11 family (2 adults and up to 4 children); free under-6s. **No credit cards**. **Map** p405 Q8.

The tower that houses this curiosity used to be part of the chapel of St Thomas's Hospital, founded on this site in the 12th century. When the hospital was moved to Lambeth in the 1860s most of the buildings were torn down to make way for London Bridge Station. The chapel was preserved, and in 1956 the atmospheric old herb garret was discovered. Visitors enter via a vertiginous wooden spiral staircase (sadly, there's no disabled access) to view the medicinal herbs on display. Further in is the centrepiece: a Victorian operating theatre with tiered viewing seats for students. Even more horrifying are the displays of operating equipment that look like implements of torture (pity the poor women faced with the cervical dilators). Other display cases hold strangulated hernias, leech jars and amputation knives. In autumn 2003 the museum celebrated 300 years, and a new display was mounted; a life-size anatomical figure with removable organs dating from the 18th century. Check the website for events (such as Victorian Surgery demonstrations) and regular lectures on a a variety of subjects.

Not for profit

You might think that only the wealthy could afford to live on the slick South Bank, but private developers haven't had it all their own way with the desirable real estate round here; the **Coin Street Community Builders**, a social enterprise and development trust, have seen to that. The Coin Street Action Group formed in 1977 in response to a proposed hotel complex on land behind the National Theatre. They campaigned for seven years before they were able to buy the 13 acres (5.3 hectares) connecting Upper Ground and Stamford Street. One of the first things the group did was to create a pleasant riverside park, **Bernie Spain Gardens**, named after one of its campaigners.

The group's mission is to make the riverside a pleasant place to live and work in. Affordable housing co-operatives are made possible by the commercial success of retail and business enterprises such as Gabriel's Wharf and Oxo Tower Wharf, both owned by the Coin Street Community.

Plans have been unveiled for a smart new neighbourhood centre with a café and restaurant on Stamford Street, to be completed in 2005. Future community work includes the building of a public leisure centre with swimming pool, next to the National Theatre, by 2006. These projects are for people struggling to bring up their children in an area rich in tourist attractions but poor in ordinary facilities. Visitors, meanwhile, continue to make use of the Community Builders' commercial ventures. **Gabriel's Wharf**, with its gourmet pizzas, wooden toys for children, gift shops and cafés, feels like a holiday camp on sunny days. The **Oxo Tower** has a cooler vibe, particularly in the eighth-floor restaurant (*see p191*). The views are free, and the ground-floor shops are trendy.

Winston Churchill's Britain at War Experience

64-6 Tooley Street, SE1 2TF (7403 3171/ www.britainatwar.co.uk). London Bridge tube/rail. **Open** *Apr-Sept* 10am-5.30pm (last entry 5pm) daily. *Oct-Mar* 10am-4.30pm daily (last entry 4pm). **Admission** £7.50; £5 concessions; £4 5-16s; £16 family; free under-5s. **Credit** AmEx, MC, V. **Map** p405 Q8.

An authentically drab and dusty exhibition calls to mind the privations endured by the British people during the Second World War. There's plenty about London during the Blitz, including real bombs, rare documents and photos. The displays on rationing, food production and Land Girls are fascinating and the huge set-piece bombsite (you enter just after a bomb has dropped on the street, and witness pyjamaed legs sticking out of the rubble – children love it) is quite disturbing. It's a funny old place, but it conjures up wartime austerity pretty well.

Tower Bridge & Bermondsey

Bermondsey tube/London Bridge tube/rail.

Walking riverside from London Bridge to Tower Bridge, you pass the pristine environs of **City Hall**, the rented home of the current London government. Designed by Norman Foster (who also did the Millennium Bridge, *see p70*), the rotund glass structure leans squiffily away from the river (to prevent it casting shade on the walkers below). It uses just a quarter of the energy of a normal office building because of its simple water cooling system (there's no air-conditioning). The building has an exhibition blowing the Mayor's trumpet on the ground floor, a café on the lower ground floor and a pleasant outdoor amphitheatre for lunch breaks and sunbathing.

Just near **Tower Bridge** a noticeboard announces when the bridge will next open (which it does about 500 times a year for tall ships to pass through). The bridge is one of the lowest crossings over the Thames, which is why the twin lifting sections ('bascules') were designed by architect Horace Jones and engineer John Wolfe Barry. The original steam-driven hydraulic machinery can still be seen if you visit the **Tower Bridge Exhibition** (*see p94*), although the lifting gear has been run by electricity since 1976.

Further east, riverside dining in gracious surroundings is now what **Butler's Wharf** is all about. There is a series of Sir Terence Conran's restaurants with river views. Here, too is the **Design Museum**, housed in a building that was once also a warehouse. Shad Thames is the main thoroughfare behind the wharves, where in days long gone dockworkers unloaded tea, coffee and spices to be stored in huge warehouses (now expensive apartments and offices). Shad Thames comes from the area's original name St John at Thames, as it was called when Knights Templars ran the area.

Up past the Design Museum across Jamaica Road and down Tanner Street is historic Bermondsey Street, site of Zandra Rhodes's labour of love, the **Fashion & Textile Museum** (*see p82*). On the way, take a peek at **St Saviour's Dock**, originally the mouth of

Sightseeing

Old Operating Theatre. *See p80.*

the old river, Neckinger, whose name comes from 'Devol's Neckenger', a reference to this spot's popularity as a place of execution for pirates. The River Neckinger was also responsible for the slime-filled tidal ditches that surrounded a deeply unwholesome part of Bermondsey once known as Jacob's Island. Charles Dickens was so appalled by the conditions here that he chose it as a suitably pestilential place for Bill Sykes to meet his end in *Oliver Twist*. Further south, around Bermondsey Square, it's all Starbucks and delis, new cobbles and hanging baskets. The Friday antiques market here is lovely (4am-2pm).

Design Museum

Shad Thames, SE1 2YD (7403 6933/ www.designmuseum.org). Tower Hill tube/London Bridge tube/rail/42, 47, 78, 100, 188 bus. **Open** 10am-5.45pm daily (last entry 5.15pm). **Admission** £6; £4 concessions, 5-15s; £16 family; free under-5s. **Credit** AmEx, MC, V. **Map** p405 S9.

This white, 1930s style building was once a warehouse but is now a fine container for exhibitions devoted to design in all its forms. Outside the main building, the Design Museum Tank is a little outdoor gallery of constantly changing installations by leading contemporary designers; it also offers a taster of exhibitions within the museum. Once inside this acclaimed shrine to design, it's hard to ignore the shop's glossy design books and chic household accessories, but remember you're here for the exhibitions. The space has frequently changing temporary shows. Exhibitions in 2004 cover home matters from anglepoise lamp to iPod in 'The History of Modern Design in the Home' (until 5 September), the architect group Archigram (3 April-4 July), 'Saul Bass On Film' (17 July-31 October) and 'Designer of the Year' (6 March-13 June), a celebration of the diversity of the UK's design talent, which everyone can join in by voting at the exhibition of work or on the website. The museum hosts a year-round programme of talks and lectures by designers from all over the world (see the website for details). On the first floor the Blueprint Café (a smart restaurant) has a balcony overlooking the Thames; the ground-floor café is run by Konditor & Cook.

Fashion & Textile Museum

83 Bermondsey Street, SE1 3XF (7407 8664/ www.ftmlondon.org). London Bridge tube/rail. **Open** 11am-5.45pm (last entry 5.15pm) Tue-Sun. **Admission** £6; £4 concessions, students, 5-16s; £16 family; free under- 5s. **Credit** DC, MC, V. **Map** p405 Q9.

Like the flamboyantly coiffed fashion designer who dreamed it up, this pink and orange museum stands out like a beacon among the grey streets of south London. It's the first exhibition space in the UK dedicated to the global fashion industry. The grand pink foyer, with its jewel-inlaid floor leads to a long gallery and exhibition hall. The core collection comprises 3,000 garments donated by Zandra Rhodes, along with her archive collection of paper designs and sketchbooks, silk screens, finished textiles, completed garments and show videos. There are plans for at least two temporary exhibitions a year: check the website for details.

All dressed up: **Fashion & Textile Museum.**

The City

Richly historic.

Maps p402-p405

The City of London was built nearly 2,000 years ago as an outpost of the Roman Empire. Thus, the first locals of what was then called Londinium were Italians, who built a fort, a temple to Diana and a 6,000-seat amphitheatre where, respectively, the **Barbican** (*see p94*), **St Paul's Cathedral** (*see p87*) and the **Guildhall** (*see p89*) now stand. Around AD 200, the Romans built a defensive wall from the bank now occupied by **Tower Bridge** around to the bank where **Blackfriars Bridge** now begins; the area enclosed by it, roughly 300 acres (121 hectares), is a portion of what, today, is known as the City. Parts of this wall still stand; a stretch was recently exposed as the centrepiece of a café terrace on Cooper's Row near Tower Hill.

The Romans stayed for four centuries, but when they left, no one really moved in. Anglo-Saxons and poorly organised tribespeople inhabited some of the ruins, but they mostly stood in awe of what they called 'the City of Giants', living outside it but occasionally pilfering it for building materials. Though the area did become a commercial hub, the Anglo-Saxons' reticence let in the French, who quickly moved into the ready-made capital after the Norman invasion and marked their arrival by building the **Tower of London** (*see p94*).

The medieval period saw the coming and going three times of Dick Whittington who, as a boy, believed the streets to be paved with gold. Metaphorically, they were; by the time Whittington was first elected Mayor in 1397, the merchants had grown more prosperous than ever, and have maintained their wealth ever since. The Plague of 1665 and the Great Fire of 1666 (*see p11*) halted progress, but only briefly. Indeed, the destruction wrought by the latter provided an opportunity to rebuild London in brick and stone as the most modern city in the world, which it duly was (albeit largely due to its medieval street plan). Despite serious damage caused by World War II, many of these 17th-century buildings remain, as do other landmarks erected in the 18th century: the **Mansion House**, the façade of the **Guildhall**, and St Paul's Cathedral, completed in 1711.

Gradually, as sea travel declined and London ceased to handle stocks of material goods, the merchants turned to the money markets, and with great success. The modern-day City has grown into one of the world's leading financial centres. This shift in priorities hasn't been the only change, however. Over 13,000 houses were burned down in the Great Fire of 1666; today, barely half that many *people* live in the City. Yet the area remains a world apart from its neighbours. Its ruling body, the arcane and fiercely independent Corporation of London, is arguably the most powerful local council in the country, and certainly the richest.

At night and on weekends, there's no quieter corner of London than the one that, hours earlier, has been its noisiest. That isn't to say there's no nightlife in the City: the cluster of restaurants and pubs around Liverpool Street Station and the fashionable bars and clubs of Smithfield bring the lie to that myth, as do the scattering of ancient pubs throughout the Square Mile. That said, this is still an area at its best during the day.

City Information Centre

St Paul's Churchyard, EC4M 8BX (7332 1456). St Paul's tube. **Open** *Apr-Sept* 9.30am-5pm daily. *Oct-Mar* 9.30am-5pm Mon-Fri; 9.30am-12.30pm Sat. **No credit cards. Map** p404 O6.

Information on sights, events, walks and talks in the Square Mile.

Along Fleet Street

Chancery Lane tube/Blackfriars tube/rail.

Fleet Street takes its name from the largest of London's lost rivers. In its heyday, the Fleet was a major inlet for trade in London; flowing into the Thames at Blackfriars Bridge, it was flanked by docks that received ships bearing coal, spice and fabrics. However, pollution of the river at its upper reaches – it rises up in Hampstead – ended its usefulness, and the river was covered over in stages during the 19th century. It now flows entirely beneath ground.

One of the arterial roads linking Buckingham Palace to the City (and the monarch to the money), Fleet Street is still famous as the home of the country's press, even though most have long since moved elsewhere. 'Media' is the perfect word to describe the industry that was first undertaken here centuries ago, when reporters mediated on the antagonism created between the City of Westminster and the City. The proximity of the law courts proved handy for settling disputes that got a little too fiery.

The journalistic tradition has its roots in Wynkyn de Worde, who set up a printing press beside the River Fleet in 1500 at **St Bride's** church; still referred to as 'the printers and journalists' church', its beautiful Wren-designed spire was the inspiration for the tiered wedding cake. Only Reuters, the press agency that began in 1850 with a basket of carrier pigeons, remains; the rest of the newspapers that once dominated the locale have moved, mostly east to Wapping or Canary Wharf. However, traces of the industry remain: in the buildings that housed the *Daily Telegraph* (No.135) and the *Daily Express* (Nos.121-8, known as the Lubianka building after the architect who gave it a glass face and an art deco interior), and in the pubs and bars that once hosted endless liquid lunches for the bibulous hacks, including El Vino (No.47) and the Punch Tavern (No.99, where satirical magazine *Punch* was founded in 1841). Other writers left their mark, too; you can still sit in Samuel Johnson's seat in Ye Olde Cheshire Cheese (*see p219*).

Dr Johnson's House

17 Gough Square, off Fleet Street, EC4A 3DE (7353 3745/www.drjh.dircon.co.uk). Chancery Lane or Temple tube/Blackfriars tube/rail. **Open** *May-Sept* 11am-5.30pm Mon-Sat. *Oct-Apr* 11am-5pm Mon-Sat. *Tours* by arrangement; groups of 10 or more only. **Admission** £4; £3 concessions; £1 5-14s; free under-5s; £9 family. *Tours* free. *Evening tours* £5-£8 per head. **No credit cards. Map** p404 N6.

The writer Samuel Johnson (1704-84) lived in this typical Georgian townhouse while working on his *Dictionary of the English Language,* published in 1755. The museum, which celebrates its 250th anniversary in 2005, is lent a tremendous atmosphere by its creaky floorboards, Queen Anne furniture and authentic sash windows; indeed, you can almost feel the old wit's presence. Johnson, though, didn't always love his job: 'To make dictionaries is dull work,' he wrote in his definition of the word 'dull'.

Around St Paul's

St Paul's tube.

Is there a finer sight in London than **St Paul's Cathedral** (*see p87*), rising majestically from the mess of cranes, half-built skyscrapers and dreary office blocks that currently passes for a City skyline? Unlikely. Its dome, familiar from a million postcards, is a serene curve in a concrete jungle of angles. At night, when it's underlit, there really isn't anything in London to touch it.

There has been a cathedral dedicated to St Paul on this site for exactly 1,400 years. After one incarnation was destroyed in the Great Fire of 1666, Sir Christopher Wren designed the present structure, and though he had to fight hard to get it built as he wanted, build it he did; in just 35 years, too, next to no time in cathedral terms. If you're passing at lunchtime, listen for the 17-ton 'Great Paul' bell, which tolls daily at 1pm from one of the baroque towers.

Alongside the cathedral sits **Paternoster Square**, re-opened to the public in September 2003 following a long development programme. St Paul's is now flanked by what *Guardian* critic Jonathan Glancey scathingly called 'a gathering of burly office blocks clad in the architectural equivalent of tweed coats.' Not everyone's happy with the new look.

Heading east, **Bow Lane** is a cosy alleyway that offers a quaint little row of shops, bistros and champagne bars. Close by sits **St Mary Aldermary**, an attempt by Wren to hark back to the pre-Great Fire perpendicular style. Inside is a little display containing oyster shells; a step up from the usual communion wafer, you might think, but they're really from the Thames and were a staple part of workmen's diets in the 17th and 18th centuries. Once the oysters were eaten, the shells were used in the walls of the buildings they were erecting. Over Queen Victoria Street, meanwhile, is **Garlick Hill**, its medieval name proving false the supposed antipathy between the English and the pungent bulb. And at the bottom of the street is Wren's **St James Garlickhythe**, which, after St Paul's has the highest roof in the City.

A little west of St Paul's, on Ludgate Hill, stands **St Martin within Ludgate**, its lead spire still visible over the surrounding buildings as Wren intended. Around the corner is the most famous court in the land, the **Old Bailey** (*see below*). However, try to detour down the delightful tangle of winding alleys that lead from St Paul's Cathedral to Blackfriars station following medieval street plans; they now conceal shops, pubs and the Wren's dinky **St Andrew by the Wardrobe**. Built between 1685 and 1695, the church's curious name dates from 1361, when the king's wardrobe (the ceremonial clothes of the Royal Family) were moved to the adjoining building.

Nearby sit two more Wren creations, **St Benet** and **St Nicholas Cole Abbey**, though they're usually closed. Facing the former across scruffy Queen Victoria Street is the neat red-brick, 17th-century mansion of the **College of Arms**, where 'heralds' examine the pedigrees of those to whom such things matter (*see p87*). And just north of Blackfriars station is the **Apothecaries' Hall**, one of several livery halls.

Central Criminal Court (Old Bailey)

Corner of Newgate Street & Old Bailey, EC4M 7EH (7248 3277). St Paul's tube/4, 8, 11, 22, 23, 25, 26 bus. **Open** *Public gallery* 10.30am-1pm, 2-4.30pm Mon-Fri. **Admission** free. No under-14s; 14-16s accompanied by adults only. **Map** p404 O6.

A tale of two cathedrals

London has two Anglican cathedrals: the north has **St Paul's** (*pictured below; see also p87*), Wren's domed masterpiece in the City, commissioned after the Great Fire of 1666 had destroyed its medieval predecessor; the south has **Southwark Cathedral** (*see p78*), a square-towered building, which Shakespeare knew as St Saviour's. These two places of worship are a short and enjoyable walk away from each other, via the Millennium Bridge. In their own holy way, they symbolise the north/south divide that has long existed on the banks of the Thames.

St Paul's is one of the greatest buildings in Christendom, an awesome sight especially if you come upon it suddenly, emerging from the winding Dickensian alleys between Ludgate Hill and Blackfriars.

Southwark is a rather modest, part-Gothic, part-Victorian building upon which you can only come suddenly because it is hidden beneath railway viaducts and behind Borough Market.

St Paul's has Roman origins, its site that of a temple to Diana. Southwark, too, has a Roman heritage in the fourth-century mosaic pavement in the south aisle.

St Paul's is wonderfully puffed up and confident, a fitting testimonial to the elevated position that the great City of London has in the world. Southwark looks solidly self-deprecating, a dependable rock for the hundreds of nervously commuting inhabitants in so many dormitory boroughs feeding the City from the south.

St Paul's has a diary of civic functions and visits by the Queen, who draws up in a golden coach at the foot of the magnificent broad steps outside the west entrance. Southwark is slightly uncomfortable with Establishment functions and has trouble accommodating the limos in its narrow cobbled streets.

St Paul's seats 6,000 with ease. Southwark seats 600 with a squeeze.

In a massive marble tomb in the crypt, St Paul's has Admiral Lord Nelson, a member of the military and one of the nation's heroes, who died prematurely at the Battle of Trafalgar. Under a makeshift slab between the choirstalls, Southwark has Shakepeare's younger brother Edmund, an actor and layabout who died prematurely after a short life of fun and poverty.

St Paul's has a world-famous choir with a continuous 800-year-old tradition. Southwark has a less well-known one with an interrupted history dating to the 14th century.

St Paul's welcomes the travellers of the world, charging them £7 for a look along its glorious nave or an ascent to the fabulous Whispering Gallery and above. Southwark is a traditional point of departure. Chaucer and his pilgrims congregated here before the long journey to Canterbury. So did the passengers and crew of the *Mayflower* before setting off on their historic pilgrimage. Today, the scuttling commuters belt through Southwark Cathedral's garden trying to catch the 6.20 to Beckenham without so much as a glance at its tranquil lavender borders.

Sightseeing

DOCKLANDS. PAST AND PRESENT.

Discover the story of London's river, port and people from the arrival of the Romans to the rise of Canary Wharf

It is a mark of success in the criminal world to be tried at the Central Criminal Court, commonly known as the Old Bailey after the street on which it sits. The courts, famous for its copper dome and golden statue representing justice, were built by Edward Mountford in 1907 on the site of the old Newgate Prison; part of the old Roman wall is preserved behind glass in the basement.

The public is welcome to visit the courts and watch British justice in action; a notice by the front door provides details of the trials taking place on any given day. High-profile cases take place in Courts 1 to 4, for which the entrance is in Newgate Street. Join the queue but note that you will not be allowed in with food, large bags, cameras or electronic equipment.

College of Arms

Queen Victoria Street, EC4V 4BT (7248 2762/ www.college-of-arms.gov.uk). St Pauls tube/ Blackfriars tube/rail. **Open** 10am-4pm Mon-Fri. *Tours* by arrangement 6.30pm Mon-Fri; prices vary. **Admission** free. **No credit cards. Map** p404 O7.

In medieval times, heralds' main role in society was to organise tournaments. The knights who took part were recognised by the arms on their shields and the crests on their helmets. The heralds got to be such experts at recognising the symbols that they became responsible for recording arms, and, eventually, for controlling their use. The practice continues within the venerable college, the present building dating from the 1670s. Only the wood-panelled entrance room is accessible to the public, although tours can be booked in order to view the Record Room and the artists working on the intricate certificates.

St Paul's Cathedral

Ludgate Hill, EC4M 8AD (7236 4128/ www.stpauls.co.uk). St Paul's tube. **Open** 8.30am-4pm Mon-Sat. *Galleries, crypt & ambulatory* 9.30am-4pm Mon-Sat. Closed for special services, sometimes at short notice. *Tours* 11am, 11.30am, 1.30pm, 2pm Mon-Sat. **Admission** *Cathedral, crypt & gallery* £7; £3 6-16s; £6 concessions; £17 family; free under-6s. **Audio guide** £3.50; £3 concessions. **Credit** *Shop* AmEx, MC, V. **Map** p404 O6.

Now undergoing the most comprehensive refurbishment programme in its 300-year history, this most famous of cathedrals continues to arouse artistic passions, as controversy surrounding the restoration of the ceiling of the Whispering Gallery threatens to put the work on permanent hold. It was, though, ever thus. Sir Christopher Wren had to fight to get his plans for the building approved (they were initially rejected), and the building process was by no means simple. However, be glad he persisted. Although some areas will be marred by scaffolding for another year or so, it truly is an impressive sight, both during the day and, illuminated, at night.

Of the millions who visit each year, many come as much for the views as anything: it's a 530-step, 280ft (85m) climb to the open-air Golden Gallery. Walk around it, taking in London in all its magnificence (and marvelling at the variety of construction cranes that surround you). En route, you'll pass the Whispering Gallery (259 steps up), which runs around the dome's interior and takes its name from the acoustically implausible but absolutely true fact that if you whisper into the dome's wall, someone at the other side of the gallery can hear you perfectly.

There's plenty to see in this vast building; buying a guidebook (£4) is imperative if you want to make the most of what you're seeing. That said, some of the monuments are easily explained, such as the one to the Americans who died in Great Britain during World War II, and the one to poet John Donne in the south aisle, the only monument in the building to have survived the Great Fire. The two most eye-catching tombs in the crypt are of the Duke of Wellington and Horatio Nelson, though among the notable figures from the arts buried here are Henry Moore, JMW Turner, Joshua Reynolds, Max Beerbohm, Arthur Sullivan and Wren himself.

North to Smithfield

Barbican or St Paul's tube.

From St Paul's, a short walk north across Cheapside takes you to Foster Lane, and another Wren church, **St Vedast** (7606 3998, open 9.15am-4.30pm Mon-Fri). Wren built it in 1673, using remnants of an earlier church destroyed in the Great Fire. Though it was gutted in 1941, Dykes Bower restored it in 1962; of the dozen churches that once stood in the immediate vicinity, it's the sole survivor. Fans claim its delicately phased tower is the prettiest in town; certainly, it contrasts beautifully with the elaborate steeple of **St Mary le Bow**.

Between Foster Lane and St Bartholomew's Hospital lies the delightful **Postman's Park**. The green space is pretty enough, but its most famous feature is the Heroes Wall, an expanse of ceramic plaques inscribed in florid Victorian style. 'Frederick Alfred Croft, Inspector, aged 31,' begins one typical thumbnail drama. 'Saved a Lunatic Woman from Suicide at Woolwich Arsenal Station, But Was Himself Run Over By the Train (Jan 11, 1878).'

St Bartholomew's Hospital has the Augustinian pilgrim Rahere to thank for its existence; he had a hospital built here in the 12th century after a near-death brush with malaria in Rome. **St Bartholomew's Hospital Museum** (7601 8152, 10am-4pm Tue-Fri), charts the hospital's history and contains epic biblical murals by William Hogarth, who was baptised in the nearby **St Bartholomew-the-Great**, the oldest parish church in the capital (*see p88*).

Today's Londoners know **Smithfield** as London's meat market. It opened for business in 1868, and trades on today. Or, rather, tonight:

Swiss Re Tower aka 'The Gherkin' (30 St Mary Axe) is part of the City scenery. *See p28.*

trucks begin to pull into the market from around midnight, with the buying and selling commencing around 3am.

Night owls have long fled here for a fix of greasy food, as the nocturnal nature of the business means there are a number of all-night caffs here. But since the addition of **Fabric** (*see p316*), the area's become fashionable among the clubbing fraternity, with other cool bars opened nearby. The **Fox & Anchor** on Charterhouse Street is one of a handful of longer-established pubs, traditional in all but its hours: it serves beers and breakfasts from 7am.

St Bartholomew-the-Great

West Smithfield, EC1A (7606 5171/www.greatstbarts.com). Barbican tube/Farringdon tube/rail. **Open** *Mid Nov-mid Feb* 8.30am-4pm Tue-Fri; 10.30am-1.30pm Sat; 8.30am-1pm, 2.30-8pm Sun. *Mid Feb-mid Nov* 8.30am-5pm Tue-Fri; 10.30am-1.30pm Sat; 8.30am-1pm, 2.30-8pm Sun. **Services** Sun 9am, 11am & 6.30pm; Tue 12.30pm; Thur 8.30am. **Admission** free; donations welcome. **Map** p402 O5.

This historic church is a remnant of a 12th-century monastic chapel, built by a courtier of Henry I as a thanksgiving for his delivery from fever, whose nave was demolished during Henry VIII's monastic purge; the gateway across the yard used to be the front door. The interior swirls with Romanesque round arches and red and yellow zigzags that once must have decorated the entire building. Benjamin Franklin trained here as a printer in 1724.

Around Bank

Mansion House tube/Bank tube/DLR.

A triumvirate of buildings – the Bank of England, the Royal Exchange and Mansion House – stake their claim to being, if not the geographical centre of the Square Mile, then its symbolic heart. This trio of imposing buildings, made from the best Portland stone, are only let down by the oddity at nearby **Number 1 Poultry**, which resembles the prow of a ship.

The **Bank of England** was founded in 1694 to fund William III's war against the French. Most of what you see today was the work of Sir Herbert Baker in the 1920s; John Soane's original building was demolished to make room for it, though a reproduction of his Stock Office was built a few years ago ostensibly to house the **Bank of England Museum** (*see below*).

The Lord Mayor of London's official residence, **Mansion House** (7626 2500; group visits only, by written application to the Diary Office, Mansion House, Walbrook, EC4N 8BH, at least two months in advance), was designed by George Dance and completed in 1753. It's the only private residence in the UK to have its own court of justice, complete with 11 prison cells; the building's pediment, by Robert Taylor, depicts London defeating envy and bringing plenty through exploitation of its Empire.

The current **Royal Exchange**, the third on the site, was opened by Queen Victoria in 1844, but within a few years a Gothic revival led to its design being viewed as somewhat outmoded. The only trading that takes place now is in the high-class shops set in the arcades. A little further west is the centre of the City's civic life: the **Guildhall**, the base of the Corporation of London and home to a library, the **Clockmakers' Museum** (for both *see below*), the church of **St Lawrence Jewry** and the **Guildhall Art Gallery** (*see below*).

Next to Mansion House stands one of the City's finest churches, **St Stephen Walbrook**, the trial run for St Paul's. Nearby is a heap of stones that once constituted the Roman **Temple of Mithras** (*see p91*). Other churches in the area include Hawskmoor's **St Mary Woolnoth** (*see p90*) and Wren's exquisite **St Mary Abchurch** off Abchurch Lane.

Bank of England Museum

Entrance on Bartholomew Lane, EC2R 8AH (7601 5491/cinema bookings 7601 3985/www.bankofengland.co.uk/museum). Bank tube/DLR. **Open** 10am-5pm Mon-Fri. *Tours* by arrangement. **Admission** free. *Audio guide* £1. *Tours* free. **Map** p405 Q6.

The life story of the national bank unfolds quite amusingly in these elegant rooms, a gleaming replica of Soane's Stock Office. As well as coin and banknote galleries and wall adornments, display cases contain Roman vases and drawing/writing instruments, including a sovereign weighing machine dating back to 1845. An iron chest dating back to the 18th century is believed to be the oldest piece of furniture in the bank; more glamorously, those with strong forearms can lift a real gold bar worth over £93,000. Entry costs nothing, though unfortunately there are no free samples. (*See also p90* **Making the world go round**.)

Clockmakers' Museum

Guildhall Library, Aldermanbury, EC2P 2EJ (Guildhall Library 7332 1868/1870/www.clockmakers.org). Mansion House or St Paul's tube/Bank tube/DLR/Moorgate tube/rail. **Open** 9.30am-4.45pm Mon-Fri. **Admission** free. **Map** p404 P6.

All types of clocks, from 6ft (1.8m) grandfathers to delicate pocket watches, tick merrily as you pass the time with a potted history of horology. A collection of the creations of 17th-century clockmaker Thomas Tompion includes curious, possibly priceless, timepieces. There's plenty to fascinate here, should you want to devote 30 minutes to watching the clocks in this neatly ordered room.

Guildhall

Gresham Street, EC2P 2EJ (7606 3030/tours ext 1463/www.corpoflondon.gov.uk). Bank tube/DLR. **Open** *May-Sept* 9.30am-5pm daily. *Oct-Apr* 9.30am-5pm Mon-Sat. Last entry 4.30pm. Closes for functions, call ahead. *Tours* by arrangement; groups of 10 or more people only. **Admission** free. **Map** p404 P6.

The centre of the City's government for more than 800 years, the Guildhall has had its tribulations in the past. The Great Hall, indeed, was damaged by the Great Fire and the Blitz, but has been restored. Banners and shields of the 100 livery companies adorn the walls, and every Lord Mayor since 1189 gets a namecheck on the windows. Meetings of the Court of Common Council (the governing body for the Corporation of London, presided over by the Lord Mayor) take place monthly, though the Guildhall is mostly used for banquets and ceremonial events.

Guildhall Art Gallery

Guildhall Yard, off Gresham Street, EC2P 2EJ (7332 3700/www.guildhall-art-gallery.org.uk). Mansion House or St Paul's tube/Bank tube/DLR/Moorgate tube/rail. **Open** 10am-5pm Mon-Sat (last entry 4.30pm); noon-4pm Sun (last entry 3.45pm). **Admission** £2.50; £1 concessions; free under-16s. Free to all after 3.30pm daily, all day Fri. **Credit** (over £5) MC, V. **Map** p404 P6.

The newest exhibit at the Guildhall Art Gallery is not a work of art at all, but the ruins in the basement of London's Roman amphitheatre that date from about AD 200; archaeologists discovered it only 15

Sightseeing

Making the world go round

Invented in 700 BC by the people of Lydia (now north-eastern Turkey), money revolutionised trade by separating the acts of buying and selling. Previously, a weak corn-seller who wished to buy a cudgel had to go in search of a hungry cudgel-vendor who wished to buy corn.

The nations with the most efficient money systems have always ruled the world. The Romans had brilliant money – the British Library catalogue of Roman coins fills three enormous volumes. The British inherited their enthusiasm for coinage from Rome and, by the first millennium, almost every medieval city in the land had its own mint. London's was in **Mint Street** inside the **Tower of London** until 1810, by which time it was coining for the whole kingdom, and thereafter across the way in **Royal Mint Street**, until 1968 when it was moved to Llantrisant in Wales. Nothing remains of the Royal Mint Street site (it was demolished in 1975 and redeveloped as a housing estate).

The gold and various other metals used in minting came from the vaults of goldsmiths. In the early 17th century those who made sizeable deposits were given paper receipts that could be passed on as if they were real money. These were the first banknotes.

These goldsmiths' banks were private concerns for a while. In the late 17th century, after years of social upheaval, it was clear that the country needed a state-controlled bank on the lines of the Bank of Amsterdam (it surely can be no coincidence that Parliament also looked for political salvation to the Dutchman William of Orange).

In 1694, a Scotsman called Paterson devised the scheme that established the Bank of England. He would raise, by public subscription, £1.2 million, which he would then lend to the government at eight per cent interest. The difference between this and other loans was that there should be no fixed period for its repayment, but that the interest should be paid in perpetuity. Paterson's ingenuity stabilised the relationship between government and finance, and ensured British trading dominance for the next 250 years.

years ago. The full extent of the oval arena is marked with a black line on the surface of Guildhall Square above; all that remains is the gladiators' entrance, a drainage gutter and a section of wall, though the ruins are beautifully presented. The amphitheatre seated around 6,000 people, which makes it about the same size as the Royal Albert Hall. Entertainment included the ritual slaughter of slaves.

The gallery contains works of mixed quality. The Pre-Raphaelites in the basement are exquisite, the Egyptian scenes hot and exotic, the bust of Clytie positively sensuous. Yet hanging between the ground and first floors is the largest painting in Britain, John Copley's *Siege of Gibraltar*, more congratulatory than great. This is true also of the official paintings, although that of the 1995 banquet for the half-century since the ending of the war contains recognisable characters and even has TV cameramen depicted among the guests.

St Mary Woolnoth

Lombard Street, EC3 (7626 9701). Bank tube/DLR. **Open** 9.30am-4.30pm Mon-Fri. **Admission** free; donations appreciated. **Map** p405 Q6.

Wulnoth, a Saxon noble, is thought to have founded this church on the site of a Roman temple to Concord. It was rebuilt often, most recently by Hawksmoor in 1716-17, and its interior, based on the Egyptian Hall of Vitruvius, is one of the architect's finest. When Bank station was built between 1897 and 1900, the church was undermined, the dead removed, and lift shafts sunk beneath the building.

The **Bank of England** (*pictured right*) is linked to the government whose monetary policy it advises and carries out. Inflation and interest rates are its concern. It does not deal with the public except in the **Bank of England Museum** around the corner (*see p89*).

At the museum, exhibits are laid out in several rooms of the original complex of buildings designed by the architect Sir John Soane. It is a clean and quiet museum, whose calm is disturbed only in school holidays, by events for children such as stories with the Roman Moneyer (*see above left*). There are ancient heavy-framed pictures showing periwigged Georgians signing documents. There is a cheque for one million pounds. There are forgeries for which a forger was hanged (in the 13th century he probably would have had his testicles chopped off). The banking hall runs touch-screen tests on your fiscal know-how. In a separate room there's a display of all the bank notes ever designed. The notes are reverently displayed in humidified glass boxes.

Temple of Mithras

On raised courtyard in front of Sumitomo Bank, Legal & General Building, Temple Court, 11 Queen Victoria Street. For further information contact the Museum of London. Mansion House tube. **Open** 24hrs daily. **Admission** free. **Map** p404 P6.

In the third century AD, the rival cults of Mithraism and Christianity were battling for supremacy. The Persian god Mithras appealed to Roman soldiers, and the troops on the British frontier built a small temple to their champion near this spot (AD 240-50). The reconstructed foundations aren't much to look at, but show the Roman influence on the later design of churches: rounded apse, central nave and side aisles. Most of the artefacts found at the site are on display at the Museum of London (*see p92*).

Around the Tower of London

Tower Hill tube/Tower Gateway DLR.

You won't find many locals near here. Around the giant sundial on the mound where public executions once took place sit tourists, munching sandwiches, waiting for friends. Few notice the bronze statue of the Emperor Trajan; fewer still wander to the Trinity Square memorial gardens, where the names of the thousands of merchant seamen who died in both World Wars are etched in stone, or wonder as to the antiquity of the nearby wall (it's Roman, part of the original wall that ringed the city; you can follow its course to the Museum of London).

The City's most famous chronicler, Samuel Pepys, lived and died close by in Seething Lane. There's a bust of him in **Seething Lane Gardens**, though he's actually buried in St Olave's Hart Street (nicknamed by Dickens 'St Ghastly Grim' after the leering skulls at the entrance). Pepys watched London burn in 1666 from **All Hallows by the Tower** (*see below*).

Along the river, between Tower and London Bridges, stand two reminders of London's great days as a port. David Lang built the **Custom House** in 1817, but the most appealing part of the building, its riverfront façade, was added by Robert Smirke a decade later. Next door is **Billingsgate Market**, for years London's fish market; trading ceased in 1982. The lanes behind the waterfront are packed with churches: **St Magnus the Martyr**, **St Mary at Hill**, **St Margaret Pattens** and **St Dunstan in the East**, the latter with lovely gardens.

Nearby sits the **Monument** (*see below*); just north-east of it is one of the City's loveliest places. 'Foreigners' (anyone from outside London) were allowed to sell poultry (and, later, cheese and butter) at **Leadenhall Market** from the 14th century. The arcaded buildings, painted in green, maroon and cream with wonderful decorative detail, are the work of Horace Jones, who built Smithfield Market. Today, a mix of shops competes for trade: alongside a Virgin selling CDs, a branch of the Jigsaw fashion chain and the requisite Body Shop sit florists and fruiterers, butchers and fishmongers, a shoeshine stall and a lovely pub (the Lamb).

Between Leadenhall and Liverpool Street rail station sit many more churches: **St Helen's Bishopsgate** (*see p93*), **St Andrew Undershaft** on St Mary Axe, **St Botolph-Without-Aldgate** and **St Katharine Cree** on Leadenhall Street, the latter an extraordinary hybrid of classical and Gothic styles. Nearby is the oldest synagogue in the country, the superbly preserved **Bevis Marks Synagogue**, built in 1701 by Sephardic Jews who had escaped from the Inquisition in Portugal and Spain, and located in a courtyard off Bevis Marks.

This area suffered considerable damage from IRA bombs in 1992 and 1993, and the tiny pre-fire church of **St Ethelburga-the-Virgin** (built 1390) was devastated. A great deal of restoration work has been undertaken, however, and the church has risen from the ashes as a peace and reconciliation centre.

All Hallows by the Tower

Byward Street, EC3R 5BJ (7481 2928/ www.allhallowsbythetower.org.uk). Tower Hill tube. **Open** *Church* 9am-5.45pm Mon-Fri; 10am-5pm Sat, Sun. *Service* 11am Sun. **Admission** free; donations appreciated. **Audio tour** £3 (suggested donation). **Map** p405 R7.

Though just the walls and a 17th-century brick tower were left standing after World War II attacks, post-war rebuilding at All Hallows has created a pleasingly light interior. A Saxon arch testifies to the church's seventh-century roots. Other relics include Saxon crosses, a Roman tessellated pavement, Tudor monuments and a superb carved limewood font cover (1682) by Grinling Gibbons.

Fishmongers' Hall

London Bridge, EC4R 9EL (7626 3531/ www.fishhall.co.uk). London Bridge tube/rail. **Open** tours only, by arrangement. **Admission** free; donations appreciated. **Map** p405 Q7.

The most interesting of the remaining City guilds or livery companies (the union HQ of once-powerful trades), this 19th-century hall displays, amid a jumble of precious loot, the dagger used by fishmonger and mayor William Walworth to stab Wat Tyler in the back and put down the Peasants' Revolt of 1381.

The Monument

Monument Street, EC3R 8AH (7626 2717/ www.towerbridge.org.uk). Monument tube. **Open** 9.30am-5pm daily. **Admission** £2; £1 5-15s; free under-5s. **No credit cards. Map** p405 Q7.

The Monument, built between 1671 and 1677 by Sir Christopher Wren and his friend Robert Hooke to commemorate the Great Fire of 1666, is little more than a 311-step spiral staircase enclosed within a 202-ft (65m) Doric column; its height is the distance from here to Farriner's bakery in Pudding Lane, where the fire began. In its day, the Monument was the tallest object for miles, as Wren had not yet started St Paul's; the golden ball of flame at the top shone in the sun, a salutary reminder of the vanity of man and the awesome power of nature. The views from the top are well worth the climb. Look out for the relief of King Charles carved in 1672 by one Caius Cibber, who'd done time in a debtors' prison. His revenge was to perch the King's finger on the nipple of a woman's exposed breast.

Museum of London

150 London Wall, EC2Y 5HN (7600 3699/recorded information 0870 444 3851/www.museumof london.org.uk). Barbican, Moorgate or St Paul's tube. **Open** 10am-5.50pm Mon-Sat; noon-5.50pm Sun. **Admission** free. **Credit** *Shop* AmEx, MC, V. **Map** p402 P5.

A new bridge and outdoor escalator have improved access to this excellent museum, which also has a larger foyer and shop. Better lifts and walkways mean that visitors may now go straight to their chosen destinations without the risk of first being distracted by other galleries; that said, if you've plenty of patience and time, you can walk the detailed, engaging displays in chronological order. Among the highlights: the Great Fire Experience, one for the kids; the walk-through Victorian street scene, like stepping into the pages of a Dickens novel; and the central garden, which presents a curious botanical history of the City. The courtyard has a café with outdoor tables and a hands-on Roman water pumping device; parked in the middle of the ground floor is the red and gold fairytale Lord Mayor's coach. Upcoming exhibitions include, until 18 July 2004, '1920s: The Decade that Changed London', and, from October 2004, the fashion-dedicated 'London Look'.

St Botolph-Without-Aldgate

St Botolph's Church, Aldgate High Street, EC3 1AD (7283 1670). Aldgate tube. **Open** 9.30am-3pm Mon-Fri; services only Sun. *Eucharist* 1.05pm Mon, Thur; *prayers* 1.05pm Tue, Wed. **Admission** free; donations appreciated. **Map** p405 R6.

This is the oldest of the three surviving churches of St Botolph, built at the old gates of Roman London as homage to the patron saint of travellers (the others are St Boltophs Without-Aldersgate and Without-Bishopsgate). Boston, Lincolnshire, and Boston, Massachusetts, are named for the saint; the name trips off the tongue more easily than Botolphstown. The present building was largely reconstructed by George Dance in 1744 and is noted for its beautiful ceiling decorated by John Francis Bentley in 1884. Daniel Defoe married here in 1683.

St Ethelburga Centre for Reconciliation & Peace

78 Bishopsgate, EC2N 4AG (7496 1610/www.centreethelburgas.org). Bank tube/DLR/ Liverpool Street tube/rail. **Open** 11am-3pm Wed; 8.45am Mon for prayers; noon-2.30pm 1st Fri of mth. **Admission** free; donations appreciated. **Map** p405 R6.

In 1994, the poet John Betjeman wrote of the tiny church of St Ethelburga, destroyed by an IRA bomb. Today, though, the debris has been put together with money from local businesses, American benefactors, the Church of England and the Corporation of London. A new east window has been created using broken stained glass from the original, an altar made from the ancient beams and a cross formed from scattered nails. Despite these ecclesiastical features, the building is no longer a church but a conference centre dedicated to world peace. The font, which survived the blast, contains the longest known ancient Greek palindrome: Niyon Anomhma Mh Monan Oyin, meaning 'Wash my sins as well as my body'.

St Helen's Bishopsgate

Great St Helen's, off Bishopsgate, EC3A 6AT (7283 2231/www.st-helens. org.uk). Bank tube/DLR/ Liverpool Street tube/rail. **Open** 9am-12.30pm Mon-Fri. *Lunchtime meetings* 1-2pm Tue, Thur. *Services* 10.15am, 7pm Sun. **Admission** free. **Map** p405 R6.

Because of the huge number of monuments and memorials within, St Helen's is known as the City's version of Westminster Abbey. It owes its unusual shape to the fact that it is really two medieval churches knocked into one. After surviving the Great Fire and the Blitz, it was damaged by terrorist bombs in the 1990s.

Tower Bridge Exhibition

Tower Bridge, SE1 2UP (7403 3761/www.towerbridge.org.uk). Tower Hill tube/London Bridge tube/rail. **Open** 9.30am-6pm daily. Last entry 5pm. **Admission** £4.50; £3 5-15s, concessions; free under-5s; £14 family. **Credit** AmEx, MC, V. **Map** p405 R8.

The main attraction, of course, is not the exhibition within it but Tower Bridge itself. In its day, the drawbridge idea was hugely ambitious, its construction a triumph of Victorian technology. Visitors ascend in the south tower, cross at the upper level,

Sightseeing

The **Tower of London**'s White Tower. *See p94.*

which has fabulous views, and descend the north tower. There are lifts part of the way. The climb is interrupted by unmanned electronic presentations that do the thinking for you while you rest.

Tower of London

Tower Hill, EC3N 4AB (0870 756 6060/ www.hrp.org.uk). Tower Hill tube/Fenchurch Street rail. **Open** *Mar-Oct* 9am-6pm Mon-Sat; 10am-6pm Sun; last admission 5pm. *Nov-Feb* 10am-5pm Mon, Sun; 9am-5pm Tue-Sat; last admission 4pm. **Admission** £13.50; £10.50 concessions; £9 5-15s; free under 5s; £37.50 family. **Credit** AmEx, MC, V. **Map** p405 R7.

The best way to see the Tower of London, which has served as a fortress, a palace and a prison over its 900-year history, is on a free tour led by one of the 40 Beefeaters, red-coated ex-soldiers picked for their public relations skills and resident within the grounds. The tales they tell are fascinating: of imprisonment, of treason, of torture and of execution. Of permanent haunting fascination is Traitor's Gate, the traditional river entrance to the Tower reserved for enemies of the state, and the chopping block on Tower Green, the traditional exit. The Crown Jewels are in the Jewel House; you'll glide past them on airport-style travelators. The Armoury, meanwhile, is in the White Tower; here you can admire Henry VIII's enormous codpiece. And wherever you are in the Tower, you're never far from a jolly costumed presentation, especially in summer.

Highlights for 2004 are led by 'Prisoners of the Tower 1100-1945', an exhibition running from 28 April to 5 September that examines the role of the Tower as state prison; inmates have included Anne Boleyn, Lady Jane Grey, Guy Fawkes and Rudolf Hess. Book ahead for the Christmas, half-term and summer events for families. Redevelopment work in 2003 means that disabled access to the Tower is very much improved. One final tip: arrive early to beat the crowds, especially in summer.

North of London Wall

Barbican tube/Moorgate tube/rail.

Running close to the impressively redeveloped Liverpool Street Station and the rather bland Broadgate Centre next to it, **London Wall** follows the northerly course of the old Roman fortifications. Part of the wall, and the remains of one of the gates into the Cripplegate Roman fort, can be seen in St Alphage Gardens, just near the Barber Surgeons Herb Garden, two pleasant little green picnicking places not far from the main road (off Fore Street).

The area just to the north of here was levelled during the Blitz. Rather than encourage office developments, the City of London and London County Council purchased a large site in 1958 to build 'a genuine residential neighbourhood, with schools, shops, open spaces and amenities'. We ended up with the **Barbican**, a vast estate of 2,000 flats and an arts complex (*see p300*) that, altogether, exudes little warmth or sense of community. Some of those who live there or regularly use the wonderful (once inside) Barbican library, cinema, theatre and concert hall defend it passionately, arguing quite rightly for the convenience of its location. But to the outsider, it's a strangely unknowable place.

Marooned amid the towering blocks is the only pre-war building in the vicinity: the heavily restored 16th-century church of **St Giles Cripplegate**, where Oliver Cromwell was married and John Milton buried. Further north-east, **Bunhill Fields** was set aside as a cemetery during the Great Plague, though it doesn't appear to have been used. Instead, apparently because the ground was never consecrated, the cemetery became popular for Nonconformist burials, gaining the name of 'the cemetery of Puritan England'. Much of the graveyard is cordoned off these days, but it's still possible for visitors to stroll through it and take a look at the monuments to John Bunyan, Daniel Defoe and William Blake. Opposite Bunhill Fields on City Road is the **Museum of Methodism** and **John Wesley's House** (*see below*) where, in 1951, the late Denis Thatcher married Margaret Hilda Roberts.

Barbican Art Gallery

Level 3, Barbican Centre, Silk Street, EC2Y 8DS (box office 7638 8891/www.barbican.org.uk). Barbican tube/Moorgate tube/rail. **Open** 10am-6pm Mon, Tue, Thur-Sat; 10am-9pm Wed; 10am-6pm Sun. **Admission** £8, £6 concessions. **Credit** AmEx, MC, V. **Map** p402 P5.

The Barbican Art Gallery reopens after refurbishment on 29 April 2004 with a retrospective of the late Helen Chadwick, whose best-known works include the controversial *Piss Flowers* and the sensual *Cacao,* a vast fountain of hot bubbling chocolate. The exhibition runs until August alongside Tina Madotti and Edward Weston: The Mexico Years; following them is an exhibition of works by 'sculptural architect' Daniel Libeskind, who won the contract to design the Freedom Tower at Ground Zero in New York.

Museum of Methodism & John Wesley's House

Wesley's Chapel, 49 City Road, EC1 1AU (7253 2262/www.wesleyschapel.org.uk). Moorgate or Old Street tube/rail. **Open** 10am-4pm Mon-Sat. *Tours* arrangements on arrival; groups of 10 or more must telephone ahead. **Admission** free. **Credit** *Shop* MC, V. **Map** p403 Q4.

John Wesley (1703-91), the father of Methodism, built this chapel beside his house in 1778. The museum in the crypt contains letters, Bibles, manuscripts and other ecclesiastical items. Wesley's house, meanwhile, contains a number of his personal effects including his nightcap, preaching gown and his personal experimental electric shock machine.

Holborn & Clerkenwell

Law and holy orders.

Holborn

Maps p399 & p401
Holborn tube.

The Inns of Court

Holborn is to lawyers what Fleet Street once was to journalists – the centre of the universe. Thousands of legal eagles are based around the four **Inns of Court**, where English common law first developed during the Middle Ages. Scattered throughout Holborn, the four Inns – Lincoln's Inn, Gray's Inn, and Inner and Middle Temple – are, combined, the spiritual heart of the British justice system. They were founded in medieval times, when they functioned as quasi-universities for the aristocracy. They are still called 'inns' because the students once lodged, ate and studied there. Over time, the inns gradually evolved into institutions where barristers are trained.

Today, they contain barristers' chambers, and a strong sense of archaic tradition: every barrister is aligned to one of the Inns, and must eat a series of meals there before they are called to the bar. The Inns are also lovely places to wander, with narrow alleys, courtyards and lawns. Most of the buildings are only open by appointment – some just for group tours – so call before you make the trip.

Of the four, **Lincoln's Inn** is the most spectacular (Lincoln's Inn Fields, 7405 1393). On a tour, you can relive scenes from *Bleak House*, Dickens's ferocious attack on the legal system, as virtually nothing has changed in hundreds of years. Its Old Hall dates from 1422, and its buildings – a mixture of Gothic, Tudor and Palladian styles – all survived bombing during the war. **Gray's Inn** (Gray's Inn Road, 7458 7800) was not so lucky: it was devastated by the Luftwaffe, and then sadly was largely rebuilt in an uninspiring style.

Further south, opposite the splendid Gothic buildings of the **Royal Courts of Justice** (*see p96*), are the other two Inns of Court: **Middle Temple** and **Inner Temple** (Middle Temple Lane, 7427 4800; Inner Temple Treasury Office, group tours £10, 7797 8241). Built around a maze of courtyards and passageways, they're especially atmospheric when gaslit after dark. The **Middle Temple Hall**, built in 1573, has a huge table made from a single oak tree donated by Queen Elizabeth I, and a smaller table made from the hatch of the original *Golden Hinde*. The Inner Temple has several fine buildings, and its lawns are a beautiful spot for picnics. Of particular note is **Temple Church** (Inner Temple, King's Bench Walk, 7353 8559); built in 1185, it combines elements of Romanesque and Gothic architecture, and is London's only surviving round church.

North of Middle Temple, on the Strand, is **Temple Bar**, a monument that divides Westminster from the City of London. In the Middle Ages, it was a barrier to the City, past which the monarch could not stray without the say so of the Lord Mayor, as the City and the royal court were in a constant power struggle. The Queen still needs permission from the Lord Mayor to enter the City, but the gate was replaced in 1878 by a fearsome bronze griffin.

A word of warning: if you want to soak up the atmosphere, Sunday isn't the best day to come, as the area is a virtual ghost town.

Aldwych

Walk west along the Strand past a slew of historic churches, including **St Clement Danes** (*see p96*) and **St Mary-le-Strand** (James Gibbs's first public building; 1714-17). On the Aldwych crescent, you'll see a trio of imperial buildings: India House, Australia House and Bush House, now home to the BBC's World Service. Back on the Strand lies King's College, its 1960s buildings sitting uneasily with Robert Smirke's 1829 originals. Easier on the eye is the regal **Somerset House** (*see p96*).

On **Temple Place**, just south of the Strand, is one of a handful of still-functioning cabmen's shelters. These green-painted sheds are a legacy of the Cabmen's Shelter Fund, set up in 1874 to provide cabbies with an alternative to pubs in which to get refreshment. On Strand Lane is the 'Roman' bath, reached via an alley off Surrey Street. Dickens's David Copperfield took many a cold plunge here. It can be viewed through a window if you miss its limited opening times (10am-12.30pm Mon-Fri, 7641 5264). Back near King's College, on the Strand and on Surrey Street, are entrances to Aldwych, one of London's ghost tube stations. Today, it's hired out for special events and movie shoots.

Prince Henry's Room

17 Fleet Street, EC4Y 1AA (7936 4004). Temple tube (closed Sun). **Open** 11am-2pm Mon-Sat. **Admission** free; donations appreciated. **Map** p404 N6.

This oak-panelled space with one of the best Jacobean plaster ceilings in the city is one of the few survivors of the 1666 Great Fire of London. Formerly used by the lawyers of Prince Henry, eldest son of King James I of England and VI of Scotland, the room was built in 1610, the same year the 14-year-old Henry became Prince of Wales. The rest of the building was once a tavern, a favourite haunt of Samuel Pepys, the famed chronicler of 17th-century London life. A collection of Pepys memorabilia is on display.

Royal Courts of Justice

Strand, WC2A 2LL (7947 6000/www.courtservice.gov.uk). Temple tube (closed Sun). **Open** 9.30am-5pm Mon-Fri. **Admission** free. **Map** p399 M6.

You can see British justice in action in these splendid Gothic buildings. Anyone is free to take a pew in the 88 courts, where the High Court presides over the most serious civil trials in the country. Lists in the central hall bear the names of the parties in cases being heard but don't give information about the proceedings; try asking the court ushers. Cameras, mobile phones and under-14s are not permitted. Note that there are few trials in August and September.

St Clement Danes

Strand, WC2 (7242 8282). Temple tube (closed Sun). **Open** 9am-4pm Mon-Fri; 9am-3pm Sat, Sun. *Services* 11am Sun. **Admission** free; donations appreciated. **Map** p399 M6.

It was, in fact, another church (St Clement Eastcheap), that gave rise to the nursery rhyme *Oranges and Lemons* (say the bells of…), but the vicar of this Wren-designed church made a theme song of it in 1920 and now the bells ring out the tune at 9am, noon, 3pm and 6pm Monday-Saturday. A German air raid razed the church in 1941, but it was restored in the 1950s as a memorial to Allied airmen; these days it's the central church of the RAF. Outside, there's a statue of Arthur Harris, the bomber of Dresden. A statue of writer Samuel Johnson is round the back.

St Dunstan in the West

186A Fleet Street, EC4A 2HR (7242 6027/www.stdunstaninthewest.org). Chancery Lane tube. **Open** 11am-3pm Tue. **Services** 12.30pm Tue. **Admission** free; donations appreciated. **Map** p404 N6.

St Dunstan was first mentioned in 1185, but the present building dates from 1831-3. John Donne was rector here (1624-31); Izaak Walton (whose *Compleat Angler* was published in the churchyard in 1653) held the posts of 'scavenger, questman and sidesman' (1629-44). In 1667 a lecherous Pepys popped in to hear a sermon and tried to fondle a local girl ('at last I could perceive her to take pins out of her pockets to prick me if I should touch her again').

Somerset House

Strand, WC2R 1LA (7845 4600/www.somerset-house.org.uk). Covent Garden or Temple tube (closed Sun). **Open** 10am-6pm daily; extended hours for courtyard & terrace. *Tours* phone for details. **Admission** *Courtyard & terrace* free; charge for exhibitions. **Credit** *Shop* MC, V. **Map** p401 M7.

This magnificent Georgian building was closed to the public for almost a century, but following a millennial makeover it is now one of London's cultural stars. Originally, there was a Tudor palace here, built in 1547 by Edward Seymour, the first Duke of Somerset and brother of Henry VIII's third wife Jane. In 1775, George III ordered Sir William Chambers to rebuild the crumbling palace in neo-classical style. The new building was later taken over by the Navy Board, then by mundane government offices such as the Inland Revenue.

Today, the tax office remains, but the rest of the building is open to the public. It houses the **Courtauld Gallery**, **Gilbert Collection** and **Hermitage Rooms** (*see below*), but the focal point is the beautiful fountain court, which is turned into an ice-skating rink in winter. There's also a little café, a posh restaurant (the Admiralty, *see p208*) and a pleasant river terrace, with views to Westminster and St Paul's.

Courtauld Gallery *Somerset House, Strand, WC2R 0RN (7848 2526/www.courtauld.ac.uk/gallery).* **Open** 10am-6pm daily (last entry 5.15pm). **Tours** phone for details. **Admission** £5; £4 concessions; free students, under-18s and to all 10am-2pm Mon. *Joint ticket with Hermitage Rooms* £8; £7 concessions. **Credit** *Shop* MC, V.

A recent study showed that, on average, gallery visitors start to lose interest after 45 minutes. In that sense, the Courtauld is the perfect gallery: it's got its fair share of famous pieces, but its compact size makes it less daunting than the National Gallery. The more famous works here include Manet's *A Bar at the Folies Bergère* and *Le Dejeuner sur L'Herbe*; Van Gogh's *Self-Portrait with a Bandaged Ear*, Degas' *Two Dancers on the Stage* and Rubens' *Landscape by Moonlight*. In 2003 the Courtauld expanded its 20th-century collection, adding works by Kandinsky, Matisse and the Fauves.

Gilbert Collection *Somerset House, Strand, WC2R 1LA (7420 9400/www.gilbert collection.org.uk).* **Open** 10am-6pm daily (last entry 5.15pm). *Tours* phone for details. **Admission** £5; £4 concessions; free students, under-18s. **Credit** *Shop* AmEx, MC, V.

Minimalists beware: this collection of gold, gem encrusted trinkets, baubles and knicknacks – some of it once owned by the likes of Napoleon and Louis XV – is truly garish. But fashion be damned. Some of these treasures, collected by the late Beverly Hills real estate magnate, Arthur Gilbert, are deliciously OTT. There is, for example, an ostentatious snuff box collection, adorned with gold, diamonds, rubies and emeralds; grotesque gilt candelabras fit for Liberace's piano; flamboyant Florentine cabinets with mosaic ornamentation of agates, amethysts,

The gorgeous fountain courtyard of **Somerset House**. *See p96.*

jasper and lapis; and a dazzling silver collection. For those who find galleries a slog, this kind of glitter tends to liven things up.

Hermitage Rooms *Somerset House, Strand, WC2R 1LA (7845 4630/www.hermitagerooms.co.uk).* **Open** 10am-6pm daily (last admission 5.15pm). **Admission** £5; £4 concessions; free students, under-18s. *Joint ticket with Courtauld Gallery* £8; £7 concessions. **Credit** *Shop* MC, V.

A taster of St Petersburg's State Hermitage Museum, the Hermitage Rooms are decorated in the same splendid imperial style. The gallery hosts rotating exhibitions from its Russian counterpart. New exhibitions arrive twice a year, with everything from paintings and drawings to decorative art and jewellery liable to be presented. For each ticket sold, £1 goes to the State Hermitage. Exhibitions in 2004 include, Heaven on Earth: Art from Islamic Lands (27 March-12 September).

Lincoln's Inn & Gray's Inn

Streets to the west of the courts are named for now-defunct inns of Chancery, such as New Inn and Clement's Inn, and are home to the one-time cradle of left-wing agitation, the London School of Economics (LSE). On **Portsmouth Street** the Old Curiosity Shop (1567) purports to have been the inspiration for the Dickens novel.

Lincoln's Inn Fields is London's largest square and Holborn's focal point. On the north side is the district's premier attraction, **Sir John Soane's Museum** (*see below*), and to the south lies the **Museums of the Royal College of Surgeons** (7869 6560), where the Hunterian Museum holds a variety of specimens but is closed until February 2005. Chancery Lane, running up from the Strand to High Holborn, is home of the Public Records Office and the Law Society. The subterranean shops of the **London Silver Vaults** (7242 3844) are at the northern end. Toward Holborn Circus, the half-timbered **Staple Inn** is a fine example of Tudor architecture.

West of here, back towards Holborn tube, **Red Lion Square** has one crumpled old building of note: just as radicalism has fallen out of fashion in these conservative times, **Conway Hall**, once a hotbed for campaigning lefties, is no longer as bustling as it once was. However, it still holds the occasional debate and fundraiser (see www.conwayhall.org.uk or call 7242 8037 to find out what's on).

Sir John Soane's Museum

13 Lincoln's Inn Fields, WC2A 3BP (7405 2107/ www.soane.org). Holborn tube. **Open** 10am-5pm Tue-Sat; 10am-9pm 1st Tue of mth. *Tours* 2.30pm Sat. **Admission** free; donations appreciated. *Tours* £3; free concessions. **Map** p399 M5.

Sir John Soane (1753-1837) was one of the leading architects and most obsessive collectors of his day. He acquired so many treasures during his lifetime, he was forced to turn his home into this museum. It's crammed to the rafters with delightful pieces: sculptures, paintings, furniture, architectural models, antiquities, jewellery and various odds and sods.

Sightseeing

Diamond lies

It was one of the greatest heists in the history of **Hatton Garden**. And nobody noticed it was happening. In June 2003 a distinguished-looking man entered the vaults at 88-90 Hatton Garden, right in the centre of London's diamond trade, at 9am on a calm Saturday morning. Dressed in a smart black suit and black hat, he spent three hours in the vaults, and emerged carrying a black holdall. In a scene straight out of the *Thomas Crown Affair*, the suave thief calmly walked past a security guard, making off with £2 million in jewellery and cash. Now the million dollar question rocking Hatton Garden is: how the hell did he pull it off?

Hatton Garden, with its sparkling windows filled with diamonds, rubies, emeralds and sapphires, has always held a fascination for thieves. But its security was considered exceptional: undercover security men prowl the streets in bulletproof vests, communicating via concealed radios. It is said that they keep tabs on every customer: as soon as you ask questions at a jewellery shop, a cadre of guards will know about you within a matter of seconds.

Which makes the gentleman thief's heist all the more audacious. Posing as an Antwerp gem merchant, the crook – who went by the alias Luis Ruben – spent eight months befriending merchants in Hatton Garden's tightly knit community. On his regular rounds, he showed jewellers his precious stones, blending into his environment and gaining their trust. At the vaults, where he hired four safe deposit boxes, he was said to be a great conversationalist.

There's no question he was a smooth operator. But experts are baffled by how the thief actually broke into the vault's safes. After all, the security system is meant to be foolproof. Not only does a CCTV camera trace your every step, but each safe requires two keys – one owned by the customer, the other by staff – and both of the keys must be used simultaneously to unlock the strongboxes. Even if the thief had managed to make a copy of the master key, he still would have needed copies of all the customers' keys. As for forcing the safes open, experts believe that is impossible: made of tungsten and thick steel, the boxes are virtually impenetrable.

Everybody's got a theory about the crime. Some say that the thief was a hypnotist, an expert locksmith or a magician; some believe he took impressions of other people's keys using wax in the palm of his hand; others insist it was an inside job involving security guards. One thing the jewellers all agree on is that it was the best-planned heist in the history of Hatton Garden.

Said one gemologist: 'if he could get away with it in the Hatton Garden vaults, no lock in the world is safe.'

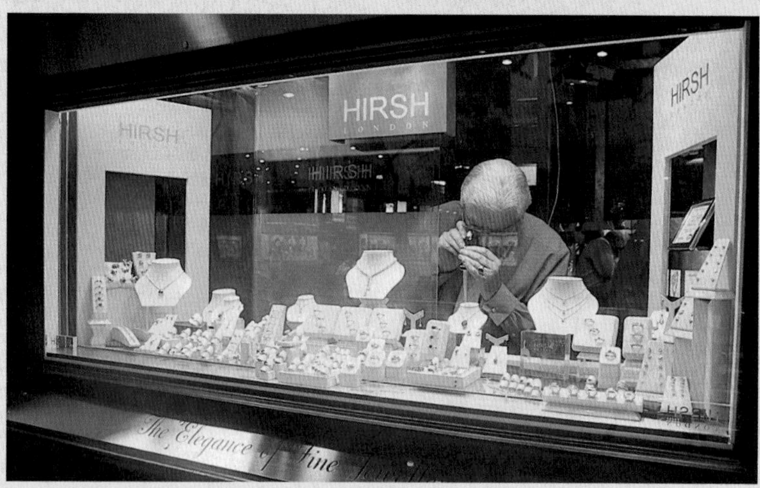

Highlights include Hogarth's *Rake's Progress*, and the 3,300-year-old sarcophagus of an Egyptian pharaoh, but there's always something curious to catch your eye: hundreds of plaster casts of Greek statues, animals, cherubs and nymphs, ornate furniture and many of Soane's architectural designs. For an atmospheric encounter, visit on the first Tuesday of the month, when the candlelit museum opens into the evening. Tickets for Saturday tours go on sale at 2pm on a first-come, first-served basis.

Exhibitions for 2004 include the architecture-themed, Maggie Centres: Masterpieces of Design by Frank Gehry, Daniel Libeskind, Zaha Hadid, Richard Rogers and others (March-June), and, Wotton: the Remarkable Story of a Soane Country House (25 June-28 August).

Clerkenwell and Farringdon

Before the 1990s, Clerkenwell was a fairly anonymous area, full of abandoned factories and office space.Then artists began colonising the place, moving into empty warehouses and converting them into lofts. In the 1990s, property developers wised up to the area's potential. Nightclubs and restaurants followed. The neighbourhood's enduring destinations include a pioneering restaurant, the splendid St John – pronounced best restaurant in the country in a recent poll (*see p193*); the gastropub the Eagle (159 Farringdon Road), Match (*see p218*), one of London's best cocktail bars, and Fabric, London's club du jour (*see p316*). These are the hangouts of workers from nearby photographic studios, advertising agencies and media companies (the *Guardian* newspaper's offices are on Farringdon Road).

For those who couldn't give a toss about gastropubs and loft conversions, Clerkenwell is an area with a rich history. It was named after Clerk's Well; first mentioned in 1174, and rediscovered in 1924, it can be viewed through a window at 14-16 Farringdon Lane. The district grew up in the 12th century around the religious foundations of the priory of St John of Jerusalem. All that remains of the priory is a gatehouse dating from 1504, now home to the **Museum and Library of the Order of St John** (*see below*). The Carthusian monastery of Charterhouse, meanwhile, was founded in 1370. It became a private boys' school – since moved to Surrey – and is now a posh old people's home. The cloisters, the 14th-century chapel and the 17th-century library survive. The area's most fascinating religious institution is the enclave of **Ely Place**, once the site of the Bishop of Ely's London palace; still standing today is **St Etheldreda** (*see below*). The private, gated road, lined by Georgian houses, is crown property and remains outside the jurisdiction of London. Pop into the Olde Mitre Tavern, on this site since 1546, up a narrow alley just off Ely Place.

Over the centuries, a strong crafts tradition grew up in Clerkenwell, as French Huguenots and other immigrants settled to practise their trades away from the City guilds. As the area has grown posher, it has not forgotten its roots: the Clerkenwell Green Association still provides affordable studios for artists and craftspeople at **Pennybank Chambers** in St John's Square and **Cornwell House** on Clerkenwell Green. Many sell their wares from their studios by appointment (see www.cga.org.uk for details).

In the early 19th century this area was favoured by Irish and Italian immigrants and radicals: Lenin used to edit his Bolshevik paper *Iskra* from a back room (which has been preserved) in the **Marx Memorial Library** at 37A Clerkenwell Green.

European Jews settled in **Hatton Garden**, and transformed it into London's diamond district (*see p98* **Diamond lies**). West of here lies **Leather Lane Market**, with its clothes, food, pirate videos and cheap caffs.

Museum & Library of the Order of St John

St John's Gate, St John's Lane, EC1M 4DA (7324 4000/www.sja.org.uk/history). Farringdon tube/rail. **Open** 10am-5pm Mon-Fri; 10am-4pm Sat. *Tours* 11am, 2.30pm Tue, Fri, Sat. **Admission** free. *Tours* £5; £3.50 concessions. **Map** p402 O4.

The history of the Order of the Hospital of St John of Jerusalem, set up during the Crusades to protect sick pilgrims from warring Muslims, is the business of this unsung little museum. A broad spectrum of medical history is covered: medieval medicine, healthcare during the Industrial Revolution, and, more recently, the Order's work during the 1991 Gulf War. In addition to the usual museum stuff – silver, furniture and weaponry – there's a multimedia exhibit about the work of the Ambulance Brigade. There are guided tours of the priory, with its Tudor Gatehouse, church and Norman crypt.

St Etheldreda

14 Ely Place, EC1N 6RY (7405 1061). Chancery Lane tube. **Open** 7.30am-7pm daily. **Admission** free; donations appreciated. **Map** p402 N5.

Built in the 1250s, this is Britain's oldest Catholic church and London's only surviving example of Gothic architecture from the 13th century. Thanks to a change in the wind, it survived the Great Fire of London, and is the last remaining building of the Bishop of Ely's palace. Today, it is a tranquil haven from the city's hustle and bustle, and its stained-glass windows are gorgeous. Quirky Ely Place facts: it's the street in which David Copperfield met Agnes Wakefield, and the strawberries once grown in the gardens here were said to be the finest in the city, receiving plaudits in Shakespeare's *Richard III*.

Bloomsbury & Fitzrovia

This is where Virginia met Leonard, and where Karl got stewed.

Bloomsbury

Map p399

Chancery Lane, Holborn or Tottenham Court Road tube/Euston or King's Cross tube/rail.

The intellectual heart of London, Bloomsbury is synonymous today with the British Museum, Virginia Woolf, publishing and academia, but it wasn't always so: back in 1086, the neighbourhood was a breeding ground for pigs. Its pretty floral name also has humdrum origins: it's taken from 'Blemondisberi', or, 'the manor of William Blemond', who acquired the area in the early 13th century. It remained rural until the 1660s, when the fourth Earl of Southampton built Bloomsbury square around his house, though none of the original architecture remains. The Southamptons intermarried with the Russells, the Dukes of Bedford, and both families developed the area as one of London's first planned suburbs. During the next couple of centuries, the families built a series of grand squares and streets, laid out in the classic Georgian grid style: check out **Bedford Square** (1775-80), London's only complete Georgian Square, and huge **Russell Square**, now an attractive public park. Gower Street is also an uninterrupted stream of classic Georgian terraced houses.

The neighbourhood's not so posh now, but its shabby grandeur is charming. It's certainly less residential – most of the Georgian terraces have been converted into offices. Still, the area is fair speckled with blue plaques, like a who's who of English literature: William Butler Yeats once lived at 5 Upper Woburn Place; Edgar Allan Poe lived at 83 Southampton Row; Mary Wollstonecraft lived on Store Street, the birthplace of Anthony Trollope (he was born at No.6). Then there's Charles **Dickens' House**, at 48 Doughty Street, now a museum (*see p101*). As for the famous Bloomsbury Group, their headquarters were at 50 Gordon Square, where EM Forster, Lytton Strachey, John Maynard Keynes, Clive and Vanessa Bell and Duncan Grant would discuss literature, art and politics. Virginia and Leonard Woolf lived at 52 Tavistock Square.

Bloomsbury's western borders, along Malet Street, Gordon Street and Gower Street, are dominated by the **University of London**. The most notable building here is **University College**, on Gower Street, founded in 1826 and built in the Greek Revival style by William Wilkins, the same architect who built the National Gallery. Inside lies one of the strangest exhibits in London: the preserved remains of philosopher Jeremy Bentham, who introduced the world to utilitarianism. The massive **Senate House**, on Malet Street, holds the university's biggest library. It was a particular favourite of Hitler's: had Germany won the war, he had planned to make his headquarters here. South of the university lies the fabled **British Museum** (*see p101*), with its collection of the world's riches, not the least of which are all the marble statues from the Acropolis in Athens.

Such grand institutions may have put Bloomsbury on the map, but aficionados claim that the real delights lie in hidden pockets. **Sicilian Place**, a pedestrianised stretch of colonnaded shops that links Bloomsbury Way with Southampton Row, is one such. Note that **St George Bloomsbury** (Bloomsbury Way, 7405 3044), a Hawksmoor church, is closed until after Christmas 2004 for much needed renovations. Services will be held just behind the church in the Lower Vestry (6 Little Russell Street, WC1). North-east of here is Lamb's Conduit Street, a convivial area with a good selection of old-fashioned pubs and stylish restaurants. At the top of this street lies wonderful **Coram's Fields** (*see p271*), a park built on the former grounds of Thomas Coram's Foundling Hospital (it provided for abandoned children). The legacy of the great Coram family is due to be revealed in what promises to be a fascinating new museum, the Foundling Museum (40 Brunswick Square, WC1, 7841 3600), which opens in May with exhibitions on the social history of the hospital, an art gallery with works by Hogarth and Gainsborough among others and memorabilia relating to Handel, who helped to found the hospital. Tucked away behind the student-land is **Mecklenburgh Square**, and to the north-west lies budget hotel-land and **Cartwright Garden**. **Woburn Walk** is a loveable stretch of shops and cafés.

It's not all Georgian grandeur. Take the **Brunswick Centre**, just opposite Russell Square tube station. When it was built in 1973, Patrick Hodgkinson's concrete jungle was hailed as the future for community living: a

Young's at heart (*see p219*) on **Lamb's Conduit Street**. *See p100.*

complex of shopping centre, flats, a cinema and an underground car park. Thirty years on, modernism's young dream has been pilloried as Bloomsbury's worst eyesore. Still, film buffs love the Renoir Cinema (*see p281*) and readers frequent Skoob Russell Square for second-hand books. For new ones, the massive Waterstone's on Gower Street is one of London's best; for alternative ones Gay's the Word (*see p231*) is world famous, and Bookmarks (1 Bloomsbury Street, 7637 1848) is all left-wing tomes.

British Museum

Great Russell Street, WC1B 3DG (7636 1555/ recorded information 7323 8783/www.thebritish museum.ac.uk). Russell Square or Tottenham Court Road tube. **Open** *Galleries* 10am-5.30pm Mon-Wed, Sat, Sun; 10am-8.30pm Thur, Fri. *Great Court* 9am-6pm Mon-Wed, Sun; 9am-11pm Thur-Sat. *Highlights tours (90mins)* 10.30am, 1pm, 3pm daily. **Admission** free; donations appreciated. *Temporary exhibitions* prices vary. *Highlights tours* £8; £5 concessions. **Credit** *Shop* AmEx, DC, MC, V. **Map** p399 K5.

Officially London's most popular tourist attraction, the museum building is a neoclassical marvel built in 1847 by Robert Smirke, one of the pioneers of the Greek Revival style. Also impressive is Norman Foster's glass-roofed Great Court, the largest covered space in Europe, opened in 2000. This £100m spectacular surrounds the domed Reading Room, where Marx, Lenin, Thackeray, Dickens, Hardy and Yeats once worked.

Star exhibits include the Ancient Egyptian artefacts – the Rosetta Stone, statues of the pharaohs, mummies – and Greek antiquities, such as the marble statues and detail from the Parthenon. The Celts gallery has the Lindow Man, killed in 300 BC and preserved in peat. In 2003 the Wellcome Gallery of Ethnography opened with an Easter Island statue and regalia from Captain Cook's travels.

In 2004 the restored King's Library is scheduled to open. Considered to be the finest neo-classical space in London, it will house a new permanent exhibition, 'Enlightenment: Rethinking the World in the 18th Century', a 5,000-strong collection devoted to the formative period of the museum.

Don't try to see everything in one day; instead, buy a souvenir guide (£6) and pick out the showstoppers. The 90-minute 'greatest hits' tour (£8, bookable at the information desk) and EyeOpener tours focus on specific aspects of the collection.

Scheduled exhibitions for 2004 include 'Treasures: Finding our Past' (until 14 March), the first major national exhibition of British archaeology in 20 years, and, from The Sudan, 'Kingdoms of the Ancient Nile: Treasures from the National Museum of Khartoum' (9 September-9 January 2005).

Dickens' House

48 Doughty Street, WC1N 2LX (7405 2127/www. dickensmuseum.com). Chancery Lane or Russell Square tube. **Open** 10am-5pm Mon-Sat; 11am-5pm Sun. *Tours* by arrangement. **Admission** £4; £3 concessions; £2 5-15s; £10 family. **Credit** *Shop* AmEx, MC, V. **Map** p399 M4.

London is scattered with plaques marking addresses where the prolific writer Charles Dickens lived but never settled, including Devonshire Terrace near Paddington and Camden's Bayhem Street, but this is the only one of the author's many London homes that is still standing. Dickens lived here for three years between 1837 and 1840 while he wrote *Nicholas Nickleby* and *Oliver Twist*. Restored to its former state, the house is packed with Dickens ephemera. There are personal letters, all sorts of manuscripts and his writing desk. Exhibitions for 2004 include 'Peake's *Bleak House*', Mervyn Peake illustrations that were intended for that novel but never used (1 June-28 September).

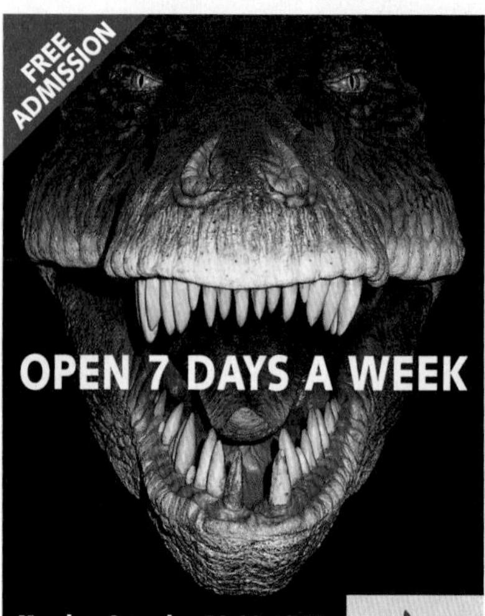

Monday-Saturday 10.00-17.50,
Sunday 11.00-17.50.
Cromwell Road, London SW7.
Underground: South Kensington.
www.nhm.ac.uk

Walk through time
GEFFRYE MUSEUM
400 Years of English Domestic Interiors

Kingsland Road London E2 8EA
Telephone 020 7739 9893
ADMISSION FREE. Open Tue-Sat 10-5,
Sun/Bank Hols 12-5,
Rail - Liverpool Street/Old Street.
Bus - 149, 242, 243, 67
www.geffrye-museum.org.uk

NEW FOR 2004
A 42-foot drop, abrupt twists and wild 180-degree turns while riders experience extreme acceleration, breaking and maneuverability.

LEGOLAND® Windsor's new roller coaster is the fastest ride in the Park, topping speeds of 26mph while zipping along 1,300 feet of steel track. It also has a higher drop than any other attraction in the Park, towering nearly five stories above the ground.

2004 Opening Dates 20th March - 31st Oct Information and booking Number 08705 040404 For more information visit www.legoland.co.uk

LEGO, the LEGO logo and LEGOLAND are trademarks of the LEGO Group. ©2003 The LEGO Group.

Percival David Foundation of Chinese Art

53 Gordon Square, WC1H 0PD (7387 3909/ www.pdfmuseum.org.uk). Euston Square or Goodge Street or Russell Square tube. **Open** 10.30am-5pm Mon-Fri. **Admission** free; donations appreciated. **Credit** *Shop* DC, MC, V. **Map** p399 K4.

Widely considered to be the finest collection of Chinese ceramics outside China, this 1,700-strong collection dates mainly from the 10th to the 18th centuries. Highlights include extremely rare Ru and Guan pieces and a striking pair of Yuan dynasty temple vases (1351). The museum is scholarly in feel – it was named after the professor who donated the collection to UCL in 1850 – but friendly to guests.

Petrie Museum of Archaeology

University College London, Malet Place, WC1E 6BT (7679 2884/www.petrie.ucl.ac.uk). Goodge Street, Warren Street or Euston Square tube. **Open** 1-5pm Tue-Fri; 10am-1pm Sat. **Admission** free; donations appreciated. **Map** p399 K4

The British Museum may have all the blockbuster exhibits from Ancient Egypt, but the Petrie Museum is no slouch when it come to Egyptian antiquities: its impressive collection focuses on the minutiae of Egyptian life. This being an academic institution – it's housed in UCL – some of the labelling is a bit dry. But there's fun to be had amongst the girly bits: make-up pots, grooming accessories, jewellery, the world's oldest dress (2800 BC). Check out the coiffured head of a mummy with eyebrows and lashes intact. The museum is hard to find – ask a security guard at UCL – but its location, coupled with a tomb-like ambience, makes it spooky.

St Pancras New Church

Euston Road (corner of Upper Woburn Place), NW1 2BA (7388 1461/www.stpancraschurch.org). Euston tube/rail. **Open** 12.45-2pm Wed; noon-2pm Thur; 9.15-11am Sat; 7.45am-noon, 5.30-7.15pm Sun; occasional lunchtimes Tue, Fri. *Services* 8am, 10am, 6pm Sun; 1.15pm Wed. *Recital* 1.15pm Thur. **Admission** free. **Map** p399 K3.

Built in 1822, this church is a spectacular example of the Greek Revivalist style. At the time of its construction, at £89,296, it was the most expensive church to be built in London apart from St Paul's Cathedral. Inspired by the Ionic Temple of Erechtheion in Athens, its most notable feature is its Caryatid porches, used as entrances to the burial vaults. The interior is more restrained but has beautiful 19th-century stained-glass windows and an impressive marble font.

Somers Town & King's Cross

Somers Town is Bloomsbury's ugly sister, situated on the north side of Euston Road, between St Pancras and Euston stations. Dickens used it as a backdrop for his darker characters, and in years gone by locals lived in fear of the 'Somers Town mob'. The area still exudes gritty realism, which means it's a dump. **Euston Station** is a bleak 1960s building that replaced Philip Hardwick's tragically beautiful Victorian structure. **St Pancras Station**, by contrast, has a gorgeous Victorian glass-and-iron train shed fronted by Sir George Gilbert Scott's Gothic hotel, the Midland Grand. This building is now **St Pancras Chambers**, and, at press time, was open to the public for tours (7304 3921), but call before you drop by.

To the east lies **King's Cross**, which is the kind of place your mother warned you about. Immortalised in Neil Jordan's *Mona Lisa* and various TV dramas, the area is notoriously seedy, and a favourite of prostitutes and junkies. It only gets worse, as north of here is pure industrial wasteland. But that's cool: there are now hip clubs springing up in the area, including the Cross Bar (*see p315*). And you can bet when the Eurostar terminal opens at St Pancras in 2007, grimy King's Cross will be gentrified beyond belief. All those run-down warehouses are just crying out to be converted into trendy loft apartments.

The British Library

96 Euston Road, NW1 2DB (7412 7332/www.bl.uk). Euston Square tube/King's Cross tube/rail. **Open** 9.30am-6pm Mon, Wed-Fri; 9.30am-8pm Tue; 9.30am-5pm Sat; 11am-5pm Sun. **Admission** free; donations appreciated. **Map** p399 K3.

Dubbed 'one of the ugliest buildings in the world' by a Parliamentary committee, the new British Library has been dogged by controversy since its opening in 1997 after moving from the British Museum. The project went over budget by £350m, and took 20 years to complete (longer than St Paul's Cathedral and 15 years behind schedule). When it finally opened, architecture critics ripped it to shreds.

But don't judge a book by its cover: the interior is spectacular, all white marble, glass and light. In the piazza sits Antony Gormley's sculpture *Planets*, a new addition in 2003. In the John Ritblat Gallery, the library's main treasures are displayed: the Magna Carta, the Lindisfarne Gospels and original manuscripts from Chaucer. There's fun stuff too: Beatles lyric sheets, first editions of *The Jungle Book* and archive recordings of everyone from James Joyce to Bob Geldof. The library is also famous for its 80,000-strong stamp collection. The focal point of the building is the King's Library, a six-storey glass-walled tower that houses George III's collection.

This is one of the greatest libraries in the world, with an astounding collection of 150 million items. Each year, the library receives a copy of every publication produced in the UK and Ireland, including maps, newspapers, magazines, prints and drawings. Contrary to myth, it's not that difficult to get a reader's pass, but to avoid disappointment, call before you go. Exhibitions for 2004 include 'The Silk Road: Trade, Travel, War and Faith' (21 April-September) and 'Regency Writers' (September-April 2005).

London's space needle

It's one of London's most curious landmarks. It's been described as an eyesore and an icon, ugly and groovy, futuristic and retro. It's survived a terrorist attack, a hurricane, and, worst of all, blistering attacks by architectural critics. In the process, it's managed to outlive most of the other icons of the Swinging '60s. And now, 30 years after it was erected, the BT Tower has achieved the impossible: it's officially been deemed a national treasure.

In 2003 the Culture Department awarded the controversial tower a Grade II listing, an accolade usually reserved for the likes of stately homes or castles, certainly not for gawky communications towers reminiscent of the skyline in an episode of *The Jetsons*.

Opened to the public in 1965, the tower – then known as the Post Office Tower – was synonymous with a supremely confident era in British history. London was swinging, and Harold Wilson famously announced his vision of a country in the 'white heat of technology'. But the great British public didn't care so much about the techie stuff: they flocked to the space-age structure because it looked really cool, it was 620 feet (189 metres) tall – London's highest building – and, above all, it had a revolving restaurant. Billy Butlin's 'Top of the Tower' made one full turn every 22 minutes, and served all the fashionable foods of the day – duck à l'orange, prawn cocktails, T-bone steaks and knickerbocker glories – to a panoramic backdrop. For Londoners, emerging from an era of postwar grimness, it didn't get much better than this.

Britain's love affair with the telephone tower came to a rude halt in 1971 when an IRA bomb destroyed the public viewing galleries. Miraculously, nobody was killed, and the tower didn't topple; its engineers, after all, had designed it to withstand nuclear war. But this was the era of disaster movies – *Towering Inferno* is a case in point – and the government took no chances: the tower was closed to the public forever. In the following years, it lost some of its lustre: in 1981 it was surpassed in height by the NatWest Tower, much of the technology it housed has become obsolete and the viewing galleries became a suite for BT corporate entertaining.

However, in an era of Austin Powers, '60s nostalgia and ugly modernist chic, the BT Tower has come full circle: it has never been more popular in the eyes of the cultural critics. And Londoners have come to rely on its quirky presence: no matter which street you turn down in Bloomsbury, Soho or Fitzrovia, the tower is there to guide you, in all its awkward, retro glory. The truth is, we'd probably be lost without it.

St Pancras Old Church & St Pancras Gardens

Pancras Road, NW1 1UL (7387 4193). King's Cross tube/rail. **Open** *Gardens* 7am-dusk daily. *Services* 9am Mon-Sat; 9.30am Mon, Sun; 7pm Tue. **Admission** free. **Map** p399 K2.

The Old Church, set on an ancient site (it may date back to the fourth century), has been ruined and rebuilt many times. The current structure is a handsome building, but it's the churchyard that delights. Restored a couple of years ago after an extended period of neglect, it merits the hike up bleak St Pancras Road. Among those buried here are writer William Godwin and his wife, Mary Wollstonecraft; over this grave, daughter Mary Godwin (author of *Frankenstein*) declared her love for poet Percy Bysshe Shelley. The grave of Sir John Soane is one of only two Grade I-listed tombs in Britain (the other is Karl Marx's, in Highgate Cemetery, *see p149*); its dome influenced Sir Giles Gilbert Scott's design of the classic British phone box.

Fitzrovia

Fitzrovia is not as famous as Bloomsbury, but its history is just as rich. Squeezed in between Gower Street, Oxford Street, Great Portland Street and Euston Road, it only became known as Fitzrovia during the 20th century. The origins of its name are hazy: some believe it got its name from Fitzroy Square, which was named after Henry Fitzroy, the son of Charles II. Others insist that the neighbourhood was named after the famous **Fitzroy Tavern** (7580 3714) at 16 Charlotte Street, ground zero for London bohemia for a good chunk of the 20th century. Once a favourite with down-at-heel artists and radicals, past regulars included Dylan Thomas, George Orwell, Aleister Crowley and Quentin Crisp.

The neighbourhood's radical roots go deep. In 1792 Thomas Paine lived at 154 New Cavendish Street – the same year he published *The Rights of Man* and incurred the wrath of the government. His friend Edmund Burke lived at 18 Charlotte Street. During the early 19th century the district became a hotbed of Chartist activity and working men's clubs. Later, Karl Marx attended meetings at Communist clubs in Tottenham Street, Charlotte Street and Rathbone Place. He was also a regular on the Tottenham Court Road pub scene: his favourites included the Rising Sun (No.46); the Court (No.108); Northumberland Arms (No.119); Mortimer Arms (No.174); and the Jack Horner (then known as the Italian, No.236).

A century later, Fitzrovia played pop. In the 1960s the Stones played gigs at the 100 Club (100 Oxford Street). A young Bob Dylan made his British debut singing at the King and Queen Pub (1 Foley Street) in 1962. Concert scenes for the Beatles' *A Hard Day's Night* were filmed at the Scala Theatre, then at 21-5 Tottenham Street. Pink Floyd and Jimi Hendrix were regulars at the Speakeasy at 50 Margaret Street. As flower power declined, punk took over. Regular performers at the 100 Club included the Sex Pistols, Siouxsie and the Banshees, the Damned and the Clash. At this time, Fitzrovia was descended upon by squatters. Boy George lived in squats on Great Titchfield Street, Warren Street and Carburton Street, while he wrote 'Do You Really Want to Hurt Me?'.

During the 1980s Fitzrovia's raffish image was transformed when the media moved in. ITN started broadcasting from 48 Wells Street, and Channel 4's first office was at 60 Charlotte Street in 1982. The BBC's simple, pared-down Broadcasting House had been on the western fringe of the area – 2-8 Portland Place – since 1922. While many of this rather fine neighbourhood's atmospheric pubs remain – the Fitzroy, the Newman Arms (23 Rathbone Street) – Fitzrovia's image has become smarter and beloved of media folk. For a bit of the old bohemian scruff, head to seedy Hanway Street, a dark alley lined with divey Spanish bars, popular with late-night drinkers.

All Saints

7 Margaret Street, W1W 8JG (7636 1788/ www.allsaintsmargaretstreet.org.uk). Oxford Circus tube. **Open** 7am-7pm daily. *Services* 7.30am-8am, 1.10pm, 6pm, 6.30pm Mon-Fri; 7.30am, 8am, 6pm, 6.30pm Sat; 8am, 10.20am, 11am, 5.15pm, 6pm Sun. **Admission** free. **Map** p398 J5.

This 1850s church was designed by William Butterfield, one of the great Gothic Revivalists. It is squeezed into a tiny site, but its soaring architecture and lofty spire – the second-highest in London – disguise this fact. Its lavish interior is one of the city's most striking, with rich marble, flamboyant tile work, and glittering stones built into its pillars.

Pollock's Toy Museum

1 Scala Street (entrance on Whitfield Street), W1T 2HL (7636 3452/www.pollocksmuseum.co.uk). Goodge Street tube. **Open** 10am-5pm Mon-Sat. **Admission** £3; £1.50 3-16s; free under-3s. **Credit** *Shop* MC, V. **Map** p398 J5.

They don't make 'em like they used to. Children's toys that is – and that's a shame. This museum is a shrine to a pre-PlayStation era. Housed in a creaky Georgian townhouse, it's crammed with vintage toys to raise a nostalgic smile in adults and a resentful stare from the Ritalin generation. Highlights include the oldest teddy bear in the world (dating from 1905), vintage Action Men, enormous dolls, even bigger dolls' houses, toy soldiers and puppets from around the world. In the shop you can buy Jack-in-the-boxes, tin toys, yo-yos, marionettes and dolls' house miniatures. The museum is also famed for its toy theatres.

Marylebone

Where Nash cut a dash and wax grabs the cash.

Sightseeing

Maps p395 & p398

Baker Street, Bond Street, Edgware Road, Great Portland Street, Marble Arch, Oxford Circus or Regent's Park tube.

The last decade or so has been good to Marylebone. For years the neighbourhood was the unfortunate filling in a sandwich of two busy thoroughfares: heaving Oxford Street to the south and thundering Marylebone Road to the north. All that has changed, partly because of clever management of Marylebone High Street by local landowners. By selecting incoming retailers and restaurateurs to make an interesting mix, Marylebone 'Village' was set on a spiral of fashionability, which shows no sign of abating.

The village has not always been as genteel as it is now. Marylebone was once made up of two ancient manors, Lileston (Lisson) and Tyburn (named after a stream that flowed through the area). In the 14th century these manors were violent places. Tyburn was the site of a famous gallows until 1783, a spot marked by a plaque on the traffic island at **Marble Arch**.

The original parish church was demolished in 1400. A new church was built halfway up what is now **Marylebone High Street**. It was called St Mary by the Bourne, a name that soon came to cover the entire village. This had been abbreviated to Marylebone by 1626.

Though nothing remains of the first two parish churches, you can see the foundations of the third – damaged in the war, demolished in 1949 – near the top of the high street, in the **Memorial Garden of Rest**. Connected with many famed figures (Francis Bacon married here in 1606, William Hogarth painted the interior in 1735, and Lord Byron was baptised here in 1788), the garden is a lovely place to take stock of what is now a desirable area.

In the 16th century the northern half of Marylebone – now **Regent's Park** – became a royal hunting ground, while the southern section was bought up by the Portman family. Two centuries later, the Portmans developed many of the elegant streets and squares that lend the locale its dignified air. Some, such as **Bryanston Square** and **Montagu Square**, have survived well; others, such as **Cavendish Square**, are less impressive. One of the squares, laid out in 1761, still bears the Portman name; another, 1776's **Manchester Square**, is home to the **Wallace Collection** (*see p107*).

Harley Street and **Wimpole Street** have been associated with highbrow medical practitioners since the mid 19th century. Elizabeth Barrett left 50 Wimpole Street in 1846 to elope with fellow poet Robert Browning; they were secretly married at **St Marylebone Parish Church**, on Marylebone Road. Dickens lived next door to the church at 1 Devonshire Terrace (demolished in 1959). Across the road, the **Royal Academy of Music**, founded in 1822 and designed by John Nash, has a glass recital building and a little museum (7873 7373; open 12.30-6pm Mon-Fri; 2-5.30pm Sat, Sun).

Portland Place, which leads up to Regent's Park, was the glory of 18th-century London. At **Langham Place**, where it links with Nash's handsome **Regent Street**, is the BBC's HQ, **Broadcasting House**. Next door is Nash's church **All Souls** (1822-4). Over the road is the Langham Hilton, the first of London's grand hotels (it opened in 1865); further north is the **Royal Institute of British Architects**.

North of Marylebone Road, the landscape gives way to '50s and '60s housing at **Lisson Grove**. The Landmark Hotel here opened as the Great Central Hotel in 1899, was the last significant Victorian hotel to be built in the golden age of steam. It was closed in 1939, used as offices, then redeveloped as a hotel in 1986.

Slightly further west, **Church Street** is a popular local food and general market that is rapidly gentrifying at its eastern end, thanks to Alfie's Antiques Market (*see p229*) and designer homewares shops round it.

St James's Spanish Place

Spanish Place (back of Manchester Square), 22 George Street, W1U 3QY (7935 0943/www.spanish place.hemscott.net). Baker Street or Bond Street tube.
Open 7am-6.45pm daily. *Services* 7.15am, 12.30pm, 6pm Mon-Fri; 10am, 6pm Sat; 8.30am, 9.30am, 10.30am, noon, 4pm, 7pm Sun. **Admission** free. **Map** p398 G5.

This Gothic edifice's Iberian connection dates back to the restoration of Charles II, when a Spanish embassy was re-established in London, first in Ormond Street, then in Manchester Square. In 1791, just after the repeal of laws affecting Catholic worship, a chapel was built on the corner of Spanish Place and Charles Street (now George Street). Most of the holy objects in today's church came from this older building, mentioned by Thackeray in *Vanity Fair*. Official Spanish links ceased in 1827 but some items, including Alfonso XIII's standard, remain.

Regent's Park is a bosky place for the **Central London Mosque**.

The present church opened in 1890, opposite the first. Its Lady Chapel was designed by JF Bentley, architect of Westminster Cathedral. Vivien Leigh wed barrister Leigh Holman here in 1932.

Wallace Collection

Hertford House, Manchester Square, W1U 3BN (7935 0687/www.the-wallace-collection.org.uk). Bond Street tube. **Open** 10am-5pm Mon-Sat; noon-5pm Sun. **Admission** free. **Credit** AmEx, MC, V. **Map** p398 G5.

The handsomely restored late 18th-century house contains a collection of furniture, paintings and Sèvres porcelain. It all belonged to Sir Richard Wallace, who, as the illegitimate heir of the Marquis of Hertford, inherited the treasures that the Marquis, a great Francophile, bought for safekeeping after the Revolution. There's room after room of Louis XIV and XV furnishings, galleries of lush paintings by Titian, Velázquez, Gainsborough and Reynolds, weapons and armour. Franz Hals's *Laughing Cavalier* is the masterpiece that most visitors delight in. A millennial renovations programme added several new galleries, which blend in beautifully. The glass-roofed restaurant, Café Bagatelle, is among the best of all the London museums.

Regent's Park

The impulse behind the creation of Regent's Park (7486 7905, open dawn to dusk daily) was hardly philanthropic. In 1811 John Nash, Crown Architect and friend of the Prince Regent, designed a private residential estate set in parklands to raise revenue for the Crown. The Regency terraces of the **Outer Circle**, the road running around the park, are still Crown property, but of the 56 villas planned, only eight were built. Development of the Royal Park, with its botanic and zoological gardens (*see p108* **Pride of London**) took a further 20 years, but rehabilitation after wartime damage and general neglect in the mid 20th century was not completed unti the late 1970s. It's lively in summer, with a boating lake, tennis courts, music, sporting leagues, a café and an open-air theatre (*see p331*). To the west of the park is the London Central Mosque, built in 1978.

Just south of the park on Marylebone Road, are **Madame Tussaud's** and **the London Planetarium** (*see p107*). Nearby, **Baker Street**, which leads to Oxford Street, is forever associated with a certain fictional detective. Just down from the tube two places dedicated to Sherlock Holmes look across the street at each other. The **Sherlock Holmes Museum** goes the whole hog (*see p108*), while the Sherlock Holmes Memorabilia Company at No.230 (7486 1426) is full of pipes, magnifying glasses, notebooks and mugs and an upstairs exhibition (£2.50) dedicated to the actor Jeremy Brett, who played Holmes on television. By the way, the fictional character lived at No.221B.

London Planetarium & Madame Tussaud's

Marylebone Road, NW1 (0870 400 3000/ www.madame-tussauds.com). Baker Street tube. **Open** 9.30am-5.30pm daily, times vary during holiday periods. **Admission** *9.30am-6pm* £18.99 ; £12.99 concessions; 5-15s; £58 family ticket (internet booking only). *5-6pm* £11; £6 5-15 concessions; £35 family. **Credit** AmEx, MC, V. **Map** p398 G4.

You can't really have the projected planets without the waxen stars now, and as the London Planetarium's show is over in 20 minutes, and the

Pride of London The Zoo

The reason mature Londoners get all misty-eyed about childish visits to the zoo aren't always that commendable. Many of us can remember the halycon days when camels gave rides and elephants ate buns and the chimps wore trousers and had tea parties. Nowadays we're all much too sensitive to see such sport and the Zoological Society of London has to make a tourist attraction out of its far more worthy *raison d'être*: conservation and breeding programmes.

With the elephants lodging at their country retreat (Whipsnade, in Bedfordshire, www.whipsnade.co.uk), a distinct dearth of any sort of bear, and the big cats lolling miserably in their enclosures, the zoo has a job on its hands. The conservationists have risen to the challenge, however. It is made

exit takes you straight into the waxworks museum, it makes sense to do this pair of visitor attractions in one noisy, bewildering hit. The Planetarium's display is projected on to the dome's ceiling every ten minutes or so and the newly revamped waiting zones are a great improvement on the rather tedious exhibition that used to be here. The new star show for 2004, in the planning stage as we went to press, promises some great 3D motion effects.

Most people are here for the waxworks, though. They join the scrum of schoolchildren draped around Beckham, they take the podium between an unrecognisable Blair and a good George Dubya and wonder whether to shell out the £6.50 for the photographer's snap; they smack J-Lo's bottom. The Blush! celebrity zone bombards you with mocked-up paparazzi hysteria as you enter the world of Geri Halliwell, Britney on a pole and the tinies: Kylie Minogue and the ickle British television duo, Ant and Dec. Below stairs, the Chamber of Horrors surrounds you with hanging corpses and eviscerated victims of torture. For £2 you can hear live actors portray more unspeakable acts of cruelty. The irredeemably kitsch 'Spirit of London Ride' is loved by children. You climb aboard a moving taxi pod for a highly coloured and rather cursory trundle through a 400 years of the city's history, taking in a bit of Shakespeare, plague, fire, Nelson's famous victory, war, Swinging '60s and finally a merry-go-round on which a waxwork of Madame Tussaud, who is responsible for all this, rides alongside various other revellers who look vaguely familiar but you can't quite place.

Sherlock Holmes Museum

221B Baker Street, NW1 6XE (7935 8866/ www.sherlock-holmes.co.uk). Baker Street tube. **Open** 9.30am-6pm daily. **Admission** £6; £4 5-16s; free under-5s. **Credit** AmEx, DC, MC, V. **Map** p398 G4.

So great is the sleuth's cult that many fans tend to forget he never really existed. This museum isn't about to disabuse them. It is atmospheric: the burning candles, flickering grates, pipe, violin and hypodermic in the first-floor study are eerily compelling. On the top two floors are waxwork figures in various murderous or cadaverous poses – all amusingly labelled – 'The Blackmailer Charles

patently clear that the tigers and leopards pacing fretfully here in London would be in danger in the wild, where they're still hunted, and it's the same story all over the zoo. Phew. That was a close one.

In fact, of the more than 600 species here, 150 are on the International Union for the Conservation of Nature's Red List of the world's most threatened species. Meanwhile, though a good captive breeding record interests many (witness the adoring crowds around a limpid-eyed mother François Langur nursing her tiny baby in the monkey house), stories of endangered moth species might not. Nonetheless, the creatures – ants, fish, cockroaches, spiders, leeches, scorpions and more – on display as part of the snappily titled B.U.G.S. (or Biodiversity Underpinning Global Survival, if you're interested) in the Millennium Conservation Centre, make it one of the most popular attractions.

Other big successes include the children's petting zoo, where goats chew meditatively on toddlers' anorak toggles, and the jolly Happy Families area, where you can watch the otters gambling on their waterslide and in their pool, or the inscrutable meerkats staring you down from their sandy kingdom.

For decades the impossibly sweet penguins have lured crowds to their Tecton and Lubetkin-designed pool for a feeding time date. A day at the zoo is measured out by such events: animal feed times, reptile petting, camel charming, small animal husbandry talks… You pick up a leaflet at the front desk to find out about the day's events and a useful route map to what is, after all, a huge site. It's worth following the route suggested: there's nothing more exhausting than getting to the café for a well-earned cup of tea and realising you've gone and missed the giraffes.

Another useful tip is to travel here by boat. Every day in spring and summer, and at weekends only in winter, the **London Waterbus Company** (7482 2550/2660) has a bargain-priced boat trip and zoo entry deal from Camden Lock (£12.70; £9.30 children) and Little Venice (£12.90; £9.40 children). You float straight into the zoo without having to get a bus from the tube or walk across the park.

London Zoo

Regent's Park, NW1 4RY (7722 3333/ www.londonzoo.co.uk). Baker Street or Camden Town tube then 274, C2 bus. **Open** *end Oct-mid Mar* 10am-4pm daily. *Mid Mar-end Oct* 10am-5.30pm daily. **Admission** £12.70; £10.20 concessions; £9 3-15s; free under-3s; £38 family. **Credit** AmEx, MC, V. **Map** p398 G2.

Augustus Milverton and the surprise assailant' and so on. There's a shop on the ground floor if you want to buy your own deerstalker, pipe or magnifying glass. Conan Doyle is conspicuous by his absence. The Sherlock Holmes Collection of books, journals, photos and filmscripts (round the corner at Marylebone Library; 7641 1039, by appointment only) is a better bet for serious Sherlockians.

South to Oxford Street

From Regent's Park, Portland Place takes you south as the northern end of Regent's Street, and chaotic Oxford Circus, the eastern end of London's nightmarish shopping stretch: **Oxford Street**. Most people come here from out of town for the department stores – or at least Selfridges (*see p234*) and John Lewis (*see p233*), many Londoners try to avoid it.

Marylebone High Street, which leads from Marylebone Road at Tussaud's down to the other end of Oxford Street, is one of London's last remaining independently minded shopping streets. Even so, the Gap and Starbucks have invaded where once there were only pleasant individuals such as Aveda (Nos.28-9), clothes boutiques like Agnès B (Nos.40-41) and furniture shops (Shaker, at Nos.72-3). It's here, too, that you'll find the area's best restaurants, among them Orrery (*see p199*) and the Providores & Tapa Room (*see p197*).

Marble Arch, another Nash creation, marks Oxford Street's western extent. This unremarkable monument was intended to be the entrance to Buckingham Palace but, discovered to be too puny, was moved to this site in 1851. Only members of the Royal Family and some military types are allowed by law to walk through the central portal. Tyburn Tree, a public execution site from 1196 to 1783, used to stand where Marble Arch does now, and a few yards from here, at 8 Hyde Park Place, is one of the buildings of Tyburn Convent, established by a group of Benedictine sisters in 1903. One of the buildings, at a mere three and a half feet (one metre) wide, is London's smallest house.

Mayfair & St James's

Handsome, haughty and bordering on the tawdry.

Mayfair

Map p400

Bond Street, Green Park, Hyde Park Corner, Marble Arch, Oxford Circus or Piccadilly Circus tube.

It has one of the prettiest names in London, but Mayfair is not as blithe as its moniker (which comes from the fact that a fair used to take place here each May). In fact, it's austere, impressive and important. Mayfair has been a smart address for centuries: Handel, Disraeli, Shelley and Jimi Hendrix all once lived here.

It is generally agreed that Mayfair is the area between Oxford Street, Regent Street, Piccadilly and Park Lane. When it was all green rolling fields at the edge of London town, it belonged to the Grosvenor and Berkeley families, who bought the land in the mid 1600s. In the 1700s they developed the pastures into a posh new neighbourhood. In particular they built a series of squares surrounded by elegant houses – the three biggest squares, Hanover, Berkeley and the immense Grosvenor, are surrounded by offices and embassies these days. The most famous of the squares, Grosvenor (pronounced 'grove-ner'), is where you'll find the drab US Embassy. Finished in 1960, it takes up one whole side of the square and its only decoration is a fierce-looking eagle, a lot of barbed wire and some heavily armed soldiers. A big statue of President Eisenhower has pride of place, although there's also a grand statue of President Franklin D Roosevelt sitting nobly in the square nearby. When in London, Eisenhower stayed at the painfully expensive hotel Claridge's (*see p49*), just a block away on Brook Street. American troops stationed in London during Word War II went to Sunday services at the **Grosvenor Chapel** on South Audley Street. It's still popular with Americans, and part of the attraction could be the beautiful **Mount Street Gardens**, which sit serenely behind it. The gardens lead to the neo-Gothic **Church of the Immaculate Conception**, on Farm Street, where the Jesuits have run things since the mid 19th century.

The toffs are still in residence elsewhere in Mayfair, and the tone of the area is still sky-high. It has always been smart: the Duke of Wellington is its most distinguished former resident – he briefly lived at 4 Hamilton Place, before moving to **Apsley House** (*see p113*) – but he has stiff competition from Benjamin Disraeli (29 Park Lane), Florence Nightingale (10 South Street), Percy Bysshe Shelley (29 Aldford Street) and Sir Robert Peel (12 Great Stanhope Street). GF Handel and Jimi Hendrix both lived at 25 Brook Street, though not at the same time. Handel's fans won the unofficial Who Gets to Turn the House into a Museum contest a couple of years ago: the address is now dedicated to his memory (*see p112*). Outraged Hendrix fans could always sing 'Cross Town Traffic' outside in protest.

With all the high-quality residents around here it's unsurprising that Mayfair is still associated with high fashion. Crowded, noisy Oxford Street to the north has high street fashion and the city's top department stores. You can spend all day in Selfridges (*see p234*) and still not shop it all. Nearby **Bond Street** is all about expensive clothes, and this is where you'll find the famous designers – tell Donna Karan (No.19) we said hi.

The most famous of Mayfair's shopping streets is **Savile Row**, the land of made to measure suits of the highest quality (*see p235* **Smart tailoring**). The shop at No.15 holds the estimable Henry Poole & Co, which, over the years, has cut suits for clients including Napoleon, Charles Dickens, Winston Churchill and Charles de Gaulle. On a different note, 3 Savile Row was the home of Apple Records, which was, in turn, the home of the Beatles. The bearded boys famously played their last gig in February 1969 on the roof.

Savile Row leads on to the equally salubrious **Conduit Street**, from where you can follow St George's Street into **Hanover Square**. Here you'll find St George's Church, built in the 1720s, and once everybody's favourite place to get married. Among the luminaries who said their vows at the altar were George Eliot and Teddy Roosevelt. Handel, who married nobody, attended services here.

While all of this is so very chi-chi, many say that it's the area around **Shepherd Market** (named after a food market set up here by architect Edward Shepherd in the early 18th century) that was the true heart of the neighbourhood. Back in the 1700s this was where the raucous May Fair was held, until it was shut down for good in the 18th century

Pride of London Piccadilly Circus

You are forgiven if, standing in the hurly-burly of Piccadilly Circus, looking at neon billboards big as houses, backpack-toting Eurotrash, actual trash, pigeons eating trash, lucky heather-clutching gypsies, surly newspaper sellers and mad kilt-wearing bagpipers, you cannot picture it as a genteel place of elegant buildings, passing carriages and class. But that was what it was meant to be.

After Piccadilly was built as one of the major highways leading out of London, the city gradually built up around it. By 1819 architect John Nash was busily at work creating Regent Street, which would intersect with Piccadilly. Clearly, with Nash involved, this would be no simple crossroads. Instead, he conceived an elegant circle in which the frontages of the buildings around it were recreated as lovely curves, with arches and columns in restrained shades of white and grey.

It was a hit, but it didn't last. By 1880, Shaftesbury Avenue crashed into the design, when it too was extended. Buildings on one side of the circle were demolished to make space for the new street, and then eventually replaced by unspectacular shops, giving the circle its odd appearance – part circle, part... not circle. To distract everyone from the mess they'd made of Nash's plans, city fathers put the delicate statue known as Eros in the middle of it all. (The monument is, in fact, the Shaftesbury Memorial Fountain; designed by Alfred Gilbert in honour of the noble Earl of Shaftesbury, a fervent Christian and campaigner against child labour. It was completed in 1893, and has long been mistaken by virtually everyone as Eros, the ancient Greek god of love. In reality, the sculptor originally meant it to depict the Angel of Christian Charity.)

Worse was to come. In 1910 shopowners discovered they could rent out the fronts of their buildings to be used as illuminated signs, much like modern billboards. Soon the noble structures were subsumed by enormous adverts for Bovril and Schweppes. Over the years the companies have changed, but the billboards have never left.

As the most recent affront, Eros was moved from its once-symmetrical centre position off to one side to facilitate traffic, giving it all an even more gangly and ungainly perspective. It's a circle only in Salvador Dalí terms now, dripping down Shaftesbury Avenue, listing aimlessly to the left and right.

With each heedless alteration, it seemed that Piccadilly lost a little more cachet. Today, it is an ignoble memorial to how urban development can go wrong. Surrounded by tourist shops, video arcades and fast food outlets, the once lovely architecture hidden by signs and dirtied by pollution, there is something lost and lonely about that angel of charity, vainly clutching his bow, poised on one foot in mid-flight, looking for all the world as if he were trying to run away.

after city leaders complained of 'drunkenness, fornication, gaming and lewdness'. Today, it's a pleasant, upscale area with a couple of fine pubs (Ye Grapes at 16 Shepherd Market and the Shepherd's Tavern at 50 Hertford Street). But, in keeping with its background, you'll often also see downmarket prostitutes working from tatty apartment blocks whose accommodation probably bears little resemblance to the clutch of sophisticated hotels – the Hilton, the Dorchester, the Metropolitan and the Inter-Continental – moments away on Park Lane.

Faraday Museum

Royal Institution, 21 Albemarle Street, W1S 4BS (7409 2992/www.rigb.org). Green Park tube. **Open** 10am-5pm Mon-Fri. *Tours* by arrangement. **Admission** £1. *Tours* £5. **Credit** MC, V. **Map** p400 J7.

This small museum in the building where Michael Faraday was professor has a re-creation of the lab where he discovered the laws of electromagnetics. It's probably of interest only to those of a scientific bent, but if you're at the Royal Institution, ask to see the prized possession, which isn't on public display: a silver cup presented to Humphry Davy by Tsar Alexander I in 1825 in gratitude for what Davy's famous lamp had done for the miners of Russia.

Handel House Museum

25 Brook Street (entrance at rear), W1K 4HB (7495 1685/www.handelhouse.org). Bond Street tube. **Open** 10am-6pm Tue, Wed, Fri, Sat; 10am-8pm Thur; noon-6pm Sun. **Admission** £4.50; £3.50 concessions; £2 6-15s; free under-5s. **Credit** MC, V. **Map** p400 J7.

George Frideric Handel moved to Britain from his native Germany aged 25 and settled in this Mayfair house 12 years later, remaining here until his death in 1759. The house has been beautifully restored with original and recreated furnishings, paintings and a welter of the composer's scores. The programme of events here is surprisingly dynamic for a museum so small: there are activities tilted at kids every Saturday and recitals most Thursdays.

Piccadilly & Green Park

One of London's grandest streets, **Piccadilly** is the city's most touristy address, linking as it does bustling **Hyde Park Corner** with the pickpocket heaven that is **Piccadilly Circus**. Its undeniably charming name comes from the fancy suit collars ('picadils') favoured by the posh gentlemen who once paraded down its length. It's not very high class any more, but you can still see remnants of its glossy past in its Victorian shopping arcades. These were designed to protect shoppers from mud and horse manure, and today they are pretty (and pricey) tiny shopping malls. One of the nicest is the **Burlington Arcade**. According to archaic laws still on the books, it is illegal to sing, whistle, carry open umbrellas or hurry in the arcade, and there are wardens (known as 'Burlington Berties') on the job to catch anybody doing any of the above. Just next door to the Arcade, the **Royal Academy of Arts** (*see p113*) lures with innovative arts exhibitions. Across Piccadilly from the academy, it's virtually impossible to pass the wonderfully overwrought mint green veneer of the department store **Fortnum & Mason**

In at No 1. **Apsley House**. *See p113.*

(*see p233*) without stopping in. Behind those heavy brass doors lies one of the best food halls in the city and a delightful place to take tea.

The simple-looking church at No.197 is **St James's** (*see p114*). This was the architect Sir Christopher Wren's personal favourite, a fact that may come as a surprise to those who might expect him to have a soft spot for the glorious St Paul's. There's often a market out front, and there's a handy coffee shop with outdoor seating tucked into a corner behind it.

A few doors further down Piccadilly, the old-fashioned uniforms sported by the doormen, and excellent 1950s-style lighted sign leave no doubt that you've reached the **Ritz**, one of the city's best-known hotels and the place to go for afternoon tea (*see p192* **Posh Tea**). The simple green expanse just beyond the Ritz is the aptly named **Green Park**. Once a plague pit, where the city's many epidemic victims were buried, it may not be able to match the grandeur of Regent's Park (*see p107*), or the sheer scale of Hyde Park (*see p138*), but this park has its charms, most evident in the spring, when its gentle slopes are covered in bright daffodils. **Buckingham Palace** and its extensive gardens lie at its southern tip. **St James's Park**, just across the Mall, with its lovely views and exotic birdlife, does rather overshadow Green Park's bland greensward. Originally a royal deer park for St James's Palace, the park's current pastoral landscape owes its influence to John Nash, who redesigned it in the early 19th century under the orders of George IV. The view of Buckingham Palace from the bridge over the lake is wonderful, especially at night when the palace is floodlit. The lake is now a sanctuary for wildfowl, among them pelicans (fed at 3pm daily) and Australian black swans.

Continuing down Piccadilly, which gets particularly noisy and hectic in short order, you work your way past the queues outside the Hard Rock Café (*see p199*) to the Duke of Wellington's old homestead, **Apsley House** and on to **Wellington Arch** (*see p114*), both at Hyde Park Corner.

Apsley House: The Wellington Museum

149 Piccadilly, W1J 7NT (7499 5676/ www.vam.ac.uk). Hyde Park Corner tube.
Open 11am-5pm Tue-Sun. *Tours* by arrangement. **Admission** £4.50 (includes audio guide); £3 concessions; free under-18s, over-60s. *Tours* £2.50 per person (min 10). **Credit** AmEx, DC, MC, V. **Map** p400 G8.

Called No.1 London because it was the first London building one encountered on the road from the village of Kensington, Apsley House was built by Robert Adam in the 1770s. The Duke of Wellington had it as his London residence from 1817 until his death in 1852. Though his descendants still live here, some rooms are open to the public and contain interesting trinkets: Goya's Wellington portrait shows the Iron Duke after he defeated the French in 1812. An X-ray of the painting in 1966 showed that Wellington's head had been brushed over that of Joseph Bonaparte, Napoleon's brother: Goya had been working on the portrait when he found out Wellington had been victorious, so he adjusted the painting accordingly.

Buckingham Palace & Royal Mews

SW1A 1AA (7766 7300/Royal Mews 7766 7302/ www.royalresidences.com). Green Park or St James's Park tube/Victoria tube/rail. **Open** *State Rooms* early Aug-Sept 9.30am-4.15pm daily. *Royal Mews* Oct-July 11am-4pm daily; Aug-Sept 10am-5pm daily. Last entry 45mins before closing. **Admission** *Palace* £12; £10 concessions; £6 5-16s; £30 family; free under-5s. *Royal Mews* £5; £4 concessions; £2.50 5-16s; free under-5s; £12.50 family. **Credit** AmEx, MC, V. **Map** p400 H9.

The world's most famous palace, built in 1703, was intended as a house for the Duke of Buckingham, but George III liked it so much he bought it for his young bride Charlotte. His son, George IV, hired John Nash to convert it into a palace. Thus construction on the 600-room palace began, but the project was beset with disaster from the start. Nash was fired after George IV's death – he was too flighty apparently – and the reliable but unimaginative Edward Blore was hired to finish the job. After critics saw the final result, they dubbed him 'Blore the Bore'. Queen Victoria, the first royal to live here, hated the place, calling it 'a disgrace to the country'.

Judge for yourself. In August and September, while the Windsors are off on their holidays, the State Apartments – the rooms used for banquets and investitures – are open to the public. After the initial thrill of being inside Buckingham Palace, it's not all that interesting, save for the Queen's Gallery, which contains highlights of Liz's art collection. An exhibition of 500 Georgian treasures entitled 'George III and Queen Charlotte: Patronage, Collecting and Court Taste', opens on 26 March 2004.

Around the corner, on Buckingham Palace Road, the Royal Mews holds those royal carriages that are rolled out for the Royals to wag their hands from on very important occasions. Top banana goes to Her Majesty's State Coach, a breathtaking double gilded affair built in 1761.

Royal Academy of Arts

Burlington House, Piccadilly, W1J 0BD (7300 8000/www.royalacademy.org.uk). Green Park or Piccadilly Circus tube. **Open** 10am-6pm Mon-Thur, Sat, Sun; 10am-10pm Fri. **Admission** varies. **Credit** AmEx, DC, MC, V. **Map** p400 J7.

Britain's first art school was founded in 1768 and moved to the extravagantly Palladian Burlington House a century later. It's best known these days for its galleries, which stage a roster of populist temporary exhibitions (there is a small permanent collection on show; make an appointment with the curator to see the rest). The Giorgio Armani exhibition runs until 18 Feb 2004, the Vuillard till April, but the Academy's biggest event is the Summer Exhibition, which for 235 years has drawn from works entered by the public. Some 12,000 pieces are submitted each year, with 10% making it past the judges. The exhibition runs s 8 June-16 August 2004.

St James's Church Piccadilly

197 Piccadilly, W1J 9LL (7734 4511/www.st-james-piccadilly.org). Piccadilly Circus tube. **Open** 8am-7pm daily. Evening events times vary. **Admission** free. **Map** p400 J7.

Consecrated in 1684, St James's is the only church Sir Christopher Wren built on an entirely new site. It's a calming building without architectural airs or graces but not lacking in charm. It was bombed within an inch of its life in World War II, but was painstakingly reconstructed. The lovely plasterwork around the sanctuary was reformed by using the bits that remained of the original as a model. It is still the building's only real frill. This is a busy church, as along with its inclusive ministry, it runs a counselling service, stages regular classical concerts (*see p302*), provides a home for the William Blake Society (the poet was baptised here) and hosts markets in its churchyard: antiques on Tuesday, arts and crafts from Wednesday to Saturday.

Wellington Arch

Hyde Park Corner, W1J 7JZ (7930 2726/www.english-heritage.org.uk). Hyde Park Corner tube. **Open** *Apr-Sept* 10am-6pm Wed-Sun. Oct 10am-5pm Wed-Sun. *Nov-Mar* 10am-4pm Wed-Sun. **Admission** £2.50; £2 concessions; £1.50 5-16s; free under-5s. **Credit** MC, V. **Map** p400 G8.

Built in the 1820s to mark Britain's triumph over Napoleonic France, Decimus Burton's Wellington Arch was moved from its original Buckingham Palace location to Hyde Park Corner in 1882. It was initially topped by a statue of Wellington, but since 1912 Captain Adrian Jones's *Peace Descending on the Quadriga of War* has finished it with a flourish. It was restored a couple of years ago, and now has three floors of displays about the history of the arch. From the balcony, you can see the Houses of Parliament and Buckingham Palace, though trees will probably obstruct your view in summer.

Piccadilly Circus & Regent Street

Probably the closest London comes to a Times Square, Piccadilly Circus is one of those places you either love or hate (*see p111* **Pride of London**). It can be a disappointment to some (the word 'circus' in this sense means only a circular intersection of streets – no lions or elephants, sadly), while for others it's the big city junction of their dreams. The tired souvenir stalls and deafening videogame arcades at the busy Trocadero were once an elegant music hall; there's progress for you.

Connecting Piccadilly Circus to Oxford Circus to the north and Pall Mall to the south, Regent Street is a broad, curving boulevard designed by John Nash in the early 1800s to separate the wealthy of Mayfair from the working classes of Soho. Seriously. The grandeur of the sweeping road is impressive – although much of Nash's architecture was destroyed in the early 20th century, some does survive – and some of the shops have retained their aura, particularly Liberty department store in its fabulous mock-Tudor building (*see p233*) and Hamleys toy shop (*see p255*). Unfortunately, the chains have moved in of late, making it a sort of Oxford Street Lite.

St James's

Maps p400 & p401

Green Park or Piccadilly Circus tube.

Not many visitors – nor many Londoners, for that matter – venture too far into St James's, which takes as its borders Piccadilly, Haymarket, the Mall and Green Park. And, that's just the way its habituées like it. For St James's is even posher than Mayfair, its comrade-in-swank, north of Piccadilly. This is a London that has remained unchanged for centuries: charming in its way, but arrogant and rich all the same.

The material needs of the venerable gents of St James's are still met by the anachronistic shops and restaurants of Jermyn Street and St James's Street. Tourists make up some of the clientele today, but it's a thrill to see the lovingly crafted goods and the timewarp shopfronts, among them cigar retailer JJ Fox (19 St James's Street) and upmarket cobbler John Lobb (No.9). To stroll around the alleys is to step back in time, and up in class.

Around the corner from Jermyn Street is the Queen Mother's old gaff: **Clarence House** (*see p115*). Now the official London residence of Prince Charles and his sons Harry and William, it recently opened to the public for the first time. Very near to Clarence House, **St James's Palace** was originally built as a residence for Henry VIII in 1532. It has remained the official residence of the sovereign throughout the centuries, despite the fact that since 1837 the monarchs have all actually lived at nearby Buckingham Palace. It has great historic significance to the monarchy: Mary Tudor surrendered Calais here, Elizabeth I lived here during the campaign against the Spanish Armada, and Charles I was confined here before his execution in 1649.

Triumphal **Wellington Arch**. *See p114.*

Today, St James's Palace is used by Prince Charles and various minor royals, and it is, essentially, the address of the now largely defunct government of the monarch. Tradition still dictates that foreign ambassadors to the UK are officially known as 'Ambassadors to the Court of St James'. Although the palace is closed to the public, you can explore **Friary Court** on Marlborough Road and attend the Sunday services at the historic **Chapel Royal** (October to Good Friday; 8.30am, 11.30am).

Two other notable St James's mansions stand nearby and overlook Green Park. The neo-classical **Lancaster House** was rebuilt in the 1820s by Benjamin Dean Wyatt for Frederick, Duke of York, and impressed Queen Victoria with its splendour. Closed to the public, it's now used mainly for government receptions and conferences. A little further north, on St James's Place, is beautiful, 18th-century **Spencer House**, ancestral townhouse of the late Princess Diana's family and now infrequently open as a museum and art gallery.

Across Marlborough Road lies the **Queen's Chapel**, which was the first classical church to be built in England. Designed by the mighty Inigo Jones in the 1620s for Charles I's intended bride of the time, the Infanta of Castile, the chapel now stands in the grounds of **Marlborough House** and is only open to the public during Sunday services (Easter to July; 8.30am, 11.30am). The house itself was built by Sir Christopher Wren.

Reached from the west via King Street or the Mall, **St James's Square** was the most fashionable address in London for the 50 years after it was laid out in the 1670s: some seven dukes and seven earls were residents by the 1720s. Alas, no private houses survive on the square today, though among the current occupants is the prestigious **London Library**. This private library was founded by Thomas Carlyle in 1841 in disgust at the inefficiency of the British Library.

Further east, overlooking the Mall, is **Carlton House Terrace**, which was built by Nash in 1827-32 on the site of Carlton House. When the Prince Regent came to the throne as George IV, he decided his home was not ostentatious enough for his elevated station and levelled what Horace Walpole had once described as 'the most perfect palace' in Europe. No.6 Carlton House Terrace, now occupied by the Royal Society, was the Germany Embassy during the Nazi era; its interior was designed by Albert Speer, Hitler's architect.

Clarence House

SW1A 1AA (7766 7303/www.royalresidences.com). **Open** *Aug-mid Oct* 9am-7pm daily (last admission 6pm). **Admission** £5; £3 5-16s; free under-5s. *Tours* All tickets for the guided tours are timed and must be pre-booked. **Credit** AmEx, MC, V.

Standing austerely beside St James's Palace, Clarence House was built between 1825 and 1827, based on designs by John Nash. It was built for Prince William Henry, Duke of Clarence, who lived there as King William IV until 1837. During its history, the house has been much altered by its many royal inhabitants, the most recent of whom was the Queen Mother, who lived there until she died in 2002. Prince Charles and his two sons have moved in and plan to hold summer openings. On display are five receiving rooms and the small but significant art collection, strong in 20th-century British art, accumulated by the Queen Mother. Among the art on display is a lovely 1945 portrait of her by Sir James Gunn. There's also a painting by Noël Coward, and others by John Piper, WS Sickert and Augustus John. Note that tickets are hard to come by – all the 2003 tickets sold out by the beginning of September.

Spencer House

27 St James's Place, SW1A 1NR (7499 8620/ www.spencerhouse.co.uk). Green Park tube. **Open** *House* Feb-July, Sept-Dec 10.30am-4.45pm Sun. *Restored gardens* spring, summer (phone to check). **Admission** Tour only £6; £5 10-16s. No under-10s. **Map** p400 J8.

Designed by John Vardy and built for John Spencer, who became Earl Spencer the year before his house was completed, this 1766 construction is one of the capital's finest Palladian mansions. The Spencers moved out just over a century ago and the lavishly restored building is used chiefly as offices and as a venue for corporate entertaining, hence the limited opening hours. However, the weekly guided tours are a splendid little Sunday diversion, especially if you get lucky and find your visit coinciding with a rare opening for the restful gardens.

Soho

A loud, brash, much-loved corner of W1, hanging on for dear life.

There's more to Soho than just sex shops, strip joints and 'Girls! Girls! Girls!'. Everybody's here: media and film stars, prostitutes, immigrants, tourists and the gay community all cosy up in W1's bohemia. Throw in a few cheeky market traders, designers, artists, drunks and junkies, and you've got London's spiciest melting pot.

It's a far cry from the Middle Ages, when the area was a rural idyll used as a hunting ground by London's aristocracy. It was after the Great Fire of 1666 that Soho became residential, when thousands were forced to relocate. Around this time, Soho also got its first wave of immigrants: Greek Christians (hence Greek Street) fleeing Ottoman persecution, and French Protestants (Huguenots) forced out of France by Louis XIV. Soon, the only trace of the neighbourhood's pastoral roots was its name: hunters used to cry 'So-ho!' when they spotted their prey.

As the immigrants poured into Soho, wealthy residents moved out. The architect John Nash encouraged this social apartheid in 1813, when he designed Regent Street to provide what he called 'a complete separation between the Streets occupied by the Nobility and Gentry [Mayfair], and the narrower Streets and meaner houses occupied by mechanics and the trading part of the community'.

With Nash's kind of thinking ruling the day, Soho became one of Britain's worst slums during the 19th century, as the Industrial Revolution, the Napoleonic Wars and the Irish potato famine brought thousands of unskilled rural labourers to London. Cheap boarding houses and tenements spread like a plague. In 1844 Frederick Engels wrote: 'the houses are occupied from cellar to garret, filthy within and without, and their appearance is such that no human being could possibly wish to live within them.' No doubt the squalid living conditions fuelled Karl Marx's revolutionary zeal: he lived in some particularly down-at-heel buildings, including Nos.28 and 64 Dean Street.

It wasn't all doom and gloom, though, as Soho's cheap rents attracted legions of artists, writers and thinkers. In addition to Marx, other famous residents included William Blake (born on Broadwick Street, he went on to live at 28 Poland Street); Charles Darwin (41 Great Marlborough Street); and one Wolfgang Amadeus Mozart (20 Frith Street).

While the rich were leaving in droves, the showgirls were starting to move in: Soho became the entertainment capital of London; theatres and music halls sprang up everywhere. A bustling restaurant trade followed in the early 20th century, while in the 1950s it was music: Ronnie Scott's jazz club opened up (and remains, *see p312*), and there was a brief skiffle boom – Adam Faith and Cliff Richard were discovered at the 2 i's Coffee Bar at 59 Old Compton Street. In 1962 Georgie Fame started his sweat-soaked residency at the Flamingo Club (33-7 Wardour Street, these days a dreary Irish pub); the nearby Marquee (then at 90 Wardour Street) hosted early gigs by Hendrix and Pink Floyd.

The sex industry expanded in the 1960s and '70s into a Soho institution. But sexy soon became seedy; the neighbourhood was drowning in smut. During the following two decades, it was the gay community who started to move in (*see p118* **Sex and Soho**). Spurred along by the pink pound, Soho was reborn as a sort of So-Homo. Pubs such as the **Golden Lion** on Dean Street had long been the haunt of gay servicemen (as well as writer Noel Coward), and now, with the arrival of a plethora of gay bars along Old Compton Street, the dirty mac brigade gradually disappeared. Today, some sex shops still exist, but most have been replaced by cafés.

But Soho may become a victim of its own success: rents are skyrocketing and chains are creeping in. We'd like to say that the neighbourhood's bohemian spirit will keep blandness at bay, but, then, look at what happened to the King's Road (*see p141*).

Around Old Compton Street

The core of Soho is Old Compton Street and its surrounding avenues and alleys. This is Soho at its most heterodox and lively: gay bars and straight boozers, well-stocked off-licences and continental delis, fashionable restaurants and low-rent strip joints. Gay highlights include **Clone Zone** (No.62), the scene's premier fetish shop, and the **Admiral Duncan** (No.54, *see p296*), a pub that was attacked by the 'London nail bomber' in 1999 and has subsequently become a gay landmark. The **Prince Edward Theatre** at No.30 is the perfect example of the mainstreaming of gay culture: the wretched

Abba musical *Mamma Mia* has been playing here for aeons (enough already, the joke's over).

Whatever your gender bent, grab a table at any of the cafés: try **Duke's Bar** (No.27), which featured in Michael Winterbottom's film *Wonderland,* and enjoy the buzz.

Just a few blocks off Old Compton Street, **Soho Square** forms the neighbourhood's northern gateway. This tree-lined quadrangle was initially called King Square, and a weather-beaten statue of Charles II stands in the centre. In summer, office workers spread out on the grass at lunchtime, or sit on the benches, one of which bears a dedication to late singer Kirsty MacColl who wrote a song about the square. The miniature mock-Tudor cottage in the middle evokes *Snow White and the Seven Dwarfs*, but it's just a tool shed. London's one remaining French Protestant church and St Patrick's Catholic church provide spiritual nourishment, but the area is dominated by the advertising and film industries: the British Board of Film Classification and 20th Century Fox both have offices here.

The streets that link Old Compton with Soho Square are rich with history. **Greek Street**, which runs through the archway of the Pillars of Hercules pub, on the corner of Manette Street, is where Casanova and Thomas de Quincey once lodged. Neighbouring **Frith Street** was home to John Constable, Mozart and William Hazlitt (at No.6); before World War I, Ezra Pound, Rupert Brooke and several other writers frequented a café at No.67; and John Logie Baird demonstrated his TV above **Bar Italia** (No.22), Soho's all-night café (*see p202*).

Neighbouring **Dean Street** has an equally colourful history, mostly composed of the bohemian characters who got drunk in its pubs. Dylan Thomas – surprise, surprise – held marathon drinking sessions at the **York Minster** (No.49), then nicknamed 'the French Pub' for its association with Charles de Gaulle and the Free French resistance movement; it's now called the **French House** (*see p220*), and still retains its louche charm.

Despite Soho's many bars, celebrities and media hacks prefer to quench their thirst and powder their noses in its members-only clubs: the **Groucho Club** (44 Dean Street) and **Soho House** (40 Greek Street). The latter made headlines in 2002 when Jude Law and Sadie Frost's two-year-old daughter swallowed an ecstasy tablet she reportedly found on the club's floor. Speaking of bad behaviour, check out what's on at the **Soho Theatre** (21 Dean Street), known for top-notch new writing.

These days, Greek, Frith and Dean streets form the heart of Soho's bar and restaurant scene. The **Gay Hussar** (2 Greek Street, *see p205*), a traditional Hungarian restaurant frequented by Labour Party politicians, celebrated its 50th anniversary in 2003. It sits near cheaper places such as **Café Emm** (17

Sex and Soho

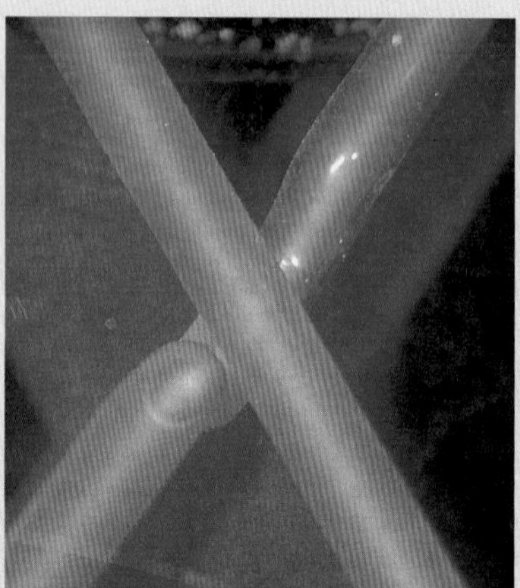

So, they're cleaning up Soho. These days, smart cafés outnumber sex shops, hip bars have replaced strip joints and po-faced offices are moving into former brothels. It's nice to see the neighbourhood thriving and everything, but enough is enough: Soho needs a bit of sex.

After all, Soho has been associated with sex since the '40s – the 1640s, that is. One of Soho's earliest recorded residents was a 'lewd woman' named Anna Clerke, who in 1641 was arrested after 'threteninge to burne the houses at So:ho'. In the 18th century a connoisseur by the name of Mr Harris published an annual guide to the area's prostitutes. Witness this description of Miss B___rn, a resident of 18 Old Compton Street in 1788: 'This accomplished nymph... plays on the pianoforte, sings, dances, and is mistress of every Maneuver in the amorous contest... In bed she is all the heart can wish; her price two pounds.' Other bawdy residents, such as Elizabeth Flint of Meard Street ('generally slut and drunkard; occasionally whore and thief'), are recounted in Judith Summers's wonderful tome, *Soho: A History of London's Most Colourful Neighbourhood.*

It wasn't always sexy, as during the 19th century grinding poverty forced scores of women on to the game. At one time, there were an estimated 80,000 prostitutes working in the area. William Gladstone, then an MP, walked the streets at night, bringing the most desperate girls home to his wife, who would cook them meals and give them a bed. (Gladstone's motives, by the way, may not have been entirely altruistic: after each encounter he reportedly whipped himself.)

Frith Street), and glamorous cocktail bars such as **Akbar** (77 Dean Street, *see p228*) and the **Sanctuary** (4 Greek Street, *see p299*). Happily, there are still some trad old boozers, such as the **Crown and Two Chairmen** (31 Dean Street).

West of here, **Wardour Street** is film industry territory, with an abundance of production companies. It's also home to the wholesome **Busaba Eathai** (no.106-110, *see p196*), for generous portions of pan-Asian food, although the best value Asian eating round here is at the wonderful **Masala Zone** (9 Marshall Street; *see p204*) and also at **Soba** (11-13 Soho Street; 38 Poland Street).

The heavily fenced churchyard at Wardour Street's southern end is **St Anne's**. It was bombed during the Blitz, and only the 19th-century tower remains. In the gardens here a bench commemorates the victims of the aforementioned Admiral Duncan pub bombing.

For those of you who miss the sleazy Soho of yore, don't despair: two tiny cut-throughs, **Tisbury Court** (linking Wardour and Rupert streets) and **Walkers Court** (from Brewer to Berwick Street) are lined with insalubrious strip joints, which promise the earth but leave you broke, and sex shops invariably fronted by ridiculous plastic streamers. Get a cheap thrill

By the 20th century it was more glam. The majority of Soho's prostitutes were French women, known as 'Fifis'. They wore elegant clothes, kept immaculate brothels and drank champagne at the French House (*see p220*).

The tone changed in 1959, when the Street Offences Act was passed, forcing prostitutes off the streets. The pimps took over, luring men into massage parlours and strip clubs, where a rendezvous would be arranged.

In the 1960s, after censorship laws were relaxed in Scandinavia, Soho was flooded with hardcore porn imports. Soho's sex industry exploded: porn barons became rich, and many policemen were paid to turn a blind eye. The streets around here were awash with video booths, peep shows and X-rated cinemas. By the 1970s there were 250 sex shops in the district.

Many residents fled, and Westminster Council talked of razing the district altogether and implementing a regeneration scheme to sanitise Soho for once and for all. But a diehard group of residents fought back, forming the Soho Housing Association in 1972. They forced the clean-up of the seedier elements of the industry. In 1986, a new licensing system ordered those wanting to open sex shops to prove they were 'of good character' and to pay a large fee. The number of sex shops dropped dramatically: by the end of the 1990s there were only 35 in the area.

But just when it looked like Soho might go a bit bland, sex put the area back on the map: more specifically, gay sex. The opening of a number of gay bars in the area gave it a new lease of life. The wave of gentrification that followed was inevitable, but worrying – rents are skyrocketing; small businesses and longtime residents are being pushed out.

Suddenly the citizens of Soho think a little sex is a good thing. When the local government announced a plan to evict prostitutes in 2003, 10,000 locals signed a petition protesting against the crackdown. The government insists that prostitution is associated with Balkan crime gangs, but the protesters accuse them of trying to sell the properties to developers to make a quick buck. They argue that prostitutes are more vulnerable working the streets than in brothels, and say that prostitutes spend their hard-earned cash locally.

The crux of the matter? Locals argue that prostitutes are an essential to Soho's character and part of the area's tolerant atmosphere. So there you have it: sex and Soho, passionately intertwined.

and then walk on, either to Rupert Street and its rash of grubby shops, or to the noisy market stalls and record shops of Berwick Street.

Broadwick Street, to the west, is famous for a couple of reasons: it was the birthplace of poet, artist and visionary William Blake, and the centre of a severe cholera outbreak in 1854. Local doctor John Snow became convinced that the disease was transmitted by polluted water and had the street's water pump closed. Snow's hypothesis proved correct, leading to a breakthrough in epidemiology. The doctor is commemorated by a handleless replica water pump and in the name of the street's pub.

West Soho

Brewer Street is the perfect microcosm of the new Soho. There are a few naughty sex shops to please the old school, a 'gay department store' (Prowler, Nos.3-7) and some fascinating speciality shops, such as **Anything Left-Handed** (No.57). The **Vintage Magazine Store** (Nos.39-43) is crammed with glorious old copies of *Smash Hits* and *NME*.

Great Windmill Street, which leads from Brewer Street to Shaftesbury Avenue, offers the perfect illustration of Soho's changing mores: in 1932 the **Windmill Theatre** started its now-

Old Compton Street, all bright and gay. *See p116.*

legendary 'revuedeville' shows with their erotic 'tableaux', which the law dictated could feature only stationary naked girls on stage. Some 70 years later, the Windmill is a lap-dancing joint. Around the corner, the **New Piccadilly** (8 Denman Street) is a British caff of the old school, with its formica surfaces and booths.

West Soho's most famous spot is **Carnaby Street**. In the 1960s it was the epitome of swinging London. Today, the shopping lane is smart, but it's lost its street cred: most of the design shops have been replaced by chains.

South of Beak Street lies the delightful **Golden Square**, the setting for Ralph Nickleby's gloomy house in *Nicholas Nickleby*.

Chinatown

Shaftesbury Avenue, which wends its way down from New Oxford Street to Piccadilly Circus, is the heart of Theatreland (*see p330*). During the late Victorian period, seven grand theatres were built here; six of them still stand. It also has Chinese shops and restaurants to mark it as the northern edge of **Chinatown**, a district that extends to Leicester Square.

Soho has always attracted immigrants, but the Chinese were relative latecomers: most arrived in the 1950s from Hong Kong. Attracted by the cheap rents along Gerrard and Lisle streets, thousands moved in, and soon the neighbourhood developed its Chinese personality. The ersatz oriental gates, stone lions and pagoda-topped phone booths suggest a Chinese theme park, but, in reality, this is a close-knit residential and working enclave. **Gerrard Street** is the glitziest spot, crammed with restaurants and twinkly lights. (For Chinatown restaurants, *see p203*)

Leicester Square

Most Londoners avoid Leicester Square, put off by the crowds, Burger Kings, crowds, Pizza Hut, crowds… Get the picture? But this is all relatively new; in the 17th and 18th centuries, this was one of London's most exclusive addresses. By the 19th century, as Soho became a ghetto, the aristos moved out. In the last few decades, it's become the city's cinema centre, and some of them are spectacular, with huge screens and star-studded film premières. But the glitz doesn't come cheap: be prepared to fork out more than £10 to see a flick. And don't come here expecting a Truffaut retrospective. For that, you should head around the corner to Leicester Place, where the **Prince Charles Cinema** (*see p284*) shows an eclectic mix of art and B-movies. Next door is the French Catholic church of **Notre Dame de France**, which contains murals by Jean Cocteau.

Along with cinemas, Leicester Square is full of tourists, buskers, teenagers and drunken louts. The square is not completely without culture: in the middle stands a statue of Charlie Chaplin, and on the south side of the square is the half-price ticket booth called **tkts**, where, if you queue on the same day, you can get cheap theatre tickets. (10am-7pm Mon-Sat; 12-3pm Sun, *see p331*). Beside the booth is London's weak attempt at a Hollywood Walk of Fame: in the pavement are a few bronzed handprints of stars like Omar Sharif and Charlton Heston.

In the midst of all of this, stands one lone outpost of intelligence, the **Westminster Reference Library**, arguably London's best public library. It's located in St Martin's Street, at the square's southern end.

Covent Garden & St Giles's

Piazza the action.

Covent Garden

Maps p399 & p401

Covent Garden, Leicester Square or Temple tube.

The boundaries that separate London's 'good' and 'bad' neighbourhoods are elusive and ephemeral. Covent Garden remains a testament to how the shifting forces of urban evolution conflate aristocratic housing with gin-soaked back alleys and brothels, even if – as here – complete degeneracy is avoided.

These days Covent Garden is home to some of London's most desirable properties, which is exactly what the Earl of Bedford had in mind when, in the 1630s, he commissioned master architect Inigo Jones to design a series of Palladian arcades based on the elegant central piazza in Livorno, Italy. A suitably well-heeled clientele were quick to claim the area as their own, but as the riotous fruit and vegetable market expanded to dominate the main square during the next century, they headed west to more assured lodgings, leaving Covent Garden foundering in an ocean of iniquity.

Less than a century after the foundations of Bedford's optimism were laid in stone, his elegant homes looked blankly on to a teeming scene of pubs, gambling dens and barely disguised brothels, strewn with the rotting debris and detritus of another day's trading. And yet these are the years that most characterised the Covent Garden we see today. Then, as now, the area was renowned for its theatres, and many of the same mannered folk who'd fled a few years earlier would regularly return, reluctantly stepping over steaming drunks to see Garrick play Hamlet to Woffington's Ophelia. The bawdy houses and coffee shops combined to create a hotbed of literary and intellectual activity, with luminaries including Charles Dickens and Thomas De Quincey periodically lodging above the arterial streets and alleys.

Eating out in central **Covent Garden.**

In 1974, when the restored market was moved south to Vauxhall, property developers pegged the area for more unwanted office blocks, and it was only through mass squats and demonstrations by Covent Garden's incumbent alternative community that the area was saved, and those first tentative steps towards regeneration were taken. A 'good' neighbourhood once again, then. It would appear that Bedford's dream has come full circle, although not without the performance years leaving their mark in the predominance of theatres and street artists, or the alternative culture – to which Covent Garden owes its very existence – which still resides in pockets (Neal's Yard, *see p209* and *p245*) among promenades otherwise dominated by trendy shoe shops.

Covent Garden Piazza

Little remains of Jones's original piazza now, although tourists flock undeterred to Covent Garden's main square for a combination of gentrified shopping and less predictable street performances. The majority of the latter take place under the portico of **St Paul's** (*see p122*). Shoppers favour the old covered market (7836 9136/www.coventgardenmarket.co.uk), now a collection of small stores, many of them with a twee, touristy appeal. The **Apple Market**, in the North Hall, has arts and crafts stalls every Tuesday to Sunday, and antiques on Monday.

Across the road, the cheaper, tackier **Jubilee Market** (7836 2139) – once a flower market – has moved on a great deal since its Eliza Doolittle days, dealing mostly in novelty T-shirts and unofficial calendars, although it, too, is filled with antiques every Monday and crafts on a weekend. The piazza is host to an abundance of cafés, tempting weary tourists with tables outdoors or shelter from the rain – just check the price list before you take them up on it.

London's Transport Museum

Covent Garden Piazza, WC2E 7BB (7379 6344/ www.ltmuseum.co.uk). Covent Garden tube. **Open** 10am-6pm Mon-Thur, Sat, Sun; 11am-6pm Fri. **Admission** £5.95; £4.50 concessions; free under-16s when accompanied by an adult. **Credit** MC, V. **Map** p401 L6.

Its efficiency may not be legendary, but London Transport still draws more than just trainspotters to this well-managed museum, which charts the history of public transport in the city centre from 19th-century horse-drawn carts to the present day, with plenty of actors and interactive displays bringing the journey to life. Kids clamber on the electric trams and pretend to drive the bus; older enthusiasts marvel at the development of a genuine urban aesthetic. There's also an exhibition of promotional posters for mass transit systems.

Royal Opera House

Covent Garden, WC2E 9DD (7304 4000/ www.royaloperahouse.org). Covent Garden tube. **Open** 10am-3.30pm Mon-Sat. **Admission** free. *Stage tours* £8; £7 concessions. **Map** p401 L7.

The last time opera made inroads into popular culture was 1990, when Nessun Dorma accompanied slow-motion replays of the World Cup's more emotional moments. In the 18th century, Handel debuted many specially commissioned works here to enormous public acclaim, but these days the mostly stylised, upper class conventions of opera just don't rest easy with the proverbial 'man in the street'. Never mind – now fully restored, it's worth wandering upstairs just to enjoy a drink in the Amphitheatre bar and restaurant, with its spectacular views across Covent Garden. Fans of the equally proverbial 'fat lady singing' – it goes without saying – will be in seventh heaven.

St Paul's Covent Garden

Bedford Street, WC2E 9ED (7836 5221/ www.actorschurch.org). Covent Garden or Leicester Square tube. **Open** 9am-4.30pm Mon-Fri; 9am-12.30pm Sun. *Services* 1.10pm Wed; 11am Sun. *Choral Evensong* 4pm 2nd Sun of mth. **Admission** free; donations appreciated. **Map** p401 L7.

Known as the Actors' Church for its association with Covent Garden's Theatreland – lining its walls are memorials to stars from Ivor Novello to Hattie Jacques – this plain Tuscan pastiche was designed by Inigo Jones in 1631. George Bernard Shaw set the first scene of *Pygmalion* under the church's portico, which will always be associated with Punch and Judy (*see p123* **Theatricality**). The first known victim of the Great Plague, Margaret Ponteous, was buried in St Paul's churchyard.

Theatre Museum

Tavistock Street (entrance Russell Street), WC2 (7943 4700/www.theatremuseum.org). Covent Garden tube. **Open** 10am-6pm Tue-Sun. Last entry 5.30pm. **Admission** free. **Credit** AmEx, MC, V. **Map** p401 L6.

The various colourful threads of Covent Garden's theatrical history are spun into a vivid tapestry in this little museum. The permanent galleries form an intriguing window into the heroes of a bygone age – David Garrick, Edmund Kean, Eliza Vestris – as well as the plays that cast them into the public eye. There are regular make-up displays, while larger exhibitions include an interactive biography of the Redgrave family and – for younger audiences – a potted history of the *Wind in the Willows*, and its journey from the paper to the stage. Phone for details of Kids Club workshops, every Saturday from 10am.

Elsewhere in Covent Garden

Elsewhere, the changing fortunes of Covent Garden are reflected to varying degrees. A cultural melting pot it certainly is: from opposite ends of **St Martin's Lane** – and the

Theatricality

It's difficult to take a step in Covent Garden without treading on a dead actor. From Garrick Street and Macklin Street, over to Betterton, Kean and Kemble streets, the names of London's many resident theatrical types have become an integral part of the city, weaving into a great stage.

Many tourists flock to Covent Garden because of the area's reputation for performance, and while this is written in a number of historical, high-profile theatres – including the **Lyceum**, **St Martin's** and the **Theatre Royal** (*see p330* and *p334*) – their often static programmes of big budget, long-running shows pale in comparison to the more spontaneous cast of have-a-go street performers occupying every corner.

Some of them, let's be fair, aren't so great. Novelty value aside, penniless crack addicts playing with traffic cones aren't going to have roads named after them in the near future, and even the string quartets invariably hammering out Pachelbel's Canon to rapturous applause in the covered market don't always sound like their hearts are in it.

But there are diamonds in the rough: the comedian Eddie Izzard is just one of many international talents who cut their teeth drawing crowds in the piazza. Performers these days hoping to become the centre of attention under the portico of St Paul's (*see p122*) must first be auditioned and then authorised by Covent Garden Market, and even then slots are booked weeks in advance. Entertainment in front of this church has a long history, after all: on May 9th 1662, the diarist Samuel Pepys described being 'mighty pleased' after witnessing the first recorded Punch and Judy show there. It's a birthday marked by an annual **May Fayre and Puppet Festival** (*see p260*).

On a grander scale, performances are conducted every summer as part of the **Royal Opera House**'s end of season celebrations: in 2003, more than 17,000 people watched *Pagliacci* being performed in the great outdoors and relayed live across the capital. Meanwhile, street performers from around the world descend on the South Bank every summer for the **Royal National Theatre**'s Watch This Space festival (*see p331*).

For more home-grown entertainment, however, Covent Garden piazza is the place to come whatever the time of year: as the authorities begin to take street performers more seriously, they are even shedding their status as 'glorified buskers'. In fact, all this legitimate, open-air cultivation of upcoming artists creates a sense that London is returning to the age when wandering musicians or 'waits' were maintained by the city for the public benefit. Still, some of today's artists are remaining underground in more ways than one: a system of auditioning and licensing buskers in tube stations, introduced in 2003, means that an era of offensively tuneless Cat Stevens covers may at last be coming to a welcome end.

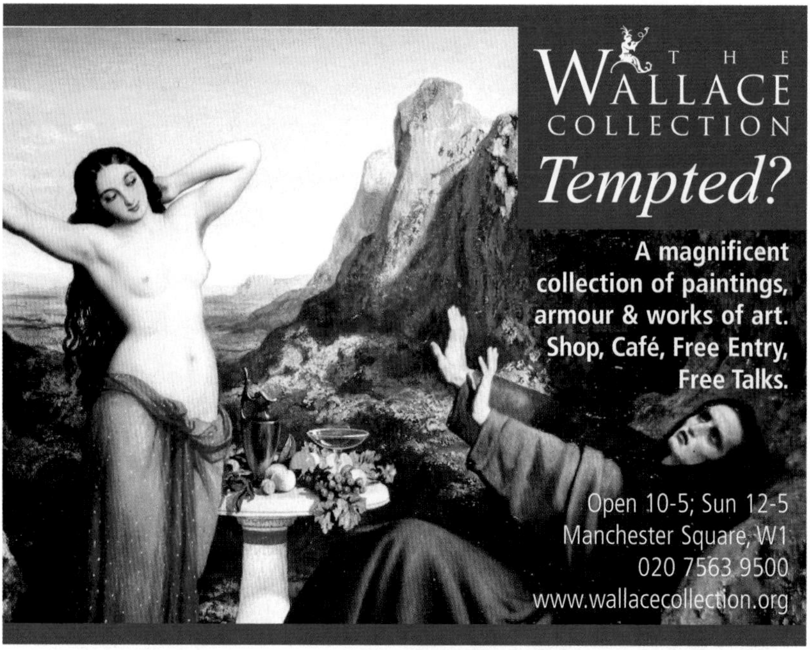

THE WALLACE COLLECTION
Tempted?
A magnificent collection of paintings, armour & works of art. Shop, Café, Free Entry, Free Talks.
Open 10-5; Sun 12-5
Manchester Square, W1
020 7563 9500
www.wallacecollection.org

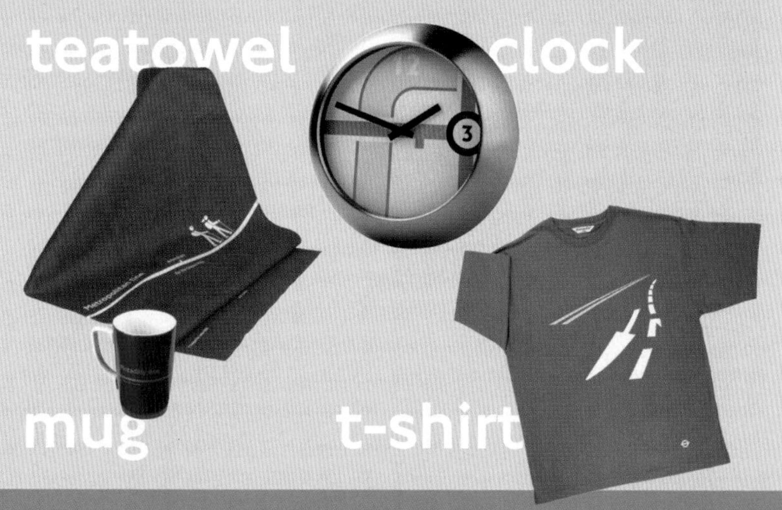

teatowel
clock
mug
t-shirt
Available from London's Transport Museum shop and online at www.ltmuseum.co.uk
London's Transport Museum
Covent Garden Piazza

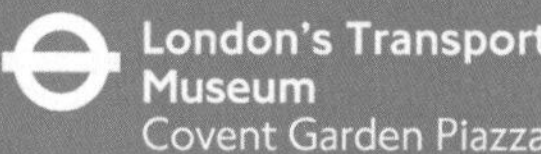

social spectrum – Stringfellows nightclub (7240 5534/www.stringfellows.com) faces down the **Coliseum** (7836 0111/www.eno.org), home of the **English National Opera** (*see p122*) and currently in a state of extensive refurbishment. Meanwhile, neighbouring alleys in the shadow of the Wyndham and Albany theatres exude an overpowering old world charm; from the nook and cranny antiques stores of Cecil Court to the clockwork-operated gas lighting of **Goodwin's Court**, which nightly illuminates a row of delightfully bow-fronted 17th-century housing.

Further towards the piazza, most of the older, more unusual shops have been superseded by a homogenous mass of cafés (although Arthur Middleton on New Row, 7836 7042 continues to stock an arcane collection of scientific instruments), and by the time you reach the far end of King Street, Covent Garden offers only token gestures towards its colourful history. High-profile fashion designers (and a few trendy up-and-comers supported by their celebrity parents) have all but domesticated **Floral Street**, **Long Acre** and, most noticeably, **Neal Street**, although more interesting shopping experiences await on **Monmouth Street** and **Earlham Street**. On the latter, a traditional butcher's and a family ironmonger's look on to cult clothing stores, specialist bookshops and a flower market.

At one end of Earlham Street is the **Seven Dials** roundabout, named after both the number of sundials incorporated into the central monument (the seventh being formed by the pillar itself) and streets branching off it. A stone's throw from Seven Dials, **Neal's Yard** remains the most faithful reminder of the alternative community that saved Covent Garden from wanton redevelopment in the 1970s. In this colourful square, co-operative cafés mingle cheerfully with herbalists, head shops and a tattoo parlour. Slam City Skates (7240 0928) is still the city's mecca for style-conscious freewheelers.

Towards Holborn, Covent Garden becomes less distinguished. **Endell Street** is perhaps most noticeable for the queues leading to legendary chippie Rock & Sole Plaice (*see p208*). These days **Drury Lane** is largely ignored even by theatre-goers: the current Theatre Royal (the first was built there in 1663) opens on to Catherine Street, with its excess of restaurants vying for the attention of pre- and post-performance diners. Meanwhile, the historical depravity of the area is remembered at the **Bow Street Magistrates Court**, home to author and one-time magistrate Henry Fielding's Bow Street Runners (original precursors to the Metropolitan Police), as well as the site of Oscar Wilde's notorious conviction, in 1895 for committing 'indecent acts'. Finally, the **Freemasons' Hall** – the impressive white building at the point where Long Acre becomes Great Queen Street (7831 9811) – is worth a peek, if only for its solemn, symbolic architecture: the only thing missing is an all-seeing eye in its imposing central tower.

If the sense of being watched is becoming creepy, have a pint in either the Salisbury on St Martin's Lane (7836 5863), the Cross Keys on Endell Street (7836 5185) or the Lamb and Flag tucked away on little Rose Street (7497 9504). There's peace in **Ching Court**, off Shelton Street, or the beautiful **Phoenix Garden** (21 Stacey Street, 7379 3187), *rus in urbs* writ large, where willow trees, fruit trees and honeysuckle attract the wildlife and lunch-time dreamers.

St Giles's

The reality of St Giles's may never have lived up to the legend, but immortalised so unfavourably in Hogarth's Gin Lane, and described with such venom by neighbour Charles Dickens, this once-squalid area can rightly be considered to have improved significantly in recent years, despite being overshadowed by the much-reviled Centrepoint office tower. Indeed, the 12 or so acres of predominantly Irish slums, which struck such fear into the heart of central London, remained a threat until the Metropolitan Board of Works scattered their inhabitants to make way for New Oxford Street in 1847. After an alarmingly effective mopping-up operation, all that remains of those dangerous days is the original church of **St Giles in the Fields** just behind Centrepoint on the High Street, which, in its current form dates

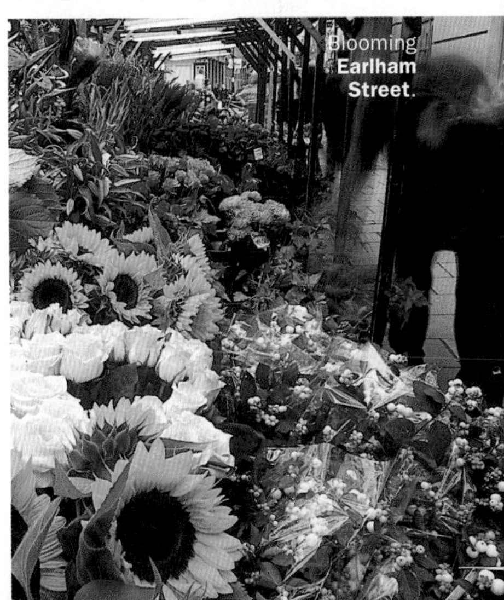
Blooming Earlham Street.

back to the early 1700s, although there's been a house of prayer on this site for more than 900 years. Just along the road, a pub known to Elizabethans simply as the Bowl mercifully offered last pints to condemned men on their short walk from Newgate to the gibbet at Tyburn. Don't be put off, however: the Angel (7240 2876), which now stands in its place, is a pleasant little watering hole you'll want to revisit, even if some never had that chance.

Beyond this, St Giles's is probably best known for the musical heritage of **Denmark Street**, affectionately known as Tin Pan Alley, and once home to Regents Sound Studios, where the Stones recorded 'Not Fade Away' and the Kinks cut their first demo. The Small Faces were signed at the Giaconda Café, where Bowie also met his first band, and the Sex Pistols wrote 'Anarchy in the UK' in what is now a guitar shop at No.6. These days, instrument sales and repairs are what Denmark Street does best (expect to be serenaded by an army of bedroom guitar soloists 'testing' the latest Fenders), although the **12 Bar Club**, which doubles up as a cheap and cheerful café in the afternoon, remains the city's most intimate songwriters' venue when the sun goes down.

Charing Cross Road means books. Bravely trying to stare out the world-famous and stubbornly traditional Foyles is the more modern Borders (for both, *see p230*). Still, the real gems are to be found in the smaller, specialised and second-hand stores including Henry Sotheran (7439 6151), Quinto (7379 7669) and Al Hoda (7240 8381), which is also a comprehensive Islamic study centre. Cult crews can snap up comics and movie memorabilia at Comic Showcase (7434 4349) or VinMagCo (7494 4064), across the road.

The Strand & Embankment

In 1292, the body of Eleanor of Castile, consort to Edward I, completed its funerary procession from Lincoln to the Westminster end of the Strand, then marked by the last of 12 elaborate crosses, reconstructed in 1863 behind the railings of Charing Cross Station. Strange to think that back then this bustling street – which connects Westminster to the City in a narrow, unbroken thread, as its name suggests – once ran directly beside the Thames.

Like much of Covent Garden, the Strand has endured its fair share of slings and arrows throughout history. As far back as the 14th century, the street was lined with waterside homes and gardens for the well-educated and well-to-do, and was still a highly reputable part of London at the time when Inigo Jones was poring over plans for the main square. Just as his piazza proved too small for the swelling market, so the Strand proved too thin for the wave of licentiousness rushing to fill the void left by the fleeing upper classes. It was a notorious blackspot for poverty and prostitution until the second half of the 19th century, when Sir Christopher Wren suggested the creation of a reclaimed embankment to ease congestion, beautify the riverside and house the main sewer (thus stopping the others from emptying directly into the Thames).

By the time George Newnes's *Strand* magazine was introducing its readership to Sherlock Holmes (1891), things were starting to look up. While never quite regaining the composure of more central parts of Covent Garden (there's little among its collection of overbearing office blocks and underwhelming restaurants to really fire the imagination today), Richard D'Oyly Carte's Savoy Theatre, created in the 1880s to host Gilbert and Sullivan operas and predating the world-famous hotel by eight years, gives some indication of how its fortunes began to change once again after the reinforced concrete Embankment was completed.

The **Embankment** itself can be approached down **Villiers Street** (from 2004, the Villiers Theatre Bar, in the atmospheric Arches shopping arcade, will be fully up and running: 7930 6601). Cut down Embankment Place to **Craven Street**, where at No.36 the American writer, scientist, philosopher and statesman Benjamin Franklin lived for 16 years from 1762. The London-based Benjamin Franklin House Foundation is working to restore the crumbling building where Franklin conducted his experiments and entertained, and make it into a museum. The house earned its blue plaque in 1914, and is expected to receive its first visitors in 2004, if the foundation can raise a further $1.4million (see www.rsa.org.uk/franklin).

Back to the Embankment, whence a number of boat tours with on-board entertainment, such as the Bateaux London restaurant (7839 3572) and the jolly Queen Mary floating nightclub (7240 9404), embark. On dry land stands **Cleopatra's Needle**, a stone obelisk first erected in Egypt under Pharaoh Tothmes III in 1500 BC, and which underwent truly epic adventures (not least of which was its being abandoned and then rescued after a storm in the Bay of Biscay in the 19th century) before being repositioned on the Thames in 1878. **Embankment Gardens**, on the opposite side of the road, is a tranquil park with an annual programme of free summer music played out on its small public stage, while among the flora you'll find statues erected to – among others – the poet Robert Burns, the political reformer Henry Fawcett and Richard D'Oyly Carte.

Westminster

Get your camera out – this is the heart of tourist London.

Maps p400 & p401

Embankment, Piccadilly Circus, Pimlico, St James's Park or Westminster tube/Charing Cross or Victoria tube/rail.

This is the London most tourists see on the postcards: Trafalgar Square, Buckingham Palace, Westminster Abbey, Big Ben – wham, bam, you've done the sights of London. It's an area where few Londoners actually live, and most don't even visit. And you can tell: the nightlife and shopping aren't exactly stellar. The tourist attractions are big stars, though. Westminster has been at the heart of the Church and monarchy for the better part of 1,000 years, since Edward the Confessor built his 'West Minster' and palace on marshy Thorney Island in the 11th century. Politics came to the fore in the 14th century, when the first Parliament met in the abbey. Today, the splendid Houses of Parliament provide an iconic backdrop for holiday photos: go on, pose in front of Big Ben.

Trafalgar Square

This classic landmark was the brainchild of the Prince Regent, later crowned George IV, who was obsessed with building monuments to celebrate imperial Britain. He commissioned his architect, John Nash, to create a grand square to pay homage to Britain's naval power, and raise the tone of the area. The square wasn't laid out until 1840, ten years after the King's death, but Nash certainly did as he was asked.

The square's star attraction is **Nelson's Column**, a tribute to the heroic Horatio, who died during the Battle of Trafalgar in 1805. This Corinthian column, designed by William Railton, is topped by a statue of Nelson, the work of neo-classical architect Charles Barry. Hitler was so impressed by the monument he ordered bombers not to touch it, hoping to erect it in Berlin once he had conquered Britain. The granite fountains at the base were added in 1845 (then redesigned by Lutyens in 1939); and the bronze lions – the work of Edwin Landseer – were added in 1868. Neo-classical buildings overlook the square: James Gibbs's **St Martin-in-the-Fields**, completed in 1726 (*see p128*), and one of the world's great art museums, the **National Gallery** (*see below*).

The square has always been one of the city's natural meeting points and is even more so since it was pedestrianised in 2003 (*see p129* **Pride of London**). Technically, this is the geographical centre of London: on a traffic island on the south side (look for the statue of King Charles I on horseback) there's a plaque to prove it. This is the point from which all distances on signposts are measured. Spiritually, too, it has always been the heart of London: the Chartists began their march here in 1848, many protest marches now finish here, and it's a boisterous spot on New Year's Eve.

National Gallery

Trafalgar Square, WC2N 5DN (7747 2885/ www.nationalgallery.org.uk). Leicester Square tube/Charing Cross tube/rail. **Open** (incl Sainsbury Wing) 10am-6pm Mon, Tue, Thur-Sun; 10am-9pm Wed. *Micro Gallery* 10am-5.30pm Mon, Tue, Thur-Sun; 10am-8.30pm Wed. *Tours* 11.30am, 2.30pm daily; 6.30pm Wed. **Admission** free. *Special exhibitions* prices vary. **Credit** *Shop* MC, V. **Map** p401 K7.

Founded in 1824, this is a national treasure. From a mere 38 paintings at the start, the collection has grown into one of the greatest in the world, with more than 2,000 classic Western European paintings. There are masterpieces from virtually every school of art, starting with 13th-century religious works and culminating in Van Gogh. You name it, they're here: Leonardo da Vinci, Raphael, Titian, Rubens, Rembrandt, Van Dyck, Caravaggio, Turner, Constable, Gainsborough, Monet, Cézanne and Picasso. You can't see everything in one visit, but there are guided tours that take in major works. The free audio guides (available at the two main entrances) offer excellent tours of the art.

The Sainsbury Wing concentrates on the early Renaissance period, with an emphasis on Italian and Dutch painters. In the North Wing, look out for masterpieces by Rubens, Rembrandt and Vermeer. The East Wing has a strong collection of English paintings, include Constable's *Hay-Wain,* Turner's romantic watercolours and works by Gainsborough, Reynolds and Hogarth. The real big ticket items, however, are the Impressionist paintings: Monet's *Water Lilies* series, Van Gogh's *Chair* and Seurat's *Bathers at Asnières* are the stars.

The gallery's plans for a £21m renovation, with a glass-roofed inner courtyard and two new entrances, received a setback in 2003 when the Duke of Northumberland announced he intended to sell Raphael's *Madonna of the Pinks*, which hangs in the

Trafalgar Square's new look. *See p129.*

National. The museum's decision to try to keep the small Raphael will cost the museum millions of pounds, and could delay the planned extension.

Exhibitions in 2004 include Bosch and Bruegel (until 4 April); El Greco (11 February-23 May); Dürer and the *Virgin in the Garden* (24 March-20 June); Russian Landscape – 19th-century paintings (23 June-12 September); Raphael (20 October-16 January 2005) and 'Art in the Making: Degas' (10 November-30 January 2005).

National Portrait Gallery

2 St Martin's Place, WC2H 0HE (7306 0055/ www.npg.org.uk). Leicester Square tube/Charing Cross tube/rail. **Open** 10am-6pm Mon-Wed, Sat, Sun; 10am-9pm Thur, Fri. *Tours* throughout Aug, times vary. **Admission** free. *Special exhibitions* £6; £4 concessions. **Credit** AmEx, MC, V. **Map** p401 K7.

Subjects for the portraits hanging here range from Tudor royalty to present-day celebrities. It's not exactly a complete history of the country, being more like a museum crossed with *Hello!* magazine, but it is entertaining. The portraits are organised chronologically from top to bottom: start on the second floor and work your way down.

One of the gallery's most prized possessions is the only known portrait of William Shakespeare. It's also a fascinating who's who of medieval monarchy: there's a room devoted to pictures of Mary, Queen of Scots, and a portrait of Henry VIII by Holbein. Dickens, Darwin and Disraeli (the latter painted by Millais) are among those on the first floor. The contemporary portraits, both painterly and photographic, run the gamut from Arthur Scargill, the miners' leader, to Margaret Thatcher, his enemy.

Exhibitions for 2004 include: a retrospective of the photographer Cecil Beaton, who photographed Marilyn Monroe, Audrey Hepburn and Andy Warhol (5 February-31 May); 'We Are the People' (3 March-20 June), a collection of Tom Phillips's portraits of life in Britain (3 March-20 June); 'Off the Beaten Track: Three Centuries of Women Travellers' (7 July-24 October); and GF Watts (14 October-9 January 2005).

St Martin-in-the-Fields

Trafalgar Square, WC2N 4JJ (7766 1100/Brass Rubbing Centre 7930 9306/box office evening concerts 7839 8362/www.stmartin-in-the-fields.org). Leicester Square tube/Charing Cross tube/rail. **Open** *Church* 8am-6.30pm daily. *Services* 8am, 8.30, 5.30 Mon-Fri; 1.05pm, 5pm Wed; 9am Sat; 8am, 10am, noon, 2.15pm, 5pm, 6.30pm Sun. *Brass Rubbing Centre* 10am-6pm Mon-Sat; noon-6pm Sun. **Admission** free. *Brass rubbing* £2.90-£15. *Evening concerts* £6-£20. **Credit** *Brass Rubbing Centre* AmEx, MC, V *Concert box office* MC, V. **Map** p401 L7.

A church has stood on this site since the 13th century, 'in the fields' between Westminster and the City; this one was built in 1726 by James Gibbs, who designed it in a curious combination of neo-classical and baroque styles. This is the parish church for Buckingham Palace (note the royal box to the left of the gallery), but it is perhaps best known for its classical music concerts (*see p302*). It also has a gem of a café (*see p209*), a small gallery, a gift shop and the London Brass Rubbing Centre. Its churchyard, home to a souvenir market, also contains the graves of painters Reynolds and Hogarth. There are plans for a £34m refurbishment that would give it wheelchair accessible lavatories and a glazed pavilion entrance.

Around the Mall

From Trafalgar Square, the grand processional route of the Mall passes under Aston Webb's 1910 **Admiralty Arch** to the **Victoria Memorial**. Contrary to appearances, the street was not designed as a triumphal entry to **Buckingham Palace** (*see p113*), which lies at its end. In fact, Charles II had the street laid out before the palace was even a royal residence, as he wanted a new place for *pallemaille*, a popular game that involved hitting a ball through a hoop at the end of a long alley. Nearby Pall Mall, had become too crowded for the sport.

As you walk along the Mall, look out on the right for **Carlton House Terrace**: the last project completed by John Nash before his death. It was built on the site of Carlton House, which was George IV's home until he decided it wasn't fit for a king and built Buckingham Palace to replace it. Part of the terrace now houses the **Institute of Contemporary Arts** (*see p130*), showcase for Brit Art.

Pride of London Trafalgar Square

This cosmetic surgery thing is getting out of hand. Society's obsession with smoothing over the blemishes has spilled over into architecture. Purists argue that these renovations remove all traces of character. But most Londoners aren't complaining. The Hungerford Bridge was recently given a spectacular facelift (*see p70*), the British Museum has been beautified beyond belief (*see p101*), and now London's greatest landmark, Trafalgar Square, has been given the make-over of the century (so far). Call us shallow, but after its £25million transformation, we've fallen in love with Trafalgar Square all over again.

That said, the biggest change is not cosmetic: it's psychological. Architect Norman Foster's 2003 pedestrianisation of the north side of the square was an act of liberation. Gone is the bus-filled, polluted gridlock, replaced by a serene expanse of elegant York stone. For those who have experienced Trafalgar Square in the past as a sea of double deckers and jostling crowds, the new spaciousness is almost dizzying: it feels like you've been let out of tourist prison. Speaking of which, a bronze statue of Nelson Mandela is scheduled to be erected here some time in 2004 – an apt choice.

As with the best facelifts, the gradual transformation of Trafalgar Square has been subtle. The simple granite steps from the National Gallery down into the square blend with the neo-classical gallery, lending the building even more gravitas. And a new café has been thoughtfully hidden under the steps, so the Costa Coffee sign won't blight the 19th-century splendour. As Foster himself remarked, 'This isn't the place for an architectural ego trip'. It is now, however, a good place for a day trip.

The new wall of steps is now one of the capital's great places to sit and watch the world go by. There are fewer pigeons to poop on you: Mayor Ken Livingstone's programme to eradicate 'rats with wings' from the square – by gradually reducing their feed – is reducing their numbers. The scavengers will probably never disappear completely, and this may be a good thing: Trafalgar Square without pigeons is like Soho without the sex – it just wouldn't be right.

Nor would Trafalgar Square be Trafalgar Square without an acrimonious debate about the empty plinth. The stone pedestal was created 160 years ago for a statue of William IV, but the project was abandoned because of lack of funds. After that, it stood empty. In recent years it has become the showcase for avant-garde sculptures, notably Rachel Whiteread's inverted perspex plinth. Traditionalists will no doubt fume at the latest shortlist of artists who may get to fill the empty space: Marc Quinn, who once made a cast of his head using his own blood; Chris Burden, an American who had himself shot in the name of performance art and Sarah Lucas, whose work revolves around sex. Still, in the case of the plinth, the enhancement won't be permanent: each sculpture will be removed after 18 months.

Meanwhile, with or without the controversial artworks, new-look Trafalgar Square basks in the glory of its architectural Botox and Londoners are again proud to be seen in the company of such beauty.

On the south side of St James's Park (*see p113*) the Wellington Barracks, home of the Foot Guards, contains the **Guards' Museum** (*see below*). At the park's southern end is Birdcage Walk, named for the aviary James I built there. Nearby are the Georgian terraces of Queen Anne's Gate and Old Queen Street.

Guards' Museum

Wellington Barracks, Birdcage Walk, SW1E 6HQ (7414 3428). St James's Park tube. **Open** 10am-4pm daily (last entry 3.30pm). **Admission** £2; £1 concessions; free under-16s. **Credit** *Shop* AmEx, MC, V. **Map** p400 J9.

The Changing of the Guards, at St James's Palace and Buckingham Palace, is one of London's great spectacles. (*see p258* **A few to catch**). This small museum, founded in the 17th century under Charles II, records the history of the British Army's five Guards regiments. It contains mainly uniforms and oil paintings, set to an accompaniment of martial music. A collection of curios includes the Guards' oldest medal (awarded by Cromwell to officers of his New Model Army at the Battle of Dunbar in 1651. The shop has a good selection of toy soldiers.

Sightseeing

ICA Gallery

The Mall, SW1Y 5AH (box office 7930 3647/ www.ica.org.uk). Piccadilly Circus tube/Charing Cross tube/rail. **Open** *Galleries* noon-7.30pm daily. **Membership** *Daily* £1.50, £1 concessions Mon-Fri; £2.50, £1.50 concessions Sat, Sun; free under-14s. *Annual* £30; £20 concessions. **Credit** AmEx, DC, MC, V. **Map** p401 K8.

The ICA basks in controversy. In 2002 Ivan Massow, the gallery's chairman, resigned after calling much of the art championed by his institution 'pretentious, self-indulgent, craftless tat'. Which raises the question: why was he chairman? After all, the ICA's *raison d'être* is to challenge traditional notions of art. Since it opened in 1948, scores of challengers have held their first exhibitions here: Henry Moore, Picasso, Max Ernst and, more recently, Damien Hirst, Helen Chadwick and Gary Hume. Its cinema (*see p281*) shows London's artiest films, its theatre stages twisted performance art, and its temporary exhibitions are always talking points. Check out the shop for cutting-edge coffee table books and critical theory tomes. In 2004 the fourth annual Beck's Futures exhibition and art prize features the best of contemporary painting, sculpture, photography, installation and video (2 Apr-16 May).

Whitehall to Parliament Square

You're in civil servant territory now. Lined with faux-imperial government buildings, the long, gentle curve of Whitehall is named after Henry VIII's magnificent palace, which burned to the ground in 1698. The street is now home to the Ministry of Defence, the Ministry of Housing and the Treasury. These buildings are closed to the public, but if you can, pop into the **Whitehall Theatre** (No.14) for a peek at its gorgeous art nouveau interior. Halfway down the street, the **Horse Guards** building faces the **Banqueting House** (*see below*), central London's first classical-style building.

Nearby is Edwin Lutyens's plain memorial to the dead of both world wars, the **Cenotaph** and, on **Downing Street** (closed off by iron security gates), the equally plain homes of the prime minister and chancellor. At the end of King Charles Street sit the **Cabinet War Rooms** (*see p131*), the operations centre used by Churchill during World War II air raids.

At the end of Whitehall, **Parliament Square** has architecture on a grand scale. Constructed in 1868, it features the fantastical neo-gothic **Middlesex Guildhall** (1906-13) on the west side, just behind it is **Westminster Central Hall**, with its great black dome. It was built on the site of the old Royal Aquarium in 1905-11 and is used for conferences (the first assembly of the United Nations was held here in 1946) as well as for Methodist church services. The buildings overlook the shady square with its statues of British politicians, such as Disraeli and Churchill, and one outsider – Abraham Lincoln, who sits sombrely to one side.

Nearby, **Westminster Abbey** (*see p133*) is resplendent in white. Similarly shaped but much smaller, **St Margaret's Westminster** (*see p132*) stands to its side: both Samuel Pepys and Winston Churchill were married here.

If it is true, as some say, that few buildings in London genuinely dazzle, the handsome **Houses of Parliament** (*see p131*) are an exception. The Gothic structures are gorgeous. Although formally still known as the Palace of Westminster, the only surviving part of the medieval royal palace is Westminster Hall (and the **Jewel Tower**, just south of Westminster Abbey, *see p132*). One note: legendary **Big Ben** is actually the name of the bell, not the Parliament's clock tower. In its shadow, at the end of Westminster Bridge, stands a statue of the warrier Boudicca (*see p7*) and her daughters gesticulating toward Parliament.

Banqueting House

Whitehall, SW1A 2ER (7930 4179/www.hrp.org.uk). Westminster tube/Charing Cross tube/rail. **Open** 10am-5pm Mon-Sat (last entry 4.30pm). **Admission** £4; £3 concessions; £2.60 5-15s; free under-5s. **Credit** MC, V. **Map** p401 L8.

Built in 1622, this was the first Italianate building in London, and the first great masterpiece of neo-classicist Inigo Jones. It is the only surviving part of Whitehall Palace, which burned down in 1698. The cool simplicity of the exterior stands in stark contrast to the glorious first-floor hall, which is adorned with ceiling paintings by Rubens. Charles I commissioned the Flemish artist to glorify his less

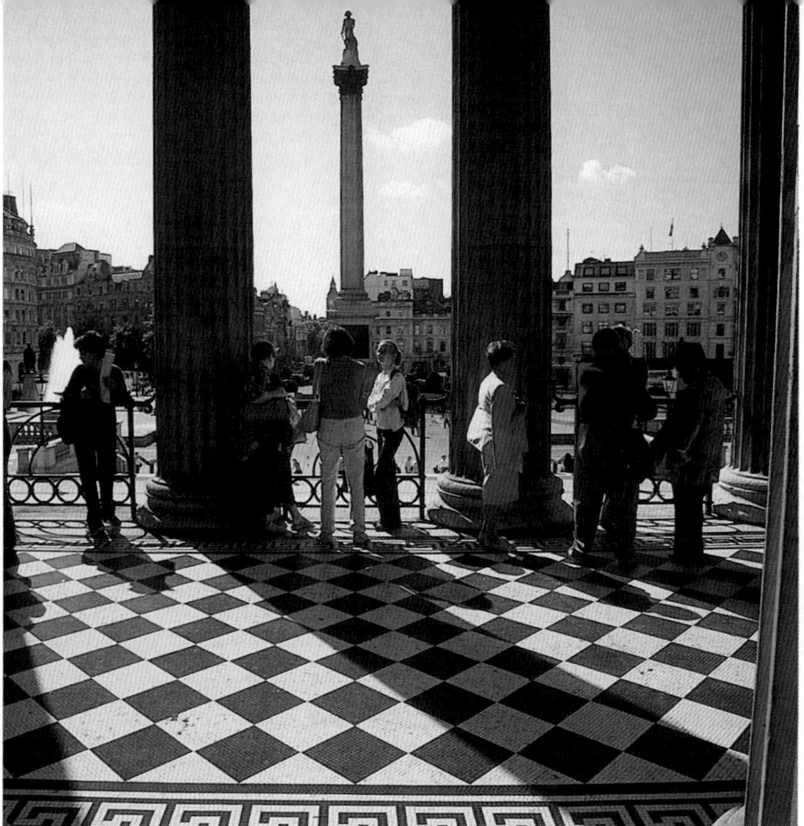

Nelson's Column framed in the **National Gallery**'s front porch. *See p127.*

than glamorous father James I and celebrate the divine right of the Stuart kings. A bust over the entrance commemorates the fact that Charles was beheaded here in 1649. The building's history is explained in an exhibition in the undercroft. Call to check the hall is open before you visit: the building is used for corporate functions and sometimes closes to accommodate them.

Cabinet War Rooms

Clive Steps, King Charles Street, SW1 2AQ (7930 6961/www.iwm.org.uk). St James's Park or Westminster tube. **Open** *Oct-Mar* 10am-6pm daily. *Apr-Sept* 9.30am-6pm daily. Last entry 5.15pm. **Admission** £7; £5.50 concessions; £3.50 disabled; free under-15s. **Credit** MC, V. **Map** p401 K9.

The secret underground HQ of Churchill during World War II, the Cabinet War rooms resemble a perfectly sealed time capsule. Virtually nothing has been touched since it was closed on 16 August 1945: every book, chart and pin in the map room remains in place, as does the BBC microphone he used when addressing the nation. Churchill's bedroom, the setting for his catnaps, displays a chamberpot and nightshirt; the Transatlantic Telephone Room had a hotline to the White House; and there's also a collection of Churchill's papers and speeches. Last year, the museum opened the Churchill Suite, private rooms that include the PM's kitchen and his wife's bedroom. The furnishings are spartan, evoking the wartime atmosphere. The audio guide's sound effects – wailing sirens, Churchill's wartime speeches – add to the nostalgia. The War Rooms are set to open a new Churchill museum in 2005.

Houses of Parliament

Parliament Square, SW1A 0AA (Commons information 7219 4272/Lords information 7219 3107/www.parliament.uk). Westminster tube. **Open** (when in session) *House of Commons Visitors' Gallery* 2.30-10.30pm Mon; 11.30am-7.30pm Tue, Wed; 11.30am-6.30pm Thur; 9.30am-3pm Fri. *House of Lords Visitors' Gallery* from 2.30pm Mon-Wed; from 11am Thur, occasional Fri. *Tours* summer recess only; phone for details. **Admission** Visitors' Gallery free. *Tours* £7; £5 concessions; free under-2s. **Credit** *Tours* MC, V. **Map** p401 L9.

This neo-gothic extravaganza is so spectacular it's enough to make you want to go into politics. Its ornate architecture is the ultimate expression of Victorian self-confidence, even if its style was a throwback to the Middle Ages. Completed in 1854,

Big Ben is the bell inside. *See p130.*

it was the creation of Charles Barry and Augustus Pugin, hired for the job after the original Houses of Parliament were destroyed by fire in 1824. Pugin hated the sober neo-classical style of the day, so added as many decorative flourishes as possible. The original palace was home to Henry VIII, until he upped sticks to Whitehall in 1532. Although the first Parliament was held here in 1275, Westminster did not become Parliament's permanent home until Henry moved out. Parliament was originally housed in the choir stalls of St Stephen's Chapel where members sat facing each other from opposite sides, and the tradition continues today. The only remaining parts of the original palace are the Jewel Tower and Westminster Hall, one of the finest medieval buildings in Europe.

In all, there are 1,000 rooms, 100 staircases, 11 courtyards, eight bars and six restaurants. None of them is open to the public, but you can watch the Commons or Lords in session from the galleries. In truth, there's not much to see: most debates are sparsely attended and unenthusiastically conducted. Visitors queue at St Stephen's Entrance (it's well signposted) and, in the high season, may have to wait a couple of hours. At most other times of year, though, you'll not wait long at all. There's no minimum age but children must be able to sign their name in the visitors' book. The best spectacle is Prime Minister's Question Time at noon on Wednesdays, but you need advance tickets for this (available through your MP or embassy). Parliament goes into recess at Christmas, Easter and summer, at which times the galleries are open only for pre-booked guided tours. To be sure you can get in, check www.parliament.uk or call before you come.

Jewel Tower

Abingdon Street, SW1P 3JY (7222 2219/ www.english-heritage.org.uk). Westminster tube. **Open** *Apr-Sept* 10am-6pm daily. *Oct* 10am-5pm daily. *Nov-Mar* 10am-4pm daily. Last entry 30mins before closing. **Admission** (EH) £2; £1.50 concessions; £1 5-16s; free under-5s. **Credit** MC, V. **Map** p401 L9.

There are no jewels inside. There used to be: the tower was built in 1365 to house Edward III's baubles. But it's still worth a look as, along with Westminster Hall, it is the only surviving part of the medieval Palace of Westminster. From 1621 to 1864 the tower stored Parliamentary records, and it contains an exhibition on Parliaments past. The records housed there can be consulted by anyone.

St Margaret's Church

Parliament Square, SW1P 3PL (7654 4840/ www.westminster-abbey.org). St James's Park or Westminster tube. **Open** 9.30am-3.45pm Mon-Fri; 9.30am-1.45pm Sat; 2-5pm Sun (times may change at short notice due to services). *Services* 11am Sun; phone to check for other days. **Admission** free. **Map** p401 K9.

Westminster Abbey.

Founded in the 12th century, this historic church was demolished in the reign of Edward III, but rebuilt from 1486 to 1523. Since then it has been restored many times. As the official church of the House of Commons since 1614, its bells are rung when a new Speaker of the House is chosen. Above the doorway is a bust of Charles I, looking across the street at a statue of his old adversary, Oliver Cromwell. Inside, the impressive east window (1509), with its richly coloured Flemish glass, commemorates the marriage of Henry VIII and Catherine of Aragon. Later windows celebrate Britain's first printer, William Caxton, buried here in 1491, explorer Sir Walter Raleigh, executed in Old Palace Yard, and writer John Milton (1608-74), who married his second wife, Katherine Woodcock, here.

Westminster Abbey

20 Dean's Yard, SW1P 3PA (7222 5152/tours 7222 7110/www.westminster-abbey.org). St James's Park or Westminster tube. **Open** *Chapter House, Nave & Royal chapels* 9.30am-3.45pm Mon, Tue, Thur, Fri; 9.30am-7pm Wed; 9.30am-1.45pm Sat. *Abbey Museum* 10.30am-4pm Mon-Sat. *Cloisters* 8a.-6pm Mon-Sat. *College Garden* Apr-Sept 10am-6pm Tue-Thur. Oct-Mar 10am-4pm Tue-Thur. Last entry 1hr before closing. *Services* 7.40am, 8am, 12.30pm, 5pm Mon-Fri; 8am, 10am, 11.15am, 3pm, 5.45pm, 6.30pm Sun. **Admission** £6; £4 concessions; free under-11s with paying adult; £12 family. **Credit** MC, V. **Map** p401 K9.

Westminster Abbey has been synonymous with British royalty since 1066, when Edward the Confessor built a church on the site, just in time for his own funeral: it was consecrated eight days before he died. Since then, a who's who of monarchy have been buried here, and, with two exceptions, every king and queen of England since William the Conqueror (1066) has been crowned in the Abbey.

Of the original abbey, only the Pyx Chamber (the one-time royal treasury) and the Norman Undercroft remain; the Gothic nave and choir were rebuilt by Henry III in the 13th century; the Henry VII Chapel, with its spectacular fan vaulting, was added in 1503-12; and Hawksmoor's west towers completed the building in 1745.

The interior is cluttered with monuments to statesmen, scientists, musicians and poets. Poets' Corner contains the graves of Dryden, Samuel Johnson, Browning and Tennyson (although it has plaques for many more, most are buried elsewhere). The centrepiece of the octagonal Chapter House is its faded 13th-century tiled floor, while the Little Cloister with its pretty garden offers respite from the crowds, especially during free lunchtime concerts (call for details). Worth a look, too, are ten statues of 20th-century Christian martyrs in 15th-century niches over the west door. Come early, late, or on midweek afternoons to avoid the crowds.

Millbank

Millbank runs along the river from Parliament to Vauxhall Bridge. Just off here is **Smith Square**, home to two old-fashioned British institutions: **St John's Smith Square**, an exuberant baroque fantasy built as a church in 1713-28, but now a venue for classical music (*see p302*) with a nice basement bar/restaurant, and the Conservative Party headquarters (at No.32). Nearby, on Lord North Street, is a clutch of fine Georgian houses – one of the most prestigious addresses in London. By the river, the Victoria Tower Gardens contain a statue of the suffragette leader, Emmeline Pankhurst, a cast of Rodin's glum-looking *Burghers of Calais* and the Buxton Drinking Fountain, which commemorates the emancipation of slaves.

Further along the river, just north of Vauxhall Bridge, stands the **Tate Britain** museum (*see p134*). With its excellent collection of British art, it occupies the former site of the Millbank Penitentiary, one of Britain's fouler Victorian prisons, which was demolished in 1890. The misery was replaced with art in 1897; a gift to the nation from sugar magnate cum philanthropist Sir Henry Tate. Overshadowing the Tate is the 387-foot (240-metre) **Millbank Tower**, erstwhile home to the Labour Party. Across the river, the cream and green-glass office block is the rather conspicuous HQ of the internal security service, MI6.

Tate Britain

Millbank, SW1P 4RG (7887 8000/www.tate.org.uk). Pimlico tube/C10, 77A, 88 bus. **Open** 10am-5.50pm daily. *Tours* 11am, noon, 2pm, 3pm Mon-Fri; noon, 3pm Sat, Sun. **Admission** free. *Special exhibitions* prices vary. **Credit** *Shop* MC, V. **Map** p401 K11.

Tate Modern (*see p78*), its younger, sexier sibling, seems to get all the attention, but don't forget the Britain: it contains London's second great collection of art, after the National Gallery (*see p127*). With the opening of the Modern, oodles of space were freed up to accommodate the collection of British art from the 16th century to the present day.

The collection fills the 'something for everyone' remit that you'd hope from a gallery whose exhibits span five centuries. It takes in works by artists such as Hogarth, the Blakes (William and Peter), Gainsborough, Constable (who gets three rooms all to himself), Reynolds, Bacon and Moore. Turner is particularly well-represented, even more so since last year, when the gallery recovered two classics – *Shade and Darkness, The Evening of the Deluge*; *Light and Colour* (Goethe's Theory) – that were stolen in 1994. And Tate Modern doesn't have a monopoly on contemporary artists: there are works here by Howard Hodgkin, Lucian Freud, and David Hockney. The shop is well stocked with posters and art books, and the restaurant highly regarded.

You can now have the best of both art worlds, thanks to a new Tate-to-Tate boat service (*pictured on p78*); this sleek catamaran decorated dottily by Damien Hirst shows videos previewing the galleries' collections as it takes you back and forth between the two. Tickets (£4.50) are available at both galleries for by calling 7887 8888.

Exhibitions planned for 2004 include 'Pre-Raphaelite Vision: Truth to Nature' (12 February-3 May); Sarah Lucas, Damien Hirst and Angus Fairhurst 'In-a-Gadda-da-Vida' (3 March-31 May); 'Michael Landy, Duveens Sculpture Commission' (28 Apr-26 Sept); 'Art of the Garden' (3 June-30 August); 'British Art in the 1960s' (3 June-3 October); 'Gwen and Augustus John' (29 September-9 January); and Turner Prize 2004 (20 October-23 January).

Victoria & Pimlico

Victoria Street, stretching from Parliament Square to Victoria Station, links political London with a rather more colourful and chaotic backpackers' London. Victoria Coach Station is a short distance away in Buckingham Palace Road; Belgrave Road provides an almost unbroken line of cheap and fairly grim hotels.

In the 18th and early 19th centuries, this area was dominated by the Grosvenor Canal, but in the 1850s much of it was buried under the new Victoria Station. A century later, many of the shops and offices along Victoria Street were pulled down and replaced by the anonymous blocks that now line it.

Not to be confused with the abbey a few blocks away, **Westminster Cathedral** (*see below*) is partially hidden by office blocks, and comes as a pleasant surprise. The striking, red-brick Byzantine church was built between 1896 and 1903, but its interior was never finished.

Continuing along Victoria Street towards Parliament Square, you come to **Christchurch Gardens**, burial site of Thomas ('Colonel') Blood, the 17th-century rogue who nearly got away with stealing the Crown Jewels. A memorial is dedicated to the suffragettes, who held meetings at Caxton Hall, visible on the far side of the gardens. **New Scotland Yard**, with its famous revolving sign, is in Broadway, but there's not much else to see there. **Strutton Ground**, on the other side of Victoria Street, has a small market. Richard Rogers's **Channel Four Building** is on the corner of **Chadwick Road** and **Horseferry Road**.

At the other end of Victoria Station from Victoria Street, smart **Pimlico** fills the triangle of land formed by Chelsea Bridge, Ebury Street, Vauxhall Bridge Road and the river. Thomas Cubitt built the elegant white stone streets and squares in the 1830s. The posh neighbourhood was immortalised in one of the great Ealing Comedies, *Passport to Pimlico*, in which the local residents discover that their district is technically part of France. In general, though, Pimlico is residential and a bit dull for tourists, filled largely with foreign embassies.

Westminster Cathedral

Victoria Street, SW1P 1QW (7798 9055/ www.westminstercathedral.org.uk). Victoria tube/rail. **Open** 7am-7pm Mon-Fri, Sun; 8am-7pm Sat. *Services* 7am, 8am, 10.30am, 12.30pm. 1.05pm, 5.30pm Mon-Fri; 8am, 9am, 10.30am, 12.30pm, 6pm Sat; 8am, 9am, 10.30am, noon, 5.30pm, 7pm Sun. **Admission** free; donations appreciated. *Campanile* £3; £1.50 concessions; £7 family. **No credit cards.** **Map** p400 J10.

Westminster Abbey is more famous, but Westminster Cathedral is spectacular in its own bizarre way. Part wedding cake, part candy cane, this neo-Byzantine confection is Britain's premier Catholic cathedral, built in 1895-1903 by John Francis Bentley, who was inspired by the Hagia Sophia in Istanbul. The land on which it is built had been a bull-baiting ring and a pleasure garden before being bought by the Catholic Church in 1884. With such a festive exterior, you'd expect an equally ornate interior. Not so: the inside was never finished. You can get a taste of what could have been from the magnificent columns and mosaics (made from more than 100 kinds of marble). Eric Gill's sculptures of the Stations of the Cross (1914-18) are world renowned. The nave is the broadest in England, and the dark wood floors and flickering candles add to the drama. The view from the 273ft (83m) bell tower is superb: best of all, it's got a lift.

South Kensington & Knightsbridge

Annexed by royalty, open to all.

South Kensington

Maps p396 & p397

The Millenium Dome may be little more than an inverted crater in Greenwich (*see p167*), but not all of London's attempts to glorify social progress have crash-landed so spectacularly. In 1851 the Great Exhibition of the Works and Industry of All Nations drew six million visitors in less than six months – more than the Dome mustered in a year. Championed by Prince Albert, the exhibition's profits went towards fulfilling his dream of founding a capital of intellectual activity and creative thought in South Kensington. That's why so many academic institutions and museums line its streets today. Imperial College (7589 5111) and the Royal College of Music (7589 3643) nestle together on Prince Consort Road (the latter with a collection of 700 instruments dating from 1480, open on Wednesdays during term time). The Royal Geographical Society (7591 3000), on Exhibition Road, has statues of explorers David Livingstone and Ernest Shackleton set into its walls. There are various international institutes (French, German, Polish, Islamic) softening the surrounding upper lip a little.

The most significant museums in the area are the **Natural History Museum** (*see below*) with its dinosaurs and dodos, the **Science Museum** (*see p136*) with its technology and inventions and the beautiful, antique-filled **Victoria & Albert** (*see p137*).

Reflections of the ancient Sophistic cultures are everywhere, not least in the enchanting fresco on the **Royal Albert Hall** (*see p302*). The mansions gloating over the venue are some indication of the effect Albert's aspirations had on surrounding land values, but it isn't all for the wealthy: 'the Proms', summer concerts here (*see p305*) bring classical music to all.

Natural History Museum

Cromwell Road, SW7 5BD (7942 5000/ www.nhm.ac.uk). South Kensington tube. **Open** 10am-5.50pm Mon-Sat; 11am-5.50pm Sun. **Tours** hourly, 11am-4pm daily. **Admission** free; tours £3; £1.50 children, concessions. **Credit** AmEx, MC, V. **Map** p397 D10.

It may be best known for the Diplodocus skeleton that has towered over generations of excited children in the entrance hall, but there's more than just dinosaurs to be seen in this architecturally stunning museum, and it's not just for kids. The main building divides roughly into Life Galleries and Earth Galleries: highlights of the former include the prehistoric lizards, of course, and the Creepy Crawlies hall, with its live ants and robotic arthropods, while the latter houses the Restless Surface exhibit, which shows how natural elements shape the planet. The odd 'supermarket shake' re-creation of the Kobe earthquake is the draw here, particularly for children. The Wildlife Garden is open to the public between May and September. Phase one of the new Darwin Centre – open for tours (every half-hour 10.30am-5pm daily, booking essential) – is home to an incredible collection of the obscure 'type' specimens from which species were first identified and named, some more than 200 years old, and all kept in eerie, temperature-controlled jars. Creepiest of all is the Tank Room, with the largest specimens – fish, snakes, monkeys – in huge jars and stainless steel tanks. An exhibition on the mightiest dinosaur ('T-Rex: The Killer Question') explodes myths until 3 May 2004. Entries for the Wildlife Photographer of the Year competition will be displayed until April 2004.

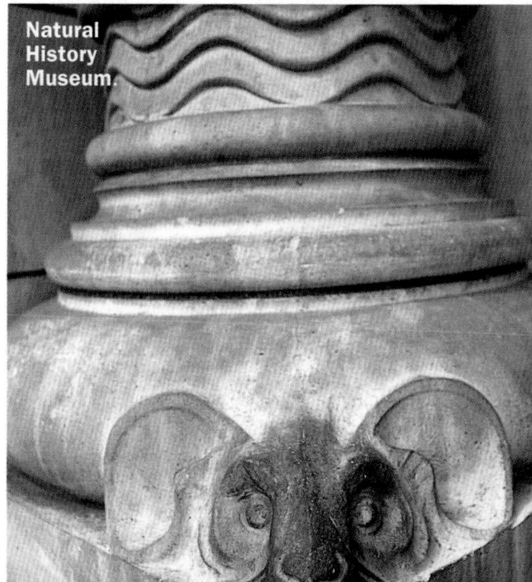
Natural History Museum.

Pride of London Scenic Serpentine

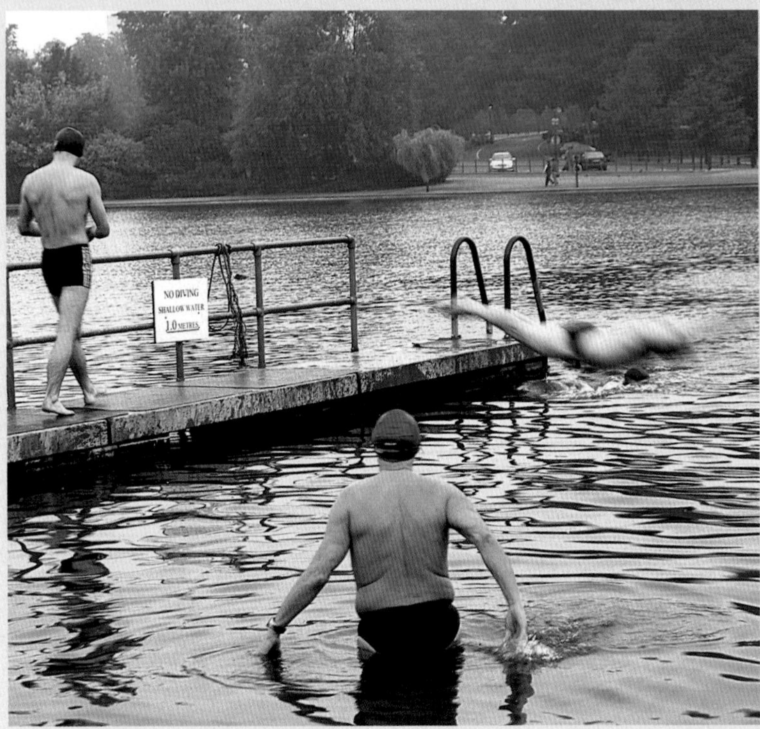

With the 200th anniversary of Nelson's victory at Trafalgar in 1805 fast approaching, plans are under way to recreate the entire battle in miniature on the surface of the **Serpentine Lake**. It won't be the first time – in 1814, crowds cheered as a flotilla of flaming three-foot (0.9 metre) replicas of the French ships sank beneath the water to strains of the national anthem. Boats haven't always found it so hard-going on the Serpentine, however. Dammed from the River Westbourne in 1730 at the behest of Queen Caroline, the lake was originally conceived as one large playground for royal yachts. These

Science Museum

Exhibition Road, SW7 2DD (7942 4454/www.sciencemuseum.org.uk). South Kensington tube. **Open** 10am-6pm daily. **Admission** free. *Temporary exhibitions* prices vary. **Credit** AmEx, MC, V. **Map** p397 D9.

If this is the most popular of South Kensington's 'big three', that's because it breathes new life into a subject frequently dismissed as boring. Over seven floors, this incredible museum takes science off the page and into reality and – through cutting-edge displays – demonstrates it as a force that can power ships and put people in space (check out the working naval engines on the ground floor, or the reconstructed Apollo landing module next door). There's interactive fun: sparks fly in the hands-on Launch Pad gallery, and there's a five-storey IMAX cinema simulating larger than life experiences from weightlessness to deep-sea diving. The Dana Centre, with its bar and restaurant, opened in November 2003. It's an informal venue for adults to voice their concerns, and raise questions, about contemporary science issues. Programming is by the Science Museum, the British Association for the Advancement of Science and the Dana Alliance. Opening 12 February 2004, 'Pain' is the fourth in a days, rowing boats can be rented by the general public (March to October, 10am to 6.30pm daily), although broadsides will be met with stern disapproval.

In 1816, Harriet Shelley, pregnant wife of poet Percy Bysshe, drowned herself in the Serpentine after learning that her husband had eloped with 16-year-old Mary Godwin (the future Mrs Shelley – they were married two weeks after he learned of Harriet's death).

Ten years later, George Rennie's prominent bridge divided the lake of the southern Serpentine from the more scenic **Long Water**, which winds its way towards **Lancaster Gate** and the **Italian Gardens**, a series of fountains in front of an ornate pumphouse.

Royal grounds are apt to establish obscure rules and regulations: whether these are deliberately aimed at starting even stranger traditions is open to debate, but there's no doubt that the **Serpentine Swimming Club** (www.serpentineswimmingclub.com) is one of the city's more amusing institutions. Since 1864 the club has capitalised on the few hours when it remains legal to go for a constitutional dip anywhere in the Serpentine. And constitutional is the word: in winter, swimmers will break holes in the ice to get their fix, and the 100-yard race held every Christmas morning is a highlight of the annual calendar, with the winner picking up the Peter Pan cup, so called because it used to be presented by the character's creator JM Barrie. Anyone with an alarm clock can join: the club assembles on the banks at 8am every Saturday morning, and newcomers are encouraged to simply turn up on the day.

For less bracing experiences, the Serpentine **Lido** (*see p323*), a buoyed off area of the lake, is open to casual swimmers between June and September, with a veranda for fair-weather frolics, a busy restaurant for refreshments and a paddling pool. Everyone loves the winsome bronze statue of Peter Pan, just to the north-east of Long Water. It was commissioned by Barrie and kept secret until its appearance, as if by magic, on the morning of 1 May 1912.

series of art-science collaborations with the Wellcome Trust. The exhibition looks at the human response to pain and dealing with it, using modern artists' work alongside the Science Museum's collections of historical medical artefacts.

Victoria & Albert Museum

Cromwell Road, SW7 2RL (7942 2000/ www.vam.ac.uk). South Kensington tube. **Open** 10am-5.45pm Mon, Tue, Thur-Sun; 10am-10pm Wed, last Fri of mth. **Tours** daily; phone for details. **Admission** free. *Temporary exhibitions* prices vary. **Credit** AmEx, MC, V. **Map** p397 E10.

Recently accused of shameless populism (for its fashion retrospectives on Gianni Versace, Coco Chanel and Ossie Clarke), it seems the V&A has trouble finding a middle ground. Not long ago it was revealed that huge swathes of the local population didn't even know what was inside its beautiful if scarred façade (the brickwork on Exhibition Road was damaged by bombs in WWII), and those that did considered it a frumpy, dusty institution. But while there is something to be said for displaying a cone-breasted catsuit by Jean Paul Gaultier a stone's throw from Italian Renaissance sculpture, the V&A's collection of decorative arts – from Britain,

Europe and Asia – is the best in the world, and reflects centuries of achievement in ceramics, sculpture, furniture making, jewellery, metalwork, textiles and dress. Around four million objects are held here, including the finest collection of Italian Renaissance sculpture outside Italy. The World Galleries span the ground floor, with displays including Chinese Imperial robes and huge Persian carpets. The British galleries are ordered chronologically from the Tudors to the Victorians and were recently restored at a cost of £31 million; they include such treasures as Henry VIII's writing desk and James II's wedding suit. Shows in 2004 will include a display of innovative domestic lighting designs (12 Feb-25 Apr), and a retrospective exhibition by British photographer Bill Brandt (18 Mar-25 July). A model of Daniel Libeskind's spiral extension to the museum (scheduled for 2007) is in the foyer.

Hyde Park & Kensington Gardens

Maps p394 & p395

During the all too fleeting London summers it can sometimes feel like the entire population has quit the city's congested streets for the green lungs of Hyde Park and Kensington Gardens. Not that it matters: whatever the weather, the parks are large and rambling enough for everyone to find a spot away from Frisbees and footballs. It wasn't always a free-for-all though. Snatched from the Church by Henry VIII for hunting grounds, the parks were first opened to the public in the reign of James I, although they were only frequented by the upper echelons of society. The most lingering royal foundations weren't laid until the end of the 17th century when William III, suffering from asthma and averse to the dank air of Whitehall Palace, relocated to the village of Kensington and made his home in Kensington Palace. A corner of Hyde Park was sectioned off to make grounds for the palace, and although today the two merge, Kensington Gardens was closed to the public until King George II opened it on Sundays to those in formal dress only – soldiers, sailors and servants were not welcome.

These days, soldiers form an integral part of the area's attraction for tourists: at 10.30am each day (9.30am on Sundays), after a brief warm up in the park, the Household Cavalry leave their high-rise barracks near the Prince of Wales Gate, and trot in full ceremonial dress to Whitehall for the Changing of the Guard.

There are plenty of less formal attractions in Hyde Park, however, not least of which is the central **Serpentine Lake** (*see p136* **Pride of London**), while several sculptures of note include GF Watts's violently animated *Physical Energy*, a delightful bronze of Peter Pan and Jacob Epstein's depiction of *Rima, Spirit of Nature*, the unabashed nakedness of which inspired such anger upon its unveiling in 1925 that it was tarred and feathered twice for its sins. That said, Hyde Park first became a hotspot for mass demonstrations in the 19th century, and remains so today – an anti-Iraq War march in 2003 was the largest in its history. Adding to its political allure, the legalisation of public assembly in the park led to the establishment of **Speakers' Corner** in 1872. This isn't the place to come for balanced, political debate: more often than not it's a case of soapbox religious mania struggling to make itself heard above a noisy mob of hecklers. Those with young children may feel more comfortable at the pristine **Diana, Princess of Wales Memorial Playground** (*see p271*), part of a commemorative seven-mile (10.5-kilometre) walk designed in memory of the Queen of Hearts. Work on Diana's long-mooted memorial fountain finally began in mid 2003.

Kensington Palace

W8 4PX(7937 9561/www.hrp.org.uk). Bayswater, High Street Kensington or Queensway tube. **Open** 10am-5pm (last entry) daily. **Admission** (LP) £10.50; £7 5-15s; £8 concessions; £31 family. **Credit** AmEx, MC, V. **Map** p394 B8.

Far more intimate than other, more resoundingly regal palaces, Kensington exudes a warm, homely feel that visitors are quick to associate with its most recent resident, Princess Diana. A series of her dresses, including a blue silk number in which she once took to the dancefloor with John Travolta at a White House party, are now permanently on display alongside the Royal Ceremonial Dress Collection, an exhibition of royal livery. If this wasn't enough, around 100 of the Queen's hats and handbags are on show until 18 April 2004. Those who'd rather avoid the high entry fees to the State Apartments (the palace itself is closed to visitors) can still enjoy a walk around the sunken gardens, or take tea in the Orangery café with its charming topiary gardens.

Serpentine Gallery

Kensington Gardens (nr Albert Memorial), W2 3XA (7402 6075/www.serpentinegallery.org). Lancaster Gate or South Kensington tube. **Open** 10am-6pm daily. *Tours* 3pm Sat. **Admission** free.

Despite its prime park location and the delicate 1930s tea pavilion in which it's housed, the Serpentine refuses to be judged by its cover. So small you could blink and miss it, the gallery nonetheless continues to court controversy with challenging exhibitions by modern artists, this year including American-born painter Cy Twombly (14 April until the end of May 2004), with work by Mexican artist Gabriel Orozco later in the summer. Also, each year, a contemporary architect is commissioned to design an outdoor pavilion, which then plays host

Prince **Albert** before his **Hall**. *See p135.*

to the annual Park Nights programme of open-air screenings, readings and talks (June to September): the 2003 pavilion was the work of Oscar Niemeyer, who helped create the UN Headquarters in New York. There's also a first-rate arts bookshop on site.

Albert Memorial

Hyde Park (opposite Royal Albert Hall), SW7 (tours 7495 0916/www.tourguides.co.uk). South Kensington tube. **Open** *Tours* 2pm, 3pm Sun. **Admission** £3.50; £3 concessions.

By all accounts Prince Albert was a self-effacing chap, so presumably he's spinning in his grave over this spectacular memorial where even the dramatic 180ft (55m) spire is inlaid with semi-precious stones. This is, however, more a testament to the man's intellectual legacy. Created by Sir George Gilbert Scott and unveiled in 1876 – 15 years after Albert's death from typhoid – the Prince is surrounded on all sides by marble statues of famous poets and painters, while pillars are crowned with depictions of the sciences, and the arts are represented in a series of intricate mosaics. Guided tours take visitors behind the protective railings.

Knightsbridge

Maps p395-p397, p400

Knightsbridge may no longer be plagued by highwaymen, but that doesn't mean people aren't still leaving with significantly lighter wallets. This is a shopper's paradise: the vogueish **Harvey Nichols** (*see p233*) still holds sway over **Sloane Street**, where urban princesses glare at each other, their heels clicking against the polished marble. The range of designer headquarters on this otherwise unremarkable street – Chanel, Yves Saint Laurent, Bulgari – let's you know you're in a moneyed neighbourhood. There are no cafés, and few places for lunch. More understated is **Beauchamp Place**, a peaceful road that was a favourite of Princess Diana, set back from the main thoroughfare and with plenty of good restaurants to break up the haute couture.

That's all well and good, of course, but this is Knightsbridge, and Knightsbridge means one thing in the eyes of the wave of tourists flooding Brompton Road each afternoon: **Harrods** (*see p233*). From its tan bricks to its olive green awning with natty yellow trim and top-hatted doormen, Harrods is an instantly recognisable retailing legend. Originally a family grocer's, the world's most famous department store now employs 5,000 people and takes over £1.5 million per day. Under owner Mohammed Al Fayed it may be ageing gracefully, but Harrods wasn't without its misspent youth: its first aeroplane was sold in 1919, and in 1967 the Prince of Albania purchased a baby elephant for Ronald Reagan.

Brompton and Belgravia serve primarily as residential catchment areas for wealthy families who imagine they couldn't survive without Harrods' dog grooming service on their doorstep. To which extent, it's strange to find a pillar of penitence like the **Oratory Catholic Church** (*see below*) amid the excess.

There's not much else in Brompton to fire the imagination, however, bar Arne Jacobson's **Danish Embassy** building (55 Sloane Street) and the prospect of peering into other people's living rooms. Belgravia is a little better, if only for the few nice pubs tucked away behind its serious marble parades: the Nag's Head on Kinnerton Street (*see p222*) and the Grenadier on Wilton Row are worth seeking out. **St Paul's Knightsbridge**, on Wilton Place, is an appealing Victorian church with scenes from the life of Jesus in ceramics tiling the nave, and a wonderful wood-beamed ceiling. Otherwise, the area is characterised by a cluster of foreign embassies all struggling to do the neighbourly thing around Belgravia Square.

Oratory Catholic Church

Thurloe Place, Brompton Road, SW7 2RP (7808 0900/www.brompton-oratory.org.uk). South Kensington tube. **Open** 6.30am-8pm daily. **Admission** free; donations appreciated. **Map** p397 E10.

Westminster Cathedral may be the biggest Catholic church in the country but this one, in second place sizewise, is the spookiest. The Oratory was completed in 1884, but many of its florid marbles, mosaics and statuary are much older. Mazzuoli's late 17th-century apostle statues, for example, once stood in Siena cathedral. The combined effect of the treasures in shimmering candlelight is awe inspiring. During the Cold War, the church was used by the KGB as a dead letter box.

Chelsea

Where punk was born, flowers now flourish, and everybody has too much cash.

Maps p396 & p397

Sloane Square tube.

A rich district, certainly, in both historical and financial terms, but Chelsea's coolness is now open to question. This once-arty, bohemian part of town chattered in the 1880s, swung in the 1960s and snarled a decade later as the home of punk. These days, however, the cost of living here has seen off the colourful painters and poets, and has dulled its cutting edge. But this doesn't detract from smart Chelsea's tourist appeal. A walk through the streets leading off the King's Road (its main thoroughfare) unearths some fetching treasures.

At the end of the **King's Road** closest to the tube station, **Sloane Square** gets its name from Sir Hans Sloane (1660-1753), a physician and canny entrepreneur who bought the Manor of Chelsea and saved the famously restorative **Chelsea Physic Garden** (*see p142*) from decline. His heirs are the Cadogans, who still own the large Chelsea Estate, and a number of other things. The **Royal Court Theatre** (*see p331*), with its reputation for avant-garde theatricals, looks imperiously down on the King's Road, past the polished department store beloved of lunching ladies from the Shires, Peter Jones (*see p211*).

Pride of London
Chelsea Pensioners

The Royal Hospital in Chelsea is not your average old folks' home, but then the Chelsea Pensioners are not your average old folks. About 350 of them live here, all of them ex-soldiers. Their quarters, the Royal Hospital, was founded in 1682 by Charles II (the inspiration for the hospital came from Louis XIV's Hôtel des Invalides in Paris). The building was designed by Sir Christopher Wren and intended to house all army pensioners. When the forces were expanded under James II, the original quadrangle was joined by further courts.

The building took a decade to complete, with later adjustments added by Robert Adam and Sir John Soane, who also designed the infirmary destroyed by bombing in 1941. A new Infirmary opened 20 years later.

The little six-square-foot oak-panelled rooms designed by Wren have been enlarged over the years to more comfortable nine-square-foot spaces. During the day, many of the hospital's residents take the air on benches on the quad, gazing at the bright red pelargoniums in the window boxes, or at the central statue of King Charles.

Sunday worship takes place in the chapel, and the magnificent Great Hall, across the passage, is where the pensioners take their meals. Retired soldiers are eligible to apply for a final posting here if they are over 65, in receipt of an Army or War Disability Pension for Army Service (this they hand over to pay for their keep) and free of obligation to support a wife and family.

The in-pensioners are organised into companies, along military lines, with a governor and other officers, including medical officers, a quartermaster and a chaplain, but they are free these days to have leave of absence or holidays. In fact, life is much easier for them now than it was in the 18th century, when they had to stand guard shifts throughout the night, to protect the road from the Royal Hospital to St James's.

Today, in-pensioners have their own club room, amenity centre, billiard rooms, library, bowling green and gardens. Some work in the museum, which tells you more about the life of a pensioner from the 17th century to the present day. Free to enter, the museum has a mock-up of an in-pensioner's room, designed by Wren, and there are ceremonial arms, medals bequeathed by former residents and uniforms on display. The museum also has a number of paintings, the most arresting of which is *The Last Muster*, which shows an old

Overall, the King's Road is not what it once was, sadly. Once the trendiest street in London, it still has a few independent boutiques and antiques markets (including Antiquarius, No.131-41), but its glory days are largely over. Back in the swinging '60s, it became a focal point for designers such as Mary Quant (whose shop, Bazaar, stood at No.138) who dared the city to wear their creations. In the 1970s it became the bedrock for the punk movement, when Vivienne Westwood's shop, Sex, made headlines with its outlandish approach to style. It was there that Malcolm McLaren famously met John Lydon and Sid Vicious, and from that shop that the Sex Pistols reportedly got their names. Westwood still has a shop there (World's End, No.430) where the floor slopes drunkenly and the clock outside counts backwards, but the fashions within don't shock like they used to, which is somewhat symbolic of the King's Road itself, which is much like a particularly posh high street these days, all Gaps and Starbucks. One of the bright spots is Bluebird (No.350), a Terence Conran restaurant with a Sainsbury's attached. That doesn't come cheap, and it's easy to imagine what Sid Vicious would think of the street now.

Between the King's Road and Chelsea Embankment, the grounds of the **Royal Hospital** are best known these days as the site of the flashy, posh celebrity-magnet Chelsea Flower Show (*see p260*), but for 51 weeks of the year the area is quiet and peaceful, as befits a place of sanctuary for retired soldiers (*see below* **Pride of London**).

The old Ranelagh Gardens are now part of the hospital grounds, and are put to good use every year for the Chelsea Flower Show. Opened in 1742, this verdant stretch once had an ornamental lake, a Chinese Pavilion and large rococo rotunda surrounded by stalls for tea and wine drinking. The surrounding shrubbery and wooded paths were meeting and posing place for nobility and society.

soldier breathing his last during service in the chapel.

The familiar scarlet coat and tricorn hat the old soldiers wear for ceremonial duties date back to the 18th century. Pensioners march redcoated to a military band, each wearing an oak leaf in his buttonhole, on Oak Apple Day. The leaves are laid at the statue of Charles II, to commemorate the day the King climbed into an oak tree to escape Cromwell's men after the Battle of Worcester. The red coats aren't in evidence when you visit the hospital on an ordinary day: dark trousers and pale blue shirts are worn for relaxing at home.

Royal Hospital Chelsea

Royal Hospital Road, SW3 4FR (7730 5282). Sloane Square tube/11, 19, 22, 137, 211, 239 bus. **Open** 10am-noon, 2-4pm Mon-Sat (*May-Sept also* 2-4pm Sun). **Admission** free. **Map** p397 F12.

Riverside Chelsea

Continuing down Royal Hospital Road toward the **Chelsea Physic Garden** (*see below*), and just past the **National Army Museum**, you pass **Tite Street**, where Whistler once had a studio, and where dramatist Oscar Wilde lived (at No.34) before his arrest for gross indecency at the Cadogan Hotel. Edwardian Chelsea, when Whistler and Wilde socialised there, was self-consciously stylish.

The heart of the original Chelsea village is **Chelsea Old Church** (*see below*), where the saint and statesman Thomas More once sang in the choir. More's river-facing home, Beaufort House, is long gone. You can still see parts of the original orchard wall bordering the gardens of the houses on the west side of Paulton's Square off Beaufort Street. More's country life ended in 1535 when he was thrown into the Tower of London by Henry VIII for refusing to swear to the Act of Succession and the Oath of Supremacy. L Cubitt Bevis's statue of the 'man for all seasons' stands outside the Old Church.

The artists and writers' community in Chelsea was centred at the western end of Chelsea Embankment, on **Cheyne Walk**, where the fashionable houses have changed little over the centuries. Blue plaques are thick on the walls: Pre-Raphaelite painter Rossetti at No.16; George Eliot at No.4; JMW Turner at No.119; James McNeill Whistler at No.96. Thomas Carlyle lived on **Cheyne Row**, north of the Walk, and his house is open to view.

Further west, the transformation of **Chelsea Harbour** from industrial wasteland into opulent offices, swish hotels, shops, restaurants and marina have made it a playground for the rich and famous. Downriver, **Lots Road Power Station** (*see map p397*) once the power behind London Underground, became a target for property developers when the last generator was turned off in October 2002 (plans for a tall apartment block there were rejected in 2003).

Carlyle's House

24 Cheyne Row, SW3 (7352 7087/www.nationaltrust.org.uk). Sloane Square tube/11, 19, 22, 39, 45, 49, 219 bus. **Open** *Apr-Oct* 2-5pm Wed-Fri; 11am-5pm Sat, Sun; last admission 4.30pm. **Admission** (NT) £3.70; £1.80 5s-16s. **Map** p397 E12.

This house witnessed lively argument and tension when the prim scholar lived here from 1834 with his long-suffering wife Jane. In the well-preserved house visitors can see the original decor, furniture, books and pictures. At the top is the windowless study where the writer insisted on complete quiet to write *The French Revolution* (the manuscript of which was thrown into the fire by a careless maid, forcing Carlyle to start all over again).

Chelsea Old Church

Cheyne Walk, Old Church Street, SW3 5DQ (7352 5627/www.domini.org/chelsea-old-church). Sloane Square tube/11, 19, 22, 49, 319 bus. **Open** 1.30-5pm Tue-Fri; 8am-1pm, 2-7pm Sun. **Admission** free; donations appreciated. **Map** p397 E12.

Most of the ancient church, which dates back to the 13th century, was destroyed by a bomb in 1941. The Thomas More Chapel remains on the south side, and legend has it that his headless body is buried somewhere under the walls, but his head, after being spiked on London Bridge (as was the custom in the brutal 16th century) was rescued and buried in a family vault in St Dunstan's Church, Canterbury.

Chelsea Physic Garden

66 Royal Hospital Road (entrance in Swan Walk), SW3 (7352 5646/www.chelseaphysicgarden.co.uk). Sloane Square tube/11, 19, 22, 239, 319 bus. **Open** *Apr-late Oct* noon-5pm Wed; 2-6pm Sun. *Tours* times vary. **Admission** £4; £2 5-16s, concessions (not incl OAPs). *Tours* free. **Credit** *Shop only* MC, V. **Map** p397 F12.

This therapeutic garden was founded in 1673 by the Worshipful Society of the Apothecaries of London, and remains a draw today. The garden's objective was to provide medical students with the means to study plants used in healing, and Sir Hans Sloane (for whom Sloane Square is named) helped to develop it in the early 18th century. The grounds are used today for research and education. Many of the beds in the 3.8 acres (1.5 hectares) are tended by students. The garden was opened to the public in 1983, but hours are limited. A free tour conducted by one of the garden's entertaining volunteers traces the history of the medicinal beds, where mandrake, yew, feverfew and other herbs are grown for their efficacy in treating illness.

National Army Museum

Royal Hospital Road, SW3 4HT (7730 0717/www.national-army-museum.ac.uk). Sloane Square tube/11, 19, 239 bus. **Open** 10am-5.30pm daily. **Admission** free. **Map** p397 F12.

This disarmingly friendly museum seems rather empty and sad these days. It must be tough having the more famous Imperial War Museum (*see p168*) as a direct competitor. But this low-key place is enthusiastically run, and boasts a full events calendar of interest to many. Children come here for workshops with historians dressed as soldiers, amateur historians come for the lectures, and wargame fanatics for the model demonstrations of famous battles. The museum is on four floors, with the art gallery at the top alongside a display with films on the developing roles of the modern army. Other galleries include the 'Road to Waterloo', where visitors can see three short films over an enormous model of the battle employing 70,000 model soldiers. There's also the skeleton, supposedly of Napoleon's favourite horse, Marengo, a trench mock-up for the 'World at War 1914-1946' exhibition and a Tudor cannon – the oldest object in the museum.

North London

Richly rustic, edgily urban, Camden Town crusty – variety is the spice of northern life.

Camden

Camden Town or Chalk Farm tube.

Like many of London's now-fashionable addresses, Camden Town has had a long association with lowlife. Cheap lodging houses dominated the area around the time when the Regent's Canal was laid out in 1816, and it was rough in Victorian times too, at least according to Charles Dickens, who grew up in Bayham Street. In later decades Irish and Greek immigrants laid down roots here, and by the 1960s this indisputably poor area had earned itself a raffish, bohemian character.

Around this time, arty types, among them writer Alan Bennett, saw the potential of the tall, spacious houses and elegant crescents, and moved into the area; white-collar professionals followed, and today Camden has a decidedly middle-class flavour. The architecture has grown more affluent with the locals: Camden folk now eschew the traditional markets and buy their provisions from Nicholas Grimshaw's high-tech 1988 Sainsbury's supermarket on Camden Road. Yet the area is still not without its edge: nightly, Camden Town tube is garlanded with exotic types, whether punks and goths in full regalia or the rather less photogenic (but basically harmless) junkies.

Teenagers and students love the area for **Camden Market** (*see p250*), but the fact that this once-alternative hangout is one of London's big tourist attractions means that the crowds can be unpleasant and bargains are few and far between. Within the market, the worthwhile stalls include collectibles in the Stables and the crafts and unusual homewares in the main Market Hall, but the overriding impression is of litter, grime and too many people trying too hard to have a good time. There is, of course, more to the neighbourhood than Camden High Street and the market, but you'd do well to explore it out of market hours to avoid the rabble.

The **Roundhouse** on **Chalk Farm Road**, built as a tram turning point and then converted into a prominent 1960s music venue, is being redeveloped as a performance space and media centre (7424 9991). It will reopen in spring 2005… if another £14 million in funding can be found. The lovely **Jewish Museum** (*see below*), just off Parkway, is a gem, and a reflection of the area's cultural diversity. However, Camden is let down by its eating and drinking options; there are loads of grim bars and restaurants round here. Try a cheap cake or seafood pasta dish from one of the Portuguese cafés on Plender Street or excellent pub food at the Engineer (65 Gloucester Avenue, 7722 0950), and then cool down with an ice-cream at Marine Ices (8 Haverstock Hill), a local institution.

Jewish Museum, Camden

129-31 Albert Street, NW1 7NB (7284 1997/ www.jewishmuseum.org.uk). Camden Town tube. **Open** 10am-4pm Mon-Thur; 10am-5pm Sun. **Admission** £3.50; £2.50 OAPs; £1.50 5-16s; free under-5s. **Credit** MC, V.

One of a pair (its sister is in Finchley; *see p152*), Camden's Jewish Museum provides a fascinating insight into one of Britain's oldest immigrant communities. Different aspects of six centuries of Jewish life are illustrated through oil paintings, artefacts from a tailor's 'sweatshop', silver and chinaware, and photographs and passports. The museum also has one of the world's finest collections of Jewish ceremonial art, including a collection of silver Hanukkah candlesticks, spice boxes and an amazing 16th-century Italian synagogue ark, brought to Britain in the 19th century by an Englishman who had picked it up while doing his European Grand Tour. Audio-visual programmes provide information on Jewish festivals and Jewish life, while the temporary exhibitions in 2004 include the 'Story of the Jews' Free School' (until 29 February).

Around Camden

Primrose Hill, to the north of Camden, is as pretty as the actors, pop stars and writers who live there. The main shopping street, Regent's Park Road, is a pleasant mix of independent cafés and smart shops. Not so far away, though, **Kentish Town**, with its bargain stores, looks rather grubby by comparison. Around these parts, traditional London boozers trade up into restaurant class before you can say 'gastropub'. Head to Highgate Road for grub and a pint at the Vine (No.86) or the Bull & Last (No.168).

South and east of Camden, bucolic **Camley Street Natural Park** (*see p269*) is the London Wildlife Trust's flagship reserve. The **Regent's**

New Camden is epitomised by Nicholas Grimshaw's starkly modern **Sainsbury's**.

Canal, which runs along one side of the park, opened in 1820 to provide a working waterway to link east and west London; the **London Canal Museum** (*see below*) has all the history. The towpath's in good shape, so you can take a stroll along it from Little Venice through Primrose Hill into Camden itself.

London Canal Museum

12-13 New Wharf Road, King's Cross, N1 9RT (7713 0836/www.canalmuseum.org.uk). King's Cross tube/rail. **Open** 10am-4.30pm Tue-Sun. **Admission** (LP) £2.50; £1.25 8-16s, concessions; free under-8s. **Credit** MC, V. **Map** p399 L2.

The warehouse containing this small museum on the Regent's Canal's Battlebridge Basin was built in the 1850s by Carlo Gatti, an Italian immigrant who made his fortune importing ice from Norway's frozen lakes to the vast ice well that's open to view in the museum floor. Photos and videos tell the Gatti story, and further footage and exhibitions give the lowdown on the hardships endured by those who made their living on the canals. There are intricate models of boats upstairs and a barge cabin in which visitors can sit.

St John's Wood

St John's Wood or Swiss Cottage tube.

Rural calm prevailed in St John's Wood until well into the 19th century, when the only development around the wooded hills and meadows were smart stucco villas. The pure air attracted artists, scientists and writers: Mary Anne Evans (aka George Eliot) often held receptions at her house here. A blue plaque marks the gloriously ostentatious house at 44 Grove End Road once owned by the artist Sir Lawrence Alma-Tadema, but the interior is sadly closed to the public.

In the 19th century, the houses, reasonably inexpensive but very pretty, suited rich men, who used them to house their mistresses. The building work carried out by the Great Central Railway in 1894 destroyed the rural calm, but sensitive redevelopment during the 1950s has left the area smart, desirable and fabulously expensive, which is reflected in chic boutiques of the exceedingly couth High Street.

Lord's, the world's most famous cricket ground (*see p145*), is the reason most people visit, but Beatles fans have their own reasons. Grove End Road leads to **Abbey Road**, made famous by the Fab Four when its recording facility was still officially called EMI Studios (No.3). The crossing outside is always busy with tourists scrawling their names on the wall.

Up the Finchley Road from St John's Wood, you'll find that a **Swiss Cottage** actually exists, its black and white timbers smiling coyly at visitors. The structure is on the site of a Swiss-style tavern at the Junction Road Toll Gate. The excitement stops at the entrance, sadly, but don't leave without sampling the superlative cakes at Louis Pâtisserie, around the corner at 12 Harben Parade.

Village green Highgate

Sit down on a bench in **Pond Square**, what remains of the old Highgate Green, and the first thing you notice is the peaceful rustling of the trees overhead. You won't see any green beneath your feet – the square's been paved with asphalt. Pond Square hasn't actually had any ponds since 1869 either, as the two dug here in the Middle Ages were filled in 1869. But some bits of the square's history endure. Every village has a ghost, and Highgate's is a chicken.

The story goes like this: one day scientist and philosopher Sir Francis Bacon – who was staying at Arundel House (now **Old Hall**, on South Grove) in the 1620s – was struck by inspiration and ordered his driver to buy and kill a chicken. Bacon stuffed the creature's body with snow, thereby inventing frozen meat. In a coup of poetic justice for animal lovers, Bacon was struck down by fatal pneumonia shortly after his discovery. No more was seen of Bacon, but the chicken is still said to haunt Pond Square.

The flapping and squawking reported by ghost-sighters would likely have gone unnoticed during much of the square's history, as until the 19th century Highgate Green was the fairground and social hub of the village. Its ponds were convenient for watering horses, so for centuries the village was a pit stop for travellers toiling up and down steep Highgate Hill between the city of London and the north. In the Middle Ages, a toll gate here was one of the three ways into the Bishop of London's great park of Haringey, or Hornsey. Nothing remains of the gate now on its former site on the High Street at Highgate West Hill, unless you count its commemoration in the name of the Gatehouse pub (8340 8054), itself a clearly branded Wetherspoon chain affair. The gate, an arch with rooms inside, linked a tavern to a burial ground; the latter is still here, and now part of the grounds of the Highgate School, on this site since 1565. Frederick Prickett, in his *History and Antiquities of Highgate* (1842), lamented the demise of many of the tall trees and of the good, clean fun – such as ball games and quoits – that had once defined the green. Today, he'd be spinning in his grave at the rumour that Pond Square is none too safe.

Another landmark is the **Highgate Literary & Scientific Institution**, at 11 South Grove. One of London's last remaining post-Reform Act cultural societies, it's been here since 1840. Members share a reading room and library. On the other side of the square, across Highgate West Hill, sharply pointed roofs mark Highgate's covered reservoir. Nearby, 3 The Grove was the home of the poet Samuel Taylor Coleridge for the last three years of his life; now, he's in St Michael's, at the bottom of South Grove. Just across the grass is the cosy Flask Tavern (77 Highgate West Hill, 8348 7346), festooned with vines and flowers. In the 18th century water from the Hampstead Wells was sold here, and the owner's hens roamed the streets. Artist regulars included William Hogarth, one of whose sketches captured the hardcore-drinker's grin on the face of a man who'd been hit in the head with a pint pot during a quarrel.

Highgate has long had the role of refreshing travellers, and it has always been dotted with pubs. Fortunately for visitors, some things haven't changed.

Lord's Tour & MCC Museum

Marylebone Cricket Club, Lord's, St John's Wood Road, NW8 8QN (7432 1033/www.lords.org). St John's Wood tube/13, 46, 82, 113, 274 bus.
Open *Oct-Mar* noon, 2pm daily. *Apr-Sept* 10am, noon, 2pm daily. **Admission** £7; £5.50 concessions; £4.50 5-15s; free under-5s. **Credit** MC, V.

Though their reputation is that of progress-fearing stick-in-the-muds, the wearers of the famous egg-and-bacon striped tie have nonetheless accepted the NatWest Media Centre, the stunning raised pod that dominates the self-proclaimed home of cricket. The Centre joins the portrait-bedecked Long Room on the guided tour (you'll need to book), along with the expected collection of battered bats, photos and blazers. There's plenty of WG Grace ephemera, a stuffed sparrow felled by a ball in 1936 and, of course, the Ashes. No matter how often the Aussies win 'em, you can rest assured that cricket's holy grail – the story of whose creation is related with appealing dryness – will remain here.

Hampstead

Golders Green or Hampstead tube/Hampstead Heath rail.

Like many rural villages on the fringes of the city, Hampstead was a popular retreat from the city in times of plague. Its undulating

A plaque on both your houses

There is one thing that unites Mahatma Gandhi with Boris Karloff, PG Wodehouse and Emile Zola: a blue plaque. These small, distinctive blue discs 19 inches (48 centimetres) in diameter have festooned buildings since 1867, when the Royal Society of Arts decided to mark the residences of the capital's famous and notorious, and put one on Byron's now-demolished house in Holles Street in Mayfair.

The earliest plaque survivors, from 1875, are all in central London, one for 17th-century poet John Dryden at 43 Gerrard Street in Soho, and one to the less-known Napoleon (Napoleon III) at 1C King Street, St James.

By the time the London County Council took over from the RSA in 1901 there were 36 brown plaques around town. English Heritage later inherited the scheme when the council was abolished in the 1980s, and now there are nearly 800 plaques about.

Anyone can propose a plaque, but EH has its rules. It won't consider anyone who's not been dead for 20 years, their names must be instantly recognisable to the man in the street (although it's quite clear that some have played fast and loose with this rule in the past), they should have made some important contribution to human welfare or happiness, or be regarded as eminent by a majority of members of their own profession.

Only the actual buildings associated with people are marked (formerly it was whatever stood on a historic site, however new) and if you've been commemorated on one building, you won't get another plaque anywhere else.

There will soon be too many markers in south London, now that Southwark Council has recently launched an annual scheme (after readers of the *Southwark News* complained that the borough wasn't getting its share of historical recognition) whereby any resident can nominate a person or spot, and the most popular 20 will be marked with a 'People's Plaque'. In 2003 Globe Theatre founder Sam Wanamaker topped the list, followed by the Clink Prison (*see p77*).

A street's blue plaques can throw together some unlikely bedfellows. Posh mid-Georgian Brook Street in Mayfair boasts Handel, the man who wrote the 'Hallellujah Chorus', as he once lived upstairs at Nos.23-5 while, in his own time, Jimi Hendrix lived downstairs at the same address. With a total of nine, Hampstead's Frognal Street is positively measled with plaques. Its erstwhile residents include Victorian illustrator Kate Greenaway at No.39, politicians Ramsey MacDonald (No.103) and De Gaulle (No.99) who lived here during his London exile 1940-42. It must have been particularly noisy at times during the 1950s with hornplayer Dennis Brain (No.37) jostling with opera singer Kathleen Ferrier (No.97).

The **Freud Museum** (*see p147*), is one of few houses to boast two plaques: one to the father of psychoanalysis, and one to his daughter Anna, a pioneer of child psychiatry.

In 2003, English Heritage's plaque picks included the controversial poet Ezra Pound at 10 Kensington Church Walk, in Kensington, and the dance band leader Henry Hall at 38 Harman Drive in West Hampstead. The cabbie Fred Hitch is commemorated at 62 Cranbrook Road in Chiswick, in recognition for the fact that he won the Victoria Cross at the age of 22 for heroism as a wounded soldier at the siege of Rorke's Drift in 1879.

thoroughfares and protected heath ensured that urbanisation never really happened here, and the village remains somewhat exclusive to this day. For centuries Hampstead has been the favoured roosting place for literary and artistic bigwigs; Keats and Constable called it home in the 19th century, while a century later, during the 1930s, modernist and surrealist artists such as Barbara Hepworth and Henry Moore lived the village London idyll here.

Hampstead tube station stands at the top of the steep High Street. The twin lines of the higgledy-piggledy terraces that make up Church Row, one of Hampstead's most beautiful streets, lead down to **St John at Hampstead** (7794 5808), a less ostentatious cemetery than its near-neighbour Highgate, but just as restful and bucolic. Among those of note buried here are Constable and, in an unmarked plot, the comedian Peter Cook, who lived near here.

Close by, on Holly Hill, is Hampstead's antique Holly Bush pub (*see p223*), which was painter George Romney's stable block until he moved to rustic Hampstead to get over his obsession with Nelson's paramour, Lady Hamilton. Another minute's climb will bring you to **Fenton House** (*see p147*), while the celestially inclined should potter round the corner to **Hampstead Scientific Society Observatory** (Lower Terrace, 8346 1056).

Take a cooling countryside dip in **Hamstead Heath's** traditional bathing ponds.

Sightseeing

East of Heath Street, a maze of attractive streets shelters **Burgh House** on New End Square, a Queen Anne house that now contains a small museum, and **2 Willow Road** (*see p149*), a residence built by émigré Hungarian architect Ernö Goldfinger for himself and his family in the 1930s. Nearby, off Keats Grove, is **Keats House** (*see p148*), where he did most of his best work. The bullet-marked Magdala pub on South Hill Park is where Ruth Ellis shot her former boyfriend in 1955 and earned her place in history as the last woman hanged in Britain; her family still campaigns for the murder charge to be commuted.

Hampstead Heath was the inspiration for CS Lewis's Narnia, and is the city dweller's countryside. The views of London from the top of **Parliament Hill** are stunning; on hot days, the murky bathing ponds (men's, women's and mixed, open daily all year) are a godsend. There are concerts here on summer Sundays; pick up an events diary at information points on the heath. Nearby is **Kenwood House** (*see p150* **The crown of Iveagh**), while the historic pub the Spaniards Inn, on the edges of the heath, has been a top choice for drinkers ever since legendary highwayman Dick Turpin galloped here for a quick pint.

Camden Arts Centre

Arkwright Road, corner of Finchley Road, NW3 6DG (7604 4504/www.camdenartscentre.org). Finchley Road tube/Finchley Road & Frognal rail. **Open** phone to check. **Admission** free. **Credit** *Shop only* MC, V.

Following a lengthy £4 million refurbishment, this innovative centre dedicated to contemporary visual art is scheduled to reopen in January 2004. The money has been spent on new galleries and studios, a café and landscaped gardens.

Fenton House

3 Hampstead Grove, NW3 6RT (7435 3471/ information 01494 755563/www.nationaltrust. org.uk). Hampstead tube. **Open** *Mar* 2-5pm Sat, Sun. *Apr-Oct* 2-5pm Wed-Fri; 11am-5pm Sat, Sun. **Tours** phone for details. **Admission** (NT) £4.50; £2.25 5-15s; free under-5s. *Joint ticket with 2 Willow Road* £6.30. **No credit cards**.

Devotees of early music will be impressed by the collection of harpsichords, clavichords, virginals and spinets housed at this William and Mary house. The bequest was made on condition that qualified musicians be allowed to play them, so you may get to hear them in action (if not, phone for details of the fortnightly summer concerts). The porcelain collection won't appeal to everyone – the 'curious grotesque teapot' certainly is, as are the poodles – but for fans, there's work by Meissen and Rockingham. The gardens are a delight (£1 unless visiting the house), with the small orchard coming into its own for October's Apple Day celebration. Out of season, enjoy the exterior: join the walking tours that begin in the '30s at 2 Willow Road (*see p149*) and go back in time through Georgian and Edwardian Hampstead to end up here (£6; 01494 755572).

Freud Museum

20 Maresfield Gardens, NW3 5SX (7435 2002/ www.freud.org.uk). Finchley Road tube. **Open** noon-5pm Wed-Sun. **Admission** £5; £2 concessions; free under-12s. **Credit** MC, V.

After Anna Freud's death in 1982, the house she and her father, Sigmund, shared for the last year of his life became a museum. The analyst's couch sits in the study, round glasses and unsmoked cigars setting the scene, and the copious library is impressive, but more intellectual or biographical context would be appreciated, especially for the uninitiated. Extracts from Freud's writings require a good deal of concentration to piece together. Upstairs, there's footage of the various branches of the Freud family,

Where the poet wrote: **Keats House**.

Anna's room (with another couch and handloom) and a gallery. This is one of the few buildings in London to have two blue plaques (*see p146* **A plaque on both your houses**): commemorating both father and daughter (she was a pioneer in child psychiatry), they were unveiled by comedian John Cleese in 2002.

Keats House

Keats Grove, NW3 2RR (7435 2062/www.keatshouse.org.uk). Hampstead Heath rail/ Hampstead tube/24, 46, 168 bus. **Open** *Apr-Oct* noon-5pm Tue-Sun. *Nov-Mar* 10am-4pm Tue-Sun. **Tours** 3pm Sat, Sun. **Admission** £3; £1.50 concessions; free under-16s. **Credit** MC, V.

From 1818 to 1820, this little house was the home of the noted Romantic poet; today, it attracts quite obscene numbers of visitors every year. The building reopened in July 2003 after a long building maintenance programme; there's now more to see (albeit most of it fascinating only to Keats fans). You can now view other rooms, attend events and talks in the poetry reading room and see a new display on Keats' sweetheart Fanny Brawne. The garden in which he wrote 'Ode to a Nightingale' is a pleasant place to wander in romantic reverie.

2 Willow Road

2 Willow Road, NW3 1TH (7435 6166/ www.nationaltrust.org.uk). Hampstead tube/ Hampstead Heath rail. **Open** *Mar, Nov* noon-5pm Sat. *Apr-Oct* noon-5pm Thur-Sat. Last entry 4pm. **Tours** noon, 1pm, 2pm. **Admission** £4.50; £2.25 5-15s; free under-5s. *Joint ticket with Fenton House* £6.30. **No credit cards.**

The National Trust's only example of international modernism, 2 Willow Road is a strange and atmospheric building. The light pouring through the windows is a feature in itself, and the perfect functionalism of original fixtures and fittings is a revelation. Designed and built by the respected Austro-Hungarian architect Ernö Goldfinger in 1939 as a terrace of three houses (the two others are still occupied), it also contains works by Max Ernst, Bridget Riley and Henry Moore, and is lined with curios brought by guests.

Highgate

Archway or Highgate tube.

Highgate's name comes from a tollgate that once stood on the site of the Gate House pub on the High Street. Dinky shops now predominate there, but a villagey vibe still remains (*see p145* **Village green**).

Legend has it that Dick Whittington, as he walked away from the city at the foot of Highgate Hill, heard the Bow bells peal out, 'Turn again Whittington, thrice Mayor of London'. The event is commemorated on the Whittington Stone, near the hospital of the same name. However, the area is today best known for **Highgate Cemetery** (*see below*), the last resting place of Karl Marx. Adjoining it is beautiful **Waterlow Park** (7272 2825), donated to Londoners by low-cost housing pioneer Sir Sydney Waterlow in 1889. It has ponds, a mini-aviary, tennis courts, and, in 16th-century **Lauderdale House**, a garden café.

Further down Swains Lane, peep through the Gothic entrance to **Holly Village**, a private village built in 1865. Hornsey Lane, on the other side of Highgate Hill, leads you to **Archway**, a Victorian viaduct offering vertiginous views of the City and of the East End. The famous **Archway Bridge** has become a sort of Suicide Point for Londoners since 1908, when the first known jumper took the leap. In recent years, though, fencing has made this vast cast-iron Victorian arch a little more difficult to use as a launching pad into the afterlife.

If this depresses you, hurry away from grim Archway east down Hornsey Lane to comfortable middle class **Crouch End**. Here, the 1895 clock tower and the **Hornsey Town Hall** preside over a pleasant community. The High Street is an eclectic mix of boutiques and excellent restaurants: try the Turkish Mazgal (19 Topsfield Parade, 8340 3194).

North of Highgate tube, shady **Highgate Woods** were mentioned (under another name) in the famed 1086 census the Domesday Book. Nowadays, this is a conservation area with a nature trail, a children's playground, and plenty of space for picnics and ball games.

Highgate Cemetery

Swains Lane, N6 6PJ (8340 1834/www.highgate-cemetery.org). Archway tube/C11, 271 bus. **Open** East Cemetery *Apr-Oct* 10am-5pm Mon-Fri; 11am-5pm Sat, Sun. Last admission 4.45pm. *Nov-Mar* 10am-4pm Mon-Fri; 11am-4pm Sat, Sun. Last admission 3.45pm. West Cemetery *tours Apr-Oct* 2pm Mon-Fri; hourly 11am-4pm Sat, Sun. *Nov-Mar* hourly 11am-3pm Sat, Sun. **Admission** *East Cemetery* £2. *West Cemetery tours* £3; £1 1st child 8-16 (others pay full price); prior booking advisable. *Camera permit* £1. No video cameras. No under-8s. **No credit cards.**

Highgate Cemetery is London's most famous graveyard, marked by its dramatic tombs of towering angels and curling roses. Celebrity spotters will be delighted with the Karl Marx and George Eliot memorials in the East Cemetery, but the West Cemetery is really the highlight. It is a breathtaking place: long pathways wind through tall tombs, gloomy catacombs and remarkably elaborate funerary architecture (plus the bones of poet Christina Rossetti and chemist Michael Faraday). Note that the cemetery closes during burials.

Islington

Map p402

Angel tube/Highbury & Islington tube/rail.

Henry VIII owned houses for hunting in this once-idyllic village, but by the 19th century it was already known for its shops, theatres and music halls. From 1820, the arrival of the **Regent's Canal** brought industrial slums, and Islington declined into one of the poorest boroughs in London. However, like so much of the city, its Georgian squares and Victorian terraces have been gentrified in the past 25 years. These days, despite stubborn pockets of poverty, this is a wealthy middle-class area, as is clear when you emerge from Angel tube and walk along Upper Street, past the glass façade of the Business Design Centre (and, opposite, hoary old Camden Passage antiques market; *see p229*), along the side of the triangular Green and up towards **Highbury**. En route, you'll take in

The crown of Iveagh

Hop off the 210 bus by the Kenwood sign, and you'll be next to one of the nicest presents ever given to the British public. Go to the right down the leafy path through the historic gardens without waking the bats slumbering in London's largest Pipistrelle maternity roost to find yourself looking at the gracious, creamy façade of **Kenwood House**.

Built in 1616 as a manor house, it was remodelled for the first Earl of Mansfield by Robert Adam in 1760. Good feng shui must have mellowed him, since it was his decision as Chief Justice in a test case in 1772 that made it illegal to own slaves in England.

The house stayed in the Mansfield family until 1924, when brewing magnate Edward Guinness bought it, saving it from developers and filling it with his art collection. He died in 1927, leaving Kenwood to the nation; two years later an Act of Parliament safeguarded the house and grounds, endorsing his wish 'that the atmosphere of a gentleman's private park should be preserved'.

Now English Heritage is in charge and the perfect interiors and gorgeous paintings are free to anyone with a stout pair of walking shoes. The great library with its blue and white decor and ceiling paintings by Zucchi is considered one of Adam's finest creations. Other rooms bear eloquent testimony to Guinness's taste: Vermeer's *The Guitar Player*, Rembrandt's self-portrait and works by Hals and Van Dyck jostle 18th- and early 19th-century Brits Reynolds, Gainsborough and Romney, and French rococo scenes by Boucher and Pater. In the green-grey music room, Gainsborough's *Countess Howe* presides over a harem of society beauties.

Outside, Humphrey Repton's landscape remains mostly unchanged from its creation in 1793. Repton meant it to be walked, and the ivy arch leading from the flower garden to a raised terrace with lovely views over the lakes is one of his famous 'surprises'. He didn't like the *trompe l'oeil* bridge over the lake at all, but fortunately it escaped his ministrations. A lover of order, he probably wouldn't have liked the section of Kenwood's grounds that is now listed as a Site of Special Scientific Interest, though four species of bat and nine Nationally Scarce Species of invertebrate do. Watch your feet, you may be treading on something important.

The outbuildings that serviced the house are still here, and the old brewhouse is now the Brew House Restaurant, and does a terrific breakfast. In July and August there are concerts by the lake (*see p304*).

Kenwood House/Iveagh Bequest

Hampstead Lane, NW3 7JR (8348 1286/ www.english-heritage.org). Hampstead tube/Golders Green tube then 210 bus. **Open** *Apr-Sept* 10am-5.30pm Mon, Tue, Thur, Sat, Sun; 10.30am-5.30pm Wed, Fri. *Oct* closes at 5pm. *Nov-Mar* closes at 4pm. *Tours* by appointment only. **Admission** free; donations appreciated. *Tours* £3.50; £2.50 concessions; £1.50 under-16s. **Credit** AmEx, MC, V.

countless boutiques, the Screen on the Green cinema, the Almeida Theatre (*see p335*) and the Union Chapel (*see p307*).

Taking this route, though, you'll miss the new N1 Centre shopping mall on Liverpool Road, near the Angel; among its many largely mainstream tenants are a Gap, a big and loud Warner Village cineplex and lots of branches of mainstream chain stores. This behemoth is but a symptom of the influx of high street names into the area over the past half-decade or more, turning a formerly unique locale into something more nondescript.

You might spy some cabbies nearby: Penton Street, at the end of Chapel Market, is where all cab drivers once chewed down a pencil trying to pass 'the Knowledge', a detailed exam based on London streets and buildings that all London's cabbies must pass before they're licensed.

On the way along Upper Street, take a detour to **Canonbury Square**, a Regency square once home to George Orwell (No.27) and Evelyn Waugh (No.17A). Worth a look is the **Estorick Collection of Modern Italian Art** (*see p152*), while to the east is the tranquil New River, beside the less than tranquil Marquess Estate. It turns out that New River is neither new nor a river, but a 17th-century aqueduct that is now a park.

Just beyond the end of Upper Street is **Highbury Fields**, where 200,000 Londoners fled to escape the Great Fire of 1666. Smart Highbury is best known as home to author Nick Hornby's beloved Arsenal football club, who play at the compact, art deco **Highbury Stadium**. There's a museum (Avenell Road, 7704 4000) and very occasional guided tours, though the team plan to move to a new ground a mile away in the not too distant future.

The **Royal Air Force Museum**.
See p152.

Estorick Collection of Modern Italian Art

39A Canonbury Square, N1 2AN (7704 9522/ www.estorickcollection.com). Highbury & Islington tube/rail/271 bus. **Open** 11am-6pm Wed-Sat; noon-5pm Sun. **Admission** £3.50; £2.50 concessions; free under-16s, students. **Credit** MC, V.

Eric Estorick was a US political scientist, writer and art collector whose interest in the Futurists began in the 1950s. The collection he amassed in this elegant Georgian townhouse includes work by some fine Italian Futurists, such as Balla's *Hand of the Violinist* and Boccioni's *Modern Idol*, as well as pieces by Carra, Marinetti, Russolo and Severini. The museum has a library with over 2,000 books on modern Italian art, a shop and a café. Temporary exhibitions in 2004 include 'Vorticism in Britain 1910-1920' (4 February-18 April).

Dalston & Stoke Newington

Dalston: Dalston Kingsland rail/30, 38, 56, 67, 149, 242, 243, 277 bus. Stoke Newington: Stoke Newington rail/73 bus.

Bishopsgate starts in the City, passes through Shoreditch and becomes Kingsland Road. This main road runs north through Dalston and Stoke Newington, past the Hassidic enclave of Stamford Hill, and out of London altogether.

Though scruffy and, at times, intimidating, **Dalston** is a vibrant place, with shops, market stalls, cafés and all-night restaurants catering to the city's immigrant communities (chiefly Afro-Caribbean and Turkish).

Stoke Newington has been labelled, not inaccurately, as the place people move to when they can't afford Islington. Stoke Newington Church Street has a number of good restaurants: Rasa (No.55) and Rasa Travancore (No.56) are famed for their vegetarian Indian cooking. For shoppers, there are second-hand bookstores and the fascinating Cookson's Junk Yard (121 Marton Road, 7254 9941). **Clissold Park** (7923 3660) is a lovely green space with a small zoo, tennis courts, a lake and a tearoom; rather more other-worldly is the wildlife-filled **Abney Park Cemetery** (7275 7557), a rambling old boneyard that's also a nature reserve. Among the notables buried within are Salvation Army founder William Booth and painter Edward Calvert. Rare butterflies, woodpeckers and bats are the live attractions for nature lovers.

Further north

The tidy suburban streets at north London's perimeter are enlivened by the immigrant communities that have made them their home. Golders Green, Hendon and **Finchley** have large Jewish communities, the latter home to north London's second **Jewish Museum** (80 East End Road, 8349 1143, *see also p143*), where the focus is on Jewish social history and there's an exhibition tracing the life of Leon Greenman, a British Jew who survived Auschwitz. He's in his 90s now but still comes in on Sundays to speak about his experiences.

Golders Green is the focus of a growing population of both Chinese and Japanese City workers, with the Oriental City shopping mall (399 Edgware Road, 8200 0009) supplying their shopping needs. There's been a Jewish cemetery on Hoop Lane since 1895; cellist Jacqueline du Pré is buried here. Meanwhile, TS Eliot, Marc Bolan and Anna Pavlova are among the many whose bodies ended up at **Golders Green Crematorium** (8455 2374).

The neighbourhoods of **Tottenham** and **Haringey** have sizeable Greek Cypriot, Turkish Cypriot and Kurdish communities; aside from occasional clashes, the groups live side by side in **Green Lanes**, where food-related business success is evident in the thriving kebab shops, bakeries and supermarkets. Finally, the unfortunate but comely **Alexandra Palace** (*see below*) is as good a reason as any to visit **Muswell Hill**.

Alexandra Park & Palace

Alexandra Palace Way, N22 7AY (park 8444 7696/ information 8365 2121/boating 8889 9089/ www.alexandrapalace.com). Wood Green tube/ Alexandra Palace rail/W3, W7, 84A, 144, 144A bus. **Open** *Park* 24hrs daily. *Palace* times vary.

'The People's Palace', when it opened in 1873, was supposed to provide affordable entertainment for all, but it burned to the ground just 16 days later. Rebuilt, it became the site of the first TV broadcasts by the BBC in 1936, but in 1980 was destroyed by fire once more. The born-yet-again palace has remained upright for the past 24 years and yields panoramic views of London. Its grounds provide a multitude of attractions – ice skating, boating, pitch-and-putt – while its entertainment and exhibition centre hosts fairs and events, such as the London Festival of Railway Modelling (27-28 Mar 2004).

Royal Air Force Museum Hendon

Grahame Park Way, NW9 5LL (8205 2266/ www.raf museum.org.uk). Colindale tube/Mill Hill Broadway rail/32, 226, 292, 303 bus. **Open** 10am-6pm daily. *Tours* times vary. **Admission** free. **Credit** MC, V.

Claiming to be the birthplace of aviation in Britain, Hendon Aerodrome currently houses more than 70 aircraft, among them WWI Fokkers, WWII Spitfires and Cold War-era Valiants, together with all manner of aviation memorabilia. Following redevelopment work at the museum, a new exhibition traces the history of aviation. There's an interactive show about the Battle of Britain and a Red Arrows flight simulator and a 'touch and try' Jet Provost cockpit.

East London

Streets prowled by Jack the Ripper and fascinating to Jack London are now cool 'Eastside' to their visitors.

Whitechapel & Spitalfields

Maps p403 & p405

Aldgate, Aldgate East, Shoreditch or Whitechapel tube.

When author Jack London sought to investigate the seamy underbelly of England a century ago, the police advised him to disguise himself as a pauper if he wanted to survive in the ever-edgy East End. Over the years, the area's poverty has been its main draw. Low rents have brought a steady influx of immigrants: Huguenots (French Protestant refugees) settled here in the 18th century, Irish and Germans came in the early 19th century, and Jewish refugees arrived from Eastern Europe from 1880 to 1914. Then, when the Jews prospered and headed to north London, Bangladeshis and Indians moved in. The textile businesses on Commercial Street and Commercial Road have simply passed from one group of immigrants to the next.

You no longer have to go undercover around here, though. It's all gone trendy, especially around **Brick Lane** and **Spitalfields Market** (*see p250*). But despite the influx of new money – rents are higher than they've ever been – the streets here, especially west of Bishopsgate and east of Vallance Road, are still gritty enough to worthily accommodate the Jack the Ripper guided walks that pass through them by night. The best, visiting sites at which the unidentified 19th-century serial killer butchered local whores, is run by Original London Walks (7624 3978/www.walks.com); an equally entertaining alternative history of the area, meanwhile, can be garnered on the Back Passages of Spitalfields tours (www.backpassageswalks.co.uk).

Whitechapel

Beside Aldgate East station sits Whitechapel's main cultural temptation: the art nouveau **Whitechapel Art Gallery**, which specialises in contemporary work. A little to the east, stallholders offer temptations of a very different kind – clothes, five lighters for a pound – at the modest market that runs along grimy, noisy Whitechapel Road.

A little further east, the **Whitechapel Bell Foundry** (*see p154*) and (on Commercial Road) the **Gunmakers' Company Proof House** give a tangible sense of the area's industrial history. Fieldgate Street, which runs behind the huge East London Mosque, is worth a detour for a look at the grim Victorian bulk of **Tower House**. Once a workhouse, it provided a mean lodging for Jack London during his sojourn, as well as for future revolutionaries Stalin and Lenin; these days, save for the occasional squatter, it's derelict.

Back on Whitechapel Road, Joseph Merrick – the Elephant Man – was exhibited at what is now the **Bombay Saree House**, before the surgeon Sir Frederick Treves spotted him and offered him a home in the hospital across the road, as described at the **Royal London Hospital Archives & Museum** (*see below*).

East End crime didn't end with the Ripper's disappearance: George Cornell was shot dead by gangster Ronnie Kray in March 1966 at the Blind Beggar pub (337 Whitechapel Road), close by Whitechapel tube. The area is also famously political: Sidney Street, opposite Cambridge Heath Road, was the site of a siege on 3 January 1911, when anarchists barricaded themselves into a house and took pot-shots at the police and soldiers (led by Winston Churchill). The house burned down and two bodies were recovered, but the gang's leader, a Russian known only as Peter the Painter, was never found.

Royal London Hospital Archives & Museum

St Philip's Church, Newark Street, E1 2AA (7377 7608/www.brlcf.org.uk). Whitechapel tube. **Open** 10am-4.30pm Mon-Fri; archives by appointment. **Admission** free; donations appreciated.

This single-room museum traces the hospital's history, from its beginnings in the 18th century as a voluntary institution. Note the 1930s X-ray machine that wouldn't be out of place in an HG Wells story, Norman Hartnell's jaunty designs for nurses' uniforms and George Washington's upper mandibular denture. The sections on the Elephant Man and Jack the Ripper are brief but interesting, the latter featuring Ripper letters and the former displaying Merrick's veiled hat.

Whitechapel Art Gallery

80-82 Whitechapel High Street, E1 7QX (7522 7888/www.whitechapel.org). Aldgate East tube/15, 25, 205, 253 bus. **Open** 11am-6pm Tue, Wed, Fri-Sun; 11am-9pm Thur. *Tours* 2.30pm Sun. **Admission** free; 1 paying exhibition a yr/phone for details. **Map** p405 S6.

Gunmakers' Company Proof House. *See p153.*

The Whitechapel Art Gallery was founded a century ago to offer east London a window in to modern art, and to this day consistently presents challenging temporary shows in a large ground-floor gallery and skylit upper gallery. Among the 2004 shows is a large scale exhibition of works by the Belgian painter Raoul de Keyser, scheduled to open in the spring. The café, designed by Turner Prize nominee Liam Gillick, is a pleasant spot.

Whitechapel Bell Foundry

32-4 Whitechapel Road, E1 1DY (7247 2599/ www.whitechapelbellfoundry.co.uk). Aldgate East or Whitechapel tube. **Open** *Museum* 9am-4pm Fri. *Foundry tours* by arrangement Sat. **Admission** (over-14s only) £8. **Credit** MC, V.

The Whitechapel Bell Foundry was established in 1420, making it the country's oldest manufacturing business in continuous operation; among the bells cast here are Big Ben and the Liberty Bell. It moved to its current site in 1738; a fascinating two-hour tour leads visitors around the grimy factory building, detailing loam-casting, bell tuning, change ringing and the art of working wrought iron (the self-taught blacksmith here may be the last with the skills to make certain repairs). Though you won't see the fire and brimstone of metal being poured, the workshop remains uncomfortably hot the day after a pouring.

Spitalfields

The only way to explore the evocative little streets north of Aldgate East is on foot. Start by getting some winkles from Tubby Isaac's stall by the corner of Whitechapel High Street and Old Castle Street, and then tuck down the latter to the new **Women's Library** (7320 2222/www.thewomenslibrary.ac.uk). Opened in 2002 in a converted Victorian washhouse, the pristine building holds an airy café and regular exhibitions. In contrast, the working class hurly-burly of **Petticoat Lane Market** (*see p251*) bustles on Sundays.

To the east, Commercial Street is a wide swathe of Victorian warehouses, most of which now house clothing wholesalers. Halfway up its length sits the covered Spitalfields Market (*see p251*), whose selection of goods (CDs, art, furniture) is highlighted by the organic food stalls that set up on Fridays and always-busy Sundays. The market is under threat from developers; check www.smut.org.uk for news on its survival. Although the area around the market is pretty spruce, after dark it exudes an air of menace, a great deal of which emanates from Hawksmoor's domineering **Christ Church Spitalfields** (Commercial Street, E1, 7247 7202; *see p151*). In its shadow, the Ten Bells pub (84 Commercial Street, E1 6LY; 7366 1721) is where the prostitutes who evaded the Ripper got ruined on cheap gin.

Fournier Street, running alongside Christ Church between Commercial Street and the now-famous **Brick Lane**, is all tall Huguenot houses, with distinctive shutters and ornate, jutting porches. Time your visit right and you'll be able to look inside one: **19 Princelet Street** (7247 5352/www.19princeletstreet.org.uk), an unrestored 18th-century silk merchant's home that's variously been a Huguenot chapel, a Methodist chapel, a synagogue and mosque, opens to the public ten days a year. Supporters are trying to attract the £3 million necessary to open the house as a permanent museum of immigration. Similar houses can be found in Elder Street and Folgate Street, north-west of Spitalfields Market, including the wonderful **Dennis Severs' House**.

Dennis Severs' House

18 Folgate Street, E1 6BX (7247 4013/www.dennissevershouse.co.uk). Liverpool Street tube/rail. **Open** 2-5pm 1st & 3rd Sun of mth; noon-2pm Mon (following 1st & 3rd Sun of mth); Mon eves (times vary). **Admission** £8 Sun; £5 noon-2pm Mon; £12 Mon eves. **No credit cards. Map** p403 R5.

The house at 18 Folgate Street has been quietly gaining international notice. It was bought in the late 1970s by Severs, a Californian, who restored it as a 'still-life drama'; when he died in 1999, the rooms

The dark side

Towering over Old Spitalfields Market, the great white spire of **Christ Church** (*see p154*) seems almost to scar heaven. Begun in 1712, it took 14 years to complete, and it's one of only three churches in the area built by the baroque architect **Nicholas Hawksmoor**, the other two are the squat, sullen **St George-in-the-East** (1712-29) and **St Anne** (1712-30) in Limehouse (*see p161*).

Hawksmoor's London churches – the three around Stepney, plus **St Alfege** in Greenwich (1712-18); **St George** in Bloomsbury (1716-31); **St Mary** in Woolnoth (1716-24); **St Luke** in Old Street, and **St John** in Horselydown (both 1727-33, the latter now demolished) – were mostly built as a result of the 50 New Churches Act of 1711. Passed by a High Tory government fearful of a growing population of poor working folk, the act raised money from a tax on coal for the construction of churches. Of the 12 churches actually built, Hawksmoor was wholly responsible for six.

Despite the conservative nationalism of the New Churches Commission, his buildings were idiosyncratic, imaginative and eclectic.

There are the monuments, for one thing. The most obvious one is the 12-foot (45-metre) high pyramid in the grounds of St Anne, Limehouse. There's a smaller pyramidal monument behind St George-in-the-East. Then there's the tower of St George, Bloomsbury, avowedly a re-creation of the Mausoleum of Halicarnassus (complete with golden statue of King George II dressed in a toga) and a profusion of obelisks, one flattened to the north wall of St Alfege and another two forming the spires of St Luke.

Many people have thus been encouraged to theorise lines of force connecting Hawksmoor's churches into pentacles, hieroglyphs or other symbols of occult power. The Luxor Brethren apparently recognised the Eye of Horus in the churches' alignment, relating it to the sites of Ripper murders. Peter Ackroyd's novel *Hawksmoor* (1985) suggested that sacrificial victims were laid in the foundations of each.

It's all in the imagination, of course. Although it has not gone unnoticed that the Freemasons Arms on Salmon Lane is in alignment with St Anne's clock tower via that pyramid. And the obelisk at Christ Church Spitalfields is on a straight line between the steeple and the Swiss Re tower. Hmmm...

were left as he had reconstructed them. Each indicates a different epoch in the history of the house, complete with appropriate smells and sounds; clinks and half-empty wine glasses in the Georgian downstairs give way to Dickensian creaks and half-empty chamber pots in the Victorian upstairs. The atmosphere throughout the house is reverential; notes request silence and encourage you to engage with your surroundings.

Brick Lane

Routinely celebrated as emblematic of Britain's multicultural cool, Brick Lane has its share of community triumphs and tensions (not the least of them the 2003 firebombing of the fine Pride of Spitalfields pub on **Heneage Street**, the pub reopened almost immediately). Londoners throng here, attracted by fashionable bars, the colourful Sunday market and the countless inexpensive curry restaurants. Despite their fame, the latter are mostly uninspiring – notable exceptions are the sleek Café Naz (Nos.46-8) and the down-home Sweet & Spicy (No.40). Brick Lane's Jewish heritage survives in the always reliable 24-hour Brick Lane Beigel Bake at No.159 (*see p213*).

An artsier and more self-conscious Brick Lane has emerged since the Truman Brewery buildings were redeveloped a few years ago. Trendier shops, restaurants and bars are still following the route marked out by the Vibe Bar (91 Brick Lane; 7377 2899), the ostentatious Les Trois Garçons restaurant (1 Club Row, E1; 7613 1924/www.lestroisgarcons.com) and its sibling bar Loungelover (1 Whitby Street, E1; 7012 1234/www.loungelover.co.uk); weekends here are gloriously chaotic affairs.

Shoreditch & Hoxton

Map p403

Old Street tube/rail.

The intersection of two Roman roads (**Old Street**, running east–west, and the north–south **Kingsland Road**) marks the beginnings of **Shoreditch**. Not quite the City and not quite the East End, the place was never terribly sure of itself. That said, some of the anecdotes that surround are colourful. James Burbage founded London's first theatre on the corner of Great Eastern Street and New Inn Yard in 1598, where it remained until – with the rent due and the landlord away for a long weekend – Shakespeare and Burbage's men removed its timbers to build the Globe (*see p77*).

The neighbourhood known as **Hoxton** (actually a section of Shoreditch north of Old Street and west of Kingsland Road), has a recorded history reaching back to the Domesday Book. In 1598 Britain's foremost playwright after Shakespeare, Ben Jonson, fought actor Gabriel Spencer at Hoxton Fields (now **Hoxton Square**) and killed him. As a clergyman, Jonson escaped the gallows, but he served a prison term, forfeited his fortune and his left thumb was branded with a felon's mark.

From Victorian times until World War II, the area was known for its overcrowded slums and boisterous music halls; the Queen of the Halls herself, Marie Lloyd, was born here in 1870. Post-war, the area went through hard times, but an influx of artists, musicians and other bohos in the 1990s gave the area an unexpected chic; up sprung commercial galleries (most notably White Cube, the commercial hub of Young British Artists' work; *see p291*) and DJ bars (*see p318*) of uneven quality but measurable attitude. Still, with young executives now slumming it here for unfathomable rents (they've tripled since 2000), many artists have headed east or north, where the cost of living is more within the realm of reason.

Geffrye Museum

Kingsland Road, E2 8EA (7739 9893/recorded information 7739 8543/www.geffrye-museum.org.uk). Liverpool Street tube/rail then 149, 242 bus/Old Street tube/rail then 243 bus. **Open** 10am-5pm Tue-Sat; noon-5pm Sun. *Almshouse tours* 11am, noon, 2pm, 3pm, 4pm of 1st Sat/mth. **Admission** *Museum* free; donations appreciated. *Almshouse tours* £2 adults; free under-16s. **Credit** *Shop* MC, V. **Map** p403 R3.

Built in 1716 with money from a bequest by former Lord Mayor Sir Robert Geffrye, these beautiful old almshouses were converted into a museum of furniture and interior design in 1914. The museum consists of a chronological series of middle class interiors from the 15th to the 20th centuries; the 20th-century rooms and exhibits are housed in an extension, with Edwardian, 1930s and 1960s living rooms and a 1990s loft conversion arranged in a loop around a staircase that leads down to the Geffrye Design Centre, a showcase for local designers. In 2004, the Geffrye is opening a Grade I-listed almshouse restored to its original condition: once a month visitors are able to tour it and see how 18th- and 19th-century pensioners lived. Outside is a delightful, walled herb garden, which affords a pleasantly scented wander in fine weather. The airy restaurant can provide a hearty lunch or at least an invigorating cup of tea and scones. The museum's Christmas festivities see rooms exquisitely decorated in seasonal style.

Bethnal Green & Hackney

Bethnal Green tube/rail, Hackney Central or Hackney Downs rail.

Notorious in Victorian times as the poorest area of London, **Bethnal Green** was targeted for wholesale slum clearance and the building of massive public housing developments during the 20th century. Despite recent gentrification, it remains largely impoverished, if increasingly trendy. The strangely interesting **Bethnal Green Museum of Childhood** opened in 1872. E Pellicci's art deco-inlaid Anglo-Italian caff (332 Bethnal Green Road) is nearly as old, it's been run by the Pellicci family for a century. A short walk away is **Columbia Road**, whose bijou shops and restaurants are supplemented on Sundays by a flower market (*see p252*).

Hackney, to the north, was originally a village, popular in the 15th and 16th centuries with merchants who wanted to live near but outside the City; its oldest residence, **Sutton House** (*see p158*), dates from this period. The area remained rural until the 19th century, when the market gardens were buried under rows of houses and stretches of workshops, these were eventually replaced after World War II by public housing.

Though the London borough that bears its name stretches to Finsbury Park in the north-west, many people associate Hackney with the area around **Mare Street**. The **Hackney Empire** (8985 2424/www.hackneyempire.co.uk), in its heyday one of London's great music halls, has been inching its way through a major restoration for years; it's expected to reopen in early 2004. It's no longer the only attraction round here: the gleaming music venue Ocean (*see p307*) creatively fills the old library building, and the thoroughly modern Technology Learning Centre with its Hackney Museum (*see p158*) sits across the street off **Town Hall Square**.

Bethnal Green Museum of Childhood

Cambridge Heath Road, E2 9PA (8983 5200/recorded information 8980 2415/www.museumofchildhood.org.uk). Bethnal Green tube. **Open** 10am-5.50pm Mon-Thur, Sat, Sun. **Admission** free; donations appreciated.

The artistry and oddity of dolls is the main focus on the ground floor of this quirky old museum, with macabre multi-faced examples and an intricately detailed Queen Victoria in full coronation attire; the excellent collection of dolls' houses, highlighted by its 1673 Nuremberg House and 2001 Kaleidoscope House, is similarly impressive. The museum also holds generous displays of puppets, clockwork and cuddly toys, boats, trains and spinning tops. The coin-operated pier-end amusements are a nice touch.

Village green Walthamstow

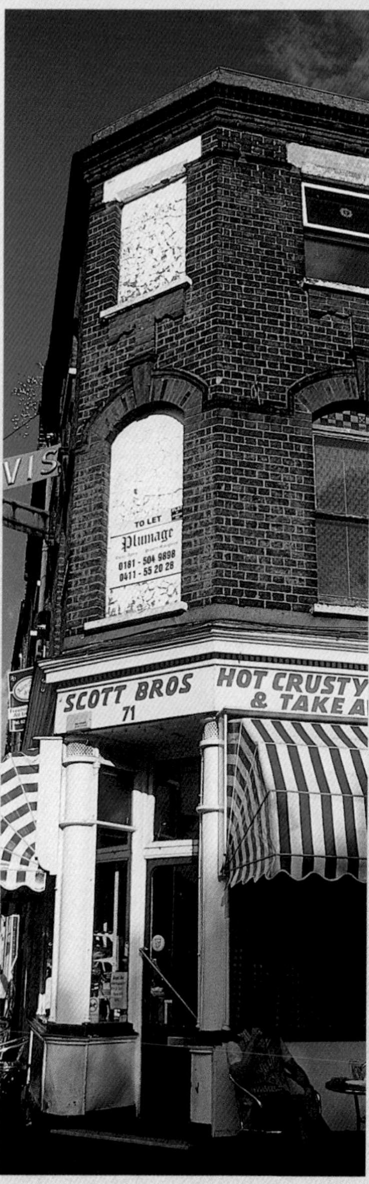

Whether you arrive by tube, train or bus, you're going to think we've sent you to the wrong place. Walthamstow Central is no place for a cucumber sandwich. But nip east across forbiddingly busy Hoe Street, stroll down St Mary's Road and...well, you'll begin to see why we sent you here.

At the end of the road the church of **St Mary Walthamstow** has overlooked the community since at least 1108, cossetted in a quiet churchyard and blissfully unaware of its urban location. Now a nature reserve, the lovely cemetery contains four Grade II-listed tombs. It has a grisly history, mind: both Black Death and Great Plague burial pits were dug here. Trenches were filled with vinegar to prevent the disease spreading; the path in front of the 18th-century Monoux Almshouses is called **Vinegar Alley** for this reason.

Vestry Road and **Orford Road** are the key thoroughfares of Walthamstow Village. On the former lie St Mary's, with the justly named half-timbered **Ancient House** opposite. Built in the 15th century, the former farmhouse was painstakingly restored in 1934. Pottering distance away is the **Vestry House Museum** (open 10am-1pm, 2-5.30pm Mon-Fri, 10am-1pm, 2-5pm Sat, 8509 1917), with its local artefacts that include Britain's first car with an internal-combustion engine, various kitchenware and an old prison cell.

Between the church and museum, the row of charming pale-brick cottages are the **Squires Almshouses**, which keep to the medieval theme with *Laus Deo* written over the portal and hooded dwarves in an alcove. You'll also find the **Walthamstow National Spiritualist Church** here, opposite the museum, but the Nag's Head (9 Orford Road, no phone) may seem a better idea. Tucked just behind the Ancient House, it was founded in 1857 as a coaching inn.

Don't get too comfortable, though. There's the quaint old **Frank Ison Ironmongery & Oil Stores** (47 Orford Road, 8520 1446), and the sweet little **Village Bakery** at No.71. **Beulah Terrace**, at the end of Orford Road, is full of prim gardens of lavender and roses, with hanging baskets and ornate stucco.

If you haven't the energy for the five-minute walk back to the Nag's Head, try the charming **Village** pub instead (31 Orford Road, 8521 9982). When the fires are lit in the wintertime, it's hard to drag yourself away.

Hackney Museum

Hackney Technology & Learning Centre, 1 Reading Lane, E8 1GQ (8356 3500/www.hackney.gov.uk/hackneymuseum). Hackney Central rail. **Open** 9.30am-5.30pm Tue, Wed, Fri; 9.30am-8pm Thur; 10am-5pm Sat. **Admission** free; donations appreciated.

That it moved this museum from its old location five years before the new place was ready tells you everything you need to know about the local government in Hackney. But all's well that ends well; now, £400,000 worth of gleaming displays cram 1,000 years of interesting history into a small space. Displays include a full-scale replica Anglo-Saxon canoe and one on the art of matchbox-making.

Sutton House

2 & 4 Homerton High Street, E9 6JQ (8986 2264/www.nationaltrust.org.uk). Bethnal Green tube then 253, 106, D6 bus/Hackney Central rail. **Open** *Historic rooms* 1-5.30pm Fri, Sat; 11.30am-5.30pm Sun. *Café, gallery, shop* 11.30am-5pm Wed-Sun. *Tours* 1.30pm, 3.30pm 1st Sun of mth. **Admission** £2.20; 50p 5-16s; free under-5s; £4 family. *Tours* free on admission. **Credit** MC, V.

The juxtaposition of this red-brick Tudor mansion, the oldest house in the East End, with its quintessentially urban setting, is striking. The house was built in 1535 for Henry VIII's first secretary of state, Sir Ralph Sadleir, who was a rising star in the court. It became home to various merchants, Huguenot silk-weavers, some Victorian schoolmistresses and Edwardian clergy, and although altered over the years, remains essentially Tudor. Visitors can view an Edwardian chapel, a 16th-century garderobe and medieval foundations in the cellar.

Mile End & Bow

Bow Church, Bow Road or Mile End tube.

Mostly common land until the 16th century, **Mile End** experienced a minor population explosion in the 1800s as industrialisation took hold. The area didn't suffer the ravages of poverty endured by neighbouring Whitechapel and Bethnal Green; nevertheless, it was here that the **Trinity Almshouses** were built for '28 decayed masters and commanders of ships' in 1695. East of the junction with Cambridge Heath Road, the attractive cottages and tiny gardens are more village than metropolis, with dinky model galleons at the gate. In the 1860s William Booth founded the Salvation Army in Mile End; his beleaguered statue near the almshouses gives up an exhortatory hand to regular vandals. Opposite, a plaque celebrates the exploits of Captain Cook.

To the south-west, **Mile End Park** borders Copperfield Road, home to the **Ragged School Museum** (*see p159*) and **Matt's Gallery** (*see p289*). Around £12 million from the Millennium Commission, matched by funding from a range of sponsors, saw the 1950s park remodelled by architects and planners Tibbalds TM2. The new park, which features a colourful bridge that connects turf-covered pavilions and ponds with terraced gardens and a children's park with a wonderful playground and go-kart track, has been a great local success.

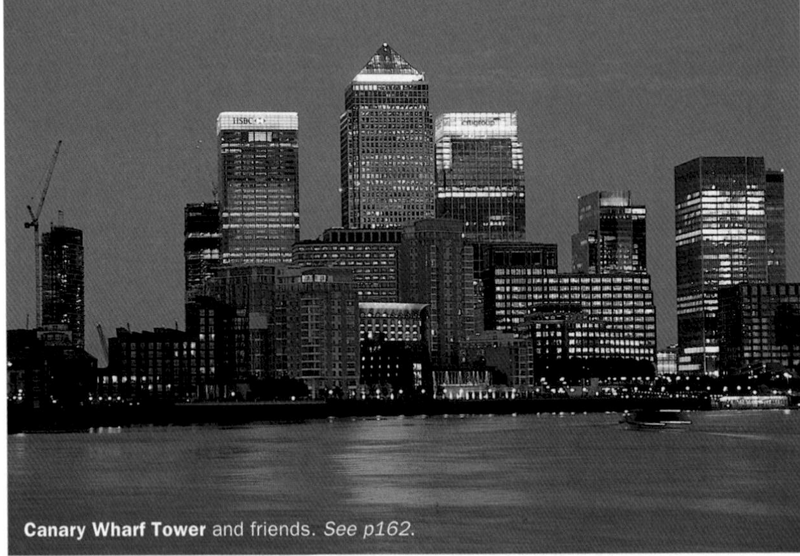

Canary Wharf Tower and friends. *See p162.*

Northwards again, where the Grand Union meets the Hertford Union Canal, the rose gardens and swans of **Victoria Park** sprawl over the neighbourhood. At the main Sewardstone Road entrance, look out for the deranged-looking Dogs of Alcibiades; they've stood here since 1912.

Bow, to the east, has played a major role in London's growth. In the 12th century, the Roman bridge over the River Lea at Old Ford was supplemented by a new bridge downriver. Its shape gave the area its name. Hertfordshire grain was unloaded at mills along the river: **Three Mills Island** survives, as does Joseph Bazalgette's Byzantine-Gothic **Abbey Mill** pumping station (built in 1868) nearby. The 19th century saw industrial works spring up, notably the Bryant & May match factory, scene of a bitter but ultimately successful match-girls' strike in 1888. Twenty five years later, Bow struck another blow for women's rights when Sylvia Pankhurst launched the East London Federation of Suffragettes.

Ragged School Museum

48-50 Copperfield Road, E3 4RR (8980 6405/ www.raggedschoolmuseum.org.uk). Mile End tube. **Open** 10am-5pm Wed, Thur; 2-5pm 1st Sun of mth. *Tours* by arrangement; phone for details. **Admission** free; donations appreciated.

Ragged schools were an early attempt at public education: here Dr Barnardo taught 900 shoeless East End urchins. This surprisingly good museum gives a history of each of the Tower Hamlets on the ground floor, touching on poverty, industry, wartime devastation and immigration through the centuries. There's a re-creation of a ragged classroom on the first floor (sometimes with modern schoolkids drilling the 3Rs for a 'teacher' in full Victorian kit), and the top floor is an early 20th-century kitchen. The museum's reliance on personal testimony provides a social history both eloquent and elegant.

Three Mills Island

Three Mills Lane, E3 3DU (8980 4626). Bromley-by-Bow tube. **Open** *May-Sept* 2-4pm Sat, Sun; *Oct* 2-4pm Sun. *Apr-Dec* 11am-4pm 1st Sun of mth. **Admission** £3; free under-16s. **No credit cards**.

The island holding the titular old mills is now an interesting museum of early industrial technology. The House Mill, built in 1776, is the oldest and largest tidal mill left standing in Britain; much of the original grinding mechanism can still be seen inside it. The Clock Mill was rebuilt in 1817 from an earlier version, and is similarly informative. The visitors' centre provides a history of the area and leaflets detailing walks nearby. A crafts market is held on the first Sunday of the month (April-December only).

Walthamstow

Walthamstow tube/rail.

Walthamstow's fortunes have recently begun to change. For decades a resolutely working class area, E17 is starting to attract the middle classes in large numbers. Small surprise: **Walthamstow Village** (*see p157* **Village green**), tucked away discreetly to the east of

Desirable properties at **Limehouse Basin**. *See p161.*

the main station, recently won *Time Out*'s search for the best village in London.

Walthamstow town centre, currently undergoing a massive facelift to further advance its desirability quotient, has a narrow, busy High Street considerably brightened by **Walthamstow Market**. Stretching a mile, it's the longest street market in Europe, and one of few such traditional markets in London. The second road through town is undulating Hoe Street, a more workaday selection of kebab shops and grocery shops.

Turn right on busy Forest Road and you'll be rewarded with a dramatic view of the art deco **Walthamstow Town Hall**, one of the most startling pieces of municipal architecture in London; turn left and you'll reach sweet little **Lloyd Park**. The 18th-century building at the park gates, with its back imperiously turned to the rest, is the **William Morris Gallery** (*see below*); behind it are an ornamental pond and aviary (with budgies, cockatiels, canaries and zebra finches), tennis courts and manicured bowling greens, a scented garden for the visually impaired, an under-sevens play area and a café (open 9.30am-4pm). To the north, just across the A406, lies **Walthamstow Stadium** (*see p323*), London's best-known greyhound track.

From Walthamstow Central station, it's just three stops by train (every 15 minutes, originating at Liverpool Street station) to Chingford, the gateway to the spectacular **Epping Forest**. That this green lung survives is thanks to the Victorians: in 1878 Parliament granted the City of London the power to buy land within 25 miles (40 kilometres) of the city centre so that urbanites could continue to enjoy it in its natural state, and this is where they put their money. Some 6,000 acres remain of the primeval forest that once covered most of East Anglia and was yet another of King Henry VIII's hunting grounds. Today the forest is perfect for walking, cycling, riding and picnicking. The friendly staff at the visitors' centre (8508 0028) can suggest walks and supply information and maps; alternatively, head to www.cityoflondon.gov.uk, and follow the links to open spaces and then to Epping Forest.

William Morris Gallery

Lloyd Park, Forest Road, E17 4PP (8527 3782/ www.lbwf.gov.uk/wmg). Walthamstow Central tube/rail. **Open** 10am-1pm, 2-5pm Tue-Sat, 1st Sun of mth. *Tours* phone for details. **Admission** free; donations appreciated. **Credit** *Shop* MC, V.

This is the only museum in Britain dedicated to the work of the influential late Victorian designer, craftsman and socialist, and several of his followers. On the ground floor, Morris's biography is expounded through his work and political writings (as well as a number of more personal items, such as his coffee cup). Exhibits include furniture, stained glass and textiles. The upstairs galleries are devoted to his associates, including Edward Burne-Jones and Dante Gabriel Rossetti.

Further north-east

Suburban **Leyton** lacks the cohesion and village charm of neighbouring **Walthamstow**. During the 18th century, this part of London was best known for its market gardening, but much of the land was covered by railways and gas works in the 19th century. Badly bombed in World War II, it was redeveloped haphazardly. But it does have the **WaterWorks Nature Reserve**, which reverses time by giving water-filter beds – built to fight a cholera epidemic in 1849 – back to nature. Open to the public on weekends and public holidays (8am-dusk), the reserve boasts over 300 plant species, grass snakes, newts and water voles, as well as 25 types of breeding bird, kingfishers and an abundance of dragonflies. The visitors' centre (8988 7566) is just off Lea Bridge Road.

Docklands

Various stops on the Docklands Light Railway.

Given its name, it's not difficult to figure out what this area of town was like back in the 18th century, when it earned its title. In fact, the docks were in continuous operation until well into the 20th century, working at full capacity even after suffering 57 consecutive nights of German bombing during the height of the Blitz.

It couldn't last, though. Labour unrest and the collapse of the Empire, exacerbated by the docks' failure to respond to the development of deep-draught container ships, led to the closure of all London's docks from Tower Bridge to Barking Creek from 1967. In 1981 the Conservative government set up the London Docklands Development Corporation (LDDC) to convert the now derelict waterfront land into offices and homes. It took time, but the project has ultimately changed the area into a sort of waterside skyscraper city. Today, some 55,000 people commute daily to work at Canary Wharf.

St Katharine's & Wapping

Just east of Tower Bridge on the north bank of the Thames, **St Katharine's** once housed more than 1,250 cottages, a brewery and the 12th-century church of St Katharine, but all were demolished to make way for a grandiose development scheme in 1828. St Katharine's Dock, built over the old settlement, remained open until 1968, then re-emerged in 1973 as St

Katharine's Haven, the first of the Docklands redevelopments. Now a yacht marina, it houses russet-sailed, century-old barges in one corner and glossy new vessels everywhere else. A fleet of upscale restaurants and pubs cater to wealthy condo and yacht owners.

North-east of the basin, an ornamental canal flows past a couple of reconstructed pirate ships into **Wapping**. In 1598 historian John Stowe saw Wapping High Street as a 'filthy strait passage, with alleys of small tenements or cottages…built and inhabited by sailors' victuallers'. Today, it's a quiet thoroughfare hemmed in by warehouses and new flats, with nary a sailors' victualler in sight. But much of the city's seafaring history can be traced to here. Until well into the 19th century, convicted pirates were taken at low tide to **Execution Dock** (near the River Police station at Wapping New Stairs), hanged and left there in chains until three tides had washed over them.

Thames Barrier Park. *See p162.*

The Captain Kidd pub (No.108) commemorates one of the most famous executionees, who was dispatched at a gibbet erected near the pub on 23 May 1701. Another historic pub, the Town of Ramsgate (No.62), is where Kidd's nemesis Judge Jeffreys was captured trying to escape to Hamburg (he died in the Tower of London), where 'Colonel' Blood was caught after attempting to steal the Crown Jewels in 1671, and where Captain Bligh and Fletcher Christian shared a pint before setting off in the HMS *Bounty*. But the oldest and, if you're spared the coachloads of tourists, most atmospheric Wapping pub is actually the Prospect of Whitby (*see p225*); it dates to 1520, counts Pepys, Dickens, Whistler and Turner among its (former) regulars, and is said in 1780 to have been where the first fuschia to enter Britain was bought from a sailor for a noggin of rum. Opposite, the red-brick London Hydraulic Power Company building (1890) is now the **Wapping Project** (*see p290*), an impressive restaurant and art space.

Sightseeing

North of the Highway, a large mural at St George's Town Hall on Cable Street commemorates the battle between working class locals and fascist Blackshirts, led by Sir Oswald Mosley, on 4 October 1936. Intending to intimidate the local Jewish population, the Blackshirts found their way blocked by a mass of people and eventually abandoned their march. West along the Highway, on Cannon Street Road, **St George-in-the-East** (*see p155*) is a brooding Hawksmoor structure.

Limehouse

Sandwiched between Wapping and the Isle of Dogs, **Limehouse** was named after its medieval lime kilns but earned its living from the sea: a 1610 census revealed that half of its working population were mariners. The straw-coloured **Sail Makers' & Ship Chandlers' Building** still stands at 11 West India Dock Road, despite squatters and vandals. The clock tower of **St Anne's Limehouse** (*see p155*) is the second highest in Britain, trailing only Big Ben, and is the only non-HM ship in the world permitted to fly the white ensign year-round.

Britain's first wave of Chinese immigrants, mainly seafarers, settled in Limehouse in the 19th century, where street names (Ming Street, Canton Street) and Chinese restaurants around West India Dock Road are their only memorial. The area was notorious in Victorian times for its gambling and drug dens: Wilde's Dorian Gray comes here to buy opium, and the area features in stories by both Sax Rohmer (creator of Fu Manchu) and Sir Arthur Conan Doyle. Dickens used the tiny, dark and still superb Grapes (*see p224*) as the model for the six jolly fellowship porters in *Our Mutual Friend* (1865).

Isle of Dogs

After two decades of development, building work on the Isle of Dogs is moving outwards from the centre, with blocks of luxury modern flats and the skeletons of yet more high-rise office blocks. That centre is still **Canary Wharf** and the 800-foot (244-metre) rocket-shaped **Canary Wharf Tower**, more properly known as One Canada Square. Designed by Cesar Pelli, it's been the tallest building in the UK since 1991. But where once it sat in splendid isolation, in 2002 it was joined by the **Citigroup Centre** to the south-east and the **HSBC Tower** to the north-east. The area is rapidly turning into a copse of skyscrapers, impressive in bulk but otherwise a bland recapitulation of boring, boxy 1980s glass architecture. Regardless, the best way to see it all is from the elevated Docklands Light Railway (DLR). The views from the trains are often spectacular, though you may find yourself waiting a while at weekends.

On a smaller scale, the developments have been more impressive. The Japanese-style garden nestled behind Canary Wharf station is a refreshing surprise, and the sculpture trail around West India Docks a charming diversion. The view through the glass-domed roof of Canary Wharf station is spectacular, and almost makes up for not being able to sample the view from the top of the building (an IRA bomb attack in February 1996 stopped public visits). However, the single most important development is the **Museum in Docklands**, which opened in 2003.

There's little about the **Isle of Dogs** that isn't subject to dispute, but perhaps the most basic argument concerns whether or not it's actually an island at all; though the main section of West India Docks effectively divides it from the 'mainland', some insist it's actually a peninsula. No one agrees on whether 'Dogs' refers to royal kennels once kept here or, via a linguistic corruption, to the dykes built by 19th-century Flemish engineers. And, more seriously, arguments still rage over whether the changes on the Isle of Dogs over the last decade show the success of business-led regeneration or the failure of big business to consider local needs.

Heading south down the Isle of Dogs, get off the train at Island Gardens for a gorgeous view across the Thames towards Greenwich, said to be Sir Christopher Wren's favourite vista during his construction of the **Old Royal Naval College** (*see p168*). Here, you'll also find one end of a 100-year-old pedestrian foot tunnel (lift service 7am-7pm Mon-Sat, 10am-5.30pm Sun) that surfaces beside the *Cutty Sark* on the south bank, a chilly and leaky reminder of the brilliance of Victorian engineering.

Museum in Docklands

No.1 Warehouse, West India Quay, Hertsmere Road, E14 4AL (recorded information 0870 444 3856/ box office 0870 444 3855/www.museumindocklands. org.uk). West India Quay DLR or Canary Wharf tube. **Open** 10am-6pm daily (last admittance 5.30pm). **Admission** (unlimited entrance for 1 year) £5, £3 concessions, free under-16s. **No credit cards**.

This museum is bigger than it looks. Housed in a carefully restored, Grade I-listed Georgian warehouse, it spreads over 12 galleries, with displays ranging from a 4,000-year-old timber figure to a discussion of the economic effects of containerisation. In the Roman galleries, Tony Robinson's enthusiastic rhetorical questions begin to grate ('Was this the end of London's story?' he asks near the start), but the story of London's docks still fascinates. Along the route are whale jawbones, a gibbet cage, a reconstructed quay and sailors' slum, cutlasses and actual rowing skiffs and pilot boats. The Docklands at War gallery is as moving as it is vivid.

Further east

Take the eastward DLR from Westferry to Beckton for views of the Dome (*see p167*) across the river; alight at Custom House station and walk across the slightly tatty white footbridge high over **Royal Victoria Dock** to admire the grandeur of the docks. On the south side, North Woolwich Road brings you to **Thames Barrier Park** (7511 4111/www.thames barrierpark.org.uk), London's first entirely new park construction in recent history. Finished in 2001, this thickly vegetated sunken garden is lined by walkways and offers a lovely spot for idling beside the futuristic **Thames Barrier** (*see p164*). Poor transport links mean you'll have the park pretty much to yourself.

North Woolwich Old Station Museum

Pier Road, E16 2JJ (7474 7244/www.newham. gov.uk). Beckton DLR/North Woolwich, Woolwich Arsenal or Woolwich Dockyard rail, then foot tunnel to North Woolwich Pier. **Open** *Jan-Nov* 1-5pm Sat, Sun. *Newham school holidays* 1-5pm daily. **Admission** free. *Rides* £1.

This converted Victorian railway station is paradise for trainspotters, its exhibits including old engines, tickets and station signs. You can hop on the miniature railway, which runs on the first and second Sundays of each month (April-October), or simply stand and watch as the Coffee Pot and Pickett steam engines chuff past.

South-east London

Up the Elephant, round the Castle and beyond to pastures green.

Rotherhithe

Rotherhithe tube.

Olde worlde *Redriffe,* as **Rotherhithe** used to be known (it means 'mariner's haven'), was the departure point for the Pilgrim ship, the *Mayflower,* in 1620. Then the shipbuilding capital of the world, the area's maritime past is evident in old warehouses, docks and riverside pubs, such as the Mayflower (*see p225*) and the 17th-century Angel (101 Bermondsey Wall East, 7237 3608), which has a smuggler's trapdoor. Around Rotherhithe Street, the most antiquated bit of neighbourhood, are two local gems. The first is **St Mary's Rotherhithe** (*see below*); the second, just down a cobbled street, is the fascinating **Brunel Engine House & Tunnel Exhibition** (Railway Avenue, SE16 4LF; 7231 3840).

The Rotherhithe Festival, which takes place usually around the second weekend in July, is held in nearby **Southwark Park**, London's oldest municipal park, which was made over in 2002 after 130 years in existence.

St Mary's Rotherhithe

St Marychurch Street, SE16 4JE (7231 2465). Rotherhithe tube. **Open** 7am-6pm Mon-Thur; 8am-6pm Sat, Sun. **Admission** free.

The captain of the *Mayflower*, Christopher Jones, is buried in this church, built by local sailors and watermen in 1715. The communion table in the Lady Chapel is made from timber salvaged from the warship *Fighting Temeraire,* the painting of which, by Turner, hangs in the National Gallery (*see p127*). Sadly, burglary and vandalism mean the interior can now only be viewed through glass, under the watchful eye of a CCTV camera.

Charlton & Woolwich

Charlton, Woolwich Arsenal or Woolwich Dockyard rail.

Highwaymen such as the notorious Dick Turpin lurked in the woods of **Shooters Hill** two centuries ago. A gibbet at the bottom of the hill stretched the necks of those who were caught. Away from such lowlife, the village of **Charlton** grew up around the splendid Jacobean manor, **Charlton House**. The area looks suburban and unremarkable now, though there's nothing unremarkable about the nearby **Thames Barrier** (*see p164*).

Due north of Shooters Hill (so called, it's said, because Henry VIII used the area for archery practice) and Charlton, **Woolwich** has an intriguing naval and military history. The Woolwich Arsenal was established in Tudor times as the country's main source of munitions and, by World War I, stretched 32 miles (52 kilometres) along the river. The arsenal was closed in 1967, but some beautiful buildings, such as the main section of the Arsenal, a cluster of Georgian houses where Wellington and Marlborough drew up battle plans, have been preserved. The chief visitor attraction is **Firepower** museum (*see p164*); south of here, the **Royal Artillery Barracks** has the longest Georgian façade in the country.

Henry VIII established the Royal Dockyard at Woolwich in 1512, initially so that *Great Harry*, his flagship, could be built there. Downriver, **Gallions Reach** was the scene of the Thames' worst ever shipping accident in 1878, when a pleasure steamer was struck broadside by a collier, with the loss of 700 lives.

The **Woolwich Ferry** crosses to **North Woolwich** every 15 minutes or so. It's a free service, and has been since 1889, when today's diesel-driven chuggers replaced the paddle steamers that had been in use until then (the ferry service dates back to the 14th century). In summer 2003, one of the vessels was torched and had to go into dock for a lengthy refurb. It will return, good as new, to ply this unloved stretch of the river, ever hopeful that intrepid tourists might want to tear themselves away from the delights of Woolwich waterfront to visit the **North Woolwich Old Station Museum** (*see p162*) on the other side.

Charlton House

Charlton Road, SE7 8RE (8856 3951). Charlton rail/53, 54, 380, 442 bus. **Open** by appointment 9am-10.30pm Mon-Fri; 10am-4pm Sat. **Admission** free.

One of the finest examples of Jacobean architecture in the country, Charlton House was built between 1607 and 1612, probably by John Thorpe, and occupied by Adam Newton, tutor to James I's eldest son Henry. The house, with its original oak staircases and ornate fireplaces and ceilings, now operates as a community centre. The redesigned grounds, with an orangery designed by Inigo Jones, a tranquil Jacobean herb garden and a mulberry tree that dates back to 1608, reopened in summer 2003.

Village green Dulwich

The ancient village of Dulwich, remembered by some as the place too sleepy for Margaret Thatcher to lay her handbag (Mrs Thatcher and her late husband briefly owned a property here), is hemmed in by costly public schools and million-pound family homes. Dulwich is often accused of a certain smugness; thinks it's God's gift to urban villages, some say. Well it is. Its fortunes are based around the success of one benefactor who founded the College of God's Gift right here. The funding for this place of learning, now known as **Dulwich College**, was raised from rather unsavoury practices.

Dulwich has always been an attractive spot. Its name does not refer to the level of excitement around here, but means 'the meadow where dill grows'. The most influential figure in the village's history was Edward Alleyn. A successful actor with a celebrity status in the 16th century, he was also an entrepreneur: the keeper of King

Firepower

Royal Arsenal, Woolwich, SE18 6ST (8855 7755/ www.firepower.org.uk). Woolwich Arsenal rail.
Open *Nov-Mar* 11am-5pm Fri-Sun (last entry 3.30pm); *Apr-Oct* 10.30am-5.30pm Wed-Sun (last entry 4pm). **Admission** £6.50; £5.50 concessions; £4.50 5-16s; free under-5s; £18 family. **Credit** MC, V.

Firepower, the lively Royal Artillery Museum, is dedicated to the Gunners and the hardware they've used across the centuries. Exhibits trace the evolution of artillery from catapults to nuclear warheads: the History Gallery interprets wars in terms of weaponry; the noisy multimedia presentation Fields of Fire covers World War I through to Bosnia; the Gunnery Hall is full of howitzers and tanks; and the Real Weapon Gallery shows you how all the guns work. The big galleries focus on the family market, and school holidays herald much entertainment for the kids: paintballing, quizzes, dressing up and talks with real soldiers are organised. There's plenty of serious information for the more mature weapons inspector however, and the medals and real-life testimonies are touching. Events during 2004 include a military fair in March, a new Cold War Gallery, opening in early April, D-Day events for 9 June, the shooting section of the British Pentathlon on 10 July, and Christmas markets during November and December (check the website for details).

Thames Barrier Visitors Centre

1 Unity Way, SE18 5NJ (8305 4188/www. environment-agency.gov.uk). North Greenwich tube/Charlton rail/161,177, 180 bus. **Open** *Apr-Sept* 10.30am-4.30pm daily. *Oct-Mar* 11am-3.30pm daily. **Admission** £1; 75p concessions; 50p 5-16s; free under-5s. **Credit** MC, V.

The world's largest adjustable dam was completed in 1982 at the cost of £535m. The nine shiny metal piers anchor massive steel gates that can be raised from the riverbed to protect London from devastating surge tides: the barrier's saved the city 67 times. The tiny visitors' centre on the south bank shows how the barrier was built and how it works, and a

James's bull mastiffs and a provider of animals for bear-, bull- and even lion-baiting. A particularly brutal sport, baiting involved blinding and tethering the creatures before setting hunting dogs on them. With the money he made out of this pastime, he established a college to provide education and shelter to 12 poor scholars in 1620. The poor dozen underprivileged youths have grown to more than 1,000 mostly rich boys, and Dulwich College is now one of the country's top private schools.

The original College of God's Gift was the small building next to the **Dulwich Picture Gallery** on Gallery Road, now used as a chapel (*pictured, right*). The gardens in front of the chapel are the original village green.

The **Pavilion Café** in nearby **Dulwich Park** is a delightful place to eat. Walking through the park to Dulwich Common Road, toward Lordship Lane, leads you to the site of the original Dulwich Wells, a mineral spring first discovered in 1739. It's now a Harvester pub.

Back in the village, the shops and cafés have a sweetly provincial look to them. There's a very busy Italian deli with tables outside on the pavement (Panino d'Oro, 37 Dulwich Village, 8693 2614), several designer clothes shops, a beauty parlour (Lesley Leale-Green at No.70 Dulwich Village 8299 2906) and, most popular with the chaps of Dulwich College, a Pizza Express (No.94 Dulwich Village; 8693 9333).

Sightseeing

map shows the bits of London that would be submerged if it stopped. Time your visit to see the barrier in action: there's a partial test-closure monthly, and a full-scale test each September (ring for details).

Deptford & Greenwich

Cutty Sark DLR for Maritime Greenwich or Deptford Bridge DLR/Greenwich DLR/rail/Deptford or Maze Hill rail.

It might not be a UNESCO World Heritage site like neighbouring Greenwich, but Deptford has a proud maritime history of its own. At **St Paul's church** (on Mary Ann Gardens), a Roman baroque church by Thomas Archer that dates back to 1730, a plaque commemorates one Myididdee, a Tahitian sailor who accompanied Captain Bligh on HMS *Providence*. Houses for naval officers of the early 18th century fill handsome Albury Street; legend has it that Nelson and Lady Hamilton lodged here.

The neighbourhood's **St Nicholas's church**, on Deptford Green, dates to 1697; known as 'the sailors' church', it has skull and crossbone carvings on its gate piers. Christopher Marlowe is buried here; he died following a brawl in a waterfront tavern on Deptford Strand. Look out for the grim carving by Grinling Gibbons called *Ezekiel in the Valley of Dry Bone*s in the church.

Deptford gets trendier by the day. Artists' studios are everywhere, and the gorgeous new **Laban Centre** (Creekside, SE8 3DZ; 8691 8600; *see p28 and p278*) and **Cockpit Arts Studios** (18-22 Creekside, SE8 3DZ; 7419 1959) can only improve the area's cultural profile. Gentrification, too, continues apace: **Convoy's Wharf** is currently being redeveloped, the renewed facility to include luxury housing, retail businesses and a recycling plant. Critics say it will further widen the gap between rich

Pride of London Trees

Greenwich Park, the oldest Royal Park, dating from 1433, is a tree-hugger's paradise. Beech, oak and chestnut lining the great Tudor avenues provide majesty. But there are also rarer delights: the Indian bean tree, paper birch and black mulberry. In the flower gardens, a more formal corner, there are cedars, sweet chestnuts and Judas trees among the lawns and flowerbeds. In this corner of the park, where toddlers look for squirrels on a winding path near the lake under foliage domestic or exotic, you can also see trees in a more intimate setting. Dells have been created, featuring a gingko and the wonderfully named 'headache tree'. One of the sweet chestnuts here is 400 years old, and along with an unusual shagbark hickory features in a list of 'Great Trees of London' by the campaigning organisation, **Trees for London**. Visiting its website you can probably find a great tree from its list somewhere near you that's well worth a visit, whether it be the giant beech in traffic-choked Islington or a forgotten boundary oak of 800 years' vintage in the suburbs.

Oak is a symbol of Englishness and royalty and evokes the antiquity of both. No leafy paradise like Greenwich Park would be complete without a very old or celebrity oak. The Queen Elizabeth oak is not far from the observatory and is thought to date from the 12th century. For hundreds of years its huge hollow trunk was famous. Henry VIII and Anne Boleyn danced round it, and for a time it was used as a lock-up for criminals. A storm brought the long-dead husk down in 1991 and next to its great twisted remains, now preserved, stands an adolescent tree planted by Prince Phillip for the Queen's jubilee.

Although Greenwich is all about strolling down an avenue with chestnuts underfoot, there's a serious side to trees as well. By absorbing carbon monoxide and other poisonous gases, they are incredibly useful. One tree can cancel out the air pollution of a car driven for ten miles, says Trees for London, and this group aims to plant a million more trees in the city by 2010. It is trying to green dreadful zones like Elephant & Castle where the twig is an endangered species. Get involved and help it plant some new ones.

Greenwich Park

Blackheath Gate, Charlton Way, SE10 (visitors centre 8293 0703/www.royalparks.co.uk). Cutty Sark DLR/Greenwich DLR/rail/ Maze Hill rail/1, 53,177, 180, 188, 286 bus/riverboat to Greenwich Pier. **Open** 6am-dusk daily.

Trees For London

7587 1320/www.treesforlondon.org.uk.

and poor in the area. But both enjoy Deptford's waterside views, which soften the otherwise edgy locale; kingfishers have been spotted at Deptford Bridge.

Greenwich, Deptford's rather more visitor-friendly neighbour, is best known for its maritime history and elegant Georgian and Regency architecture, but it was also a playground for Tudor royalty. Henry VIII and his daughters Mary I and Elizabeth I were all born here, and Greenwich Palace was Henry's favourite residence. The palace fell into disrepair under Cromwell; during the reign of William and Mary, who preferred Hampton Court and Kensington, it was designated as the Royal Naval Hospital. The hospital is now the **Old Royal Naval College** (*see p168*).

The most picturesque way of arriving is by taking a boat to Greenwich Pier, where you'll disembark in the shadow of the **Cutty Sark**. A great many tourist boats dock at Greenwich Pier, which in summer looks for all the world like a seaside resort. However, a cheaper option is to take a commuter boat from St Katharine's Pier, just by Tower Bridge, to the Masthouse Terrace Pier on the other side of the river at Island Gardens. From here it's a mere ten-minute walk east to the Greenwich Foot Tunnel, through which you can stroll under the Thames to Greenwich Pier. However you reach it, **Greenwich Tourist Information Centre** (0870 608 2000), based in Pepys House beside the *Cutty Sark*, is a useful first point of call.

Walk past the Old Royal Naval College with the river on your left, and you'll reach the Trafalgar Tavern, a favourite haunt of Thackeray, Dickens and Wilkie Collins. Tiny **Crane Street**, on the far side of the pub, leads to Trinity Hospital, which in 1617 provided a home to '21 retired gentlemen of Greenwich'. The path continues as far as the attractive Cutty Sark Tavern, dating from 1695.

Back in town, busy **Greenwich Market** (*see p251*) pulls in yet more tourists at weekends, but the area's loveliest bits are away from the centre of town, either along the riverside walk or around the prettiest of the Royal Parks, tree-filled **Greenwich Park** (*see p166* **Pride of London**). In 1616 James I commissioned Inigo Jones to rebuild the Tudor Greenwich palace, Henry VIII's birthplace, within Greenwich historic park. The palace became **Queen's House** (*see p168*), England's first Palladian villa. The parkland was later redesigned by André Le Nôtre, who landscaped Versailles for Louis XIV. At the southern end of the park is the **Ranger's House** (*see p168*).

Climb the hill in Greenwich Park (or take the shuttle bus – £1.50 from the *Cutty Sark* Apr-Sept; 8859 1096) for views of the city. The main attraction up here is the Wren-designed **Royal Observatory** (*see p168*). Greenwich Mean Time, introduced in 1890, sets the world's clocks, and just outside the observatory you can straddle the Greenwich Meridian Line, one foot in each of the world's hemispheres.

Two different worlds lie at opposite points of the compass from Greenwich. To the north, on the curve of the river, sits the empty shell of the **Millennium Dome**, which, just three years after its pricey construction, is in line for a £4 billion make-over into a sports arena. To the south, though, things get more pastoral. **Maze Hill** runs south from Trafalgar Road, forming the eastern boundary of Greenwich Park. The castle-like house on the hilltop was built by architect and playwright John Vanbrugh, who lived here from 1719 to 1726.

Maze Hill leads to the kite-fliers' paradise of **Blackheath**, home to some of Britain's earliest sports clubs: the Royal Blackheath Golf Club (1745), the Blackheath Hockey Club (1861) and the Blackheath Football Club (which actually plays rugby; 1862). Among the homes that surround the heath, the **Paragon** is special. Built in the late 18th century to draw the right sort of people to the area (then plagued by bandits), this beautiful crescent of prestigious colonnaded houses was bombed in World War II, but has since been restored to become the area's most desirable address.

Cutty Sark

King William Walk, SE10 9HT (8858 3445/ www.cuttysark.org.uk). Cutty Sark DLR/Greenwich DLR/rail. **Open** 10am-5pm daily (last entry 4.30pm). **Admission** £3.95; £2.95 concessions; free under-5s; £9.80 family. **Credit** MC, V.

The last surviving tea clipper, built by Hercules Linton in 1869, is looking a bit forlorn. Its future seems uncertain, as millions of pounds are required if it is to remain ship-shape. However, the Heritage Lottery Fund has stumped up £50,000 towards the bill, and designer and TV presenter Lawrence Llewelyn-Bowen has become the figurehead of the campaign to save the ship. The lower decks house an extensive exhibition on the clipper's history, and paintings, models and the world's largest collection of carved and painted figureheads. Summer holiday and weekend activities are organised for families.

Fan Museum

12 Crooms Hill, SE10 8ER (8305 1441/www.fan-museum.org). Cutty Sark DLR/Greenwich DLR/ rail. **Open** 11am-5pm Tue-Sat; noon-5pm Sun. **Admission** £3.50; £2.50 concessions; free under-7s (free OAPs, disabled 2-5pm Tue). **Credit** MC, V.

This museum is one of only two permanent exhibitions of hand-held folding fans in the world. There are some 3,000 fans, dating back to the 11th century, though only a part of the collection is on view because the fans need to be rested to avoid damage.

National Maritime Museum

Park Row, SE10 9NF (8858 4422/information 8312 6565/www.nmm.ac.uk). Greenwich DLR/rail/Maze Hill rail. **Open** *July, Aug* 10am-6pm daily. *Sept-June* 10am-5pm daily. **Admission** free. **Credit** MC, V.

One of London's most elegant and, given that it charts the nation's seafaring history, relevant museums, the National Maritime Museum is essential viewing when in Greenwich. However, note that there is a lot to get around, even if you eschew the special exhibitions (which usually charge admission). Among them, running 31 Mar-5 September, 2004, is an exhibition on the nautical adventures of Tin Tin, held to mark the 75th anniversary of the creation of the comic strip boy detective.

Of the permanent galleries, Explorers is devoted to pioneers of sea travel, Passengers is a paean to glamorous old ocean liners, and Maritime London tells the capital's nautical history through old prints and model ships. Upstairs, Seapower covers naval battles from Gallipoli to the Falklands and the Art of the Sea is the world's largest maritime art collection. Kids can learn to send Morse code, navigate Viking longboats or steer a modern passenger ferry.

Old Royal Naval College

King William Walk, SE10 9LW (8269 4747/ www.greenwichfoundation.org.uk). Cutty Sark DLR/ Greenwich DLR/rail. **Open** 10am-5pm daily. **Admission** free. **Credit** MC, V.

Sir Christopher Wren's 1696 naval hospital is an elegant and majestic pair of neo-classical buildings, neatly framing Inigo Jones's Queen's House (*see below*). In 2003, a £34m refurbishment project finally came to a end and the scaffolding came down to reveal a reroofed Painted Hall and Dome, restored friezes, a regilded weather vane and repaired windows. After the Navy left in 1997, the University of Greenwich took over some of the building, but the public can still visit the chapel and the Painted Hall.

Queen's House

Park Row, SE10 9NF (8312 6565/www.nmm.ac.uk). Greenwich DLR/rail/Maze Hill rail. **Open** 10am-5pm daily. **Admission** free. **Credit** MC, V.

Designed by Inigo Jones in 1616 for James I's wife, Anne of Denmark, the Queen's House was his first attempt at Palladian architecture. The lavish interior contains the National Maritime Museum's art collection, with works by Hogarth and Gainsborough. A magnificent colonnade connects the building to the National Maritime Museum (*see above*). A monographic exhibition of work by 18th-century landscape painter William Hodges, the first professional landscape painter to visit India, opens on 6 July 2004.

Ranger's House

Chesterfield Walk, SE10 8QX (8853 0035/ www.english-heritage.org.uk). Cutty Sark DLR/ Greenwich DLR/rail/Blackheath rail. **Open** *Nov-Dec, Mar* 10am-4pm Wed-Sun. *Apr-Sept* 10am-6pm Wed-Sun. *Oct* 10am-5pm Wed-Sun. **Admission** (EH) £4.50; £3.50 concessions; £2.50 5-15 yrs. **Credit** MC, V.

Once a 'grace and favour' home to the Greenwich park ranger, this pretty 18th-century villa had been converted into council-owned changing rooms by 1902. English Heritage eventually refurbished the place, which now houses the Wernher Collection, displaying crafts dating from 3 BC, Old Masters, 18th-century French furniture and Britain's largest private collection of Renaissance jewellery.

Royal Observatory

Greenwich Park, SE10 9NF (8312 6565/www.rog. nmm.ac.uk). Greenwich DLR/rail/Maze Hill rail. **Open** 10am-5pm daily. **Admission** free. **Credit** MC, V.

The Royal Observatory was built by Wren in 1675 on the orders of Charles II. The museum explains the remarkable search for longitude, from 45 years of celestial observation by Royal Astronomer John Flamsteed to John Harrison's creation of the first maritime clock. Other exhibits examine the origins of astronomy and the history of timekeeping from sundials to atomic clocks. The planetarium holds regular star-gazing shows; call ahead to book.

Kennington & the Elephant

Kennington tube/Elephant & Castle tube/rail.

Kennington Park is the remains of a common where, during the 18th and 19th centuries, John Wesley and other preachers addressed large audiences. Nowadays the Surrey faithful gather at the **AMP Oval** (*see p322*) to watch their team – and, several times a year, the national side – play cricket. Off Kennington Lane are some elegant streets; Cardigan Street, Courtenay Street and Courtenay Square all have neat neo-Georgian terraced houses. Across Kennington Road lies pretty Cleaver Square, while another gem, Walcot Square, lies further to the north-east.

A short walk north takes you to the **Imperial War Museum** (*see below*), beyond which lies the rubicund fright known as the **Elephant & Castle**. Rumour has it this shabby shopping centre will be demolished and replaced by all sorts of loveliness by 2012, but the planners' grandiose dreams are forever facing setbacks.

Imperial War Museum

Lambeth Road, SE1 6HZ (7416 5000/www.iwm. org.uk). Lambeth North tube/Elephant & Castle tube/rail. **Open** 10am-6pm daily. **Admission** free. **Credit** AmEx, MC, V. **Map** p404 N10.

More than just displays of military hardware, this affecting museum casts the visitor into the thick of 20th-century warfare. Inevitably, the tanks, rockets and planes in the ground-floor exhibition hall make for a bombastic first impression, but the sections on World Wars I and II are the main attractions, with the Trench and Blitz Experiences, maps, film footage and artefacts providing absorbing testimony to the hardships endured at home and abroad. In a new extension, a moving permanent exhibition is devoted to the Holocaust, with footage of Hitler's speeches, models of concentration camps and survivors' testimonials. Conflicts Since 1945 explains wars (such as the Korean War), while the Secret War deals with intrigue and espionage. The Art of World War I and II, on the second floor, includes works by Henry Moore and Stanley Spencer.

To mark the 60th anniversary of D-Day, which falls in June 2004, a free temporary exhibition opens in the spring, looking at the personal experiences of some of those who took part using film, photos, documents and mementoes. 'Women and War' (£7; £5 concs) runs until 18 April 2004.

Camberwell & Peckham

Denmark Hill or Peckham Rye rail.

A typically congested south London crossroads surrounds beleaguered Camberwell Green; it may sound bucolic, but this sour little patch of greensward is mostly alcoholic (hard drinking gentlemen of the road tend to congregate here). **St Giles church**, just east of the green, is a typically imposing early Victorian structure by Sir George Gilbert Scott of St Pancras Station fame (*see p33*). The trendy bars and cafés of Church Street lend it a bohemian air, as does Camberwell College of Arts (Peckham Road, 7514 6300), London's oldest art college.

Linking Camberwell to Peckham, **Burgess Park** was created by filling in the Grand Surrey Canal and razing rows of houses. Walking through it to Peckham takes you to a canal path cycleway that runs past the peculiar looking Peckham Library, for which architect Will Alsop won awards. **Peckham Rye Common**, once nothing more than grazing land, is an airy stretch with ornamental gardens. At the top, Honor Oak and Forest Hill look down over suburban south-east London and Kent. The **Horniman Museum** (*see below*) is the best reason for taking to these hills.

Horniman Museum

100 London Road, SE23 3PQ (8699 1872/ www.horniman.ac.uk). Forest Hill rail/363, 122, 176, 185, 312, 356, P4, P13 bus. **Open** 10.30am-5.30pm daily. **Admission** free; donations appreciated. **Credit** MC, V.

A £13m renovation in 2002 gave this Forest Hill landmark a smart café, an absorbing music room and, newest of all, an 'environment' room, with bees in an observation hive. All the stuff that once had it filed firmly under 'eccentric' in guidebooks is still here, though: an overstuffed walrus presides over hundreds of other more accurate taxidermic specimens in the main gallery; the ornate Apostle clock sometimes chimes entertainingly (there's a fund to get it mended); and there are exotic fish and masks, puppets and curiosities. The museum exists thanks to the collecting passion of the tea trader Frederick Horniman, who opened it in 1901. The gardens, with their animal enclosure and elegant conservatory, are quite lovely, especially in the summer when there are family shows here.

The dinosaurs are listed Victorian structures at **Crystal Palace Park**. *See p170.*

Dulwich & Crystal Palace

Crystal Palace, East Dulwich, Herne Hill, North Dulwich or West Dulwich rail.

Well-heeled and picture-pretty Dulwich Village (*see p164* **Village green**), complete with its ye-olde-village signposts, is home to England's first public art gallery, the **Dulwich Picture Gallery** (*see below*). West of it, Herne Hill provides a leafy halfway point between posh, white, middle-class Dulwich and multicultural Brixton (*see p171*); **Brockwell Park**, with its fabulous if financially straitened lido (*see p323*), is on the way.

If you head down College Road from Dulwich, you'll reach **Crystal Palace Park**. The palace, which was built in Hyde Park (*see p138*) for the Great Exhibition of 1851 and then moved south to Sydenham, burned down in 1936, but the park, with its hornbeam maze and dinosaurs – now classified as listed buildings – still bears its name. A seemingly endless programme of refurbishments promises new gardens and animal enclosures. The **National Sports Centre** (*see p322*) is in the south-east corner of the park. **Crystal Palace Museum** (8676 0700; open 11am-5pm Sun and bank holidays) is housed in the former engineering school where John Logie Baird invented TV.

Dulwich Picture Gallery

Gallery Road, SE21 7AD (8693 5254/www.dulwichpicturegallery.org.uk). North Dulwich or West Dulwich rail. **Open** 10am-5pm Tue-Fri; 11am-5pm Sat, Sun and bank holidays. **Admission** £4; £3 concessions; free under-16s, students, unemployed, disabled. **Credit** MC, V.

The tiny size of England's original public art gallery in no way reflects its importance. First, there's Sir John Soane's perfect neo-classical building, which inspired the National Gallery's Sainsbury Wing and the Getty Museum in Los Angeles. Inside is a roll-call of greats: Rubens, Van Dyck, Cuyp, Poussin, Rembrandt, Gainsborough, Raphael and Reynolds. The gallery's critically acclaimed revamp in 2000 added a lovely café and a new gallery. Images of Crystal Palace, Sydenham, an exhibition running 4 February to 18 April 2004, brings remnants of the original palace to the gardens, as well as prints from its heyday. Henry Moore's sculptures and drawings are exhibited 12 May-19 September 2004.

Further south-east

Reasons for plunging deeper into suburban south-east London may not be immediately apparent, but, bleak stretches of public housing aside, there are prizes for those who venture beyond the beaten tourist track. The bland town of Eltham has **Eltham Palace**, while way over in Bexleyheath, the **Red House**, designed by young architect Philip Webb for William Morris, finally opened to the public in 2003 (*see below*).

The area around Eltham and Bexley is dotted with meadows and ancient woodlands, such as **Oxleas Wood** (accessible from Falconwood rail station); many of them are connected by the **Green Chain Walk** (8921 5028, www.greenchain.com for maps). Heading further south into Kent, the village of **Chislehurst** has its very own Druids' caves (8467 3264/www.chislehurstcaves.co.uk) to tempt day trippers underground.

Eltham Palace

Court Yard, off Court Road, SE9 (8294 2548/www.english-heritage.org.uk). Eltham rail. **Open** *Apr-Sept* 10am-6pm Wed-Fri, Sun. *Oct* 10am-5pm Wed-Fri, Sun. *Nov-Mar* 10am-4pm Wed-Fri, Sun. **Admission** (EH) *House & grounds (incl audio tour)* £6.50; £5 concessions; £3.50 5-16s; free under-5s; £16.50 family (2+3). *Grounds only* £4; £3 concessions; £2 5-16s; free under-5s. **Credit** MC, V.

The moat and medieval remains surround an art deco feast. Stephen Courtauld, a member of the textile family and patron of the arts (*see also p96* Courtauld Gallery), built this country house in the mid 1930s. The interior is sleek, with polished veneer walls, modish abstract carpets and a circular entrance hall housing drinks trays, glass cigarette boxes and white furniture under a concrete-and glass-domed ceiling. In sharp contrast, the 15th-century great hall, the second largest of its kind in England, is all that's left of the original palace, and is cleverly incorporated into the modern building.

Red House

13 Red House Lane, Bexleyheath, Kent DA6 8JF (01494 755588/www.nationaltrust.org.uk). Bexleyheath rail, then 15min walk or taxi from station. **Open** (pre-booked guided tour only) *Oct-Feb* 11am-3.30pm Wed-Sun, bank holidays. *Mar-Sept* 11am-4.15pm Wed-Sun. **Admission** (NT) £5 £2.50 concessions; £12.50 family.

It's fitting that the man who founded the Society for the Protection of Ancient Buildings in 1877, part of a movement that gave rise to the National Trust, should have his old house preserved. William Morris, who lived here for five years until 1864, commissioned a young architect friend to design this building, and it became a landmark in the development of the Arts and Crafts movement.

With Webb, Rossetti and Burne-Jones, Morris furnished and decorated Red House using medieval styles and influences, and this work formed the basis of the manufacturing and decorating firm of Morris & Co, which had a profound influence on interior design and decoration. Many of the original furnishings are on display at the Victoria & Albert Museum (*see p137*) although some furniture, stained glass and wall paintings remain in the house. Visits are by pre-booked guided tour only. There's a tea room but no toilets on site at present.

South-west London

This side of the beautiful south is sophisticated – it has the tube to prove it.

Shrine to a 20th-century boy at **Barnes Common**. *See p173.*

Vauxhall, Stockwell & Brixton

Vauxhall tube/rail, Stockwell tube or Brixton tube/rail.

Back in the 18th century, when **Vauxhall** was still a pretty southern village, Vauxhall Pleasure Gardens drew well-to-do crowds to take the air. All that remains of that heyday now is a scruffy small park, renamed Spring Gardens; rather nicer is Bonnington Square's Pleasure Garden, reclaimed, developed and maintained by the residents with a lavender-filled garden and a 30-foot Victorian waterwheel. Otherwise, the area holds little of interest for the visitor.

The railway boom of the 1840s and subsequent urban expansion woke up the sleepy village of **Stockwell** and ate up all of the commonland around it. Nowadays, it's an unappealing stretch of housing estates and heavy traffic. A blue plaque at 87 Hackford Road tells us it was Vincent van Gogh's home from 1873 to 1874. Further north, between Prima Road and Camberwell New Road, is **St Mark's church**, built in 1824 on the site of a gallows; many of the Jacobite rebels of 1745 were hanged, drawn and quartered here.

Brixton was a marshy wasteland until the construction of Vauxhall Bridge in 1816 improved access to central London and planted the seeds for suburban development. Brixton Prison, which opened in 1820 off Jebb Avenue, soon gained a reputation as one of the harshest in London, a reputation that remains to this day. The first treadmill, invented by Sir William Cubitt, was used there to grind corn until 1921.

The railways and trams of the 1860s made a commuter town of Brixton and Electric Avenue, later immortalised in Eddy Grant's song, became one of the first shopping streets lit by electricity. As wealthier residents moved out between the wars, their large houses were turned into cheap boarding houses popular with theatre folk: former prime minister John Major was raised here by his circus-performer father.

Brixton's personality changed dramatically during the 1950s and '60s with the arrival of immigrants from the West Indies. A generation later, tensions between black residents and police reached boiling point. The infamous riots of 1981, 1985 and 1995 centred on the area around Railton Road and **Coldharbour Lane**, which became known as the 'Front Line'. Problems remain, particularly drug-related ones, and contribute to the edginess of the area.

Despite this, the mood in Brixton is upbeat and the atmosphere buzzing. Gentrification – pop into Trinity Gardens for a glimpse of genteel Brixton – hasn't yet pushed out anarchists and artists who've been squatting here since the '70s, and the sizeable black population, almost a third of Brixton's residents, lives alongside a growing gay community.

By day, Brixton's mixed-up craziness is best experienced by strolling chaotic **Brixton Market** (*see p249*). On your wanderings, pop into the Black Cultural Archives (378 Coldharbour Lane, 7738 4591), the Brixton Art Gallery (35 Brixton Station Road, 7733 6957) or the Juice Bar (407 Coldharbour Lane, 7738 4141). Clubs and bars of note include the Fridge

A dog's best friend

When she founded the Temporary Home for Lost and Starving Dogs in 1860, Mary Tealby was subjected to growls of displeasure from Victorian society. At the time, it was thought 'immoral' to spend time and money on dumb animals when there were so many humans suffering poverty. Tealby, however, was dogged, and her canine collection flourished in a stable yard in Holloway, north London.

After her death in 1865, a new home was found for the dogs. **Battersea Dogs' Home** is now a world famous institution, providing temporary shelter for lost cats and dogs and arranging new homes for thousands of abandoned or unwanted pets every year.

Long-term shelter residents have large, clean enclosures, toys and regular meals, and are taken for walks in Battersea Park. Yet they all appreciate a visit, and live in hope that someone will find them irresistible. It's as likely as not to be the dog's previous master: the Battersea Lost Dogs Line helps reunite 40 per cent of the animals brought here with their owners.

People who are willing to give a dog or cat a new home embark on a sort of computer dating process, which presents potential new owners with a list of animals that would be suitable for their needs. Each dog brought into the home is given a behavioural assessment, so that staff can gauge what sort of home would best suit it. Once a new owner has been found, they pay a fee (£40 for cats; £70 for dogs) to cover the shelter's costs.

Even if you don't plan to give a dog a home, Battersea is an interesting place to visit, with its wall of dedications to dear, departed dogs and dog lovers. Visitors are guided by a series of coloured pawprints and should be prepared to have their heart strings tugged.

Battersea Dogs' Home

4 Battersea Park Road, SW8 4AA (7622 3626/www.dogshome.org). Battersea Park or Queenstown Road rail. **Open** *Viewings* 10.30am-4.15pm Mon-Wed, Fri; 10.30am-3.15pm Sat, Sun. **Admission** £1; 50p concessions, under-16s; free under-5s. **Credit** *Shop* MC, V.

(*see p316*), Tongue & Groove (*see p226*) and the venerable party palace Dogstar (*see p319*).

A glimpse of village history still survives, however. Walk up Brixton Hill and turn right down Blenheim Gardens to Brixton's Grade II-listed windmill. It was built in 1815, when the concrete jungle was still fields of wheat.

Battersea

Clapham Junction rail.

Battersea derives its name from *Batrices Ege* (Badric's Island), the small Saxon settlement that stood here more than 1,000 years ago. Until the 19th century, the chief occupation in the area was market gardening, but the coming of the railways changed that: **Clapham Junction** was soon the city's bustling transport hub (it's still one of the busiest stations in the world), and the fields became factories.

The industrial buildings have mostly given way to luxury flats, notably Richard Rogers' wedge-shaped glass tower Montevetro, yet the most distinctive piece of architecture on the horizon is **Battersea Power Station** Sir Giles Gilbert Scott's landmark structure completed in 1933. The new owners of the building, which closed in 1983, have obtained planning permission to convert it into a business and entertainment complex, but as yet, work has yet to really begin on the project. There are more signs of life nearby at **Battersea Dogs Home** (*see p172* **A dog's best friend**).

A short walk west, the area now known as **Battersea Park** was once a rough old place; in the early 19th century, it was popular with duellers, gamblers, drunkards and criminals. However, the Public Parks Commission relandscaped the country park in the mid 19th century; nearly a century later, in 1951, it became the site of the Pleasure Gardens for that year's Festival of Britain. More relandscaping went on over the Millennium, and the riverside promenades, Peace Pagoda (built by Japanese monks and nuns in 1985 to commemorate Hiroshima Day), boating lake and fountains all look lovely. The Children's Zoo (closed winter; 8871 7539), another Festival of Britain creation, has been threatened with closure, but a number of other zoos have offered to run it. The park also has a gallery (the Pumphouse, 7350 0523).

From the park, social climbers can choose from two bridges for their route to Chelsea Embankment. We recommend the **Albert Bridge**, just beyond the Peace Pagoda. Heed the notice before you cross: 'All troops must break step when marching over this bridge'. A little further west is Battersea Bridge; built in 1886-90 to Joseph Bazalgette's designs, it replaced the wooden structure that was the subject of Whistler's moody *Nocturnes*. Not far from here is **St Mary's Battersea**, where Blake was married, where the American traitor Benedict Arnold was buried, and from where Turner used to sit and paint the river.

Clapham & Wandsworth

Clapham Common tube/Wandsworth Common or Wandsworth Town rail.

People fleeing the Plague and the Great Fire in the 17th century sought sanctuary in the 'village on the hill' (*see p16*); for years afterwards, Clapham's clean air won it many fans. The air's not so pure now, but the area is still desirable.

The heart of the neighbourhood lies around **Clapham Common**. The smart shops and cafés of Abbeville Village, south-east of the station, and **Clapham Old Town**, north-east of the common, centre on the attractive 18th-century pubs and shops of the Pavement. In the 19th century, the Clapham Sect, a group of wealthy Anglicans known for their 'muscular Christianity', worshipped at **Holy Trinity Church** on the edge of the common. Popular with joggers and footballers by day, after dark parts of the common become a gay cruising ground.

To the south-west, **Wandsworth Common** forms, along with Clapham Common, the borders of 'Nappy Valley', so called because of the recent proliferation of young, middle class families in the neighbourhood. The north side of Wandsworth Common is dominated by a big old Victorian heap, the Gothic **Royal Victoria Patriotic Building**, surrounded by modern tower blocks. The building was originally an asylum for orphans of the Crimean War; during World War II, it became a POW camp.

Putney, Barnes & Kew

Putney Bridge tube, Barnes rail, Kew Gardens tube/rail or Kew Bridge rail.

Peaceful, riverside **Putney** was an anonymous fishing and farming community until it became popular with Tudor celebrity commuters such as Thomas Cromwell. These days it's familiar to millions as the starting point of the annual Varsity Boat Race (*see p260*). The river takes on a semi-rural aspect at Putney Bridge; looking back down the Thames, you can catch glimpses of London's skyline, but upstream, it's all trees.

The **WWT Wetland Centre** (*see p175*) lies on the other side of **Barnes Common**. The main road across the expanse, Queen's Ride, humpbacks over the railway line below. It was here, on 16 September 1977, that singer Gloria Jones drove her Mini off the road, killing her passenger, T-Rex singer Marc Bolan. The slim trunk of the sycamore tree hit by the car is now

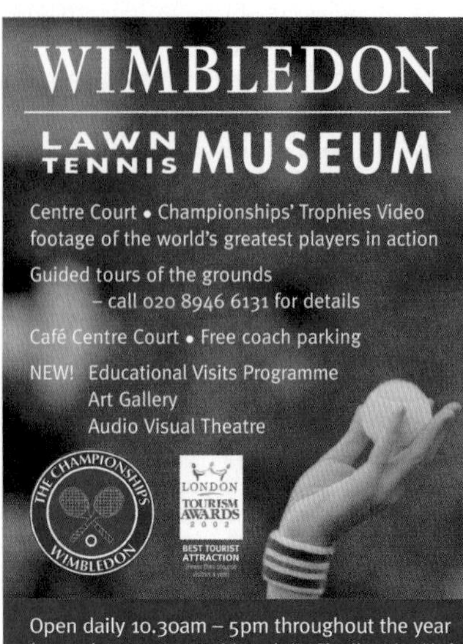

WIMBLEDON
LAWN TENNIS MUSEUM
Centre Court • Championships' Trophies Video footage of the world's greatest players in action
Guided tours of the grounds – call 020 8946 6131 for details
Café Centre Court • Free coach parking
NEW! Educational Visits Programme
Art Gallery
Audio Visual Theatre
THE CHAMPIONSHIPS WIMBLEDON
LONDON TOURISM AWARDS 2002
BEST TOURIST ATTRACTION
Open daily 10.30am – 5pm throughout the year
(open only to tournament visitors during The Championships)
Call 020 8946 6131 for further details and rates
Centre Court, The All England Lawn Tennis & Croquet Club, Church Road, Wimbledon, London SW19 5AE
Nearest Tube Southfields
www.wimbledon.org/museum

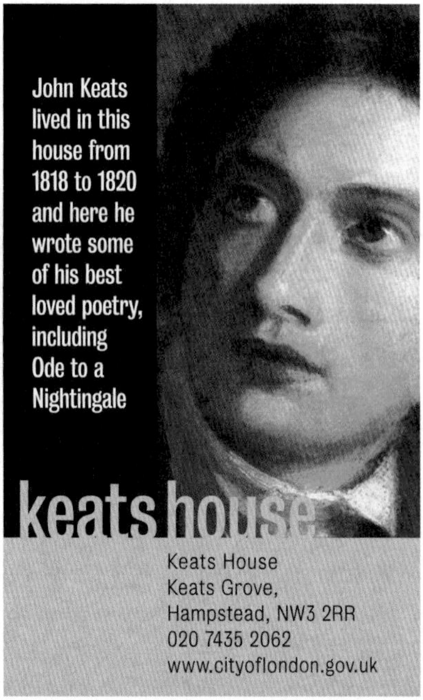

John Keats lived in this house from 1818 to 1820 and here he wrote some of his best loved poetry, including Ode to a Nightingale
keats house
Keats House
Keats Grove,
Hampstead, NW3 2RR
020 7435 2062
www.cityoflondon.gov.uk

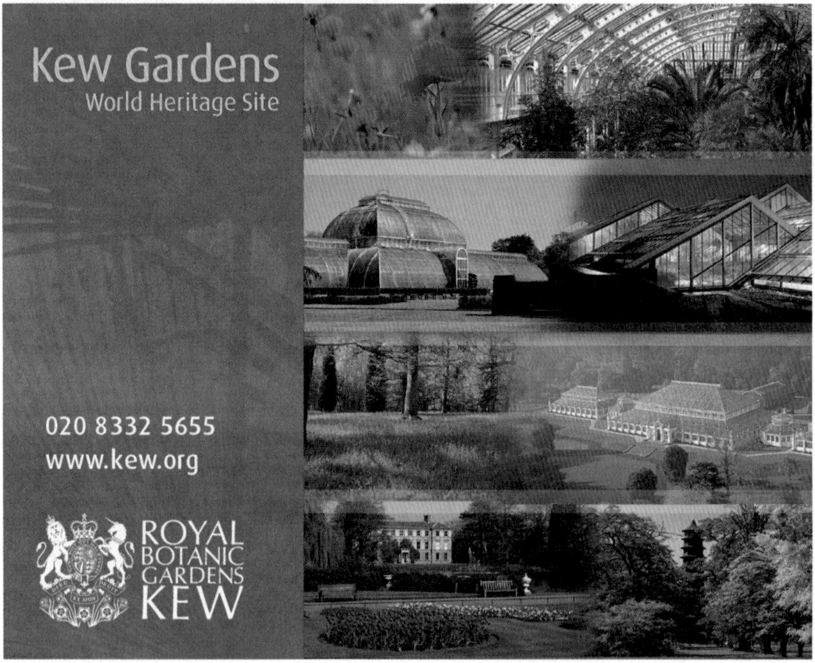

Kew Gardens
World Heritage Site
020 8332 5655
www.kew.org
ROYAL BOTANIC GARDENS KEW

covered with notes, poems and declarations of love. Steps lead to a bronze bust of the star.

Much further west of here, **Kew** is famed for its gardens (properly known as the **Royal Botanic Gardens**; *see below*) and its royal, bucolic air (*see p176* **Village green**).

Royal Botanic Gardens

Kew, Richmond, Surrey, TW9 3AB (8332 5655/ information 8940 1171/www.kew.org). Kew Gardens tube/rail/Kew Bridge rail/riverboat to Kew Pier. **Open** *End Mar-Aug* 9.30am-6.30pm Mon-Fri; 9.30am-7.30pm Sat, Sun, bank holidays. *Sept-Oct* 9.30am-6pm daily. *End Oct-beginning Feb* 9.30am-4.15pm daily. *Beginning Feb-end Mar* 9.30am-5.30pm daily. **Admission** (LP) £7.50; £5.50 concessions; free under-16s. **Credit** AmEx, MC, V.

UNESCO appointed Kew Gardens a World Heritage Site in July 2003. It's regarded internationally as a centre for horticultural research and its history is noble; the roots of the vegetation here (the biggest plant collection in the world) are almost 300 years old. The gardens, which now cover 300 acres (121 hectares), were developed in the 17th and 18th centuries in the grounds of Kew Palace, landscaped by Lancelot 'Capability' Brown in the 1770s.

To do the most exotic collections justice, a visit to each of the various giant, mostly Victorian, glasshouses, is in order. For nearly two centuries Kew botanists have been able to create conditions suitable to make any plant in the world feel at home. In sultry Palm House (Decimus Burton and Richard Turner, 1848) lurk the record breakers: the slow-growing *encephalartos altensteinii*, the oldest pot plant in the world, and the tallest palm under glass (a Chilean wine palm, planted in 1775). Not too far away, the Temperate House is the world's largest ornamental glasshouse with the worlds largest permanent orchid display. The star of the show is *pendiculata sanderina*, the Holy Grail for orchid-hunters, whose petals grow to 3ft (0.9m) long.

On the eastern border of the gardens is the Marianne North Gallery, housing paintings by this Victorian artist. To the south-west stands Queen's Cottage, built as a summer house for Queen Charlotte in 1771; it's open occasionally during August and May. The Great Pagoda, built in 1762, is too unstable to enter these days, but still makes a useful mustering point. For a view of forest canopy, take to the aerial walkway in the forest just west of the pagoda – it's 33ft (10m) high, 328ft (100m) long and takes you into another world entirely.

You can just wander the site at will, or take the Kew Explorer road train, which runs from the Victoria Gate (£3; £1.50 concessions) for a restful 35-minute tour of the site's curiosities. You can board and disembark as often as you like. Highlights at Kew during 2004 include the Summer Festival (29 May-26 September), a celebration of garden loveliness, and Making Spirits Bright (27 November 2004-4 January 2005), a lantern-lit display with carol singing and other special, family-oriented events.

WWT Wetland Centre

Queen Elizabeth's Walk, SW13 9WT (8409 4400/ www.wwt.org.uk). Hammersmith tube then 283 bus/Barnes rail/33, 72 bus. **Open** *Mar-Oct* 9.30am-6pm daily (last entry 5pm). *Nov-Feb* 9.30am-5pm daily (last entry 4pm). **Admission** £6.75; £5.50 concessions; £4 4-16s; free under-4s; £17.50 family. **Credit** MC, V.

The WWT Wetland Centre is just four miles (6.5km) from the West End, but feels miles from London. A sea of paths through ponds, rushes, reed beds and wildflower gardens culminates in two raised look-out points from which to gaze at the centre's teeming birdlife. London's wildlife equivalent of King's Cross station, the Wetland Centre is home to 150 species of bird, 300 varieties of moth and butterfly, 20 types of dragonfly, four species of bat and water vole, 300,000 aquatic plants and 27,000 trees.

It wasn't always this pretty. Until 1989 the site consisted of four huge concrete reservoirs owned by Thames Water. But when the reservoirs were made redundant, naturalist Sir Peter Scott got permission from the water company to transform the 105 acres (42 hectares) into wetland habitat. The concrete boxes were converted into a marshy oasis and the place became an avian five-star hotel and a twitcher's paradise: little ringed plovers, black-tailed godwits, kingfishers, willow warblers, herons, geese and swans stay here, with the cast of characters changing by the season.

Wimbledon

Wimbledon tube/rail.

Once the tennis tournament (*see p261*) is over, wealthy residents reclaim smart houses rented to players and SW19 reverts to leafy, sleepy type. Wimbledon's **Centre Court** shopping centre holds many high street chains; the handsome, Edwardian **Wimbledon Theatre** is big on Christmas pantomime (seasonal plays for children) and touring musicals.

The area is best known among Londoners for **Wimbledon Common,** a huge, partly wooded expanse crossed with paths, cycleways and horse tracks. The common also has a windmill with a volunteer-run tearoom (Windmill Museum, Windmill Road, 8947 2825), where Robert Baden-Powell wrote *Scouting for Boys* in 1908. The villagey bit of Wimbledon is to the east, as is attractive **Wimbledon Park** and the **All England Lawn Tennis Club**.

Wimbledon Lawn Tennis Museum

Centre Court, All England Lawn Tennis Club, Church Road, SW19 5AE (8946 6131/www.wimbledon.org/ museum). Southfields tube/39, 93, 200, 493 bus. **Open** 10.30am-5pm daily; spectators only during championships. **Admission** (LP) £5.50; £4.50 concessions; £3.50 5-16s; free under-5s. **Credit** MC, V.

Those who think the championships don't come around often enough will be pleased to hear that at

Village green Kew Green

There's a certain disjunction between perfectly manicured Kew Green and the heavy traffic ploughing relentlessly through it on the A205. This has long been a transport route: the name Kew first appears in local records in the 14th century, although excavated coins suggest a settlement existed here much earlier – 'Kew' is a derivative of Saxon 'Cayho' – and from the first it was the ease of transport across a ford in the Thames that marked this out as favourable land.

Fewer vehicles back then had surfboards strapped to their roofs (the M4 now starts on the far side of Kew Bridge), but today this remains one of London's prettiest village greens. Tall trees border the common, casting a handful of benches in dappled shade. The grass forms a picturesque ground for **Kew Cricket Club** (8940 9155, www.kewcc.co.uk). Its squat, wooden clubhouse shelters under elderly trees, and typifies the parish charm of this small but perfectly formed community green.

Such understated elegance is all the more unusual in the light of the area's royal associations. Kew's proximity to Richmond Palace meant that courtiers lived here from the 16th century onwards, and in the late 18th century it wasn't unusual to see members of the Royal Family descending from their carriages for tea in one of the Georgian cottages that still frame the green, some now upmarket restaurants and bars.

A more permanent reminder of regal eating habits exists further down Kew Road, at The Original Maids of Honour restaurant (8940 2752). Henry VIII loved 'Maid of Honour' cakes and is supposed to have locked the recipe in an iron box in Richmond Palace. Whatever truth underlies such legend, the Newens family has guarded the recipe for more than 150 years, and continues to turn out these fabled fancies from their rickety building, with its quaint gold lettering and gabled window boxes.

The relationship between court and village life in Kew is best expressed by **St Anne's church** on the green. Although dating from 1714, a place of worship existed here solely for the use of the local manor as far back as the 16th century. At the start of the 18th century, Queen Anne – then Lady of the Manor – bowed to public demand, and set aside £100 of her own money for the construction of a parish church on the 'waste known as Kew Green' (her words). Over the

the Lawn Tennis Museum, they never really end. Open all year, the museum is home to historical memorabilia, starting from the years of starchy, serious-looking Victorian players and leading to the foul-mouthed celebrities of today; items on show include dresses worn by the Williams sisters and the racket with which Martina Navratilova won her record 20th Wimbledon title in 2003. A theatre endlessly replays classic matches, and a gallery showcases tennis-related art from across the generations in special exhibitions: 'The Golden Age of the Tennis Poster, 1890-1940' is on until March 2004. Guided tours take fans behind the scenes, where they soak up the atmosphere on the main courts.

Richmond

Richmond tube/rail.

Although home to its fair share of generic, high-street shops (and more than its fair share of low-flying planes), Richmond nevertheless manages to embody an idyll of the Great Outdoors in far west London that can make you wonder if the District line hasn't gone and dropped you in Cambridge by mistake. Once known as Shene, the area has been linked with royalty for centuries: Edward III had a riverside palace here in the mid 1300s, and in 1501 Henry VII completed Richmond Palace, so besotted with its surroundings that he renamed them after his favourite Yorkshire earldom.

These days, all that's left of the palace where Elizabeth I spent her last few summers (she died here in 1603) is the gateway on **Richmond Green**, once the site of royal jousting tournaments and now most notable for the antiquated alleyways liberally peppered with old, cloistered pubs that branch off it, and for the elegant **Richmond Theatre**, nestling against an eerily boarded-up church on the green's east side. Also of interest is the **Church of St Mary Magdalene**, on Paradise Road, with its blend of architectural styles and tranquil gardens, lent a Gothic air by the grand trees looming over ancient tombs.

Branching off Hill Street, and running alongside Richmond's old town hall, Whittaker Avenue leads amblers to the riverside, where the delightful White Cross pub (8940 6844), with its 'entrance at high tide' (the river floods regularly), has watched the waters run by since 1835. **Richmond Bridge**, built in 1774 and the

years, the graveyard became a final home for the painters Gainsborough and Zoffany, while the organ is believed to have once belonged to Handel. The grounds are currently in a state of some disrepair, although the many children's paintings and family photographs lining the walls highlight the central role they still play in Kew's community life. Teas are served every Sunday from 1.30pm.

Similarly bucolic is the local newsagents, Horton's, where antiquated Jason Donovan puzzles gather dust among soft footballs and faded notebooks. There's a duck pond to amuse toddlers, a playground and public tennis courts at nearby **Westerly Ware**. In 1987 an association was founded to resurrect the historic Kew Fayre (*pictured*), which sees the green covered with stalls on the first Saturday of September, and every August bank holiday weekend marks the Kew Horticultural Society's annual Summer Show: 2004 will be its 60th anniversary, with more fruit, vegetables and flower displays than ever. For refreshment, try the timber-beamed Coach & Horses (8940 1208), where there's a good menu, delightful beer garden and some decent bedrooms for those who can't face rolling themselves home.

oldest surviving crossing on the Thames, has cafés tucked beneath it and magnificent, sweeping views up top. The river promenade is otherwise dominated by chain pubs such as the Pitcher & Piano and the Slug & Lettuce.

The area is perhaps most famous for the rugged beauty of **Richmond Park**, the largest park in London, and, along with Epping Forest, one of the last vestiges of the magnificent oak woodland that once encircled the city. It's wonderfully uncultivated, as suited to riding, rambling and off-road cycling as to more organised sports. The park also forms a natural habitat for wildlife, such as free-roaming red and fallow deer. Buildings include **Pembroke Lodge**, the childhood home of philosopher Bertrand Russell (now a café), and the Palladian splendour of **White Lodge**; **Isabella Plantation** offers a winding walk through landscaped gardens with streams and ponds.

Museum of Richmond

Old Town Hall, Whittaker Avenue, Richmond, Surrey TW9 1TP (8332 1141/www.museumofrichmond.com). Richmond tube/rail. **Open** *May-Sept* 11am-5pm Tue-Sat; 1-4pm Sun. *Oct-Apr* 11am-5pm Tue-Sat. **Admission** free. **No credit cards**.

Housed in Richmond's old town hall, a lovely late 19th-century building 98ft (30m) from the riverside, this small but well-maintained museum charts the development of the surrounding area as a royal resort and fashionable haven for high society. The life of 'sensationalist' local author Mary Elizabeth Braddon is the subject of a display until 24 April 2004. Following that, there's a model soldiers extravaganza from 12 May to 29 August 2004, and an Alice in Wonderland special from 8 September to 30 October; ring or check the website for more details.

Further south-west

If the water table allows, follow the river from Richmond on a pastoral walk to Petersham and Ham, or take in one of a handful of country villas in the area; among them are **Orleans House**, **Ham House** (*see p178*) and **Marble Hill House** (*see p179*). Further along, the river meanders around Twickenham to **Strawberry Hill** (8240 4224), home of Horace Walpole and the first significant building of the Gothic Revival, and, after a leisurely trip through suburban Kingston, arrives at **Hampton Court Palace** (*see below*).

Hampton Court Palace and grounds.

Sightseeing

Ham House

Ham, Richmond, Surrey TW10 7RS (8940 1950/ www.nationaltrust.org.uk/hamhouse). Richmond tube/rail then 371 bus. **Open** *Gardens* 11am-6pm or dusk Mon-Wed, Sat, Sun. *House Apr-Oct* 1-5pm Mon-Wed, Sat, Sun. **Admission** £7; £3.50 5-15s; £17.50 family (2+2). Garden only £3; £1.50 5-15s; £7.50 family (2+2); free under-5s. **Credit** MC, V.

One of the most outstanding Stuart properties in the country, this red-brick retreat for counts and countesses is now a lavish window into the lives of history's rich and famous. The building alone is a treasure, built in 1610 for a courtier of James I and extended in the 1670s under the extravagant Countess of Dysart, a political schemer. The grand interior has period furnishings: rococo mirrors, ornate tapestries and a table in the dairy supported on sculptures of cows' legs. The formal grounds attract the most attention: there's a delightful trellised Cherry Garden dominated by a statue of Bacchus. The tea-room in the old orangery turns out historic dishes (lavender syllabub, anyone?) using ingredients from the restored Kitchen Gardens.

Hampton Court Palace

East Molesey, Surrey KT8 9AU (0870 751 5175 24hr information 0870 752 7777/advance tickets 0870 753 7777/www.hrp.org.uk). Hampton Court rail/riverboat from Westminster or Richmond to Hampton Court Pier (Apr-Oct). **Open** *Palace* Apr-Oct 10.15am-6pm Mon; 9.30am-6pm Tue-Sun. Nov-Mar 10.15am-4.30pm Mon; 9.30am-4.30pm Tue-Sun (last entry 45mins before closing). *Park* dawn-dusk daily. **Admission** (LP) *Palace, courtyard, cloister & maze* £11.50; £8.50 concessions; £7.50 5-15s; £34 family (max 5 people); free under-5s. Maze only £3.50; £2.50 5-15s. **Credit** AmEx, MC, V.

There's hardly a footnote in British history that doesn't in some way work itself back to Hampton Court. Seized by Henry VIII from Cardinal Wolsey in the early 16th century, this formidable palace went on to form a backdrop for some of the most famous scenes in the last few centuries, as well as serving as a stage for its most infamous players. Charles I was held here as a prisoner of Oliver Cromwell's army (he escaped after three months, and Cromwell went on to use the palace as his home). The grounds have seen royal births (Henry VIII's only son, Edward), deaths (Jane Seymour, his mother, days later, and in 1702 William III, after falling from a horse), and in the 1980s barely escaped complete disaster when fire destroyed much of the King's Apartments.

It was first opened to the public by Queen Victoria in 1838, and visits include six separate guided tours, variously taking in highlights including Henry VIII's Great Hall, with hammer-beam roof and windows stained in the crests of his unfortunate wives; the reputedly haunted Renaissance Picture Gallery, home to works by artists as eminent as

Correggio and Titian; and the Tudor Kitchens, where costumed actors create period dishes and charm children silly. Outside, Lancelot 'Capability' Brown's Great Vine continues to runneth over: planted in 1768, it still yields 500-700lb (230-320kg) of grapes a year. Adults and children both can amuse themselves for an hour (possibly much, much longer) in the world-famous maze.

Marble Hill House

Richmond Road, Twickenham, Middx TW1 2NL (8892 5115/www.english-heritage.org.uk). Richmond tube/rail/St Margaret's rail/33, 90, 490, H22, R70 bus. **Open** *Apr-Sept* 10am-6pm daily. *Oct* 10am-5pm daily. **Admission** £3.50; £2.50 concessions; free under-5s. **Credit** MC, V.

So perfect an example of Palladian architecture did George II demand this place to be that he almost went to war with Spain over their objections to his cutting down Honduran mahogany for its grand staircase. It says something about his feelings for Henrietta Howard, the mistress for whom he was having the house built in 1724, although more famous than any of its residents are some of the guests entertained over the centuries in the opulent Great Room; Alexander Pope, Jonathan Swift and Horace Walpole, for example.

The 66-acre (27 hectares) grounds of Marble Hill House are home to England's oldest black walnut tree (which would, in itself, make a formidable staircase). Picnic parties are welcome here, as are those looking to take advantage of the on-site sports facilities (tennis, putting, cricket). Ferries regularly cross the river to neighbouring Ham House (*see p178*). A programme of concerts and events plays out in the summer months.

Orleans House Gallery

Riverside, Twickenham, Middx TW1 3DJ (8831 6000/www.richmond.gov.uk/orleanshouse). St Margaret's rail or Richmond tube then 33, 490, H22, R68, R70 bus. **Open** *Apr-Sept* 1-5.30pm Tue-Sat; 2-5.30pm Sun. *Oct-Mar* 1-4.30pm Tue-Sat; 2-4.30pm Sun. **Admission** free. **Credit** MC, V.

Peacefully secluded in six acres (6.4 hectares) of gardens, this lovely Grade I-listed riverside house was constructed in 1710 for James Johnson, the then-secretary of state for Scotland, but it actually takes its name from Louis-Philippe, Duke of Orleans, who lived here between 1800 and 1817 in exile from Napoleonic France (he would later make something of a comeback by returning and claiming the throne for himself). Although it was partially demolished in 1926, the building retains James Gibbs's neoclassical Octagon Room, housing the impressive Richmond-upon-Thames art collection, a soothing pictorial record of the surrounding countryside from the early 1700s to the present. Elsewhere, temporary exhibitions tend to be less dusty than you might imagine, and include plenty of modern and contemporary work. Until 14 February 2004, decorative art by Duncan Grant (1885-1978) will be on display in the main gallery.

Rugby Museum/ Twickenham Stadium

Twickenham Rugby Stadium, Rugby Road, Twickenham, Middx TW1 1DZ (8892 8877/ www.rfu.com). Hounslow East tube then 281 bus/Twickenham rail. **Open** *Museum* 10am-5pm Tue-Sat; 11am-5pm Sun (last entry 4.30pm). *Tours* 10.30am, noon, 1.30pm, 3pm Tue-Sat; 1pm, 3pm Sun. **Admission** £8; £5 concessions; £25 family. **Credit** AmEx, MC, V.

The impressive Twickenham Stadium is the home of English rugby union (*see p324*). Tickets for the domestic and international games held here are hard to come by, but this little museum offers some compensation if you can't get any. Tours take in the England dressing room ('sights, sounds and smells' indeed), where visitors experience the rush of adrenaline standing in the players' tunnel, and even drop in on the Members Lounge, the Presidents Suite and the Royal Box. A permanent collection of memorabilia charts the game's development from the late 19th century, with the oldest jersey in existence (1871) on display alongside the Calcutta Cup (created from the silver rupees remaining after the Calcutta Rugby Club disbanded in the 1920s), while video snippets recall classic matches. Temporary exhibitions change roughly every six months, and recently included a celebration of the life of rugby legend Jimmy Peters.

West London

The winds of cool blow westerly, from Paddington, through Notting Hill, even unto the leafy suburbs of appealing Ealing.

Paddington & Bayswater

Maps p394 & p395

Bayswater, Lancaster Gate or Queensway tube/ Paddington tube/rail.

Paddington derives its name from Padda, an ancient Anglo-Saxon chieftain who chose to settle here. The area was a rural backwater, isolated from the rest of London for centuries; for a while in the 18th century, it served as a haven for French Huguenots. However, its role changed with the building of Paddington Station in 1838. The original station was built of wood, but the magnificent structure designed by Isambard Kingdom Brunel replaced it in 1854.

The area soon descended into seediness, rushed there by overcrowding and poverty in Victorian times. The grim situation persisted throughout the 20th century, but today, those behind the massive Paddington Basin project, one of the most high-profile urban regeneration projects in Europe, are hoping to reverse the area's fortunes. The areas around West End Quay, the Point and Waterside are already gleaming; by 2006 a new urban quarter will feature restaurants, offices and other businesses.

The area known as **Bayswater**, to the south and west of Paddington, started life as a grand estate for the Bishop of London's trustees. However, the original crescent was abandoned, its smart houses built into pretty squares that became fashionable during Victorian times. Inevitably, the huge houses became too dear to maintain, and many were sold off or demolished; these days the area is a mishmash of grubby-fronted hotels, expensive apartments, and touristy shops and restaurants. At the southern edge runs Bayswater Road, a straight, tree-lined thoroughfare facing **Hyde Park**. A blue plaque to Sir James Barrie, of *Peter Pan* fame, adorns No.100, on the corner of Leinster Terrace.

A left turn at the northern end of busy **Queensway** leads into trendy **Westbourne Grove**. At its eastern extremity sit a number of splendid restaurants, including excellent Middle Eastern options and the Argentinian eaterie Rodizio Rico (*see p216*), and interesting shops. But the Grove's western end, towards Notting Hill (*see p182*), is markedly posher, with delis, antiques shops and, particularly on Ledbury Road, posh clothes boutiques.

Alexander Fleming Laboratory Museum

St Mary's Hospital, Praed Street, W2 1NY (7886 6528). Paddington tube/rail/7, 15, 27, 36 bus.
Open 10am-1pm Mon-Thur. By appointment 2-5pm Mon-Thur; 10am-5pm Fri. **Admission** £2; £1 concessions, 5-16s; free under-5s. **No credit cards**. **Map** p395 D5.

Stand in the room in which Alexander Fleming discovered penicillin in 1928 before watching a ten-minute video detailing his pioneering work. Among the artefacts preserved from Fleming's day is the fungus infested petri dish in which he first saw his miraculous 'mould juice' in action.

Maida Vale & Kilburn

Kilburn, Kilburn Park, Maida Vale or Warwick Avenue tube.

Leading from Marble Arch up past Paddington, the **Edgware Road** is a long, straight, traffic-clogged thoroughfare, its southernmost end – Marble Arch to Praed Street – interesting for its colourful collection of Middle Eastern businesses, including arguably the best kebab shops in London. North of St John's Wood Road, Edgware Road turns into **Maida Vale**, the road – and the neighbourhood it splits – named after the British victory against the French at the Battle of Maida in southern Italy in 1806.

It's affluent round here, and prettified immeasurably by the locks around the area known as **Little Venice**. From here, you can walk or take a waterbus along the canal to **London Zoo** (*see p108*). Aside from the waterway, the area's main point of interest is a large pub called Crocker's Folly (24 Aberdeen Place, 7286 6608). It was built as a hotel in 1898 by entrepreneur Frank Crocker, who'd received a tip-off that a new rail terminus was to be built opposite. When a Marylebone area half a mile away was instead chosen for the station site, a distraught Crocker threw himself off the roof.

Sprinting through the green **Paddington Recreation Ground**, where Roger Bannister practised for his four-minute mile, you'll reach **Kilburn**, whose **High Road** is well known for its pubs packed with Irish expats. This is the best place in town for a proper St Patrick's Day celebration. However, its best feature is undoubtedly the excellent **Tricycle** (*see p283*), a theatre, gallery and cinema.

Village green Acton Green Common

In 1642 the Battle of Turnham Green took place on **Acton Green Common**, when King Charles I attempted to enter London but was met by the Earl of Essex's army. As those forces were twice the size of his own, the king withdrew from Turnham Green and went to Kingston. Acton Green Common has remained a peaceful little corner of London ever since, and a large wooden sign at the edge of the green tells the tale in detail.

Nowadays, an overhead railway bridge cuts the green in two and Acton Green Common sits prettily outside Turnham Green tube station. Despite the rumblings above and below, this piece of Chiswick has a relaxed air. Its perimeter is bounded by some smart Victorian houses, and in fair weather the greensward is dotted with picnickers. There are some battered old tennis courts, and, as if to seal its claim to idyllic *rus in urbe* vibe, a defunct drinking fountain and cattle trough.

Bedford Park, on its northern edge, was London's first garden suburb, becoming a commuting village as soon as the station was built in 1869. Opposite the Common, at the junction of **Turnham Green Terrace** and **Bath Road**, the impressive exterior of **St Michael and All Angels church** was designed by Norman Shaw in 1887 and is distinguished by a huge porch, palisaded gates and a spectacular lantern between the nave and the transepts. Ornamental gardens separate it from the road. Shaw also designed the **Tabard Inn** (2 Bath Road, 8995 6035) opposite. The bar inside the Tabard divides the space in two, and it has a little theatre upstairs.

More quality evening entertainment comes in the shape of **Headliners**, west London's first purpose built comedy club, a five-minute walk from the common (*see p275*).

Loungers in the park get the ingredients for their picnic from the **Indigo** 'delicafé' (98 Turnham Green Terrace, 8995 9000). There are other nice cafés and cake shops nearby, including the split-level **Trinity's** next to the Tabard, and the larger **Maison Blanc** (26-8 Turnham Green Terrace, 8995 7220).

Sightseeing

Notting Hill

Map p394

Notting Hill Gate or Westbourne Park tube.

Originally farmland, old *Knottynghull* has gone from gracious (18th century) to poor, white working class (through the 1950s) through bohemian (the 1960s to the 1980s) and finally to stratospherically expensive (ever since the movie *Notting Hill*, really). **Notting Hill Gate**, into which you'll emerge from the tube station, will disappoint those expecting the vibrant streets of the Hugh Grant film, despite the presence of one of the best pub theatres in town (the tiny Gate Theatre above the Prince Albert pub; *see p336*). However, fear not: the Notting Hill you want is not far away.

From Notting Hill Gate, follow Pembridge Road to **Portobello Road**, a narrow, snaking thoroughfare that's home to a number of cafés, bars, restaurants, delis and shops, the revamped Electric Cinema (*see p281*) and, towards the northern end on Fridays and Saturdays, a flea market with modish used clothes, shoes and accessories (*see p250*). Some of the area's best shops are actually just off Portobello Road; at its northern end, for instance, **Golborne Road** has excellent antiques shops and Portuguese pâtisseries such as the Lisboa. The street also has the **Trellick Tower**; built in 1973 by Ernö Goldfinger, it's seen by some as a hideous carbuncle and by others as a seminal piece of modern architecture.

Besides the film, Notting Hill is chiefly famous for the Notting Hill Carnival (*see p264*). The event was introduced in 1959 as a celebration of the West Indian immigrants who first moved to the area in the 1950s, when it was dominated by slums. The carnival continues, even though most of the immigrant families who first created the event have long since been priced out of the area by the trendification of the pretty, tree-lined neighbourhood with its elegant rows of houses.

East of Portobello Road, the **Westbourne Park** area is scruffy but hip, especially around All Saints Road, which has been colonised by quirky little boutiques. Up at the top of Ladbroke Grove, meanwhile, is one of London's famously spooky boneyards, **Kensal Green Cemetery**.

Kensal Green Cemetery

Harrow Road, Kensal Green, W10 4RA (8969 0152/www.kensalgreen.co.uk). Kensal Green tube. **Open** *Apr-Sept* 9am-6pm Mon-Sat; 10am-6pm Sun. *Oct-Mar* 9am-5pm Mon-Sat; 10am-5pm Sun. *Tours* 2pm Sun; *tours incl catacombs* 2pm, 1st & 3rd Sun of mth (bring a torch). **Admission** free. *Tours* £5 donation; £4 concessions. **No credit cards**.

The Duke of Sussex, sixth son of King George III, made it clear his remains should not be buried in the usual place (Windsor). Instead, he chose Kensal Green Cemetery for his resting place, his patronage making it a socially acceptable venue for the lofty dead. The scale of the monuments shows that the wealthy were happy to invest in stonemasonry. William Makepeace Thackeray, Isambard Kingdom Brunel and Anthony Trollope lie here, but many of the most eye-catching graves are of less famous folk.

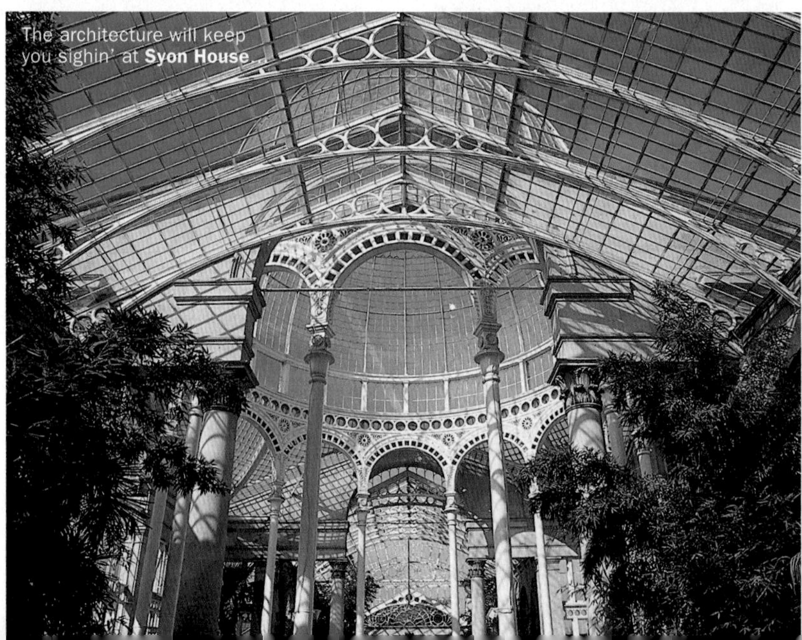

The architecture will keep you sighin' at **Syon House**...

Kensington & Holland Park

Maps p394-p397

High Street Kensington or Holland Park tube.

From fertile farmland (*Chenesit*) listed in the Domesday Book of 1086, to prosperous rural parish favoured for its proximity to London in the 17th century, **Kensington** has attracted the well-off for years. The district first grew up around Holland House (1606) and Campden House (1612), and the area was described by one historian in 1705 as a place 'inhabited by gentry and persons of note, with an abundance of shopkeepers and artificers'. It's as smart today as it's always been.

The section around Kensington High Street offers a lively mix of shops stretching along the busy main road, while the nearby streets and squares are lined by large townhouses. The most famous of the squares is just behind the art deco splendour of Barker's department store (built 1905-13); **Kensington Square** still looks noble, and sports a generous display of plaques for its residents of distinction, such as Thackeray (No.16) and John Stuart Mill (No.18).

At the foot of Kensington Church Street is the church of **St Mary Abbots**, designed by Sir George Gilbert Scott and built in 1872, and one of the finest examples of Victorian Gothic style. It has the tallest spire in London (250 feet/85 metres), as well as fine stained-glass windows that include the famous 'Healing' window funded by the Royal College of Surgeons.

Further west is the famously romantic **Holland Park**, whose 1991 Kyoto Garden is now being refurbished in authentic Japanese style. Beautiful woods and formal gardens surround the reconstructed Jacobean **Holland House**, named after an early owner, Sir Henry, Earl of Holland. The house suffered serious bomb damage during World War II and only the ground floor and arcades survived. The restored east wing contains the most dramatically sited youth hostel in town (*see p64*), and the summer ballroom has been converted into a stylish contemporary restaurant, the Belvedere. Open-air operas are staged in the park under a canopy during the summer, and for children there's an adventure playground with tree-walks and rope swings. Among the historic houses worth a visit are **Leighton House** (*see below*) and **Linley Sambourne House** (*see p184*).

Leighton House

12 Holland Park Road, W14 8LZ (7602 3316/ www.rbkc.gov.uk/leightonhousemuseum). High Street Kensington tube. **Open** 11am-5.30pm Mon, Wed-Sun. Last admission 5pm. *Tours* 2.30pm Wed, Thur; by appointment other times (min group of 12). **Admission** £3; £1 concessions. **Credit** MC, V.

One-time residence and studio of Victorian artist Frederic, Lord Leighton (1830-96), this is a breathtakingly beautiful Victorian house. Its highly decorative rooms and halls are hung with paintings and drawings by Lord Leighton, including *The Death of Brunelleschi* and *Clytemnestra from the Battlements of Argos*. Other works of art are by Leighton's contemporaries, such as John Everett Millais and

...as will the lush interiors. See p188.

Tag along

The thin line between vandalism and commercial art is increasingly hard to see. At a time when the Turner Prize can be handed to a man made famous for scrunching up pieces of paper, well, who can say that a scrawl on a wall isn't art? As a movement, modern graffiti can be traced back to Jean-Michel Basquiat, who first made his name by scribbling 'SAMO' on the streets in 1970s New York. These days, such semi-anonymous 'tags' are everywhere in London (FUME, KNOWN, MESME), and the somehow organic nature of the elaborate murals they leave behind – the way they interact with and replace other murals while having a threatened life-expectancy of their own – gives the city a kind of second skin, constantly shed and regenerated.

Enthusiasts can drop in on legalised graffiti walls known as 'Halls of Fame', including the Pit at Westbourne Park (in a basketball court on Wornington Road). Easier (and safer) may be to wait for the **Notting Hill Carnival** *(see p264)*, where legal graffiti displays are organised by the likes of SHOK1 (www.shok1.com), a 'writer' whose intricate designs offer more ammunition in the war against what Culture Minister Kim Howells called the 'cold, mechanical, conceptual bullshit' that dominates the prestigious Turner Prize for modern art.

But while noone is being forced at gunpoint to coo appreciative comments at artist Tracey Emin's unmade beds, residents in London have no choice but to consider the square acres of often illegible scrawls that sully their streets: several local councils have formed resident graffiti-bashing units. Recently, the London Assembly recommended stricter enforcement of city codes against graffiti, and fines of up to £5,000.

The ideology of graffitism for many of the painters – including most of the more fundamental 'bombing' crews that regularly risk life and limb painting around on train lines – is all about the idea of reclaiming parts of the city from the 'authorities'. And while most of these are mere territorial pissings, some use their ambiguous legality with more thought-provoking results. Bristolian artist Banksy (www.banksy.co.uk) pulled in celebrities from Jamie Oliver to Pulp's Jarvis Cocker for his 2003 Turf War exhibition, but he's best known for spraying innovative stencil designs across the capital, from his Mujahedin Mona Lisa complete with rocket launcher (now painted over), to his official-looking 'Designated Graffiti Area' notice, pasted on walls that are anything but. In 1999, before the Turner Prize ceremony, he memorably stencilled every step at Tate Modern with: 'Mind the crap'.

Edward Burne-Jones. The house was designed in 1864 by Leighton in collaboration with the architect George Aitchison. In addition to the permanent displays and temporary exhibitions, there are regular talks, tours and recitals.

Linley Sambourne House, about ten minutes' walk away (18 Stafford Terrace), was the home of cartoonist Edward Linley Sambourne. Classical Italianate in style, Stafford Terrace was built in the 1870s. Sambourne and his wife furnished their home in the fashionable artistic style of the period, and the basic decorative scheme remains the same today as they'd planned it. The house can be visited only by booking a guided tour through the Leighton House switchboard (*see p183*).

Earl's Court & Fulham

Maps p396 & p397

Earl's Court, Fulham Broadway or West Brompton tube.

What's in a name? In the case of Earl's Court, a lot: the district started life as the courthouse of the earls of Warwick and Holland, who owned the area. The two earls are immortalised in the naming of **Warwick Road** and **Holland Park** in neighbouring Kensington.

Grand landowners notwithstanding, the area was a mere hamlet up until the 1860s, when the Metropolitan Railway bought some of the farmland nearby to build Earl's Court station. A fairground was built on some derelict land near to the tracks in 1887, and its founder JR Whitley can take the blame for sowing the seeds of this country's obsession with Ferris wheels, having erected the country's first – also, at that time, the world's largest – in the mid 1890s. The site now houses the massive Earl's Court Exhibition Centre, built in 1937 and now host of trade shows, pop concerts and large-scale events such as the Ideal Home Show (*see p259*).

During the early 1900s, many of Earl's Court's residential properties were turned into flats, attracting a large immigrant population to the area. The biggest was the Australian influx of the 1950s, '60s and '70s, which earned Earl's Court the nickname 'Kangaroo Valley'. Today, it's still popular among the Antipodean population, and a clutch of budget hotels, hostels and pubs continue to fly the flag.

In the 1970s the area glammed up a bit and became a popular gay haunt; Queen frontman Freddie Mercury called Logan Place home, before moving to Stafford Terrace in the 1980s. The gay scene has since moved on, in the most part to Soho, Stoke Newington and Vauxhall, but busy men's bar Brompton's (corner of Old Brompton Road and Warwick Road, 7370 1344) still holds court.

Just south-east of Earl's Court station, connecting Old Brompton Road and Fulham Road, is **Brompton Cemetery**. This huge Victorian burial ground, consecrated in 1840, has elaborate stonemasonry and grand funereal architecture, and is the final resting place of suffragette Emmeline Pankhurst. The grounds are a lovely spot in which to wander. However, it's not only the dead who get laid here: this is a favoured trysting place among gay men, so ignore any rustlings in the undergrowth.

Nearby neighbourhoods **Parson's Green** and **Fulham** are both affluent. The former is centred around a small green that once supported – of course – a parsonage, the existence of which was first recorded in 1391. This was considered the aristocratic part of Fulham in the 1700s, housing the great and good of both the royal court and commerce. Nearby, the Queen's Club reigns, this is where the annual pre-Wimbledon Stella Artois tennis tournament is held. Also in the area is **Fulham Palace** (*see below*), which is inside pretty **Bishop's Park**, along the Thames Path.

Fulham Palace

Bishop's Avenue, off Fulham Palace Road, SW6 6EA (7736 3233). Putney Bridge tube/14, 74, 220, 414, 430 bus. **Open** *Mar-Oct* 2-5pm Wed-Sun. *Nov-Feb* 1-4pm Thur-Sun. *Tours* 2pm, 2nd & 4th Sun of mth. **Admission** free; under-16s must be accompanied by adult. *Tours* £3; free under-16s. **No credit cards**.

The foundations of Fulham Palace can be traced back to 704, when the property was granted to Bishop Wealdheri. Sadly, tours of the palace as it stands now – a hotchpotch of architectural styles having been the home of successive Bishops of London for around 700 years – are only available on certain Sundays. For the rest of the time, a small museum goes a little way in satiating curiosity, housing a number of artefacts and ephemera. The surrounding Bishop's Park makes for a nice riverside stroll.

Shepherd's Bush & Hammersmith

Goldhawk Road, Hammersmith or Shepherd's Bush tube.

The focus of Shepherd's Bush remains its triangular, eight-acre patch of grass generally known as Shepherd's Bush Green. In truth, this is only the name of the road that bounds it on two sides, the grassy area itself being officially called Shepherd's Bush Common. Either way, there's not much to it; it's just a slightly scruffy traffic island that separates Uxbridge Road to the north and Goldhawk Road to the south.

Back in the late 1700s, Shepherd's Bush became famous after the highwayman Sixteen-String Jack was captured here. Nowadays, the common's main draws are the **Bush Theatre**, a highly regarded centre for new writing (*see p336*), the **Shepherd's Bush Empire**, one of London's leading music venues (*see p307*), and **Shepherd's Bush Market** (just east of the railway viaduct off Goldhawk Road), which offers stalls selling African and Caribbean food and clothing every day except Sunday. The raucous Walkabout Inn (8740 4339), a huge Aussie pub next door to the Empire, is there to remind you that the area's popularity with Antipodean travellers is undying.

Thanks to a large chunk of council and EU funding, this neighbourhood – known for its tatty shops, ankle-deep litter and obvious social problems – is undergoing major redevelopment. The W12 shopping centre has been made over, and a number of restaurants and a 12-screen cinema have opened. More interesting is the proposed West London Tram Project; if approved, it will link Shepherd's Bush with nearby western neighbourhoods by 2009.

To the north of Shepherd's Bush is White City, home of the absolutely massive **BBC Television Centre** (*see p186*), now recovered from a Real IRA bombing in March 2001. The centre offers backstage tours to those who book ahead. Across the road, developers are building what is likely to be one of Europe's biggest retail parks: 1.4 million square feet (427,000 square metres) in size, it's due to open in 2007.

If you're to the manor born, everything is grand...

To the north of White City, **Wormwood Scrubs** is infamously home to an imposing Victorian jail. To brighten things a bit, part of the extensive parkland outside the prison walls has been designated a nature reserve.

South of Shepherd's Bush is the altogether more lively **Hammersmith** area. On Saturday nights, don't be surprised to find it thronging with overexcited (and drunk) twenty- and thirtysomethings dressed as schoolkids; they're just here for the bizarre ritual that is School Disco club night (Hammersmith Palais, 230 Shepherds Bush Road, 0871 872 1234, www.schooldisco.com).

Close to the main roundabout are a number of other entertainment venues. On Queen Caroline Street is the **Carling Apollo Hammersmith**, which hosts live music events; some alternative theatrical work comes courtesy of the handy **Lyric Hammersmith** (*see p336*), whose main auditorium has a gloriously old-fashioned interior and a grand proscenium arch; while the **Riverside Studios** (*see p284*) is home to three theatre spaces, a gallery and a rep cinema. But the area's main attraction is the beautiful, over-the-top **Hammersmith Bridge**, the oldest suspension bridge in the city.

BBC Television Centre Tours

Wood Lane, W12 7RJ (0870 603 0304/ www.bbc.co.uk/tours). White City tube. **Tours** by appointment only Mon-Sat. **Admission** £7.95; £6.95 concessions; £5.95 10-16s, students; £21.95 family. No under-9s. **Credit** MC, V.

Tours of the BBC include visits to the news desk, the TV studios and the Weather Centre and more, though you must book ahead to secure a place. To be part of a TV audience when a show is being filmed for TV or recorded for radio, log on to www.bbc.co.uk/whatson/tickets, where you can see performance schedules and apply for free tickets.

Chiswick

Turnham Green tube, Chiswick rail.

Turning your back on the tarmacked swoops of Hammersmith and walking west alongside the river from Hammersmith Bridge, you'll eventually reach the elegantly aloof **Chiswick Mall**, a mile-long riverside stretch of grand 17th- to 19th-century townhouses with colourful flowers and wrought-iron verandas that heralds your arrival in the wealthy suburb of Chiswick. The nearby **Fuller's Griffin Brewery**, just off Chiswick Mall on Chiswick Lane South, has stood on the same site since the 17th century (for tours, *see p224*). Just a few hundred yards away, Chiswick Mall ends at **St Nicholas Church**. Only the ragstone tower of the 15th-century building remains, the rest of the church being 19th century. Gravestones commemorate local painters Hogarth and Whistler, but they're actually buried elsewhere.

Other Chiswick attractions include the Palladian **Chiswick House** and **Hogarth's House**; further west is the **Kew Bridge Steam Museum** (for all *see p187*). The

... see for yourself at **PM Gallery & House**. *See p188.*

much-loved **Musical Museum** is currently in the middle of a move from an old, damp church building into a new custom-built premises. It should reopen during 2004; for full details, see www.musicalmuseum.co.uk.

South of here, overlooking Kew Gardens from the opposite side of the river, is **Syon House** (*see p188*). A pretty riverside promenade, just east of Kew Bridge on the north side of the river, runs by the mini-village of Strand-on-the-Green, which offers two splendid pubs in the shape of the Bell & Crown and the City Barge.

Chiswick House

Burlington Lane, W4 2RP (8995 0508/www.english-heritage.org.uk). Turnham Green tube then E3 bus to Edensor Road/Hammersmith tube/rail then 190 bus/Chiswick rail. **Open** *Apr-Sept* 10am-6pm Wed-Fri, Sun; 10am-2pm Sat. *Oct* 10am-5pm Wed-Fri, Sun; 10am-2pm Sat. Last entry 30mins before closing. Closed Nov-Mar. **Admission** (EH) £3.50; £3 concessions; £2 5-16s; free under-5s. **Credit** MC, V.

This lovely Palladian villa was designed by Richard Boyle, third Earl of Burlington, in 1725. As a leading patron of the arts, he built the villa to be a temple of culture in which he could entertain the cream of society. Among those he supported were the writers Pope, Swift, Gay and Thomson, the composer Handel and the artists Kent, Leoni and Rysbrack. Sculptures by Rysbrack of Burlington's heroes, Inigo Jones and Palladio, stand in front of the house.

William Kent was responsible for much of the interior. The gorgeous reception rooms interconnect with a magnificent domed central saloon. The grounds, designed by Lord Burlington with William Kent and Charles Bridgeman, are a triumph of early 18th-century garden design. There's plenty to admire, including a gateway originally designed by Inigo Jones in 1621 and erected at Chiswick in 1738.

Hogarth's House

Hogarth Lane, Great West Road, W4 2QN (8994 6757). Turnham Green tube/Chiswick rail. **Open** *Apr-Oct* 1-5pm Tue-Fri; 1-6pm Sat, Sun. *Nov, Dec, Feb, Mar* 1-4pm Tue-Fri; 1-5pm Sat, Sun. **Admission** free; donations appreciated. **No credit cards**.

This early 18th-century house was the country retreat of painter, engraver and social commentator William Hogarth. Fully restored in 1997 for the 300th anniversary of Hogarth's birth, it now functions as a gallery displaying most of his well-known engravings, including *Gin Lane*, *Marriage à la Mode* and a copy of *Rake's Progress*.

Kew Bridge Steam Museum

Green Dragon Lane, Brentford, Middx TW8 0EN (8568 4757/www.kbsm.org). Gunnersbury tube/Kew Bridge rail/65, 237, 267, 391 bus. **Open** 11am-5pm daily. **Admission** *Mon-Fri* £3.60; £2.70 concessions; £1.50 5-15s; free under-5s; £8 family. *Sat, Sun* £4.60; £3.70 concessions; £2.50 5-15s; free under-5s; £11.95 family. **Credit** MC, V.

Housed in a Victorian riverside pumping station, this museum looks at the city's use and abuse of water. The highlight, for some at least, is a walk through a section of the London ring main water-pipe. On weekends (11am-5pm) the engines are in steam; one of the biggest working examples in the world, a Cornish beam engine built in 1845 for use in the tin mines, stirs into motion at 3pm.

Syon House

Syon Park, Brentford, Middx TW8 8JF (8560 0883/ www.syonpark.co.uk). Gunnersbury tube/rail then 237, 267 bus. **Open** *House (24 Mar-31 Oct only)* 11am-5pm Wed, Thur, Sun, bank holidays. Last entry 4.15pm. *Gardens (year-round)* 10.30am-dusk daily. *Tours* by arrangement. **Admission** *House & gardens* £7.25; £5.95 concessions; £16 family. *Gardens only* £3.75; £2.50 concessions; £9 family. *Tours* free. **Credit** AmEx, MC, V.

The land around this turreted Tudor mansion, embellished by successive incumbents during the 16th century, belonged to the Syon Monastery. It was dedicated to the Bridgettine order in 1415 and remained so until the Dissolution of the Monasteries by Henry VIII. It was here that Catherine Howard, Henry's fifth wife, spent a miserable Christmas before her execution in 1542.

The building was remodelled as a house in 1547 for the Duke of Northumberland, who still uses it as his London home; the neo-classical interior was created by Robert Adam in 1761. Paintings by Van Dyck, Gainsborough and Reynolds hang inside, but the duke's most valuable painting, *Madonna of the Pinks* by Raphael, has hung in the National Gallery (*see p127*) for years. It's become a bone of contention: claiming he needs the funds to maintain Syon, and Alnwick (his place in Northumberland), the duke plans to sell the painting, so the gallery has to come up with millions of pounds to purchase it.

A collection of 1960s buildings in the grounds house the London Butterfly House (8560 7272), where more than 1,000 specimens flutter and settle. There's also a walk-in aviary of tropical birds, and the Aquatic Experience (8847 47300), which counts crocodiles and piranhas among its largely pescatorial residents. Both will soon close, though, when a large hotel is built in the park. The house's glittering film career includes an appearance in *Gosford Park*.

Further west

The birthplace of the British film industry and the first purpose-built film studios in the country, **Ealing Studios** put the westerly suburb of Ealing on the map. A consortium of filmmakers and developers owns the old site, where classic comedies like *Kind Hearts and Coronets* were produced, and has converted the historic buildings into offices and production units. More mundanely, Ealing offers handy shopping (the Broadway Centre lies at its heart) and eating and drinking, which makes the long tube ride west to see gems such as **Walpole Park**, home to **Pitzhanger Manor**, more inviting. Further west still, in the middle of Osterley Park, is **Osterley House** (for both *see below*), another Robert Adam project.

Just north of here, **Southall** has been given a new lease of life by Indian immigrants, their presence promising authentic cuisine in countless restaurants lining the Broadway. The golden dome of the **Sri Guru Singh Sabha Southall** can be seen from all over London; cover your head with a scarf and remove your shoes to enter what is, with capacity for 3,000 people, the largest Sikh place of worship outside India.

To the north, **Wembley** is best known as the home of the famous stadium, which closed in October 2000. Construction of the new 90,000-seater **Wembley National Stadium** has been dogged by controversy and financial problems, but is due to be completed in 2006; the new building will contain a museum remembering the glory days of the old stadium. For details, check www.wembleynationalstadium.co.uk.

Nearby **Neasden** is famous for the multi-billion-rupee **Shri Swaminarayan Mandir** temple, built here by a Hindu sect in 1995. It required 5,000 tons of marble and limestone and the work of around 1,500 sculptors for an enterprise unprecedented in this country since cathedral-building in the Middle Ages. As well as a large prayer hall, the complex contains a conference hall, a marriage suite, sports facilities, a library and a health clinic. All visitors here should dress discreetly.

Osterley House

Osterley Park, off Jersey Road, Isleworth, Hounslow, Middx TW7 4RB (8232 5050/recorded information 01494 755566/www.nationaltrust.org.uk). Osterley tube. **Open** *Park* 9am-7.30pm daily, year-round. *House Mar* 1-4.30pm Sat, Sun. *Apr-Nov* 1-4.30pm Wed-Sun. **Admission** (NT) *House* £4.50; £2.25 5-15s; free under-5s; £11.20 family. *Park* free.

In 1761, Scottish architect Robert Adam was commissioned to transform Osterley from a crumbling Tudor mansion into a swish neo-classical villa. He did so in spectacular style, creating friezes, pilasters and ornate ceilings over the course of 19 years. The National Trust oversee a number of events throughout the year, from ghost walks to conservation mornings; ring or check the website for details. From April to October, the Jersey Galleries stage contemporary art exhibitions.

PM Gallery & House

Walpole Park, Mattock Lane, Ealing, W5 5EQ (8567 1227/www.ealing.gov.uk/pmgallery&house). Ealing Broadway tube/rail. **Open** 1-5pm Tue-Sat. *Tours* by arrangement. **Admission** free.

Though one early wing (the west one) was designed by George Dance, Pitzhanger House is the work of Sir John Soane (*see p31*), who bought the house as his weekend retreat in 1800 and proceeded to reconstruct it. After Soane sold it in 1810, the house was owned by a number of notables, among them Spencer Perceval, the only British prime minister to have been assassinated. To celebrate the 250th anniversary of Soane's birth in 2003, the property honoured him with a special exhibition, and the house and gallery were given a new title.

Eat, Drink, Shop

Features

Restaurants

Eat your way around the world without ever leaving town.

Welcome to one of the world's great culinary capitals. There are restaurants in London to fit every wallet, to satisfy every craving, to tantalise every food obsession. There is food here from every corner of the globe – from Afghanistan to Mexico. In fact, some of the biggest news on the food front in the last year has come from new top-notch international restaurants, among them **Chintamani** (*see p201*), a Turkish gem. And the restaurant *Time Out* named as the best of 2003 was French (**Racine**, *see p211*).

The best is not always the most famous, of course. Sometimes fame is a product solely of itself – celebrity for celebrity's sake. Thus, we have Jordan and places like the **Ivy** (*see p208*), where there's paparazzi out front, and homely British comfort food inside.

On the other hand, some restaurants deserve their headlines. You'll have nearly as much trouble getting a reservation at **Gordon Ramsay**, whether in Claridge's hotel (*see p201*) or in Chelsea (*see p211*), as you will at the Ivy, but the food makes it worth the time spent on hold. And the same can be said of chef Jamie Oliver's new venture, **Fifteen** (*see p213*) – the subject of a television documentary in both the US and Britain before it opened, it is booked up months in advance, but not only is the food stellar, it's all for a very good cause.

The best Restaurants

For outrageously filling fry-ups
Goodfellas. *See p193.*

For offally good meat
St John. *See p193.*

For organically sourced veg
Mildred's. See *p207.*

For orgasmically rich puddings
Cecconi's. *See p201.*

For orientally spiced delights
Nahm. *See p210.*

For perfection on a plate
Racine. *See p211.*

DOS AND DON'TS

Not all London restaurants insist on reservations, so we've indicated the places where booking is essential, but it's always best to reserve in advance where possible.

Some London places are entirely non-smoking and others allow smoking anywhere; some set aside sections for smokers. If you're passionate either way, it's best to call ahead.

Tipping is standard practice; ten to 15 per cent is usual. Some add service to the bill, so double-check or you may tip twice.

We've listed a range of meal prices for each place. However, restaurants often change their menus, so these prices are only guidelines.

For the best places to eat with kids, *see p268*; For more information on all aspects of eating out in London, buy the annual *Time Out Eating & Drinking Guide* (£9.99).

The South Bank & Bankside

Cafés & brasseries

Konditor & Cook

10 Stoney Street, SE1 9AD (7407 5100/ www.konditorandcook.com). London Bridge tube/ rail. **Open** 7.30am-6pm Mon-Fri; 8.30am-4pm Sat. **Main courses** £1.95-£4.25. **Credit** MC, V. **Map** p404 P8.

This upmarket mini-chain is one for connoisseurs of cake. Slices, biscuits and truffles in delicate packaging line the shelves. Seating is limited.

Southwark Cathedral Refectory

Southwark Cathedral, Montague Close, SE1 9DA (7407 5740/www.digbytrout.co.uk). London Bridge tube/rail. **Open** 10am-5pm daily. **Main courses** £5.95-£6.50. **Credit** MC, V. **Map** p404 P8.

Tucked away in the modern wing of the cathedral, this little café offers substantial meals, a wide selection of cakes and even an ale brewed for the cathedral. Try the rocket and potato soup, salmon cakes or the grilled aubergine and halloumi.

Tate Modern Café: Level 2

2nd floor, Tate Modern, Sumner Street, SE1 9TG (7401 5014/5020/www.tate.org.uk). Southwark tube/London Bridge tube/rail. **Open** 10am-6pm daily. **Main courses** £7.50-£12. **Credit** AmEx, DC, MC, V. **Map** p404 O/P8.

Streamlined service is the priority here – and quite right, too, as the place can get busy, especially when art lovers begin to flag around lunchtime. Bright lighting and functional seating seem designed to move you swiftly on, but desserts – apple crumble with maple clotted cream – may encourage you to forego browsing and extend your pit stop.

Fish

Livebait

41-5 The Cut, Waterloo, SE1 8LF (7928 7211/www.santeonline.co.uk/livebait. Southwark tube/Waterloo tube/rail. **Open** noon-11.30pm Mon- **Main courses** £7.95-£19.75. **Credit** AmEx, DC, JCB, MC, V. **Map** p404 N8.

The menu is this clean, tiled restaurant centres on fresh fish served in fast and unfussy style to a young and trendy crowd. The quality of the fish is high; the seafood platters are exuberant and expensive.

Other locations: throughout the city.

Global

Baltic

74 Blackfriars Road, SE1 8HA (7928 1111/ www.balticrestaurant.co.uk). Southwark tube. **Open** noon-3pm, 6-11pm Mon-Fri; 6-11pm Sat; noon-3pm, 6-10.30pm Sun. **Main courses** £11-£12.50. **Credit** AmEx, MC, V. **Map** p404 N8.

Gorgeous Baltic has modern East European food on the menu: blinis and herring are offered alongside Georgian lamb and Latvian fish dishes. Desserts are divine, especially the white chocolate cheesecake.

Tas

72 Borough High Street, SE1 1XF (7403 7200/ www.tasrestaurant.com). London Bridge tube/rail. **Open** noon-11.30pm Mon-Sat; noon-10.30pm Sun. **Main courses** £4.95-£14.45. **Credit** AmEx, MC, V.

Modern and rather chic, this large, noisy restaurant packs in a lot of people without seeming crowded. The spacious non-smoking basement helps. The food is excellent with varied choice for vegetarians.

Other locations: 72 Borough High Street, Bankside, SE1 (7403 7200).

Modern European

Oxo Tower Restaurant, Bar & Brasserie

Top floor, Oxo Tower Wharf, Barge House Street, SE1 9PH (7803 3888/www.harveynichols.com). Blackfriars or Waterloo tube/rail. **Open** noon-2.45pm, 5.30-11.30pm Mon-Sat; noon-3.45pm, 6-11pm Sun. **Main courses** *Brasserie* £10.25-£17. *Restaurant* £17.50-£26. **Credit** AmEx, DC, JCB, MC, V. **Map** p404 N7.

Perched atop the Oxo Tower with sweeping views along the Thames, glass walls make sure you see it all. The restaurant is extremely posh – staff wear bow ties and absurd little jackets – the brasserie is cheaper and more casual. In both, food is excellent, from the crab meat on yuzu jelly starter to venison, veal sweetbreads and guinea fowl mains.

Busy eaters at **Busaba Eathai**. *See p196.*

People's Palace

Level 3, Royal Festival Hall, South Bank Centre, SE1 8XX (7928 9999/www.peoplespalace.co.uk). Embankment tube/Charing Cross or Waterloo tube/rail. **Open** noon-3pm, 5.30-11pm daily. **Main courses** £12.50-£17. **Credit** AmEx, DC, MC, V. **Map** p401 M8.

The menu at this smart place in the South Bank Centre gives you luxury if you want it, simple if you don't. The food is diverse and creative: butternut squash and mozzarella tarte tatin, honey roast duck.

The City

Cafés & brasseries

De Gustibus

53-5 Carter Lane, EC4V 5AE (7236 0056). St Paul's tube/Blackfriars tube/rail. **Open** 7am-5pm Mon-Fri. **Main courses** £4.95-£8. **Credit** MC, V. **Map** p404 O6.

Its situation between St Paul's and the river ensures De Gustibus a booming trade with the business crowd who love the delicious artisan sandwiches.

Other locations: 53 Blandford Street, Marylebone, W1U 7HL (7486 6608); 4 Southwark Street, Borough, SE1 1TQ (7407 3625).

Japanese

Miyama

38 Clarges Street, W1Y 7PJ (7493 3807/7499 2443). Green Park tube. **Open** noon-2.30pm, 6-10.30pm Mon-Fri; 6-10.30pm Sat, Sun. **Main courses** £9-£25. **Credit** AmEx, DC, JCB, MC, V. **Map** p400 H7/8.

A calm, traditional Japanese restaurant with a sushi bar in the basement. Expect wonderful sushi and sashimi – the slivers of tuna, salmon and sea bass melt in your mouth. Service is seamless.

Posh tea

Everything stops for tea, of course, and so it should, if you're spending £30 a head for a brew and buns somewhere smart. The apotheosis of afternoon tea, pioneered by the seventh Duchess of Bedford and taken up with enthusiasm by everyone thereafter, is still the preserve of London's deluxe hotels. The **Savoy Hotel** (*see p51*) was one of the first to hit upon the idea of the 'tea dance', at which ladies and gents dressed up, danced to a four-piece orchestra and drank a cup or two. Sadly, tea dances are long gone, but afternoon tea at the Savoy is still a big draw. For £24 (weekdays, £27 weekends), smartly dressed visitors can drink as much tea as they can, soaked up with lavish amounts of sandwiches and cakes.

Similarly, tea at the **Ritz** is legendary. To enjoy cucumber sandwiches and scones with cream in the fashionable Palm Court, book at least two weeks in advance and be prepared to fork out £29 for sandwiches, scones, pastries and tea. At **Claridge's** (*see p49*), afternoon tea is taken either in the foyer or the reading room. For £28.60, you get sandwiches, scones with cream and strawberry jam, tea cakes and pastries along with the hot beverages. Adding champagne to that little lot brings up the price to £38.50. At the **Lanesborough**, tea and sandwiches, scones and pastries await in the lovely conservatory and cost £24.50 (or £32 for the Belgravia, with added strawberries, cream and a glass of champagne).

The best-value posh hotel tea is served at the **Cadogan Hotel** (75 Sloane Street, SW1, 7235 7141), however, where just £12.50 buys you a variety of splendid sandwiches, scones, fruit cake and tea.

All hotels require men to wear a jacket and tie and women to look smart – denim is a no-no. Most hotel teas are served between 3 and 6pm and should be booked ahead. If you want to wear whatever the heck you like and take afternoon tea whenever you choose (as long as it's during opening hours), the **Bramah Museum of Tea & Coffee** (*see p75*) does a nice line in scones, sandwiches, cakes and the best cup of tea in town for just £7 (£9 if you want toasted teacakes and crumpets too). To combine the cup that cheers with gardens fit for a queen, take tea at the **Orangery** in Kensington Gardens (7376 0239), a frightfully civilised, airy venue for scones, tea and the richest fruit cake since George III. Set teas here cost from £6.25.

Yokoso Sushi

40 Whitefriars Street, EC4Y 8BH (7583 9656). Blackfriars tube/rail. **Open** 11am-8pm Mon-Fri. **Main courses** *Set meals* £7.50-£12. **Credit** AmEx, JCB, MC, V. **Map** p404 N6.

Tucked away down a set of stairs near Fleet Street, this small, brightly lit, spotlessly clean sushi bar is best for lunch, when the food is very fresh and the service efficient. Prices here beat the pants off most Japanese places around the City.

Mediterranean

Eyre Brothers

70 Leonard Street, EC2A 4QX (7613 5346/ www.eyrebrothers.co.uk). Old Street tube/rail. **Open** noon-3pm, 6.30-11pm Mon-Fri; 6.30-11pm Sat. **Main courses** £13-£25. **Credit** AmEx, DC, MC, V. **Map** p403 Q4.

This place is a blast of fresh air. Prices aren't modest, but combinations of food are enticing: try stuffed sardines, followed by a Portuguese fish stew mixing hunks of lobster with white fish.

Modern European

Bonds

Threadneedles, 5 Threadneedle Street, EC2R 8AY (7657 8088/www.theetongroup.com). Bank tube/ DLR. **Open** noon-2pm, 6.30-10.30pm Mon-Fri. **Main courses** £19.75-£23. **Credit** AmEx, DC, MC, V. **Map** 405 Q6.

Overlooking the Bank of England and the Stock Exchange, this is business client territory. In the vast dining hall, menu options include tender pink veal carpaccio and warm salad niçoise in a pastry cage. The huge, diver-caught scallops are fabulous.

1 Lombard Street

1 Lombard Street, EC3V 9AA (7929 6611/ www.1lombardstreet.com). Bank tube/DLR. **Open** *Brasserie* 7.30-11pm Mon-Fri. *Restaurant* noon-3pm, 6-10pm Mon-Fri. **Main courses** *Brasserie* £12.50-£27.50. *Restaurant* £27.50-£29.50. **Credit** AmEx, DC, JCB, MC, V. **Map** p405 Q6/7.

This is the temple of the power lunch. The menu is of the carrot velouté with crab beignet variety. Or try the carpaccio of smoked scallops. Service is attentive. FYI: it seems customers in the noisy, cheaper brasserie have more fun.

Vegetarian & organic

The Place Below

St Mary-le-Bow, Cheapside, EC2V 6AU (7329 0789/www.theplacebelow.co.uk). St Paul's tube/Bank tube/DLR. **Open** 7.30-10.30am, 11.30am-3.30pm Mon-Fri. **Main courses** £5.50-£7.50. **Credit** MC, V. **Map** p404 P6.

This is a deservedly popular lunch spot for the business crowd. The dramatic setting of Norman domed ceilings and alcoves makes an unusual location in which to enjoy a meat-free lunch. The daily changing menu features leafy salads, quiches and soups (split green pea and mint, say) with good bread, and excellent pastries and coffee too.

Holborn & Clerkenwell

British

St John

26 St John Street, EC1M 4AY (7251 0848/ www.stjohnrestaurant.com). Farringdon tube/rail. **Open** noon-3pm, 6-11pm Mon-Fri; 6-11pm Sat. **Main courses** £10-£18. **Credit** AmEx, DC, MC, V. **Map** p402 O3.

St John is used to praise. The kitchen's inventive approach to British cuisine attracts the curious to his often offally dishes. It's not all red meat, though: there's squid served fennel, or roast chicken in broccoli vinaigrette. Desserts are hearty, the wine great. **Other locations**: St John Bread & Wine, 94-6 Commercial Street, E1 6LZ (7247 8724).

Cafés & brasseries

Flâneur Food Hall

41 Farringdon Road, EC1M 3JB (7404 4422). Farringdon tube/rail. **Open** 9am-10pm Mon-Sat; 9am-6pm Sun. Brunch served 9am-4pm Sun. **Main courses** £9-£11.90. **Credit** AmEx, DC, JCB, MC, V. **Map** p402 N4/5.

A food hall and restaurant in a grim part of the Farringdon Road. The deli extends back into the dining room, where the tables are squashed in. The creative menu may list pea, mint and pancetta soup, and braised shoulder of Gloucester Old Spot (pork) with cream and sage. Prices are reasonable.

Goodfellas

50 Lamb's Conduit Street, WC1N 3LH (7405 7088). Chancery Lane or Holborn tube. **Open** 8.30am-5pm Mon-Fri; 10am-5pm Sat. **Main courses** £3.39-£4.25. **No credit cards. Map** p399 M4/5.

Goodfellas has it all – ciabatta sandwiches filled with anything from minty lamb to parma ham, a lunchtime buffet (£3-£4) with pasta, cooked meats and salads, and New York breakfasts with bacon, perfect eggs and butter-soft pancakes.

French

Club Gascon

57 West Smithfield, EC1A 9DS (7796 0600). Barbican tube/Farringdon tube/rail. **Open** noon-2pm, 7-10pm Mon-Fri; 7-10.30pm Sat. **Main courses** £4-£15. **Credit** AmEx, MC, V. **Map** p402 O5.

This place specialises in fine French food served in creative tapas style: wild smoked salmon is wrapped around a pine twig and served on a piece of slate with herbed sorbet. The foie gras and cassoulet are both good, the service is reassuringly French and the wine list is unlikely to disappoint.

delicious noodles, fabulous rice dishes, freshly squeezed juices, wine, sake and japanese beers

bloomsbury WC1A
4a streatham st tube | tottenham court rd

soho W1R
10a lexington st tube | piccadilly circus

west end W1H
101a wigmore st tube | bond st / marble arch

camden NW1
11 jamestown rd tube | camden town

kensington W8
26 kensington high st
tube | high st kensington

knightsbridge SW1X
harvey nichols lower ground floor
tube | knightsbridge

covent garden WC2E
1a tavistock st tube | covent garden

leicester square WC1H
14a irving st tube | leicester square

haymarket SW1Y
8 norris st tube | piccadilly circus

citypoint EC2V
citypoint moor lane tube | moorgate

fleet street EC4A
109 fleet st tube | st pauls / blackfriars

islington N1
the n1 centre parkfield st tube | angel

old broad street EC2N
by tower 42 22 old broad st tube | liverpool st

tower hill EC3N
2b tower place london

canary wharf E14
jubilee place 45 bank st

for menu and chatroom visit: www.wagamama.com
london | dublin | amsterdam | sydney

wagamama and positive eating + positive living are registered trademarks of wagamama ltd

positive eating + positive living

Global

Gaucho Grill

125-6 Chancery Lane, WC2A 1PU (7242 7727/ www.thegauchogrill.co.uk). Chancery Lane tube. **Open** noon-11pm Mon-Fri. **Main courses** £9-£20. **Credit** AmEx, DC, JCB, MC, V. **Map** p399 M5, p404 N6.

Only the cowskin seats evoke the pampas of Argentina at these grills; this is a slick lounge of cool black and white spaces. Food varies from humdrum to classy, but most comes at aristocratic prices. The 200g steaks are petite compared to their South American cousins. Still, it's endlessly popular with the post-work/birthday party crowd.

Other locations: throughout the city.

Modern European

Bank Aldwych

1 Kingsway, WC2B 6XF (7379 9797/www.bank restaurants.com). Holborn or Temple tube. **Open** 7.30-10.30am, noon-3pm, 5.30-11.30pm Mon-Fri; 11.30am-3.30pm, 5.30-11.30pm Sat; 11.30am-3.30pm, 5.30-10pm Sun. **Main courses** £10.80-£21. **Credit** AmEx, DC, MC, V. **Map** p399 M6.

The decor is dated, but the food has kept pace with the times. A lengthy menu offers a diverse range of dishes. Try the creamy crab and leek tart, or the grilled asparagus with sauce mousseline. The pan-roasted venison with beetroot marmalade is above par, and the set meal is excellent value.

Smiths of Smithfield

67-77 Charterhouse Street, EC1M 6HJ (7251 7950/ www.smithsofsmithfield.co.uk). Farringdon tube/rail. **Open** 7am-11pm Mon-Fri; 9am-11pm Sat; 9am-10.30pm Sun. **Main courses** £10.50-£28. **Credit** AmEx, DC, MC, V. **Map** 402 O5.

Smiths is a great big place, and its funky industrial decor – sandblasted walls, massive beams, oak furniture – betrays its warehouse origins. As you move upstairs, the formality rises. The ground-floor bar serves a café menu and outstanding breakfasts until 5pm; the food is homely and top rate. On the next floor, the Dining Room is a little quieter and serves things like duck salad with papaya. Upstairs, the smart Top Floor restaurant is the posh part. Popular without being hyper-fashionable.

Spanish

Cigala

54 Lamb's Conduit Street, WC1N 3LW (7405 1717/www.cigala.co.uk). Holborn or Russell Square tube. **Open** noon-3pm, 6-10.45pm Mon-Fri; 12.30-3.45pm, 6-10.45pm Sat; 12.30-9.30pm Sun. **Main courses** £11-£17. *Tapas* £2-£8. **Credit** AmEx, DC, MC, V. **Map** p400 H7/J6.

This is a slick operation, with attentive service, high-quality food and classy surroundings. Black-clad wait staff whisk around tapas like oak-smoked cured beef with mini gherkins, and king prawns in white wine, garlic and chilli sauce. The wine list has plenty of characterful vintages for under £30.

Moro

34-6 Exmouth Market, EC1R 4QE (7833 8336/ www.moro.co.uk). Farringdon tube/rail/19, 38 bus. **Open** 12.30-2.30pm, 7-10.30pm Mon-Fri; 7-10.30pm Sat. **Main courses** £13.50-£16.50. **Credit** AmEx, DC, MC, V. **Map** p402 N4.

Tapas at this modern and modish place is served all day at the long zinc bar, but the full menu owes as much to North Africa and the Middle East as it does to Spain. Mains make much use of the wood-fired oven and charcoal grill, producing perfectly cooked sea bass (from the grill) with saffron rice, tahini sauce and a cooling chickpea and cucumber salad. The wine list is short but nifty. A terrific place.

Fitzrovia

Global

Archipelago

110 Whitfield Street, W1T 5ED (7383 3346). Goodge Street or Warren Street tube. **Open** noon-2.30pm, 6-10.30pm Mon-Fri; 6-10.30pm Sat. **Main courses** *Set lunch* £24.50 2 courses, £29.50 3 courses. *Set dinner* £32.50 2 courses, £38.50 3 courses. **Credit** AmEx, DC, JCB, MC, V. **Map** p398 J4.

It's all about exotica at this theatrical restaurant where kangaroo, crocodile and insects are on the menu. The 'Love Bug' salad is well-dressed leaves topped with a few frazzled locusts – the taste of which didn't match up to their startling appearance. With dinner costing well over £100 for two, you certainly pay for the bizarre experience.

Eagle Bar Diner

3-5 Rathbone Place, W1T 1HJ (7637 1418/ www.eaglebardiner.com). Tottenham Court Road tube. **Open** 8am-11pm Mon-Fri; 11am-11pm Sat; 11am-7pm Sun. **Main courses** £4-£8.75. **Credit** MC, V. **Map** p399 K5.

The Eagle is an upscale version of a US-style joint that, come sundown, morphs into a cocktail bar. This is diner chic: it looks, tastes and hits your wallet like a roadside diner in Beverly Hills. Burgers are prime beef or grilled tuna and served with gourmet cheeses and good bread. Milkshake flavours include banana and peanut butter, Martinis come in marshmallow and liquorice. There are also rare beers, such as Brooklyn Lager, from across the pond.

Indian

Rasa Samudra

5 Charlotte Street, W1T 1RE (7637 0222/ www.rasarestaurants.com). Goodge Street tube. **Open** noon-3pm, 6-10.45pm Mon-Sat; 6-10.45pm Sun. **Main courses** £6.25-£12.95. **Credit** AmEx, DC, JCB, MC, V. **Map** p398 J5.

This branch of the Rasa chain has terrific Keralan vegetarian and seafood dishes. The set feasts offer an introduction to the cuisine. Top mains are crab *varuthathu* (cooked dry with ginger, curry leaves and mustard seeds) and *chemeen theeyal* (prawns in coriander, chilli and coconut sauce).
Other locations: throughout the city.

Italian

Carluccio's Caffè

8 Market Place, off Oxford Circus, W1W 8AG (7636 2228/www.carluccios.com). Oxford Circus tube. **Open** 8am-11pm Mon-Fri; 10am-11pm Sat; 11am-10pm Sun. **Main courses** £4.85-£10.95. **Credit** AmEx, MC, V. **Map** p398 J6.
Excellent food and coffee, combined with all-day convenience, friendly service, a lively atmosphere and reasonable prices make this upmarket café a winner. Mouth-waterers such as seasonal risottos and chargrilled tuna with sautéd spinach are glorious.
Other locations: throughout the city.

Sardo

45 Grafton Way, W1T 5LA (7387 2521/www.sardo-restaurant.com). Warren Street tube. **Open** noon-3pm, 6-11pm Mon-Fri; 6-11pm Sat. **Main courses** £8.90-£18. **Credit** AmEx, DC, JCB, MC, V. **Map** p398 J4.
London's only dedicated Sardinian restaurant, this place has excellent dishes like sun-dried tuna fillet with fresh beans and sun-dried tomatoes, and fregola (like giant couscous) cooked with courgette and sprinkled with exquisitely fresh white crab meat. On wines, your best move is to be guided by the gregarious owner, who is constantly looking for bottles with which to tantalise customers.

Modern European

Pied à Terre

34 Charlotte Street, W1T 2NH (7636 1178/ www.pied.a.terre.co.uk). Goodge Street or Tottenham Court Road tube. **Open** 6.15-11pm Mon, Sat; 12.15-2.30pm, 6.15-11pm Tue-Fri. **Main courses** £27. **Credit** AmEx, MC, V. **Map** p398 J5.
The food here takes good ingredients, partners them ideally and presents them creatively. Doughy German pasta is pillow light, glossed in a buttery hazelnut emulsion, studded with dark and luscious *trompettes de mort*. Desserts are even better. Were you a visitor to London with just one night to spare, you couldn't do better than to eat here.

Oriental

Busaba Eathai

22 Store Street, WC1 7DS (7299 7900). Goodge Street or Tottenham Court Road tube. **Open** noon-11pm Mon-Thur; noon-11.30pm Fri, Sat; noon-10pm Sun. **Main courses** £5.10-£9.80. **Credit** AmEx, JCB, MC, V. **Map** p399 K5.
All dark wood from walls to ceiling to communal tables, this is a brisk place for busy people to eat great Thai food. The menu lists noodles rice plates, curries, stir-fries and numerous veggie options.
Other locations: 106-10 Wardour Street, W1F OTR (7255 8686)

Hakkasan

8 Hanway Place, W1P 9DH (7907 1888). Tottenham Court Road tube. **Open** noon-3.15pm, 6-11.30pm Mon-Wed; noon-3.15pm, 6pm-12.30am Thur, Fri; noon-4.30pm, 6pm-12.30am Sat; noon-4.30pm Sun. **Main courses** £5.90-£40; £3.50-£16 dim sum. **Credit** AmEx, MC, V. **Map** p399 K5.
This Michelin-starred restaurant is incredibly stylish: a slinky assembly of black furniture on black tiles. Both dim sum and full menus are full of novel interpretations of traditional dishes: meltingly light taro croquettes; delectable Chinese chive dumplings. Prices are high, but food is of the highest order.

Han Kang

16 Hanway Street, W1T 1UE (7637 1985). Tottenham Court Road tube. **Open** noon-3pm, 6-11pm Mon-Sat. **Main courses** £6.50-£28. **Credit** AmEx, DC, MC, V. **Map** p399 K5.
One of the best Korean restaurants in central London, Han Kang's chive pancakes are packed with green onions, and marinated beef barbecue is redolent with garlic and sesame. Angler fish involves large pieces of fish robed in sweet chilli sauce. Noisy and smoky, this place tastes of Korea.

Marylebone

Fish & chips

Golden Hind

73 Marylebone Lane, W1U 2PN (7486 3644). Bond Street tube. **Open** noon-3pm, 6-10pm Mon-Fri; 6-10pm Sat. **Main courses** £5-£10.70. **Credit** AmEx, JCB, MC, V. **Map** p398 G5/H6.
A dear little restaurant where friers have been serving good stuff to Marylebone folk since 1914. Traditional delights of fish cakes, cod, haddock and skate are served alongside mussels in batter and king prawns in garlic. Service is friendly.

Global

Original Tajines

7A Dorset Street, W1H 3SE (7935 1545/ www.originaltagines.com). Baker Street tube. **Open** noon-3pm, 6-11pm Mon-Fri; 6-11pm Sat. **Main courses** £8.95-£11. **Credit** MC, V. **Map** p398 G5.
The varieties of Moroccan tagines (and couscous) here go far beyond the norm. There's a superb sweet and sour melding of lamb and thinly sliced pear, and a butter-soft chicken kedra (stewed slowly with raisins and chickpeas). The almost exclusively Moroccan wine list has obligingly wallet-friendly prices. Staff are efficient and charming.

Providores & Tapa Room

109 Marylebone High Street, W1U 4RX (7935 6175/www.theprovidores.co.uk). Baker Street or Bond Street tube. **Open** 9-11.30am, noon-2.45pm, 6-10.45pm Mon-Fri; 10am-3pm, 6-10.45pm Sat; 10am-3pm, 6-10pm Sun. **Main courses** *Tapas* £1.50-£9. Cover £1.50 (lunch Sat, Sun). **Credit** AmEx, MC, V. **Map** p398 G4/5.

A café and wine bar with a first-class fusion restaurant attached. The global tapas range is expansive, from simple grilled chorizo to elaborate dishes such as beetroot, sorrel and parmesan risotto.

Six-13

19 Wigmore Street, W1U 1PH (7629 6133/www.six13.com). Bond Street or Oxford Circus tube. **Open** noon-3pm, 5.30-10.30pm Mon-Thur. **Main courses** £17-£24. **Credit** AmEx, MC, V. **Map** p398 G6.

Sophisticated, modern, kosher cuisine; dishes here are presented with style, given the limitations of *kashrut*. Salmon ceviche, foie gras or Mediterranean vegetable terrine are all tempting. With a broadly selected wine list, it adds up to a pleasurable, if expensive, experience.

Italian

Locanda Locatelli

8 Seymour Street, W1H 7JZ (7935 9088/www.locandalocatelli.com). Marble Arch tube. **Open** noon-3pm, 7-11pm Mon-Thur; noon-3pm, 7-11.30pm Fri, Sat. **Main courses** £16-£30. **Credit** AmEx, JCB, MC, V. **Map** p395 F6.

It's hard not to be excited by the prospect of dinner at this sensuously styled restaurant headed by celebrity chef Giorgio Locatelli and rated one of the city's best restaurants by *Time Out*. Ingredients such as ox tongue and pig's head are listed alongside; guinea fowl with shaved black truffle and guinea fowl liver crostini lures. Desserts are experimental, such as the chocolate fondant with a bright and bitter yellow saffron liquid centre.

Middle Eastern

Levant

Jason Court, 76 Wigmore Street, W1U 2SJ (7224 1111/www.levantrestaurant.co.uk). Bond Street tube. **Open** noon-11.30pm Mon-Fri; 5.30-11.30pm Sat, Sun. **Main courses** £12.50-£22.50. **Credit** AmEx, DC, JCB, MC, V. **Map** p398 G6.

From the dramatic entrance (down stone-clad stairs strewn with rose petals, lit by lanterns) to the entertainment (belly dancers), Levant strives for the exotic Eastern effect. It's all very partyish and pricey. Food is a combination of standard Lebanese meze dishes and main courses, plus some European-inspired plates with a Lebanese slant.

Patogh

8 Crawford Place, W1H 5NE (7262 4015). Edgware Road tube. **Open** 1pm-midnight daily. **Main courses** £5-£9.50. **No credit cards**. **Map** p395 E5/F5.

The menu in this tiny place is minimal – seven varieties of kebab – but food is always prime quality fare: the freshest salads, thick yoghurt dip with

Chintamani. *See p201.*

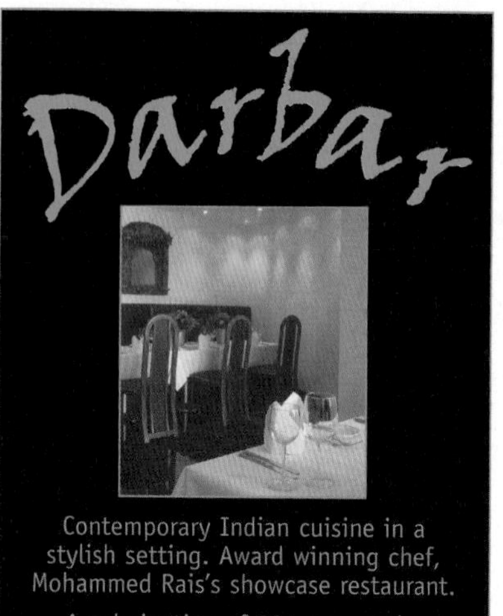

Contemporary Indian cuisine in a stylish setting. Award winning chef, Mohammed Rais's showcase restaurant.

A culmination of 20 years at the top of his profession.

Open Monday to Saturday for lunch and dinner.

92 – 94 Waterford Road, Fulham, SW6 2HA
Tel: 020 7348 7373

mint leaf

Mint Leaf has become one of the most exciting additions to London's restaurant scene.

Serving Indian food in a beautifully designed contemporary environment, the restaurant seats 140 people offering a wonderful sense of occasion and spectacle.

Mint Leaf also features a large cocktail bar serving light snacks and drinks until 1am. A spacious and discreet private room, the Jaipur Lounge,seats a further 60 people and 90 for any other special events and functions.

Situated on Suffolk Place, near Trafalgar Square.
Mint Leaf offers 'Business Lunch' and 'Pre-Theatre'menu starting at £13.50.
Open Mon-Fri 12pm-3pm & Mon-Wed 5.30pm-12am
Thurs-Sat 5.30pm-1am, Sun 6pm-11pm

Mint Leaf, Suffolk Place, London SW1Y 4HX
Tel: 020 7930 9020
Fax: 020 7930 6205
Email: reservation@mintleafrestaurant.com
Website: www.mintleafrestaurant.com

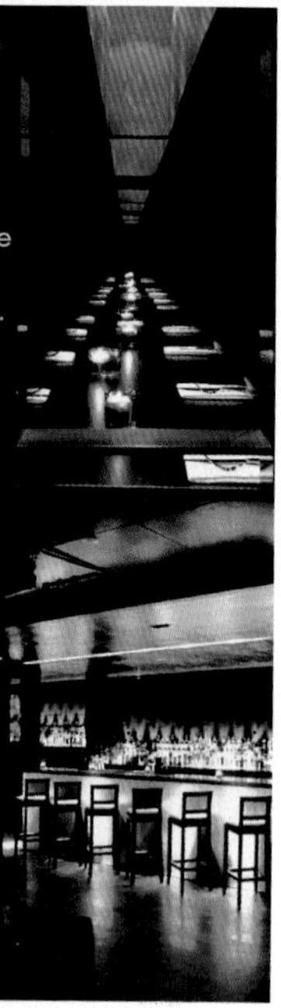

shallots, tender lamb and chicken. The hot wheels of flatbread are particularly good and so big they cover the whole table. Television chef Nigella Lawson recently confided to *Time Out* magazine that Patogh is one of her favourite cheap eats. Although this is not the place to take a hot date unless he or she is Iranian, homesick and very hungry, it's a little gem, and always full.

Modern European

Orrery

55 Marylebone High Street, W1M 3AE (7616 8000/www.orrery.co.uk). Baker Street or Regent's Park tube. **Open** noon-3pm, 7-11pm Mon-Sat; 7-10.30pm Sun. **Main courses** £14.50-£26. **Credit** AmEx, DC, JCB, MC, V. **Map** p398 G4/5.

This upmarket Conran-owned place is a class act, with an appetising Francophile menu, a top-notch wine list and prices that reflect its haute cuisine aspirations. Dishes like watercress velouté with poached duck egg and truffle, and lasagne of Dorset crab with courgette are little miracles of taste and texture. Fish dishes are wonderfully good; fresh and cooked with great sensitivity. Light dishes, such as sweet soufflés and truffles, are always winners. The French waiters jump at every opportunity to replenish glasses, shake down napkins and light cigarettes.

Oriental

Royal China

40 Baker Street, W1M 1DA (7487 4688). Baker Street tube. **Open** noon-11pm Mon-Thur; noon-11.30pm Fri, Sat; 11am-10pm Sun. Dim sum noon-5pm daily. **Main courses** £7-£30; £2.20-£4.50 dim sum. **Credit** AmEx, MC, V. **Map** p398 G4/5.

The Royal China chain is renowned for exquisitely presented and delicious dim sum; steamed dumplings are an art form here. Try shark's fin asparagus dumplings, crab dumplings in soup or pan-fried water chestnut cake and glutinous rice in lotus leaves. Expect queues and quite a bit of noise at weekends.

Other locations: throughout the city.

Wagamama

101A Wigmore Street, W1H 9AB (7409 0111/ www.wagamama.com). Bond Street or Marble Arch tube. **Open** noon-11pm Mon-Sat; 12.30-10.30pm Sun. **Main courses** £5.25-£8.50. **Credit** AmEx, DC, JCB, MC, V. **Map** p398 G6.

This chain of cheap and cheerful noodle bars offers filling, tasty food in a bustling, smoke-free environment. You sit on benches at long tables, close to other diners. The menu includes items like chicken *katsu* curry and *kare lomen* (a big bowl of spicy sauce-based ramen noodles with lemongrass, coconut milk and char-grilled king prawns). Drinks, such as green tea and fresh juices, are wholesome.

Other locations: throughout the city.

Mayfair & St James's

The Americas

Hard Rock Café

150 Old Park Lane, W1K 1QZ (7629 0382/ www.hardrock.com). Hyde Park Corner tube. **Meals served** 11.30am-midnight Mon-Thur, Sun; 11.30am-1am Fri, Sat. **Main courses** £6.25-£14.95. **Credit** AmEx, DC, MC, V. **Map** p400 G8.

As much a tourist attraction as a restaurant, this place always has a queue outside. Inside, the rock music blasts at unpleasant levels and it's all very impersonal. The famed Hard Rock nachos are as huge, cheesy and good as their reputation. The Hard Rock burger is less impressive: rather small and flavourless. Chicken fajitas are a better option; they're juicy, flavoursome and generously proportioned.

Planet Hollywood

13 Coventry Street, W1D 7DH (7287 1000/ www.planethollywood.com). Piccadilly Circus tube. **Meals served** noon-1am Mon-Sat; noon-11.30pm Sun. **Main courses** £9.95-£19.95. **Credit** AmEx, DC, MC, V.

Listen, if you can endure the barrage of noise and primary colours swirling around the restaurant's walls of televisions, you can indulge in a pretty darn good spinach and cheese dip starter, served with crispy corn tortilla chips, or spicy buffalo wings with cool blue cheese dressing. Mains from the Marco Pierre White menu may include Moroccan lamb with couscous or Asian chicken salad. We've always enjoyed our burgers here, so we can see why it's so popular.

British

Dorchester Grill Room

The Dorchester, 53 Park Lane, W1A 2HJ (7317 6336/www.dorchesterhotel.com). Hyde Park Corner tube. **Open** 7-11am, 12.30-2.30pm, 6-11pm Mon-Sat; 7.30-11am, 12.30-2.30pm, 7-10.30pm Sun. **Main courses** £21-£30. **Credit** AmEx, DC, JCB, MC, V. **Map** p400 G8.

Whatever you think of Flemish tapestries and velvet banquettes, there's no risk of being underwhelmed here. Typical starters might be Cornish crab with cider jelly, or cured duck breast with quail's egg. Items from the grill remain a favourite, as does the pudding trolley. Waiters are partial to such remarks as 'a fine choice, sir', but then this is, after all, the Dorchester.

Wiltons

55 Jermyn Street, SW1Y 6LX (7629 9955/ www.wiltons.co.uk). Green Park or Piccadilly Circus tube. **Open** 12.30-2.30pm, 6.30-10.30pm Mon-Sat; 12.30-2.30pm Sun. **Main courses** £15.90-£29.75. **Credit** AmEx, DC, JCB, MC, V. **Map** p400 J7.

To eat and drink in the formal hush of Wiltons, you must look smart. Prices are, at times, almost comically high (£21 for a starter of smoked salmon).

The food is good – rich terrine of duck, pork and foie gras, omelette Arnold Bennett – the atmosphere traditional, but it's hard to justify the bill.

Cafés & brasseries

Victory Café

Basement, Gray's Antiques Market, South Molton Lane, W1K 5AB (7499 6801). Bond Street tube. **Open** 10am-6pm Mon-Fri. **Main courses** £2.75-£4.95. **No credit cards**. **Map** p398 H6.

In true 1950s style, this nostalgic basement café calls itself a 'milk bar'. There's an old Wurlitzer jukebox and the yellow walls display images of post-war England. Fear not: there's no post-war theme to the food: breakfast fry-ups and sandwiches, sausage and mash, smoked haddock and quiches.

French

Deca

23 Conduit Street, W1S 2XS (7493 7070). Oxford Circus tube. **Open** noon-3pm, 5.30-11pm Mon-Sat. **Main courses** £12.50-£18.50. **Credit** AmEx, DC, MC, V. **Map** p400 H7/J6.

Low-key sophistication is the keynote of this converted townhouse. It's a perfect setting for the long menu of French classics. Expect starters such as grilled scallops with garlic butter and rocket, or terrine of foie gras with green peppercorns. Mains might be chicken breast with wild mushrooms, ravioli of foie gras or charcoal-grilled john dory fillets with thyme olive oil. It's not cheap, but all the details are just so. This was rated by *Time Out* as one of the city's best new restaurants in 2003.

Global

Mô

23 Heddon Street, W1B 4BH (7434 4040/ www.momoresto.com). Piccadilly Circus tube. **Open** 11am-9.45pm Mon-Wed; noon-10.30pm Thur-Sat. **Main courses** £7-£8.50. **Credit** AmEx, MC, V. **Maps** p400 J7.

Most of what you see in this place is for sale (bauble lights, lanterns and chandeliers, raffia bags, jewellery and antiques), but it is first and foremost a café, and a great spot for lunch. Food includes meze, North African-style sandwiches, delicious smoothies and fruit juices squeezed to order.

Light lunch

When you get right down to it, the problem is that London simply has too much to offer. You're looking for a little bite to eat, or a nice place for a mid-morning refuel that won't break the bank, and you're passing 10,000 places with Lithuanian chefs specialising in Malaysian cuisine with Ethiopian sauces, and one copycat pub after another offering 'hot food all day'.

Where do you turn?

To us, of course. Here's a compilation of our favourite places for a light but satisfying lunch: coffee and cakes, tea and buns, crumble and custard, soup and sandwiches or, if you're virtuous, salad and fruit juice.

You're welcome.

If you're wandering around Trafalgar Square, and you think all the restaurants are going to be too touristy for words... well, you're right. But the best of the tourist-centric lot is to be found underneath the church of St Martin's-in-the-Fields, in the form of the rather cool **Café in the Crypt** (*see p209*). It offers affordable hot dishes and cool salads, as well as a good cup of tea and traditional desserts in a grand atmosphere.

Soho offers two stellar options. **Pâtisserie Valerie** on Old Compton Street (*see p202*) – much beloved for its exquisite pastries and cakes – offers good hot lunches, along with great coffee, teas and fruit juices. Not far away on Greek Street, the antique and charming **Maison Bertaux** (*see p202*) has some of the best croissants in town.

Just south of the river, you should head over towards Borough Market to **Konditor & Cook** (*see p190*). Its fresh-baked pizzas, sandwiches and excellent cakes make for a fabulous, and wallet-friendly, lunch. Just across from the market, the food in the **Southwark Cathedral Refectory** (*see p190*) is almost as irresistible.

Shopping down King's Road way? Duck into the ever-reliable Peter Jones department store, and take the escalator to the **Top Floor** (*see p211*) self-service brasserie for lunch. The good, fresh sandwiches and salads and decadent desserts are served in elegant surroundings with a view of the high-priced real estate of Sloane Square. And prices are shockingly reasonable.

Finally, if you're checking out Spitalfields Market and Brick Lane in the east, you'll find the freshest bagels in the country at **Brick Lane Beigel Bake** (*see p213*). The simple food here is cheaper than chips, the staff and customers are real characters, and you're all but guaranteed a good time.

Indian

Tamarind

20 Queen Street, W1J 5PR (7629 3561/ www.tamarindrestaurant.com). Green Park tube. **Open** noon-3pm, 6-11.30pm Mon-Fri; 6-11.30pm Sat; noon-2.30pm Sun. **Main courses** £14.50-£22. **Credit** AmEx, DC, JCB, MC, V. **Map** 400 H7.

This dignified basement establishment is mainly North Indian with an emphasis on gentle spicing. Tandoori *kumbh chaat*, a medley of mushrooms dipped in ginger-infused yoghurt and seared in the tandoor, is delicious. Delicate *roomali rotis* are ideal for dipping into creamy lentils simmered with tomatoes, cream and butter. Even with all tables taken, service never misses a beat.

Italian

Cecconi's

5A Burlington Gardens, W1S 3EP (7434 1500). Green Park tube. **Open** noon-3pm, 6.30-11pm Mon-Fri; noon-3pm, 7-11pm Sat. **Main courses** £10-£28. **Credit** AmEx, DC, JCB, MC, V. **Map** p400 J7.

The bright staff and sexy leather interior give this place all the chic of a Prada handbag. The bar is terrific, and the approachable sommelier puts a friendly face on the intimidating wine list. Fish is filleted table-side; a plate of mixed grilled fish has nutrient- packed nuggets of tuna, salmon, monkfish and scallops. Desserts are deadly good.

Middle Eastern

Al Sultan

51-2 Hertford Street, W1J 7ST (7408 1155/1166/ www.alsultan.co.uk). Green Park or Hyde Park Corner tube. **Open** noon-midnight daily. **Main courses** £10-£12. **Credit** AmEx, DC, MC, V. **Map** p400 H8.

The discreetly anonymous decor sets the scene for this upscale Lebanese restaurant. Meze is the forte, with an extensive choice offered: creamy *labneh*, sour pickled baby aubergines, piquant *muhamara*, satin-smooth houmous topped with tender pieces of lamb and plump spinach-filled pastries. Round the meal off with cardamom-scented Lebanese coffee.

Chintamani

122 Jermyn Street, SW1Y 4UJ (7839 2020). Green Park or Piccadilly Circus tube. **Open** 12.30-3pm, 6-11.30pm Mon-Sat. **Main courses** £14-£22. **Credit** AmEx, DC, JCB, MC, V. **Map** p400 J7.

This striking establishment redefines the top end of Turkish dining in a luxurious, informal and relaxed setting. The wine list is global and extensive. Starters of veal dumplings in yoghurt, and mussels with rice and pine kernels are creative. Mains of harissa-crusted cod are superb. A meal for two can easily cost more than £100, but, if you can afford it, the adventurous menu and the fresh ingredients make this one of the city's best restaurants.

Modern European

Le Caprice

Arlington House, Arlington Street, SW1A 1RT (7629 2239). Green Park tube. **Open** noon-3pm, 5.30pm-midnight Mon-Sat; noon-3.30pm, 6pm-midnight Sun. **Main courses** £12-£23. Cover £1.50. **Credit** AmEx, DC, MC, V. **Map** p400 J8.

This hugely influential, utterly reliable restaurant knocks out simple but beautifully executed bistro dishes to its business, media and political regulars. Should you crave char-grilled squid with Italian bacon, a spicy steak tartare or even a top burger and chips (sorry, chopped steak americaine with pomme allumettes), you won't find better in London.

Gordon Ramsay at Claridge's

55 Brook Street, W1A 2JQ (7499 0099/ www.gordonramsay.com). Bond Street tube. **Open** noon-2.45pm, 5.45-11pm Mon-Fri; noon-3.15pm, 5.45-11pm Sat; noon-3.15pm, 6-10.30pm Sun. **Main courses** *Set lunch* £25 3 courses. *Set dinner* £50 3 courses, £60 6 courses. **Credit** AmEx, JCB, MC, V. **Map** p398 H6.

The hotel's glamour steps up as you enter the plush restaurant Gordon Ramsay. Less daunting than it may sound, the six-course 'prestige' menu is a light, modestly portioned affair designed to offer as many flavour contrasts as possible. Tuck into velvety pumpkin velouté with parmesan, artichoke and truffle; foie gras with saffron and pear chutney; tiger prawn and scallop raviolo on creamy lemongrass and chive sauce. Lunch is particularly good value.

The Ritz

150 Piccadilly, W1J 9BR (7493 8181 ext 3370/ www.theritzlondon.com). Green Park tube. **Open** 12.30-2.30pm, 6-11pm Mon-Sat; 12.30-2.30pm, 6.30-10pm Sun. **Main courses** £25-£56. **Credit** AmEx, JCB, MC, V. **Map** p400 J8.

With tail-coated waiters, silver bedecked tables and bow-tied trio lightly stringing out *Putting on the Ritz*, there's an air of period drama about the Ritz. Prices are impressive, with entrées and roasts from £25 to £56 and desserts to a whopping £48 for two. Wine prices are likewise angina-inducing. For your money you get asparagus and morel risotto, ballottine of ham hock with white beans, or sea bass with fennel and vanilla. Still, dining here is grand and glitzy and doesn't have to cost a fortune.

Oriental

Kaya

42 Albemarle Street, W1S 3FE (7499 0622/0633). Green Park tube. **Open** noon-3pm, 6-11pm Mon-Sat; 6-11pm Sun. **Main courses** £7.50-£17. **Credit** AmEx, DC, JCB, MC, V. **Map** p400 J7.

Kaya is the most formal – and most expensive – of London's Korean restaurants. The look is easy on the eye; staff are decked out in traditional, voluminous Korean garb. Table-top grilling is popular, but you can also get *panch'an* (cabbage

Roguish **Gay Hussar**. *See p205.*

kimch'i, sesame leaf and salty fried squid pickles), jellyfish and seafood in mustard sauce, *yuk hwe,* with slices of raw beef with raw egg yolk, pine nuts, pear and sesame seeds. All very authentic.

Kiku

17 Half Moon Street, W1J 7BE (7499 4208). Green Park tube. **Open** noon-2.30pm, 6-10.15pm Mon-Sat; 5.30-9.45pm Sun. **Main courses** £10-£28. **Credit** AmEx, JCB, MC, V. **Map** p400 H8.
Kiku is similar to restaurants you find on the top floors of Tokyo department stores – spotless and bright with blonde wood, bamboo blinds and tinkling background music. It offers fine sushi beautifully presented: silky tuna, scallop and perky salmon roe, and other (cooked) delights.

Nobu

19 Old Park Lane, W1K 1LB (7447 4747/www.nobu restaurants.com). Hyde Park Corner tube. **Open** noon-2.15pm, 6-10.15pm Mon-Thur; noon-2.15pm, 6-11pm Fri; 6-11pm Sat; 6-9.30pm Sun. **Main courses** £5-£27.50. **Credit** AmEx, DC, MC, V. **Map** p400 G8.
A stream of celebrity customers has kept Nobu in the news, but it's often packed with family groups and tourists. Part of an exclusive international chain set up by chef Nobuyuki Matsuhisa, this one takes up the first floor of the Metropolitan Hotel (*see p49*). Food features traditional favourites with a Nobu twist. Dishes include *toro* (fatty tuna), *wagyu* (beef tartar with caviar) and tuna tempura rolls. Of the Nobu special dishes, the famous black cod with miso has a distinctive sweet, aromatic flavour.

Soho & Chinatown

Cafés & brasseries

Bar Italia

22 Frith Street, W1V 5PS (7437 4520/www.baritalia soho.co.uk). Leicester Square, Piccadilly Circus or Tottenham Court Road tube. **Open** 24hrs Mon-Sat; 7am-4am Sun. **Credit** (noon-3am only) AmEx, DC, MC, V. **Map** p399 K6.
This place has administered round-the-clock caffeine fixes for decades, catering to every clique and freak that's ever followed their vices to Soho. Pizza, panini and croissants with various toppings and fillings lead the menu. It's always bustling, but peak time is 3am. The mops are out at five for an hour's cleaning – and then they do it all over again.

Maison Bertaux

28 Greek Street, W1V 5LL (7437 6007). Leicester Square, Piccadilly Circus or Tottenham Court Road tube. **Open** 8.30am-8pm daily. **Main courses** £1.30-£2.90. **No credit cards**. **Map** p399 K6.
Another year passes, and nothing's changed at this gem. Happily, the stasis extends to the food (as ever, magnificent) and the welcome (warm). Savoury snacks stretch to slices of pizza and terrific quiches. Sweet things range from the fruity to the creamy, the croissants are legendary, the coffee up to scratch.

Pâtisserie Valerie

44 Old Compton Street, W1D 4TY (7437 3466/ www.patisserie-valerie.co.uk). Leicester Square, Piccadilly Circus or Tottenham Court Road tube. **Open** 7.30am-8.30pm Mon-Sat; 9.30am-6.30pm Sun. **Main courses** £3.75-£7.95. **Credit** AmEx, DC, MC, V. **Map** p399 K6.
Valerie's has been around since 1926. A mouth-watering display of croissants, fruit tarts and French gâteaux fill the window, and formica-topped tables and Toulouse-Lautrec cartoons decorate inside. Breakfast includes smoked salmon and scrambled eggs and lovely grilled snacks.
Other locations: throughout the city.

Star Café

22 Great Chapel Street, W1F 8FR (7437 8778). Tottenham Court Road tube. **Open** 7am-4pm Mon-Fri. **Main courses** £4.55-£7.25. **No credit cards**. **Map** p399 K6.
With its cheeky staff and informal atmosphere, the Star is a local fave. The clientele is Soho folk, the menu pasta, sandwiches and hot dinners. Some are good, some are bad, but it's all affordable and friendly. This isn't a place that boasts about its food, but the atmosphere will keep you coming back.

Chinese

Imperial China

White Bear Yard, 25A Lisle Street, WC2H 7BA (7734 3388). Leicester Square tube. **Open** noon-11.30pm Mon-Sat; noon-10.30pm Sun. *Dim sum* noon-8pm Mon-Fri; noon-5pm Sat, Sun. **Main courses** £6-£22.50; £2.80-£5 dim sum. **Credit** AmEx, MC, V. **Map** p401 K7.

A dramatic refit has made the former China City into the smartest place in Chinatown. The menu includes both conventional dishes and more interesting concoctions such as steamed *choi sum* with preserved vegetables and ginger, and a fruity stew of pork belly. Sadly, we found the waiting staff know little about the food that tastes so good.

ECapital

8 Gerrard Street, W1D 5PJ (7434 3838). Leicester Square or Piccadilly Circus tube. **Open** noon-11.30pm Mon-Thur, Sun; noon-midnight Fri, Sat. **Main courses** £6-£22. **Credit** AmEx, DC, JCB, MC, V. **Map** p401 K6/7.

Specialising in food from the eastern seaboard of China, this is a bright little space with a long menu. Pressed pig's ear, delicate wheat-gluten folds of vegetarian goose, and smoked fish typify the cuisine. Family Shanghai banquet soup, a warming meaty mushroomy broth, is recommended. Ask the staff to translate the Chinese menu: eastern treats hide there.

Fook Sing

25 Newport Court, WC2 (7287 0188). Leicester Square tube. **Open** 11am-10.30pm daily. **Main courses** £3.50-£12.50. **No credit cards. Map** p401 K7.

Fook Sing has barely a dozen tables but the food is bigger than that. A sign in the window lists the dishes in English – take a notebook or you'll be limited to the few dishes on the English menu. You'd miss out on purple seaweed soup, slippery noodles in peanut sauce, tangy consommé of 'special fish ball with meat inside' and the whelks and vegetables in curry sauce. Few other than Chinese eat here, yet the informative staff are helpful and friendly.

Mr Kong

21 Lisle Street, WC2H 7BA (7437 7341/9679). Leicester Square or Piccadilly Circus tube. **Open** noon-2.45am daily. **Main courses** £5.90-£26. **Credit** AmEx, DC, JCB, MC, V. **Map** p401 K7.

Cheerful and unpretentious, Mr K is a favourite among the Chinese for steamed crab in sauces like Shaoxing wine or ginger and spring onion. Chef's specials include steamed scallops with glass noodles and sandstorm aubergine and beancurd (the 'sand', crispy golden-fried garlic). Another superbly named dish, dragon whistlers, was delicate green pea leaves flavoured with scallops.

New Diamond

23 Lisle Street, WC2H 7BA (7437 2517/7221). Leicester Square tube. **Open** noon-3am daily. **Main courses** £5.80-£22. **Credit** AmEx, DC, MC, V. **Map** p401 K7.

A bright and shiny restaurant with a helpful English translation for both its regular and its specials menus. The fresh razor-clams steamed with garlic and chilli in light soy have become a signature dish. Also good: the crisp-skinned pigeon, the winter melon soup with vegetables, pork and seafood, and fresh squid fried with chilli and salt. The yeung saam bou ('stuffed three precious') dish of peppers, aubergine and beancurd is also especially delicious.

New World

1 Gerrard Place, W1D 5PA (7734 0396). Leicester Square or Piccadilly Circus tube. **Open** 11am-11.45pm Mon-Sat; 11am-11pm Sun. *Dim sum* 11am-6pm daily. **Main courses** £4.90-£10.50, £1.80-£5.10 dim sum. **Credit** AmEx, DC, MC, V. **Map** p401 K7.

This mighty, unchanging hangar of a dim sum restaurant is fast becoming a retro gem. Metallic dragons coil around the chandeliers. The waitresses wear silk and push trolleys about. In uncertain English they offer steamed dumplings, deep-fried snacks such as yam croquettes, soup noodles, pork and chive dumplings and sweet titbits. Point at what you want. The full menu is a tome. Come in a group and relish the atmosphere as hundreds of local Chinese dig in.

Yming

35-36 Greek Street, W1D 5DL (7734 2721/ www.yming.com). Leicester Square, Piccadilly Circus or Tottenham Court Road tube. **Open** noon-11.45pm Mon-Sat. **Main courses** £5-£10. **Credit** AmEx, DC, JCB, MC, V. **Map** p399 K6.

An enticing menu, helpful staff and a serene atmosphere make Yming a welcome refuge from the hurly-burly of nearby Chinatown. Top items include 'Village duck', a concoction of duck, lily flowers and shiitake mushrooms; fish in Chinese rice wine sauce with wood ear fungus; and 'aubergine delight' topped with black bean sauce.

French

L'Escargot Marco Pierre White

48 Greek Street, W1D 4EF (7437 2679). Leicester Square or Tottenham Court Road tube. **Open** noon-2.15pm, 6-11.30pm Mon-Fri; 6-11.30pm Sat. **Main courses** £12.95-£17.95. **Credit** AmEx, DC, JCB, MC, V. **Map** p399 K6.

L'Escargot remains a Very Serious Institution. Its rooms are immaculate, its clientele largely black-jacketed and its staff and menu formal. Thankfully, the menu was recently translated from the French. The menu features snails 'bordelaise', crab bisque, and cod with spinach and champagne. Haute cuisine with a side of hauteur.

La Trouvaille

12A Newburgh Street, W1F 7RR (7287 8488/ www.latrouvaille.co.uk). Oxford Circus tube. **Open** noon-3pm, 6-11pm Mon-Sat. **Main courses** £12.50-£17.95. **Credit** AmEx, DC, JCB, MC, V. **Map** p398 J6.

La Trouvaille is some find: slightly crazy, thoroughly inspired French food served by slightly crazy, adrenaline-fired French staff. How about a flower salad with fiddlehead fern fritters, or liquorice bisque with beef skirt, or a mature cheddar milk-shake with strawberry charlotte? Suspend your disbelief, ask for the waiter's recommendations and prepare yourself for a witty yet ungimmicky and thoroughly memorable meal. A real winner.

Indian

Masala Zone

9 Marshall Street, W1F 7ER (7287 9966). Oxford Circus tube. **Open** noon-2.45pm, 5.30-11pm Mon-Fri; noon-3pm, 5-11pm Sat; 12.30-3.30pm, 6-10.30pm Sun. **Main courses** £5-£11. **Credit** MC, V. **Map** p398 J6.

The large dining hall here is a deserved success. Its pan-Indian menu encompasses rare ingredients in authentic regional dishes. The Malabar seafood bowl has flat noodles, tender squid and big prawns in a coconut milk-based soup. Samosas are freshly fried, kebabs featured mousse-light flavoursome meat. Equally praiseworthy are the side dishes, just 75p.

Other locations: 80 Upper Street, Islington, N1 0NP (7359 3399).

Red Fort

77 Dean Street, W1D 3SH (7437 2115/ www.redfort.co.uk). Tottenham Court Road tube. **Open** noon-2.15pm, 5.45-11.15pm Mon-Fri; 5.45-11.15pm Sat. **Main courses** £12.50-£28. **Credit** AmEx, DC, MC, V. **Map** p399 K6.

The chef here takes pride in recreating spice blends from the royal kitchens of Awadh (a historical region around Lucknow). Highlights include *biriani samudra,* spinach leaves flash-fried with mild chilli powder, garlic and onions. The Red Fort's attention to the finer aspects of traditional cooking makes it London's top Indian restaurant.

Italian

Quo Vadis

26-29 Dean Street, W1T 6LL (7437 9585/ www.whitestarline.org.uk). Leicester Square, Piccadilly Circus or Tottenham Court Road tube. **Open** noon-2.30pm, 5.30-11.30pm Mon-Fri; 5.30-11.30pm Sat. **Main courses** £5.50-£19.50. **Credit** AmEx, DC, JCB, MC, V. **Map** p399 K6.

Quo Vadis doesn't keep skeletons in its closet, it puts them out on display in a design that's a disconcerting blend of Brit Art, Arts and Crafts and art deco styling. The menu also blends styles freely. Modern Italian dominates, but other European touches (such as foie gras terrine with raisins) provide welcome juxtaposition. The food is hit or miss, but the atmosphere is what you're paying for.

Modern European

Alastair Little

49 Frith Street, W1D 4SG (7734 5183). Leicester Square or Tottenham Court Road tube. **Open** noon-3pm, 6-11.30pm Mon-Fri; 6-11.30pm Sat. **Main courses** £16.50-£18.50. **Credit** AmEx, JCB, MC, V. **Map** p399 K6.

Although the restaurant still bears his name, Alastair Little has nothing to do with it. You'd never guess it to eat here, though. The atmosphere is unpretentious, the decor calming, the staff accommodating, and the restaurant as a whole one of London's nicest. Typical dishes include sizzling prawns, crab and avocado pâté, and cod steak with salsa and beans.

Andrew Edmunds

46 Lexington Street, W1F 0LW (7437 5708). Oxford Circus or Piccadilly Circus tube. **Open** 12.30-3pm, 6-10.45pm Mon-Fri; 1-3pm, 6-10.45pm Sat, Sun. **Main courses** £7.95-£13. **Credit** AmEx, MC, V. **Map** p398 J6.

The close-set tables and church pew seating beg the question: bistro chic or consciously created discomfort? Whatever your view, the food is imaginative, and deceptively simple. Dishes like strawberries with roast beetroot, mint and balsamic vinegar, and mackerel with harissa and flageolet beans allow the ingredients to shine through.

Having it all

If you're ever in a London restaurant on a weeknight between 6pm and 8.30pm and you're wondering why it's all but empty, here's the scoop: everybody's at the pub. It is a London tradition to head straight from work to the local boozer to drink on an empty stomach. And it was ever thus, until those cool Britannia days of the early 1990s, when one pub changed everything.

At this time many public houses were being sold off cheaply by big breweries affected by the deregulation of the industry, a number of young chefs saw the redundant premises as a way of opening a restaurant cheaply. The idea was to combine convivial pub culture with big plates of hearty gourmet food and an upscale atmosphere (big windows, exposed pine floors and brushed steel everything else). Farringdon pub the **Eagle** started the fashion of the (now ubiquitous) gastropub.

Now this is one of those either love-it-or-hate-it creations, but it's certainly hard to deny that it was a good idea. Since the Eagle opened in 1991 (159 Farringdon Road, 7837 1353), innumerable imitations have sprung up across the city. Some are good, most are poncey and a select few are fab, but all share certain characteristics: the aforementioned decor is markedly common, as are organic beer, extensive wine lists emphasising California and a blackboard menu featuring foods with a colourful Mediterranean slant and/or a revisionist approach to traditional British cuisine. (Vegetarian shepherd's pie, for instance. Or grilled cod and roasted sweet potato chips. Etc.)

Most, sadly, are not centrally located, although a few of the best are easy to reach. Among these is the **Endurance** in Soho (90 Berwick Street, 7437 2944), where the menu's short length is directly proportional to its high prices, and the ambience is in strict opposition to the earthy surrounding marketplace. Then there's the **Perseverance** on Lamb's Conduit Street near Holborn tube, so trendy you have to book a table (in a pub!!) if you expect to eat.

Other than those, though, you'll have to take the tube, but not far, especially as the **Duke of Cambridge** is very near Angel tube (30 St Peter's Street, 7359 3066). A sort of condensed gastropub, it's got all the options – enormous windows, bare wood absolutely everywhere and a holier-than-thou all-organic menu from the food right down to the beer and wine.

The lack of tube makes getting to **Lots Road Pub & Dining Rooms** (114 Lots Road, SW10, 7352 6645), *Time Out*'s Best Gastropub award winner of 2002, a bit of a chore, but that doesn't stop its top drawer grub pulling in the crowds every evening; do book. Back in Islington, as most gastropubs seem to be, The **Social** (Arlington Square 7354 5809) has a big, bustling gastropub kitchen filled with perspiring chefs and culinary promise. Its brother in town is at 5 Little Portland Street, W1 (7636 4992). Canonbury's The **House** (63-9 Canonbury Road, N1, 7704 7410) is absolute yuppie heaven; the satisfying food and friendly service make up a real class act.

You'd expect chic pub grub to gain a foothold in smart Primrose Hill, so it has, with the pleasantly bohemian **Lansdowne** (90 Gloucester Avenue, (7483 0409), where the wine list is classy and the food snacky, well presented and Mediterranean.

One of the best places to find a gastropub is, predictably, over Notting Hill way, where the cheerful **Cow** is restaurateur Tom Conran's excellent foray into posh-pub life (89 Westbourne Park Road, 7221 5400), and the achingly cool **Golborne House** (36 Golborne Road, 8960 6260) makes a creamy butternut squash risotto so good you'll wonder how anybody ever got by before the *gourmetpub* (ahem) was invented.

Gay Hussar

2 Greek Street, W1D 4NB (7437 0973). Tottenham Court Road tube. **Open** 12.15-2.30pm, 5.30-10.45pm Mon-Sat. **Main courses** £9.50-£16.50. **Credit** AmEx, DC, JCB, MC, V. **Map** p399 K6.

This legendary political venue feels like a private club. The Hungarian menu inspires confidence with its authenticity: unpronounceable Hungarian classics are carefully and precisely described. There's a lot of veal, pork and goose fat, and for vegetarians, very little action indeed. Starters can be light – fish terrine with beetroot sauce – but are often heavy, such as marinated fillet of herring with sour cream, and grilled chicken breast with potato and onion salad. 'Gypsy Quick Dish' (medallions of pork with diced bacon, onions, potatoes and green paprika) is surprisingly good. The wine list is excellent, and the Hungarian house red comes by the carafe. Noise and smoke levels, however, can get irritating. Political types tend to pontificate in the corner.

162 Clapham High Street,
London SW4 7UG

020 7978 1108

4 Market Row, Electric Lane,
Brixton SW9 8LD

020 7738 3021

www.ecorestaurants.com

Oriental

Kulu Kulu

76 Brewer Street, W1F 9TX (7734 7316). Oxford Circus tube. **Open** noon-2.30pm, 5-10pm Mon-Fri; noon-3.45pm, 5-10pm Sat. **Main courses** £1.20-£3. **Credit** JCB, MC, V. **Map** p397 E10.

Customers at this branch of the kaiten-zushi chain sit shoulder to shoulder on small stools around a conveyor belt and grab whatever takes their fancy. Beer, saké or soft drinks are delivered by hand (or you can help yourself to green tea). Once you've finished, the stack of colour-coded plates is carried to the till and the bill added. But the conveyor belt tends to dry out the sushi, although the temaki sushi, made with crisp, tasty nori and filled with goodies such as avocado, vegetable tempura and salmon were pretty good. Even though there's a good selection on the belt, you're better off with the fresh, made-to-order noodle dishes straight from the chef.

Other locations: 39 Thurlow Place, South Kensington, SW7 (7589 2225).

Melati

21 Great Windmill Street, W1D 7LQ (7437 2745). Piccadilly Circus tube. **Open** noon-11.30pm Mon-Thur, Sun; noon-12.30am Fri, Sat. **Main courses** £5.65-£8.45. **Credit** AmEx, MC, V. **Map** p401 K7.

As much a Soho stalwart as the neighbouring strip-clubs, Melati is all about Indonesian food, with a menu offering well over 100 dishes. *Kretoprak*, deep-fried tofu, noodles and beansprouts, and mackerel *bumbu bali* are good options. But this place is more about filling your stomach than fine dining.

Ramen Seto

19 Kingly Street, W1B 5PY (7434 0309). Oxford Circus tube. **Open** noon-3pm, 6-10pm Mon-Sat. **Main courses** £5-£8.50. **Credit** JCB, MC, V. **Map** p398 J6.

With pop tunes pumping out of the corner speakers and peels of paint creeping down the walls, Ramen Seto is avowedly no-nonsense. Japanese diners slurp down their noodles seriously and don't linger long. There are other options – like gyoza dumplings and tempura – but you'd be best doing the same.

Saigon

45 Frith Street, W1D 4SD (7437 7109). Leicester Square tube. **Open** noon-11.30pm Mon-Sat. **Main courses** £3-£13.75. **Credit** AmEx, DC, MC, V. **Map** p399 K6.

Though situated in the heart of bustling Soho, Saigon's interior resembles a forgotten corner of Vietnam, with dark wooden tables, a bamboo-roofed bar and a slowly rotating ceiling fan. The staff are dressed in traditional costume and the menus are beautifully presented. Good choices are the Vietnamese spring rolls with pork and prawn with a fantastic spicy dipping sauce, stir-fried prawns, dry stir-fried lamb with pepper and mint, and chicken simmered with ginger and fish sauce. Saigon is great both for food and atmosphere.

Vegetarian & organic

Mildred's

45 Lexington Street, W1F 9AN (7494 1634). Oxford Circus or Piccadilly Circus tube. **Open** noon-11pm Mon-Sat. **Main courses** £5.20-£6.90. **No credit cards**. **Map** p399 K6.

Good food and service in relaxed, unpretentious surroundings have earned this place a loyal following, so it can get pretty crowded at lunchtime. Ingredients are organic where possible (including wine, smoothies and soft drinks), with vegan and wheat-free options. Choose from 12 flavour-packed starters and mains, plus specials: spring rolls with chilli jam, soup, pasta and stir-fries. Energising, detoxing salads are the virtuous options; more enjoyable is the beery mushroom and ale pie, served with mushy peas and wonderfully chunky, fluffy inside and crispy outside chips.

Covent Garden & St Giles's

Belgian

Belgo Centraal

50 Earlham Street, WC2H 9LJ (7813 2233/ www.belgo-restaurants.com). Covent Garden or Leicester Square tube. **Open** noon-11pm Mon-Thur; noon-11.30pm Fri, Sat; noon-10.30pm Sun. **Main courses** £8.75-£17.95. **Credit** AmEx, DC, JCB, MC, V. **Map** p399 L6.

This Belgian theme restaurant had its moment a few years back, when its waiters dressed like monks and open kitchens were all the rage. Its star has faded, but it's still a fun place for Belgian beer and dishes like the wild boar sausages and mash, or mussels steamed with white wine and garlic. The best thing in the house is the fries.

Other locations: 72 Chalk Farm Road, Camden, NW1 8AN (7267 0718).

British

The Savoy Grill

The Savoy, Strand, WC2R 0EU (7420 2065/ www.savoy-group.com). Covent Garden or Embankment tube/Charing Cross tube/rail. **Open** noon-2.45pm, 5.45-11pm Mon-Fri; noon-3.15pm, 5.45-11pm Sat, Sun. **Main courses** *Set meal* (5.45-6.45pm Mon-Sat) £25 3 courses. *Set dinner* £35 3 courses, £45 tasting menu (7-11pm Mon-Sat). **Credit** AmEx, JCB, MC, V. **Map** p399 L6.

The dining room has shimmering staff and old world clientele, and the menu, shoved into the 21st century by the arrival of new executive chef Marcus Wareing, has haute cuisine overtones. Starters include roasted scallops with fresh pea purée, and caramelised calves' sweetbreads on pancetta. Mains include inventive combinations, such as braised pork belly with sautéd jerusalem artichoke, and tender, rare pigeon with foie gras and sautéd ceps. The wine list tends toward 'oh my God' prices.

Simpson's-in-the-Strand

100 Strand, WC2R 0EW (7836 9112/www.simpsons-in-the-strand.com). Embankment tube/Charing Cross tube/rail. **Open** 7.15-10.30am, 12.15-2.30pm, 5.30-10.45pm Mon-Fri, 12.15-2.30pm, 5.30-10.45pm Sat; noon-3pm, 6-8.30pm Sun. **Main courses** £19.50-£23.50. **Credit** AmEx, DC, JCB, MC, V. **Map** p400 L7.

On the ground floor the wood-panelled dining room plays host to serious suits and tourists with its mix of old world ceremony and traditional British dining (roasts, carved from the trolley, are still the favourite choice). Upstairs is a lighter affair, brighter and more spacious, and the food veers toward haddock with a poached egg and cheese sauce.

Cafés & brasseries

Zoomslide Café

The Photographers' Gallery, 5 Great Newport Street, WC2H 7HY (7831 1772/www.photonet. org.uk). Leicester Square tube. **Open** 11am-5.30pm Mon-Sat; noon-5.30pm Sun. **Main courses** £1.65-£4.25. **No credit cards. Map** p401 K6.

As you'd expect for a café in the centre of a gallery, the atmosphere here is calm, cultured and fresh. It's an excellent place for a light and relaxed lunch – the salads and generously filled rolls (brie and salad, Mexican tuna, mozzarella and sun-dried tomato) are fresh and tasty, and very reasonably priced.

Fish

J Sheekey

28-32 St Martin's Court, WC2N 4AL (7240 2565). Leicester Square tube. **Open** noon-3pm, 5.30pm-midnight daily. **Main courses** £9.75-£29.95. Cover £1.50. **Credit** AmEx, DC, MC, V.

Like its better-known sister, the Ivy (*see below*), the interior here is beautiful – elegant, restrained, comfortable – the food is simple but of the highest quality, and the prices are reasonable. Unlike the Ivy, you won't be bombarded by celebrity-chasing rubbernecks and you won't have to book months in advance. Food includes the best fish pie in town, squid with chorizo, and wafer-thin tuna carpaccio with fennel. This is one of London's finest.

Fish & chips

Rock & Sole Plaice

47 Endell Street, WC2H 9AJ (7836 3785). Covent Garden tube. **Open** 11.30am-10pm Mon-Sat; noon-10pm Sun. **Main courses** £7-£13. **Credit** JCB, MC, V. **Map** p399 L6.

This black and white tiled Covent Garden institution has juicy haddock, cod and plaice, and solid chips. More unusual specials may be tuna, trout or mackerel. It's Turkish-run, so there's also taramasalata, Efes beer and pitta. Takeaways are half-price, but you risk the staff's wrath if you try to eat them on the benches outside.

French

The Admiralty

Somerset House, Strand, WC2R 1LA (7845 4646/www.somerset-house.org.uk). Embankment or Temple tube/Charing Cross tube/rail. **Open** noon-2.30pm, 6-10.30pm Mon-Sat; noon-2.30pm Sun. **Main courses** *Set lunch* £28 4 courses. *Set dinner* £28 2 courses, £33 3 courses, £37 5 courses (vegetarian), £42 5 courses (dégustation). **Credit** AmEx, DC, JCB, MC, V. **Map** p401 L7.

The location makes this place special, in gorgeous Somerset House, with restrained nautical decor and fantastical chandeliers. The menu is nicely conceived, typical dishes would be snail ravioli with artichokes, poached garlic and wine butter; or tender pigeon with puy lentils, pommes anna, onion soubise and red wine jus. It's all-round good food in a spectacular setting.

Modern American/European

Christopher's

18 Wellington Street, WC2E 7DD (7240 4222/www.christophersgrill.com). Covent Garden tube. **Open** noon-3.45pm, 5pm-midnight Mon-Fri; 11.30am-4pm, 5pm-midnight Sat; 11.30am-4pm Sun. **Main courses** £12-£28. **Credit** AmEx, DC, MC, V. **Map** p401 L6/7.

This upscale US restaurant – reached by a glorious, Italianate staircase – is a low-key place for a simple, good meal. Options include lean steaks, broiled lobster and excellent Maryland crabcakes. Desserts are similarly traditional and comforting.

The Ivy

1 West Street, WC2H 9NQ (7836 4751). Leicester Square tube. **Open** noon-3pm, 5.30pm-midnight daily. **Main courses** £8.75-£21.75. Cover £1.50 (lunch). **Credit** AmEx, DC, JCB, MC, V. **Map** p399 K6.

As it's still London's most famous restaurant, it's best to view the Ivy as a private club to which civilians are occasionally allowed access. The tortuous booking process can turn you off the place before you've even tasted the food. If you get in, you'll find a reasonably priced menu of comfort food: potted shrimps with granary toast, corned beef hash with fried egg and the famous salmon fish cake. It all comes with a line of paparazzi waiting outside.

Vegetarian & organic

Food for Thought

31 Neal Street, WC2H 9PR (7836 9072). Covent Garden tube. **Open** 9.30am-8.30pm Mon-Sat; noon-5pm Sun. **Main courses** £3-£8. **No credit cards. Map** p399 L6.

This café dishes out tasty, inviting fare in unpretentious surroundings. You'll have to share a table if you eat in, and queues are long at lunch, but the daily changing global menu might include

The **Rock & Sole Plaice**. *See p208.*

Indonesian curry and noodles, Middle Eastern bake with roasted veg, or portobello mushrooms stuffed with rocket pesto risotto. There are always vegan, wheat- and dairy-free choices.

World Food Café

First floor, 14 Neal's Yard, WC2H 9DP (7379 0298/www.worldfoodcafe.com). Covent Garden tube. **Open** 11.30am-4.30pm Mon-Fri; 11.30am-5pm Sat. **Main courses** £4.85-£7.95. **Credit** MC, V. **Map** p399 L6.

Global influences permeate this café, where eats include Indian thalis, African sweet potato in a spicy nut sauce and Mexican refried beans with guacamole. Soups and specials add variety.

Westminster

British

Shepherd's

Marsham Court, Marsham Street, SW1P 4LA (7834 9552). Pimlico or Westminster tube. **Open** 12.30-2.45pm, 6.30-11pm Mon-Fri. **Main courses** £18.50. **Credit** AmEx, DC, JCB, MC, V. **Map** p401 K10.

Alive with the whisperings of the Parliamentarians who arrive in droves from across the street, Shepherd's provides the kind of sober, atmosphere in which affairs of state and business can be discussed over traditional British nosh. The wine list is notable for its sensible prices, and the waiters are masters of the discreet Jeevesian shimmy.

Cafés & brasseries

Café in the Crypt

Crypt of St Martin-in-the-Fields, Duncannon Street, WC2N 4JJ (7839 4342/www.stmartin-in-the-fields.org). Embankment tube/Charing Cross tube/rail. **Open** 11.30am-3pm, 5-7.30pm Mon-Wed; 11.30am-3pm, 5-10.30pm Thur-Sat; noon-3pm, 5-7.30pm Sun. **Main courses** £5.95-£7.50. **No credit cards**. **Map** p401 L7.

Underneath St Martin-in-the-Fields, this café is a stone's throw from Whitehall, the Mall and the National Gallery. The restaurant is atmospheric, with tables arranged between solid stone pillars. Self-service, limited choice and simplicity are the keys. Vegetarian or meat-and-two veg, the food is sensible stuff and the apple crumble is lovely.

Indian

Cinnamon Club

The Old Westminster Library, Great Smith Street, SW1P 3BU (7222 2555/www.cinnamonclub.com). St James's Park or Westminster tube. **Open** 7.30-10am, noon-3pm, 6-11pm Mon-Fri; 6-11pm Sat. **Main courses** £11-£31. **Credit** AmEx, DC, MC, V. **Map** p401 K9.

Located in a former Victorian library, the Cinnamon Club is a popular haunt for Westminster suits, power brokers and others on expense accounts. The food caters for a well-travelled clientele, and dresses-up dishes with Western-style presentations. Bombay spiced vegetables with cumin pao is fab, roast turbot with Bengali dopiaza sauce a winner. The extensive wine list has some lofty prices.

Quilon

St James's Court Hotel, 41 Buckingham Gate, SW1E 6AF (7821 1899/www.thequilonrestaurant.com). St James's Park tube. **Open** noon-2.30pm, 6-11pm Mon-Fri; 6-11pm Sat. **Main courses** £7.50-£20. **Credit** AmEx, DC, MC, V. **Map** p400 H9/J9.

Never mind the less than tropical feel to this business hotel dining hall – Quilon's South Indian coastal cooking is a saviour for Indians (and others) blessed with good taste and deep pockets. Dishes like sumptuous mussels mappas, served on the shell with pounded ginger, tart sun-dried fish with tamarind and coconut milk are top-drawer stuff. This is one of the city's best curry houses.

Oriental

Nahm

The Halkin, Halkin Street, SW1X 7DJ (7333 1234). Hyde Park Corner tube. **Open** noon-2.30pm, 7-11pm Mon-Fri; 7-11pm Sat; 7-10pm Sun. **Main courses** £24-£29. **Credit** AmEx, DC, JCB, MC, V. **Map** p400 G9.

You don't come here for the look of the place, which is like airport-mall chic; you come for David Thompson's food. The startling interpretations of 'Royal Thai' cuisine make Nahm extraordinary. Try the appetiser-sized *miang* (betel leaf-wrapped savoury confections), the 'sour orange curry' of halibut, bursting with hot spices, or the surprising textures of tender 'caramelised' shredded beef.

Knightsbridge & South Kensington

Global

Jakob's

20 Gloucester Road, SW7 4RB (7581 9292). Gloucester Road tube. **Open** 8am-10pm Mon-Sat; 8am-5pm Sun. **Main courses** £5.50-£8.50. **Credit** AmEx, MC, V. **Map** p396 C9.

Jakob's is a friendly deli with a restaurant out the back, which has a lovely, summery feel with its conservatory-style glass roof. The front counter

Let's make a deal

When the deal really matters, or when money really doesn't, there are a select few formal, stiff-backed restaurants where everything is designed to facilitate the smooth progress toward the handshake and the bottom line. In their plush environs corporations are bought and sold, new laws are contemplated and 'get out of jail free' cards are issued. It all makes sense in a way, since, when it comes to privilege, patronage and profligacy, there's simply no better place than London.

Celebrating its 50th anniversary in 2003, the **Gay Hussar** (*see p205*) is still one of the most important restaurants for the political crowd. The photos on the walls of prime ministers past and present clue you in to the Hussar's position on the political spectrum. Those who don't make it from Westminster to Hussar's Soho location head to **Shepherd's** (*see p209*) to whisper behind one another's backs and plan future political shenanigans.

With expense accounts the size of the gross domestic products of third-world countries, corporate bigwigs have their choice of London restaurants, and many choose the over-the-top luxury of the **Savoy Grill** (*see p207*) and the glitz of the **Ritz** (*see p201*) when they want to impress international clients. Those looking for tradition along with their cabernet and contracts head to venerable establishments like **L'Escargot Marco Pierre White** (*see p204*), **Simpson's-in-the-Strand** (*see p208*), **Dorchester Grill Room** (*see p199*) and one of the grandest of them all, **Wiltons** (*see p199*). At the latter, the dress code is so strictly enforced that if a gentleman removes his jacket during the meal, he will be told politely but firmly to return it to his shoulders.

This doesn't sit well with the younger generation, so executives under 40 tend to avoid such stuffy restaurants, and frequent more nouveau posh places like **J Sheekey** (*see p208*) and **Le Caprice** (*see p201*), where they can drop their Armani jackets on a hot day without fear of rebuke.

offers a host of great Armenian salads alongside traditional meze like excellent couscous and grilled courgette, and a slow-cooked aubergine and pepper bake. The Middle Eastern cakes are moist, sweet and moreish. There's a good selection of wine and beer, plus non-alcoholic organic drinks.

French

Racine

239 Brompton Road, SW3 2EP (7584 4477). Knightsbridge or South Kensington tube/14, 74 bus. **Open** noon-3pm, 6-10.30pm daily. **Main courses** £9.50-£18.75. **Credit** AmEx, JCB, MC, V. **Map** p397 E10.

Racine is not flashy – the decor is plain but elegant – it's just very, very good at what it does. This is a French restaurant for the 21st century: tomatoes baked with basil and crème fraîche with toasted brioche make a subtle precursor to grilled calf's kidney with cabbage, onion and emmenthal mash. Exemplary puddings such as the delicate pot de crème de vanille aux pruneaux are hard to pass up. This lovely place was *Time Out's* New Restaurant of the Year in 2003 for good reasons.

Japanese

Zuma

5 Raphael Street, SW7 1DL (7584 1010/www.zumarestaurant.com). Knightsbridge tube. **Open** noon-2pm, 6-11pm Mon-Sat; noon-2.30pm Sun. **Main courses** £3.50-£28.50. **Credit** AmEx, DC, MC, V. **Map** p397 F9.

Zuma opened in 2002 to great reviews. It's got a good look: the stylish dining area is bounded by a golden wood-grained screen illuminated from behind. The dishes are composed of top ingredients: spicy beef is meltingly soft; tuna tataki (small rolls of flash-grilled tuna in ponzu) are sublime, vegetable tempura is excellent, and a raspberry version of chawan mushi creative. A brilliant place.

Spanish

Cambio de Tercio

163 Old Brompton Road, SW5 0LJ (7244 8970). Gloucester Road or South Kensington tube. **Open** 12.30-2.30pm, 7-11.30pm Mon-Sat; 12.30-2.30pm, 7-11pm Sun. **Main courses** £13.50-£15.50. **Credit** AmEx, MC, V. **Map** p396 C11.

Cambio's mixed chic-and-kitsch decor may be a bit battered, but this hasn't stopped the place being full of a buzzy, international crowd attracted by the tapas, especially when the doors are opened on to the street on a warm summer evening. Reliable options include the potato purée with octopus, prawns fried in almonds with a garlic emulsion, and the exquisitely tender grilled tuna with leeks, broad beans and Burgos cheese. Try the amazing 'textures of white chocolate' dessert. Service can be erratic.

Chelsea

Cafés & brasseries

Top Floor at Peter Jones

Peter Jones, Sloane Square, SW1 8EL (7730 3434). Sloane Square tube. **Open** 9.30am-7pm Mon-Sat. **Main courses** £3.50-£13. **Credit** MC, V. **Map** p400 G11.

This place resembles a posher version of the canteen on a cross-Channel ferry. In mitigation, the salmon is nicely grilled, and there are fantastic views towards Hyde Park. Dishes (sandwiches, salads and ready-poured glasses of wine) are in chilled displays. Hot dishes are made to order. You have to queue with plastic trays and pay in advance, though.

Indian

Chutney Mary

535 King's Road, SW10 0SZ (7351 3113/www.realindianfood.com). Fulham Broadway tube/West Brompton tube/rail/11, 22 bus. **Open** 12.30-2.30pm, 6.30-11pm daily. **Main course** £12.50-£24. **Credit** AmEx, DC, JCB, MC, V. **Map** p397 C13.

Always busy, this spot has a loyal clientele of dapper American business suits and well-to-do Chelsea types. It gives street food a glam make-over, and sits raunchy salads next to delicacies from royal Indian palaces. Especially memorable are the *nihari* soup (lamb stock with cardamom and crisp puff pastry) and the Goan green chicken curry. Service is faultless and the wine list well chosen.

Modern European

Bibendum

Michelin House, 81 Fulham Road, SW3 6RD (7581 5817/www.bibendum.co.uk). South Kensington tube. **Open** noon-2.30pm, 7-11pm Mon-Fri; 12.30-3pm, 7-10.30pm Sat, Sun. **Main courses** £19-£26.50. **Credit** AmEx, DC, MC, V. **Map** p397 E10.

This is one classy dining room. Set on the first floor of the Michelin building, it's decorated in cream, with colour coming from stained glass and the blue slip-covers on the chairs. Much of the menu occupies the same urbane, crowd-pleasing territory: haddock and (golden, thin) chips, and deep-fried calf's brain with sauce gribiche. Finish with the likes of rich chocolate and praline parfait.

Gordon Ramsay

68-9 Royal Hospital Road, SW3 4HP (7352 4441/3334/www.gordonramsay.com). Sloane Square tube. **Open** noon-2pm, 6.30-11pm Mon-Fri. **Main courses** *Set lunch* £35 3 courses. *Set meal* £65 3 courses, £80 7 courses. **Credit** AmEx, DC, JCB, MC, V. **Map** p397 F12.

God and Gordon Ramsay alone know the secret of his (not His) confounded booking system, but all hassles are forgotten once you're seated in the cool purple-hued room. The restaurant is full of food lovers drawn by the Skye scallops with oyster velouté, salad of Scottish lobster tail, and tender cannon of pink Cornish lamb with confit shoulder. The coffee soufflé with tiramisu sauce is sublime.

Oriental

Hunan

51 Pimlico Road, SW1 8NE (7730 5712). Sloane Square tube. **Open** noon-2.30pm, 6-11pm Mon-Sat. **Main courses** £8-£30. **Credit** AmEx, DC, MC, V. **Map** p400 G11.

Ignore all we've said about Chinese set meals and order the 'leave it to us feast' when booking here. The resulting repast is dish after exquisite, bijou dish of Hunan delicacies. This is the only venue in London dedicated to the Hunan region's cuisine. Highlights are piquant pickles, stuffed baby squid with bitter melon, succulent 'water chicken' (frogs' legs), tempura-like french beans in a light batter and salmon and white fish rolls in a fabulously tangy dressing. One of the best.

Eat, Drink, Shop

North London

Global

Afghan Kitchen

35 Islington Green, Islington, N1 8DU (7359 8019). Angel tube. **Open** noon-3.30pm, 5.30-11pm Tue-Sat. **Main courses** £4.50-£6. **No credit cards. Map** p402 O2.

This little place takes minimalism to the extreme: from the green and white interior to the pared-down menu, with just four meat and four veggie choices. Dishes include chicken in yoghurt, and lamb with potatoes, both with subtle spicing and succulent meat. Service is sweet, and prices reasonable.

Mango Room

10 Kentish Town Road, Camden, NW1 8NH (7482 5065). Camden Town tube. **Open** 6pm-midnight Mon; noon-3pm, 6pm-midnight Tue-Sat. **Meals served** noon-11pm Sun. **Main courses** £9-£12. **Credit** MC, V.

'Caribbean with a global twist' describes not only the cuisine but the service. The menu contains an enticing selection of dishes. You can't go wrong with options like seared salmon fillet with pickled mango sauce with fried plantain, or the warm ackee and avocado salad. A wide selection of drinks is available, including glorious cocktails.

Mediterranean

Café Corfu

7 Pratt Street, Camden, NW1 0AE (7267 8088/ www.cafecorfu.com). Camden Town tube. **Open** noon-10.30pm Tue-Thur, Sun; noon-11.30pm Fri; 5-11.30pm Sat. **Main courses** £7.95-£12.95. **Credit** MC, V.

Quirky Café Corfu offers a delightfully modern and imaginative menu. Top marks to the sweet and succulent *papoutsáki* (stuffed aubergines) and beautifully presented *kalamarákia tiganta* (crisped baby squid in a pastry basket), delicious organic wild boar and *tsipoura* (grilled sea bream) with spinach. The organic Greek wines are equally good.

Iznik

19 Highbury Park, Highbury, N5 1QJ (7354 5697). Highbury & Islington tube/rail/4, 19, 236 bus. **Open** 10am-4pm, 6.30pm-midnight Mon-Fri; 6.30pm-midnight Sat, Sun. **Main courses** £7.50-£9.50. **Credit** MC, V.

Iznik serves some of the best Turkish food of its type. Authentic stews and bakes are the speciality here – dishes such as aubergines stuffed with minced lamb and baked in tomato sauce, are supplemented with fresh salads and *kisir* (cracked wheat with tomatoes, peppers and lemon juice). Puddings are notable, especially the pears stuffed with pistachios. The atmosphere is congenial.

Sariyer Balik

56 Green Lanes, Stoke Newington, N16 9NH (7275 7681). Bus 141, 341. **Open** 5pm-1am daily. **Main courses** £6.50-£10. **No credit cards.**

Sariyer Balik doesn't look much from the outside – small and dark, with its name painted on the window – but you won't get better Turkish fish dishes in London. The menu is entirely fish-based and includes some beautifully tender kalamar soaked in vodka, tasty mussels in beer, and simple grilled mackerel and bass, perfectly done.

Oriental

The New Culture Revolution

43 Parkway, Camden, NW1 7PN (7267 2700). Camden Town tube. **Open** noon-3.30pm, 5.30-11pm Mon-Fri; 1-11pm Sat, Sun. **Main courses** £4.60-£10. **Credit** AmEx, JCB, MC, V.

This establishment is really about noodles in soup, and the steaming bowls draw 'oohs' of wonder from the customers. The fish cooked in yellow bean sauce with fresh beancurd is also a good choice, and the pork-filled *guo-tier* (pot-sticker dumplings) are succulent. It's inexpensive and worth a visit.

Vegetarian & organic

Heartstone

106 Parkway, Camden, NW1 7AN (7485 7744). Camden Town tube. **Open** noon-9pm Tue; 10am-9pm Wed-Sat; 10am-4pm Sun. **Main courses** £9.50-£15. **Credit** MC, V.

This is a rare treat: a stylish, modern, north London eaterie with good, wholesome, honest food. Generous portions of spinach salad come with cubes of fried cheese, grilled swordfish is tender and tasty. A super-chilled-out staff give diners the feeling they've been invited round to someone's house.

Chutney Mary for Indian food with flair. *See p211.*

East London

Cafés & brasseries

Brick Lane Beigel Bake

159 Brick Lane, Spitalfields, E1 6SB (7729 0616). Liverpool Street tube/rail/8 bus. **Open** 24hrs daily. **No credit cards**. **Map** p403 S4.

At any time of day or night you can feast on London's best-value (and, many consider, best-tasting) bagels. Buy them plain, or filled with any of the traditional favourites: smoked salmon, salt beef, egg and onion, or chopped liver.

Jones Dairy Café

23 Ezra Street, Bethnal Green, E2 7RH (7739 5372). Bethnal Green tube/26, 48, 55 bus. **Open** 9am-3pm Fri, Sat; 8am-3pm Sun. **Main courses** £2-£5. **No credit cards**. **Map** p403 S3.

This sweet little café is at its busiest on Sunday mornings, when most of east London seems to turn up to buy bouquets and bedding plants at Columbia Road Flower Market (*see p251*). The menu is basic but wholesome, with bagels, fabulous home-made breads, soup, organic lemonade and coffee. A wood-burning stove ensures a wonderful cosy atmosphere on a cold winter's day.

Global

Arkansas Café

Unit 12, 107B Commercial Street, Old Spitalfields Market, Spitalfields, E1 6AA (7377 6999). Liverpool Street tube/rail. **Open** noon-2.30pm Mon-Fri; noon-4pm Sun. **Main courses** £5-£14.50. **Credit** MC, V. **Map** 403 R5.

This US barbecue joint is a rough and ready sort of a place tucked away inside Spitalfields Market, and artfully equipped with throwaway furniture. But the food could not be better: the barbecue platter features succulent roast chicken, tender brisket and sagey sausage with beans, tart coleslaw, tangy purple cabbage and mash: all for less than a tenner.

The Real Greek

15 Hoxton Market, Hoxton, N1 6HG (7739 8212/ www.therealgreek.co.uk). Old Street tube/rail/26, 48, 55, 149, 243 bus. **Open** noon-3pm, 5.30-10.30pm Mon-Sat. **Main courses** £12.90-£15.90. **Credit** MC, V. **Map** p403 R3.

Food-wise, forget what you think you know about pitta bread, souvláki and retsina. Here they appear in their finest incarnation. Grilled meats and souvláki are displayed in many guises: traditional style on a skewer, encased in warm rye sourdough, with chicken or smoked sausage.

Other locations: 140-2 St John Street, EC1V 4UA.

Indian

Café Spice Namaste

16 Prescot Street, Whitechapel, E1 8AZ (7488 9242/ www.cafespice.co.uk). Tower Hill tube/Tower Gateway DLR. **Open** noon-3pm, 6.15-10.30pm Mon-Fri; 6.30-10.30pm Sat. **Main courses** £9.95-£15.95. **Credit** AmEx, DC, JCB, MC, V. **Map** p405 S7.

Although all dishes here rely on traditional techniques to good effect, purists may baulk at the chef's use of the unusual (such as venison tikka and wild boar sausages). Seafood samosa encloses crab meat and chopped prawns in the traditional Keralan manner. King scallops with ginger and chilli arrive with garlic pilau and a small bowl of thin coconut curry. Fellow diners are suited City types affluent enough (or on expense accounts) to afford the prices.

Modern Europe

Fifteen

15 Westland Place, Hoxton, N1 7LP (7251 1515/ www.fifteenrestaurant.com). Old Street tube/rail. **Open** 8.30am-12.30pm, 12.30-3.30pm, 6pm-midnight Mon-Sat; 8.30am-5pm Sun. **Main courses** £22-£28. **Credit** AmEx, JCB, MC, V. **Map** p403 Q3.

Celeb chef Jamie Oliver's bar-restaurant opened in a torrent of publicity in 2002 after a documentary followed his efforts to create it as a combination school/eaterie where he would train underprivileged youth. It's still going great guns: the basement restaurant is booked months in advance, but the airy ground-floor bar (which serves breakfasts, deli snacks and antipasti) can usually squeeze you in. If you get a seat, you'll find surprisingly good cooking for trainees: line-caught sea bass steamed with courgettes and Florence fennel, for example, or wild Irish salmon with mashed purple potatoes. Prices are sky high, but it's a happening place and all profits go to Oliver's Cheeky Chops Charity, which takes on unemployed youngsters to train as chefs.

South-east London

Modern European

Belair House

Gallery Road, Dulwich, SE21 7AB (8299 9788/ www.belairhouse.co.uk). West Dulwich rail. **Open** noon-2.30pm Tue-Sun. Dinner served 7-10.30pm Tue-Sat. **Main courses** *Set lunch* (Tue-Sat) £18 2 courses, £22 3 courses; (Sun) £27 3 courses. *Set dinner* £32 3 courses. **Credit** AmEx, DC, JCB, V.

The restaurant is set in an elegant white 1785 mansion in its own grounds. Summer lunches on the terrace are unforgettable, especially if you can afford a good bottle from the wine list (which has little under £20). Expect handsome posh-peasant-grub treats such as crispy pork belly on superb salad to start, and a rich earthy daube of Scottish beef, or Bresse pigeon for mains. Puddings are lovely.

Inside

19 Greenwich South Street, Greenwich, SE10 8NW (8265 5060/www.insiderestaurant.co.uk). Greenwich rail/DLR. **Open** noon-2.30pm, 6.30-11pm Tue, Thur-Sat; noon-2.30pm Wed; noon-3pm Sun. **Main courses** £10.95-£16. **Credit** MC, V.

Local restaurants don't come much better than this tiny little place. The regularly changing menu is the sort where just about every dish appeals. Start, perhaps, with a subtle tomato and tarragon consommé with beef raviolini, and try mains of roasted barbary duck breast with a substantial puy lentil salad and strong garlic confit, or roast sea bass with thyme chips. End with soft pistachio meringue with mascarpone cream and strawberries.

South-west London

Cafés & brasseries

The Lavender

171 Lavender Hill, Battersea, SW11 5TE (7978 5242). Clapham Junction rail. **Open** noon-11pm Mon-Sat; noon-10.30pm Sun. **Main courses** £7-£10.50. **Credit** AmEx, MC, V.

This bastion of Battersea is popular, particularly at weekends, although the food – chosen from a chalkboard above the bar – can be variable. Options include smoked salmon with horseradish dressing or homely and tasty calf's liver and sautéd potatoes. Prices are reasonable, there's outside seating and the service is friendly and efficient.

Other locations: 112 Vauxhall Walk, Vauxhall, SE11 (7735 4440); 24 Clapham Road, Clapham, SW9 (7793 0770); 61 The Cut, South Bank, SE1 (7928 8645).

Enoteca Turi. *See p215.*

Global

Bamboula

12 Acre Lane, Brixton, SW2 5SG (7737 6633). Brixton tube/rail. **Open** 11am-11pm Mon-Fri; noon-11pm Sat; 1-6pm Sun. **Main courses** £5.95-£7.50. **Credit** MC, V.

Bamboula aims to please. The menu at this Caribbean joint has stayed much the same over the past few years. Snacks include patties (chicken, mutton or vegetable), plantain, and jerk chicken sandwiches. Full meals of ackee and saltfish, goat curry with rice and peas, and jerk fish are all filling.

Canyon

The Towpath, Richmond Riverside, Richmond, Surrey TW10 6UJ (8948 2944). Richmond tube/rail. **Open** noon-3.30pm, 6-11pm Mon-Fri; 11am-3.30pm, 6-11pm Sat, Sun. **Main courses** £10-£18. **Credit** AmEx, DC, MC, V.

With its big terrace overlooking the river, wide windows and sweeping views, Canyon has long been the perfect fair-weather restaurant for those to whom money is little object, and for whom good modern American food matters. It is worth the trip because of starters like Asian pear salad with roast pumpkin seeds and sliced avocado, and for mains like the basil-stuffed chicken breast with herb couscous. Staff are pleasant, and the wine list is quality.

Italian

Enoteca Turi

28 Putney High Street, SW15 1SQ (8785 4449). East Putney tube/Putney Bridge rail/14, 74, 270 bus. **Open** noon-2.30pm, 6.30-11pm daily. **Main courses** £14-£17. **Credit** AmEx, DC, MC, V.

This spacious and stylishly cosmopolitan venue could hold its own in the West End. There's bold modern art on the walls and a sophisticated list of seasonal foods on the menu, but perhaps most notable is the huge wine selection. On the menu: seared tuna with peas and artichokes; grilled squid with tomato, carrot salad and toast; gnocchi with courgettes and prawns. Desserts are excellent.

Modern European

The Glasshouse

14 Station Parade, Kew, Surrey TW9 3PZ (8940 6777). Kew Gardens tube/rail. **Open** noon-2.30pm, 7-10.30pm Mon-Sat; 12.30-2.45pm, 7-10.30pm Sun. **Main courses** *Set lunch* £17.50 3 courses, (Sun) £25 3 courses. *Set dinner* £30 3 courses. **Credit** AmEx, MC, V.

One of London's most genteel neighbourhoods, Kew is perhaps the ideal location for a restaurant as sophisticated and unassuming as this one. The cooking is ambitious, yet affordable. The menu features: pea soup with smoked bacon chantilly, ragoût of prawns and salmon with scallop agnolotti, roast suckling pork with apple, sage and choucroute tarte. The reasonable wine list is another attraction.

Thyme

14 Clapham Park Road, Clapham, SW4 7BB (7627 2468/www.thymeandspace.com). Clapham Common tube. **Open** 6.30-10.30pm Tue-Sat. **Main courses** £6-£11. **Credit** AmEx, MC, V.

This is a slick, well-organised operation with a quirky culinary approach, which deserves to do well. Here, every dish is served as a trio of mini-dishes, arranged on a long, rectangular plate. So, you could order a delicate parcel of sole flanked by crunchy roast cockles and scallops. The staff know their stuff and there's a choice of set menus.

Oriental

Tsunami

5-7 Voltaire Road, Clapham, SW4 6DQ (7978 1610). Clapham North tube. **Open** 6-11pm Mon-Thur; 6-11.30pm Fri; noon-11.30pm Sat. **Main courses** £7.95-£16.50. **Credit** MC, V.

This is one of the best, most professionally run Japanese restaurants in town. It's difficult to say which dishes Tsunami does best, but the sushi is not to be missed. Specials might include *wagyu* beef, sea urchin and shiso leaf tempura. Some dishes, such as foie gras and chive roll with eel sauce, stray into fusion territory, but the underlying current remains Japanese. It's not cheap, but it is excellent value.

West London

Cafés & brasseries

Lisboa Patisserie

57 Golborne Road, Ladbroke Grove, W10 5NR (8968 5242). Ladbroke Grove or Westbourne Park tube/23, 52 bus. **Open** 8am-8pm Mon-Sat; 8am-7pm Sun. **Credit** MC, V.

There's a wide selection of cakes, at this popular pâtisserie, and all are cooked on the premises. The custard tarts and rice cakes are fantastic, but try a pastry filled with sweet creamed beans. At 35p to 50p an item, you can't go wrong. Savouries include potato and cod cakes and croquettes.

Lucky 7

127 Westbourne Park Road, Westbourne Park, W2 5QL (7727 6771). Royal Oak or Westbourne Park tube. **Open** 7am-11pm Mon-Sat; 9am-10.30pm Sun. **Main courses** £4.25-£7.95. **No credit cards**. **Map** p394 A5.

With its smooth booths and 1950s-style formica tables, Tom Conran's diner is such a perfect imitation you'd be hard-pressed to find so authentic a joint in America itself. The menu is short and basic – sandwiches, burgers, shakes and salads – but the food is cooked with real style. The enormous beer-batter onion rings are crisp and generous.

Fish & chips

Geales

2 Farmer Street, Notting Hill, W8 7SN (7727 7528). Notting Hill Gate tube. **Open** noon-3pm, 6-11pm Mon-Sat; 6-10.30pm Sun. **Main courses** £7.25-£11.50. Cover 50p. **Credit** AmEx, MC, V. **Map** p394 A7.

White and blue walls and a concertina front window opening on to the street make this one chic chippy. Claudia Schiffer, Mick Jones and Vernon Kay have been recent noshers. The attraction? The satisfying fish soup and tasty salmon fish cakes, as well as the caviar, and moules marinière. Watch out for the extras: 50p per head cover, 60p for tartare sauce.

French

La Trompette

5-7 Devonshire Road, W4 2EU (8747 1836). Turnham Green tube. **Open** noon-2.30pm, 6.30-10.30pm Mon-Sat; 12.30-3pm, 7-10pm Sun. **Main courses** *Set lunch* £21.50 3 courses, (Sun) £25 3 courses. *Set dinner* £30 3 courses. Service 12.5%. **Credit** AmEx, JCB, MC, V.

The room is discreetly luxurious, and staff are exemplary, even when lovely la Trompette is packed to the gills. The modern French menu offers a mix of light dishes and heartier, meatier options. Try the dozen rock oysters, the ragoût of sea bream or the shellfish in crème fraîche and champagne. The set dinner is a bargain for cooking of such quality.

Global

Mandalay

444 Edgware Road, Paddington, W2 1EG (7258 3696). Edgware Road tube. **Open** noon-2.30pm, 6-10.30pm Mon-Sat. **Main courses** £3.90-£6.90. **Credit** AmEx, DC, JCB, MC, V. **Map** p395 E4.

The capital's only Burmese restaurant is modestly housed in cosy premises on the down-at-heel northern stretch of Edgware Road. Tasty shrimp and beansprout fritters, chicken with lemongrass in coconut milk sauce, and satisfying twice-cooked fish curry are all good options.

Rodizio Rico

111 Westbourne Grove, Bayswater, W2 4UW (7792 4035). Bayswater tube. **Open** 6-11.30pm Mon-Fri. noon-4.30pm, 6-11.30pm Sat; 12.30-10.30pm Sun. **Main courses** *Set buffet* £11.70 vegetarian, £17.90 barbecue. **Credit** MC, V. **Map** p394 B6.

This must be the simplest restaurant in town. It follows the Brazilian rodizio model: one price, one meal, a few blokes with skewers doling out meat, serve-yourself buffet salads and stews, and that's about it. The great reddish rump steaks are cooked to perfection, crispy and salty round the edges. Sadly, the prices aren't as low key as the food.

Indian

Zaika

1 Kensington High Street, Kensington, W8 5NP (7795 6533/www.zaika-restaurant.co.uk). High Street Kensington tube. **Open** noon-2.45pm, 6.30-10.45pm Mon-Fri, 6.30-10.45pm Sat; noon-2.45pm, 6.30-9.45pm Sun. **Main courses** *Set lunch* £14.95 2 courses, £17.95 3 courses. *Set meals* £38 6 courses, £58 9 courses. **Credit** AmEx, DC, JCB, MC, V. **Map** p394 C8.

Located in a former bank, Zaika's impressive flower arrangements and Moghul-style low seating add opulence to this already sumptuous restaurant. It serves contemporary Indian dishes with flair: *murgh tukde* (cardamom-scented chicken with saffron) is seared to perfection. Service is as smooth as silk.

Italian

Assaggi

39 Chepstow Place, Notting Hill, W2 4TS (7792 5501). Notting Hill Gate tube. **Open** 12.30-2.30pm, 7.30-11pm Mon-Fri; 1-2.30pm, 7.30-11pm Sat. **Main courses** £15.95-£19.50. **Credit** DC, JCB, MC, V. **Map** p394 B6.

Assaggi is one of the most inviting and informal of London's upmarket Italian venues. Most of the menu is written in Italian, necessitating an entertaining run-through of the options from the maîtresse d'. Top options include pear, pecorino and walnut salad to start, followed by roast guinea fowl with pea purée and shaved black summer truffles, and tagliolini with clams and *bottarga* (dried mullet roe).

Rosmarino

1 Blenheim Terrace, St John's Wood, NW8 0EH (7328 5014). St John's Wood tube. **Open** noon-2.30pm, 7-10.30pm Mon-Fri; noon-3pm, 7-10.30pm Sat, Sun. **Main courses** *Set lunch* (Mon-Thur) £19.50 2 courses, £25 3 courses. *Set meal* (lunch Fri-Sun; dinner daily) £23.50 2 courses, £28 3 courses, £33 4 courses, £35 5 courses. **Credit** AmEx, DC, MC, V.

Haute cuisine touches lend a formal air to meals here, but the atmosphere is certainly not stuffy. The menu extends from staples – creamy buffalo mozzarella with fresh tomatoes and basil oil – to more experimental ingredients including cured sea bass roe and delicious chestnut pasta.

Oriental

E&O

14 Blenheim Crescent, Ladbroke Grove, W11 1NN (7229 5454). Ladbroke Grove or Westbourne Park tube. **Open** noon-3pm, 6-11pm Mon-Sat; 1-3pm, 6-10.30pm Sun. **Main courses** £6-£19.50. **Credit** AmEx, DC, MC, V.

This joint has the kind of front bar you can imagine film stars draping themselves over. The menu here is varied and was ranked by *Time Out* in 2003 as the city's best restaurant for vegetarians. Along with dim sum, salads, tempura, sashimi, curries and specials, are fabulous fruit and veg mixed to create flavour-packed food. The E&O kitchen leaves your body feeling healthy and your spirit indulged.

Mandarin Kitchen

14-16 Queensway, Bayswater, W2 3RX (7727 9012). Bayswater or Queensway tube. **Open** noon-11.30pm daily. **Main courses** £5.90-£25. **Credit** AmEx, DC, JCB, MC, V.

They say more lobsters are served here than at any other restaurant in Britain, and this is certainly the place for a seafood extravaganza, with steamed scallops, razor–clams, sea bass and exquisite roasted baby squid. In fact, a meal here can be the stuff of dreams. The decor is nothing to write home about, but that's not the point, the food is.

Vegetarian & organic

The Gate

51 Queen Caroline Street, Hammersmith, W6 9QL (8748 6932/www.gateveg.co.uk). Hammersmith tube. **Open** noon-3pm, 6-10.45pm Mon-Fri; 6-10.45pm Sat. **Main courses** £7.95-£11.50. **Credit** AmEx, DC, JCB, MC, V.

Dine in the secluded, leafy courtyard, or ascend to the airy loft for some of the best vegetarian cooking in town. Spinach, blue cheese and walnut tart might precede baby aubergines stuffed with pine nuts, goat's cheese, spinach and puy lentils. There are vegan dishes as well. Go on, have a cappuccino brûlée for pudding if it's on the menu.

Other locations: 72 Belsize Lane, Belsize Park, NW3 (7435 7733).

Pubs & Bars

Ours is a pint of London Pride. Cheers.

Some trends in publand are to be welcomed. Some are not. Among the former: the trend toward gastropubs (*see p205* **Having it all**), and pubs in general serving food that isn't bland, pre-fab or downright awful. Also in the good column: the growing (if still limited) popularity of cocktails for those nights when you just don't feel like a pint. Another plus: real ale is growing again in popularity after two decades in which the so-called 'proper beer' was put on the back shelf in favour of sparkly alcopops and European lagers promoted in aggressive television advertising campaigns in the 1980s and '90s.

Other ongoing trends, though, fall in among the cons. London's streets are still tainted by an endless series of characterless chain pubs: the flat-packed and polished blandness of the All Bar One, Pitcher & Piano and Slug & Lettuce chains, the loud and lairy Aussie-themed Walkabout Inns and the faux Oirishery of O'Neill's are to drinkers what Pizza Hut and KFC are to gourmets. Even those pubs that escape branding are not immune to ruin. Over the last few years too many London pubs have been blighted by ham-fisted refits involving what should be illegal amounts of light pine, country kitchen furniture and brown leather. And if the rebranding proves a flop, there's always money to be made selling off old pubs to property redevelopers.

Thankfully, though, plenty of pubs have been permitted to carry on as if nothing has changed in the last few centuries, thus allowing fans of social history to have a fine old time exploring London's recent (and not so recent) history through the architecture, memorabilia and the lined and worn faces of some of the locals in the city's heritage boozers.

While you're here, should you find your drinking rudely interrupted by a ringing bell and the cry of 'Time, please!' we apologise. There's not an adult in London who has not been frustrated by the arcane law that means, without a special licence, pubs may only open between the hours of 11am-11pm (or noon-10.30pm on Sunday). A bill to reform the law and allow late pub hours is being considered by Parliament, but we're not holding our breath. For a full survey of London drinking options we suggest that you pick up a copy of the annual *Time Out Pubs & Bars Guide* (£6.99).

Central London

The South Bank & Bankside

Anchor Bankside

34 Park Street, SE1 9EF (7407 1577). London Bridge tube/rail. **Open** 11am-11pm Mon-Sat; noon-10.30pm Sun. **Credit** AmEx, DC, MC, V. **Map** p404 P8.

This riverfront boozer positively creaks with its past. A labyrinthine layout holds countless bars and alcoves – including the Johnson Room, where the great man wrote parts of his dictionary. The terrace is always busy in summer, and understandably so.

Market Porter

9 Stoney Street, SE1 9AA (7407 2495). London Bridge tube/rail. **Open** 6-8.30am, 11am-11pm Mon-Fri; noon-11pm Sat; noon-10.30pm Sun. **Credit** AmEx, MC, V. **Map** p404 P8.

A smashing little hideaway, this, recommendable not just for its early opening hours (it unlocks early for the benefit of traders at Borough Market) but for its genial atmosphere and terrific beer choices.

Royal Oak

44 Tabard Street, SE1 4JU (7357 7173). Borough tube/London Bridge tube/rail. **Open** 11.30am-11pm Mon-Fri. **Credit** MC, V. **Map** p404 P9.

Recently restored (the mahogany gleams, the etched glass sparkles like new), this is a strong candidate for London's best pub. The full range of Harvey's cask-conditioned canon is on offer, from Mild to Old.

The best Pubs & bars

For the grub
Queen's. *See p223.*

For the buzz
Tongue & Groove. *See p226.*

For the view
Twentyfour. *See p218.*

For the brew
White Horse. *See p228.*

For wine
Guinea. *See p220.*

For spirits
Boisdale. *See p221.*

The **Counting House** – one of the most beautiful boozers in London.

The City

Black Friar

174 Queen Victoria Street, EC4V 4EG (7236 5474). Blackfriars tube/rail. **Open** 11.30am-11pm Mon-Sat; noon-10pm Sun. **Credit** AmEx, MC, V. **Map** p404 O6.
An extraordinary wedge-shaped pub with an art nouveau façade, and Edwardian marble, mosaics and pillared fireplaces inside. There's also some decent beer and, more often than not, a sizeable crowd of City suits on hand to enjoy it.

Counting House

50 Cornhill, EC3V 3PD (7283 7123). Monument tube/Bank tube/DLR. **Open** 11am-11pm Mon-Fri. **Credit** AmEx, DC, MC, V. **Map** p405 Q6.
Once the headquarters of NatWest Bank, when it was converted into a boozer this place became the first ever pub to win a City Heritage award. With bare-board floors, marble walls and huge, gilt-framed mirrors and portraits, it's easy to see why. This is a Fuller's pub, so there's a full selection of that brewery's beers, and it's in the City, so there's a full selection of banking types at the tables.

Jamaica Wine House

St Michael's Alley, off Cornhill, EC3 9DS (7929 6972). Bank tube/DLR. **Open** 11am-11pm Mon-Fri. **Credit** AmEx, MC, V. **Map** p405 Q6.
London's first coffee house, this place was rebuilt after the Great Fire and converted into a pub at the end of the 19th century, hence the nicely aged mahogany interior.

Twentyfour

Level 24, Tower 42, 25 Old Broad Street, EC2N 1HQ (7877 7703/www.twenty-four.co.uk). Bank tube/DLR/Liverpool Street tube/rail. **Open** noon-11pm Mon-Fri (last admission 10pm). Booking essential. **Credit** AmEx, DC, MC, V. **Map** p402 N5.
The decor might be nice and modish and the cocktails might have been immaculately mixed, but all the suits are here for the views, 24 floors up.

Smiths of Smithfield

67-77 Charterhouse Street, EC1M 6HJ (7251 7950/ www.smithsofsmithfield.com). Farringdon tube/rail. **Open** *Main bar* 11am-midnight Mon-Sat; noon-10.30pm Sun. *Cocktail bar* 5.30pm-1am Mon-Sat. **Credit** AmEx, DC, MC, V. **Map** p402 O5.

Bang opposite Smithfield Market, this impressive warehouse dating back to 1886 used to service meat traders with butchers' supplies. It still contains many of the building's original features, so walking through the front door is like walking on to the world's poshest factory floor. Doors open bright and early for the breakfast crowd, while in the evening the cosy velvet booths upstairs do banner business.

Ye Olde Cheshire Cheese

145 Fleet Street, EC4A 2BU (7353 6170/ www.yeoldecheshirecheese.com). Blackfriars tube/ rail. **Open** 11.30am-11pm Mon-Fri; noon-3pm, 5.30-11pm Sat; noon-3pm Sun. **Credit** AmEx, DC, MC, V. **Map** p404 N6.

This place might look closed but it probably isn't: its anonymous dark frontage thoroughly conceals the unprepossessing alleyway entrance. Inside, it's a warren of wooden settles, boards and sawdust, once familiar to Dickens, Thackeray and Johnson.

Holborn & Clerkenwell

Bleeding Heart Tavern

Bleeding Heart Yard, off Greville Street, EC1N 8SJ (7242 8238). Chancery Lane tube/Farringdon tube/rail. **Open** noon-11pm Mon-Fri. **Credit** AmEx, DC, MC, V. **Map** p402 N5.

With its gory past of bloody murders and royal weddings safely behind it (we could go into it, but you'll get quite enough of it from the information posted all around the pub), this City yard plays host to claret of a different kind. The wine list is extensive, the surroundings are warm and comfortable, and the food is modern, French and tasty. This is one of the City's best offerings.

Café Kick

43 Exmouth Market, EC1R 4QL (7837 8077/ www.cafekick.co.uk). Farringdon tube/rail. **Open** noon-11pm Mon-Sat; noon-10.30pm Sun. **Credit** MC, V. **Map** p402 N4.

A little slice of continental Europe in Clerkenwell, Café Kick's thing is football, both televised and played on a table (there are three lovely *baby foot* tables here). Beer and coffee accompany the action. **Other locations**: Bar Kick 127 Shoreditch High Street, E1 (7739 8700).

Jerusalem Tavern

55 Britton Street, EC1N 5MA (7490 4281/ www.stpetersbrewery.co.uk). Farringdon tube/ rail. **Open** 11am-11pm Mon-Fri. **Credit** MC, V. **Map** p402 O5.

This small, intimate tavern looks as if it's been preserved from the days of the Young Pretender. The sole London outpost of St Peter's Brewery out in Suffolk, it has half a dozen of its beers on draught.

Seven Stars

53-4 Carey Street, WC2A 2JB (7242 8521). Chancery Lane, Holborn or Temple tube. **Open** 11am-11pm Mon-Fri; noon-11pm Sat. **Credit** AmEx, MC, V. **Map** p399 M6.

Behind the Royal Courts of Justice and within easy strolling distance of the old bankruptcy court, it's not surprising that the majority of customers at this low-beamed, historic pub (it was built in 1602) are lawyers. Add a few visiting Soho eccentrics and those attracted by the historic associations and this small, narrow pub can get mighty crowded.

Bloomsbury & Fitzrovia

Bradley's Spanish Bar

42-4 Hanway Street, W1P 9DE (7636 0359). Tottenham Court Road tube. **Open** noon-11pm Mon-Sat; 3-10.30pm Sun. **Credit** MC, V. **Map** p399 K6.

Tucked away on one of central London's most charmingly shabby streets, this is a bar out of time: the furniture is worn, the two floors are tiny and the jukebox is all-vinyl. Among the best bars in town.

Lamb

94 Lamb's Conduit Street, WC1N 3LZ (7405 0713). Holborn or Russell Square tube. **Open** 11am-11pm Mon-Sat; noon-4pm, 7-10.30pm Sun. **Credit** AmEx, MC, V. **Map** p399 M4.

One of London's most celebrated pubs, the Lamb is a central London flagship for the Young's brewery. The decor is carefully restored Victorian, with three wood-panelled drinking areas, the beer is immaculately kept, and the atmosphere is convivial.

Mash

19-21 Great Portland Street, W1W 8QB (7637 5555). Oxford Circus tube. **Open** 11am-midnight Mon,Tue; 11am-2am Wed-Sat. **Credit** AmEx, MC, V. **Map** p398 J5.

If you believe that irony is second only to sarcasm as the lowest form of wit, you'll hate the knowingly retro decor here. Happily, the beers (brewed on site) are no joke – and the food's usually pretty darn good too. DJs play four nights a week.

Match

45-7 Clerkenwell Road, EC1M 5RS (72504002/www. matchbar.com). Farringdon tube/rail. **Open** 11am-midnight Mon-Fri; 5pm-midnight Sat. **Credit** AmEx, MC, V. **Map** p402 N4.

Pete, the bartender, has more than 200 cocktail recipes in his head, and many stories to tell. Staff are inspirational in their love for drinks like Bees Knees, the Blood and Sand, Beneath the Sheets, Stolipolitan and, above all, the Wibble. An excellent bar with other locations in the West End (37-8 Margaret Street, 7499 3443) and Shoreditch (*see p225*).

Nordic

25 Newman Street, W1P 3HA (76313174/www.nordicbar.com). Tottenham Court Road tube. **Open** noon-11pm Mon-Fri; 6-11pm Sat. **Credit** AmEx, MC, V. **Map** p398 J5.

A Scandinavian bar with Scandinavian food (meatballs!), Scandinavian drinks (including Danish lager Red Erik) and Scandinavian prices. No matter: it might be a stylish place, but it's not unwelcoming.

Soho & Leicester Square

Alphabet

61-3 Beak Street, W1RF3LF(74392190/ www.alphabetbar.com). Oxford Circus or Piccadilly Circus tube. **Open** noon-11pm Mon-Fri; 5-11pm Sat. **Credit** AmEx, MC, V. **Map** p400 J6.

The media-mobbed bar of 1997, this place has since slipped into its comfy jeans and a sweatshirt, and it's all the better for it. It's a combination of chic and shack, with two floors to sprawl on, and imports including Pilsner Urquell, Hoegaarden and Negra Modelo. DJs raise the volume later in the evening.

Coach & Horses

29 Greek Street, W1 5LL (7437 5920). Leicester Square tube. **Open** 11am-11pm Mon-Sat; noon-10.30pm Sun. **Credit** MC, V. **Map** p399 K6.

A shambolic Soho boozer blessed – if that's the right word – with a shambolic clientele of chancers, bores, wannabes, geniuses and serious drinkers. Don't expect brushed pine furniture and rocket salad; this is a proper pub. Long may it thrive.

Cork & Bottle

44-6 Cranbourn Street, WC2H 7AN (7734 6592). Leicester Square tube. **Open** 11am-midnight Mon-Sat; noon-10.30pm Sun. **Credit** AmEx, DC, MC, V. **Map** p401 K7.

A nondescript doorway is all that's visible at street level of this cosy underground burrow. There's a big, juicy wine list, along with blackboards and flyers announcing assorted bin ends, wines of the month, and the like.

French House

49 Dean Street, W1D 5GB (7437 2799). Leicester Square tube. **Open** noon-11pm Mon-Sat; noon-10.30pm Sun. **Credit** AmEx, DC, MC, V. **Map** p399 K6.

The restaurant above it has gone, but this Soho institution remains unchanging as the years past. One of the most historically and artistically important of all the Soho dives, during the war this beautiful old bar was a meeting place for the French Resistance in London; later, it was a home from home to the Soho bohos of the 1950s and 1960s. In its time, it was the louche dive of choice for Brendan Behan, Francis Bacon, Samuel Beckett and Dylan Thomas. In continued opposition to British boorishness, staff still refuse to serve pints (halves only).

Lab

12 Old Compton Street, W1D 4TQ (7437 7820/ www.lab-bar.com). Leicester Square or Tottenham Court Road tube. **Open** 4pm-midnight Mon-Sat; 4-10.30pm Sun. **Credit** AmEx, MC, V. **Map** p399 K6.

The cocktail list at this Soho bar is as weighty as your average computer manual, but fortunately it's much more comprehensible and makes for lip-smacking reading. Sit at the space-age bar to watch the mixologists at work.

Marylebone

Dusk

79 Marylebone High Street, W1U 7JZ (7486 5746). Baker Street tube. **Open** 10am-11pm Mon-Sat; 10am-10.30pm Sun. **Credit** AmEx, DC, MC, V. **Map** p398 G4.

A recent makeover transformed this old corner boozer into Marylebone High Street's first designer bar. And nice it is, with beautiful arched windows, polished wood floor and brushed aluminium bar. Drinks are designer, too – Affligem and Dutch Wieckse Witte beers, plus New and Old World wine by the glass or bottle. Food runs the gamut from confit of duck to burgers.

Windsor Castle

29 Crawford Place, W1H 4LQ (7723 4371). Edgware Road tube. **Open** 11am-11pm Mon-Sat; noon-10.30pm Sun. **Credit** MC, V. **Map** p395 F5.

Leaving aside the Thai food on the menu, the Windsor is as British as boozers get. Royal memorabilia fills the walls satisfyingly, with pictures of Winston Churchill and wartime crooner Vera Lynn also on display. Somehow, it still avoids being the tackiest pub in town.

Mayfair & St James's

Guinea

30 Bruton Place, W1J 6NL (7409 1728). Green Park tube. **Open** 11am-11pm Mon-Fri; 6.30-11pm Sat. **Credit** AmEx, DC, MC, V. **Map** p400 H7.

The Guinea, a cosy little wood-soaked boozer, is a Young's pub, so the beers are lovely. This being Mayfair, though, the wine list's outstanding. You'll need to book to eat in the acclaimed Grill here.

Red Lion

23 Crown Passage, off Pall Mall, SW1Y 6PP (7930 4141). Green Park tube. **Open** 11am-11pm Mon-Sat. **Credit** MC, V. **Map** p400 J8.

Both the pub and its regulars are old-fashioned sorts. The saloon bar is all dark woods and velvet-effect banquettes; the sandwiches are sturdy and stomach-packing; the staff are genial and rightly proud of their cirrhosis-inducing range of whiskies. A joy.

Covent Garden & St Giles's

Bunker

41 Earlham Street, WC2H NLX (7240 0606/www.bunkerbar.com). Covent Garden tube. **Open** noon-midnight Mon-Sat; noon-10.30pm Sun. **Credit** AmEx, MC, V. **Map** p399 L6.

The highlight of a visit to this surprisingly large (so big that you can often find a table, even on busy weeknights) Covent Garden hangout is, of course, the beer: we especially like the pale ale, which goes most of the way towards compensating for the so-so bar food and noisy atmosphere. The handy location is not bad either.

Gordon's

47 Villiers Street, WC2N 6NE (7930 1408/ www.gordonswinebar.com). Covent Garden or Embankment tube/Charing Cross tube/rail.
Open 11am-11pm Mon-Sat; noon-10pm Sun.
Credit MC, V. **Map** p401 L7.
Large on atmosphere, light on spring-cleaning, and perennially busy, this basement wine bar is a London landmark. Wine, cheese, candlelight and chaos: a place to bring an illicit lover.

Lamb & Flag

33 Rose Street, WC2E 9EB (7497 9504). Covent Garden tube. **Open** 11am-11pm Mon-Thur; 11am-10.45pm Fri, Sat; noon-10.30pm Sun. **No credit cards**. **Map** p401 L7.
We've always relished the fact that this venerable boozer (built in 1623) was once known as the Bucket of Blood. What a name! Why'd they change it? Today, it's one of London's last wooden-framed buildings, and one of the very few bearable boozers in Covent Garden, but alwyas very busy and noisy.

Lowlander

36 Drury Lane, WC2B 5RR (7379 7446/ www.lowlander.com). **Open** noon-11pm Mon-Sat; noon-10.30pm Sun. **Credit** AmEx, MC, V.
Map p399 L6.
Drink and food from Belgium and the Netherlands is the gimmick at this very civilised and understandably popular spot. The beers are good, but for a real treat try a small sip of jenever or two.

Westminster

Boisdale

15 Eccleston Street, SW1W 9LX (7730 6922/ www.boisdale.co.uk). Victoria tube/rail. **Open** *Back bar* noon-11pm Mon-Fri. *Macdonald bar* noon-1am Mon-Fri; 7pm-1am Sat. **Credit** AmEx, DC, MC, V.
Map p400 H10.
The Boisdale's range of whiskies: some 250 of them in total, has to be sampled. Entry after 10pm is £10.
Other locations: Swedeland Court, 202 Bishopsgate, EC2M 4NR (7283 1763).

Red Lion

48 Parliament Street, SW1A 2NH (7930 5826). Westminster tube. **Open** 11am-11pm Mon-Sat; noon-7pm Sun. **Credit** MC, V. **Map** p401 L9.
There's been a tavern here since 1434, but this incarnation has existed since 1900, hence the mahogany and etched-glass fittings. The silent TV screens are tuned to the BBC Parliamentary Channel, which gives a good indication of who the regulars are.

When is a pub not a pub?

Not so very long ago drinkers in London knew where (or, rather, in what) they stood. A bar served cocktails and returned change in a silver dish; a pub was awash with warmish draught beer and dim lighting meant it was perpetually 10.30pm, whatever the time might have been outside.

Over just the last few years, though, those boundaries have been blurred. Take somewhere like **Dusk** on Marylebone High Street (*see p220*). Opened in 2002, it looks like a pub (until recently it *was* a pub) but the beer is sidelined now in favour of good wine and posh cocktails. Food gets prominent billing, starting with breakfast from 10am and going through lunch and dinner right up until closing time. Out goes 'two pints of lager and a packet of crisps, luv', in comes 'a half of Dutch Wieckse White, a glass of Chardonnay and a leek tart'.

It's all down to reinvention.

In fact, the traditional pub is struggling. Its crusty, laddish image is distinctly unappealing when held against those cool bars in the TV ads: the banging places where everyone necks Bacardi Breezers in a crush of beautiful people, teeth flashing, eyes twinkling, hips slinking. So goodbye hand pumps, formica and red leather upholstery, and hello designer bottles of pre-mixed drinks and cases of pricey imported beer, DJ decks and ironic bar snacks. You'll find all of that and more at Camden's **Lock Tavern** and Belsize Park's the **Hill** (for both *see p223*), two sexy new venues that are neither pub nor bar but something in between, aimed at a crowd that is generally too old for alcopops but too young for real ale.

London's other fast-spreading pub hybrid is the gastropub – a pub in which the food takes priority over the booze (*see p205* **Having it all**). Opinion remains divided on the phenomenon: *Time Out* magazine's letters column recently blazed against 'the transformation of unpretentious local boozers into bland gastropubs', which the reader reckons are 'overpriced and full of wankers'.

That's one point of view. The fact is, gastropubs come in both good and bad varieties, some of which are a definite improvement on the shabby, smoky old geezers' haunts that they've replaced.

So, does the rise of the glitzy pub-bar and cool gastropub mean that the death of the traditional London boozer is nigh? Don't you believe it. It's called a renaissance.

Everything's legal at **Seven Stars**. *See p219.*

Knightsbridge & South Kensington

Nag's Head

53 Kinnerton Street, SW1X 8ED (7235 1135). Hyde Park Corner tube. **Open** 11am-11pm Mon-Sat; noon-10.30pm Sun. **No credit cards. Map** p400 G9.
Perhaps the floor of this pint-sized saloon has been raised or that of the bar lowered, but the net result is that staff address your navel. Still, the superbly eccentric decor and the diminutive downstairs snug make this one of SW1's loveliest watering holes.

Townhouse

31 Beauchamp Place, SW3 1NU (7589 5080/ www.lab-townhouse.com). Knightsbridge tube. **Open** 4pm-midnight Mon-Thur; noon-midnight Fri, Sat; 4-11.30pm Sun. **Credit** AmEx, MC, V. **Map** p397 F10.
The myriad house Martinis at comfortable, quietly stylish Townhouse will convert you to a fan in no time. A word of warning, though: drinks can only be served with food after 11pm.

Chelsea

Lots Road Pub & Dining Room

114 Lots Road, SW10 0RJ (7352 6645). Fulham Broadway or Sloane Square tube then 11, 19, 22 bus. **Open** 11am-11pm Mon-Sat; noon-10.30pm Sun. **Credit** AmEx, MC, V. **Map** p396 C13.
The gastropub cult reached its apogee with this pleasant if fairly generic refurbishment, and while the location isn't ideal for visitors – it's quite a way from the nearest tube – the effort it takes to get here is just about worth it for the excellent beer and food.

Phene Arms

9 Phene Street, SW3 5NY (7352 3294). Sloane Square or South Kensington tube. **Open** 11am-11pm Mon-Sat; noon-10.30pm Sun. **No credit cards. Map** p397 E12.
For years, the Phene Arms was footballer George Best's local, though alcoholism isn't a prerequisite for those wanting to drink at this democratic Chelsea boozer. It gets busy in summer, but with a terrace this terrific that's no surprise.

North London

Albion

10 Thornhill Road, Islington, N1 1HW (7607 7450/ www.thealbion.net). Angel tube. **Open** 11am-11pm Mon-Sat; noon-10.30pm Sun. **Credit** AmEx, MC, V. **Map** p402 N1.
The Albion is villagey, preternaturally quaint and an absolute joy. Come in winter for Sunday lunch, and in summer for the garden.

Clifton

96 Clifton Hill, St John's Wood, NW8 0JT (7372 3427). St John's Wood tube. **Open** noon-11pm Mon-Sat; noon-10.30pm Sun. **Credit** AmEx, MC, V.

Blending in perfectly with the surrounding houses, the Clifton can be hard to spot (except in summer, when its outside tables are packed to overflowing). Inside is all manner of carved wood, a Gothic-looking bar, ornate fireplaces and snug corners.

Duke of Cambridge

30 St Peter Street, Islington, N1 8JT (7359 3066/ www.singhboulton.co.uk). Angel tube. **Open** noon-11pm Mon-Sat; noon-10.30pm Sun. **Credit** MC, V. **Map** p402 O2.

This was London's first organic pub (the owners now have another: the Crown on Victoria Park, 223 Grove Road, 8981 9998), and it enjoys a lovely corner location. All the beers and food are organic, and tasty with it, though you pay for the privilege.

Embassy

119 Essex Road, Islington, N1 2SN (7359 7882). Angel tube. **Open** 5-11pm Mon-Thur; 5pm-1am Fri, Sat; 5-10.30pm Sun. **Credit** MC, V. **Map** p402 O1.

The Medicine Bar (181 Upper Street, 7704 9536) rolls on, the Salmon & Compasses (58 Penton Street, 7837 3891) is more popular than ever, but this is the best DJ bar in Islington, beautifully decorated and offering some splendid music (call to see what's on, as the schedule changes frequently and special guests are not uncommon).

Flask

77 Highgate West Hill, Highgate, N6 6BU (8348 7346). Archway or Highgate tube. **Open** 11am-11pm Mon-Sat; noon-10.30pm Sun. **Credit** MC, V.

Purportedly dating back to 1663, and preserved pretty well by a series of sympathetic refurbishments over the years, this is one of north London's loveliest old pubs, and also one of its busiest. Don't confuse it with the rather earthier – but just, in its own way, as enjoyable – Flask nearby in Hampstead (14 Flask Walk, 7435 4580).

The Hill

94 Haverstock Hill, NW3 2BB (7267 0033). Belsize Park or Chalk Farm tube. **Open** noon-midnight Mon-Sat; noon-11pm Sun. **Credit** MC, V.

Entering the bar, winking fairy lights and candles illuminate wingback leather armchairs and sofas. Staff are charming enough to make up for the generally mainstream beers (Staropramen and the like).

Hollybush

22 Holly Mount, Hampstead, NW3 6SG (7435 2892). Hampstead tube. **Open** noon-11pm Mon-Sat; noon-10.30pm Sun. **Credit** MC, V.

One of the oldest and most picturesque drinking haunts in the area, the Hollybush is well hidden up a tiny backstreet. It has four bars, low ceilings, wood and plaster walls, and a real coal fire that is great for toe-warming after winter walks.

Lock Tavern

35 Chalk Farm Road, Camden, NW1 8AJ (7482 7163). Camden Town or Chalk Farm tube. **Open** noon-11pm Mon-Sat; noon-10.30pm Sun. **Credit** MC, V.

Smart money (some of it belonging to DJ Jon Carter) has reinvented this place from an old dive into the very essence of a modern public house. It's roomy and laid-back, with polished leather banquettes and big tables, and an open kitchen serving pies, snacks and excellent roasts. Expect big crowds on weekends looking for the faint whiff of celebrity.

Monkey Chews

2 Queen's Crescent, Camden, NW5 4EP (7267 6406/www.monkeychews.com). Chalk Farm tube. **Open** 5-11pm Mon-Fri; noon-midnight Sat; noon-10.30pm Sun. **Credit** MC, V.

Situated at the right end of Camden – as far from the market and the High Street as possible – this is a visually stunning bar, a wild cross between opium den and beach hut. Cocktails are cheap, and the regular DJs don't hurt the ears: try the excellent Moon Palace every first Sunday of the month.

Queen's

49 Regent's Park Road, Primrose Hill, NW1 8XD (7586 0408). Chalk Farm tube. **Open** 11am-11pm Mon-Sat; noon-10.30pm Sun. **Credit** MC, V.

A north London gastropub that's a cut above the rest in every department. Food, served in the upstairs dining room, is terrific; drinks come from the Young's brewery. The Queen's oozes civility; it may be the nicest pub in Primrose Hill.

Shakespeare

57 Allen Road, Stoke Newington, N16 8RY (7254 4190). Bus 73. **Open** 5-11pm Mon-Fri; noon-11pm Sat; noon-10.30pm Sun. **Credit** MC, V.

The most welcoming boozer in Stokey has retained its homey atmosphere thanks to a location just a little off the beaten track, a terrific and very wide range of beers, a friendly vibe and one of the best jukeboxes you'll find in London.

East London

Cantaloupe

35-42 Charlotte Road, Shoreditch, EC2A 3PD (7613 4411/www.cantaloupe.co.uk). Old Street tube/rail. **Open** 11am-midnight Mon-Fri; noon-midnight Sat; noon-11.30pm Sun. **Credit** AmEx, DC, MC, V. **Map** p403 R4.

Credit where it's due: this bar opened before the Shoreditch area got turned into style-mag central. It's no longer as cutting edge as it was, but thank Christ for that: it's now 'just' a nice, buzzy place to have a drink and something to eat in an area where nice, buzzy places are few and far between.

Charlie Wright's International Bar

45 Pitfield Street, Hoxton, N1 6DA (7490 8345). Old Street tube/rail. **Open** noon-1am Mon-Wed; noon-2am Thur-Sun. **Credit** AmEx, MC, V. **Map** p403 Q3.

Mr Wright is a Nigerian powerlifter. His bar is an institution. DJs play Thursday to Sunday and the beer's exceptional, but you come to Charlie's for the other customers, a gloriously eccentric cavalcade of chancers and wits, locals and travellers.

Pride of London The two brewers

Londoners, famous for their love of beer, have a particular, and long-standing, affection for the capital's two breweries, **Fuller's** and **Young's**. Although a certain amount of partisan loyalty exists among those who live close to one brewery or the other, there is really little difference between the two historic brew companies.

Both are family firms founded in the first half of the 19th century, and both have used Thames water as their main ingredient. Water, as any beer expert knows, is what makes a beer distinct. London beer, for example, was a thick, dark Guinness-like drink called 'porter' after the people who were most frequently seen drinking it.

The particular gypsum-rich quality of the River Trent in North-east England created a lighter beer that travelled well enough for export to India for the colonial market. When the empire-builders returned to England, they brought with them a taste for 'bitter' or 'India Pale Ale', which was soon being brewed in Burton-on-Trent. Before long, brewers across the country were adapting their own recipes to satisfy the demand.

In 1959 Fuller's took the name 'London Pride' for its most successful ale, a national prize-winner that is still popular today. In the last decade output has increased threefold. The brewery now sells 200,000 barrels of London Pride a year or 57.6 million pints. Most of these are drunk in the brewery's London pubs. Until recently, London Pride was the only beer you could purchase at Harrod's. That is changing, though. In the 1990s, the Monopolies and Mergers Commission forced pubs to dispense other beers as well as their own brews, and Fuller's has since begun nation-wide distribution. Fuller's is the only canned ale available on British Airways and Virgin Atlantic flights, and it has allied itself with sport by sponsoring the international Rugby Sevens tournament at Twickenham. It is also the official payment for London's cartoonist laureate, Martin Rowson. Famously, upon his appointment to the post, he asked only for one or more pints of Fuller's annually in exchange for his work making fun of the mayor.

Young & Co's most famous drinker was the late Queen Mother, who died in 2002 at the age of 101. Pictures of Her Majesty pulling herself a royal pint hang in all the brewery's pubs. In 2003 the company revamped the image of its two best known beers, Ordinary and Special, by smartening the logo of the former and changing the recipe of the latter. At the same time it introduced an award-winning new bottled lager called 'Champion'. It has allied itself with the game of cricket, in an advertising campaign using the company's symbol, a well-endowed ram. The company attracted complaints after making light of the animal's genitalia in an advertising campaign, although no legal action was ultimately taken.

Indeed, the firm is famous for its animal husbandry. It keeps a company ram named

Ferry House

26 Ferry Street, Docklands, E14 3DT (7537 9587). Island Gardens DLR. **Open** 2-11pm Mon-Fri; 11am-11pm Sat; noon-10.30pm Sun. **Credit** AmEx, MC, V.

As the name suggests, the Ferry House began life as the ferry master's residence, with the present building going up in 1823. These days it's an old-fashioned family boozer, with cheap booze and a traditional London Fives dartboard. A good place to hang out, if you happen to find yourself in Docklands of a night.

Grapes

76 Narrow Street, Limehouse, E14 8BP (7987 4396). Limehouse or West Ferry DLR. **Open** noon-3pm, 5.30-11pm Mon-Fri; noon-11pm Sat; noon-10.30pm Sun. **Credit** AmEx, DC, MC, V.

This superb little pub is steeped in Dickensian charm, and is a real treat in summer if you can find space on the small riverside deck. Best of all, there's no music to disturb the convivial hubbub.

Home

100-106 Leonard Street, Shoreditch, EC2A 4RH (7684 8618/www.homebar.co.uk). Old Street tube/rail. **Open** 5pm-midnight Mon-Sat. **Credit** AmEx, MC, V. **Map** p403 Q4.

It's not quite as welcoming as its name suggests – not least because you wouldn't want to arrive back at your flat to find some of its customers in your living room – but sink into one of the comfy armchairs with a cocktail and you'll find it terribly hard to leave. There are DJs most nights.

Lounge Lover

1 Whitby Street, off Club Row, E1 (70121234/ www.lounge lover.co.uk). Liverpool Street tube/rail. **Open** 6pm-midnight Tue-Sat. **Map** p403 S4.

This is a high camp bar in Shoreditch where the drinks list is an impressive 16 pages long. Its good cocktails and a fantastic-looking interior make this singular venue one to remember for special occasions. Prices reflect the bar's sophistication.

Ram Rod (you can meet him on the tour, *see below*) as well as a fleet of big dray horses that – in wonderfully quaint London fashion – make the daily beer deliveries to all of the pubs within a two-mile radius of the brewery.

So when you're out in a London pub, don't be afraid to turn your back, at least briefly, on the usual lagers, and try the local ales. It's very good stuff.

Fuller's Smith & Turner plc

Griffin Brewery, Chiswick Lane South, W4 2QB (tour line 8996 2063). Stamford Brook tube. **Tours** 11am, noon, 1pm, 2pm Mon, Wed-Fri. **Admission** £5, £2.50 concessions; no children under 14; advance booking essential.

Fuller's brewery tour includes a beer-tasting session (age 18 and over) and a pint of your favourite (soft drinks for minors). Book ahead.

Young & Co Brewery

The Brewery Tap Visitors Centre, 68 Wandsworth High Street SW18 4LB (8875 7005). Wandsworth Town rail. **Tours** noon, 2pm Tue-Thur, Sat. **Admission** £5.50; £4.50 concessions.

Booking is essential for the Young's tour, which takes in the stableyard and the resident dray horses. Visitors are rewarded with a pint, or a bottled beer to take away. Ring for details of health restrictions.

Mother Bar

333 Old Street, Shoreditch, EC1V 9LE (7739 5949/www.333mother.com). Old Street tube/rail. **Open** 8pm-3am Mon-Wed; 8pm-4am Thur; 8pm-5am Fri, Sat; 6pm-4am Sun. **Credit** MC, V. **Map** p403 R3.

With the Shoreditch Electricity Showrooms (*see p318*) having become something of a cliché for the fashionistas, this cosy bar is currently the boozer's bar of choice down Shoreditch. Beware, though, the lengthy queues and rather erratic door policy make you wonder just whose mother runs this place.

Pride of Spitalfields

3 Heneage Street, Spitalfields, E1 5LJ (7247 8933). Aldgate East tube. **Open** 11am-11pm Mon-Sat; noon-10.30pm Sun. **No credit cards. Map** p403 S5.

This is a genial family-run pub that's resisted the local trend towards DJ nights; unsurprising, given its fantastically mixed clientele (from businessmen and medical students to builders and seniors). The beer's good, as it should be.

Prospect of Whitby

57 Wapping Wall, Wapping, E1W 3SH (7481 1095). Wapping tube. **Open** 11.30am-11pm Mon-Sat; noon-10.30pm Sun. **Credit** AmEx, DC, MC, V.

Built in 1520 and last remodelled in 1777, this historic pub has aged gracefully. The pewter-topped counter, stone-flagged floors, giant timbers and pebbled windows have all been preserved. Enjoy the river views but beware the coach parties.

Sir Alfred Hitchcock Hotel

147 Whipps Cross Road, Leytonstone, E11 1NP (8530 3724). Leytonstone tube. **Open** 11am-11pm Mon-Sat; noon-10.30pm Sun. **Credit** MC, V.

Hitchcock was from around these parts, and portraits of the old curmudgeon line the walls here. In summer, you'd do well to grab one of the outside tables, which afford enticing views of Epping Forest.

Sosho

2 Tabernacle Street, Shoreditch, EC2A 4LU (7920 0701/www.sosho3am.com). Moorgate or Old Street tube/rail. **Open** 11.30am-10pm Mon; 11.30am-midnight Tue, Wed; 11.30am-1am Thur; 11.30am-3am Fri; 7pm-3am Sat; 8pm-2am Sun. **Admission** £3-£5 after 9pm Thur-Sat; £5 after 8pm Sun. **Credit** AmEx, DC, MC, V.

Peerlessly discerning, Sosho comes into its own as soon as the cocktail shaker appears, wielded by bar tenders of rare dexterity. The spacious lounge is decorated with glam touches, while DJs mix it up as confidently as their bar colleagues.

South-east London

Greenwich Union

56 Royal Hill, Greenwich, SE10 8RT (8692 6258). Greenwich DLR/rail. **Open** 11am-11pm Mon-Sat; noon-10.30pm Sun. **Credit** MC, V.

The beers in this cheery pub – owned by the Meantime Brewing Company – are simply one revelation after another. From the Vienna-style Amba lager, through the raspberry-flavoured Red down to the Chocolate beer, this place is beer heaven.

Mayflower

117 Rotherhithe Street, Rotherhithe, SE16 4NF (7237 4088). Rotherhithe tube/188, P11, P13 bus. **Open** noon-3pm, 6-11pm Mon-Sat; noon-10.30pm Sun. **Credit** MC, V.

A historic seafaring inn with rickety wooden floors, small wood-partitioned areas and narrow settles (the timbers are reputed to have come from the *Mayflower* ship). Greene King bitters are on offer.

Trafalgar Tavern

Park Row, Greenwich, SE10 9NW (8858 2437/www.trafalgartavern.co.uk). Cutty Sark DLR/Greenwich or Maze Hill rail. **Open** noon-11pm Mon-Sat; noon-10.30pm Sun. **Credit** MC, V.

This historic pub on the site of the Old George Inn was built in 1837 as a tribute to naval hero Horatio Nelson. There's mahogany panelling, stone fireplaces and the like, plus a riverside terrace.

South-west London

Bread & Roses

68 Clapham Manor Street, Clapham, SW4 6DZ (7498 1779). Clapham Common or Clapham North tube. **Open** noon-11pm Mon-Sat; noon-10.30pm Sun. **Credit** MC, V.

A spacious hostelry with a minimalist interior and a traditional pub atmosphere. There's good beer, music, poetry and comedy events, and a tasty, affordable African buffet on Sundays. Children are welcome; there are toys and activities at weekends.

Dogstar

389 Coldharbour Lane, Brixton, SW9 8LQ (7733 7515/www.dogstarbar.co.uk). Brixton tube/rail. **Open** noon-2am Mon-Thur, Sun; noon-4am Fri, Sat. **Credit** AmEx, MC, V.

Where the Brixton revival began, offering late beverages and loud sounds to twentysomethings bored with the prices and pretensions of the West End. Less hip than it was, but no less busy.

Fire Stables

27-9 Church Road, Wimbledon, SW19 5DQ (8946 3197). Wimbledon tube/rail then 200, 93 bus. **Open** 11am-11pm Mon-Fri; 10.30am-11pm Sat; 10am-10.30pm Sun. **Credit** AmEx, MC, V.

It used to be a dire boozer called the Castle, but these days the Fire Stables is an upmarket, minimalist bar with sophisticated cooking. Well worth the schlep it takes to get here; try to book if you're eating.

Inigo

642 Wandsworth Road, Battersea, SW8 3JW (7622 4884/www.inigobar.com). Clapham Common tube. **Open** 6pm-2am Mon-Fri; noon-2am Sat, Sun. **Credit** MC, V.

The punters at this revamped pub will groove anywhere they can find the space. There are queues out front every weekend after 11pm. DJs kick off at 8pm daily; turn up between 6pm and 10pm (6-9pm Fri-Sun) and you can snack on decent pizza as well.

Sand

156 Clapham Park Road, Clapham, SW4 7DE (7622 3022/www.sandbarrestaurant.co.uk). Clapham Common tube. **Open** 5pm-2am Mon-Sat; 5pm-1am Sun. **Credit** MC, V.

The decor's easy on the eye, the listening (Sinatra, Bacharach) easy on the ear, and candles, spotlights and intimate (usually reserved) alcoves make it all very cosy. DJs spin at weekends, though.

Ship

41 Jew's Row, Wandsworth, SW18 1TB (8870 9667/www.theship.co.uk). Wandsworth Town rail. **Open** 11am-11pm Mon-Sat; noon-10.30pm Sun. **Credit** AmEx, DC, MC, V.

The summer pub to end all summer pubs: there's a lovely riverside beer garden and a barbecue when the sun comes out. On the other 363 days of the year, dine on solid pub food and sup on Young's ales or, on Sundays, a knockout Bloody Mary.

Kitschy **South London Pacific.**

South London Pacific

340 Kennington Road, SE11 4LD (7820 9189/ www.southlondonpacific.com). Oval tube. **Open** 6pm-midnight Tue, Wed; 6pm-1am Thur; 6pm-2am Fri, Sat; 6pm-midnight Sun. **Credit** MC, V.

From the blue-painted Easter Island totems outside to the carvings of distorted faces and hula girls within, this is a colourful, tongue-in-cheek, psychedelic homage to beach living. Beers are standard Beck's, Stella, et al, but the cocktails are things like Pago Pago, Royal Hawaiian and Bahama Mama.

Tongue & Groove

50 Atlantic Road, Brixton, SW9 (7274 8600/ www.tongueandgroove.org). Brixton tube/rail. **Open** 8pm-3am Wed-Sun. **Admission** £3 after 11pm Fri, Sat. **Credit** AmEx, MC, V.

This wanton bar is packed most nights, and while it's not worth queuing outside, as many do on weekends, it's great if you're inside. Pornographic murals adorn the walls, cocktails fill the stomachs.

West London

Albertine

1 Wood Lane, Shepherd's Bush, W12 7DP (8743 9593). Shepherd's Bush tube. **Open** 11am-11pm Mon-Fri; 6.30-11pm Sat. **Credit** MC, V.

It's not about gimmicks at this unassuming hangout: it's purely about wine. This place gets very busy with the post-work crowd, but you can usually find a table as the night wears on. Even better, is the friendly owner who is often on hand to help you navigate the lengthy menu.

Anglesea Arms
35 Wingate Road, Shepherd's Bush, W6 0UR (8749 1291). Goldhawk Road or Ravenscourt Park tube. **Open** 11am-11pm Mon-Sat; noon-10.30pm Sun. **Credit** MC, V.
Dark wooden floors, exposed brick walls, big leather sofas. You've probably seen it all before, but the Anglesea is still an attractive, comfortable boozer serving fine food with a splendid wine list. It's a pleasant place to while away an evening.

Archery Tavern
4 Bathurst Street, Paddington, W2 2SD (7402 4916). Lancaster Gate tube. **Open** 11am-11pm Mon-Sat; noon-10.30pm Sun. **Credit** MC, V. **Map** p395 D6.
This genteel pub sticks to most of the traditional formulae: plates on the walls, bunches of dried hops, and regulars who commandeer their favourite seat and ask the staff by name to turn the music down.

Canvas
177 Portobello Road, Ladbroke Grove, W11 2DY (7727 2700). Ladbroke Grove or Notting Hill tube. **Open** 5-11pm Tue-Sun. **Credit** AmEx, MC, V.
Canvas is cool as this review is being written but, such is the short attention span of the Notting Hill style-mag posse, it may be over before you arrive. No matter: its 21st-century take on 1970s retro chic is nicer than most.

Churchill Arms
119 Kensington Church Street, Kensington, W8 7LN (7727 4242). High Street Kensington or Notting Hill Gate tube. **Open** 11am-11pm Mon-Sat; noon-10.30pm Sun. **Credit** AmEx, MC, V. **Map** p394 B8.
Lepidopterists will want to check out the boxed butterflies on display at the back of this pub; others might wonder why they weren't left alone to fly. But everybody can agree on the quality of the ales and the good, cheap Thai food on offer.

Dove
19 Upper Mall, Hammersmith, W6 9TA (8748 5405). Hammersmith tube. **Open** 11am-11pm Mon-Sat; noon-10.30pm Sun. **Credit** AmEx, MC, V.
More than 300 years old and gloriously dishevelled, the Dove has three small split-level rooms around a central bar – one room, at 3.35sq ft (3.12sq m), is the smallest bar in England – and a pretty ivy-clad riverside terrace. A gem, all told.

Grand Union
45 Woodfield Road, Westbourne Park, W9 2DA (7286 1886). Westbourne Park tube. **Open** noon-11pm Mon-Sat; noon-10.30pm Sun. **Credit** MC, V.
A fashionable crowd frequent this much-loved local. Expect good gastropub food and beer, DJs on Sundays and a covered patio for al fresco boozing.

Lonsdale
44-8 Lonsdale Road, W11 2DE (7228 1517/www.genevieveuk.com). Notting Hill Gate or Westbourne Park tube. **Open** noon-midnight Mon-Sat; noon-11.30pm Sun. **Credit** AmEx, MC, V.
The interior here is a knockout: walls are studded with antiqued-bronze hemispheres; floor and bar are sleek, glossy black. Further in there's lush red carpet and fake fur upholstery. Luckily, the mood is a bit more relaxed than the decor. The drinks selection is posh but not extensive; cocktails run from £7.

Westbourne

101 Westbourne Park Villas, Notting Hill, W2 5ED (7221 1332). Royal Oak tube. **Open** 5-11pm Mon; noon-11pm Tue-Sat; noon-10.30pm Sun. **Credit** AmEx, DC, MC, V. **Map** p394 B5.

The only way to get an outside table at this terminally hip and almost invariably ram-jammed pub is to turn up when it's chucking it down. Otherwise you'll be sitting inside on a sunny day, glaring at the lucky few. Still, a good range of wines and beers, as well as smoothies, make it worth the squeeze.

White Horse

1-3 Parson's Green, Fulham, SW6 4UL (7736 2115/ www.whitehorsesw6.com). Parson's Green tube. **Open** 11am-11pm Mon-Sat; 11am-10.30pm Sun. **Credit** AmEx, MC, V.

This imposing multi-bar Victorian boozer has been pleasantly modernised and comfortably decked out with sofas and chunky wooden furniture. More than 100 fine wines are stocked, plus real ale and every available Trappist brew. It makes for a comfortable, pretty place to take friends or family.

White Swan

Riverside, Twickenham, Middx TW1 3DN (8892 2166). Twickenham rail. **Open** *Apr-Sept* 11am-11pm Mon-Sat; noon-10.30pm Sun. *Oct-Mar* 11am-3pm, 5.30-11pm Mon-Thur; 11am-11pm Fri, Sat; noon-10.30pm Sun. **Credit** MC, V.

This legendary riverside pub attracts connoisseurs from miles around. On matchdays at Twickenham, the place gets overrun with rugby fans before and after the game gets underway. Raised to avoid flooding (an omnipresent problem in this area), the White Swan overlooks Eel Pie Island, the infamous, one-time 1960s rock hangout that is still a last refuge for keepers of alternative culture. But that counter culture attitude stays on the island. The Swan is all about having a beer and relaxing.

After hours

Most boozers still chuck you out at 11pm. They have to, according to the still sadly unchanged (as we go to press) licensing laws. Increasing numbers of bars are opting to get a licence to stay open till midnight or 1am, but many will charge admission – or a great deal for a bottle of beer – just for the privilege of drinking for a while inside their late-opening portals.

The central London bars listed below don't charge admission, but expect drink prices to be comparatively high in the smart hotel places, such as **Blue Bar** and **Mandarin Bar**. For more late places, check a copy of the *Time Out Pubs& Bars Guide* (£6.99). Other late-opening bars can be found in the **Nightlife** chapter, *see p313*.

Akbar *77 Dean Street, Soho, W1D 3SH (7437 2525).* **Open** 5pm-1am Mon-Sat.

Amber *6 Poland Street, Soho, W1S 8PS (7734 3094).* **Open** 5pm-1am Mon-Sat.

Atlantic Bar & Grill *20 Glasshouse Street, Covent Garden, W1B 5DJ (7734 4888).* **Open** noon-3am Mon-Fri; 6pm-3am Sat.

Bar Soho *23-5 Old Compton Street, Soho, W1V 5PJ (7439 0439).* **Open** 4pm-1am Mon-Thur; 4pm-3am Fri, Sat; 4pm-12.30am Sun.

Blue Bar *Berkeley Hotel, Wilton Place, Knightsbridge, SW1X 7RL (7235 6000). Hyde Park Corner or Knightsbridge tube.* **Open** 4pm-1am Mon-Sat.

Café Bohème *13-17 Old Compton Street, Soho, W1D 5KQ (7734 0623).* **Open** 8am-3am Mon-Sat; 8am-11pm Sun.

Café Lazeez *21 Dean Street, Soho, W1V 5AH (7434 9393).* **Open** 11am-1am Mon-Sat.

Cuba *11-13 Kensington High Street, Kensington, W8 5NP (7938 4137).* **Open** 5pm-2am Mon-Thur; noon-2am Fri, Sat; 5-10.30pm Sun.

Detroit *35 Earlham Street, Covent Garden WC2H 9LD (7240 2662).* **Open** 5pm-midnight Mon-Sat.

Eclipse *113 Walton Street, South Kensington, SW3 2HP (7581 0123).* **Open** 5.30pm-1am Mon-Fri; 2pm-1am Sat; 2pm-12.30am Sun.

The Langley *5 Langley Street, Covent Garden, WC2H 9JA (7836 5005).* **Open** 4.30pm-1am Mon-Sat; 4-10.30pm Sun.

Mandarin Bar *Mandarin Oriental Hotel, Hyde Park, 66 Knightsbridge, SW1X 7LA (7235 2000).* **Open** 11am-2am Mon-Sat; 11am-10.30pm Sun.

Mash *19-21 Great Portland Street, W1W 8QB (7637 5555).* **Open** 11am-1am Mon, Tue; 11am-2am Wed-Sat.

Point 101 *101 New Oxford Street, St Giles's, WC1A 1DB (7379 3112).* **Open** 11am-2.30am Mon-Sat; 6pm-midnight Sun.

Sevilla Mia *22 Hanway Street, Fitzrovia, (7637 3756).* **Open** 7pm-1am Mon-Sat; 7pm-midnight Sun.

Steam *1 Eastbourne Terrace, Marylebone, W2 1BA (7850 0555).* **Open** 9am-1am Mon-Wed; 9am-2am Thur, Fri; 11am-1.30am Sat.

Zander *45 Buckingham Gate, Victoria, SW1 6BS (7379 9797).* **Open** noon-11pm Mon, Tue; noon-1am Wed-Fri; 5pm-1am Sat.

Shops & Services

Everything you want to buy is here, if you can afford it.

London is known for many things, but cheap shopping just isn't one of them. The killer combination of generally high prices and an often unfavourable exchange rate can give you a scary credit card bill to remember your trip by. On the other hand, you can find just about anything you want here, and some things are worth paying for in this sprawling metropolis.

What you're looking for will determine where you should go to find it. The teeming, noisy crush of **Oxford Street** has the best selection of chain stores and department stores. Try **Covent Garden** or **Knightsbridge** for expensive designer fashion, **Soho** for music and funky clothes, **Charing Cross Road** for bookstores (new and antiquarian) and the **King's Road** for (expensive) homewares and kids' stuff. Your adolescent children may want to skulk around **Camden**, but most adult Londoners avoid this tourist attraction.

THE BASICS

Central London shops are open late one night a week, usually till 7pm or 8pm. Those in the West End (Oxford Street to Covent Garden) are open until late on Thursdays, while Wednesday is late opening in Chelsea and Knightsbridge.

For more listings and reviews, the extensive *Time Out Shopping Guide* (£8.99) is available from good bookshops and newsagents.

Antiques

Islington, Kensington and Chelsea are the three antiques centres in London. *Antiques Trade Gazette* (www.antiquestradegazette.com), the *Collector* (www.artefact.co.uk) and *Antique Collecting* (www.antique-acc.com) have listings on dealers, plus details of auctions. **Greenwich Market** (*see p250*) has a sizeable antiques section, as does **Portobello Road** (*see p251*).

Alfie's Antique Market

13-25 Church Street, Marylebone, NW8 8DT (7723 6066/www.alfiesantiques.com). Edgware Road tube/Marylebone tube/rail. **Open** 10am-6pm Tue-Sat. **Credit** varies. **Map** p395 E4.

Refurbishment of the basement area is currently blamed for the chaotic look at Alfie's, but in truth the place has needed reorganising for years. Over three or more floors (mezzanines complicate matters) you'll see a disproportionate amount of '50s furniture, along with textiles, costume jewellery and great furniture. The top floor is the best.

Antiquarius

131-41 King's Road, Chelsea, SW3 5EB (7351 5353). Sloane Square tube then 11, 19, 22 bus. **Open** 10am-6pm Mon-Sat. **Credit** varies. **Map** p397 E12.

Since not every unit here is devoted to antiques (especially the ones with windows on the street), it's hard to judge what may be beyond, but browsers who persevere will be rewarded with interesting finds. There's a great deal of jewellery, along with specialist dealers in field sports, wooden boxes and luggage. Everything is negotiable.

Camden Passage

Camden Passage, off Upper Street, Islington, N1 5ED (73590190/www.antiquesnews.co.uk/camdenpassage). Angel tube. **Open** *General market* 7am-4pm Wed; 7am-5pm Sat. *Book market* 8.30am-6pm Thur. **Credit** varies. **Map** p402 O2.

The market held in this pedestrianised backstreet near Angel majors in costume jewellery, silver plate and downright junk – but that doesn't mean you can't find rare items at good prices. More interesting are the dealers in the surrounding arcades, who open to coincide with the market.

Grays Antique Market & Grays in the Mews

58 Davies Street & 1-7 Davies Mews, Mayfair, W1K 5AB (7629 7034/www.graysantiques.com). Bond Street tube. **Open** 10am-6pm Mon-Fri. **Credit** varies. **Map** p398 H6.

The section closest to Oxford Street is where dozens of antique jewellery dealers arrange stunning glittering displays leavened by some fine porcelain and

The best Shops

For hunger pangs
& Clarke's. *See p244.*

For feeding your face
Kiehl's. *See p247.*

For finding your way
Stanfords. *See p231.*

For losing track of time
Alfie's Antique Market. *See p229.*

For suiting yourself
Ozwald Boateng. *See p244.*

Beautifully chaotic: **Alfie's Antique Market**. *See p229.*

textiles. Prices reflect the age and rarity of the pieces, although some repro stock has crept in. Try Wimpole Antiques (stand 338-349) on the ground floor for honest advice (most stock costs from £500-£5,000). A second building in the Mews has more varied dealers and is a better hunting ground for affordable presents.

Books

General

Blackwell's

100 Charing Cross Road, St Giles's, WC2H 0JG (7292 5100/www.blackwell.co.uk). Tottenham Court Road tube. **Open** 9.30am-8pm Mon-Sat; noon-6pm Sun. **Credit** AmEx, MC, V. **Map** p399 K5.

This is a solid branch of the academic book chain, whose stores are being given a makeover to give them a lighter, brighter feel. It's particularly good for cheap versions of classics, but it also has all the bestsellers, many at £1 off the listed price.
Other locations: throughout the city.

Books etc

421 Oxford Street, Oxford Circus, W1C 2PQ (7495 5850/www.booksetc.co.uk). Bond Street tube. **Open** 9.30am-8pm Mon-Thur; 9.30am-8.30pm Fri, Sat; noon-6.30pm Sun. **Credit** AmEx, DC, MC, V. **Map** p399 J6.

This utilitarian chain is very handy for those seeking bestsellers, the latest from celebs such as Jamie Oliver and Nigella Lawson, pretty reprints of classics and the like. Some branches have a café.
Other locations: throughout the city.

Borders Books & Music

197-203 Oxford Street, Oxford Circus, W1R 1AH (7292 1600/www.borders.com). Oxford Circus tube. **Open** 8am-11pm Mon-Sat; noon-6pm Sun. **Credit** AmEx, MC, V. **Map** p398 J6.

When you're in a hurry and you need to know a certain book will be there, this is the place to go. It has chairs, so you can read before you buy, a Starbucks coffee shop and a good selection of CDs. Staff actually seem to read the books, so they can help you find that Jonathan Franzen you heard was so good.
Other locations: throughout the city.

Foyles

113-19 Charing Cross Road, Soho, WC2H 0EB (7437 5660/www.foyles.co.uk). Tottenham Court Road tube. **Open** 9.30am-8pm Mon-Sat; noon-6pm Sun. **Credit** AmEx, DC, MC, V. **Map** p399 K6.

This is a massive, meandering behemoth of a book store, with a huge collection spread out across a large old building. It can be difficult to navigate, but if what you want is to lose yourself in towering shelves of books, this is the place.

London Review of Books

14 Bury Place, Bloomsbury, WC1A 2JL (7269 9030). Tottenham Court Road tube. **Open** 10am-6.30pm Mon-Sat; noon-6pm Sun. **Credit** AmEx MC, V. **Map** p399 L5.

If heaven were a bookshop, this would be it. Half-owned by the eponymous literary-political journal, this beautiful shop is all clean, polished wood, quiet conversations, seats on which to linger and the best books in the world. Given its small size, the selection is extraordinary, from Dave Eggers' latest to the most recent doorstop biography of Lyndon Johnson. There's no coffee shop and no CD section; just books for those who love them best.

Waterstone's

82 Gower Street, Bloomsbury, WC1E 6EQ (7636 1577/www.waterstones.co.uk). Goodge Street or Warren Street tube. **Open** 9.30am-8pm Mon, Wed-Fri; 10am-8pm Tue; 9.30am-7pm Sat; noon-6pm Sun. **Credit** AmEx, DC, MC, V. **Map** p399 K4.
Devotees of literature will have heated debates over whether this branch of the bookselling giant or the one on Piccadilly (Nos.203-6) reigns supreme. Both have outstanding selections – particularly of best-sellers – and offer three-for-two deals. Once a famous Dillons, the Gower Street store is prettier and has an excellent selection of second-hand books, but the Piccadilly one is bigger with a better café.
Other locations: throughout the city.

Specialist

Cinema Bookshop

13-14 Great Russell Street, Bloomsbury, WC1B 3NH (7637 0206). Tottenham Court Road tube. **Open** 10.30am-5.30pm Mon-Sat. **Credit** MC, V. **Map** p399 K5.
With biographies of Katharine Hepburn, Alfred Hitchcock and Woody Allen sitting alongside more voluminous technical tomes, this crowded, dusty little store is one of the best resources in the city for those interested in the film industry. Along with books, there are lobby cards and boxes of stills.

French's Theatre Bookshop

52 Fitzroy Street, Fitzrovia, W1T 5JR (7387 9373/ www.samuelfrench-london.co.uk). Warren Street tube. **Open** 9.30am-5.30pm Mon-Fri; 11am-5pm Sat. **Credit** AmEx, MC, V. **Map** p398 J4.
As you would imagine, this theatrical bookstore is crammed with plays, biographies and general books on theatre, along with plenty of magazines, creative cards and souvenirs.

Gay's The Word

66 Marchmont Street, Bloomsbury, WC1N 1AB (7278 7654/www.gaystheword.co.uk). Russell Square tube. **Open** 10am-6.30pm Mon-Sat; 2-6pm Sun. **Credit** AmEx, DC, MC, V. **Map** p399 L4.
Since 1979, this excellent gay and lesbian bookshop has been spreading the word. Its shelves include gay-themed fiction, travel books and counselling, and the atmosphere is down to earth.

Helter Skelter

4 Denmark Street, St Giles's, WC2H 8LL (7836 1151/www.helterskelterbooks.com). Tottenham Court Road tube. **Open** 10am-7pm Mon-Fri; 10am-6pm Sat. **Credit** MC, V. **Map** p399 K6.
If someone were to set a film in a music bookshop, this would make the ideal location. It's the archetypal book store for music lovers, with biographies of Dylan, Bono and Lennon, rows of fanzines and stacks of music mags all lying around.

High Stakes

21 Great Ormond Street, Bloomsbury, WC1N 3JB (7430 1021/www.highstakes.co.uk). Russell Square tube. **Open** 11am-6pm Mon-Wed, Fri. **Credit** MC, V. **Map** p399 L5.
The UK's only book store dedicated to gambling is spick and span. Minimalist shelves are neatly stacked with fascinating books on poker, horse racing, greyhounds and spread betting.

Murder One

71-3 Charing Cross Road, Leicester Square, WC2H 0AA (7734 3483/www.murderone.co.uk). Leicester Square tube. **Open** 10am-7pm Mon-Wed; 10am-8pm Thur-Sat. **Credit** AmEx, MC, V. **Map** p401 K6.
This sprawling shop specialises in the literary equivalent of fast food – crime (true and fiction) and mystery novels, dark-toned sci-fi books, grisly horror novels and pastel-hued romances.

Persephone Books

59 Lamb's Conduit Street, Bloomsbury, WC1N 3NB (7242 9292/www.persephonebooks.co.uk). Holborn or Russell Square tube/King's Cross tube/rail. **Open** 9am-6pm Mon-Fri; noon-5pm Sat. **Credit** AmEx, MC, V. **Map** p399 M4.
This brilliant shop is owned by the eponymous publishing house that finds obscure or forgotten works by women writers and gives them new life. The beautifully printed books are published in elegant – and affordable – paperback form. No matter how thick the book, it will cost £10, or £27 for three.

Shipley

70 Charing Cross Road, Leicester Square, WC2H 0BQ (7836 4872/www.artbook.co.uk). Leicester Square tube. **Open** 10am-6pm Mon-Sat. **Credit** AmEx, MC, V. **Map** p401 K6.
One of the best traditional booksellers in Charing Cross, Shipley sells a gorgeous selection of new and antiquarian arts titles. It's run by people who really know what you're talking about, so no wonder this is where the experts go when they need the best.

Stanfords

12-14 Long Acre, Covent Garden, WC2E 9LP (7836 1321/www.stanfords.co.uk). Covent Garden or Leicester Square tube. **Open** 9am-7.30pm Mon, Wed-Fri; 9.30am-7.30pm Tue; 10am-7pm Sat; noon-6pm Sun. **Credit** MC, V. **Map** p401 L6.
A London institution beloved of travel editors. It's a beautiful shop that makes you want to go somewhere – anywhere. The range of guides and maps is vast, covering just about any place you've ever heard of. Now that the store is expanding to cover three floors, this selection will keep on growing.

Used & antiquarian

Along with the stores listed below, there's also the weekly **Riverside Walk Market** (10am-5pm Sat, Sun and irregular weekdays) on the South Bank under Waterloo Bridge, where you'll find plenty of cheap paperbacks.

MERTON ABBEY MILLS

The uncommon market

A bustling weekend market in South Wimbledon full of crafts and exotic things, lovely food, a riverside pub, childrens' theatre and historic waterwheel. Market every Saturday and Sunday 10-5, shops open weekdays too. Opposite the Savacentre on A24 Merantun Way, near Colliers Wood tube, plenty of free parking.

If you love shopping you'll love the Mills!

Enquiries 020 8543 9608

WELCOME TO THE HOME
OF EXCLUSIVE TRAINERS
MYTRAINERS

9 Short Gardens, Thomas Neal's Covent Garden, London WC2

t: 020 7379 9700

f: 020 7379 9400

w: www.mytrainers.com

e: mytrainers@hotmail.com

"buy where the dealers buy"

ALFIES

ANTIQUE MARKET

London's biggest & busiest antique market

vintage fashion 20thC design dolls & toys art deco art nouveau memorabilia silver militaria brass & pewter linen & lace objets d'art clocks & watches ephemera books & maps posters & prints frames & mirrors paintings jewellery furniture etc

...and don't forget the rooftop restaurant!

OPEN TUES-SAT 10-6

13 Church Street, Marylebone
London NW8
Tel 020 7723 6066

www.alfiesantiques.com

INTOXICA!

Second-hand & new vinyl bought sold and exchanged

soundtracks
jazz latin
60s beat & psych
soul r'n'r
punk weird stuff
70s funk hiphop

t: 020 7229 8010
f: 020 7792 9778
intoxica@intoxica.co.uk

231 PORTOBELLO ROAD
LONDON W11 1LT

www.intoxica.co.uk

open 7 days a week

mon-sat: 10.30am-6.30pm
sun: midday-4.30pm

international mail order service
all major credit cards accepted

Any Amount of Books

56 Charing Cross Road, Leicester Square, WC2H 0QA (7836 3697/www.anyamountofbooks.com). Leicester Square tube. **Open** 10.30am-9.30pm Mon-Sat; 11.30am-7.30pm Sun. **Credit** AmEx, MC, V. **Map** p401 K6.

More like a massive amount of books, piled high and ripe for browsing – especially the treasure trove of £1 books on the trolleys outside. The selection covers almost any area you'd care to think of.

Skoob Books

10 Brunswick Centre, off Bernard Street, Bloomsbury, WC1N 1AE (7278 8760/www.skoob.com). Russell Square tube. **Open** 11am-7pm Mon-Sat; noon-5pm Sun. **Credit** AmEx, MC, V. **Map** p399 L4.

Ever-popular Skoob specialises in philosophy and mathematics, although it has something to match just about any college course. Paperbacks (arranged by publishing house) start at around £3.

Ulysses

40 Museum Street, Bloomsbury, WC1A 1LU (7831 1600). Holborn tube. **Open** 10.30am-6pm Mon-Sat. **Credit** AmEx, MC, V. **Map** p399 L5.

If the name and the location aren't enough to draw you in, consider that this is one of the premier London bookshops for modern firsts. Prices begin at reasonable levels, but rocket depending on the desirability and scarcity of a book – a beautifully illustrated *Twelfth Night* commands £2,000.

Department stores

Fortnum & Mason

181 Piccadilly, St James's, W1A 1ER (7734 8040/www.fortnumandmason.co.uk). Green Park or Piccadilly Circus tube. **Open** 10am-6.30pm Mon-Sat. **Credit** AmEx, MC, V. **Map** p400 J7.

The ground-floor food hall here is wonderfully over the top, with marble pillars, chandeliers and long rows of tea, coffee, chocolates and other giftables, many at surprisingly reasonable prices. Upstairs are top fashions for women and men, and an excellent perfumery, while the basement is a treasure trove of Limoges, Ginori and Hermès china. Those in the know book in advance for F&M's wonderful afternoon teas, served 3-5.30pm and priced from £18.50. *See also p238* **Pride of London**.

Harrods

87-135 Brompton Road, Knightsbridge, SW1X 7XL (7730 1234/www.harrods.com). Knightsbridge tube. **Open** 10am-7pm Mon-Sat. **Credit** AmEx, DC, MC, V. **Map** p397 F9.

On the surface at least, all is as it should be in this mother of all upscale department stores. There are still teddy bears with the Harrods insignia for souvenirs and floor after floor of expensive designer clothes overseen by surprisingly friendly staff who know you can't afford to buy, but don't seem to mind you looking. Linger amid the designs by MaxMara, Joseph, Armani, Dolce & Gabbana and Moschino, or giggle at the over-the-top glitz that helped make the Harrods name. The food hall is justifiably famous, even more so now that Krispy Kreme doughnuts have arrived.

Harvey Nichols

109-125 Knightsbridge, Knightsbridge, SW1X 7RJ (7235 5000/www.harveynichols.com). Knightsbridge tube. **Open** 10am-8pm Mon-Fri; 10am-7pm Sat; noon-6pm Sun. **Credit** AmEx, DC, MC, V. **Map** p397 F9.

This refined Knightsbridge retailer can't compete with Selfridges (*see p234*) in size and sheer showbiz, but it continues to introduce lesser-known, exclusive labels that fit in with its elegant urban image, making it a manageable one-stop shop for front-line fashion. Hot designers clamour to be sold here, and names like Narciso Rodriguez, Michael Kors and Peter Som (whose clothes have appeared in *Sex and the City*) all feature. The excellent shoe department includes a swanky Jimmy Choo salon. Recharge in a choice of eating spots – from the sunny café to the posh Fifth Floor restaurant.

John Lewis

278-306 Oxford Street, Oxford Circus, W1A 1EX (7629 7711/www.johnlewis.co.uk). Bond Street or Oxford Circus tube. **Open** 9.30am-7pm Mon-Wed, Fri, Sat; 9.30am-8pm Thur. **Credit** MC, V. **Map** p398 H6.

What this all-around favourite lacks in glamour it makes up in choice and wonderful anachronisms, such as an entire display devoted to white handkerchiefs. This is the place to come for essential items, especially homewares – there are 2,500 furnishing fabrics. Although it has some fashion lines (such as Fenn Wright Manson and Phase Eight for women; French Connection and Farhi for men), the clothes and accessories remain predominantly conservative. The spacious cosmetics hall includes Crème de la Mer, Sisley and Bobbi Brown.

Other locations: Brent Cross Shopping Centre, Brent Cross, NW4 3FL (8208 6535); Wood Street, Kingston-upon-Thames, Surrey KT1 1TE (8547 3000).

Liberty

210-220 Regent Street, Oxford Circus, W1B 5AH (7734 1234/www.liberty.co.uk). Oxford Circus tube. **Open** 10am-6.30pm Mon-Wed; 10am-8pm Thur; 10am-7pm Fri, Sat; noon-6pm Sun. **Credit** AmEx, DC, MC, V. **Map** p398 J6.

Made up of two interlinked buildings, the store can be tricky to navigate, as sometimes you have to walk outside to get to the section you want. Just ask, though, and the friendly staff will help you get there. The wide-ranging cosmetics department is in the original Tudor House on Great Marlborough Street. Elsewhere, an eclectic fashion taste is embodied in collections by Dries Van Noten, Issey Miyake, Yohji Yamamoto and other new designers. In Regent House, the menswear section has some exclusives. The company's history of Far Eastern trade is clear in the basement and on the third floor, laden with sumptuous oriental rugs.

Marks & Spencer

458 Oxford Street, Marylebone, W1C 1AP (7935 7954/www.marksandspencer.co.uk). Marble Arch tube. **Open** 9am-9pm Mon-Fri; 8.30am-8pm Sat; noon-6pm Sun. **Credit** AmEx, DC, MC, V. **Map** p398 G6.

Where England goes to buy its knickers (and ready-made meals), M&S feels like part of the family around here. In this big, bustling branch the clothes are well displayed upstairs, while downstairs is a good little food market. The lingerie range has a number of lines, and excellent choice at good prices. For women, Per Una, Autograph (with designs by Betty Jackson and Philip Treacy) offers good, if conservative, options. Menswear is also reliable, the quality is dependable, and you can't argue with the prices.

Other locations: throughout the city.

Selfridges

400 Oxford Street, Oxford Circus, W1A 1AB (0870 837 7377/www.selfridges.com). Bond Street or Marble Arch tube. **Open** 10am-8pm Mon-Fri; 9.30am-8pm Sat; noon-6pm Sun. **Credit** AmEx, DC, MC, V. **Map** p398 G6.

The ground floor is a heaving cosmetics and fragrance marketplace where you can't swing a Fendi bag without bumping into a display for Stila, MAC, Christian Dior, Bobbi Brown, Nars or Benefit. Expensive names are big business here, and you could blow your budget within seconds of stepping in the door. The ground floor is for teens and the very young at heart. The second floor houses the major designer labels. Kids Universe is on the third floor. You can lose yourself in the excellent lingerie department up here too. Men have acres of accessories on the ground floor, and clothes on floor one. The vast food hall, with aisles of delectables from around the world, is legendary.

Electronics

Tottenham Court Road is practically wall to wall with electronics and computer shops.

Computers & games

Computer Exchange

32 Rathbone Place, Fitzrovia, W1T 1JJ (7636 2666/ www.cex.co.uk). Tottenham Court Road tube. **Open** 10am-7pm Mon-Wed, Sat; 10am-8pm Thur, Fri; 11am-6pm Sun. **Credit** MC, V. **Map** p399 K5.

This well-stocked shop has everything you need from Game Boy Advance to PlayStation 2 – some new, some second-hand, some imported. There's a massive retro section with games from the 1980s like Donkey Kong and Space Invaders. Excellent.

Gultronics

264-7 Tottenham Court Road, Fitzrovia, W1T 7RH (7436 4120/www.gultronics.co.uk). Goodge Street or Tottenham Court Road tube. **Open** 10am-7pm Mon-Sat; 11am-5pm Sun. **Credit** AmEx, MC, V. **Map** p399 K5.

A rich source of top-of-the-line Toshiba and Sony laptops, Gultronics also features a wealth of PC accessories. Prices vary according to the particular package and the specials of the moment – on offer at the time of writing was an HP laptop with a 1.67GHz processor for £699. Staff say they will match other shops' prices.

Micro Anvika

245 Tottenham Court Road, Fitzrovia, W1T 7QT (7467 6000/www.microanvika.co.uk). Goodge Street or Tottenham Court Road tube. **Open** 9.30am-6pm Mon-Wed, Fri, Sat; 9.30am-6.30pm Thur; 11am-5pm Sun. **Credit** AmEx, MC, V. **Map** p399 K5.

This sleek, modern chain has a good selection of Mac packages, with stock ranging from iMacs to G5s. There are gadgets and accessories galore, not to mention Sony, Toshiba and IBM laptops, although prices sometimes reflect the chic surroundings. The 90-day technical support policy is a bonus. There's also an outlet in Selfridges (*see above*).

General & audio-visual

HMV and **Virgin Megastore** (*see p251*) also have the latest music, videos, DVDs, minidiscs, accessories and computer games.

Ask

248 Tottenham Court Road, Fitzrovia, W1T 7QZ (7637 0353/www.askdirect.co.uk). Tottenham Court Road tube. **Open** 9am-6pm Mon-Wed, Fri, Sat; 10am-8pm Thur; noon-6pm Sun. **Credit** AmEx, DC, MC, V. **Map** p399 K5.

A well-stocked electronics superstore, Ask offers an up-to-date range of quality goods from brands such as Sony, Panasonic and Pioneer. The whole spectrum of audio-visual gear is covered, from digital cameras and laptops through to mini hi-fi systems and personal stereos. Staff are knowledgeable and aren't afraid to offer honest opinions.

Dixons

88 Oxford Street, Fitzrovia, W1D 1BX (7636 8511/ www.dixons.com). Tottenham Court Road tube. **Open** 10am-7pm Mon-Fri; 9.30am-6.30pm Sat; noon-6pm Sun. **Credit** AmEx, DC, MC, V. **Map** p399 J6.

Another one-stop electronics shop, there's a good selection of portable and personal stereos, mini hi-fis, DVD players, camcorders, cameras, PCs and printers on offer, as well as a smaller choice of TVs and VCRs. Prices aren't exactly the lowest, but are reasonably competitive. The salespeople don't always inspire confidence, so you're better off doing your own research.

Other locations: throughout the city.

Photography

Jacobs Photo, Video & Digital

74 New Oxford Street, St Giles's, WC1A 1EU (7436 5544/www.jacobs-photo.co.uk). Tottenham Court Road tube. **Open** 9am-6pm Mon-Wed, Fri, Sat; 9am-8pm Thur. **Credit** AmEx, MC, V. **Map** p399 L5.

Smart tailoring

The traditional slim silhouette and nipped-in waist that defines the classic bespoke suit paraded by the dandies of Edwardian London is a look that has endured. Then, as now, Mayfair's Savile Row (*see also p110*) was the traditional home of men's tailoring.

A fresh wave of interest in tailored fashion during the 1960s returned bespoke tailoring to the forefront of fashionable dress and inspired a celebrity following: Mick Jagger, Elton John and Twiggy all modelled the sharp suit, with varying degrees of success.

Should you decide to try one yourself, generally, you can expect it to take six to eight weeks for your suit to be made, and to attend up to three fittings to ensure a perfect fit. Prices throughout the Row tend to start at about £1,400 for a traditional two-piece suit.

Many of the businesses on Savile Row have been around for a century. The oldest, founding tailor **Henry Poole & Co** (15 Savile Row, 7734 5985), makes the best of all sizes (prices start at £1,880 for a two-piece).

The most expensive service on offer is at **Huntsman & Sons** (11 Savile Row, 7347 4411), where prices start at £3,000 for a two-piece, but you're paying for quality. The company is renowned for its one-button suit jacket and, like many tailors on the Row, now caters for women as well as men.

Anderson & Sheppard Ltd (30 Savile Row, 7287 1169), one of the most respected names, prefers a soft-tailored method (a popular look among 1930s film stars), with a soft, comfortable fit on the shoulders.

Steven Hitchcock (13 New Burlington street,7287 2492), once an apprentice at Anderson, is one of the youngest tailors in the area. He also adopts the old school, soft-tailoring method, and has dressed Bryan Ferry and Malcolm McClaren.

Among the new generation of young tailors, **Ozwald Boateng** (*see p244*) fuses modern design with traditional tailoring.

If you are looking for something for a formal occasion, specialist tailors **Dege and Skinner** (10 Savile Row, 7287 2941) and **Denman & Goddard Ltd** (13 New Burlington Street, 7734 6371) are experts in military, hunting and formal attire. **Airey & Wheeler** (9 Savile Row, 7734 7461) has a wide range of light-weight fabrics ideal for tropical climates.

For a limitless choice of the finest in English and Italian cloth, **Maurice Sedwell** (19 Savile Row, 7734 0824) is the location. Official tailor to the Queen, **Hardy Amies** died in 2003, but his talent lives on at 14 Savile Row (7734 2436), where tailors produce finery of all sorts, from wedding dresses to leather jackets.

This nationwide chain carries an excellent range of compact and SLR cameras, and accessories and plenty of digital options. Prices are competitive. The second-hand department is worth checking out. Next-day colour film processing is £4.99.

Jessops

63-9 New Oxford Street, St Giles's, WC1A 1DG (7240 6077/www.jessops.com). Tottenham Court Road tube. **Open** 9am-7pm Mon, Tue, Fri; 9.30am-7pm Wed; 9am-8pm Thur; 9am-6pm Sat; 11am-5pm Sun. **Credit** AmEx, DC, MC, V. **Map** p399 L5.
With nearly 250 stores nationwide, Jessops is well on the way to UK domination. This, the largest of 23 locations, has everything from writable DVDs, graphics tablets and good digital software to darkroom equipment and chemicals and tripods, plus compact, SLR, APS and digital cameras.
Other locations: throughout the city.

Kingsley Photographic

93 Tottenham Court Road, Fitzrovia, W1T 4HL (7387 6500/www.kingsleyphoto.co.uk). Goodge Street or Warren Street tube. **Open** 9am-5.30pm Mon-Fri; 10am-5.30pm Sat. **Credit** AmEx, MC, V. **Map** p399 K5.
For such a tiny place, this small shop manages to squeeze in a surprisingly large range, and if something isn't in stock, it can be ordered. A family business, the store is staffed by keen and helpful photographers. Along with the new equipment, there's a repair service and second-hand gear.

Fashion

Boutiques

Browns

23-7 South Molton Street, Mayfair, W1K 5RD (7514 0000/www.brownsfashion.com). Bond Street tube. **Open** 10am-6.30pm Mon-Wed, Fri, Sat; 10am-7pm Thur. **Credit** AmEx, DC, MC, V. **Map** p398 H6.
Joan Burstein's venerable store has reigned supreme over London's boutiques for close to 30 years. Diane von Furstenberg, Marc Jacobs, Dries Van Noten, Carlos Miele, Hussein Chalayan, Eley Kishimoto and Dolce & Gabbana are currently stocked, alongside to die for shoes and bags from Dior, Celine and Fendi.
Other locations: 6C Sloane Street, Knightsbridge, SW1X 9LE (7514 0000).

electrum
Electrum Gallery
21 South Molton Street
London W1K 5QX
Tel: 020 7629 6325
Mon-Fri 10-6, Sat10-5
18ct gold ringset on stand by WENDY RAMSHAW,CBE
ba ngle by ANGELA O'KELLY, rings by EVA WERNER
CHRISTINA SOUBLI AND ZWETELINA ALEXIEVA
for unique
and exciting contemporary
JEWELLERY

SOFT TAILORING
FOR STYLE AND COMFORT

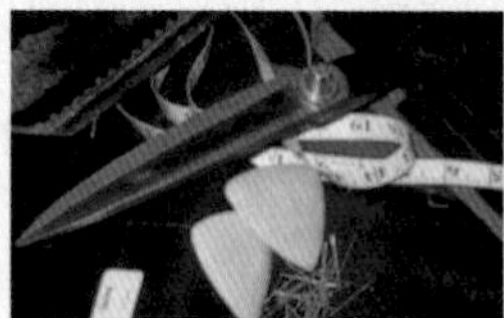

Steven Hitchcock
Savile Row • Master Tailor
13 New Burlington Street, Savile Row,
London W1S 3BG
Tel/Fax: +44 (0) 20 7287 2492

Steven Hitchcock has owned and run his own bespoke tailoring company in London's Savile Row since September 1999.
This unique style of hand-crafted tailoring was originally championed by such noted dressers as Cary Grant and the Duke of Windsor. But the skills required to create this style have only been revealed to a selected generation of Savile Row tailors, of which he is the latest member. His success in soft tailoring has been such that in the time he has been in business, he has made suits for a number of leading musicians and international businessmen.

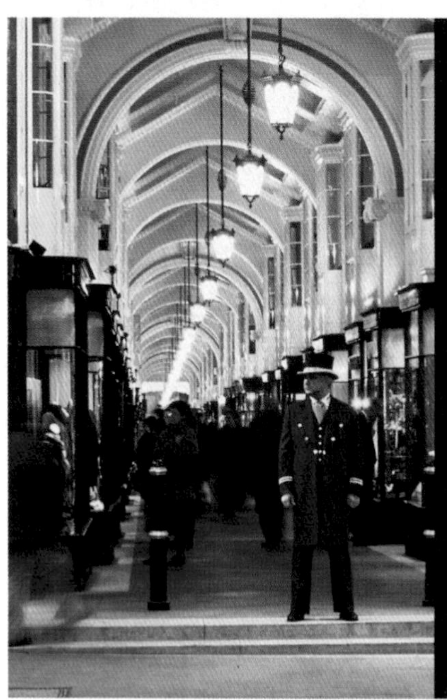

BURLINGTON
ARCADE

The height of stylish
shopping in the heart of
London's West End

Burlington Arcade Piccadilly, London W1
www.burlingtonarcade.com

The Cross

141 Portland Road, Holland Park, W11 4LR (7727 6760). Holland Park tube. **Open** 11am-5.30pm Mon-Sat. **Credit** AmEx, MC, V.

This stellar store has long been the fashion editors' fave. Its continuing appeal lies not only in its considered approach to stock – clothes by Boyd, Missoni, Alice Lee, Luisa Beccaria, and accessories courtesy of Anya Hindmarch, Michel Perry, Rodolphe Menudier and Johnny Loves Rosie – but also in its enviable celeb following.

Koh Samui

65-7 Monmouth Street, Covent Garden, WC2H 9DJ (7240 4280). Covent Garden tube. **Open** 10am-6.30pm Mon, Tue, Sat; 10.30am-6.30pm Wed, Fri; 10.30am-7pm Thur; 11am-5.30pm Sun. **Credit** AmEx, DC, MC, V. **Map** p399 L6.

This store's reputation as one of the capital's premier cutting-edge clothes emporia precedes it – and we've yet to be disappointed. A recent visit had us lusting after threads by Balenciaga, Stella McCartney and Eley Kishimoto, along with Clements Ribeiro, Matthew Williamson and the omnipresent Marc by Marc Jacobs.

Budget

All of these are chains with numerous locations around London.

Dorothy Perkins

189 Oxford Street, Oxford Circus, W1D 2JY (7494 3769/www.dorothyperkins.co.uk). Tottenham Court Road tube. **Open** 10am-8pm Mon-Wed, Fri, Sat; 10am-9pm Thur; noon-6pm Sun. **Credit** AmEx, MC, V. **Map** p399 K6.

Dorothy Perkins – which also has a glamorous new store above Bond Street tube – is good for casual modern styles, with contemporary-cut trousers in menswear fabrics (grey wool, herringbone, pinstripe) from just £15. They even come in three lengths, so you won't need to get them altered. Jackets are from £40 and skirts at around £12.

French Connection

396 Oxford Street, Oxford Circus, W1C 7JX (7629 7766/www.frenchconnection.com). Bond Street tube. **Open** 10am-8pm Mon-Wed, Fri; 10am-9pm Thur; 10am-7pm Sat; noon-6pm Sun. **Credit** AmEx, MC, V. **Map** p398 J6.

As its cheeky double-take name suggests, this chain aspires to a cool, urban image with plenty of FCUK-off attitude. The clothes, while not cutting-edge, are good quality. Well-cut mannish trousers (from £70), neat, dark denim jackets (£70) and little fitted sweaters (from around £40) are fab.

Gap

223-25 Oxford Street, Oxford Circus, W1R 1AB (7734 3312/www.gap.com). Oxford Circus tube. **Open** 10am-8pm Mon-Wed, Sat; 10am-9pm Thur, Fri; noon-6pm Sun. **Credit** AmEx, MC, V. **Map** p398 J6.

You don't have to walk far between each outlet of American giant Gap on London's busiest shopping street. It's still hard to beat when it comes to good-quality, reasonably priced T-shirts and countless variations on jeans, chinos and cords. This location is a superstore that sells kids' stuff as well.

H&M

261-71 Regent Street, Oxford Circus, W1R 7PA (7493 4004/www.hm.com). Oxford Circus tube. **Open** 10am-8pm Mon-Wed, Fri, Sat; 10am-9pm Thur; noon-6pm Sun. **Credit** AmEx, MC, V. **Map** p398 J6.

This Swedish stalwart makes the Gap seem pricey. £3.99 will buy you a basic tee here. The ground floor is given over to trendy teens, while womenswear is in the basement. You have to wade through some pretty dire fashions to find the treasures, though.

Jigsaw

126-27 New Bond Street, Oxford Circus, W1A 9AF (7491 4484/www.jigsaw-online.com). Bond Street tube. **Open** 10am-6.30pm Mon-Wed, Fri, Sat; 10am-7.30pm Thur; noon-6pm Sun. **Credit** AmEx, MC, V. **Map** p398 H6.

Good-quality cottons and knitwear in a subdued, sophisticated colour palette give Jigsaw a more expensive feel than many of its competitors. Women of all ages rely on the cotton T-shirts (from £22), georgette bias-cut dresses (around £80) and fine wool tailoring (£140 for a jacket; £70 for trousers).

Kookaï

257-9 Oxford Street, Oxford Circus, W1R 2DD (7408 2391/www.kookai.co.uk). Oxford Circus tube. **Open** 10am-7pm Mon-Wed, Sat; 10am-8pm Thur, Fri; noon-6pm Sun. **Credit** AmEx, DC, MC, V. **Map** p398 J6.

Ooh la la! The shapes and detailing may change with the catwalk trends, but Kookaï's range of jersey halter necks, lace-trim strappy tops and vampy skirts – pencil, mini, slit up the thigh – exudes a timeless Parisian sex appeal. Bombshells can expect to pay around £20 for a top and £40 for a skirt.

Mango

233 Oxford Street, Oxford Circus, W1D 2LP (7534 3505/www.mango.es). Oxford Circus tube. **Open** 10am-8pm Mon-Wed, Fri, Sat; 10am-9pm Thur; noon-6pm Sun. **Credit** AmEx, MC, V. **Map** p398 J6.

Occupying three floors of blond wood and glass, this very trendy Spanish chain offers rail upon rail of laid-back, body-conscious tops, knits and trendy trousers at moderate prices. The suede and leather jackets for under £100 are especially good value.

Miss Selfridge

36-8 Great Castle Street (entrance on Oxford Street), Oxford Circus, W1W 8LG (7927 0214/www.miss-selfridge.net). Oxford Circus tube. **Open** 9am-8pm Mon-Wed, Fri, Sat; 9am-9pm Thur; noon-6pm Sun. **Credit** MC, V. **Map** p398 J6.

This trendy store for teens offers vividly coloured, body-hugging fashions with pounding music on top. This year, patterns from the store's archives are

Pride of London Fortnum & Mason

Even if you've never heard of this esteemed London landmark, you're still likely to walk past its polite, top-hatted doormen and into its plush environs, if only for a peek (for listing, *see p233*). The draw is not just the frilly Victorian frontage, with plasterwork swirls, sconces shaped like human hands and elaborate window settings. No, there's just something about the place. It exudes exclusivity, history and class.

And so it should, of course. This is one of those many true pillars of London – a store that has been around for so long it's become as much a part of the local fabric as St Paul's or Big Ben.

Fortnum and Mason first began as a modest grocery store started by William Fortnum and Hugh Mason in 1707. With members of the Fortnum family in service to the Queen, and others working for the East India Company, soon it began importing spices and teas from the east, and providing exotic little titbits to the Royal family. Almost immediately, it had found its niche as the country's most elegant supplier of fine foods.

Today, it is still the grocer and tea supplier to the Royal family, while its famous hampers have been enlivening British holidays with their pretty collections of food and drink since the mid-1800s. It was around that time that it became known for packaging even the most mundane purchases in beautiful boxes and bags, and even today something as simple as a box of biscuits seems somehow exceptional if carried in one of Fortnum's big, square mint-green bags.

It is best known for its wide array of teas and coffees (sold under its own label, in charming jars and canisters that make excellent gifts), but you can find everything from handmade jams to Egyptian scorpions pickled in jelly in its ground floor food hall.

Of course, most people go no further than the chocolate counters here, and that's a shame, for on its upper floors it holds one of the city's best upscale department stores.

being resurrected to recreate designs from a particular decade; if you like frills, look out for '80s New Romantic designs.

New Look

500-2 Oxford Street, Oxford Circus, W1C 7LH (7290 7860/www.newlook.co.uk). Bond Street tube. **Open** 10am-10pm Mon-Fri; 9am-8pm Sat; noon-6pm Sun. **Credit** MC, V. **Map** p398 H6.

This place caters to the pre-pubescent market, with cheap and cheerful takes on the latest trends. Top marks are deserved for keeping up with trends.

Oasis

12-14 Argyll Street, Oxford Circus, W1F 7NT (7434 1799/www.oasis-stores.com). Oxford Circus tube. **Open** 10am-7pm Mon-Wed, Fri, Sat; 10am-8pm Thur; noon-6pm Sun. **Credit** AmEx, MC, V. **Map** p398 J6.

This endlessly popular chain offers a good mix of smart-looking key pieces targeting young career women. Especially attractive are the 1960s-style graphic black and white shifts for £50 and the neat leather biker jacket in white, hot pink or black for £120. Clothes suit the young and nubile – skirts tend to be impressively short.

Topshop

36-8 Great Castle Street, Oxford Circus, W1W 8LG (7636 7700/www.topshop.co.uk). Oxford Circus tube. **Open** 9am-8pm Mon-Wed, Fri, Sat; 9am-9pm Thur; noon-6pm Sun. **Credit** AmEx, DC, MC, V. **Map** p398 J6.

A fashion hotspot for teenyboppers, this is a (noisy) city in itself, with 180,000 shoppers a week, a blaring sound system and huge video screens. Designers like Sophia Kokosalaki, Markus Lupfer and Zandra Rhodes create tiny fashions for this vast place.

You won't find much that's cheap up there, but you will find designer clothes for men and women, and Limoges and Hermès china, sold in rooms in which the store's private collection of museum-quality art hangs on the walls.

It's this attention to detail, and the mingling of elegance with shopping, that sets Fortnum above the rest. This is how shopping in London should be.

Whistles

12 St Christopher's Place, Oxford Circus, W1U 1NQ (7487 4484). Bond Street tube. **Open** 10am-6pm Mon-Wed, Fri, Sat; 10am-7pm Thur; noon-5pm Sun. **Credit** AmEx, MC, V. **Map** p398 H6.

Beautiful, hand-finished tailoring, directional cuts and handcrafted details such as beadwork and embroidery characterise the style of this well-loved label. Price-wise, you're looking at £40 for a viscose top, £89 for trousers, £165 for a jacket.

Zara

118 Regent Street, Oxford Circus, W1B 5SE (7534 9500/www.zara.com). Piccadilly Circus tube. **Open** 10am-7pm Mon-Wed, Fri, Sat; 10am-8pm Thur; noon-6pm Sun. **Credit** AmEx, DC, MC, V. **Map** p398 J6.

This Spanish chain seems set for global domination, with three huge stores in the vicinity of Oxford Circus alone. Take your pick of the latest sleek catwalk knock-offs. The menswear collection is one of the high street's best; both suits (£129-£165) and separates (trousers £50; shirts £29) are good for smartening up your wardrobe on the cheap. For both genders, sizes run small.

Children

Child

49 Shelton Street, Covent Garden, WC2H 9HE (7240 8484) Covent Garden tube. **Open** 10.30am-6pm Mon-Fri; 11am-6pm Sat. **Credit** MC, V. **Map** p399 L6.

Located away from the tourist throngs, this independent shop strives to offer unusual clothes and accessories for newborns through to six-year-olds. Clothing labels tend to be European and include the likes of Simple Kids, Garçon, Jules et Julie and No Added Sugar. Prices are slightly higher than you'll find at Gap.

Daisy & Tom

181-3 King's Road, Chelsea, SW3 5EB (7352 5000/www.daisyandtom.com). Sloane Square tube then 11, 319, 22 bus. **Open** 9.30am-6pm Mon-Wed, Fri; 10am-7pm Thur, Sat; 11am-5pm Sun. **Credit** AmEx, MC, V. **Map** p397 E12.

A veritable children's wonderland, with a traditional carousel in the centre of the ground floor and a colouring table. The best bit is the book room, which has a wide and impressive selection of stock. Upstairs are expensive designer labels such as Elle, Catimini and IKKS, along with Daisy & Tom's own-brand baby clothing. An on-site hairdresser can complete your child's makeover.

Gap Kids

122 King's Road, Chelsea, SW3 4TR (7823 7272/www.gap.com). Sloane Square tube. **Open** 9.30am-7pm Mon-Sat; noon-6pm Sun. **Credit** AmEx, MC, V. **Map** p397 E12.

Widely considered to have the best children's sale rail, the Chelsea Gap offers cosy hoodies, puffas, cardies and striped tights at knockdown prices.

Gymboree

198 Regent Street, Oxford Circus, W1R 6BT (7494 1110/www.gymboree.com). Oxford Circus tube. **Open** 10am-7pm Mon-Wed, Fri, Sat; 10am-8pm Thur; 11am-6pm Sun. **Credit** AmEx, MC, V. **Map** p399 J6.

With its spiral marble staircase and wrought-iron lift, the clothes in this central London store sit squarely midway between French conservative and American casual. There are little woollen coats with velvet collars (about £50) in winter or vast quantities of colourful spotty leggings and vivid appliquéd T-shirts (for about £20) in summer.

Trotters

34 King's Road, Chelsea, SW3 4UD (7259 9620/ www.trotters.co.uk). Sloane Square tube. **Open** 9am-7pm Mon-Sat; 10.30am-6.30pm Sun. **Credit** AmEx, MC, V. **Map** p397 F11.

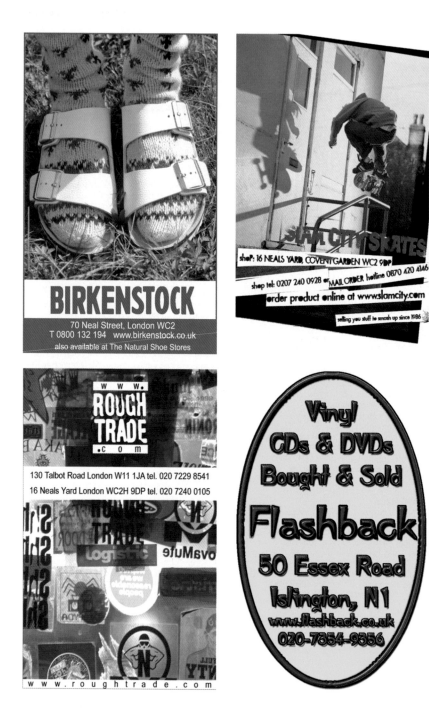

BIRKENSTOCK
70 Neal Street, London WC2
T 0800 132 194 www.birkenstock.co.uk
also available at The Natural Shoe Stores

SLAM CITY SKATES
shoP: 16 NEALS YARD, COVENT GARDEN WC2 9DP
shop tel: 0207 240 0928 or MAIL ORDER hotline 0870 420 4146
order product online at www.slamcity.com
selling you stuff to smash up since 1986

www.
ROUGH
TRADE
.com
130 Talbot Road London W11 1JA tel. 020 7229 8541
16 Neals Yard London WC2H 9DP tel. 020 7240 0105

www.roughtrade.com

Vinyl
CDs & DVDs
Bought & Sold
Flashback
50 Essex Road
Islington, N1
www.flashback.co.uk
020-7354-9356

There's a range of colourful gear for up to ten-year-olds sporting labels such as Diesel, Chipie, Oilily and Miniman. Kids can get fitted for sensible Start-rite shoes and then get their hair cut in the kiddie-themed in-store hairdresser's.

Street

Carhartt

56 Neal Street, Covent Garden, WC2H 9PA (7836 5659/www.thecarharttstore.co.uk). Covent Garden tube. **Open** 11am-6.30pm Mon-Wed, Fri, Sat; 11am-7pm Thur; noon-5pm Sun. **Credit** MC, V. **Map** p399 L6.

This is a great store for durable casuals and trendy separates. Tops are workwear-style check shirts (£35), retro logo T-shirts (£25) and stylish trousers, heavy cotton shirts, T-shirts, hoodies and sweats.

Diesel

43 Earlham Street, Covent Garden, WC2H 9LX (7497 5543/www.diesel.com). Covent Garden tube. **Open** 10am-7pm Mon-Wed, Fri, Sat; 10am-8pm Thur; noon-6pm Sun. **Credit** AmEx, MC, V. **Map** p399 L6.

The clothing at this Italian fashion staple never deviates too far from the tried-and-tested formula of quality denims and separates. For men, slim-cut shirts with floral embellishments go for around £80 and T-shirts from £40. Jeans start at £60.

Duffer of St George

29 Shorts Gardens, Covent Garden, WC2H 9AP (7379 4660/www.thedufferofstgeorge.com). Covent Garden tube. **Open** 10.30am-7pm Mon-Fri; 10.30am-6.30pm Sat; noon-5pm Sun. **Credit** AmEx, MC, V. **Map** p399 L6.

Though our experience of staff snootiness and hefty prices are black marks against Duffer, the label turns out quality urban men's clothing. Style mixes English (slim shirts and fine knitwear) with retro American (sloganned T-shirts and faded jeans).

Maharishi

19A Floral Street, Covent Garden, WC2E 9HL (7836 3860/www.emaharishi.com). Covent Garden tube. **Open** 10am-7pm Mon-Sat; noon-5pm Sun. **Credit** AmEx, MC, V. **Map** p399 L6.

Much imitated in high street stores, Maharishi's remain the best. Its draw is the embellished combats known as 'snow pants'. Girls' start at £120 and go as high as £250; men's stick around the £125 mark.

Quiksilver

Units 1 & 23, Thomas Neal Centre, Earlham Street, Covent Garden, WC2H 9LD (7836 5371/www.quiksilver.com). Covent Garden tube. **Open** 10am-7pm Mon-Sat; noon-6pm Sun. **Credit** AmEx, MC, V. **Map** p399 L6.

This place stocks everything you're ever likely to need by this long-established Aussie surf label. Stock is devoted to surfing equipment – the usual surf boards, board bags, wetsuits and cans of board wax. The clothes on offer include your basic surf-related T-shirts, baggy long shorts, cargo pants and sweats of the kind you see tousle-haired dudes sport on just about every beach.

Shop

4 Brewer Street, Soho, W1R 3FP (7437 1259). Leicester Square or Piccadilly Circus tube. **Open** 10.30am-6.30pm Mon-Fri; 11am-6.30pm Sat. **Credit** AmEx, MC, V. **Map** p400 J7.

This small basement boutique revels in its slightly seedy Soho location. Inside, it's a lot more chic than you might expect, with labels like Eley Kishimoto and Marc Jacobs. For fans of more full-on streetwear there's also fashions by Silas and Shopgirl.

Skate of Mind

Unit 26, Thomas Neal Centre, Earlham Street, Covent Garden, WC2H 9LD (7836 9060). Covent Garden tube. **Open** 10am-7pm Mon-Sat; noon-6pm Sun. **Credit** MC, V. **Map** p399 L6.

A shop for the serious skater, populated by skinny teenagers discussing the finer points of the ollie kick-flip. There's also some pretty cool clothing: serious skate brands Flip and Zoo New York as well as Unabomber. T-shirts (£20 plus), hoodies (upwards of £50) and denim (around £40) lead the way.

Underwear

Agent Provocateur

6 Broadwick Street, Soho, W1V 1FH (7439 0229/ www.agentprovocateur.com). Oxford Circus tube. **Open** 11am-7pm Mon-Sat. **Credit** AmEx, MC, V. **Map** p397 F10.

The most talked-about lingerie shop in the world, what with its saucy window displays, and staff in nurses' uniforms. There are sexy corsets (from £185), bras (from £40), knickers (from £25) and baby doll slips (from £80). Bras are sized from A to F cup. You're encouraged to try everything on.

Other locations: 16 Pont Street, Knightsbridge, SW1X 9EN (7235 0229); Royal Exchange, Threadneedle Street, City, EC3V 3LL (7623 0229).

Aware

182 King's Road, Chelsea, SW3 5XP (7351 6259/www.awareunderwear.co.uk). Sloane Square tube. **Open** 10am-7pm Mon-Sat; noon-6pm Sun. **Credit** AmEx, MC, V. **Map** p397 E12.

French ex-barrister Olivier Gazay's specialist men's underwear venture has proved so popular he now has several branches. Boxers and briefs are by Calvin Klein, Hugo Boss, DKNY, D&G, the Gallic Hom brand and the Swiss label Hanro.

Coco de Mer

23 Monmouth Street, Covent Garden, WC2H 9DD (7836 8882/www.coco-de-mer.co.uk). Covent Garden tube. **Open** 11am-7pm Mon-Wed, Fri, Sat; 11am-8pm Thur; noon-6pm Sun. **Credit** AmEx, MC, V. **Map** p399 L6.

This erotic shop is more sumptuous Victorian bordello than sexy lingerie retailer. There are books, CDs, art and antiques, and designer sex toys. The exclusivity of some of the stock, from designer names like Roberto Cavalli, Damaris Evans, and jeweller Betony Vernon, is reflected in the prices (bras start at £45, rising to £180).

Rigby & Peller

22A Conduit Street, Knightsbridge, W1R 9TB (7491 2200/www.rigbyandpeller.com). Oxford Circus tube. **Open** 9.30am-6pm Mon-Wed, Fri, Sat; 9.30am-7pm Thur. **Credit** AmEx, DC, MC, V. **Map** p397 F9.

This is the official corsetière to the Queen, so staff are experts in made-to-order lingerie, and can alter bras to suit your shape. There is also a ready-to-wear range, in sizes 30A to 40E, with bras from £45.

Other locations: 2 Hans Road, Knightsbridge, SW3 1RX (7589 9293).

Vintage

Annie's Vintage Clothes

12 Camden Passage, Islington, N1 8ED (7359 0796). Angel tube. **Open** 11am-6pm Mon, Tue, Thur, Fri; 9am-6pm Wed, Sat. **Credit** AmEx, DC, MC, V. **Map** p402 O2.

Annie's is a brilliant stop-off for 1930s bias-cut chiffon dresses (from £150), floral 1940s day dresses (around £48) and bias-cut silk slips (£78-£95), which can double as evening wear.

Bertie Wooster

284 Fulham Road, Fulham, SW10 9DW (7352 5662/www.bertie-wooster.co.uk). Earl's Court or Fulham Broadway tube. **Open** 10am-6pm Mon, Wed, Fri; 10am-7pm Tue, Thur; 10am-5pm Sat. **Credit** AmEx, MC, V.

This is the place for canny socialites, because it specialises in the best of all possible second-hand clothes. It has gorgeous vintage morning coats for £120 (new and end-of-lines for £150), shooting coats for £175 and overcoats for £125. A small basement alcove has white-tie gear, while the main stock on the ground floor consists of Savile Row suits (£150), city shirts (£30) and even boxer shorts. Made to measure is another resource. You will not find better deals on better clothes than this.

The Girl Can't Help It/ Cad Van Swankster

Alfie's Antique Market, 13-25 Church Street, Marylebone, NW8 8DT (7724 8984/www.sparkle moore.com). Edgware Road tube/Marylebone tube/rail. **Open** 10am-6pm Tue-Sat. **Credit** MC, V. **Map** p395 E4.

This award-winning emporium of vintage clothing and homewares has pink satin negligées for £75-£165, boxed stockings from £18 to £30 a pair and substantially built swimsuits at around £50.

Fashion accessories & services

General

Accessorize

22 The Market, Covent Garden, WC2E 8HB (7240 2107/www.accessorize.co.uk). Covent Garden tube. **Open** 9am-8pm Mon-Fri; 10am-8pm Sat; 11am-7pm Sun. **Credit** AmEx, DC, MC, V. **Map** p401 L6.

This ubiquitous chain is probably the best of the high street shops specialising in top-to-toe necessities: hats, bags, scarves and jewellery. Prices start at just a few pounds, and most shops have a children's stand and cosmetics bar.

Other locations: throughout the city.

Gorgeous detail at **Whistles**. *See p239.*

Dry cleaning & laundry

Perkins Dry Cleaners

28 Thayer Street, Marylebone, W1 5LJ (7935 3072). Bond Street tube. **Open** 8.15am-7pm Mon-Wed, Fri; 8.15am-6pm Thur; 8.30am-3pm Sat. **Credit** AmEx, MC, V. **Map** p398 G5.
Perkins offers a reliable service at moderate prices (gentlemen's suits can be dry cleaned from £12.50). The laundry can hand-finish anything.

Seven Dials Dry Cleaners

37 Monmouth Street, Covent Garden, WC2H 9DD (7240 9274). Leicester Square or Covent Garden tube. **Open** 8am-6pm Mon-Fri; 9am-2pm Sat. **Credit** AmEx, MC, V. **Map** p399 L6.
Staff at Seven Dials are experts in cleaning delicate and designer clothing. Garments are hand finished and a same-day service is available. Shirts are laundered from £3; dry cleaning a suit costs from £14.

Jewellery

Angela Hale

Royal Arcade, 28 Old Bond Street, Mayfair, W1S 4SE (7495 1920/www.angelahale.co.uk). Green Park tube. **Open** 10am-6pm Mon-Sat. **Credit** AmEx, MC, V. **Map** p400 J7.
Angela Hale's Bond Street boutique gleams with romantic, glamorous, elegant and classical jewellery. A green and violet crystal, baroque-style necklace is £165. It's an ideal place to buy a special gift for a girlfriend as prices are reasonable, and purchases are packaged in a pretty pink box.

Cartier

175-6 New Bond Street, Mayfair, W1S 4RN (7408 5700/www.cartier.com). Green Park tube. **Open** 10am-6pm Mon-Fri; 10am-5pm Sat. **Credit** AmEx, MC, V. **Map** p399 H6.
The name Cartier is synonymous with sophistication, and this wood-panelled store does the brand justice. Class doesn't come cheap, of course: a pink-gold Menotte bracelet starts at £1,800; a pink-gold, amethyst and turquoise ring costs £625. The popular Trinity ring is a cheaper option, from £395. But giving a gift in a Cartier box is simply priceless.
Other locations: 188 Sloane Street, Knightsbridge, SW1X 9QR (7235 9023); 40-41 Old Bond Street, Mayfair, W1S 4RN (7408 5700).

Garrard

24 Albemarle Street, Mayfair, W1Y 4HT (7758 8520/www.garrard.com). Bond Street or Green Park tube. **Open** 10am-5.30pm Mon-Sat. **Credit** AmEx, DC, MC, V. **Map** p400 J7.
Established in 1735 and crown jeweller to Queen Victoria, Garrard is now keen to shake off its fusty image – and how better to do so than by appointing Jade Jagger as its creative director? Check out her Superstyle range – which is plenty of diamond studded, plate-like pendants on big chains (starting from around £2,300) – if you can afford them.

Kaleido

11 Long Acre, Covent Garden, WC2E 9LH (7836 3444). Leicester Square tube. **Open** 11am-6.30pm Mon-Sat; noon-5pm Sun. **Credit** AmEx, MC, V. **Map** p401 L7.
This funky steel-and-glass shop sells mainly silver jewellery, with a few gold exceptions. Popular buys include the huge, silver 'rock rings' adorned with chunks of turquoise aqua aura (£60). Rotation rings, which have moving parts, start from £85.

Mikimoto

179 New Bond Street, Oxford Circus, W1S 4RJ (7629 5300/www.mikimoto.com). Green Park tube. **Open** 10am-5.30pm Mon-Sat. **Credit** AmEx, DC, MC, V. **Map** p399 H6.
Pearls have always been Mikimoto's speciality and its latest range – Pearls in Motion – is an elegant combination of white Japanese and black Tahitian pearls (from £1,100 for earrings). If you can't quite stretch to that, a pair of simple, small pearl studs is always classy; they begin at £90.

Tiffany & Co

25 Old Bond Street, Mayfair, W1S 4QB (7409 2790/www.tiffany.com/uk). Green Park tube. **Open** 10am-6pm Mon-Fri; 10am-5.30pm Sat. **Credit** AmEx, MC, V. **Map** p400 J7.
What woman on the planet doesn't yearn for one of Tiffany's little blue boxes, preferably containing a Lucida rectangular diamond engagement ring (from £2,000) or an Elsa Peretti gold open-heart pendant necklace (from £365). But hey – we'd settle for the silver open-heart pendant necklace (£85).
Other locations: Royal Exchange, Threadneedle Street, City, EC3V 3LQ (7495 3511).

Shoes

Most of the shops below are parts of chains with outlets all over town.

Aldo

3-7 Neal Street, Covent Garden, WC2H 9PU (7836 7692/www.aldoshoes.com). Covent Garden, Holborn or Leicester Square tube. **Open** 10am-7pm Mon-Sat; noon-6pm Sun. **Credit** AmEx, MC, V. **Map** p399 L6.
This vast Canadian shoe shop has a dizzying variety of styles, from dressy Mary Janes to funky wedges for women, and variations on the loafer and lace-up for men. Prices hover around £50.

Camper

Royal Arcade, 28 Old Bond Street, Mayfair, W1X 3AB (7629 2722/www.camper.com). Green Park tube. **Open** 10am-6pm Mon-Wed, Fri, Sat; 10am-6.30pm Thur. **Credit** AmEx, MC, V. **Map** p400 J7.
This ethically minded Majorcan company produces cute, comfortable, walkable shoes that have a loyal international following. The collection features mainly round-toed shoes and boots (from around £75) with solid soles; recent additions include the delicate and pretty Casi Casi, which was based on the design of a ballet slipper.

Church's Shoes
201 Regent Street, Oxford Circus, W1B 4NA (77342438/www.churchsshoes.com). Oxford Circus tube. **Open** 10am-6.30pm Mon-Wed, Fri, Sat; 10am-7.30pm Thur; noon-6pm Sun. **Credit** AmEx, MC, V. **Map** p398 J6.
Now owned by Prada, Church's is still synonymous with classic British quality – the shoes have been made in Northamptonshire since 1873. Brogues, Oxfords and loafers start at £235, rising to £1,800.

Jimmy Choo
169 Draycott Avenue, Chelsea, SW3 3AJ (7584 6111/www.jimmychoo.com). South Kensington tube. **Open** 10am-6pm Mon, Tue, Thur-Sat; 10am-7pm Wed; 1-6pm Sun. **Credit** AmEx, MC, V. **Map** p397 E10.
A Chelsea townhouse is a fitting temple for Choo's footwear, with plush purple sofas for A-list bottoms. Buyers splashing out upwards of £290 can rest assured their purchase has fashion staying power. There are some spectacular evening shoes, such as satin sandals with real pearl clusters.

Manolo Blahnik
49-51 Old Church Street, Chelsea, SW3 5BS (7352 3863). Sloane Square tube then 11, 19, 22 bus. **Open** 10am-5.30pm Mon-Fri; 10.30am-5pm Sat. **Credit** AmEx, MC, V. **Map** p397 D11.
The celebrated designer's exclusive salon (you have to ring a bell to be admitted) has occupied the same spot for 30 years – and has a loyal clientele. Shoes cost from £300 upwards, and the choice of options and colours is dazzling. There are dyed and shaved ponyskin shoes with lizard ankle straps (£575) and high-heeled shearling knee boots (£650).

Natural Shoe Store
21 Neal Street, Covent Garden, WC2H 9PU (7836 5254/www.thenaturalshoestore.com). Covent Garden tube. **Open** 9.45am-6pm Mon, Tue; 9.45am-7pm Wed-Fri; 9.45am-6.30pm Sat; 11.45-5.30pm Sun. **Credit** AmEx, MC, V. **Map** p399 L6.
This Covent Garden stalwart was once a haven of hippiedom. Foot-friendly designs from European shoemakers Arche, Birkenstock, Ecco and Trippen line the cut-log shelves. Expect to pay £60-£100.

Office
57 Neal Street, Covent Garden, WC2H 4NP (7379 1896/www.officelondon.co.uk). Covent Garden tube. **Open** 10am-7.30pm Mon-Wed, Fri; 10am-8pm Thur; 10am-7pm Sat; noon-6pm Sun. **Credit** AmEx, MC, V. **Map** p399 L6.
Men can try the hip variations on traditional styles (from £50) and streamlined designs by Paul Smith (from around £125). The women's collection explodes with colour and creativity – pumps in leopard print or polka dots (from £39.99).

Shellys
266-70 Regent Street, Marylebone, W1B 3AH (7287 0939/www.shellys.co.uk). Oxford Circus tube. **Open** 10am-7pm Mon-Wed, Fri, Sat; 10am-8pm Thur; noon-6pm Sun. **Credit** AmEx, MC, V. **Map** p398 J6.
If you want to sport the latest looks without shelling out three figures, take a tip from Kylie and Sadie Frost and come here. Shellys collaborates with designers such as Peter Jensen and Jessica Ogden. The range includes fabulous boots, and shoes from T-bars to disco brights (£50-£100).

Tailors

Since the middle of the 19th century, **Savile Row**, Mayfair, W1, has been the traditional home of men's tailoring. *See also p235.*

Ozwald Boateng
9 Vigo Street, Mayfair, W1X 1AL (7437 0620). Green Park tube. **Open** 10am-6pm Mon-Wed; 10am-7pm Thur-Sat. **Credit** AmEx, MC, V. **Map** p400 J7.
Staff here are happy to talk about their brushes with fame – Daniel Day Lewis gave his acceptance speech at the 2003 Oscars in a Boateng suit; other clients include Spike Lee, Lennox Lewis, Ray Winstone and Anthony Hopkins. The recently refurbished shop has bespoke suits starting at £2,500, made to measure at £1,500 and ready to wear at £895.

Timothy Everest
32 Elder Street, Spitalfields, E1 6BT (7377 5770/www.timothyeverest.co.uk). Liverpool Street tube/rail. **Open** 9am-6pm Mon-Fri; 9am-4pm Sat. **Credit** AmEx, MC, V. **Map** p403 R5.
What do Jarvis Cocker, Tom Cruise and David Beckham have in common? A fondness for hand-made suits by Timothy Everest. Everest rejects the rigidity of more conventionally 'classic' cuts for easier styles of suit in a range of soft fabrics such as mohair. Bespoke two-pieces start at £1,395, but a made-to-measure suit can cost as little as £695.

Food & drink

Many department stores (*see p233*) have fabulous food halls. For food markets, *see p251*.

Bakeries & pâtisseries

Along with those listed here, there are others in the **Restaurants** chapter (*see p190-216*). There are plenty of pâtisseries in Soho, including on Old Compton Street, **Amato Caffe/ Pasticceria** (No.14, 7734 5733) and **Pâtisserie Valerie** (No.44, 7437 3466).

& Clarke's
122 Kensington Church Street, Kensington, W8 4BH (7229 2190/www.sallyclarke.com). Notting Hill Gate tube. **Open** 8am-8pm Mon-Fri; 8am-4pm Sat. **Credit** AmEx, MC, V. **Map** p394 B8.
This bakery makes, shapes and bakes over 2,000 loaves a night, using top-quality ingredients. Breads include honey wholewheat, fig and fennel, sourdough, onion, raisin, rye and ficelle. Croissants (almond/cheese/chocolate) and brioches are also dished up at breakfast time.

Paul Bakery & Tearoom

115 Marylebone High Street, Marylebone, W1U 4SB (7224 5615). Bond Street tube. **Open** 8am-7pm Mon-Fri; 9am-7pm Sat, Sun. **Credit** MC, DC, V. **Map** p398 G4.

Dating back to 1889, this bakery has more than 200 outlets in France, two in London and one in Dubai. Fruit tarts (around £11.50), such as *tarte aux myrtilles* (blueberry), sit next to a range of breads, including *fougasses,* six-grain and *pain de campagne.* Light meals and pastries are served in the tearoom. **Other locations**: 9 Bedford Street, Covent Garden, WC2E 9ED (7836 3304).

Confectioners

Charbonnel et Walker

Royal Arcade, 28 Old Bond Street, Mayfair, W1S 4BT (7491 0939/www.charbonnel.co.uk). Green Park tube. **Open** 10am-6pm Mon-Wed, Fri, Sat; 10am-6.30pm Thur. **Credit** AmEx, MC, V. **Map** p400 J7.

Founded in 1875, this celebrated confectioner has followed the same traditional recipes ever since. Rose and violet crèmes and luxurious drinking chocolate are enduring favourites; recent additions include delicately flavoured 65% cocoa bars.

The Chocolate Society

36 Elizabeth Street, Chelsea, SW1W 9NZ (7259 9222/www.chocolate.co.uk). Sloane Square tube. **Open** 9.30am-5.30pm Mon-Sat: 9.30am-4pm Sun. **Credit** MC, V. **Map** p400 G10.

This temple to chocolate is dedicated to proving there's a huge difference between mass-marketed confectionery and gourmet chocolate. Valhrona comes in all shapes and sizes – as lovely handmade truffles or in huge slabs for cooking (from £18/kg). The shop doubles as a café in summer, serving ice-cream, hot chocolate and sundaes.

Pierre Marcolini

6 Lancer Square, Kensington, W8 4EH (7795 6611). High Street Kensington tube. **Open** 10am-7pm Mon-Sat. **Credit** AmEx, MC, V.

This company is one of the few to develop its own chocolate from the selection of the bean to the final product, pralines being the pièce de résistance. The most decadent are the ones moulded into the shape of golf balls (white chocolate encasing a shelled walnut in liquid caramel).

Delicatessens

Flâneur Food Hall

41 Farringdon Road, Farringdon, EC1M 3JB (7404 4422). Farringdon tube/rail. **Open** 9am-10pm Mon-Sat; 9am-6pm Sun. **Credit** AmEx, DC, MC, V. **Map** p402 N4.

This huge deli, which also has a restaurant at the back, stocks a mind-boggling variety of preserves, honeys, chocolate, oils, vinegars, sauces and caviar, stacked on shelves that seem to reach out of sight to the very high ceiling. Breads, cakes and pastries (dark chocolate and strawberry tart, apple streusel cake) are made on site. The meats and cheeses are mostly sourced from smaller producers.

The Grocer on Elgin

6 Elgin Crescent, Notting Hill, W11 2HX (7221 3844/www.thegroceron.com). Ladbroke Grove or Notting Hill Gate tube. **Open** 9am-9pm Mon-Fri; 9am-7pm Sat, Sun. **Credit** MC, V.

This minimalist shrine to ready meals combines practicality with style. Three chilled cabinets contain a changing menu of freshly made mains, side dishes and desserts. Expect the likes of cassoulet, duck curry, wild mushroom risotto and red lentil dhal, along with basics such as mixed vegetables.

Le Pont de la Tour Food Store

Butlers Wharf Building, 36D Shad Thames, Borough, SE1 2YE (7403 4030/www.conran.com). London Bridge tube/rail. **Open** 8.30am-8.30pm Mon-Fri; 10am-6pm Sat, Sun. **Credit** AmEx, MC, V. **Map** p405 R8.

This deli gets the same fresh produce as the kitchen of the eponymous Conran restaurant round the corner. Bread, which can be made to order, comes fresh from the on-site bakery, as do the cakes and pastries. Daily changing produce includes the likes of fresh salmon and Scottish fillet steaks. The deli also sells fresh fruit and veg, handmade pasta, tea and freshly ground coffee. Sandwiches and soups are sold from noon to 3pm.

Wines & spirits

Booze store **Oddbins** (www.oddbins.com for locations around London) is also hard to beat.

Gerry's

74 Old Compton Street, Soho, W1 (7434 4215). Leicester Square tube. **Open** 9am-6.30pm Mon-Fri; 9am-5.30pm Sat. **No credit cards**. **Map** p399 K6.

Gerry's shop has the weird and wonderful of the spirit and liqueur world: an Eiffel Tower-shaped bottle of absinthe, for example, or more than 100 vodkas, including a cannabis-flavoured version.

Milroy's of Soho

3 Greek Street, Soho, W1 (7437 9311/ www.milroys.co.uk). Tottenham Court Road tube. **Open** 11am-7pm Mon-Sat. **Credit** AmEx, MC, V. **Map** p399 K6.

London's most famous whisky specialist has been around for almost 40 years, and stocks around 650 types. There is virtually no version of the spirit that you cannot find here.

Gifts & stationery

Some museum and gallery shops are also great for gifts. Try the **National Gallery** (*see p127*) for cards and stationery; the **British Museum** (*see p101*) for souvenirs and the **Science Museum** (*see p136*) for children's toys.

Craft complexes

Maybe you were born to shop, but your joy's been sapped by the sameness of the high street. Or perhaps you're an art collector but want to browse before buying. Either way, if you don't yet know about London's design-retail spaces, you're in for a treat.

In these big buildings, often converted from industrial use, artists and designers of all stripes hire studio space. Visitors are welcome, especially those intending to buy finished work or commission special pieces.

The easiest time to go – and the best way to get an overview of what's on offer – is on open days. Most spaces hold these twice yearly, around late November and early December and again in late June or early July. You can also visit by appointment.

Oxo Tower Wharf on the South Bank (Bargehouse Street, *see p73*), is the exception: its 33 studios are open to the public Tuesday to Sunday from 11am to 6pm. Tenants range from children's clothiers **Little Badgers** (whose cool designs have been bought by Madonna and Bono) to **Bodo Sperlein**, the acclaimed maker of austere china and home accessories.

The adjacent **Gabriel's Wharf** is more craft than art, but here, too, you can catch artists at work and commission pieces.

Popular for bespoke work is **Cockpit Arts** (Cockpit Yard, Northington Street, 7419 1959). Contemporary silver jewellery by Cockpit artist **Fiona Bellars** is much in demand, and so is the textile work of **Claire Kitchener**, who specialises in embroidery. The more than 100 Cockpit artists also include witty knitwear designer **Hikaru Noguchi** (www.hikarunoguchi.com), who weaves everything from socks to bikinis, and **Scott King**, whose perspex cuff and pink visor Kylie Minogue wears.

At **Great Western Studios** (The Lost Goods Building, Great Western Road, 7221 0100), a vast complex tucked away behind a bus garage, the main emphasis is on the fine arts. Tenants include painter **Sophie Smallhorn**, who's been called the new Bridget Riley, and stone sculptor **Belinda Eade**, who makes everything from bowls to garden grottoes. You can visit the spaces of 160 artists on twice-yearly open days, or call for an appointment.

Open studio days are also held at the **Clerkenwell Green Association**, whose artists continue the area's jewellery-making tradition, and the **Chocolate Factory** in Dalston, which is strong on ceramics and housewares (Farleigh Place, 7503 6961).

Eat, Drink, Shop

Mont Blanc

60-61 Burlington Arcade, Piccadilly, W1J 0QP (7493 6369/www.montblanc.com). Green Park or Piccadilly Circus tube. **Open** 9.30am-5.30pm Mon-Sat. **Credit** AmEx, MC, V. **Map** p400 J7.

The name needs no introduction. Mont Blanc is well known for its posh pens (fountain pens from £159), as well as basic luxury goods: lambskin platinum-plated wallets, sunglasses, watches and belts.

Other locations: 13 Old Bond Street, Piccadilly, W1S 4DL (7629 5883); Royal Exchange, Threadneedle Street, City, EC3V 3LL (7929 4200); Canary Wharf, Docklands, E14 5AH (7719 1919.

Paperchase

213-15 Tottenham Court Road, Fitzrovia, W1T 9PS (7467 6200/www.paperchase.co.uk). Goodge Street tube. **Open** 9.30am-7pm Mon, Wed, Fri, Sat; 10am-7pm Tue; 9.30am-8pm Thur; noon-6pm Sun. **Credit** AmEx, MC, V. **Map** p399 K5.

This three-storey superstore is crammed with useful, tasteful and silly items, from calendars and invitations to cards and notepaper. Upstairs there's a more upmarket range, from Lexon accessories, posh pens, Filofaxes and a growing selection of furniture.

Other locations: throughout the city.

Smythson

40 New Bond Street, Oxford Circus, W1S 2DE (7629 8558/www.smythson.com). Bond Street tube. **Open** 9.30am-6pm Mon-Wed, Fri; 10am-6pm Thur, Sat. **Credit** AmEx, DC, MC, V. **Map** p399 H6.

An elegant selection of fine stationery and gifts is sold here, with classy (and pricey) items covering diaries, photo albums, wallets and more.

Other locations: 135 Sloane Street, Knightsbridge, SW1X 3AX (7730 5520).

Health & beauty

Beauty services

The Dorchester Spa

Dorchester Hotel, Park Lane, Mayfair, W1A 2HJ (7495 7335/www.dorchesterhotel.com). Green Park or Hyde Park Corner tube. **Open** 7am-9pm daily. **Credit** AmEx, DC, MC, V. **Map** p400 G8.

The Dorchester (*see also p49*) is traditional luxury at its best, and its five-star service and treatments are reasonably priced. A day's use of the sauna, steamroom, gym and whirlpool is £15 with a treatment, £35 without; massages are about £65.

The Refinery

60 Brook Street, Mayfair, W1K 5DU (7409 2001/ www.the-refinery.com). Bond Street tube. **Open** 10am-7pm Mon, Tue; 10am-9pm Wed-Fri; 9am-6pm Sat; 11am-5pm Sun. **Credit** MC, V. **Map** p398 H6.

This spa within an impressive Mayfair townhouse is designed entirely for men. The Refinery aims for a 'clubby' feel, and the expert staff cater for the likes of Pierce Brosnan, as well as a loyal following of businessmen and travellers. Treatments range from quick massages and facials (£20) to LaStone therapy (£100 for 90mins) and therapeutic massage.

The Sanctuary

12 Floral Street, Covent Garden, WC2E 9DH (0870 063 0300/www.thesanctuary.co.uk). Covent Garden tube. **Open** 9.30am-6pm Mon, Tue; 9.30am-10pm Wed-Fri; 10am-8pm Sat, Sun. **Credit** AmEx, DC, MC, V. **Map** p401 L6.

In an effort to get away from its '80s image, this famous women-only spa has had a makeover. The emphasis here is on relaxation, with spa pools, a steamroom and space for chilling. The reflexology (£49) is excellent. On the downside, you may be given a hard sell with the Sanctuary's own products.

SPAce.NK

127-31 Westbourne Grove, Notting Hill, W2 4UP (7727 8002/www.spa-nk.com). Notting Hill Gate tube. **Open** 10am-7pm Mon, Fri, 9am-9pm Tue-Thur; 9am-7pm Sat; 10am-5pm Sun. **Credit** AmEx, DC, MC, V. **Map** p394 B6.

The menu of treatments at SPAce.NK is extensive (allow the therapists to help you choose which one to have). The shiatsu facial (£65 for 75mins) is great for dry skin, leaving it soft and blemish-free for weeks.

Other locations: throughout the city.

Urban Retreat

5th floor, Harrods, 87-135 Brompton Road, Knightsbridge, SW1X 7XL (7893 8333/www. harrods.com). Knightsbridge tube. **Open** 10am-7pm Mon-Sat. **Credit** AmEx, DC, MC, V. **Map** p397 F9.

This once-tired old salon has recently been transformed into a shrine to beauty. Still, the biggest news is the advent of the world's first Crème de la Mer facials (from £95 for an hour). Treatments use products such as Guinot, Thalgo and La Prairie. Specialist massages include the Hydrotherm Massage (£80 for an hour), during which warm water bags support you, so you don't turn over.

Cosmetics, skincare & perfume

Department stores (*see p233*) are the places to go for most upmarket make-up brands.

Aveda Lifestyle Institute

174 High Holborn, Holborn, WC1V 7AA (7759 7355). Holborn tube. **Open** 9am-7pm Mon-Fri; 9am-6.30pm Sat. **Credit** AmEx, MC, V. **Map** p398 G5.

Environmentally friendly, luxury products are Aveda's *raison d'être*. As well as the famous hair salon, treatment rooms and an organic café, this gorgeous flagship store has the full range of lovely shampoos, skin-care and cosmetics products.

Other locations: 28-9 Marylebone High Street, W1 (7224 3157).

Boots

75 Queensway, Bayswater, W2 4QH (7229 9266/ www.wellbeing.com). Bayswater tube. **Open** 9am-10pm Mon-Sat; 2-10pm Sun. **Credit** MC, V. **Map** p394 C6.

The ubiquitous Boots chain is still going strong as the place to pick up your deodorant and cotton buds. In the larger stores you'll find beauty ranges like Ruby & Millie along with the Rimmel, but it's Boots' own No7 collection that's worth checking out for good budget alternatives to pricey brands.

Other locations: throughout the city.

Kiehl's

29 Monmouth Street, Covent Garden, WC2H 9DD (7240 2411/www.kiehls.co.uk). Covent Garden or Leicester Square tube. **Open** 10.30am-7pm Mon-Sat; noon-5pm Sun. **Credit** AmEx, DC, MC, V. **Map** p399 L6.

The original pharmacy in New York was founded in 1851 but the company moves with the times. It has built its enviable reputation by offering free consultations and lots of samples. The lip balms and the Pineapple Papaya Face Scrub are both popular.

MAC Cosmetics

109 King's Road, Chelsea, SW3 4PA (7349 0022/ www.maccosmetics.com). Sloane Square tube. **Open** 10am-6.30pm Mon-Sat; noon-6pm Sun. **Credit** AmEx, MC, V. **Map** p397 F11.

MAC is a favourite among make-up artists, for products like the Spray Fix for foundation, and Strobe Cream, which gives skin a subtle sheen. The cosmetics collection features a huge range of colours.

Other locations: 28 Foubert's Place, Soho, W1F 7PR (7534 9222); 38 Neal Street, Covent Garden, WC2H 9PS (7379 6820).

Neal's Yard Remedies

15 Neal's Yard, Covent Garden, WC2H 9DP (7379 7222/www.nealsyardremedies.com). Covent Garden or Leicester Square tube. **Open** 10am-7pm Mon-Sat; 11am-6pm Sun. **Credit** AmEx, MC, V. **Map** p399 L6.

Rows of big glass jars full of natural herbs line one wall of this attractive shop, a long-standing favourite. A new men's range includes a shaving oil, as well as moisturiser and organic cologne.

Other locations: Chelsea Farmers' Market, Sydney Street, Chelsea, SW3 6NR (7351 6380); 6 Northcote Road, Battersea, SW11 1NT (7223 7141); 9 Elgin Crescent, Notting Hill, W11 2JA (7727 3998).

Origins

51 King's Road, Chelsea, SW3 4ND (7823 6715/ www.origins.com). Sloane Square tube. **Open** 10am-6.30pm Mon, Tue, Thur, Fri; 10am-7pm Wed, Sat; noon-6pm Sun. **Credit** AmEx, MC, V. **Map** p397 F11.

It's hard to leave Origins empty-handed – the products all smell so good and work so well. Look out for the Never A Dull Moment and Perfect World ranges, in particular the latter's bestselling White Tea Skin Guardian (£25). The Paradise Found body scrub (£20) contains coconut-shell flakes. There's a very pretty make-up range too.

Shu Uemura

55 Neal Street, Covent Garden, WC2H 9PJ (7240 7635). Covent Garden tube. **Open** 10.30am-7pm Mon-Sat; noon-5pm Sun. **Credit** AmEx, DC, MC, V. **Map** p399 L6.

Shu Uemura's colourful skincare and make-up products stand out against this flagship store's white and glass decor. Major sellers include the recently reformulated cult cleansing oils (£19.50). We also like the Pleasures of Japan bath oils (£15). The extensive make-up range comes in a tempting array of colours, from palest nude to vivid aquamarine.

Hairdressers

Daniel Hersheson

45 Conduit Street, Oxford Circus, W1S 2YN (7434 1747/www.danielhersheson.com). Oxford Circus tube. **Open** 8.30am-7pm Mon-Sat. **Credit** AmEx, MC, V. **Map** p400 H7.

Despite being known as a celebrity salon (Gwyneth Paltrow is just one of those to have their tresses seen to here), this salon isn't intimidating. For women, a cut by the man himself costs £200, or from £45 to £80 with a stylist (men from £30 to £60).

Diverse Hair

280 Upper Street, Islington, N1 2TZ (7704 6842). Angel tube/Highbury & Islington tube/rail. **Open** 11am-6pm Mon-Fri; 10am-5pm Sat. **No credit cards.**

A very friendly unisex salon, where all-comers are made welcome. Gently groovy music plays (handy if you don't feel like chatting) and there's a laid-back atmosphere. Basic cuts cost £35; a half-head of highlights starts at £56.

Geo F Trumper

9 Curzon Street, Mayfair, W1J 5HQ (7499 1850/www.trumpers.com). Green Park tube. **Open** 9am-5.30pm Mon-Fri; 9am-1pm Sat. **Credit** AmEx, DC, MC, V. **Map** p400 H7.

Old-style gentility is reflected in the curtained barbering booths, dark wood panelling, green leather chairs and red velvet curtains. Striving to remain unchanged since it was founded in 1875, Trumper's has earned the loyalty of its male clients. Haircuts and wet shaves both cost from £26.50, facials are £25 and £45, and shaving lessons from £45.

Mr Topper's

13A Great Russell Street, Bloomsbury, WC1B 3NH (7631 3233). Tottenham Court Road tube. **Open** 9am-6.30pm Mon-Sat; 11am-5.30pm Sun. **No credit cards. Map** p399 K5.

The large sign advertising cuts for £6 (after years at £5, it recently went up) draws in a steady stream of traffic. Customers are waved towards a chair, the clippers come out, and the whole process is over in less than ten minutes. In terms of speed and humourlessness it's slightly reminiscent of a sheep-shearing station, but the cuts are good enough, and the place is constantly busy.

Other locations: throughout the city.

Michaeljohn

25 Albemarle Street, Mayfair, W1S 4HU (7629 6969/www.michaeljohn.co.uk). Green Park tube. **Open** 8am-6.30pm Mon, Sat; 8am-8pm Tue-Fri. **Credit** MC, V. **Map** p400 H7.

Along with a few other famous types, Tony Blair has his hair done at this swanky Mayfair salon. Michaeljohn's client list includes Natalie Imbruglia, Nigella Lawson, Anna Wintour and Dido. Cuts cost £45-£144 (ladies) and £35-£99 (gents), while the technical design team tints and colours from £60.

Opticians

Specsavers

Unit 6, 6-17 Tottenham Court Road, Fitzrovia, W1T 1BG (7580 5115/www.specsavers.com). Tottenham Court Road tube. **Open** 10am-8pm Mon-Fri; 10am-7pm Sat; noon-6pm Sun. **Credit** AmEx, DC, MC, V. **Map** p399 K5.

'Inoffensive' sums up Specsavers – from the decor and the service to the range of products on offer. But with prices starting at £30 for (albeit drab) plastic frames, who's arguing? To get something a bit more stylish, you have to move up to the £75 mark.

Other locations: throughout the city.

Spex in the City

1 Shorts Gardens, Covent Garden, WC2H 9AT (7240 0243/www.spexinthecity.com). Covent Garden or Leicester Square tube. **Open** 11am-6.30pm Mon-Sat; 1-5pm Sun. **Credit** DC, MC, V. **Map** p399 L6.

This funky, independent optician has an idiosyncratic array of styles ranging from the quirky to the sophisticated, with Alain Mikli, Philippe Starck, Porsche and Brit designers Booth & Bruce. Mention the website and you get an eye test for just £15.

Homewares

Conran Shop

Michelin House, 81 Fulham Road, Fulham, SW3 6RD (7589 7401/www.conran.com). South Kensington tube. **Open** 10am-6pm Mon, Tue, Fri; 10am-7pm Wed, Thur; 10am-6.30pm Sat; noon-6pm Sun. **Credit** AmEx, MC, V. **Map** p397 E10.

The Conran Shop reflects a type of lifestyle – slick, cosmopolitan and seductive. Everything from food and furniture to style books are sold under one roof. Lighting is strong and has a few upbeat specimens like Star Wars-style light sabres (£55).

Other locations: throughout the city.

eatmyhandbagbitch

37 Drury Lane, Covent Garden, WC2B 5RR (7836 0830/www.eatmyhandbagbitch.co.uk). Covent Garden or Holborn tube. **Open** 10am-6pm Mon-Sat. **Credit** AmEx, MC, V. **Map** p399 L6.

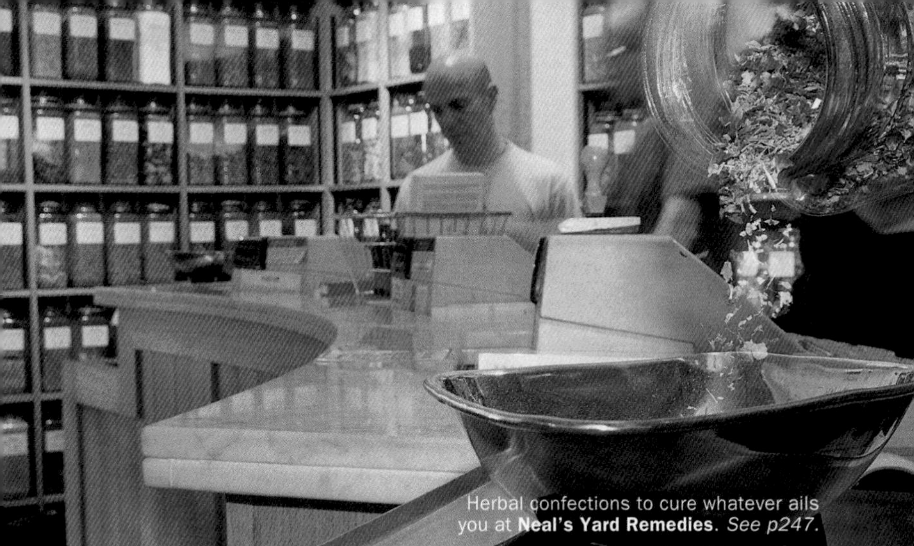
Herbal confections to cure whatever ails you at **Neal's Yard Remedies**. *See p247.*

Despite the name of the shop, the owners take a very serious approach to 20th-century design. A new line in custom-made leather goods can create anything from a set of six coasters (£75) to that must-have accessory, a travelling bar (£13,000). Although prices go into the thousands, repro versions of Baron Albrizzi's acrylic 1968 designs are priced from £75.

Habitat

196 Tottenham Court Road, Fitzrovia, W1T 7LG (7631 3880/www.habitat.net). Goodge Street tube. **Open** 10am-6pm Mon-Wed; 10am-8pm Thur; 10am-6.30pm Fri; 9.30am-6.30pm Sat; noon-6pm Sun. **Credit** AmEx, MC, V. **Map** p399 K5.

This trendy shopping beacon employs the hippest designers to turn out the best looks. Pieces to track include the Daisy Light (£15), the sturdy Cube storage unit, and the enduring Verdi chair (from £89).
Other locations: throughout the city.

Heal's

196 Tottenham Court Road, Fitzrovia, W1T 7LQ (7636 1666/www.heals.co.uk). Goodge Street tube. **Open** 10am-6pm Mon-Wed; 10am-8pm Thur; 10am-6.30pm Fri; 9.30am-6.30pm Sat; noon-6pm Sun. **Credit** AmEx, DC, MC, V. **Map** p399 K5.

Although pricier and generally less cutting edge than Habitat, Heal's produces stylish furniture and housewares. Among the choicest pieces are Matthew Hilton's glass and steel Flipper table (£630). Glassware and kitchenware are particularly fine.
Other locations: 234 King's Road, Chelsea, SW3 5UA (7349 8411); 49-51 Eden Street, Kingston-upon-Thames, Surrey KT1 1BW (8614 5900).

Markets

The markets listed below are the most famous in the capital, and not too far away from the centre, or the tourist areas. There are some fantastic markets in more far-flung places. Down south in Battersea, **Northcote Road Market** (9am-5pm Thur-Sat) has lovely food stalls; in Hackney **Ridley Road Market** (open 7am-5pm Mon-Sat) is fine for African specialities. Also notable for Afro/Caribbean goodies is **Shepherd's Bush Market** (*see p185*); while for sheer length and variety, try the traditional street market way up in Walthamstow (*see p160*).

General

Brick Lane Market

Brick Lane – north of railway bridge, Cygnet Street, Sclater Street, E1; Bacon Street, Cheshire Street, Chilton Street, E2. Aldgate East or Shoreditch tube/Liverpool Street tube/rail. **Open** 8am-2pm Sun. **Map** p403 S5.

A traditional flea market, Brick Lane's stalls and shops sell cheap soaps and razors, magazines, bagels, bric-a-brac, odd second-hand clothes, old furniture and seafood. The market spreads out along a number of narrow streets that are now lined with trendy clothes boutiques and expensive home accessories stores, which contrast with the profusion of utter tat. The most browsable bit is the warehouse on Cheshire Street selling microwaves, TVs, kitchen equipment, bric-a-brac, CDs, DVDs, furniture, glasses and everything else under the sun.

Brixton Market

Electric Avenue, Pope's Road, Brixton Station Road, Atlantic Road, SW9. Brixton tube/rail. **Open** 8am-6pm Mon-Fri; 8am-5.30pm Sat.

Visiting Brixton's thronging market is like being plunged into another country. Electric Avenue is packed with stalls piled high with exotic fruit and veg, while permanent stores are packed with halal meats and fish. As the market moves into Atlantic Road it turns more towards clothes, towels, toys,

It's not as cool as it used to be, but **Camden Market** still tries.

cheap wallets and mobile phone covers, and on Saturdays a few stalls of rather jumbly second-hand clothes appear along Brixton Station Road.

Camden Market

Camden Market *Camden High Street, junction with Buck Street, NW1 (7278 4444).* **Open** 9.30am-5.30pm daily.
Camden Lock *off Chalk Farm Road, NW1 8AF (7485 3459).* **Open** 10am-6pm daily.
Stables Market *off Chalk Farm Road, opposite junction with Hartland Road, NW1 8AH (7485 5511).* **Open** 9.30am-5.30pm daily.
Camden Canal Market *off Chalk Farm Road, south of junction with Castlehaven Road, NW1 9XJ (7485 8355).* **Open** 9am-6.30pm Fri-Sun.
Electric Market *Camden High Street, south of junction with Dewsbury Terrace, NW1.* **Open** 10am-6pm Sun.
All Camden Town tube.

Camden Market has changed beyond all recognition in the past decade. While the section just next to the tube station continues to sell clubby T-shirts, trendy platform shoes and cheap interpretations of current fashions, the rest bears little resemblance to the cutting-edge place it was years ago. The Electric Market sells second-hand clothes and young designers' wares, but it's neither cheap nor particularly exciting. In the building beside the Lock and its courtyard are crafty goods including jewellery, funky handmade boxes, candles, picture frames and mirrors. The Stables Yard is now full of permanent clothes and food huts. In the railway arches, upmarket, permanent retro stalls and clubwear outlets have taken over. Beside the canal, an avenue of food stalls sends out enticing smells, from Indian to Mexican. Here you'll also find interesting craft stalls selling bags and accessories. In the Stables at the Chalk Farm end are antiques and design furniture.

Greenwich Market

Antiques Market *Greenwich High Road, SE10.* **Open** 9am-5pm Sat, Sun.
Central Market *off Stockwell Street, opposite Hotel Ibis, SE10.* **Open** *Outdoor* 7am-6pm Sat; 7am-5pm Sun. *Indoor* 10am-5pm Fri, Sat; 10am-6pm Sun.
Crafts Market *College Approach, SE10.* **Open** *Antiques & collectibles* 7.30am-5.30pm Thur. *Arts & crafts* 9.30am-5.30pm Thur-Sun.
Food Market *off Stockwell Street, opposite Hotel Ibis, SE10.* **Open** 10am-4pm Sat.
All Greenwich rail/DLR.

Heading into the town centre from the station you come first to the antiques market, a collection of bric-a-brac and junk that varies from tat to treasures. Next along is the Village Market, where a second-hand clothes market mingles Chinese silk dresses, home furnishings and lighting, CDs and more. Passing the food court, you come to the covered Crafts Market, Greenwich's jewel in the crown. Ideal for gift-hunting, it sells all manner of crafts, from the usual (hand-knitted jumpers), through the eclectic (paper lampshades, candles) to the just plain bizarre (framed dead beetles and butterflies).

Petticoat Lane Market

Middlesex Street, Goulston Street, New Goulston Street, Toynbee Street, Wentworth Street, Bell Lane, Cobb Street, Leyden Street, Strype Street, Old Castle Street, Cutler Street, E1. Liverpool Street tube/rail. **Open** 10am-2pm Mon-Fri; 9am-2pm Sun. **Map** p405 R6.

Selling mainly cheap clothes, toys and electronic goods, Petticoat Lane is the best place to come to buy smart women's clothes and high street brands at knock-down prices. Recent bargains included a linen suit for £30 and a quality woollen overcoat for £40. The market moves with the seasons and is packed with unmissable bargains.

Portobello Road Market

Portobello Road, W10, W11; Golborne Road, W10. Ladbroke Grove, Notting Hill Gate or Westbourne Park tube. **Open** *General* 8am-6.30pm Mon-Wed, Fri, Sat; 8am-1pm Thur. *Antiques* 5.30am-4.30pm Sat. **Map** p394 A6.

Portobello Road is like several markets in one. Starting at the Notting Hill end are mainly antiques and general Victoriana. Further up you come to food stalls, ranging from traditional fruit and veg to tasty cheeses, stuffed olives, organic crackers and crêpes. Next up come clothes and jewellery. The cafés under the Westway are a good place to rest before plunging into the new designer clothes and vintage wear along the walkway to Ladbroke Grove, near a random selection of bric-a-brac, old typewriters, antique military uniforms and photographs of Hitler.

Spitalfields Market

Commercial Street, between Lamb Street & Brushfield Street, E1 (7247 8556). Liverpool Street tube/rail. **Open** *General market* 10am-4pm Mon-Fri; 9am-5pm Sun. *Fashion market* 10am-4pm Thur. **Map** p403 R5.

Getting trendier by the week, Spitalfields Market is in that little bit of the East End rapidly being bulldozed and replaced by bright shiny buildings. The big indoor market is surrounded by cool shops and good pubs, while inside, stalls offer anything from stamps, CDs and books to jewellery, handmade cards and aromatherapy products. Fashion varies from second-hand clothes to the work of young designers. There are cake and bread stalls, and stands selling grub at bargain prices.

Flowers

Columbia Road Market

Columbia Road, between Gosset Street & the Royal Oak pub, Bethnal Green, E2. Bus 26, 48, 55. **Open** 8am-1pm Sun. **No credit cards**. **Map** p403 S3.

Every Sunday, hundreds of London gardeners make an early-morning pilgrimage to Columbia Road. The keenest gardeners arrive at the crack of dawn, but there's plenty still here later on. Half the stalls are dedicated to cut flowers, and the rest offer potted plants, bedding plants and trees, and everything from pak choi to purple basil at £1 a pot.

Food

Farmers' Markets are the way forward for city folk who want to buy food that has been grown, reared and prepared by the stallholder, and produced reasonably locally. The most central ones are in **Marylebone** (Cramer Street car park, 7704 9659; open 10am-2pm Sun) and **Pimlico** (Orange Square, corner of Pimlico Road and Ebury Street, 7704 9659; open 9am-1pm Sat). For more, phone 01225 787914, or try www.farmersmarkets.net.

Borough Market

Between Borough High Street, Bedale Street, Stoney Street & Winchester Walk, SE1 1TL (www.boroughmarket.org.uk). London Bridge tube/rail. **Open** noon-6pm Fri; 9am-4pm Sat. **Map** p405 P8.

It's not only celebrity chefs who adore this place. Borough Market was recently voted top tourist attraction in a London survey, and if you love food you'll know why. There are stalls of organic breads, cakes, honeys, cheeses, meats, fruit and veg, as well as smoothies and savouries.

Music

Megastores

HMV

150 Oxford Street, Oxford Circus, W1D 1DJ (7631 3423/www.hmv.co.uk). Oxford Circus tube. **Open** 9am-8pm Mon, Wed, Fri, Sat; 9.30am-8pm Tue; 9am-9pm Thur; 11.45am-6pm Sun. **Credit** AmEx, DC, MC, V. **Map** p398 J6.

This place is enormous, with CDs, books, DVDs, videos, games and posters in the thousands. The emphasis is clearly on shifting bucketloads of goods, but underground dance, trance and hip hop (often on vinyl) are getting more of a look-in these days. **Other locations**: throughout the city.

Tower Records

1 Piccadilly Circus, Piccadilly, W1J 0TR (7439 2500/www.towerrecords.co.uk). Piccadilly Circus tube. **Open** 9am-11pm Mon-Sat; noon-6pm Sun. **Credit** AmEx, MC, V. **Map** p400 J7.

Tower does a tad better than its competitors on new releases, with an impressive dance and techno section on vinyl. You're also better off here if you're after jazz, classical, world music, folk or opera. Other than that it's just a corporate flagship (this is the only store left since it was bought by Virgin).

Virgin Megastore

14-16 Oxford Street, Fitzrovia, W1N 9FL (7631 1234/www.virgin.com). Tottenham Court Road tube. **Open** 10am-8.30pm Mon-Wed, Fri, Sat; 10am-9pm Thur; noon-6pm Sun. **Credit** AmEx, MC, V. **Map** p399 K6.

The Virgin empire is alive and well on Oxford Street, where this place is always teeming. Music-wise,

there's a massive range on CD that even squeezes in relatively obscure dance, hip hop and soul. Fans of jazz, folk, classical and opera are also well served. Videos and DVDs have their own floor now, and there are plenty of games, magazines, books, T-shirts and accessories.
Other locations: throughout the city.

Specialist music shops

Soho's Berwick Street is a CD and LP mecca – **Selectadisc** (No.34) and **Sister Ray** (No.94) are strong on indie and mainstream, while **Reckless** (No.30) is good for mainstream; there's Jamaican music at **Daddy Kool** (No.12) and cut-price CDs at **Mr CD** (No.80).

Intoxica!

231 Portobello Road, Notting Hill, W11 1LT (7229 8010/www.intoxica.co.uk). Ladbroke Grove tube. **Open** 10.30am-6.30pm Mon-Sat; noon-5pm Sun. **Credit** AmEx, DC, MC, V.
Favourites from the '50s, '60s and '70s come on collectable LP and 45 originals and re-issues at this place. Pretty much anything from these eras goes: from '60s rock, soul and funk via punk, new wave and garage. There's a small selection of books, plus soundtracks and original posters from old movies.

Harold Moores Records

2 Great Marlborough Street, Soho, W1F 7HQ (7437 1576/www.hmrecords.co.uk). Oxford Circus tube. **Open** 10.30am-6.30pm Mon-Sat, noon-6pm Sun. **Credit** AmEx, MC, V. **Map** p398 J6.
One of London's most venerable classical record stores keeps its best section downstairs, where careful previous owners have kept the 70,000 mostly classical LPs in near-mint condition. There's also an estimable selection of classical concerts on DVD and video, and a mail-order service.

Honest Jon's

278 Portobello Road, Notting Hill, W10 5TE (8969 9822/www.honestjons.com). Ladbroke Grove tube. **Open** 10am-6pm Mon-Sat; 11am-5pm Sun. **Credit** AmEx, DC, MC, V. **Map** p394 A6.
The jazz and world music floor at this long established shop is the centre of attention, with plenty of vinyl rarities alongside the contemporary CDs. Newer tastes are catered for on the reggae floor, which features a quality range of soul, hip hop, funk, Latin, breaks and R&B amid the Marleys.

MDC Classic Music

437 The Strand, Covent Garden, WC2R 0RN (7240 2157/www.mdcmusic.co.uk). Embankment tube/ Charing Cross tube/rail. **Open** 9am-7pm Mon-Sat; noon-6pm Sun. **Credit** AmEx, MC, V. **Map** p401 L7.
'Consumer classical' might be the term that best describes the range at this large West End store. Contemporary releases, mainly on CD, are well represented; prices start at around a fiver, but go up from there. Recordings of West End concerts and musicals are also sold here.

Rough Trade

130 Talbot Road, Notting Hill, W11 1JA (7229 8541/www.roughtrade.com). Ladbroke Grove tube. **Open** 10am-6.30pm Mon-Sat; 1-5pm Sun. **Credit** AmEx, MC, V. **Map** p394 A5.
Keeping the sound of the underground alive and kicking, as it has done for a quarter of a century, Rough Trade serves obscurity-hunters well with indie releases on CD and vinyl. Sublime or ridiculous, most nascent trends are here.

Pharmacies

High street chemists **Boots** (*see p247*) also runs pharmacies in many of its central locations, some of which stay open late.

Bliss Chemist

5-6 Marble Arch, Marylebone, W1 (7723 6116). Marble Arch tube. **Open** 9am-midnight daily. **Credit** AmEx, MC, V. **Map** p395 F6.
This handy store has a late-night pharmacy.

Sport & adventure

Action Bikes

23-6 Embankment Place, Covent Garden, WC2N 6NN (7930 2525/www.actionbikes.co.uk). Embankment tube. **Open** 9am-6pm Mon-Wed, Fri; 9am-7pm Thur; 9.30am-5.30pm Sat. **Credit** AmEx, MC, V. **Map** p401 L7.
The flagship store of this great-value chain of bike shops has the UK's only Oakley concession, with the full complement of the brand's kit and clothing. Other names stocked include Marin and Trek, with excellent offers across all makes. Folding and city bikes are particularly big business.
Other locations: throughout the city.

Blacks

10-11 Holborn, Holborn, EC1N 2LE (7404 5681/www.blacks.co.uk). Chancery Lane tube. **Open** 9.30am-6pm Mon-Wed, Fri; 9.30am-7pm Thur; 9.30am-5.30pm Sat; 11am-5pm Sun. **Credit** AmEx, MC, V. **Map** p398 G5
An excellent-value outdoor, travel and ski shop with a comprehensive selection of camping gear, foul-weather wear and sturdy brands such as Berghaus, Sprayway and Lowe Alpine. Competitively priced skiing equipment is sold in season.
Other locations: throughout the city.

Lillywhites

24-36 Lower Regent Street, St James's, SW1Y 4QF (0870 333 9600/www.sports-soccer.co.uk). Piccadilly Circus tube. **Open** 10am-9pm Mon-Sat; noon-6pm Sun. **Credit** AmEx, DC, MC, V. **Map** p401 K7.
Since being bought by the Sports Soccer group, Britain's most famous sports store now caters for fewer activities. On the plus side, the emphasis is now on value for money, so you can pick up all the gear you need for basics such as cricket, golf, football, and racket sports at very competitive prices.

Fun and funky **Spitalfields Market** calls you to the East End. *See p251.*

NikeTown

236 Oxford Street, Oxford Circus, W1W 8LG (7612 0800/www.nike.com). Oxford Circus tube. **Open** 10am-7pm Mon-Wed; 10am-8pm Thur-Sat; noon-6pm Sun. **Credit** AmEx, MC, V. **Map** p399 J6.

The stock of sports footwear and clothing here is very technical (apart from the ground floor, which carries accessories and seasonal lines such as beachwear). As might be expected, football boots and trainers are a particular strength.

Toys & games

In addition to the shops listed in this section, also check out the toy and game sections at the department stores (*see p233*). For computer games, *see p234*.

Benjamin Pollock's Toyshop

44 The Market, Covent Garden Piazza, Covent Garden, WC2E 8RF (7379 7866/www.pollocks-coventgarden.co.uk). Covent Garden tube. **Open** 10.30am-6pm Mon-Sat; 11am-4pm Sun. **Credit** AmEx, MC, V. **Map** p401 L7.

This colourful store is legendary in London. In its wonderful, old-fashioned rooms it holds numerous hand-made toys that would look familiar to many grandparents but that still charm children today. Pollock's is best known for its elaborate toy theatres; one of the best-selling paper theatres for kids to assemble is Jackson's theatre (an affordable £5.95), with its set of and characters from the ballet *Cinderella*. Beautiful French musical boxes with a circus theme (£37.50) are among the popular christening presents.

Cheeky Monkeys

202 Kensington Park Road, Notting Hill, W11 1NR (7792 9022/www.cheekymonkeys.com). Ladbroke Grove tube. **Open** 9.30am-5.30pm Mon-Fri; 10am-5.30pm Sat. **Credit** MC, V.

These lovely, independently owned shops (check the phone book for other locations) feature charming vintage cars, pedal aeroplanes, and wooden dolls' houses alongside paint-your-own bird boxes and some of London's best fancy dress costumes (from smart soldiers and tigers to frogs). Flying off the shelves in this branch is the popular Zamiloo range of houses (£28), people and railways (£30), all designed as a set of stackable cardboard bricks to be assembled by children.

Other locations: throughout the city.

Hamleys

188-96 Regent Street, Soho, W1B 5BT (0870 333 2455/www.hamleys.com). Oxford Circus tube. **Open** 10am-8pm Mon-Sat; noon-6pm Sun. **Credit** AmEx, MC, V. **Map** p400 J7.

If there aren't bubbles or balloons spewing out of Hamleys' entrance on Regent Street, the crowds of jostling youngsters will alert you to its location. The (allegedly) largest toy shop in the world is first and

Shops by area

The City

Flâneur Food Hall (Food & drink, *p245*); **Petticoat Lane Market** (Markets, *p250*).

Holborn & Clerkenwell

Aveda Lifestyle Institute (Health & beauty, *p247*); **Black's** (Sport & adventure, *p252*).

Bloomsbury & Fitzrovia

Ask (Electronics, *p234*); **Cinema Bookshop** (Books, *p231*); **Computer Exchange** (Electronics, *p234*); **Dixons** (Electronics, *p234*); **French's Theatre Bookshop** (Books; *p231*); **Gay's the Word** (Books, *p231*); **Gultronics** (Electronics, *p234*); **HMV** (Music, *p251*); **Habitat** (Homewares, *p249*); **Heal's** (Homewares, *p249*); **High Stakes** (Books; *p231*); **Kingsley Photographic** (Electronics, *p235*); **London Review of Books** (Books; *p230*); **Micro Anvika** (Electronics, *p234*); **Mr Topper** (Health & beauty, *p248*); **Paperchase** (Gifts & stationery, *p246*); **Persephone Books** (Books; *p231*); **Skoob Russell Square** (Books, *p233*); **Specsavers** (Health & beauty, *p248*); **Ulysses** (Books, *p233*); **Virgin Megastore** (Music, *p251*); **Waterstone's** (Books, *p231*).

Marylebone & Oxford Circus

Alfie's Antiques Market (Antiques, *p229*); **Bliss Chemist** (Pharmacies, *p252*); **Books Etc** (Books, *p230*); **Borders** (Books, *p230*); **Cartier** (Fashion accessories, *p243*); **Daniel Hersheson** (Health & beauty, *p248*); **Dorothy Perkins** (Fashion, *p237*); **French Connection** (Fashion, *p237*); **The Girl Can't Help It/Cad van Swankster** (Fashion, *p242*); **Gymboree** (Fashion, *p239*); **H&M** (Fashion, *p237*); **John Lewis** (Department stores, *p233*); **Marks & Spencer** (Department stores, *p234*); **Mikimoto** (Fashion accessories, *p243*); **Miss Selfridge** (Fashion, *p237*); **New Look** (Fashion, *p238*); **NikeTown** (Sport & adventure, *p253*); **Paul Bakery & Tearoom** (Food & drink, *p245*); **Perkins Dry Cleaners** (Fashion accessories, *p243*); **Selfridges** (Department stores, *p234*); **Shellys** (Fashion accessories, *p244*); **Smythson** (Gifts & stationery, *p246*); **Topshop** (Fashion, *p238*); **Whistles** (Fashion, *p239*).

Mayfair & St James's

Angela Hale (Fashion accessories, *p243*); **Browns** (Fashion, *p235*); **Camper** (Fashion accessories, *p243*); **Charbonnel et Walker** (Food & drink, *p245*); **Church's Shoes** (Fashion accessories, *p244*); **Dorchester** (Health & beauty, *p246*); **Fortnum & Mason** (Department stores, *p233*); **Garrard** (Fashion accessories, *p243*); **Geo F Trumper** (Health & beauty, *p248*); **Grays Antiques Market & Grays in the Mews** (Antiques, *p229*); **Jigsaw** (Fashion, *p237*); **Lillywhites** (Sport & adventure, *p252*); **Michaeljohn** (Health & beauty, *p248*); **Mont Blanc** (Gifts & stationery, *p246*); **Ozwald Boateng** (Fashion accessories, *p244*); **The Refinery** (Health & beauty, *p247*); **Tiffany & Co** (Fashion accessories, *p243*); **Tower Records** (Music, *p251*); **Zara** (Fashion, *p239*).

Soho & Leicester Square

Any Amount of Books (Books, *p233*); **Foyles** (Books, *p230*); **Gerry's** (Food & drink, *p245*); **Hamleys** (Toys & games, *p254*); **Harold Moores Records & Video** (Music, *p252*); **Liberty** (Department stores, *p233*); **Milroy's of Soho** (Food & drink, *p245*); **Murder One** (Books, *p231*); **Shipley** (Books, *p231*); **Shop** (Fashion, *p241*).

Covent Garden & St Giles's

Accessorize (Fashion accessories, *p242*); **Action Bikes** (Sport & adventure, *p252*);

foremost a loud, frenetic, exciting experience – and you can get most of the products you're looking for here. The ground floor is where the latest fun toys are demonstrated and a mountain of soft toys is accommodated. The basement is the Cyberzone, full of games and consoles and high-tech gadgets. The first floor is the place for items of a scientific bent, plus a sweet factory and bear depot. On second is everything for pre-schoolers. Third is girlie heaven – aka Barbie World. Fourth has some incredibly large remote-controlled vehicles, plus die-cast models. Fifth, if you can make it that far, has its own café and resident Darth Vader in the Star Wars area.

Mystical Fairies

12 Flask Walk, Hampstead, NW3 1HE (7431 1888). Hampstead tube. **Open** 10am-6pm Mon-Sat; 11am-6pm Sun. **Credit** MC, V.

If you don't believe in fairies already, you'll surely be convinced once you've stepped into this magical shop on this delightful cobbled street in Hampstead. The mythical creatures hang from the ceiling on beaded swings and lend their wings to little girls' rucksacks. Fairy costumes are available in great profusion, and are understandably popular. Some of the costumes incorporate animal faces on the bodice (prices range from £13 to £40).

Agent Provacateur (Fashion, *p241*); **Aldo** (Fashion accessories, *p243*); **Benjamin Pollock's Toyshop** (Toys & games, *p253*); **Blackwell's** (Books, *p230*); **Carhartt** (Fashion, *p241*); **Child** (Fashion, *p239*); **Coco de Mer** (Fashion, *p241*); **Diesel** (Fashion, *p241*); **Duffer of St George** (Fashion, *p241*); **eatmyhandbagbitch** (Homewares, *p248*); **Gap** (Fashion, *p237*); **Helter Skelter** (Books, *p231*); **Jacobs Photo, Video & Digital** (Electonics, *p234*); **Jessops** (Electronics, *p235*); **Kaleido** (Fashion accessories, *p243*); **Kiehl's** (Health & beauty, *p247*); **Koh Samui** (Fashion, *p237*); **Kookaï** (Fashion, *p237*); **MDC Classic Music** (Music, *p252*); **Maharishi** (Fashion, *p241*); **Mango** (Fashion, *p237*); **Natural Shoe Store** (Fashion accessories, *p244*); **Neal's Yard Remedies** (Health & beauty, *p247*); **Oasis** (Fashion, *p238*); **Office** (Fashion accessories, *p244*); **Quiksilver** (Fashion, *p241*); **The Sanctuary** (Health & beauty, *p247*); **Seven Dials Dry Cleaners** (Fashion accessories, *p243*); **Shu Uemura** (Health & beauty, *p248*); **Skate of Mind** (Fashion, *p241*); **Spex in the City** (Health & beauty, *p248*); **Stanford's** (Books, *p231*).

Knightsbridge & South Kensington

Harrods (Department stores, *p233*); **Harvey Nichols** (Department stores, *p233*); **Rigby & Peller** (Fashion, *p242*); **Urban Retreat** (Health & beauty, *p247*).

Chelsea

Antiquarius (Antiques, *p229*), **Aware** (Fashion, *p241*); **The Chololate Society** (Food & drink, *p245*); **Conran Shop** (Homewares, *p248*); **Daisy & Tom** (Fashion, *p239*); **Gap Kids** (Fashion, *p239*); **Jimmy Choo** (Fashion accessories, *p244*); **MAC Cosmetics** (Health & beauty, *p247*); **Manolo Blahnik** (Fashion accessories, *p244*); **Origins** (Health & beauty, *p247*); **Trotters** (Fashion, *p239*).

The South Bank & Bankside

Borough Market (Markets, *p251*); **La Pont de la Tour Food Store** (Food & drink, *p245*).

North London

Annie's Vintage Clothes (Islington, Fashion, *p242*); **Camden Market** (Camden, Markets, *p250*); **Camden Passage Antiques Market** (Islington, Antiques, *p229*); **Diverse Hair** (Health & beauty, *p248*); **Mystical Fairies** (Hampstead, Toys & games, *p255*).

East London

Brick Lane Market (Spitalfields, Markets, *p249*); **Columbia Road Market** (Bethnal Green, Markets, *p251*); **Spitalfields Market** (Markets, *p251*); **Timothy Everest** (Spitalfields, Fashion accessories, *p244*).

South London

Brixton Market (Brixton, Markets, *p249*); **Greenwich Market** (Greenwich, Markets, *p250*).

West London

& Clarke's (Kensington, Food & drink, *p244*); **Bertie Wooster** (Fulham, Fashion, *p242*); **Boots** (Bayswater, Health & beauty, *p247*); **Cheeky Monkeys** (Notting Hill, Toys & games, *p254*).**The Cross** (Holland Park, Fashion, *p237*); **The Grocer on Elgin** (Notting Hill, Food & drink, *p245*); **Honest Jon's** (Music, *p252*); **Intoxica** (Music, *p252*); **Pierre Marcolini** (Food & drink, *p245*); **Portobello Road Market** (Notting Hill, Markets, *p250*); **Rough Trade** (Notting Hill, Music, *p252*); **SPAce.NK** (Notting Hill, Health & beauty, *p247*).

TAKE A TRIP INTO A NEW DIMENSION

WALT DISNEY PICTURES
PRESENTS
A JAMES CAMERON FILM

GHOSTS OF THE ABYSS

EVEREST

A MACGILLIVRAY FREEMAN FILM
Presented by Polartec

SPACE STATION 3D

Presented By
LOCKHEED MARTIN

Box Office 020 7902 1234

Book online www.bfi.org.uk/imax

bfi London IMAX® Cinema, South Bank, London SE1

Waterloo

Supported by

© IMAX® is the registered trademark of IMAX Corporation

Arts & Entertainment

Features

Festivals & Events

There's always something going on in busy London Town.

If there is one thing London does well, it's throw a party. It doesn't really matter the reason – the Notting Hill Carnival lost its point years ago, and yet it remains one of the biggest festivals in Europe. Every season has its speciality: in the spring it's all about boat races (the Oxford and Cambridge race, *see p259*), in summer it's (multi)culture festivals (Notting Hill, *see p264*), in autumn it's history (Guy Fawkes, *see p265*) and winter sees the city covered in fairy lights and Christmas trees, and ringing with carols.

For more details on cultural festivals in the world of: Dance, *see p277*; Film, *see p284*; and Music, *see p304*. Many of the big museums and galleries, such as the British Museum (*see p101*), often hold their own events. Check the current issue of *Time Out* magazine for details. For public holidays in the UK, *see p373*.

January-March 2004

London International Boat Show

ExCeL, 1 Western Gateway, Royal Victoria Dock, E16 1XL (7069 5000/www.schroderslondonboat show.com). Custom House DLR. **Date** 8-18 Jan.

There must be more amateur sailors around than we think, because for 50 years this maritime convention has been showing off leisure boats to keen crowds. This year it relocates to spacious Docklands and promises dockside exhibits and big boats.

London International Mime Festival

Various venues (7637 5661/www.mime fest.co.uk). **Date** 10-25 Jan.

Surely the quietest festival the city has to offer, this is for all you drama school dropouts who miss those wacky parties where you would all guess what

Catch them if you can

Ceremony of the Keys

Tower of London, Tower Hill, The City, EC3N 4AB (08707 515177/www.hrp.org.ukk). Tower Hill tube. **Date** daily. Maximum *Apr-Oct* party of 7, *Nov-Mar* party of 15. **Map** p405 R7.

Dating back 700 years, this is the ceremony in which the Yeoman Warders lock the entrances to the Tower of London at 9.53pm every evening. The ticketed public assembles at the West Gate at 9pm, and it's all over by 10pm, when the last post sounds. To watch, apply in writing for free tickets giving a choice of three dates (Ceremony of the Keys Office, HM Tower of London, EC3N 4AB) with a stamped self-addressed envelope (UK only, international stamps are not accepted) at least two months in advance.

Changing of the Guard

Buckingham Palace, SW1A 1AA (09068 663344/www.royal.gov.uk). Green Park or St James's Park tube/Victoria tube/rail. **Ceremonies** *Apr-Aug* 11.15am daily. *Sept-Mar* alternate days (may be cancelled in wet weather). **Map** p400 H9. **Horse Guards Arch** *Horse Guards & St James's Palace, SW1A 1BQ* 11am Mon-Sat; 10am Sun. **Map** p401 K8.

One of the regiments of Foot Guards, in their scarlet coats and bearskin hats (*pictured*) – line up in the forecourt of Wellington Barracks, from 10.45am; at 11.27am they march, accompanied by their regimental band, to Buckingham Palace for the changing of the sentries, in the palace forecourt. At Horse Guards in Whitehall, the Household Cavalry mount the guard (10am-4pm daily); they then ride to Whitehall via the Mall from Hyde Park for the daily changeover.

Gun Salutes

Green Park, Mayfair & St James's, W1, & Tower of London, The City, EC3. **Dates** 6 Feb (Accession Day); 21 Apr (Queen's birthday); 2 June (Coronation Day); 15 June (Trooping the Colour); State Opening of Parliament (*see p265*). **Map** p400 H8.

The King's Troop of the Royal Horse Artillery makes a mounted charge through Hyde Park, sets up the guns and fires a 41-gun salute (at noon, except for on the occasion of the State Opening of Parliament) opposite the Dorchester Hotel. Not to be outdone, the Honourable Artillery Company fires a 62-gun salute at the Tower of London at 1pm.

everyone else was. In order to brighten things up, there are also animation, puppetry and other not-really-mime forms of mime.

Chinese New Year Festival

Around Gerrard Street, Chinatown, W1 (7439 3822/www.chinatown-online.co.uk). Leicester Square or Piccadilly Circus tube. **Date** 25 Feb 2004. **Map** p401 K7.

In this generally traditional event you can join the crowds that follow the Chinese 'dragons' as they snake through the streets, gathering gifts of money and food. There are fireworks galore.

London Art Fair

Business Design Centre, 52 Upper Street, Islington, N1 0QH (tickets 0870 739 9500/www.londonartfair.co.uk). Angel tube. **Date** 14-18 Jan 2004. **Map** p402 N2.

More than 100 galleries get involved in this contemporary art fair. Millions of pounds will change hands during the five-day event.

Great Spitalfields Pancake Day Race

Spitalfields Market (entrance on Commercial Street or Brushfield Street), Spitalfields, E1 6AA (7375 0441). Liverpool Street tube/rail. **Date** 24 Feb 2004. **Map** p403 R5.

This traditional tomfoolery starts at 12.30pm, with teams of four tossing pancakes as they run. Call several days in advance if you want to take part, or just show up if all you're after is seeing any number of pancakes hit the pavement.

Ideal Home Show

Earl's Court Exhibition Centre, Warwick Road, Earl's Court, SW5 9SY (box office 0870 606 6080/ groups 0870 241 0272/www.idealhomeshow.co.uk). Earl's Court tube. **Date** 10 Mar-4 Apr; 8-18 Oct. **Map** p396 A11.

This one empties the suburbs every year. It's the country's biggest consumer show, and it's all about kitchens. Well, kitchens, renovations and extensions – everything that obsesses the home-owning Briton is here. Whole houses are reconstructed to give you ideas. Even whole neighbourhoods. And experts are on hand to give advice.

St Patrick's Day

Date 17 Mar.

Even with the third biggest Irish population of any city in the world, until 2002 there was no St Patrick's Day celebration in London. In 2003 a small but enthusiastic parade wandered around Trafalgar Square, and a party was held on the South Bank. It's possible the same thing could happen again, but, either way, the Irish, and those who love them, will crowd into the city's Irish pubs. The biggest celebrations are held at the pubs in Irish-centric Kilburn in north London.

Head of the River Race

Thames, from Mortlake to Putney Bridge (01932 220401/www.horr.co.uk). Mortlake rail. **Date** 20 Mar.

As impressive as the Oxford & Cambridge faceoff (*see below*) but much less well known, the Head of the River is raced over the same four-mile (7km) course by more than 400 crews. The race moves very quickly, and is quite exciting. The best views are from Hammersmith Bridge or at Putney. The race starts from Mortlake at 3.30pm.

Oxford & Cambridge Boat Race

Thames, from Putney to Mortlake (01225 383483/ www.theboatrace.org). Putney Bridge tube. **Date** 28 Mar.

Huge crowds line the Thames from Putney to Mortlake for this annual elitist grudge match, with the riverside pubs in Mortlake and Hammersmith the most popular (read: obscenely crowded and packed with toffs) vantage points. Those who did not go to either university might hope that both boats tip over, but just in case you're nicer, Oxford is in the dark blue and Cambridge is in the light blue.

April-June 2004

London Marathon

Greenwich Park to the Mall via the Isle of Dogs, Victoria Embankment & St James's Park (7620 4117/hotline 7902 0189/www.london-marathon.co.uk). Maze Hill rail. **Date** 18 Apr.

One of the world's biggest metropolitan marathons, this one attracts 35,000 starters, including a few in outrageous costumes. Would-be runners must apply by the previous October to be entered in the ballot.

London Harness Horse Parade

Battersea Park, Albert Bridge Road, Battersea, SW11 (01737 646132). Battersea Park or Queenstown Road rail/97, 137 bus. **Date** 12 Apr.

An Easter Monday parade of working nags with their various commercial and private carriages.

May Fayre & Puppet Festival

St Paul's Church Garden, Bedford Street, Covent Garden, WC2E 9ED (7375 0441/www.alternative arts.co.uk). Covent Garden tube. **Date** 9 May. **Map** p401 L7.

Celebrating the first recorded sighting of Mr Punch in England (by Pepys, in 1662), this free event offers puppetry galore from 10.30am to 5.30pm. *See also p264* Punch & Judy Festival.

Chelsea Flower Show

Grounds of Royal Hospital, Royal Hospital Road, Chelsea, SW3 4SR (7649 1885/www.rhs.org.uk). Sloane Square tube. **Date** 25-28 May. **Map** p397 F12.

You would not believe the hysteria that builds up around this annual flower show. Fight your way past the rich old ladies to see perfect roses bred by experts, or to get ideas for your own humble plot of soil. But not on the first two days, as those are open only to Royal Horticultural Society members; the show closes at 5.30pm on the final day, with display plants sold off from 4.30pm.

Coin Street Festival

Bernie Spain Gardens (next to Oxo Tower Wharf), SE1 9PH (7401 2255/www.coinstreetfestival.org). Southwark tube/Waterloo tube/rail. **Date** June-Aug.

London's biggest free festival of music, dance and performance is now in its 12th year. Events include Community Celebration, held on the South Bank between the National Theatre and Tate Modern.

Victoria Embankment Gardens Summer Events

Victoria Embankment Gardens, Villiers Street, Westminster, WC2 (7375 0441/www.alternative arts.co.uk). Embankment tube. **Date** 30 May-20 July. **Map** p399 L7.

Free open-air events include the Latin American Fiesta da Cultura (30 May), Open Dance Festival (5-6 June), Jazz Plus (12.30-2pm Tue & Thur June-July), Out of Africa (20 June) and Out of Asia (27 June).

Royal Academy Summer Exhibition

Royal Academy of Arts, Burlington House, Piccadilly, Mayfair, W1J 0BD (7300 8000/www.royal academy.org.uk). Green Park or Piccadilly Circus tube. **Date** 8 June-16 Aug. **Map** p400 J7.

This is a fun, if hit or miss, showcase drawn from around 12,000 works submitted by artists of all styles and standards. A panel of art experts boils the choices down to around 1,000 entries for display.

Derby Day

Epsom Downs Racecourse, Epsom Downs, Surrey KT18 5LQ (01372 470047/www.epsomderby.co.uk). Epsom rail then shuttle bus. **Date** 5 June.

The most important flat race of the season has a carnival mood, but if you want comfort or a good view, be prepared to pay for it. *See also p324.*

London Garden Squares Day

Various venues (7839 3969). **Date** 12-13 June.

All those enchanting little private parks around the wealthy parts of town that tempt you but then lock you out are opened up for this event only. Maps are available to guide you to the green oases all over London (gardens vary from from Japanese-style retreats to secret 'children-only' play areas).

Meltdown

South Bank Centre, Belvedere Road, South Bank, SE1 8XX (7960 4242/www.rfh.org.uk). Embankment tube/Waterloo tube/rail. **Date** 8-30 June. **Map** p401 M8.

This relatively new and enormously successful festival of contemporary culture at the South Bank Centre invites a guest curator each year. A varied selection of bosses in recent years have included Scott Walker, Nick Cave and David Bowie. Given that, it is perhaps unsurprising that the gigs and special events tend towards the unpredictable and are occasionally brilliant.

Trooping the Colour

Horse Guards Parade, Whitehall, Westminster, SW1A 2AX (7414 2479). Westminster tube/Charing Cross tube/rail. **Date** 12 June. **Map** p401 K8.

Though the Queen was born on 21 April, this is her official birthday celebration. At 10.45am she makes the 15-minute journey from Buckingham Palace to Horse Guards Parade, then scurries back home to watch a midday Royal Air Force flypast and receive a gun salute from Green Park. Crowds gather on the Mall and cheer until they're red, white and blue in the face. So sweet.

Beating Retreat

Horse Guards Parade, Whitehall, Westminster, SW1A 2AX (booking 7839 5323/7414 2271). Westminster tube/Charing Cross tube/rail. **Date** 2-3 June. **Map** p401 K8.

This ineffably patriotic ceremony begins at 7pm, with the 'Retreat' beaten on drums by the Mounted Bands of the Household Cavalry and the Massed Bands of the Guards Division.

Royal Ascot

Ascot Racecourse, Ascot, Berkshire SL5 7JX (01344 622211/www.ascot.co.uk). Ascot rail. **Date** 15-19 June.

This society horse bash, held at the best flat-racing course in the country, even has some races thrown in. Tickets are most in demand for Ladies' Day (19 June), when the Queen swings by. This is the one that tradition demands ladies spend lots of money buying posh hats to wear, hoping that the *Daily Mail* will take photos. *See also p324.*

Bankers' holidays

If you've arrived in May or August, you may find yourself on the wrong side of closed doors, as all of Britain heads off cheerfully to the countryside on something called a 'bank holiday', and leaves you behind.

The strange name is basically meaningless – the nation certainly does not celebrate its financial institutions with regular national holidays – but virtually every holiday in Great Britain that does not concern Christmas or Easter is called a 'bank holiday', in a kind of *Brazil*-like bureaucratese that dates back to the Bank Holidays Act of 1871. This law established a series of national public holidays, and with an uncharacteristic lack of creativity, Britain has never got round to changing the rather prosaic term.

As they generally fall on Mondays, bank holidays have led to bank holiday weekends – three days of freedom for locals, but three days in which quite a few shops are closed for visitors. For many Londoners, the quaint notion of a sunny family weekend spent eating ice-cream or supping beer outside a riverside pub has given way to the 72-hour party marathon. London clubland erupts into action each bank holiday, over Easter (9-12 April 2004) and the early May and spring holidays (1-3 May 2004, 29-31 May 2004), with most events concentrated around the farewell-to-summer August bank holiday weekend (28-30 August 2004).

If you want to go where most locals are on those weekends, head to the Spanish coastal resorts. Those who couldn't get plane tickets, though, will be in the city's parks or pubs, so you won't be completely alone.

The ultimate bank holiday celebration in London is surely the legendary, if faded, **Notting Hill Carnival** (*see p264*), but for clubbers, the best bank holiday parties are held on the Thames. House music collectives **Faith** (www.faithfanzine.com), **Sancho Panza** (www.sanchopanza.org) and **Soulbrew** (www.soulbrew.com) are much loved by clubbing types for their holiday boat parties. Amid all the music and madness, these last at least retain the old bank holiday spirit of messing about in boats.

For a full list of public holidays, see p373.

Wimbledon Lawn Tennis Championships

PO Box 98, Church Road, Wimbledon, SW19 5AE (8944 1066/recorded information 8946 2244/ www.wimbledon.org). Southfields tube/Wimbledon tube/rail. **Date** 21 June-4 July.

The world's most prestigious tennis tournament and, when it's not raining, the best. Heck, even when it *is* raining. *See also p324.*

City of London Festival

Venues across the Square Mile, EC2-EC4 (information 7377 0540/box office 7638 8891/ www.colf.org). **Date** 21 June-13 July.

Now in its 42nd year, the City of London Festival takes place in some of the finest buildings in the Square Mile. The three-week programme includes traditional classical music, such as concerts from the London Symphony Orchestra, as well as more unusual offerings from the worlds of jazz, dance, visual art, literature and theatre.

Henley Royal Regatta

Henley Reach, Henley-on-Thames, Oxfordshire RG9 2LY (01491 572153/www.hrr.co.uk). Henley-on-Thames rail. **Date** 30 June-4 July.

First held in 1839, Henley is now a five-day affair, and about as posh as it gets. Boat races range from open events for men and women through club and student crews to junior boys.

July-September 2004

Mardi Gras

7494 2225/www.londonmardigras.com. **Date** (tbc) end of June or beginning of July.

It may be misnamed ('Mardi Gras' does have a meaning, you know), but it's fun nonetheless as London's proud-to-be-gays and lesbians throw their annual, good-natured bash that usually features a colourful and festive march during the day and a very groovy party in the evening. They're here, they're queer, have a beer.

Rhythm Sticks

South Bank Centre, Belvedere Road, South Bank, SE1 8XX (7960 4242/www.sbc.org.uk). Embankment tube/Waterloo tube/rail. **Date** 17-25 July. **Map** p401 M8.

Each year, Rhythm Sticks takes a week to celebrate everything that bangs, crashes and, indeed, pings. Performers come from all corners of the world and play in the widest possible range of styles.

Greenwich & Docklands International Festival

Various venues Greenwich & Docklands (8305 1818/ www.festival.org). **Date** 2-25 July.

An occasionally interesting array of theatrical and musical events are held down by the river, combining community arts with grander projects.

Turn up sober and early...

Soho Festival

St Anne's Gardens & part of Wardour Street, W1D 6AE (7439 4303/www.thesohosociety.org.uk). Tottenham Court Road tube. **Date** 11 July. **Map** p401 K7.

The famous Waiter's Race, a spaghetti-eating competition and an alpine horn blowing contest bring locals and guests together in aid of the Soho Society.

Swan Upping on the Thames

Various points along the Thames (7236 1863/ 7197/www.royal.gov.uk). **Date** 19-23 July.

An archaic ceremony in which groups of herdsmen round up, divide up and mark all the cygnets on particular stretches of the Thames as belonging to the Queen, the Vintners' or the Dyers' livery companies. The route and departure times change daily.

BBC Sir Henry Wood Promenade Concerts

Royal Albert Hall, Kensington Gore, SW7 2AP (box office 7589 8212/www.bbc.co.uk/proms). Knightsbridge or South Kensington tube/9, 10, 52 bus. **Date** 16 July-11 Sept. **Map** p397 D9.

This annual event brings together an eclectic range of mostly classical concerts over the course of two months. Most are televised, but there's nothing like seeing them in person. *See also p305.*

...to see costumed lovelies like this at the **Notting Hill Carnival**. *See p264.*

Respect Festival

Venue tbc (hotline 7983 6554/www.respect festival.org.uk). **Date** 17 July.

This free anti-racist music and entertainment festival was revived at Finsbury Park in 2001, before moving to Victoria Park in 2002.

Jazz on the Streets Midsomer Festival

Streets around the West End (01932 340718/ www.jazzonthestreets.co.uk). **Date** 18-25 July.

Music, out of doors, unstaged and acoustic is at the heart of this four-year-old festival. The squares and gardens of the West End turn into natural theatres, while shoppers, office workers and tourists become an appreciative audience. Keep an eye out, or check the website, for more details.

South East Marine Week

Various locations in London and the South East (7261 0447/www.southeastmarine.org.uk).
Date 7-15 Aug.

A week dedicated to introducing urban tykes to the marine environment. The week includes 50 free events, among them beach parties on the foreshore of the Thames and themed boat trips. Field trips and craft sessions for all ages are based around the fragile ecology of the Thames Estuary.

Great British Beer Festival

Olympia, Hammersmith Road, Kensington (01727 867201/www.gbbf.org). Kensington (Olympia) tube/rail. **Date** 3-7 Aug.

Oh, yes. If ever there was a city that could host a beer fest, it's this one. Tens of thousands of visitors are expected to sample over 300 British ales and ciders at this boozetastic event. Hiccups and belches are guaranteed. As are hangovers.

Notting Hill Carnival

Notting Hill, W10, W11 (8964 0544/www.lnhc.org.uk). Ladbroke Grove, Notting Hill Gate or Westbourne Park tube. **Date** 29-30 Aug.

It calls itself Europe's biggest street party, and that may be true, as thousands of revellers show up each year to drink warm beer and wander about in posh Notting Hill. There is occasional live music and relentless and unavoidable sound systems (loaded on to trucks, followed by unglamorous dancers in T-shirts). There's a costume parade, but all too often you miss it because of the crowds (and probably a surfeit of warm beer). Terrible loos and bad press about street crime, as well as criticism of the quality of the festival, lowered crowds in 2003.

Great River Race

Thames, from Ham House, Richmond, Surrey, to Island Gardens, Greenwich, E14 (8398 9057/www.greatriverrace.co.uk). **Date** 11 Sept.

More than 250 'traditional' boats, from Chinese dragon boats and shallops to Viking longboats and Cornish gigs, vie in the UK traditional boat championship over a 22-mile (35km) course.

Brick Lane Festival

Brick Lane Market, Brick Lane, E1 (7655 0906/www.visitbricklane.com). Aldgate East tube. **Date** 5-12 Sept. **Map** p404 S5/6.

This colourful annual celebration of Spitalfields' multicultural communities past and present is everything the Notting Hill Carnival isn't. It is a festive, enjoyable event of food, music, dance and performance, rickshaw rides, stiltwalkers, clowns and jugglers. The main stage showcases world music acts, while the children's area has funfair rides, inflatables and workshops.

Regent Street Festival

Regent Street, W1 (7440 5530/www.regent-street.co.uk). Oxford Circus or Piccadilly Circus tube. **Date** 5 Sept. **Map** p399 J6.

Celebrate central London with fairground attractions, theatre, street entertainers and storytelling, as well as a variety of live music.

Mayor's Thames Festival

Between Westminster & Blackfriars Bridge (7928 8998/www.thamesfestival.org). Blackfriars tube/rail/Waterloo tube/rail. **Date** 11-12 Sept.

Always fun and occasionally spectacular, this waterfest is highlighted by a lantern procession and firework finale on Sunday evening. Prior to the pyrotechnics, there are food and crafts stalls in a riverside market, environmental activities and creative workshops, and assorted dance and music performances. Just pray it doesn't rain or there'll be damp squibs all round.

Chelsea Antiques Fair

Chelsea Old Town Hall, King's Road, Chelsea, SW3 1SS (0870 350 2442/www.penman-fairs.co.uk). Sloane Square tube. **Date** 17-26 Sept. **Map** p397 E12.

This gathering of *Antiques Roadshow* addicts in posh Chelsea may not have too many bargains, but hey, you can dream, right? People come from all over the south of England with their hearts set on Regency chamberpots and Victorian china. Experts ensure the goods weren't made last week in Taiwan.

London Open House

Various venues (www.londonopen house.org). **Date** 18-19 Sept.

An annual event that allows architecture lovers free access to more than 500 fascinating buildings all over the capital, from palaces to pumping stations. Part of the European Heritage Days initiative, the weekend-long event gets you into places you would never otherwise see.

Horseman's Sunday

Church of St John & St Michael, Hyde Park Crescent, Paddington, W2 2QD (7262 1732). Edgware Road tube/Paddington tube/rail. **Date** 19 Sept. **Map** p395 E6.

A surreal event in which a horseback vicar blesses more than 100 horses before they all trot through Hyde Park. You'd imagine it was an ancient rite, but the ceremony actually dates back only to 1969, when local riding stables held an open-air service to protest against threats of closure.

October-December 2004

Punch & Judy Festival

Covent Garden Piazza, Covent Garden, WC2 (7836 9136/www.coventgardenmarket.co.uk). Covent Garden tube. **Map** p401 L7. **Date** early Oct 2004.

More funny-voiced domestic incidents involving the crocodile, policeman and Mr Punch punching Judy (and, happily, vice versa). This special puppet fest celebrates the shows so beloved of Samuel Pepys. *See also p260* May Fayre & Puppet Festival.

Pearly Kings & Queens Harvest Festival

St Martin-in-the-Fields, Trafalgar Square, Westminster, WC2N 4JJ (7766 1100/www.pearlysociety.co.uk). Charing Cross tube/rail. **Map** p401 L7. **Date** 3 Oct.

Pearly kings and queens – so-called because of the shiny white buttons sewn in elaborate designs on their dark suits – have their origins in the 'aristocracy' of London's early Victorian costermongers, who elected their own royalty to safeguard their interests. Now charity representatives, today's pearly monarchy gathers for this 3pm thanksgiving service in their traditional 'flash boy' outfits.

Trafalgar Day Parade

Trafalgar Square, Westminster, WC2 (7928 8978/ www.sea-cadets.org). Charing Cross tube/rail. **Date** 26 Oct 2004. **Map** p401 K7.

To commemorate Nelson's victory at the Battle of Trafalgar (21 Oct 1805), 500 sea cadets parade with marching bands and musical performances. The culmination is the laying of a wreath at the foot of Nelson's Column.

London Film Festival

National Film Theatre, South Bank, SE1 8XT (7928 3535/www.lff.org.uk). Embankment tube/Waterloo tube/rail. **Date** mid Oct-early Nov. **Map** p401 M8.

Attracting big-name actors and directors and offering the public the chance to see around 150 new British and international features, the LFF centres on the NFT (*see p284*) and the Odeon West End (*see p281*). For other London film festivals, *see p284*.

State Opening of Parliament

House of Lords, Palace of Westminster, Westminster, SW1A 0PW (7219 4272/www.parliament.uk). Westminster tube. **Date** mid Nov-early Dec (tbc). **Map** p401 L9.

In a ceremony that has changed little since the 16th century, the Queen officially reopens Parliament after its summer recess. You can only see what goes on inside on telly, but if you join the throngs on the streets, you can watch HRH arrive and depart in her Irish or Australian State Coach, attended by the Household Cavalry.

London to Brighton Veteran Car Run

From Serpentine Road, Hyde Park (01753 681736/ www.msaevents.co.uk). Hyde Park Corner tube. **Date** 7 Nov. **Map** p395 E8.

Get up at the crack of dawn to catch this parade of vintage motors setting off from Hyde Park at 7.30am, aiming to reach Brighton before 4pm. Otherwise, join the crowds lining the rest of the route, which wends down via Westminster Bridge.

Bonfire Night

Date 5 Nov.

This annual pyrotechnic frenzy sees Brits across the country gather – usually in inclement weather – to burn a 'guy' (an effigy of Guy Fawkes, who notoriously failed to blow up James I and his Parliament in the Gunpowder Plot of 1605) on a giant bonfire, and set off loads of fireworks. Most public displays are held on the weekend nearest 5 November; among the best in London are those at Primrose Hill, Alexandra Palace and Crystal Palace. Alternatively, try to book a late ride on the relevant nights on the British Airways London Eye (*see p70*).

Lord Mayor's Show

Various streets in the City (7332 1456/www.lord mayorsshow.org). **Date** 10 Oct.

Today's the day when, under the conditions of the Magna Carta of 1215, the newly elected Lord Mayor of London is presented to the monarch or to their justices for approval. Amid a procession of about 140 floats, the Lord Mayor leaves Mansion House at 11am and travels through the City to the Royal Courts of Justice on the Strand, where he makes some vows before returning to Mansion House by 2.20pm. The event is rounded off by a firework display from a barge moored on the Thames between Waterloo and Blackfriars Bridges.

Remembrance Sunday Ceremony

Cenotaph, Whitehall, Westminster, SW1. Westminster tube/Charing Cross tube/rail. **Date** 9 Nov. **Map** p401 L8.

In honour of those who lost their lives in World Wars I and II, the Queen, the Prime Minister and other dignitaries lay wreaths at the Cenotaph, Britain's memorial to 'the Glorious Dead'. After a minute's silence at 11am, the Bishop of London leads a service of remembrance.

Christmas Lights & Tree

Covent Garden (7836 9136/www.covent gardenmarket.co.uk); Oxford Street (7629 2738/ www.oxfordstreet.co.uk); Regent Street (7440 5530/ www.regent-street.co.uk); Bond Street (7821 5230/ www.bondstreetassociation.com); Trafalgar Square (7983 4234/www.london.gov.uk). **Date** Nov-Dec.

Though the Christmas lights on London's main shopping streets are an increasingly commercialised proposition (those on Regent Street are almost always switched on by a jobbing B-list celebrity in early November), much of the childhood wonder still remains in the glittering lights on St Christopher's Place, Marylebone High Street, Bond Street and Kensington High Street. The giant fir tree in Trafalgar Square each year is a gift from the Norwegian people, in gratitude for Britain's role in liberating their country from the Nazis.

International Showjumping Championships

Olympia, Hammersmith Road, Kensington, W14 8UX (7370 8202/www.olympiashowjumping.com). Kensington (Olympia) tube/rail. **Date** 16-20 Dec.

This annual jamboree for equestrian enthusiasts has more than 100 trade stands. The events include everything from international riders' competitions to the Shetland Pony Grand National.

New Year's Eve Celebrations

Date 31 Dec.

Celebratory events in London tend to be local in nature, though Trafalgar Square has traditionally been an unofficial gathering point at the turn of the year for those without party invites. Otherwise, many of the city's nightclubs hold expensive New Year parties. If you're feeling up to it the next morning, the extremely raucous New Year's Day Parade through central London includes more than 10,000 performers, from marching bands to clowns. The parade starts at Parliament Square at noon, and finishes at Berkeley Square taking in Whitehall, Trafalgar Square, Lower Regent Street and Piccadilly along the way.

Children

Capital kids' adventures.

The Children pages in *Time Out* magazine give weekly listings, while *Time Out London for Children* (£8.99) is a comprehensive guide.

Area guide

For complete reviews of family favourites listed in the Central London chapters, see the relevant pages listed in brackets below.

The South Bank to Bankside p70

British Airways London Eye (*see p70*) for views worth the queues. The **Golden Hinde** (*see p77*) for pirate games. **HMS Belfast** (*see p77*) for war games. **London Aquarium** (*see p73*) opposite the Eye has shoals of interest for children of all ages. The **BFI London IMAX Cinema** (*see p284*) has a year-round programme of 3D films for children, while the **London Dungeon** will freak them out; it's best for children of ten and over (*see p79*). The **National Theatre** (*see p331*) has school-holiday events and a summer open-air festival, and the **Royal Festival Hall** (*see p302*) has a number of weekend music workshops as well as children's shows and concerts.

The City p83

The **Tower of London** (*see p94*) has enough for children to merit its high admission charge, and the **Tower Bridge Exhibition** (*see p93*), offers the best views this side of the Eye. The **Museum of London** (*see p92*) can fill a day with the city's colourful past, and The **Barbican Centre** (*see p94 and p300*), has a terrific children's library and kids' films on Saturdays, plus free foyer events.

Covent Garden p121

The **Theatre Museum** (*see p122*) has free events and workshops in the school holidays, while the **London's Transport Museum** (*see p122*) has trails, quizzes and free events

Holborn & Clerkenwell p95

Somerset House (*see p96*) has free weekend family activities and an open courtyard with dancing fountains in which to play.

Trafalgar Square p127

The **National Gallery** (*see p127*), has free paintings trails and artist-led activities on the second Saturday and Sunday of every month, and the **National Portrait Gallery** (*see p128*) has an interactive IT gallery and weekend 'Talk and Draw' activities. **St Martin-in-the-Fields** (*see p128*), has the Brass Rubbing Centre and a fine café in the crypt.

South Kensington p135

The **Natural History Museum** (*see p135*), has dinosaurs, bugs and natural phenomena, the **Science Museum** (*see p136*), is a hands-on technological adventure for all ages, and the beautiful **V&A** (*see p137*) has weekend and holiday art and craft sessions.

Greenwich p167

Come by train from Charing Cross, walk under the river in the foot tunnel from Island Gardens, travel by DLR through Docklands or sail in by boat (*see p359*) – getting here is half the fun. The **National Maritime Museum** (*see p168*) has stories, crafts and play during the hols, the **Cutty Sark** (*see p167*) has activities on summer weekends, and the **Royal Observatory** (*see p168*) has plenty of busy school holiday workshops and lots of storytelling.

Childcare & advice

Parentline (0808 800 2222, www.parentline plus.org.uk) gives confidential, free advice; **Simply Childcare** (7701 6111, www.simply childcare.com) offers childcare listings.

Check www.kidslovelondon.com, a family entertainment website produced by the tourist board. Events in South-west and West London can be found at www.fun4families.org.

Childminders

6 Nottingham Street, Marylebone, W1U 5EJ (7935 3000/2049/www.babysitter.co.uk). **Open** 8.45am-5.30pm Mon-Thur; 8.45am-5pm Fri; 9am-4.30pm Sat. **Rates** £5.20-£6.90/hr. **Credit** AmEx, MC, V. **Map** p398 G5.

A large agency with more than 1,500 babysitters, mainly nurses, nannies and infant teachers (all with references), who live in London or the suburbs.

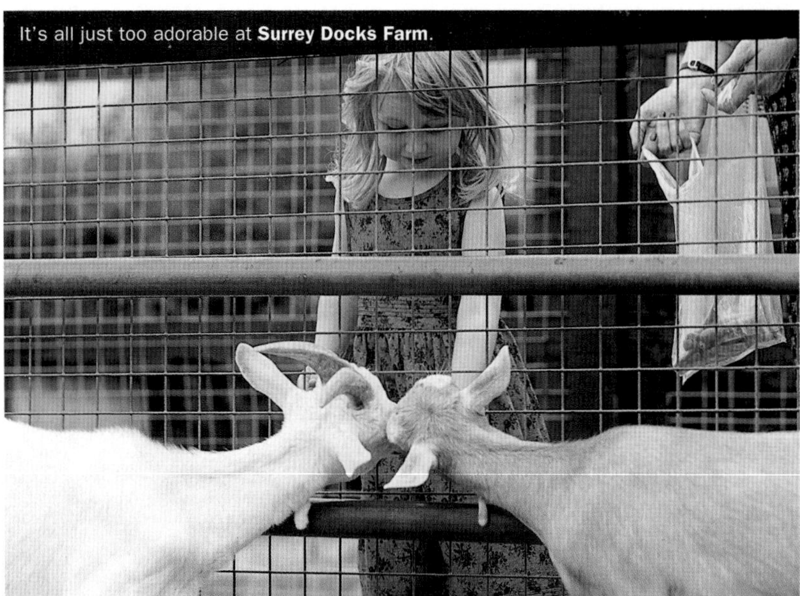
It's all just too adorable at **Surrey Docks Farm**.

Pippa Pop-ins
430 Fulham Road, Chelsea, SW6 4SN (7385 2458/www.pippapopins.com). **Open** 8.15am-6pm Mon-Fri. **Fees** *Sessions* £37-£75. **Credit** MC, V. **Map** p396 B13.
A famously friendly nursery school and kindergarten. The fully qualified staff host parties, holiday activities and a crèche.
Branch: 165 New King's Road, Chelsea, SW6 1DU (7731 1445).

Universal Aunts
Daytime childminding 7738 8937/evenings 7386 5900. **Open** 9.30am-5pm Mon-Thur; 9.30am-4pm Fri. **Rates** *Agency fee* from £15. *Childminding* from £8.50/hr. *Babysitting* from £5/hr. **No credit cards**.
This London agency, founded in 1921, provides reliable people to babysit, to meet children from trains, planes or boats, or to take them sightseeing.

City farms

When you're ready to forage further afield, Contact the British Federation of City Farms (0117 923 1800, www.farmgarden.org.uk) for a complete list of places in and around London.

Freightliner's City Farm
Paradise Park, Sheringham Road, off Liverpool Road, Barnsbury, N7 8PF (7609 0467/ www.freightlinersfarm.org.uk). Holloway Road tube/Highbury & Islington tube/rail. **Open** *Winter* 10am-4pm Tue-Sun. *Summer* 10am-5pm Tue-Sun. **Admission** free; donations appreciated.
Rare breeds are a speciality at Freightliners: there are Dexter cattle, Tamworth pigs and exotic Chilean hens as well as rabbits, geese, sheep and goats.

Mudchute City Farm
Pier Street, Isle of Dogs, E14 3HP (7515 5901). Crossharbour, Mudchute or Island Gardens DLR. **Open** 9am-4pm daily. **Admission** free; donations appreciated.
This Docklands farm has cattle, sheep, pigs, llamas and more, plus a riding school and a Young Farmers' club for little urban rustics.

Surrey Docks Farm
Rotherhithe Street, Surrey Quays, SE16 5EY (7231 1010). Canada Water or Surrey Quays tube. **Open** 10am-5pm Tue-Thur; 10am-1pm, 2pm-5pm Sat, Sun. **Admission** free; donations appreciated.
This organic farm was opened to the public in the early 1970s in an attempt to bring a bit of nature to a depressed neighbourhood. Its residents now include a herd of milking goats, sheep, cows, pigs, poultry, donkeys and bees. There's a classroom in the shape of an enchanted forest, a dairy and a forge.

Vauxhall City Farm
24 St Oswald's Place, Tyers Street, Vauxhall, SE11 (7582 4204). Vauxhall tube/rail. **Open** 10.30am-4pm Tue-Thur, Sat, Sun. **Admission** free; donations appreciated.
The biggest crowd pullers at this excellent small farm are the gentle giant Shire horse Charlie and whopping British Giant rabbits. Modestly sized goats, pigs, chickens and guinea pigs also live here.

Eating & drinking

If you're feeding a number of children, the city's many chains can come to the rescue. At **Belgo** (www.belgo-restaurants.com), children eat free; **Café Rouge** (www.caferouge.co.uk) and **Caffè Uno** (www.caffeuno.co.uk) as well as **Nando's** (www.nandos. co.uk) all have handy and inexpensive kids' menus. **Pizza Express** (www.pizzaexpress.co.uk), **Wagamama** (*see p199*) and **Yo! Sushi** (locations throughout the city; www.yosushi.com) have dishes with child, and parent, appeal.

Boiled Egg & Soldiers

63 Northcote Road, Battersea, SW11 1NP (7223 4894). Clapham Junction rail. **Open** 9am-6pm Mon-Sat; 10am-4pm Sun. **Main courses** £4-£7. **No credit cards**.

An institution with the buggy-brigade. It's nursery food, such as eggs with toast and home-made cakes, all comforting stuff.

Carluccio's Caffè

8 Market Place, Marylebone, W1N 7AG (7636 2228/www.carluccios.com). Oxford Circus tube. **Open** 8am-11pm Mon-Fri; 10am-11pm Sat; 10am-10pm Sun. **Main courses** £5.25-£10.75. **Credit** AmEx, MC, V.

The Carluccio's chain is renowned for fine Italian cooking, glorious puddings and indulgent service for the *bambinos*. There are many branches – we've listed the central ones here.

Other locations: St Christopher's Place, Marylebone (7935 5927); 12 West Smithfield, Farringdon (7329 5904); Fenwick, 63 New Bond Street, Oxford Circus (7629 0699).

Dexter's Grill

20 Bellevue Road, Wandsworth, SW17 7EB (8767 1858). Wandsworth Common rail. **Meals served** noon-11pm Mon-Fri; 10am-11pm Sat. **Main courses** £5-£15. **Credit** AmEx, MC, V.

An organic section on the menu lists curly wurly chicken, broccoli pasta and shepherd's pie. The main menu has burgers, baby back ribs, fish and chips or all-day breakfasts. Dexter's won Best Family Restaurant in the *Time Out* Eating Awards in 2003.

Other locations: 1 Battersea Rise, Battersea (7924 4935).

Giraffe

46 Rosslyn Hill, Hampstead, NW3 1NH (7435 0343/ www.giraffe.net). Hampstead tube. **Open** 8am-4pm, 5-11pm Mon-Fri; 9am-5pm, 6-11pm Sat, Sun. **Main courses** £7-£12. **Credit** AmEx, MC, V.

Another *Time Out* award-winner, with other locations in Clapham, Marylebone and Islington. The eclectic menu includes veggie options for kids, plus huge shakes and juices.

Other locations: 29-31 Essex Road, Islington (7359 5999); 6-8 Blanford Street, Marylebone (7935 2333); 30 Hill Street, Richmond (8332 2646); 7 Kensington High Street, Kensington (7938 1221).

Marine Ices

8 Haverstock Hill, Hampstead, NW3 2BL (7482 9003). Chalk Farm tube/31, 168 bus. **Meals served** 10am-3pm, 6-11pm Mon-Fri; 10am-11pm Sat; 10am-10pm Sun. **Main courses** *Restaurant* £6.15-£11.35. **Credit** DC, MC, V.

An institution founded by the Mansi family, which started life as a *gelateria*. Once you've struggled to get your children away from the ice cream window and bagged your table (book at weekends), the menu offers a range of Italian pasta dishes and pizzas.

Smollensky's on the Strand

105 Strand, Covent Garden, WC2R 0AA (7497 2101/www.smollenskys.co.uk). Covent Garden or Embankment tube/Charing Cross tube/rail. **Meals served** noon-midnight Mon-Wed; noon-12.30am Thur-Sat; noon-5.30pm, 6.30-10.30pm Sun. **Main courses** £11-£16. **Set meal** (noon-7pm, after 10.30pm Mon-Fri) £10 2 courses, £12 3 courses. **Credit** AmEx, DC, MC, V. **Map** p319 L7.

Lunchtimes are jolly, and there's entertainment at weekends for children. Smollensky's steaks are good, and the children's menu – macaroni cheese, chicken breast, fish and chips, spag bol, burgers – are attractively presented. Check the website for other locations.

Sticky Fingers

1A Phillimore Gardens, Kensington, W8 7QB (7938 5338/www.stickyfingers.co.uk). High Street Kensington tube. **Meals served** noon-11pm Mon-Sat. **Main courses** £8.95-£18.95. **Credit** AmEx, DC, MC, V. **Map** p314 A9.

Come on a Sunday and you can get your face painted as well as ketchup-smeared at this raucous, kid-friendly burger joint. It was once co-owned by Rolling Stone Bill Wyman, so teenage rock fans will be impressed by Stones memorabilia – guitars and signed posters – strategically placed. The children's menu (£7.25) gives them nuggets, burgers and pasta. Dessert and a soft drink is included.

Entertainment

Cinema

The **Barbican**, **Electric**, **Everyman**, **NFT** and **Rio** cinemas all have programmes for kids. The **Clapham Picture House** and the **Ritzy** have parent and child film slots. For all *see p280-4*.

Puppets

Puppet fans will find that they are cheerfully welcomed to the resource centre in the excellent **Battersea Arts Centre** (BAC, *see p335*). Staff there are expert makers and manipulators of puppets, and there's plenty to entertain both adults and children (kids can have a go themselves on Saturday afternoons). Phone for upcoming gigs in central London.

Little Angel Theatre

14 Dagmar Passage, Islington, N1 2DN (7226 1787/www.littleangeltheatre.com). Angel tube. **Show times** 4.30pm Thur, Fri; 11am, 2pm Sat, Sun. **Tickets** £7.50; £5 children. **Credit** MC, V.

This place has a worldwide reputation for puppetry and is an important training ground for puppeteers. The tiny proscenium-arch stage is the only permanent performance space in Britain for traditional long-stringed marionettes. Rescued from closure by donors, the Little Angel still relies on your support to keep going. Check the website for the programme.

Puppet Theatre Barge

Opposite 35 Blomfield Road, Little Venice, W9 2PF (7249 6876/summer 07836 202745/www.puppetbarge.com). Warwick Avenue tube. **Show times** 3pm Sat, Sun. *School holidays* 3pm daily. **Tickets** £7; £6.50 children/concessions. **Credit** MC, V.

London's other dedicated puppet stage floats off to Berkshire every June, but the Barge stays safely moored at Little Venice during the autumn and winter. The intimacy of the place demands advance booking and an attentive audience.

Theatre

The **BAC**, **Lyric Hammersmith** and **Tricycle** theatres have weekend performances for children, while the **Open Air Theatre** in Regent's Park runs a children's show every summer. *See chapter* **Theatre** *pp329-36.*
See also below **Dramatic development**.

Jackson's Lane Community Centre

269A Archway Road, Highgate, N6 5AA (box office 8341 4421/www.jacksonslane.org.uk). Highgate tube. **Show times** 11am, 2pm Sat. **Tickets** £4.50. **Credit** (£1 fee for usage) MC, V.

Saturday children's shows are put on by various touring companies. These can include abridged Shakespeare, nursery rhymes, and myths dramatised through the medium of puppetry.

Polka Theatre

240 The Broadway, Wimbledon, SW19 1SB (8543 4888/www.polkatheatre.com). Wimbledon tube/rail. **Open** 9.30am-4.30pm Mon; 9am-6pm Tue-Fri; 10am-5pm Sat. **Tickets** £6-£13; £5-£13 children; £5-£8 concessions. **Credit** AmEx, MC, V.

This popular and busy children's theatre has been staging top-quality shows for more than 20 years. The main theatre is for over-fives, while pre-schoolers have a theatre downstairs. There are also playgrounds, a café and courses, workshops and competitions. Polka has recently moved into the world of teens: *Hey There, Boy with the Bebop*, running until 13 March 2004, is for 12-16s.

Science & nature

Camley Street Natural Park

12 Camley Street, King's Cross, NW1 0PW (7833 2311). King's Cross tube/rail. **Open** *May-Sept* 9am-5pm Mon-Thur; 11am-5pm Sat, Sun. *Oct-Apr* 9am-5pm Mon-Thur; 10am-4pm Sat, Sun. **Admission** free. **Map** p399 K2.

Dramatic development

The **Unicorn** is the country's oldest children's theatre, founded in 1947. Its first home was at the controversial Arts Theatre on Newport Street, where, in 1967, producer Caryl Jenner introduced a good programme of children's productions and events by day, in marked contrast to the Arts Theatre's rather more adult fare in the evenings. When it moved out of its central London home after 22 years the Unicorn suddenly found itself without a stage.

Years of stagehopping and fundraising followed as the company sought to find the money to build a world-class theatre for children. In autumn 2003 work started on an acclaimed building designed by Keith Williams. The brand new Unicorn will have a 350-seat auditorium, a 120-seat studio theatre, a rehearsal studio and a café.

As far as the theatre's staff and fans are concerned, it is nothing short of a miracle to have a dedicated children's theatre in the centre of London, accessible to millions.

The establishment of the Unicorn Theatre more than 50 years ago was driven by a passionate belief in the transforming power of art in children's lives. Today, the need for that power is greater than ever, and this new centre of theatrical excellence for four- to twelve-year-olds will make its valuable work accessible to more children than ever.

The Unicorn hopes to be safely stabled in its new home at some point in 2005, but the shows will go on until then in venues around town. Already booked for spring 2004 is a touring production of *Clockwork*, which will play at the Royal Opera House's Linbury Studio.

Unicorn Theatre for Children

St Mark's Studios, Chillingworth Road, Islington, N7 8QJ (7700 0702/www.unicorntheatre.com). Holloway Road tube. **Phone enquiries** 10am-6pm Mon-Fri. **Tickets** £5-£10. Box office locations vary; check website for further details.

Getting hands-on at **Little Angel Theatre**. *See p269.*

There's plenty to do here, and environmentalists aged between eight and 14 can take part in a bat walk, go pond dipping or create homes for fauna when they join Wildlife Watch at the London Wildlife Trust's flagship reserve. Camley Park has marshlands and meadows, ponds and woodland glades, as well as a visitors' centre.

London Wildlife Trust Centre for Wildlife Gardening

28 Marsden Road, Dulwich, SE15 4EE (7252 9186/www.wildlondon.org.uk). East Dulwich rail. **Open** 10.30am-4.30pm Tue-Thur, Sun. **Admission** free.

This pleasant South London space has a wildlife meadow, woodland, marsh and herb gardens, along with a lush and lovely nursery filled with native plants and trees. In one corner there are buzzing beehives, in another plant collections. There's a play area and sandpit, and the visitors' centre – where school parties congregate – has tanks full of fish and stick insects.

Royal Gunpowder Mills

Beaulieu Drive, Waltham Abbey, Essex EN9 1BN (01992 767022/www.royalgunpowdermills.com). Waltham Cross rail then 211, 212, 213, 240, 250, 505, 517 bus. **Open** *24 Apr-25 Sept* 11am-5pm (last entry 3.30pm) Sat, Sun. **Admission** £5; £4 concessions; £2.50 5-16s; free under-5s; £15 family. **Credit** AmEx, DC, MC, V.

The big watermills here – all powered by the strength of the River Lea – produced gunpowder for centuries (from the 1660s until 1981). Now they host an interesting visitors' centre and an educational programme. When the centre is shut for winter, you can still explore the surrounding parkland and the lovely River Lea Country Park.

Museums & galleries

It may seem as if they are the province of adults, but there's lots for kids to do at museums in London. The top museums have programmes aimed to introduce youth to the arts in an appropriately creative, and hands-on fashion.

Resident artists at **Tate Modern** (*see p78*) run 'Arts Mixx' workshops on Saturdays. Sunday's activity provides a map, bag and a puzzle kit for an educational exploration of the vast galleries. Every third Saturday, a storyteller leads improvised performances based around a work of art.

On Sundays (and on Thursdays during school holidays), **Tate Britain** (*see p134*) hosts sculpture games and Art Trolley fun.

At the **British Museum**, Young Friends of the British Museum (*see p101*) get holiday fun and sleepovers with Egyptian mummies.

The **Museum of Childhood** at Bethnal Green (*see p156*) has art and craft workshops, games and soft play sessions at weekends and during holidays. The **Ragged School Museum** (*see p159*) has a recreated Victorian classroom and activities, from workshops to treasure hunts.

The **Horniman Museum** (*see p169*), in the south-east, has a fantastic music room, changing exhibitions and free shows for children during summer. In the south-west the **Wimbledon Lawn Tennis Museum** (*see p175*) offers an inspired range of activities.

Up north, the **Royal Air Force Museum Hendon** (*see p152*) has an imaginative and absorbing programme for young visitors.

Parklife

This is a particularly green city, with lots of open spaces, and plenty of activities for kids. The following parks in particular merit a day's visit. They all have well-equipped playgrounds, ice-cream booths and cafés.

Central London

Coram's Fields (*see below*) makes Bloomsbury a perfect sunny-day destination.

Kensington Gardens has one of the best playgrounds in London, thanks to the memory of Princess Diana (*see below*).

Regent's Park (*see p106*) has two boating lakes (one just for children), three playgrounds and a theatre, as well as the **London Zoo**.

St James's Park (*see p113*) is justifiably famous for its flocks of exotic wildfowl.

North London

Alexandra Park (*see p152*) has wonderful views and an ice rink.

Hampstead Heath (*see p147*) is great, both for views and kite-flying.

Highbury Fields (*see p150*) has a well-designed playground and tennis courts.

East London

Victoria Park (*see p159*) is well equipped playwise, and boasts an animal enclosure.

Mile End Park (*see p158*) has go-karts, a state-of-the-art children's playground and the 'Green Bridge' over Mile End Road.

South-east London

Crystal Palace Park (*see p170*) has huge model dinosaurs, a maze and a playground.

Dulwich Park (*see p170*) offers a wonderful café, bikes for hire and a terrific playground.

Greenwich Park (*see p166*) has a boating lake, shows in the summer and a deer enclosure.

South-west London

Battersea Park (*see p173*) may yet get new management for its much-loved children's zoo and its playground is heaven for little monkeys.

Richmond Park (*see p177*) is best for cycling, deer-spotting and rambling.

West London

Holland Park (*see p183*) is pretty and has a smart one o'clock club for pre-schoolers.

Queen's Park (*Kingswood Avenue, 8969 5661*), efficiently run by the Corporation of London, is a lovely big park with lots to do and a good school holiday events programme.

Ravenscourt Park (*Ravenscourt Road, W6*) has a paddling pool, a challenging adventure playground and an inexpensive café.

Playgrounds

Just about every neighbourhood in London has one or two, but some are better than others. To find out about safe, supervised play areas, get in touch with **Kidsactive Info** (7736 4443, www.kids-online.org.uk), which has six playgrounds across London where disabled and able-bodied children aged 5-15 can play safely.

Outdoors

Coram's Fields

93 Guilford Street, Bloomsbury, WC1N 1DN (7837 6138). Russell Square tube. **Open** 9am-dusk daily. **Admission** free (adults only admitted with an under-16). **Map** p399 M4.

The adventure playground – with a climbing tower, helter-skelter, swings and assault-course pulley – is the focus here, but there are also huge sandpits, football pitches, a basketball court, a toddlers' gym, fenced-off play areas and a café. For under-threes, the drop-in centre provides daily painting sessions and occasional summer visits by clowns.

Diana, Princess of Wales Memorial Playground

Near Black Lion Gate, Broad Walk, Kensington Gardens, Kensington, W2 4RU (7298 2117/recorded information 7298 2141). Bayswater or Queensway tube. **Open** 10am-6.45pm daily. **Admission** free (adults only admitted with child, or 9.30-10am daily). **Map** p394 C7.

Peter Pan is the theme in this fairytale playground – a pirate ship sits in a sea of white sand. There's a mermaids' fountain, wigwams and tree-houses. Much of the equipment has been adapted for children with special needs. Unaccompanied children are not allowed.

Kimber Adventure Playground & BMX Track

King George's Park, Kimber Road, SW18 4NN (8870 2168). Earlsfield Road rail. **Open** 3.30-7pm Tue-Fri; 11am-6pm Sat. *School holidays* 11am-6pm Mon-Sat. **Admission** free.

Kimber has a BMX track, basketball and the usual rope swings and platforms, as well as arts-and-crafts rooms, kitchens and ping pong.

Indoors

Bramley's Big Adventure

136 Bramley Road, Notting Hill, W10 6TJ (8960 1515/www.bramleysbig.co.uk). Latimer Road tube. **Open** 10am-6pm Mon-Fri; 10am-6.30pm Sat, Sun. **Admission** *Mon-Fri* £3.20-£4.20 1hr 30mins. Babies & adults free. *Weekends, holidays* £3.60-£4.60 1hr 30mins. **Credit** AmEx, MC, V.

With three separate play areas for babies and toddlers, small children and older adventurers, Bramley's has a little something for everyone.

Clown Town

222 Green Lanes, Palmers Green, N13 5UD (8886 7520). Palmers Green rail. **Open** 10am-7pm daily. **Admission** free; £3.50 children. **No credit cards.** Height restrictions; children must be under 4ft9in (1.3m) for admission.

With ball ponds, net climbs, slides, a toddler area and much more, this is fun town.

Spike's Madhouse

Crystal Palace National Sports Centre, Ledrington Road, Crystal Palace, SE19 2BB (8778 9876/ www.crystalpalace.co.uk). Crystal Palace rail. **Open** 10am-5pm Sat, Sun. *Holidays* noon-4pm Mon-Fri. **Admission** £2/hr; £1/30mins. **Credit** (over £5) MC, V.

Four storeys of facilities include ball pools, scramble nets, slides and biff 'n' bash bags.

Sport & leisure

Karting & motor sports

Playscape Pro Racing

390 Streatham High Road, Streatham, SW16 6HX (8677 8677/www.playscape.co.uk). Streatham rail. **Open** 10am-10pm daily. **Tickets** from £20. **Credit** AmEx, MC, V.

This centre can be booked either for parties or for half-hour taster sessions. Children must be over eight years old to be admitted. They can join the Playscape Cadet School, a founder member of the RAC's Association of Racing Kart Schools. The school operates on the first Saturday of each month (8.30am-12.30pm; cost £30).

Revolution Karting

422-4 The Arches, Burdett Road, Mile End, E3 4AA (7538 5195/www.revolutionkarting.com). Mile End tube. **Open** 10am-10pm Mon-Sat; 11am-6pm Sun. **Tickets** from £10. **Credit** DC, MC, V. Height restriction; must be over 5ft (1.5m).

The East End's newest kart track can be enjoyed by individual drivers (from £10 for eight laps) or, for groups of children, fun hours can be booked ahead.

Skateboarding

PlayStation Skate Park

Bay 65-6, Acklam Road, Notting Hill, W10 5YU (8969 4669/ www.pssp.co.uk). Ladbroke Grove tube. **Open** 11am-4pm, 5-9pm Mon-Fri; 10am-9pm Sat, Sun. **Admission** £6-£7. **No credit cards.**

Sheltered beneath the A40 are two half-pipes, a long mini-ramp and funboxes, grind boxes, ledges and rails. There's also an onsite shop.

Stockwell Park

Stockwell Road (next to Brixton Cycles), Brixton, SW9 9TP (no phone). Brixton tube/rail. **Open** 24hrs daily.

Stockwell Park is a concrete wonderland made up of an unbroken series of bumps, hips, waves, bowls and lips: perfect for tricks and carve-ups.

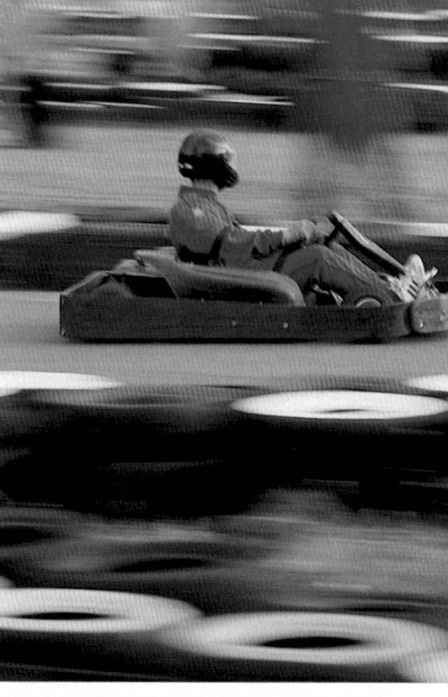

Swimming

A selection of leisure pools with flumes and slides is listed below. For lidos, *see p323.*

For lessons, contact the **Dolphin Swimming Club** (8349 1844) and **Swimming Nature** (0870 900 8002, www.swimmingnature.co.uk).

Britannia Leisure Centre

40 Hyde Road, Hoxton, N1 (7729 4485). Old Street tube/rail. **Open** 9am-6.45pm Mon-Fri; 9am-6pm Sat, Sun. **Admission** £2.10-£2.90; £1.40 concessions. **Credit** MC, V.

Latchmere Leisure Centre

Burns Road, Battersea, SW11 5AD (7207 8004/ www.kinetika.org). Clapham Common tube then 345 bus/Clapham Junction rail then 49, 319, 344 bus. **Open** 7am-9.30pm Mon-Thur, Sun; 7am-6pm Fri; 7am-7.30pm Sat. **Admission** £3.17; £2.37 parent & baby; £2.12 5-16s, concessions; free under-5s. **Credit** (over £5) MC, V.

Leyton Leisure Lagoon

763 High Road, Leyton, E10 5AB (8558 4860/ www.gll.org). Leyton tube. **Open** 7am-10pm Mon-Fri; 8am-4.15pm Sat; 8am-6pm Sun. **Admission** £2.35-£3.65; 75p-£1.60 concessions. **Credit** MC, V.

Waterfront Leisure Centre

High Street Woolwich, Woolwich, SE18 6DL (8317 5000/www.gll.org). Woolwich Arsenal rail/177, 180, 472 bus. **Open** 7am-11pm Mon-Fri; 9am-10pm Sat; 9am-9.30pm Sun. *Wet & Wild Adventure Park* 3-8pm Mon-Fri; 9am-5pm Sat; 9am-5pm, 6-8pm Sun. **Admission** £2.25-£4.50; 95p-£3.15 3-16s; free under-3s; additional charge for activities. **Credit** MC, V.

They'll feel a need for speed at **Revolution Karting**. See p272.

Wavelengths Leisure Centre

Giffin Street, Deptford, SE8 4RJ (8694 1134). Deptford rail. **Open** 8am-10pm Mon-Thur; 8am-9pm Fri; 9am-6pm Sat, Sun. **Admission** £2.90; £1.50 children. **Credit** AmEx, MC, V.

Theme parks

There are a surpising number of theme parks in the area just outside London proper, but if you don't want to spend the whole day queuing for a white-knuckle ride, try visiting on a rainy weekday outside school holidays (and check online for advance booking).

Chessington World of Adventures

Leatherhead Road, Chessington, Surrey KT9 2NE (0870 444 7777/www.chessington.com). By train: Chessington South rail. By car: M25 or A3 (Junction 9). **Open** *Apr-Aug* 10am-5pm/7pm daily. *Sept, Oct* days & times vary. **Admission** £19-£25; £15.50-£19 4s-12s; £12-£16 concessions; £52-£65 family; check the website for online advance bookings that give fast-track entry. **Credit** MC, V. Height restrictions vary on rides. **Map** p389.

Intrepid stomachs find thrills on the Samurai, Vampire and Rameses' Revenge rides, but there are interactive adventures for little'uns. Hocus Pocus Hall is an animated mansion teeming with goblins. For small children there are carousels and crazy cars in Toytown and Professor Burp's Bubble Works.

Legoland

Winkfield Road, Windsor, Berks SL4 4AY (0870 504 0404/www.legoland.co.uk). By train: Windsor & Eton Riverside or Windsor Central rail. By car: J3 M3 or J6 off M4; B3022 Windsor-Ascot Road. **Open** *Apr-Aug* 10am-5pm/7pm daily. *Sept, Oct* days & times vary. **Admission** £19-£23; £16-£20 3s-15s; £13-£17 concessions. **Credit** AmEx, MC, V. **Map** p389.

With its scaled-down Lego versions of the London Eye and Buckingham Palace, it'll feel as if you've never left the city. Alternatively, you could take a trip on the Lego safari, or chase Lego Chinese dragons. The beauty of this park is the creativity that its designers have put into the use of the adaptable plastic bricks. Anything is possible, from fantasy castles to space exploration, and although very few of the attractions will leave you white-knuckled, they're as much of a joy to look at as to ride. On the down side, queues tend to be enormous: if at all possible, visit outside British school holidays.

Thorpe Park

Staines Road, Chertsey, Surrey KT16 8PN (0870 444 4466/www.thorpepark.co.uk). By rail: Staines rail then 551 bus. By car: M25 (Junction 11 or 13). **Open** *Mar-Oct* days and times vary. **Admission** £19-£26; £15.50-£19.50 4-12s, concessions; free-under-4s; £54-£68 family. **Credit** AmEx, MC, V. Height restrictions vary on rides. **Map** p389.

Nemesis Inferno (high-speed suspended rollercoaster), Colossus (loop rollercoaster) and Detonator (a 75mph drop from 100ft) are the scream inducers. Amity Cove (downhill through a tidal wave) is the main soaker. Thorpe is great for all ages. Young children adore the gentle rides, such as the swinging seashells. On sunny days sandy Neptune's Beach, with its shallow pool, slides and fountains, is a boon. A short waterbus or land train ride away is Thorpe Farm and goats, llamas, cows and pigs.

Comedy

London's best medicine.

Headliners. *See p275.*

Comedy in London is a fine thing. Oodles of clubs, oodles of performers… in fact, the only ones with complaints about such a surfeit are the promoters and performers. For everyone else it means that the city offers vast choice in fast-paced stand-up, sketch shows, improv, character comedy and political satire.

The legendary **Comedy Store** is the circuit's equivalent of the National Theatre. Along with the **Bound & Gagged** venues – **Lee Hurst's Backyard** and the **Jongleurs** chain – it offers the biggest names in town.

If you're in London in June and July, you can catch comics testing material for August's Edinburgh Festival. Look out, too, for the **London Comedy Festival** in May (0870 011 9611/www.londoncomedyfestival.com).

Major venues

Amused Moose Soho

Moonlighting, 17 Greek Street, Soho, W1D 4DR (8341 1341/www.amusedmoose.co.uk). Leicester Square or Totttenham Court Road tube. **Shows** 7.45pm Thur, Fri; 7.30pm Sat. **Admission** £9-£12. **No credit cards**. **Map** p399 K6.

This well-established club is located underneath one of Soho's most popular gay bars. In recent years, *Time Out* Live Award-winners Eddie Izzard, Adam Bloom and Noel Fielding have appeared here.

Banana Cabaret

The Bedford, 77 Bedford Hill, Balham, SW12 9HD (8673 8904/www.bananacabaret.co.uk). Balham tube/rail. **Shows** 9pm, 11pm Fri, Sat; 8.30pm 2nd Sun of mth. **Admission** £7-£14. **No credit cards**.

Mark Thomas used to warm up for his politically charged TV shows here. Skilful and experienced comics take up most nights. At the same venue but not part of the Banana Cabaret is the New Act Night at the Bedford (Tue), when Ed Balls MCs and new names on the circuit test the water.

Bearcat Club

Turk's Head, 28 Winchester Road, Twickenham, Middx TW1 1LF (8891 1852/ www.bearcatcomedy.co.uk). St Margaret's rail. **Shows** 8.45pm Sat. **Admission** £10 non-members; £9 members. **No credit cards**.

The Bearcat, generally known for churning out strong talent to the largely well-to-do denizens of Twickenham, was the first place to give Perrier nominee Omid Djalili an open spot back in 1996.

Bound & Gagged

The Fox, 413 Green Lanes, Palmers Green, N13 4JD (8450 4100/www.boundandgaggedcomedy.com). Palmers Green rail/329, W2, W6 bus. **Shows** 8.15pm doors 9.15pm show Fri. **Admission** £8; £5 concessions. **No credit cards**.

This club's management roster ranges from the sublime (Jenny Eclair) to the ridiculous (Aaron Barschak – who invaded Prince William's 21st birthday bash).

Canal Café Theatre

Bridge House, Delamere Terrace, Little Venice, W2 6ND (7289 6054). Warwick Avenue tube. **Shows** 9.30pm Thur-Sat; 9pm Sun. **Admission** £5-£10; £4-£8 concessions. **No credit cards**. **Map** p394 C4.

The Canal Café is famed for its long-running Newsrevue, a constantly updated political satire performed through a series of sketches and songs. At other times, it plays host to longer shows, as opposed to short stand-up sets.

Chuckle Club

Three Tuns Bar, London School of Economics, Houghton Street, Holborn, WC2A 2AL (7476 1672/ www.chuckleclub.com). Holborn tube. **Shows** 7.45pm Sat. **Admission** £10; £8 concessions. **No credit cards**. **Map** p399 M6.

This friendly 18-year-old club is held in the student union bar. Expect three main spots, three open spots, the 'Chuckle Club Song', performed by compère Eugene Cheese (real name Paul), and cheap beer.

Comedy Café

66-68 Rivington Street, Shoreditch, EC2A 3AY (7739 5706/www.comedycafe.co.uk). Liverpool Street or Old Street tube/rail. **Shows** 8.30pm Wed-Sat. **Admission** £14 Sat; £10 Fri; £5 Thur; free Wed. **Credit** MC, V. **Map** p403 R4.

This purpose-built club is one of the city's leading venues. You may not recognise all the names on the bills here, but expect a good mix of the experienced, talented and inventive.

Comedy Store

1A Oxendon Street, St James's, SW1Y 4EE (Ticketmaster 08700 602 340/www.thecomedystore.co.uk). Leicester Square or Piccadilly Circus tube. **Shows** 8pm Tue-Thur, Sun; 8pm, midnight Fri, Sat. Occasional Mon shows. **Admission** £13-£15; £8 concessions. **Credit** MC, V. **Map** p401 K7.

This legendary comedy club first made its name in the 1970s, when it was the home of alternative comedy. Today, the bills are top-notch. Wednesday and Sunday are improv time, while Tuesday is the topical and innovative Cutting Edge show.

Downstairs at the King's Head

2 Crouch End Hill, Crouch End, N8 8AA (pub 8340 1028/office 01920 823265). Finsbury Park tube/rail, then W7 bus. **Shows** 8.30pm Thur, Sat, Sun. **Admission** £4-£8. **No credit cards**.

On Wednesdays, it's the Sketch Club, a weekly showcase of sketch and character-led comedy. On Thursdays 16 newish comics take to the stage, and more established ones try out material.

Ha Bloody Ha

Ealing Studios, Ealing Green, St Mary's Road, Ealing, W5 5EP (8566 4067/www.headlinerscomedy.biz). Ealing Broadway tube/rail. **Shows** 8.45pm Fri, Sat. **Admission** £8. **No credit cards**.

On the same site as the famous Ealing Studios – home of the classic Ealing Comedies – HBH offers a predominantly stand-up bill.

Hampstead Clinic

Downstairs at the White Horse, 154 Fleet Road, Hampstead, NW3 2QX (7485 2112). Belsize Park tube/Hampstead Heath rail. **Shows** 9pm Sat. **Admission** £7; £5 concessions. **Credit** MC, V.

This intimate, atmospheric basement venue tends to steer clear of open spots, instead offering stand-up bills filled with tried and tested performers.

Headliners

The George IV, 185 Chiswick High Road, Chiswick, W4 2DR (8566 4067/www.headlinerscomedy.biz). Turnham Green tube. **Shows** 9pm Fri; 8.30pm Sat. **Admission** £10.

West London's first purpose-built comedy club has gone down a treat in its first year. Expect lively audiences and strong stand-up bills.

Jongleurs Comedy Club

Battersea *Bar Risa, 49 Lavender Gardens, SW11 1DJ. Clapham Junction rail.* **Bow** *221 Grove Road, E3 1AA. Mile End tube.* **Camden** *Dingwalls, Camden Lock, Chalk Farm Road, NW1 8AB. Chalk Farm tube.* **All** *Information 0870 787 0707/box office 7564 2500/www.jongleurs.com.* **Shows** *Battersea* 8.45pm Fri, Sat. *Bow* 8.30pm Fri, Sat. *Camden* 8.15pm Fri, Sat. **Admission** *Battersea* £15. *Camden* £16. *Bow* £15. **Credit** AmEx, MC, V.

The first Jongleurs venue sprang up in 1983. Since then, the chain has grown so fast, you could call it the Starbucks of comedy (hell, there's even a branch in Magaluf). Love it or loathe it, the format is the same at each venue: quality comedy bills, plus a restaurant, and a disco afterwards.

Lee Hurst's Backyard Comedy Club

231 Cambridge Heath Road, Bethnal Green, E2 0EL (7739 3122/www.leehurst.com). Bethnal Green tube/rail. **Shows** 8pm Thur; 8.30pm Fri, Sat. **Admission** £5 Thur; £10-£12 Fri; £11-£13 Sat. **Credit** AmEx, MC, V.

Comedian Lee Hurst made his name on the popular TV game show *They Think It's All Over*. His relative fame and clout helps his east London venue attract top names. Hurst is there most nights.

Red Rose Comedy Club

129 Seven Sisters Road, Finsbury Park, N7 7QG (7281 3051/www.redrosecomedy.co.uk). Finsbury Park tube/rail. **Shows** 9pm Sat. **Admission** £7; £5 concessions. **No credit cards**.

Situated at the back of a Labour club, Red Rose is run by outspoken host Ivor Dembina. It has a 'no-frills' policy: no meals, no disco, drinks at pub prices and cheap admission, as well as top-notch comedy.

Up the Creek

302 Creek Road, Greenwich, SE10 9SW (8858 4581/www.up-the-creek.com). Greenwich DLR/rail. **Shows** 9pm Fri; 8.30pm Sat. **Admission** £10-£14; £6-£10 concessions. **Credit** AmEx, MC, V.

Some say audiences here are the most discerning on the circuit; others argue that they're just the rowdiest. Whatever they are, Up the Creek regulars come in droves, as it were, expecting strong bills that focus on stand-up sets. And they get them, usually. Both Up the Creek and Up the Creek Too were co-founded by eccentric London comedy legend Malcolm Hardee.

Other venues

For every comedy club that opens, another meets its maker. Be prepared for the details below to be ever-changing, and always phone the venues first. *Time Out* magazine's weekly Comedy pages contain even more listings to tickle your fancy.

Brixton Comedy Club *The Hobgoblin, 95 Effra Road, Brixton, SW2 1DF (7633 9539/www.brixton comedy.co.uk). Brixton tube/rail.* **Shows** 8.30pm Sun.

Comedy Brewhouse *Camden Head, 2 Camden Walk, Camden Passage, Islington, N1 8DY (7359 0851). Angel tube.* **Shows** 9pm Fri, Sat.

Covent Garden Comedy Club *20 Upper St Martins Lane, Covent Garden, WC2 (07960 071340). Leicester Square tube.* **Shows** 8.30pm Fri, Sat.

Hackney Empire Bullion Rooms *117 Wilton Way, Hackney, E8 1BH (8985 2424/www.hackney empire.co.uk). Hackney Central rail.* **Shows** days vary.

Hampstead Comedy Club *The Washington, 50 England's Lane, Hampstead, NW3 4UE (8299 2601/www.hampsteadcomedy.co.uk). Belsize Park or Chalk Farm tube.* **Shows** 9pm Sat.

Hen & Chickens Theatre *109 St Paul's Road, Highbury Corner, Highbury, N1 2NA (7704 2001/www.hen andchickens.com). Highbury & Islington tube/rail.* **Shows** 8pm Mon, Sun.

Laughing Horse Camden *Liberties Bar, 100 Camden High Street, Camden, NW1 0LU (07796 171 190/www.laughinghorse.co.uk). Camden Town tube.* **Shows** 8.30pm Wed.

Laughing Horse Richmond *Britannia, 5 Brewers Lane, Richmond, Surrey TW9 1HH (bookings 07796 171190/www.laughinghorse.co.uk). Richmond tube/rail.* **Shows** 8pm Sun.

Laughing Horse Soho *Coach & Horses, 1 Great Marlborough Street, Soho, W1F 7HG (bookings 07796 171 190/www.laughinghorse.co.uk). Oxford Circus tube.* **Shows** 8.30pm Tue, Sat.

Laughing Horse Wimbledon *267 The Broadway, Wimbledon, SW19 1SD (Bookings 07796 171 190/ www.laughinghorse.co.uk).* **Shows** 8.30pm Fri.

Mirth Control West Hampstead *Lower Ground Bar, 269 West End Lane, West Hampstead, NW6 1QS (7431 2211/www.mirthcontrol.co.uk). West Hampstead tube/rail.* **Shows** 8pm Wed.

Oxford Street Comedy Club *The Wheatsheaf, 25 Rathbone Place, Fitzrovia, W1T 1JB (7580 1585). Tottenham Court Road tube.* **Shows** 9pm Sat.

Pear-Shaped in Fitzrovia *Fitzroy Tavern, 16 Charlotte Street, Fitzrovia, W1T 2LY (7580 3714). Goodge Street tube.* **Shows** 8pm Wed.

Up the Creek Too *3 Brighton Road, Croydon, Surrey CR2 6EA (8680 5363/www.up-the-creek.com). South Croydon rail.* **Shows** 9pm Fri, 8.30pm Sat.

Cleaning up the act

The success of London's oldest comedy club is well documented: the **Comedy Store** (*see p275*) started life in 1979 above a Soho strip joint and soon became the home of alternative comedy. Eventually, it shifted to its current slick, high-tech, no-frills basement venue near Leicester Square, proving that insalubrious locations and bad sightlines were no hindrance to good entertainment. Indeed, back in the '80s, clubs in smoky basements, pub back rooms and at the ends of piers all kept the laughs coming.

Then in 1983 London's second purpose-built comedy club, **Jongleurs** (*see p275*), came along. Its founder took the idea of a comedy venue in the opposite direction with a mantra of 'Eat, Drink, Laugh, Dance'. Now there was comedy, real food, drinks and a disco after the show. Critics have described the chain as the McDonald's of comedy, but it has been very successful.

Thankfully, though, there are still plenty of down-to-earth clubs – for every Jongleurs, there's an **Up the Creek** (*see p276*) – and there are venues to ensure that comedy is a good night out – hell, you can even take a date to some of them, although you'd be advised not to sit in the front row.

A number of places have undergone serious refurbishment programmes in recent years (**Bound and Gagged**, *see p275*, looks very smart after its makeover). In 2002, Fuller's spent close to £400,000 converting the George IV pub for **Headliners** (*see p275*), and its promoter, Simon Randall, reckons it was worth every penny: 'If something is a bit smarter, people want to bring their friends to impress them. Since it opened it's been packed out almost every Saturday. I thought it would take a year or two to get to that point.' Sounds like they're laughing all the way to the bank down in Chiswick.

Dance

See the best moves, learn some fancy footwork.

London has one of the most sophisticated dance scenes in the world. Savvy programming by major venues, supplemented by activities at a number of smaller spaces, ensure that it thrives.

Apart from being a professional mecca, the city is bursting with classes for dance lovers, in genres from flamenco, Egyptian, African, street and swing to all varieties of Latin dance, including salsa and tango. Check the dance pages in *Time Out* magazine for the most comprehensive, up-to-date information on what to see and where to go, or try the website www.londondance.com.

The restoration work on the Coliseum, home to the English National Opera, has curtailed summertime visits by major dance companies. The English National Ballet, however, is scheduled to be back there by Christmas 2004.

Major venues

Barbican Centre

Silk Street, The City, EC2Y 8DS (7638 8891/ www.barbican.org.uk). Barbican tube/Moorgate tube/rail. **Box office** 10am-8pm Mon-Sat; noon-8pm Sun. **Phone bookings** 9am-8pm daily. **Tickets** £5-£30. **Credit** AmEx, MC, V. **Map** p402 P5.

The Barbican International Theatre Event (BITE) programme, now in its seventh year, has gradually turned this arts centre into a major player on London's dance scene. Contemporary moves from East, West and South Africa are spotlighted in January 2004. Israel's Batsheva company arrives with the gripping *Naharin's Virus* the week of 26 April 2004. Early October 2004 sees the return of American master Merce Cunningham's troupe, and in late November 2004 Taiwan's Cloud Gate Dance Theatre brings *Bamboo Dreams*.

The Place

17 Duke's Road, WC1H 9PY (7387 0031/ www.theplace.org.uk). Euston tube/rail. **Box office** 10.30am-6pm Mon-Fri; noon-6pm Sat; 8pm on performance evenings. **Tickets** £5-£15.**Credit** MC, V. **Map** p399 K3.

This internationally recognised dance venue provides top-notch professional training as well as classes in all genre for all levels. The 300-seat theatre presents innovative contemporary dance from around the globe. The 2004 seasons opens with *Resolution!*, a lively platform for emerging artists that can boast a different triple-bill nightly (5 Jan-14 Feb). Each autumn the venue is used by Dance Umbrella, the UK's top dance festival.

Royal Opera House

Bow Street, Covent Garden, WC2E 9DD (box office 7304 4000/textphone 7212 9228/www.royal operahouse.org). Covent Garden tube. **Box office** 10am-8pm Mon-Sat. **Tickets** £3-£170. **Credit** AmEx, DC, MC, V. **Map** p401 L7.

This magnificent theatre's main stage is home to the Royal Ballet, where you can see stars of the calibre of Carlos Acosta, Alina Cojocaru and Sylvie Guillem. In 2004 Monica Mason's first full season as artistic director honours 19th-century traditions via ballet warhorses *Giselle* (opens mid-Jan 2004) and *The Sleeping Beauty* (late Feb 2004). It also recognises artistic inroads made in the 20th century in a triple-bill by George Balanchine (from late Jan 2004), an exceptional tribute to Russian Serge Diaghilev (May 2004), Kenneth MacMillan's sensual dramas *Mayerling* (mid Mar 2004) and *Anastasia* (Apr 2004) and John Cranko's tragic *Onegin* (late May 2004).

Ticket prices start cheap (standing room or restricted views) and end high. The building has two more affordable spaces: the Linbury Studio Theatre, a 420-capacity theatre, a reputable mid-scale, West End venue for music and dance, and the Clore Studio Upstairs, for rehearsals, workshops and experimental performances. Programming responsibility for both lies with ex-Royal dancer Deborah Bull.

South Bank Centre

Belvedere Road, South Bank, SE1 8XX (box office 7960 4242/recorded information 7921 0973/ www.rfh.org.uk). Embankment tube/Waterloo tube/rail. **Box office** 11am-8pm daily; 11am-9pm on performance evenings. **Phone bookings** 9am-8pm daily. **Tickets** £6-£60. **Credit** AmEx, MC, V. **Map** p401 M8.

This multi-building complex regularly presents British and international dance companies in three

The best Venues

To look at

Laban Centre. *See p278.*

To see the best

Sadlers Wells. See p279.

To be amazed

The Place. *p277.*

To be stretched

Greenwich Dance Agency. *See p278.*

theatres: the huge Royal Festival Hall, the medium-sized Queen Elizabeth Hall and the pocket-sized Purcell Room. Highlights for 2004 include the return of *Vivisector*, a bewitching blend of dance and video from Austria (21-22 Feb), British ensemble CandoCo in new work by the inventive duo Protein Dance and American hot-shot Stephen Petronio (March 3-4), a bill shared by SBC resident artists Stephanie Schober and Robert Tannion (6-7 May), Lea Anderson's groups The Cholmondeleys and The Featherstonehaughs (20-21 May) and Belgian-Moroccan *wunderkind* Sidi Larbi Cherkaoui's ambitious, politically aware dance-theatre piece *Foi* (10-11 June). Each January the SBC is one of the prime venues for the London International Mime Festival (*see p259*). Annually, it hosts Free Summer on the South Bank, a huge and varied programme of community-aimed workshops, lectures and performances and, later in the year, some higher-profile Dance Umbrella festival events.

Other venues

Chisenhale Dance Space

64-84 Chisenhale Road, Bow, E3 5QZ (8981 6617/ www.chisenhaledancespace.co.uk). Bethnal Green/ Mile End tube. **Open** *Enquiries* 10am-6pm Mon-Sat. **Tickets** free-£5. **No credit cards**.

This seminal research centre for contemporary dance and movement-based disciplines runs workshops, community projects and a summer school.

The Circus Space

Coronet Street, N1 6HD (76134141/ www.thecircusspace.co.uk). Old Street tube/rail. **Open** 9am-10pm Mon-Fri, Sun; 10.30am-6pm Sat. **Classes** phone for details. **Membership** free. **Credit** MC, V.

Courses and workshops in all types of circus arts, from casual juggling to red-nose training for staff development, take place in this Hoxton venue. It also presents physical, choreographed performances in its impressive space (a gigantic former turbine hall).

Greenwich Dance Agency

Borough Hall, Royal Hill, Greenwich, SE10 8RE (8293 9741/www.greenwichdance.org.uk). Greenwich DLR/rail. **Box office** 9.30am-5.30pm Mon-Fri. **Classes** £3.75-£5. **Tickets** £7-£12 **Credit** MC, V.

Several of the country's best young companies and dance artists reside in this handsome old venue, where a variety of classes and workshops are complemented by an inventive programme of shows.

ICA

The Mall, Westminster, SW1Y 5AH (box office 7930 3647/www.ica.org.uk). Piccadilly Circus tube/Charing Cross tube/rail. **Box office** noon-9.30pm daily. **Tickets** £5-£20. **Membership** *Daily* £1.50, £1 concessions. *Weekend* £2.50; £1.50 concessions. Free under-14s. **Credit** AmEx, MC, V. **Map** p401 K8.

This trend-setting arts centre sometimes hosts movement-based theatre and performance with an avant-garde or technological bent.

Jacksons Lane

269A Archway Road, Highgate, N6 5AA (8341 4421/www.jacksonslane.org.uk). Highgate tube. **Open** 10am-11pm daily. **Phone bookings** 10am-7pm daily. **Tickets** £4.50-£10. **Credit** MC, V.

This community centre puts on many performances and activities, including contemporary dance. Zone 3, an autumn showcase of commissioned work from some of the UK's brightest new choreographers, may be spread through the year in 2004.

Laban Centre

Creekside, Lewisham, SE8 3TZ (information 8691 8600/tickets 8469 9500/www.laban.org). Deptford/Greenwich DLR. **Open** 9am-5.30pm Mon-Sat; until 8pm on performance evenings. **Tickets** £1-£15. **Credit** *Box office only* MC, V.

This independent conservatoire for contemporary dance training and research runs undergraduate and postgrad courses. Its £22 million premises include an intimate auditorium for shows by resident company Transitions, and dance performances by students and visiting companies.

Shobana-Jeyasingh Dance Company at **The Place**. *See p277.*

Pride of London Sadler's Wells

Sadler's Wells attracts world-class dance companies to its ultra-modern facilities. The current healthy crop of co-productions and collaborations can only enhance its status as the UK's leading dance house, which also occasionally presents opera and high-profile music theatre. The roster of dance artists is as exciting as it is eclectic.

Organisations like the Wells know that they must hook 'em while they're young. In that vein the Netherlands' **Introdans Ensemble** appears in the family-oriented entertainment *Beasts* (21-22 February).

March 2004 starts a balletic phase, with the **Moscow Dance Theatre** , then **Northern Ballet Theatre**'s *A Midsummer Night's Dream*. **Dance Theatre of Harlem** (29 March-10 April), which scored a bull's-eye when last at the Wells, returns with programmes slanted towards classics by Balanchine. **Royal New Zealand Ballet** makes its Wells debut at the end of April, with a triple-bill from British-based choreographers Mark Baldwin, Javier De Frutos and Christopher Hampson.

One of the Wells' most promising projects in 2004 is an international hip hop festival, curated by Brit Jonzi D and headlined by **Rennie Harris Puremovement**'s *Facing Mekka* (10-16 May). There's also a mixed bill from the **Rambert Dance Company** (25-29 May), after which Wells' resident company **Random** materialises in artistic director Wayne McGregor's *AtaXia*, a work by collaborators from the worlds of neuroscience, psychology and virtual design (3-5 June). Also in June, there's a celebration of the 20th anniversary season of the maverick **Bill T Jones/Arnie Zane Dance Company** (15-19 June).

Ten years ago the Wells premiered **Matthew Bourne**'s *Swan Lake*, a production that subsequently made West End history before touring the world, and he's going to do it all again (13 July-4 September).

Sadler's Wells/Peacock Theatre

Rosebery Avenue, Islington, EC1R 4TN (7863 8000/textphone 7863 7863/www.sadlers-wells.com). Angel tube. **Box office** 10am-8.30pm Mon-Sat. *Phone bookings* 9am-8.30pm Mon-Sat. **Tickets** £10-£45. **Credit** AmEx, MC, V. **Map** p402 N3.

Peacock Theatre

Portugal Street, off Kingsway, Holborn, WC2A 2HT (7863 8222/www.sadlers-wells.com). Holborn tube. **Box office** 10am-6.30pm Mon-Sat; 10am-8.30pm performance days. *Phone bookings* 9am-8.30pm Mon-Sat. **Tickets** £10-£35. **Credit** AmEx, MC, V. **Map** p399 M6.

Riverside Studios

Crisp Road, Hammersmith, W6 9RL (8237 1000/ box office 8237 1111/www.riversidestudios.co.uk). Hammersmith tube. **Box office** noon-9pm daily. **Tickets** £4.50-£12. **Credit** MC, V.

This arts and media centre occasionally presents British and international contemporary dance and physical theatre in three auditoria.

Dance classes

As well as all-rounders like the Greenwich Dance Agency (*see p278*) and Danceworks, London has a number of educational specialists. Cecil Sharp House offers fun classes in a variety of folk dance styles from around the world, while the London School of Capoeira teaches that Brazilian fusion of dance, gymnastics and martial arts.

Cecil Sharp House *English Folk Dance & Song Society, 2 Regent's Park Road, NW1 7AY (7485 2206/www.efdss.org). Camden Town tube.* **Open** *Enquiries* 9.30am-5.30pm Mon-Fri. **Classes** £5-£8.50. **No credit cards**.

Dance Attic *368 North End Road, Fulham, SW6 1LY (7610 2055). Fulham Broadway tube.* **Open** 9am-10pm Mon-Fri; 10am-5pm Sat, Sun. **Classes** £4-£6. *Membership* £1.50/day; £30/6mths; £50/yr. **Credit** MC, V. **Map** p396 A12.

Danceworks *16 Balderton Street, Mayfair, W1K 6TN (7629 6183/www.danceworks.co.uk). Bond Street tube.* **Open** 8am-10.15pm Mon-Fri; 9am-6.15pm Sat, Sun. **Classes** £4-£10. *Membership* £2-£4/day; £40/mth; £60-£120/yr. **Credit** AmEx, MC, V. **Map** p398 G6.

Drill Hall *16 Chenies Street, Fitzrovia, WC1E 7EX (7307 5060/www.drillhall.co.uk). Goodge Street tube.* **Open** 10am-9.30pm daily. **Classes** £5-£25; *Courses* £30-£100. **Credit** AmEx, MC, V. **Map** p399 K5.

London School of Capoeira *Units 1 & 2, Leeds Place, Tollington Park, Finsbury Park, N4 3RQ (7281 2020/www.londonschoolofcapoeira.co.uk). Finsbury Park tube/rail.* **Classes** 7.30-9.30pm Mon-Fri. **Fees** *Beginners' course* (4 lessons) £80; £60-£70 concessions. **No credit cards**. **Map** p399 K3.

Pineapple Dance Studio *7 Langley Street, Covent Garden, WC2H 9JA (78364004/www.pine apple.uk.com). Covent Garden tube.* **Open** 9am-9.30pm Mon-Fri; 9am-6pm Sat; 10am-6pm. **Classes** £5-£8. *Membership* £2/day; £4/evening; £60-£120/yr. **Credit** AmEx, MC, V. **Map** p399 L6.

Film

The pick of the flicks.

If you believe the movies, then you think that you can walk from Tower Bridge to Richmond Park in minutes, stopping off at Primrose Hill by way of Brick Lane. As anyone who's ever tried to circumnavigate the city will testify, this is more than optimistic. It's just plain bonkers. A fantastic voyage of a celluloid kind is possible, though, thanks to central London's Cinemascope-wide spectrum of picture houses. From the pile' em high multiplexes screening blockbusters, prequels and sequels, to exclusive members-only bars/cinemas, the film scene in London town is pretty varied.

This is not the case outside the city centre, though. Research by the London Assembly discovered in September 2003 that there are boroughs in London that have fewer cinemas than the national average – poor old Lewisham in south London hasn't a single picture house.

Only if you're a Bollywood fan is it worth travelling out of the centre. The racy potboilers and all-singing, all-dancing romances unfold mostly in the suburbs, and places like the Grade II-listed **Himalaya Palace** (*see p284*) justify a long journey in search of the exotic.

In the city centre, though, there are a number of first-run cinemas whose varied programmes stand out from the crowd. The **Renoir** and the **Barbican** (*see p281 and below*), both sitting plushly within grey 1960s developments, offer refined viewing, while the **ICA** (*see p281*) can be relied upon to provide arty, edgy, rare screenings. The **Riverside** (*see p284*) wears its silver-screen heritage proudly, but with the **National Film Theatre** (*see p284*) opting for more specialised seasons it's a little tougher to catch the old stuff. The **Prince Charles** (*see p284*) screens films over and over, offering the chance to see things you missed when all the other cinemas were showing them.

For cinema news see *Time Out* magazine each week. Time Out also publishes a fat and fantastic *Film Guide* (£19.99).

Films released in the UK are classified under the following categories: **U** – suitable for all ages; **PG** – open to all, parental guidance is advised; **12A** – under-12s only admitted with an over-18; **15** – no one under 15 is admitted; **18** – no one under 18 is admitted.

The best Cinemas

For lots of choice
Odeon Covent Garden has comfy seats, plenty of screens and cheaper tickets than in Leicester Square. *See p281.*

For watching with baby
The **Clapham Picture House**'s Thursday Parents and Babies screenings. *See 281.*

For audience participation
The **Prince Charles Cinema** (*see p284*) lets you sing your heart out with the *Singalong Wizard of Oz.*

For oldies and rarities
The **Riverside Studios** and the **National Film Theatre** (for both *see p284*).

First-run cinemas

In general the closer you are to Leicester Square, the more you're going to pay. Many cinemas charge less if you go on Mondays or before 5pm from Tuesday to Friday; call them for details. Book ahead if you're planning to see a blockbuster on the weekend of its release: new films emerge in the UK on Fridays.

Central London

Barbican

Silk Street, EC2Y 8DS (information 7382 7000/ bookings 7638 8891/www.barbican.org.uk). Barbican tube/Moorgate tube/rail. **Screens** 3. **Tickets** £7; £5.50 concessions; £4.50 Mon. **Credit** AmEx, MC, V. **Map** p402 P5.

Chelsea Cinema

206 King's Road, SW3 5XP (7351 3742). Sloane Square tube. **Screens** 1. **Tickets** £7.50-£8.50. Early shows £5.50; £3.50 concessions. **Credit** AmEx, MC, V. **Map** p397 E12.

Curzon

Mayfair *38 Curzon Street, W1J 7TY (7495 0500/ www.curzoncinemas.com). Green Park or Hyde Park Corner tube.* **Screens** 2. **Tickets** £8.50; £5.50 concessions (select times). Early shows £5.50. **Credit** AmEx, MC, V. **Map** p400 H8.

Soho *99 Shaftesbury Avenue, W1D 5DY (information 7439 4805/bookings 7734 2255). Leicester Square or Piccadilly Circus tube.*

Arts & Entertainment

Screens 3. **Tickets** £8.50; £5.50 concessions (at select times). Early shows £5.50. **Credit** AmEx, MC, V. **Map** p401 K6.

Empire
Leicester Square, WC2H 7HA (0870 010 2030/ www.uci-cinemas.co.uk). Leicester Square or Piccadilly Circus tube. **Screens** 3. **Tickets** £7.50-£9.50; £5-£6 concessions (select times). Early shows £5-£6. **Credit** AmEx, MC, V. **Map** p401 K7.

ICA Cinema
Nash House, The Mall, SW1Y 5AH (information 7930 6393/bookings 7930 3647/www.ica.org.uk). Piccadilly Circus tube/Charing Cross tube/rail. **Screens** 2. **Tickets** £6.50, £5.50 concessions. Early shows £4.50. Membership £20-£30/yr. **Credit** AmEx, DC, MC, V. **Map** p401 K8.

Renoir Brunswick Centre
Brunswick Square, WC1N 1AW (7837 8402). Russell Square tube. **Screens** 2. **Tickets** £7.50. Early shows £5; £3.50 concessions. **Credit** MC, V. **Map** p401 L4.

Screen on Baker Street
96 Baker Street, W1U 6TJ (information 7486 0036/bookings 7935 2772/www.screen cinemas.co.uk). Baker Street tube/Marylebone tube/rail. **Screens** 2. **Tickets** £6.80. Early shows £4.50. **Credit** MC, V. **Map** p398 G5.

Odeon
Covent Garden *135 Shaftesbury Avenue, WC2H 8AH (0870 505 0007/www.odeon.co.uk). Leicester Square or Tottenham Court Road tube.* **Screens** 4. **Tickets** £8.50; £5.50 concessions (select times). Early shows £5.50. **Credit** AmEx, MC, V. **Map** p399 K6.

Leicester Square *Leicester Square, WC2H 7LP (0870 505 0007/www.odeon.co.uk). Leicester Square tube.* **Screens** 1. **Tickets** £10.50-£12. Early shows £6-£7. **Credit** AmEx, MC, V. **Map** p401 K7.

Mezzanine *next to Odeon Leicester Square, WC2H 7LP (0870 505 0007/www.odeon.co.uk). Leicester Square tube.* **Screens** 5. **Tickets** £8. Early shows £5. **Credit** AmEx, MC, V. **Map** p401 K7.

Marble Arch *10 Edgware Road, W2 7DN (0870 505 0007/www.odeon.co.uk). Marble Arch tube.* **Screens** 5. **Tickets** £8.90; £5.70 concessions (select times). Early shows £5.70. **Credit** AmEx, MC, V. **Map** p395 F6.

Panton Street *11-18 Panton Street, SW1Y 4DP (0870 505 0007/www.odeon.co.uk). Piccadilly Circus tube.* **Screens** 4. **Tickets** £8; £5.50. Early shows £5.50. **Credit** AmEx, MC, V. **Map** p401 K7.

Tottenham Court Road *Fitzrovia, W1T 1BX (0870 505 0007/www.odeon.co.uk). Tottenham Court Road tube.* **Screens** 3. **Tickets** £8.20; £5.50 concessions. Early shows £5.50. **Credit** AmEx, MC, V. **Map** p399 K5.

Wardour Street *10 Wardour Street, Soho, W1D 6QF (0870 505 0007/www.odeon.co.uk). Leicester Square or Piccadilly Circus tube.* **Screens** 4. **Tickets** £7.50; £5.50 concessions. Early shows £5.50. **Credit** AmEx, MC, V. **Map** p401 K7.

West End *Leicester Square, WC2H 7LP (0870 505 0007/www.odeon.co.uk). Leicester Square tube.* **Screens** 2. **Tickets** £10.50; £6 concessions (select times). Early shows £6. **Credit** AmEx, MC, V. **Map** p401 K7.

The Other Cinema
11 Rupert Street, W1V 7FS (information 7437 0757/bookings 7734 1506/www.picturehouse-cinemas.co.uk). Leicester Square or Picadilly Circus tube. **Screens** 2. **Tickets** £8; £4.50 concessions (select times). Early shows & Mon £4.50. No concessions available Fri-Sun. **Membership** £25 single; £43 joint; £15 students; £6 mailing list. **Credit** MC, V. **Map** p401 K7.

UGC
Haymarket *63-5 Haymarket, SW1Y 4RQ (0870 907 0712). Piccadilly Circus tube.* **Screens** 3. **Tickets** £7.90; £5 concessions (select times). Early shows £4 before noon, £5 before 5pm. **Credit** AmEx, MC, V. **Map** p401 K7.

UGC Shaftesbury Avenue *Trocadero, W1D 7AQ (0870 907 0716). Piccadilly Circus tube.* **Screens** 7. **Tickets** £7.90; £5 concessions (select times). Early shows £4. **Credit** AmEx, MC, V. **Map** p401 K7.

UGC Chelsea *279 King's Road, SW3 5EW (0870 907 0710). Sloane Square tube then 11, 19, 22, 319 bus.* **Screens** 4. **Tickets** £8.30; £4.90 concessions. £5.50 before 5pm Mon-Fri. **Credit** AmEx, MC, V. **Map** p397 E12.

Warner Village West End
Leicester Square, WC2H 7AL (0870 240 6020/ www.warnervillage.co.uk). Leicester Square tube. **Screens** 7. **Tickets** £10-£11; £7.50 concessions. *Early shows* £8.50. **Credit** MC, V. **Map** p401 K7.

Outer London

Clapham Picture House
76 Venn Street, Clapham, SW4 0AT (information 7498 2242/bookings 7498 3323/www.picture houses.co.uk). Clapham Common tube. **Screens** 4. **Tickets** £7; £4 concessions; no concessions Fri-Sun; £5 for all before 6pm Tue-Sun; £4 all day Mon. **Credit** MC, V.

Electric Cinema
191 Portobello Road, W11 2ED (information 7908 9696/www.the-electric.co.uk). Ladbroke Grove or Notting Hill Gate tube. **Screens** 1. **Tickets** £10-£12.50; £5-£7.50 Mon. **Credit** AmEx, MC, V.

Everyman Hampstead
5 Hollybush Vale, Hampstead, NW3 6TX (08700 664777/www.everymancinema.com). Hampstead tube. **Screens** 2. **Tickets** £8 (luxury £15); £7 concessions (select times). **Credit** MC, V.

Gate Cinema
87 Notting Hill Gate, Notting Hill, W11 3JZ (7727 4043/www.gatecinema.co.uk). Notting Hill Gate tube. **Screens** 1. **Tickets** £7; £3.50 concessions (select times). Early shows £5. **Credit** MC, V. **Map** p394 A7.

Puttin' on the Ritzy

Question: how do you get Hollywood hunks Denzel Washington and George Clooney to deepest south London?
Answer: The **Ritzy** cinema (*see p282*).
But the historic picture house at the top of humble Coldharbour Lane is no hip members bar hang-out. Instead, the cherished former fleapit is the epitome of a local London cinema done good. Its five screens provide a shimmering heart to an area known and loved for its diversity.

'We've tried to make the cinema an integral part of the neighbourhood,' says general manager Lynn Morrison, 'and I think we're a real asset. If multiplexes are the Starbucks of cinema, providing choice but little else, we're trying to be Bar Italia, with taste and tradition.'

Tradition makes the Ritzy special. Opened as the Electric Pavilion on 11 March 1911, it was one of the country's first purpose-built cinemas, with more than 750 seats in the single auditorium. Many of the original fittings remain, and the façade, reception and Screen 1 (which now seats 352) are all Grade II listed.

Walking into the principal auditorium, with its nine proscenium arches supporting the egg-shell curve of the ceiling, it seems almost a shame to sit in the dark. It's a good thing, then, that a varied programme lights up the room. A mix of first-run blockbusters, art-

Notting Hill Coronet

103 Notting Hill Gate, Notting Hill, W11 3LB (7727 6705). Notting Hill Gate tube. **Screens** 2. **Tickets** £7; £4.50 concessions (select times). Early shows £4.50. **Credit** MC, V. **Map** p394 A7.

Odeon

Camden Town *14 Parkway, Camden, NW1 5EL (0870 505 0007/www.odeon.co.uk). Camden Town tube.* **Screens** 5. **Tickets** £7; £4-£5 concessions (select times). £5 Tue. Early shows £5. **Credit** AmEx, MC, V.

Holloway Road *419-27 Holloway Road, Holloway, N7 5ND (0870 505 0007/www.odeon.co.uk). Holloway Road tube.* **Screens** 8. **Tickets** £6.70; £4.50 concessions (select times). Early shows £4.50. **Credit** AmEx, MC, V.

Kensington *263 Kensington High Street, Kensington, W8 6NA (0870 505 0007/www.odeon.co.uk). High Street Kensington tube.* **Screens** 6. **Tickets** £8.90; £5.50 concessions (select times). Early shows (before 3pm) £5.50. **Credit** AmEx, MC, V. **Map** p396 A9.

Putney *26 High Street, Putney, SW15 1SN (0870 505 0007/www.odeon.co.uk). Putney Bridge tube.* **Tickets** £7.20; £4.50. **Credit** AmEx, DC, V.

Swiss Cottage *96 Finchley Road, Swiss Cottage, NW3 5EL (0870 505 0007/www.odeon.co.uk). Swiss Cottage tube.* **Screens** 6. **Tickets** £7.20; £4.50-£5.20 concessions (select times). Early shows £4.70. **Credit** AmEx, MC, V.

Phoenix

52 High Road, Finchley, N2 (information 8883 2233/bookings 8444 6789/www.phoenixcinema.co.uk). East Finchley tube. **Screens** 1. **Tickets** £4-£6; £3.50-£4 concessions (select times). Early shows £3.50-£4.50. **Credit** MC, V.

Rio Cinema

107 Kingsland High Street, Dalston, E8 2PB (7254 6677/www.riocinema.org.uk). Dalston Kingsland rail/30, 38, 56, 76, 149, 236, 242, 243, 277 bus. **Screens** 1. **Tickets** £7; £5.50 concessions; £5 Mon. Early shows £5; £4 concessions. **Credit** AmEx, MC, V.

Ritzy

Brixton Oval, Coldharbour Lane, Brixton, SW2 1JG (bookings 7733 2229). Brixton tube/rail. **Screens** 5. **Tickets** £7; £4 concessions; £4.50 Mon. Early shows £5. **Credit** MC, V.

Screen on the Green

83 Upper Street, Islington, N1 0NU (7226 3520/www.screencinemas.co.uk). Angel tube. **Screens** 1. **Tickets** £6.80. Early shows £4.50. **Credit** MC, V. **Map** p402 O2.

Screen on the Hill

203 Haverstock Hill, Belsize Park, NW3 4QG (7435 3366/www.screencinemas.co.uk). Belsize Park tube. **Screens** 1. **Tickets** £8; £5 concessions (select times); £5.50 Mon. Early shows £5.50. **Credit** MC, V.

house pictures, matinées, special seasons and discount shows combine to mark the cinema as something of a local hero.

You don't just have to watch films, either. For £195 – even less for the unemployed and students – you can make a movie in a day by scripting, shooting, editing and then viewing a short film in 24 hours using the Ritzy's glitzy new editing suites. So you can jump head first into film. This is one of only two UK cinemas to own a digital projection system. That's real star quality.

Tricycle Cinema

269 Kilburn High Road, Kilburn, NW6 7JR (information 7328 1900/bookings 7328 1000/ www.tricycle.co.uk). Kilburn tube. **Screens** 1. **Tickets** £7; £6 concessions (select times); £4.50 Mon. **Credit** MC, V.

UCI

Surrey Quays *Surrey Quays Leisure Centre, Redriff Road, Surrey Quays, SE16 7LL (0870 010 2030/www.uci-cinemas.co.uk). Surrey Quays tube.* **Screens** 9. **Tickets** £6; £4 concessions. Early shows £5 (select times). **Credit** AmEx, MC, V.

Whiteleys *2nd floor, Whiteleys Shopping Centre, Queensway, Bayswater, W2 4YL (0870 010 2030/ www.uci-cinemas.co.uk). Bayswater or Queensway tube.* **Screens** 8. **Tickets** £8; £4-£5 concessions (select times). Early shows £5.75. **Credit** AmEx, MC, V. **Map** p394 C6.

UGC

Fulham Road *142 Fulham Road, Chelsea, SW10 9QR (0870 907 0711). South Kensington tube.* **Screens** 6. **Tickets** £8.10; £4.50 concessions (select times). Early shows £5. **Credit** AmEx, MC, V. **Map** p397 D11.

UGC Hammersmith *207 King Street, Hammersmith, W6 9JT (0870 907 0718). Ravenscourt Park tube.* **Screens** 4. **Tickets** £6; £4-£4.90 concessions. Early shows £4.90. **Credit** AmEx, MC, V.

Warner Village

Finchley Road *255 Finchley Road, Swiss Cottage, NW3 6LU (0870 240 6020/www.warnervillage.co.uk). Finchley Road tube.* **Screens** 8. **Tickets** £7.80; £4.50-£5.50 concessions. Early shows £5.40. **Credit** MC, V.

Islington *Parkfield Street, Islington, N1 7AL (0870 240 6020/www.warnervillage.co.uk). Angel tube.* **Screens** 8. **Tickets** £8.10; £5.50 concessions. Early shows £5.80. **Credit** MC, V.

Shepherd's Bush *West 12 Centre, Shepherd's Bush Green, Shepherd's Bush, W12 0PA (0870 240 6020/www.warnervillage.co.uk). Shepherd's Bush tube.* **Screens** 12. **Tickets** £6.90; £4.20-£5 concessions. Early shows £5. **Credit** MC, V.

Repertory cinemas

In addition to the spots listed below, there are several cinemas (detailed earlier) that often offer a more limited selection of rep-style fare. These include venues such as the **Curzon Soho**, the **Electric**, the **Phoenix**, the **Rio**, the **ICA** and the **Ritzy**.

Ciné Lumière I

Institut Français, 17 Queensberry Place, South Kensington, SW7 2DT (7073 1350/www.institut. ambafrance.org.uk). South Kensington tube. **Screens** 1. **Tickets** £7; £5 concessions; £4 members. **Credit** MC, V. **Map** p397 D10.

National Film Theatre (NFT)

South Bank, SE1 8XT (information 7633 0274/ bookings 7928 3232/www.bfi.org.uk/nft). Embankment tube/Waterloo tube/rail. **Screens** 3. **Tickets** £6.50; £4.70 concessions. **Credit** AmEx, MC, V. **Map** p401 M7.

Prince Charles

7 Leicester Place, Leicester Square, WC2H 7BY (information 0901 272 7007 premium rate/bookings 7494 3654/www.princecharlescinema.com). Leicester Square tube. **Screens** 1. **Tickets** £3-£4 non-members; £1.50-£3 members. **Credit** MC, V. **Map** p401 K7.

Riverside Studios

Crisp Road, Hammersmith, W6 9RL (8237 1111/ www.riversidestudios.co.uk). Hammersmith tube. **Screens** 1. **Tickets** £5.50; £4.50 concessions. **Credit** MC, V.

Watermans Arts Centre

40 High Street, Brentford, Middx TW8 0DS (8232 1010/www.watermans.org.uk). Brentford or Kew Bridge rail. **Screens** 1. **Tickets** £6.50 non-members; £5.85 members; £4.50 concessions. **Credit** MC, V.

Bollywood cinemas

Boleyn Cinema

11 Barking Road, Newham, E6 1PW (8471 4884). Upton Park rail. **Tickets** £5; £3.50 Tue. Early shows £3.50. **No credit cards**.

Cineworld Wood Green

High Street, Wood Green, N22 6LU (8829 1400/ www.cineworld.co.uk). Wood Green tube. **Tickets** £5.50; £3.70 concessions. Early shows £3.20. £1 Kids Club (10am Sat). **Credit** MC, V.

Himalaya Palace

14 South Road, Southall, Middx UB1 3AD (8813 8844/www.himalayapalacecinema.com). Southall rail. **Tickets** £5.50 Mon-Thur; £5.95 Fri-Sun. **Credit** MC, V.

Safari Cinema, Harrow

Station Road, Harrow, Middx HA1 2TY (8426 0303/www.safaricinema.com). Harrow & Wealdstone tube/rail. **Tickets** £6; £4 concessions. Early shows £4. **Credit** AmEx, MC, V.

Uxbridge Odeon

The Chimes Shopping Centre, Uxbridge, Middx UB8 1GD (0870 505 0007/www.odeon.co.uk). **Tickets** £6; £5 concessions. Early shows £5. **Credit** AmEx, MC, V.

IMAX

BFI London IMAX Cinema

1 Charlie Chaplin Walk, South Bank, SE1 8XR (7902 1234/www.bfi.org.uk/imax). Embankment tube/Waterloo tube/rail. **Screens** 1. **Tickets** £7.50; £4.95-£6.20 concessions; free under-3s. **Credit** AmEx, MC, V. **Map** p401 M8.

This great 480-seater, drum-shaped building near Waterloo station has the biggest screen in the country for your 3-D delectation.

Science Museum IMAX Theatre

Exhibition Road, South Kensington, SW7 2DD (0870 870 4868/www.sciencemuseum.org.uk). South Kensington tube. **Screens** 1. **Tickets** £7.10; £5.95 concessions. **Credit** AmEx, MC, V. **Map** p397 D9.

A big noise in a big museum, *see also p136.*

Festivals

Human Rights Watch International Film Festival

Primarily based in Ritzy Cinema, see p282 (bookings 7733 2229/www.hrw.org). Brixton tube/rail. **Dates** 18-25 Mar 2004.

Screens fiction, documentary and animated films and videos with a distinctive human rights theme.

London Lesbian & Gay Film Festival

National Film Theatre, South Bank, SE1 8XT (7928 3232/www.llgff.org.uk/www.bfi.org.uk). Embankment tube/Waterloo tube/rail. **Dates** 24 Mar-7 Apr 2004. **Map** p401 M7.

Screens 186 new and restored films from around the world, plus a range of special events.

Rushes Soho Shorts Festival

Venues around Soho, W1 (7851 6207/ www.sohoshorts.com). Leicester Square, Piccadilly Circus or Tottenham Court Road tube. **Dates** TBA.

Around 60 short films and music videos by new directors are screened for free at venues across Soho, from cafés to cinemas.

BFM International Film Festival

Venues around London (8531 9199/www.bfm media.com). **Dates** 10-20 Sept 2004.

This *Black Filmmaker*-programmed festival shows a variety of works from both inside and outside the cinematic mainstream.

Latin American Film Festival

The Other Cinema, see p281 (7851 7042/www.latin americanfilmfestival.com). Leicester Square tube. **Dates** Sept 2004. **Map** p401 K7.

New movies from Latin America are showcased, but it's perpetually threatened, so call ahead to check if it got funding this year.

Raindance

Venues around London (7287 3833/www.rain dance.co.uk). Leicester Square tube. **Date** 20 Oct-7 Nov 2004.

Britain's largest indie film festival concentrates on first-time directors.

London Film Festival

Venues around London (7928 3232/www.lff.org.uk). **Dates** Oct/Nov 2004.

The biggest film festival in the UK, now in its 47th year, is a broad church; for further details, *see p265.*

Galleries

London's more interesting spaces.

Two major events in 2003 saw London really mature into its role as a world-class centre for contemporary art. The opening in April of the **Saatchi Gallery** at County Hall (*see p73*) gave museum status to the YBAs – Damien Hirst, Tracey Emin, Jake & Dinos Chapman, Gavin Turk – who put contemporary British art on the map. And, held in October, the **Frieze Art Fair** drew important galleries from Europe and America – the first time in recent memory that a London art fair has managed to attract major players on the international scene.

London's rising profile in the contemporary art market has been reflected in high-key gallery openings, such as **Sprüth Magers Lee** (*see p287*), a London branch for German gallerists Monika Sprüth and Philomene Magers, which opened in January.

This activity has to some extent revived the flagging central London scene, and the capital's big commercial galleries are buoyant. London's alternative, non-profit-making and artist-run spaces, however, continue to struggle. High rents in the centre of town have pushed those that survive further out to the fringes. Starved of much-needed new talent, London is in danger of becoming a more conservative city.

The galleries listed below are only a sample of what's on offer. Bigger spaces are listed in the Sightseeing chapters. They include the **Barbican** (*see p94*), **Camden Arts Centre** (*see p147*), the **Courtauld Gallery** (*see p96*) and **Hermitage Rooms** (*see p97*), the **Dulwich Picture Gallery** (*see p170*), the **Hayward Gallery** (*see p73*), the **ICA** (*see p130*), the **National Gallery** (*see p127*), the **Royal Academy of Arts** (*see p113*), the **Saatchi Gallery** (*see p73*), the **Serpentine Gallery** (*see p138*), **Tate Britain** (*see p134*), **Tate Modern** (*see p78*) and the **Whitechapel Art Gallery** (*see p153*).

Some galleries close in August; many also have little to see between shows: phone ahead or consult *Time Out* magazine. A free brochure, *New Exhibitions of Contemporary Art*, is available at galleries or at www.newexhibitions.com.

The best Galleries

For installation art
Matt's Gallery. *See p289.*

For emerging talent
Vilma Gold. *See p290.*

For cock-snooking Brit Art
White Cube. *See p291.*

For Bond Street chic
Haunch of Venison. *See p287.*

Central

Anthony Reynolds Gallery

60 Great Marlborough Street, Mayfair, W1F 7BG (7439 2201). Oxford Circus tube. **Open** 10am-6pm Tue-Sat. **No credit cards. Map** p398 J6.

Richard Billingham and Mark Wallinger are two high-profile artists represented by Anthony Reynolds. In 2002 the gallery moved to this beautifully converted building.

aspreyjacques

4 Clifford Street, Mayfair, W1S 2LG (7287 7675/ www.aspreyjacques.com). Green Park or Piccadilly Circus tube. **Open** 10am-6pm Tue-Sat. **No credit cards. Map** p400 J7.

Charles Asprey and Alison Jacques opened this elegant space in 1998, with the aim of looking outside London to emerging centres of contemporary art such as Berlin. The 2004 programme includes work by LA-based artists Jeff Ono and Jon Pylypchuk as well as selections from the estate of photographer Robert Mapplethorpe.

Entwistle

6 Cork Street, Mayfair, W1S 3EE (7734 6440/ www.entwistlegallery.com). Green Park or Piccadilly Circus tube. **Open** 10am-5.30pm Tue-Sat. **Credit** MC, V. **Map** p400 J7.

Entwistle shows a mixed bag of overseas and home-grown talent. Typical of the eclectic programme in 2003 were Conrad Shawcross's machine/sculptures and the group exhibition 'Paris is Burning', which also featured Jennie Livingstone's documentary about New York subcultures. Another significant exhibition was 'House and Garage' by rising London-based artists Oliver Payne and Nick Relph. For current exhibitions, check the website.

FA Projects

1-2 Bear Gardens, Southwark, SE1 9ED (7928 3228/www.faprojects.com). Southwark tube. **Open** 10am-6pm Tue-Fri; noon-5pm Sat. **No credit cards.** MC, V. **Map** p404 P7.

TATE

Two great galleries in the heart of London. Outstanding art, spectacular buildings, live events and an ideal place to meet friends or escape.

TATE BRITAIN
The world's greatest collection of British art from 1500 to the present day
Admission free
⊖ Pimlico

BP Displays at Tate Britain

TATE MODERN
The leading gallery of international modern and contemporary art
Admission free
⊖ Southwark

For further information **call 020 7887 8008** or visit www.tate.org.uk and sign up to free monthly email bulletins.

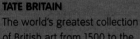

Flexibility is the philosophy behind FA Projects. Here since 2001, the gallery works as a commercial venture, a platform for emerging artists, initiates external projects and hosts a residency programme.

Frith Street Gallery

59-60 Frith Street, Soho, W1D 3JN (7494 1550/ www.frithstreetgallery.com). Tottenham Court Road tube. **Open** 10am-6pm Tue-Fri; 11am-4pm Sat. **No credit cards. Map** p399 K6.

Frith Street's interlinked rooms have hosted some great shows in recent years. The gallery represents a growing band of international figures, including Marlene Dumas, Tacita Dean and Callum Innes.

Gagosian

8 Heddon Street, Mayfair, W1B 4BS (7292 8222/ www.gagosian.com). Oxford Circus or Piccadilly Circus tube. **Open** 10am-6pm Tue-Sat; by appointment Mon. **No credit cards. Map** p400 J7.

US superdealer Larry Gagosian ('Go-Go' to his friends), opened this London branch in 2000, and has since brought over a wealth of big names – not the least of them being Andy Warhol, Jasper Johns – as well as lesser-known US and European artists. Brits represented include painters Peter Davies and Dexter Dalwood. The gallery will announce details of new premises in spring/summer 2004; check the website for details.

Haunch of Venison

6 Haunch of Venison Yard, Mayfair, W1K 5ES (7495 5050/www.haunchofvenison.com). Bond Street tube. **Open** 10am-6pm Mon-Wed, Fri; 10am-7pm Thur; 10am-5pm Sat. **Credit** AmEx, MC, V. **Map** p398 H6.

Previously leased as a project space by Anthony d'Offay (who retired in 2001), Haunch is now run by Harry Blain, a founder of nearby Blains Fine Art, and Graham Southern, ex-director of the Anthony d'Offay Gallery. First up was an exhibition by sculptor Rachel Whiteread, followed by photographs by filmmaker Wim Wenders. Highlights of the 2004 programme include work by LA-based artist Robert Therrien, known for his enlarged furniture.

Jerwood Space

171 Union Street, Bankside, SE1 0LN (7654 0171/ www.jerwoodspace.co.uk). Borough or Southwark tube. **Open** 10am-6pm daily (during exhibitions; phone to check). **No credit cards. Map** p404 O8.

Just when we'd given up hope of ever again seeing cutting-edge contemporary art at the Jerwood Space, a new initiative was announced: a platform for young artists based on nominations by critics and curators. The gallery also hosts the annual Jerwood Painting Prize, which with a first prize of £30,000 is the most valuable award for painting in the UK.

Lisson

29 & 52-4 Bell Street, Marylebone, NW1 5DA (7724 2739/www.lissongallery.com). Edgware Road tube. **Open** 10am-6pm Mon-Fri; 11am-5pm Sat. **Credit** MC, V. **Map** p395 E5.

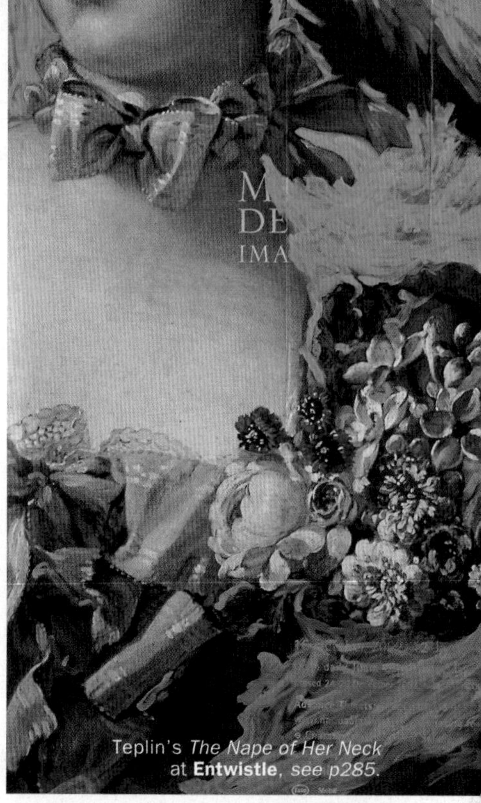

Teplin's *The Nape of Her Neck* at **Entwistle**, *see p285*.

Tony Fretton's 1991 building is one of London's most beautiful spaces, a superb platform for artists including Douglas Gordon, Dan Graham and the 'Lisson Sculptors': Anish Kapoor, Richard Wentworth, Tony Cragg and Richard Deacon. Names new to the stable, such as Roddy Buchanan, Ceal Floyer and Jemima Stehli, prove that founder Nicholas Logsdail isn't resting on his laurels. In 2002 a second space opened in Bell Street. Expect Julian Opie, Jason Martin and John Baldessari in 2004.

Sadie Coles HQ

35 Heddon Street, Mayfair, W1B 4BP (7434 2227/ www.sadiecoles.com). Oxford Circus or Piccadilly Circus tube. **Open** 10am-6pm Tue-Sat. **No credit cards. Map** p400 J7.

Sarah Lucas, Elizabeth Peyton, John Currin... Sadie Coles represents some of the hippest artists from both sides of the Atlantic and continues to scour the globe for new names, so this space gets the hottest names in the business. Last year, the gallery was extended into an upstairs space, making room for a larger main gallery and an additional viewing area.

Sprüth Magers Lee

12 Berkeley Street, Mayfair, W1J 8DT (7491 0100/ www.spruethmagerslee.com). Green Park tube. **Open** 9.30am-6pm Mon-Fri; 11am-4pm Sat. **No credit cards. Map** p400 H7.

Rotunda Gallery: Jake and Dinos Chapman, Tracey Emin, Damien Hirst, Sarah Lucas, Ron Mueck, Chris Ofili, Jenny Saville, Marc Quinn
Boiler Room: New Young Artists
Display Galleries: Duane Hanson, Paula Rego Cecily Brown, Peter Doig, Ashley Bickerton
Permanent Installation: Richard Wilson Oil Room

Saatchi Gallery: 020 7823 2363
County Hall, South Bank London SE1 Next to London Eye
Entrances on Riverside and Belvedere Road
⊖ Waterloo/Westminster. Daily 10am-8pm
Fri & Sat till 10pm. £8.50, concs. £6.50
Family Ticket: £25.00 Groups: £5.00 - 020 7928 8195
Advanced Tickets: 0870 1660 278
www.saatchi-gallery.co.uk

Sponsored by Time Out London

THE SAATCHI GALLERY

Royal Academy of Arts

Situated in the heart of the West End, the RA has a packed programme of exhibitions

Highlights for 2004 include

The Art of Philip Guston (1913-1980)
24 January - 12 April

Vuillard: From Post Impressionist to Modern Master 31 January - 18 April

Tamara de Lempicka:
The Art Deco years 15 May - 30 August

Summer Exhibition 2004
8 June - 16 August

And in March the RA's **Fine Rooms** open to the public for the first time and for no charge

See listings for details

www.royalacademy.org.uk

Open from 10am-6pm, 10pm on Fridays.
Tickets available daily at the RA, online or from 0870 848 8484
⊖ Green Park, Piccadilly Circus

Tamara de Lempicka, *La convalescente*, 1932. Private Collection. Photo courtesy of Barry Friedman Ltd., New York. © ADAGP, Paris and DACS, London 2004

Monika Sprüth and Philomene Magers oversee galleries in Cologne and Munich, where they represent major names such as Richard Artschwager, John Baldessari and Ed Ruscha. Their London branch opened last year with works by American minimalist master Donald Judd, followed by an installation by Barbara Kruger. Cindy Sherman, Stephen Shore and George Condo will show in 2004.

Stephen Friedman

25-8 Old Burlington Street, Mayfair, W1S 3AN (7494 1434/www.stephenfriedman.com). Green Park or Piccadilly Circus tube. **Open** 10am-6pm Tue-Fri; 11am-5pm Sat. **No credit cards. Map** p400 J7.

A shopfronted space, showing a range of inter national artists, including Yinka Shonibare, Vong Phaophanit and Stephan Balkenhol. Look forward to photographs by Catherine Opie and Tom Friedman's sculpture in 2004.

Timothy Taylor Gallery

24 Dering Street, Mayfair, W1J 6LS (7409 3344/ www.timothytaylorgallery.com). Oxford Circus or Bond Street tube. **Open** 10am-6pm Mon-Fri; 11am-5pm Sat. **No credit cards. Map** p398 H6.

The gap left in Dering Street by the closure in 2001 of Anthony d'Offay Gallery has been partly filled by Timothy Taylor's new joint, which opened in 2003 with a group show of gallery artists – including painters Fiona Rae, Alex Katz and Sean Scully, and photographer Mario Testino.

Waddington Galleries

11 Cork Street, Mayfair, W1S 3LT (7437 8611/ www.waddington-galleries.com). Green Park or Piccadilly Circus tube. **Open** 10am-5.30pm Mon-Fri; 10.30am-1.30pm Sat. **No credit cards. Map** p400 J7.

If it's a selection of blue-chip stock you're after, head to Waddington Galleries. You're likely to find a smörgåsbord of British and American modernism in the gallery's changing displays, as well as solo shows by UK and US big guns.

East

The Approach

Approach Tavern, 1st floor, 47 Approach Road, Bethnal Green, E2 9LY (8983 3878/www.the approachgallery.co.uk). Bethnal Green tube. **Open** noon-6pm Wed-Sun; also by appointment. **No credit cards.**

By referring to the Approach as 'a great pub with a gallery attached', most commentators get the measure of this place entirely wrong. Certainly, the Approach Tavern is a fine East End boozer but the gallery located on the first floor is the draw – with a stable that includes Turner Prize nominee Michael Raedecker and Beck's Future's winner Tim Stoner.

Chisenhale Gallery

64 Chisenhale Road, Bow, E3 5QZ (8981 4518/ www.chisenhale.org.uk). Mile End tube/D6, 8, 277 bus. **Open** 1-6pm Wed-Sun. **No credit cards.**

This former factory contains a dance space, artists' studios and a large gallery. One of the few truly independent spaces in the East End and a vital part of the scene, Chisenhale has a reputation for spotting the stars of tomorrow and continues to commission work by young or lesser-known artists.

Counter Gallery

44A Charlotte Road, Shoreditch, EC2 (7684 4518/www.countergallery.com). Old Street tube. **Open** noon-6pm Thur-Sat. **No credit cards. Map** p403 R4.

Responsible for such seminal shows as 'Modern Medicine' in 1990, Carl Freedman is an old hand at promoting young British art and, from this smart Shoreditch gallery, continues to focus his attention on new and emerging artists. Along with the gallery, Freedman co-ordinates Counter Editions, which produces prints and editions by YBAs including Tracey Emin and Jake & Dinos Chapman.

Flowers East

82 Kingsland Road, Hoxton, E2 8DP (7920 7777/ www.flowerseast.com). Old Street tube. **Open** 10am-6pm Tue-Sat; 11am-5pm Sun. **Credit** AmEx, MC, V. **Map** p403 R3.

British painting dominates at Flowers East, and at its four other spaces: Piccadilly's Flowers Central (21 Cork Street), Flowers Madison Avenue and Flowers West (beyond our remit in New York City and Santa Monica, LA). The Kingsland Road branch in East London also contains Flowers Graphics.

Interim Art

21 Herald Street, Bethnal Green, E2 6JT (7729 4112). Bethnal Green tube. **Open** 11am-6pm Wed-Sun; also by appointment. **No credit cards. Map** p403 R3.

Here since 1999, Maureen Paley's Interim Art represents Turner Prize-winners Wolfgang Tillmans and Gillian Wearing, Paul Noble (best known for drawings of the fictitious town, Nobson) along with sculptor Rebecca Warren.

Matt's Gallery

42-4 Copperfield Road, Mile End, E3 4RR (8983 1771/www.mattsgallery.org). Mile End tube. **Open** noon-6pm Wed-Sun; also by appointment. **No credit cards.**

There are few galleries in town as well respected as Matt's. Over two decades, it has commissioned installations as memorable as *20:50*, Richard Wilson's expanse of sump oil (now in the Saatchi Gallery) and Mike Nelson's *Coral Reef.* Installation continues to be the gallery's forte, with work by Lucy Gunning and Nathaniel Mellors in 2004.

The Showroom

44 Bonner Road, Bethnal Green, E2 9JS (8983 4115/www.theshowroom.org). Bethnal Green tube. **Open** 1-6pm Wed-Sun. **No credit cards.**

The Showroom has gained a reputation over the years for its commitment to young artists. And, in fact, it often commissions large-scale works at early

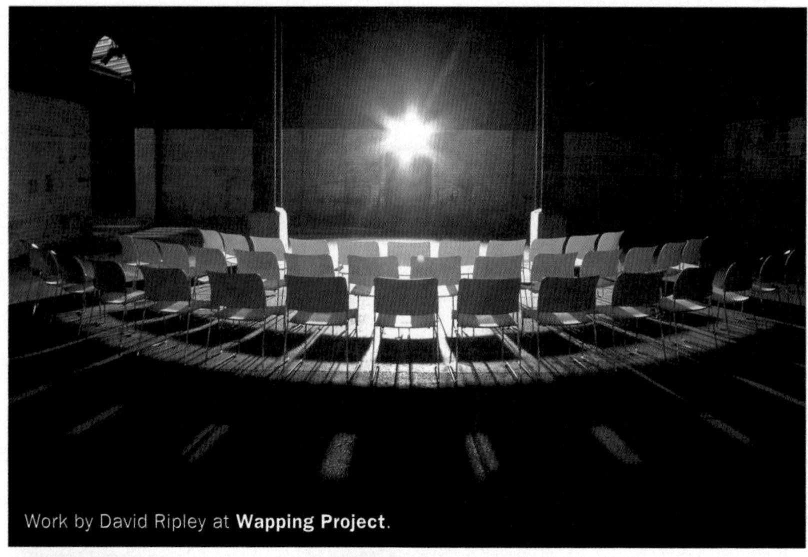
Work by David Ripley at **Wapping Project**.

stages in artists' careers. The triangular space here isn't easy to fill successfully, but it occasionally works perfectly. For instance, it responded particularly well in 2003 to interventions by Argentinian artists Dolores Zinny and Juan Maidagan. For 2004, the typically diverse programme includes a found-object installation by New Delhi-based artist Subodh Gupta, as well as new works by the Birmingham collective, Juneau Projects.

Victoria Miro

16 Wharf Road, Islington, N1 7RW (7336 8109/ www.victoria-miro.com). Angel tube/Old Street tube/ rail. **Open** 10am-6pm Tue-Sat. **Credit** MC, V. **Map** p402 P2.

One of the most fabulous art spaces anywhere, this huge converted Victorian factory is always worth a visit. Back-to-back painting shows – by Verne Dawson, Tal R and Chantal Joffe – were followed in 2003 by film installations by Isaac Julian and Doug Aitken. Expect more along those lines.

Vilma Gold

66 Rivington Street, Shoreditch, EC2 3AY (7613 1609/www.vilmagold.com). Liverpool Street or Old Street tube/rail. **Open** noon-6pm Thur-Sat. **No credit cards**. **Map** p403 R4.

Rachel Williams and Steven Pippet have a magic touch. The cognoscenti flock here for such fashionable fare as the neo-neo-expressionist paintings of Sophie von Hellermann and Markus Vater, or Andrew Mania's conglomerations of drawings, paintings, sculpture and found photographs.

Wapping Project

Wapping Hydraulic Power Station, Wapping Wall, Wapping, E1W 3ST (7680 2080). Wapping tube. **Open** noon-11pm Tue-Sat; noon-6pm Sun. **Credit** AmEx, DC, MC, V.

This magnificent converted hydraulic power station was originally intended to attract those working with film, video and the digital arts, but Richard Wilson's *Butterfly* – a time-based installation during which a light aircraft 'emerged' from a ball of crushed metal – was a highlight of 2003. The space also houses a good restaurant.

White Cube

48 Hoxton Square, Hoxton, N1 6BP (7930 5373/ www.whitecube.com). Old Street tube. **Open** 10am-6pm Tue-Sat. **Credit** AmEx, MC, V. **Map** p402 P4.

A rooftop extension has made room for a project space – 'Inside the White Cube' – with its own curator to be changed annually. Downstairs, the gallery hosted, in 2003, paintings by Carroll Dunham, Chuck Close and Neal Tait, a video installation by Christian Marclay and new work by Damien Hirst. The commercial hub of YBA art, White Cube plans to open a further space in a former London Electricity substation in Mason's Yard, Piccadilly.

Wilkinson Gallery

242 Cambridge Heath Road, Bethnal Green, E2 9DA (8980 2662/www.wilkinsongallery.com). Bethnal Green tube. **Open** 11am-6pm Thur-Sat; noon-6pm Sun; also by appointment. **No credit cards**.

A series of smallish rooms over three floors, this excellent gallery, run by Anthony Wilkinson, represents mainly British and European artists, including Bob & Roberta Smith (aka Patrick Brill) whose knockabout text pieces and sculptures poke gentle fun at the art world, and artist/writer/curator Matthew Higgs. The 2004 programme is a painting-heavy line-up that includes solo showings for rising German stars Matthias Weischer, Tilo Baumgartel and Martin Kobe.

South-east

Corvi-Mora

1A Kempsford Road, Kennington, SE11 4NU (7383 2419/www.corvi-mora.com). Kennington tube. **Open** 11am-6pm Tue-Sat. **No credit cards**.

Italian gallerist Tommasso Corvi-Mora brings a wealth of international art to this small space, which has become known for its multinational offerings. The flavour continues in 2004 with paintings by Glenn Sorensen and sculpture by Eva Marisaldi.

Gasworks

155 Vauxhall Street, Oval, SE11 5RH (7582 6848/www.gasworks.org.uk). Oval tube. **Open** noon-6pm Wed-Sun. **No credit cards**.

Part of the Triangle Arts Trust, this space comprises both a gallery and a collective of artists' studios, three of which are reserved for artists taking part in an ambitious international residency programme. So far, 100 artists from more than 50 countries have taken part in the programme. The gallery provides a platform for artists who have had limited exposure in London. Following refurbishment, Gasworks will open in spring 2004 with a month of performances, films, and music-based work by AK Dolven, Susan Philipsz and others.

Hales Gallery

70 Deptford High Street, Deptford, SE8 4RT (8694 1194/www.halesgallery.com). New Cross tube/Deptford Bridge DLR/Deptford rail. **Open** 10am-5pm Mon-Sat. **Credit** AmEx, DC, MC, V.

Run by Paul Hedge and his team, Hales represents Spencer Tunick, Judith Dean, Danny Rolph, Ben Ravenscroft and a number of other respected artists, and has helped to put Deptford on the art map. However, at time of writing, plans were afoot to move to the Tea Building, on the corner of Shoreditch High Street and Bethnal Green Road, which could take it right back off again, so check the website for details before making a special trip.

South London Gallery

65 Peckham Road, Camberwell, SE5 8UH (7703 9799/www.southlondongallery.org). Oval tube, then 436 bus/Elephant & Castle tube/rail then 12, 171 bus. **Open** 11am-6pm Tue, Wed, Fri; 11am-7pm Thur; 2-6pm Sat, Sun. **No credit cards**.

Built in 1891 as a philanthropic venture, this is a cathedral-like space that has become one of the capital's foremost venues for contemporary art, host to a remarkably varied programme. Closed for refurbishment until spring 2004, the gallery reopens with disabled access and improved facilities.

Other spaces

A number of museums are also listed in sightseeing chapters. These include the **Design Museum** (*see p82*), the **Geffrye Museum** (*see p156*) and the **V&A** (*see p137*).

Architectural Association

36 Bedford Square, Fitzrovia, WC1B 3ES (7887 4000/www.aaschool.ac.uk). Tottenham Court Road tube. **Open** 10am-7pm Mon-Fri; 10am-3pm Sat. **Credit** MC, V. **Map** 399 K5.

Talks, events, discussions and exhibitions: four good reasons for visiting these elegant premises. During the summer, the gallery shows work by graduating students of the AA School.

Crafts Council

44A Pentonville Road, Islington, N1 9BY (7278 7700/www.craftscouncil.org.uk). Angel tube. **Open** 11am-6pm Tue-Sat; 2-6pm Sun. **No credit cards**. **Map** p402 N2.

The Council showcases the nation's craft output and recently has begun to stage exhibitions that examine the crossovers between art and design. The finalists of the Jerwood Applied Art Prize are usually shown in autumn. In 2004 the Council will launch 'Collect', a new art fair, at the Victoria & Albert Museum (*see p137*).

Royal Institute of British Architects

66 Portland Place, Marylebone, W1B 1AD (7580 5533/www.architecture.com). Great Portland Street or Regent's Park tube. **Open** 10am-6pm Mon-Fri; 10am-5pm Sat. **Credit** MC, V. **Map** p398 H5.

Based in a monumental edifice built by Grey Wornham in 1934, the Royal Institute of British Architects (aka RIBA) has a gallery that celebrates the profession's great and good and checks emerging architecture from around the world.

For art, go east

Bolstered by the arrival in recent years of high-profile galleries like **White Cube** (*see p291*) and **Victoria Miro** (*see p290*), the East End has secured its place as the centre of the London art world. But what exactly do we mean by the East End? Encompassing Old Street, Hoxton and Whitechapel on the edge of the City, Bethnal Green and Bow to the east and Hackney to the north, the area takes up a vast chunk of the capital, and each pocket of the East End has its own distinctive flavour.

Home to White Cube and **Counter Gallery** (*see p289*), Hoxton is awash with fashionable restaurants, bars and clubs. A short hop to Bethnal Green offers a different, some would argue more authentic, East End experience. Here well-established commercial galleries like the **Approach**, **Interim Art** (for both *see p289*) and **Wilkinson Gallery** (*see p291*) rub shoulders with independent spaces such as **Chisenhale**, the **Showroom** (for both *see p289*) and **Ibid Projects** (www.ibidprojects.org).

Making it all easier is F-EST, an annual celebration of the East End's cultural life aimed at both Londoners and visitors. With late-night openings, gallery introductions and guided tours, the event offers an excellent introduction to East End life and culture by suggesting the best places to shop and eat en route as well.

The real beauty of F-EST, at least in terms of independent creativity, is its championing of the smaller, artist-run venues on which London depends. Places like **Radio City Cars**, a former minicab office just off the City Road that, in 2003, staged a raft of shows by up-and-coming artists. Or **Keith Talent Gallery**, which operates out of an industrial space near London Fields. Many of these so-called 'alternative spaces' just seem to spring up overnight, and often disappear just as quickly. But seek them out; they might be in less salubrious neighbourhoods, but this is where you will find the next generation of young British artists testing the boundaries, and experimenting with ideas. The next time you see them they might be in the Saatchi.

The next F-EST is scheduled to take place in October 2004 but even if your visit doesn't coincide, the website – www.f-est.com – is an invaluable resource, providing links to gallery websites, downloadable maps and suggested routes that will tempt you east to experience the wealth and diversity of London's far-flung but brilliant art scene.

Photography

Photofusion

17A Electric Lane, Brixton, SW9 8LA (7738 5774/ www.photofusion.org). Brixton tube/rail. **Open** 10am-6pm Tue, Thur, Fri; 10am-8pm Wed; 11am-6pm Sat. **Credit** MC, V.

This place is the largest independent photography resource centre in town. Among 2003's impressive exhibitions were 'Ten Thousand Li', which explored the experience of British life by Chinese artists. More of the same is expected in 2004.

Photographers' Gallery

5 & 8 Great Newport Street, Covent Garden, WC2H 7HY (7831 1772/www.photonet.org.uk). Leicester Square tube. **Open** 11am-6pm Mon-Sat; noon-6pm Sun. **Membership** £30/yr; £20/yr concessions. **Credit** AmEx, DC, MC, V. **Map** p401 K6.

A giant among photography galleries, this space hosts a huge range of diverse shows each year, while promoting photography around the country. From January until March 2004, it will again host the annual Citibank Photography Prize, the largest prize for photography in the UK. Plans to relocate will be announced in autumn 2004.

Shine Gallery

3 Jubilee Place, Chelsea, SW3 3TD (7352 4499/ www.shinegallery.co.uk). Sloane Square tube. **Open** noon-6pm Tue-Sat; or by appointment. **Credit** AmEx, MC, V. **Map** p397 E11.

Michael Hoppen's small second-floor white space and his first-floor photography gallery (7352 3649) are located above the Hulton Getty Picture Library (7376 4525). For February and March there's an exhibition by Daido Moriyama, while April and May is Desiree Dolron's turn. Photography wise, Michael Hoppen hosts a mixed show of masterwork in February and March, with William Claxton's work showing in April and May. Check the website for details of shows from June.

Zelda Cheatle Gallery

99 Mount Street, Mayfair, W1K 2TQ (7408 4448/ www.zcgall.demon.co.uk). Bond Street or Green Park tube. **Open** 10am-6pm Tue-Fri; 11am-5pm Sat. **Credit** AmEx, MC, V. **Map** p400 G7.

The Imogen Cunningham show in 2003 was typical of the high standards set and met by this specialist in the exhibition and sale of vintage and contemporary photography. Exhibitions for 2004 include James Morris's photos of the mud architecture of West Africa and George Tice's urban landscapes.

Gay & Lesbian

Look around: this scene means business.

Even jaded scene veterans admit that London is a gay consumer's paradise. These days, the competition for your pink pound is fiercer than ever. The last few years have seen yuppie demand sated by new upmarket venues, and in reaction, anti-aspirational alternatives have mushroomed *(see p298* **Ghetto blaster**). It seems as if gay angst has come to this: where do you spend your dough?

The traditional hub of gay life, **Soho**, has looked askance at the increasing popularity of **Vauxhall**'s growing gay village. For after-hours partying, gay men can go on a weekend-long bender without leaving the latter. Many do. **Old Compton Street**, meanwhile, feels like the gay equivalent of Oxford Street these days: tacky, crowded and much too popular with too many tourists.

Politically, there has been much to celebrate. The much-hated Section 28 that prevented local councils 'promoting' homosexuality was quietly killed off. And maybe just as significantly, the government's White Paper on Civil Partnership Registration has finally recommended that same-sex couples should get the some of the same legal rights as married couples.

The staging of Mardi Gras 2003 in Hyde Park was another solid achievement: a location more prestigious and central than the previous year's effort on Hackney marshes. A new celebration known as **Soho Pride** scored great success in 2003, and will be back on 4 July 2004. The event helped ensure that lesbian visibility continues to grow on the London scene.

However, you can still rely on organised religion to hit a bum note, as it were. In the summer of 2003, the prospective Bishop of Reading was forced to turn down the post after his sexuality became public knowledge. The Church of England tore itself apart over the issue, proving that it remains a controversial one within the Church.

On a more positive note, London delivers the goods on cultural events. Gay movie-goers have the huge annual **London Lesbian & Gay Film Festival** (*see p284*) at the National Film Theatre and other venues in the two weeks before Easter. Otherwise, you can look out for listings at the **Other Cinema** (*see p281*) where the programme often incorporates excellent gay indies. Theatre-wise, the **Soho Theatre** (*see p336*) performs a similar function.

The best Gay scene

For pumped-up muscle
Action. *See p294.*

For dressed-down punks
Nag Nag Nag. *See p296.*

For bar loungers
Edge. *See p297.*

For light lunches
First Out. *See p294.*

For smart girls
Candy Bar. *See p297.*

For up-to-the-minute information on events in and around London, as well as a comprehensive list of local venues across the city, *Time Out* magazine is a good bet. Freesheets *Boyz* and *QX* are available in most gay venues and can give a detailed rundown of where to find what. On newsagents' shelves, gay lifestyle is covered by *Gay Times*, the men's mag *Attitude* and the dyke bible *Diva*.

Those surfing the web for no-strings sex have the popular www.m4m4sex.com and the phenomenon that is www.gaydar.co.uk. The website www.outintheuk.com is rather more community minded. For lesbians the best place is www.gingerbeer.co.uk.

Lesbian and gay flat-seekers should try **Accommodation Outlet** (*see p66*).

Cafés & restaurants

This is a big city, so you're simply unlikely to encounter prejudice in any London restaurant. There's plenty of choice out there, but if you're looking for somewhere with a primarily gay slant, try one of these below.

Balans

60 Old Compton Street, Soho, W1D 4UG (7439 2183/www.balans.co.uk). Leicester Square or Piccadilly Circus tube. **Open** 8am-5am Mon-Thur; 8am-6am Fri, Sat; 8am-2am Sun. **Admission** £3 after midnight. **Credit** AmEx, MC, V. **Map** p399 6K.
Eat at virtually any time of the day in the stylish brasserie chain for mainly gay clientele.

First Out

52 St Giles High Street, St Giles's, WC2H 8LH (7240 8042/www.firstoutcafebar.com). Tottenham Court Road tube. **Open** 9am-11pm Mon-Sat; 11am-10.30pm Sun. **Credit** MC, V. **Map** p399 K6.

A friendly and popular café that's more favoured by London's gay women than men, good daytime destination and a popular pre-club venue on Friday evenings. Easygoing with healthy options.

Old Compton Café

34 Old Compton Street, Soho, W1V 5PD (7439 3309/www.balans.com). Leicester Square tube. **Open** 24hrs daily. **Credit** AmEx, MC, V. **Map** p399 6K.

Now owned by the folks behind Balans, the Old Compton Café is the Soho institution that never sleeps. Pre- and post-clubbers fill up here on sandwiches, soup and snacks. Buzzy and friendly, it's the best place on this stretch to people-watch, even more so if you're lucky enough to get one of the outdoor tables in the summertime.

Clubs

This town moves quickly, and its attention span is quite short, so even hardy club nights can suddenly bite the dust: recent examples include the infamous Fist. So check local magazines for the latest, although surely only an earthquake would stop G.A.Y. or Heaven.

Bear in mind that clubbing in London is expensive. You will pay in excess of £10 for the trendiest venues, then the drinks are pricey, and the taxi home won't come cheap. Why do we do it? Because it's just so much fun.

Action

The Renaissance Rooms, off Miles Street, Vauxhall, SW8 NB (07973 233377/www.actionclub.net). Vauxhall tube/rail. **Open** 11pm-6am 1st & 3rd Sat of mth. **Admission** £15; £10 members; £12 before midnight with flyer.

The muscle boys' club of choice, and London's biggest after-hours event. Huge dance arena, heated outside terrace, cruise room and chilled-out second dance area. Very popular, with queues to match if you get there early.

A:M

Fire, South Lambeth Road, Vauxhall, SW8 1RT (07905 035682). Vauxhall tube/rail. **Open** 3am-noon Sat. **Admission** £10; £8 with flyer.

Saturday morning after-hours party. Expect funky tech house and a committed crowd.

Club Kali

The Dome, 1 Dartmouth Park Hill, North London, N19 (7272 8153). Tufnell Pk tube. **Open** 10pm-3am 1st and 3rd Fri of mth. **Admission** £7; £5 concessions.

The world's largest gay Asian club night is a fortnightly affair. Whenever it's on, the big, barn-like venue echoes to a varied collection of Bhangra, Bollywood and Western sounds. It attracts a friendly, mixed crowd and if you're lucky, features some amazing displays of South Asian dancing.

Crash

Arch 66, Goding Street, Vauxhall, SE11 (www.crashlondon.co.uk). Vauxhall tube/rail. **Open** *Club* 10.30pm-6am Sat. **Admission** £10; £8 with flyer or members. **Credit** AmEx, DC, MC, V.

Keep your trousers on at the **Ghetto**. *See p296*

This is where the Vauxhall muscle marys and friends start their Saturday nights. Under the arches are four bars, two dancefloors and two chillout areas. There are go-go dancers and top DJs too.

Discotec

The End, 18 West Central Street, St Giles's, WC1A 1JJ (7419 9199/www.discotec-club.com). Holborn or Tottenham Court Road tube. **Open** 10pm-4am Thur. **Admission** £7; £5 before midnight. **Credit** *Bar only* MC, V. **Map** p399 L6.

This is a dressy mixed night in a classy venue. If you come here you'll find that you start the weekend early – and in style.

Dolly Mixtures

Candy Bar, 4 Carlisle Street, Soho, W1D 3BJ (7494 4041/www.candybar.easynet.co.uk). Tottenham Court Road tube. **Open** 9pm-2am Sat. **Admission** £5. **Credit** *Bar only* MC, V. **Map** p399 K6.

Top dykes' night with DJ Slamma playing house and soul in London's premier lesbian venue.

DTPM

Fabric, 77A Charterhouse Street, Clerkenwell, EC1M 6HJ (7749 1199www.dtpm.net). Barbican tube/ Farringdon tube/rail. **Open** 10pm-late Sun. **Admission** £14; £10 members, concessions; £8 before 11pm with flyer. **Credit** *Bar only* MC, V. **Map** p402 O5.

A mixed set of dedicated clubbers gather here, at one of London's biggest and best nightclubs, for R&B, house, hip hop and disco.

Duckie

Royal Vauxhall Tavern, 373 Kennington Lane, Vauxhall, SE11 5HY (7737 4043). Vauxhall tube/rail. **Open** 9pm-2am Sat. **Admission** £5.

The lighter side of Vauxhall clubbing. Expect a diverse set, including a cabaret of mixed ability, and a varied crowd in this endearing south London dive.

Exilio Latino

Houghton Street, Holborn, WC2 2AA (07956 983230/www.exilio.co.uk). Holborn tube. **Open** 10pm-3am Sat. **Admission** £7; £6 before 11.30pm. **No credit cards. Map** p399 M6.

Crowded Spanish-themed night in a studenty venue. If you don't salsa, don't worry, someone will take you in hand. Plenty of Enrique, Ricky and J-Lo are thrown in for a mixed clientele of all ages.

Fiction

The Cross, King's Cross Goods Yard, off York Way, King's Cross, N1 (7749 1199/www.club-fiction.net). King's Cross tube/rail. **Open** 11pm-5am Fri. **Admission** £14; £10 concessions; £8 before 11.30pm; £10 before midnight with flyer. **Credit** *Bar only* MC, V. **Map** p399 L2.

Top night in one of London's best venues, though the crowd is increasingly straight. Three dancefloors play various house grooves. It all gets very busy, especially in the summer when the outdoor terrace comes into its own.

G.A.Y.

Astoria & Mean Fiddler, 157 Charing Cross Road, Soho, WC2 (www.g-a-y.co.uk). Tottenham Court Road tube. **Open** 10.30pm-4am Mon, Thur; 11pm-4am Fri; 10.30pm-5am Sat. **Admission** £3-£10; reductions with flyer. **Map** p399 K6.

Here's where young disco bunnies unite to worship Kylie. The large arena is a bit of a dump, but the crowds don't stop movin' to the poppiest tunes. Mondays and Thursdays are Pink Pounder nights

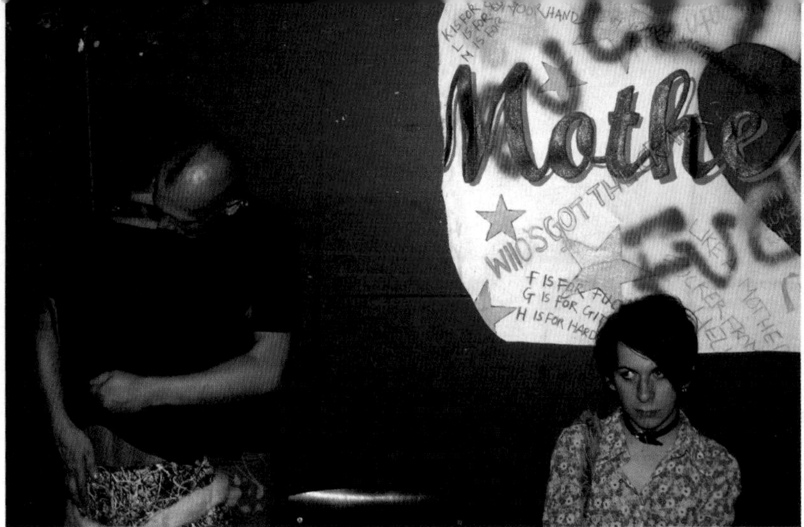

Motherfucker (*see p298* **Ghetto blaster**)...

with cheap drinks and entry, Friday is the larger-scale Camp Attack, and Saturdays feature guest appearances from big chart acts.

Ghetto

5-6 Falconberg Court, (behind the Astoria), Soho, W1 (www.ghetto-london.co.uk). Tottenham Court Road tube. **Open** 10.30pm-3am Mon-Thur, Sun; 10.30pm-4.30am Fri; 10.30pm-5am Sat. **Admission** £3-£7. **Map** p399 K6.

This intimate, central club heads the backlash against London's snootier venues (*see p298* **Ghetto blaster**). There's Nag Nag Nag for electro fans on Wednesday, while the Cock puts the spunk back into Soho on Fridays, on Saturdays it's long-running trash night Wig Out and Detox on Sunday.

Heaven

The Arches, Villiers Street, Charing Cross, WC2N 6NG (7930 2020/www.heaven-london.com). Embankment tube/Charing Cross tube/rail. **Open** 10.30pm-3am Mon, Wed; 10.30pm-5am Fri; 10pm-5am Sat. **Admission** £1-£12. **Credit** *Bar only* AmEx, DC, MC, V. **Map** p401 L7.

When did you first go to Heaven? Popcorn (Mondays) and Fruit Machine (Wednesdays) offer upbeat early-week fun, but Heaven really comes alive on Saturdays, with commercial house to a packed set of gay revellers.

Popstarz

Scala, 275 Pentonville Road, King's Cross, N1 9NL (7833 2022/www.scala-london.co.uk). King's Cross tube/rail. **Open** 10pm-5am Fri. **Admission** £8; £7 with flyer after 11pm; £5 members, students. Free before 11pm with flyer. **Credit** *Bar only* MC, V. **Map** p399 L3.

A diverse, relaxed and mixed crowd lap up indie classics on the main floor, R&B/funk in the Love Lounge, or pop trash in the Rubbish Room. An early queue forms for free entry. Students, eh?

Substation South

9 Brighton Terrace, Brixton, SW9 8DJ (7737 2095). Brixton tube/rail/N2, N3, N37, N109 bus. **Open** 10.30pm-3.30am Mon; 10.30pm-2am Tue; 10.30pm-3am Wed; 10.30pm-late Thur; 10.30pm-5am Fri; 10.30pm-6am Sat; 10pm-late Sun. **Admission** £3-£10. **No credit cards**.

Substation South is a popular south London fixture. Monday is underwear-only night with Y-Front; Tuesday is Sub FC, for those who have a penchant for sportswear; Wednesday is pure uniform, leather, rubber and boots at Boot Camp; Thursday is the electroclash night Rock 'n' Roll Fag Bar; Friday is Dirty Dishes, with funky house attitude; Queer Nation's New York-style house and garage takes place on Saturday; and it's popular indie night, Marvellous, on Sunday.

Pubs & bars

Most of London's bars are open to gay men and lesbians, although some divey pubs might not attract them. In our reviews below, we've tried to (tactfully) indicate where a given place has less to offer either male or female drinkers.

Admiral Duncan

54 Old Compton Street, Soho, W1V 5PA (7437 5300). Leicester Square tube. **Open** noon-11pm Mon-Sat; noon-10.30pm Sun. **Credit** MC, V. **Map** p399 K6.

The location of a homophobic bomb attack in 1999, but a doughty old survivor on Old Compton Street. Expect a slightly older, down-to-earth, male crowd in the darkened surroundings.

Barcode

3-4 Archer Street, Soho, W1D 7AP (7734 3342/ www.bar-code.co.uk). Piccadilly Circus tube. **Open** 4pm-1am Mon-Sat; 4-10.30pm Sun. **Admission** £3 after 11pm Fri, Sat. **Credit** MC, V. **Map** p401 K7.

...'a mission to give polysexual misfits everywhere a new home.'

Barcode combines cheap prices with a particularly masculine clientele and an expectant atmosphere. The cruisy basement serves two functions: packed disco and handy meat market.

Black Cap

171 Camden High Street, Camden, NW1 7JY (7428 2721/www.theblackcap.com). Camden Town tube. **Open** noon-2am Mon-Thur; noon-3am Fri, Sat; noon-12.30am Sun. **Credit** MC, V.

Camden's gay drinking den is a north London institution. The upstairs bar and beer garden offer typical pub surroundings, and in the evenings the basement opens up for drag shows and partying. Particularly popular on Sunday night.

The Box

Seven Dials, 32-4 Monmouth Street, Covent Garden, WC2H 9HA (7240 5828/www.boxbar.com). Leicester Square tube. **Open** 11am-11pm Mon-Sat; noon-10.30pm Sun. **Credit** MC, V. **Map** p399 L6.

This busy bar and café serves drinks, coffee and food to scene queens. Remains very popular with muscle boys and their admirers.

Bromptons

294 Old Brompton Road, Earl's Court, SW5 9JF (7370 1344/www.bromptons.info). Earl's Court tube. **Open** 5pm-2am Mon-Sat; 3pm-midnight Sun. **Admission** £1 10-11pm, £3 thereafter Mon-Thur; £1 10-11pm, £5 thereafter Fri, Sat; £1 after 10pm, £2 thereafter Sun. **Credit** MC, V. **Map** p396 B11.

Two big, bustling bars and a noisy cabaret stage make Brompton's a popular destination for the Earl's Court male set.

Candy Bar

4 Carlisle Street, Soho, W1D 3BJ (7494 4041/ www.candybar.easynet.co.uk). Tottenham Court Road tube. **Open** 5-11.30pm Mon-Thur, Sun; 5pm-2am Fri, Sat. **Admission** £5 after 9pm Fri, Sat; £3 after 10pm Thur. **Credit** *Bar only* MC, V. **Map** p399 K6.

London's flagship gay women's establishment is popular with lesbians, bisexual women and their male guests. It has regular DJs and extended opening hours for its upbeat clientele.

Compton's of Soho

51-3 Old Compton Street, Soho, W1V 5PN (7479 7961/www.comptons-of-soho.co.uk). Piccadilly Circus tube. **Open** noon-11pm Mon-Sat; noon-10.30pm Sun. **Credit** AmEx, MC, V. **Map** p399 K6.

Raw and rugged Compton's is the place if you like your men to be blokey. Shaved heads and bomber jackets predominate.

The Edge

11 Soho Square, Soho, W1D 3QE (7439 1313/ www.edge.uk.com). Tottenham Court Road tube. **Open** 11.30am-1am Mon-Sat; 11.30am-10.30pm Sun. **Credit** MC, V. **Map** p399 K6.

This is gay Soho drinking for men and women at its best. The Edge is relaxed and sociable in the perfect location just off Soho Square.

Escape Bar

10A Brewer Street, Soho, W1F 0SU (7734 2626/ www.kudosgroup.com). Leicester Square tube. **Open** 4pm-3am Mon-Sat. **Admission** £2 after 11pm Tue-Sat. **Credit** AmEx, MC, V. **Map** p401 K7.

A friendly crowd drink, chat and jiggle to music videos. For the most part, Escape's male and female clientele are attitude-free and up for a good time.

Friendly Society

Basement, 79 Wardour Street (entrance in Tisbury Court), Soho, W1D 6QB (7434 3805). Leicester Square, Oxford Circus or Tottenham Court Road tube. **Open** 4-11pm Mon-Fri; 2-11pm Sat; 2-10.30pm Sun. **Credit** MC, V. **Map** p398 J6.

This is a hip yet friendly designer bar with a cool retro-futuristic decor. It's egalitarian in its gender approach, and popular with both gay men and women. DJ sets in the evenings.

Ghetto blaster

Bar wars on the scene are nothing new, but this time it's ideological. When the club formerly known as the Tube re-opened as the **Ghetto**, it set out its alternative credentials. By explaining that it was going to 'squeeze some sense into Soho', it took aim at the city's many upmarket venues that all felt too much like casting couches for *Sex & The City*. The Ghetto promised not to have models behind the bar, and railed at the 'high prices and lack of originality' of many Soho venues. Instead, promoter Simon Hobart came up with a plan for offering friendly service alongside cheap entry and cheap drinks.

The A-gay backlash had begun.

It's the second kick up the arse Hobart has given London clubland. The first was the launch of **Popstarz** (*see p296*) in the mid 1990s. Popstarz brought indie music on to the scene. This time round, Hobart has a potent weapon in the form of 'electroclash' – a new wave synth sound that makes the prevailing funky house scene seem faceless (*see p320* **Electro go go**).

Electroclash nights at The Ghetto (*see p296*) include **Nag Nag Nag** on Wednesdays and the **Cock** on Fridays. They attract punks and freaks who dress down to dress up. The venue is down-to-earth, divey and intimate.

The club's success has spawned a new-new-wave. Nights such as **Rock 'n' Roll Fag Bar** at Substation South (*see p296*) on Thursdays, the hedonistic, polysexual **Motherfucker** (www.clubmotherfucker.com) every third Friday at Garage (*see p309*) and **Bad Arse Muthas** on Sundays at the Candy Bar (*see p297*) are, just as the names suggest, anti-materialistic, anti-sophistication, and pro having a good time.

But the swanky hangouts are fighting a rearguard action. Paul Richardson, who first launched the **Shadow Lounge** (pictured), has unveiled **Sanctuary Soho** (*see p297*). With a piano bar on the top floor and a clubby feel on other levels, it appeals to all tastes.

This is a battle of attrition, however. And it's early days. Let's see who's still standing when the smoke clears.

G.A.Y. Bar

30 Old Compton Street, Soho, W1V 5TD (7494 2756/www.g-a-y.co.uk). Leicester Square or Piccadilly Circus tube. **Open** noon-midnight Mon-Sat; noon-10.30pm Sun. **Credit** AmEx, MC, V. **Map** p399 K6.

In a central location formerly used by Manto Soho, this place packs them in night after night. Basically, if you like the Astoria's ever-popular G.A.Y. club (*see p295*), and you probably do, then you'll love this. If you don't, you won't. Girls Go Down is the new women's bar in the basement.

Glass Bar

West Lodge, Euston Square Gardens, 190 Euston Road, Bloomsbury, NW1 (7387 6184/www.glass bar.ndo.co.uk). Euston tube/rail. **Open** 5pm-late Mon-Fri; 6pm-late Sat. **Admission** £1-£2. **No credit cards**. **Map** p398 J4.

No, your eyes do not deceive you. This friendly and stylish women-only venue is located in one of the stone lodges just outside Euston Station. It can be hard to find, so phone from the station if you're not sure where to go. Dress is smart-casual.

The Hoist

Railway Arch, 47B&C South Lambeth Road, Vauxhall Cross, Vauxhall, SW8 (7735 9972). Vauxhall tube/rail. **Open** 10pm-3am Fri; 10pm-4am Sat; 9pm-2am Sun. **No credit cards**.

This is London's premier leather, rubber and uniform bar. Adhere to the dress code and relax with a pint before indulging in whatever takes your fancy.

King William IV

77 Hampstead High Street, Hampstead, NW3 1RE (7435 5747/www.kw4.co.uk). Hampstead tube. **Open** noon-11pm Mon-Sat; noon-10.30pm Sun. **Credit** MC, V.

This is an old-fashioned local in the swanky North London neighbourhood of Hampstead. It tends to fill nightly with a vaguely affluent and relaxed crowd.

Kudos

10 Adelaide Street, Covent Garden, WC2 4HZ (7379 4573/www.kudosgroup.com). Charing Cross tube/rail. **Open** noon-11pm Mon-Sat; noon-10.30pm Sun. **Credit** AmEx, MC, V. **Map** p401 L7.

Two floors of fun for fashionable scene queens and suits with music videos in the basement.

Retro Bar

2 George Court, off Strand, Charing Cross, WC2N 6HH (7321 2811). Charing Cross tube/rail. **Open** noon-11pm Mon-Fri; 5-11pm Sat; 5-10.30pm Sun. **Credit** AmEx, MC, V. **Map** p401 L7.

Unpretentious, relaxed and friendly, the Retro Bar's two floors are a respite from style-conscious Soho. Music is '70s, '80s and modern alternative, and there are regular theme nights and quizzes.

Rupert Street

50 Rupert Street, Soho, W1 (77292 7141). Leicester Square or Piccadilly Circus tube. **Open** 9.30pm-3am Mon-Wed, 8pm-3am Sat; noon-10.30pm Sun. **Credit** AmEx, MC, V. **Map** p401 K7.

This is an upmarket, pricey bar for both the image-conscious and the professional sets.

Sanctuary Soho

4-5 Greek Street, Soho, W1. (7434 3323).Tottenham Court Road tube. **Open** noon-3am Mon-Sat, noon-1am Sun. **Credit** AmEx, MC, V. **Map** p399 K6.
An upmarket venue spread over three floors, this place looks like a private members' club upstairs, and has a more typical bar and dance area on the ground floor, with an intimate basement.

The Shadow Lounge

5 Brewer Street, Soho, W1F 0RF (7287 7988/ www.theshadowlounge.co.uk). Piccadilly Circus tube. **Open** 10pm-3am Mon-Wed; 9pm-3am Thurs-Sat. **Admission** £3 after 11pm Mon-Wed; £5 after 10pm Thur; £5 before 10.30pm, £10 thereafter Fri, Sat. **Credit** AmEx, MC, V. **Map** p401 K7.
Still top of the list for A-gays. Air-conditioning and funky decor for those who like to lounge in classy, expensive surroundings.

Two Brewers

114 Clapham High Street, Clapham, SW4 7UJ (7498 4971/www.the2brewers.com). Clapham Common tube. **Open** 5pm-2am Mon-Thur; 5pm-3am Fri, Sat; 4pm-12.30am Sun. **Admission** £2 after 10pm Mon-Thur; £3 9.30-11pm; £5 after 11pm Fri, Sat; £3 after 7pm Sun. **Credit** AmEx, MC, V.
South London's finest cabaret bar and club remains popular with locals and visitors.

Vespa Lounge

Upstairs at The Conservatory Bar, 15 St Giles High Street, St Giles's, WC2H 8LN (7836 8956). Tottenham Court Road tube. **Open** 7-11pm Wed-Sat. **Credit** MC, V. **Map** p399 K6.
A centrally located, easy-to-find bar for laid-back girls and their male guests.

Village Soho

81 Wardour Street, Soho, W1V 3DG (7434 2124). Piccadilly Circus tube. **Open** 4pm-1am Mon-Sat; 1-10.30pm Sun. **Admission** £2 after 11pm Fri, Sat. **Credit** MC, V. **Map** p398 J6.
Village Soho offers three floors of mostly male bar action for fun-loving young guys. Upstairs is chilled, and offers a superb view over the gay strip, while the basement has a busy dancefloor.

The Yard

57 Rupert Street, Soho, W1V 7HN (7437 2652/ www.yardbar.co.uk). Piccadilly Circus tube. **Open** noon-11pm Mon-Sat; noon-10.30pm Sun. **Credit** AmEx, MC, V. **Map** p401 K7.
Summer's choice for relaxed drinking, the Yard has a courtyard and a comfortable loft in addition to its small, buzzy main bar. Mainly for men.

Saunas

In recent years it seems as if London's sauna scene has turned ultra-competitive. The biggest of them all, **Chariots**, boasts Europe's largest sauna and has opened a branch in Waterloo to rival popular nearby **Pleasuredrome**.

Chariots

Fairchild Street, EC2A 3NS (7247 5333/ www.gaysauna.co.uk). Liverpool Street tube/rail. **Open** noon-9am daily. **Admission** £13; £11 concessions. **Credit** AmEx, MC, V. **Map** p403 4R.
This place is big, with attitude to match. With two steamrooms, two saunas, a Jacuzzi, a Roman-style pool, quiet rooms, an extensive dark area, a bar and a gym, there are plenty of distractions.
Other location: 101 Lower Marsh, Waterloo, SE1 7AB (7247 5333).

Pleasuredrome

Arch 124, Cornwall Road, Waterloo, SE1 8XE (7633 9194/www.pleasuredrome.com). Waterloo tube/rail. **Open** 24 hrs. **Admission** £11. **Credit** DC, MC, V.
This newly refurbished sauna right by Waterloo Station never closes its doors, so there's always somewhere to go shower.

The Sauna Bar

29 Endell Street, Covent Garden, WC2H 9BA (7836 2236/www.thesaunabar.com). Covent Garden tube. **Open** noon-11pm Mon-Thur; 24hrs from noon Fri-11pm Sun. **Admission** £13; £10 concessions. **Credit** MC, V. **Map** p399 L6.
A relatively small men-only sauna with a comfortable bar, a steam room, sauna, splash pool and showers, plus private rooms, if you get to them first.

Music

Argue who dares, London is the world's greatest music city.

Classical & Opera

In the 20th century music in London grew big. Immigration and the recording industry fuelled the growth – while other nations kicked their musicians out, London took them in. Views and techniques were swapped and music became a medium for the city's polyglot culture. The orchestras became world famous; the richest of them, the **London Symphony Orchestra**, celebrates its 100th birthday in 2004.

In the 1930s the BBC, still full of idealism, broadcast nightly concerts to which culture-starved citizens of mistrustful dictatorships secretly tuned in on crackly receivers. For a time just after the second World War it was thought that recording would be the future of music. Major labels based themselves here. The EMI studios at Abbey Road became well known. Talented musicians and record companies flocked to town. The first concert hall to be built anywhere in the world after the war was the **Royal Festival Hall** (*see p302*), and international orchestras lined up to perform there. Many of them were invited to play at the **Proms** (*see p305*) in the **Royal Albert Hall** (*see p302*) when they started in the 1950s, and London's annual summer music festival soon became a world event.

The Early Music movement grew up here, and gave rise to a vast new category on the shelves of record stores. Meanwhile, Londoners who had once considered opera a continental and rather silly form of art came increasingly to love it. Today, Covent Garden's **Royal Opera House** (*see p303*) ranks with La Scala in Milan and the Met in New York as one of the world's greatest opera houses. Its grand lottery-funded renovation in 2000 also made it one of the most luxurious nights out money can afford.

At the same time, professional and amateur singing also prospered. Some of the finest children's choirs in the world thrive here in the choirs of St Paul's and Westminster.

Each of these things alone would make the city an extraordinary music centre, but combined it means that this is truly Britain's music capital.

TICKETS AND INFORMATION

Tickets for most classical and opera events in London are available direct from the venues: book ahead for good seats. Many major venues have online booking systems in addition to the telephone box offices.

A number of venues, such as the Barbican and the South Bank, operate standby schemes, in which unsold tickets are sold off at cut-rate prices to students, seniors and others who are eligible for discounted rates hours before the show. Call the venues for full details.

The best Live music

By candlelight
St-Martin-in-the-Fields. *See p302.*

With a picnic
Kenwood Lakeside Concerts. *See p304.*

On a small (unamplified) scale
Union Chapel. *See p307.*

For home-grown indie talent
Borderline. *See p308.*

For pick 'n' mix programming
Spitz. *See p309.*

Classical venues

Barbican Centre

Silk Street, The City, EC2Y 8DS (7638 4141/box office 7638 8891/www.barbican.org.uk). Barbican tube/Moorgate tube/rail. **Box office** 9am-8pm daily. **Tickets** £6.50-£35. **Credit** AmEx, MC, V. **Map** p402 P5.

This 21-year-old arts complex is the home of the London Symphony Orchestra (LSO), the richest if not the best of the capital's international orchestras. It plays 90 concerts a year here, tours the world and records prolifically for both film and CD. Its rivals include the BBC Symphony Orchestra, which also performs here at subsidised rates. In 2004 the Great Performers series brings such stars as Maxim Vengerov, Alfred Brendel, Yo-Yo Ma, the Berlin Philharmonic and the Philadelphia Orchestra. Meanwhile, the modern music programming, taking in jazz, rock, world and country, continues to find ever larger audiences. There is occasional free music in the foyer, and the centre also has cinemas, galleries, theatres, restaurants and a library (*see p73*).

A musical force

The London Symphony Orchestra (LSO) first began life on Thursday 9 June 1904 with a 3pm concert at which top-hatted gents smoked. The Centenary Gala Concert on the same date in 2004 permits no smoking but features some of the world's greatest artists, including Maxim Vengerov, Mstislav Rostropovich, Alfred Brendel, Jose Cura, Sarah Chang, Riccardo Chailly, Antonio Pappano, Michael Tilson Thomas, Richard Hickox, and John Williams – the *Star Wars* composer whose loyalty to the orchestra has made the sound of this exceptional ensemble one of the best known on the planet, if not in the entire galaxy.

It might never have been. The orchestra was booked on the *Titanic* in 1912 for its first US tour before a change of concert dates postponed departure. Thirty years later, the orchestra again had a lucky escape when a bomb destroyed its Queen's Hall home. It remained homeless until securing the Barbican residency in 1969.

For 50 years the LSO was a solid London orchestra that enjoyed relationships with leading British figures such as Elgar, Delius, Menuhin, Vaughan Williams and Beecham. Then, in the 1960s, it became an international force after embarking on a world tour in 1964 (the first by any British orchestra) and appointing the young and very charismatic American André Previn principal conductor in 1968. The orchestra then became known for TV appearances and relationships with Previn's friends in Hollywood.

The permanent home at the Barbican enabled the LSO to begin to develop its distinctive sound, characterised by the bright-edged brasses and smooth high-tension strings which have inspired people worldwide, and featured in *Star Wars* and other films (including *Harry Potter* and *Notting Hill*).

The Barbican has also given the LSO access to the London business community – the orchestra's major sponsor is Shell UK – while the Corporation of London matches the Arts Council's annual grant of £1.5 million, making the LSO by far the richest of all British orchestras and able to programme more concerts and field more soloists than any other.

The LSO is currently enjoying a golden age. With Principal Conductor Sir Colin Davis it has made Grammy- and Gramophone-award winning albums. Its own record label, LSO Live, has been a runaway success, and it has invested £14 million in an Education Centre in a redundant Hawksmoor church in Islington.

The centenary could not have come at a more propitious time. Celebrations include tours to the Far East and almost every capital city in Europe, including a show in Athens for the Olympics. Rostropovich, Gergiev, Haitink and Previn will all conduct birthday concert series, and a set of commissioned works from such disparate contemporary London-based composers as Dmitri Smirnov, Huw Watkins and Karl 'Adiemus' Jenkins is to feature the LSO's famous principal instrumentalists as soloists.

May the Force be with them.

Bush Hall

310 Uxbridge Road, Shepherds Bush, W12 7LJ (8222 6955/6933/www.bushhallmusic.co.uk). Shepherd's Bush tube. **Box office** 10am-5pm Mon-Fri. **Tickets** £6-£25. **Credit** AmEx, MC, V.

Opened in 1904 as the Carlton Ballroom (the plasterwork is dotted with musical motifs) and then used as a snooker hall, Bush Hall was refurbished as a plush music venue in 2000. It stages an even spread of chamber music concerts and low-key, often acoustic, rock shows.

Royal Albert Hall

Kensington Gore, South Kensington, SW7 2AP (information 7589 3203/box office 7589 8212/ www.royalalberthall.com). South Kensington tube/ 9, 10, 52 bus. **Box office** 9am-9pm daily. **Tickets** £4-£50. **Credit** AmEx, MC, V. **Map** p397 D9.

This grand 6,000-seat rotunda is the home of the Proms (*see p305*), which occupy the building during the summer months each year. Otherwise, the hall, built as a memorial to Queen Victoria's husband, is a venue for all forms of public event including opera, rock, jazz, tennis, wrestling, business conventions and awards ceremonies. Recent refurbishment has introduced discreet air-conditioning, modernised the backstage area and moved the main entrance to the south side, facing the Royal College of Music.

St James's Church Piccadilly

197 Piccadilly, St James's, W1J 9LL (7734 4511/ www.st-james-piccadilly.org). Piccadilly Circus tube. **Open** 8am-6.30pm daily. **Admission** free-£17; tickets available at the door 1hr before start of performances. **No credit cards**. **Map** p400 J7.

The only Wren church outside the City, this lovely, simply designed building hosts free lunchtime recitals (Mon, Wed, Fri) and a less regular programme of evening concerts. The church also hosts conventions and lectures by leading world figures. It has a decent café and a courtyard craft market around a spreading Indian Bean tree. It's worth dropping by to pick up a programme and see what upcoming events are scheduled (*see also p113*).

St John's, Smith Square

Smith Square, Westminster, SW1P 3HA (7222 1061/www.sjss.org.uk). Westminster tube. **Box office** 10am-5pm Mon-Fri, or until start of performance on concert nights; from 1hr before start of performance Sat, Sun. **Tickets** £5-£30. **Credit** MC, V. **Map** p401 K10.

This elegant 18th century ex-church hosts a nightly programme (except for during the summer months) of orchestral and chamber concerts with occasional vibrant recitals on its magnificent ten-year-old Klais organ. There's also a wonderfully secluded restaurant in the crypt where you can stop in for a bite, whether or not any musical events are scheduled. In an interesting historic note, the café is called 'the Footstool', which has been the building's nickname ever since Queen Anne was asked how she would like the new church to look when complete and, kicking hers over, said, 'Like that!'.

St Martin-in-the-Fields

Trafalgar Square, Westminster, WC2N 4JJ (concert information 7839 8362/www.stmartin-in-the-fields.org). Charing Cross tube/rail. **Box office** 10am-5pm Mon-Sat, or until start of performance. **Admission** *Lunchtime concerts* donations requested. *Evening concerts* £6-£18. **Credit** MC, V. **Map** p401 L7.

Overlooking Trafalgar Square, St Martin's hopelessly romantic candlelight concerts (Thursday-Saturday) are popular with both locals and visitors, while its frequently wonderful free lunchtime recitals (Monday and Tuesday) are one of the best bargains in town.

South Bank Centre

Belvedere Road, South Bank, SE1 8XX (7960 4242/ www.rfh.org.uk). Embankment tube/Waterloo tube/rail. **Box office** *In person* 11am-8pm. *By phone* 9am-9pm Mon-Sat; 9.30am-9pm Sun. **Tickets** £5-£75. **Credit** AmEx, MC, V. **Map** p401 M8.

The South Bank Centre has three concert halls: the 3,000-seat Royal Festival Hall for major orchestral concerts, the slightly smaller Queen Elizabeth Hall for piano recitals and the little Purcell Room for chamber groups and contemporary music concerts. First called the Festival Hall, it was originally the centrepiece of the 1951 Festival of Britain, the most advanced concert hall of its day. Orchestras from all over the world begged to play here. At first, the appetite for classical music ensured that nothing else was played here, but from the 1960s the hall has given itself more and more to populist forms of entertainment. Even so, it is still home to six classical music ensembles, including the Philharmonia and the London Philharmonic Orchestras, the unique period instrument Orchestra of the Age of Enlightenment, the Alban Berg String Quartet and London Sinfonietta, the country's leading contemporary music ensemble. It has regular free concerts in the foyer, a bookshop and record store, several cafés, bars and restaurants, including the beautiful Peoples Palace overlooking the Thames, and the Poetry Library with a performance room.

Wigmore Hall

36 Wigmore Street, Marylebone, W1U 2BP (7935 2141/www.wigmore-hall.org.uk). Bond Street tube. **Box office** *In person* Apr-Oct 10am-8.30pm Mon-Sat; 10.30am-7.30pm Sun. Nov-Mar 10am-8.30pm Mon-Sat; 10.30am-4pm Sun. *By phone* Apr-Oct 10am-7pm Mon-Sat; 10.30am-6.30pm Sun. Nov-Mar 10am-7pm Mon-Sat; 10.30am-4pm Sun. **Tickets** £8-£35. **Credit** AmEx, DC, MC, V. **Map** p398 G6.

Built in 1901 as the display and recital hall for Bechstein Pianos, this is the jewel of London's music venues. With its perfect acoustic, discreet art nouveau decor and excellent basement restaurant, it remains one of the world's top concert venues. Unlike the 'supermarket' venues where too much choice robs the individual event of its cachet, the Wigmore behaves as if nothing in the world were more important than the day's concert. The Monday lunchtime recitals are especially good value.

Holy (rock 'n') rollers, at **Union Chapel**. *See p307.*

Lunchtime concerts

A great tradition of midday performing mainly by talented music students and burgeoning young professionals has grown up in London's beautiful churches. Admission to most of these events is either free or by donation. Those listed below are all centrally located in the City but there are many more around town. See *Time Out* magazine for comprehensive coverage.

In addition to those below, regular organ recitals are held at **Temple Church** (off Fleet Street, 7353 8559), **Grosvenor Chapel** (South Audley Street, 7499 1684, *see also p110*), **St James's** (Clerkenwell Close, 7251 1190) and **Southwark Cathedral** (*see p75*).

St Anne & St Agnes *Gresham Street, The City, EC2V 7BX (7606 4986). St Paul's tube.* **Performances** 1.10pm Mon, Fri. **Map** p404 P6.

St Bride's *Fleet Street, The City, EC4Y 8AU (7427 0133). Blackfriars tube/rail.* **Performances** 1.15pm Tue, Fri (except Aug, Advent, Lent). **Map** p404 N6.

St Lawrence Jewry *Guildhall, The City, EC2V 5AA (7600 9478). Mansion House or St Paul's tube/ Bank tube/DLR.* **Performances** 1pm Mon, Tue. **Map** p404 P6.

St Margaret Lothbury *Lothbury, The City, EC2R 7HH (7606 8330). Bank tube/DLR.* **Performances** 1.10pm Thur. **Map** p405 Q6.

St Martin within Ludgate *40 Ludgate Hill, The City, EC4M 7DE (7248 6054). St Paul's tube.* **Performances** 1.15pm Wed. **Map** p404 O6.

St Mary-le-Bow *Cheapside, The City, EC2V 6AU (7248 5139/www.stmarylebow.co.uk). Mansion House tube.* **Performances** 1.05pm Thur. **Map** p404 P6.

Opera houses

English National Opera

The Coliseum, St Martin's Lane, Covent Garden, WC2N 4ES (box office 7632 8300/credit card bookings 7379 1264/www.eno.org). Leicester Square tube/Charing Cross tube/rail. **Box office** *By phone* 24hrs daily; day tickets can be purchased from 10am on day of performance or by phone from 12.30pm on day of performance. **Tickets** £5-£85. **Credit** AmEx, DC, MC, V. **Map** p401 L7.

The Coliseum, the traditional home of English National Opera (ENO), re-opens after a refurb on 4 February 2004 with *Nixon in China*, by John Adams. The company was peripatetic while the builders were in, and press reports about sacked chorus members did not enhance its reputation. The argument between those who say opera must be made profitable and others who believe it cannot be (and that it is by nature an extravagance) rages on.

Royal Opera

Royal Opera House, Covent Garden, WC2E 9DD (7304 4000/www.royaloperahouse.org.uk). Covent Garden tube. **Box office** 10am-8pm Mon-Sat. **Tickets** £3-£170. **Credit** AmEx, MC, V. **Map** p399 L6.

Covent Garden is one of the great opera houses of the world, and a hugely expensive refurbishment in 2000 only made it better. The conversion of Floral Hall, the old flower warehouse, into a restaurant and bars is one of London's wonders. The discreetly air-conditioned auditorium and comfy new seating makes a night out at the opera a positive prospect whatever the production. In a nod to the proletariat, a new system allows passers-by in the piazza outside to hear the music. A highlight for 2004 is Welsh bass-baritone Bryn Terfel tackling Wagner.

Getting experienced at **Metro**. *See p309.*

Festivals

In addition to the annual festivals listed below, the **Barbican** (*see p300*), the **South Bank** (*see p302*) and **Wigmore Hall** (*see p302*) all present events throughout the year.

City of London Festival

Venues in & around the City (information 7377 0540/box office 7638 8891/www.colf.org).
Date 21 June-13 July 2004. **Box office** 9am-8pm daily. **Tickets** free-£40. **Credit** AmEx, MC, V.
This rich event continues to expand, but the core of its annual programme remains chamber music concerts in the beautiful halls of ancient livery companies, such as the Ironmongers' and Goldsmiths', which the public never otherwise see. Concerts, talks and exhibitions also take place in churches as well as the Barbican and great St Paul's Cathedral itself.

Hampton Court Palace Festival

Hampton Court, East Molesey, Surrey (Ticketmaster 0870 534 4444/www.hamptoncourtfestival.com). Hampton Court rail/riverboat from Westminster or Richmond to Hampton Court Pier (Apr-Oct).
Date Mid June 2004 (ring for exact date). **Tickets** £15-£85. **Credit** AmEx, MC, V.
Cardinal Wolsey built this vast luxury home for himself but later gave it to King Henry VIII who frolicked here with Anne Boleyn. The air of idle pleasure persists in the annual summer festival, where overtures and operatic arias have supper intervals during which audiences picnic on the grass or loiter in champagne tents while stilt-walkers, tumblers and jugglers wander among them (*see also p178*).

Holland Park Theatre

Holland Park, Kensington High Street, Kensington, W8 6LU (7602 7856/www.operahollandpark.com). High Street Kensington or Holland Park tube.
Date June-early Aug 2004. **Tickets** £20-£42. **Credit** AmEx, MC, V. **Map** p394 A8.
This open-air, canopied theatre hosts a summer season of opera where the experience can be magical whatever the weather. Although it is harder for the performers in the rain, the audience is correspondingly more appreciative. The cries of unseen peacocks beyond the wall add a surreal touch.

Kenwood Lakeside Concerts

Kenwood House, Hampstead Lane, Highgate, NW3 (information 8233 7435/box office 7413 1443/ www.picnicconcerts.com). Golders Green or East Finchley tube, then courtesy bus on concert nights.
Date 3 July-29 Aug 2004. **Tickets** £15-£32 (approx). **Credit** AmEx, MC, V.
A pleasant programme of tried-and-tested acts by the lake in the expansive grounds of Kenwood House on Hampstead Heath where the views over London are superb. Programmes tend to be lightweight and populist, best enjoyed on a tartan rug with a chilled Chablis on one of the firework nights.

It's best to buy a festival programme from a bookshop and plan ahead: the choice is wide. Tickets for the hilariously over-the-top Last Night, when normally well-behaved grown-ups act like schoolchildren, throwing paper darts and parping klaxons at inappropriate moments, are difficult to get hold of, but a secondary event is staged simultaneously in Hyde Park, where there's plenty of room.

Spitalfields Festival

Christ Church Spitalfields, E1 or Shoreditch Church, E1 (7377 1362/www.spitalfieldsfestival.org.uk). Liverpool Street tube/rail. **Dates** 9-19 Dec 2003; 7-25 June 2004. **Box office** 10am-5.30pm Mon-Fri. **Tickets** free-£27. **Credit** MC, V. **Map** p403 S5.
After a renovation, this beautiful Restoration church hosts highlights including Richard Rodney Bennett in cabaret, harpsichordist Gary Cooper playing Part II of The 48, a Community Cantata from composer and artistic director Jonathan Dove, and the Russian Patriarchate Choir putting the church's wondrous acoustic to the test.

Resources

British Music Information Centre

10 Stratford Place, Marylebone, W1C 1BA (7499 8567/www.bmic.co.uk). Bond Street tube. **Open** noon-5pm Mon-Fri. **Credit** MC, V. **Map** p398 H6.
A mine of information on British music: books, scores and recordings (audio and video).

National Sound Archive

British Library, 96 Euston Road, King's Cross, NW1 2DB (7412 7440/www.bl.uk). Euston or Kings Cross tube/rail. **Open** 10am-6pm Mon, Thur; 10am-8pm Tue, Wed; 10am-5pm Fri, Sat. **Map** p399 K3.
From music to drama and from vox pops to wildlife sounds, it's all here, along with books, magazines and journals covering every aspect of recorded sound. Listening is free, though membership of the British Library is required and it's advisable to call ahead with your request.

Marble Hill Concerts

Marble Hill Park, Richmond Road, Twickenham, Middx (information 8233 7435/box office 7413 1443/www.picnicconcerts.com). St Margaret's rail/ Richmond tube/rail then 33, 490, H22,R68, R70 bus. **Date** July, Aug 2004. **Tickets** £10-£20 (approx). **Credit** AmEx, MC, V.
As at Kenwood, the general rule is that you picnic while an amplified orchestra plays across the grass.

The Proms

Royal Albert Hall, Kensington Gore, South Kensington, SW7 2AP (information 7765 5575/ box office 7589 8212/www.bbc.co.uk/proms). South Kensington tube/9, 10, 52 bus. **Date** 16 July-11 Sept 2004. **Box office** 9am-9pm daily. **Tickets** £4-£35. **Credit** AmEx, MC, V. **Map** p397 D9.
The BBC Sir Henry Wood Promenade Concerts, or Proms for short, is arguably the world's finest orchestral music festival. Running annually from mid July until mid September, it features 70 concerts of both staple repertoire and newly commissioned works. The Proms began in 1895 with the aim of occupying idle musicians during the summer holidays and of informally educating those Londoners who could not afford to take vacations. Audiences paid a minimal ticket price provided they were prepared to do without a seat. The tradition continues today, as you can buy reserved seats in advance, but many prefer to queue on the day for cheap tickets for the seatless promenade area in front of the stage.

Rock, Dance Roots & Jazz

Grumble all you like about the frequently substandard sound, the bar prices and the local music press's increasingly tiresome build-'em-up-and-knock-'em-down search for the Next Big Things – we won't argue with you. But even with all of that, London's music scene is still one of the best. Each night, the capital is crowded with an intoxicating selection of acts local and international, famous and unknown, who between them bring an impossibly diverse range of music to an equally impossibly diverse audience. There is so much on offer here that, put simply, if you don't find something you like, you're not looking.

Get down at the **Bull & Gate**. *See p310.*

TICKETS AND INFORMATION

Your first stop should be the weekly *Time Out* magazine, which details hundreds of gigs in London. Most venues have websites detailing future shows, and some have online booking.

Prices vary wildly: on any given night, you could pay £45 for the privilege of watching Justin Timberlake at Earl's Court, or catch a perfectly serviceable jazz act free in a bar or restaurant. Look out, too, for the regular free signings in the Virgin Megastore, HMV (for both *see p251*) and Rough Trade (*see p252*). As a rule of thumb, though, it'll cost you £20-£40 to catch a world-famous act in one of London's larger (10,000-plus capacity) venues, £12-£20 to see acts the next rung down the ladder in rooms such as the **Astoria** or **Brixton Academy** (for both *see below*), £6-£12 to hear relatively obscure names at clubby venues such as the **Borderline** (*see p308*), and a fiver for bands whose own parents haven't heard of them.

Most pub venues – the **Water Rats** and **Barfly** (*see p311 and p310*) are the main exceptions – don't sell advance tickets, and for most roots and some jazz venues (such as the **Bull's Head** and the **Vortex**, for both *see p312*) you can just pay on the night. For everywhere else, buy tickets in advance if possible. Not all shows sell out, but it's tough to predict which will. And whether heavy metal or jazz, headline acts come on at around 9-10pm.

Buy tickets with cash direct from the venue's box office if you want to avoid insidious, needlessly inflated booking fees and charges, which can add 30 per cent to the ticket price. If the venue has sold out, try a ticket agency: the big three are **Ticketmaster** (0870 534 4444, www.ticketmaster.co.uk), **Stargreen** (7734 8932, www.stargreen.com) and **Ticketweb** (08700 600 100, www.ticketweb.co.uk). Avoid buying from the scamming, violent chancers otherwise known as ticket touts and scalpers who hang around outside bigger venues: you'll pay a fortune, and your ticket may be forged.

Rock & dance venues

Major venues

In addition to the venues listed below, the **South Bank Centre** (*see p302*), **Royal Albert Hall** (*see p302*) and **Barbican Centre** (*see p300*) all stage major gigs on a regular basis. In summer, **Hyde Park** (*see p137*) stages sizeable outdoor shows, while the beautiful courtyard at **Somerset House** (*see p96*) hosts shows from ineffably cool acts that draw up to 3,000 people.

Astoria

157 Charing Cross Road, Soho, WC2H 0EL (information 8963 0940/box office 7344 0044/ www.meanfiddler.com). Tottenham Court Road tube. **Box office** *In person* 10am-6pm Mon-Sat. *By phone* 24hrs daily. **Tickets** £8-£19.50. **Credit** AmEx, MC, V. **Map** p399 K6.

After a five-month battle, this none-more-central alt-rock hall won back its licence in March 2003. Westminster Council had turned down the venue's original application on safety grounds. We're more offended by the grubby decor, hopeless air-conditioning and atrocious sound. Revealing of the depressingly low standards held by London's indie kids, this is simultaneously one of London's most disappointing and most popular venues.

Blackheath Halls

23 Lee Road, Blackheath, SE3 9RQ (8463 0100/ www.blackheathhalls.com). Blackheath rail/54, 89, 108, 202, N53 bus. **Box office** 10am-7pm Mon-Sat; 11am-5pm Sun. **Tickets** £2.50-£18.50. **Credit** AmEx, MC, V.

South-east London's premier music venue presents a variety of different styles, from classical to rock. Though not as transport-accessible as other major venues, it still attracts top performers.

Carling Academy Brixton

211 Stockwell Road, Brixton, SW9 9SL (information 7771 3000/box office 08700 600 100/www.brixton-academy.co.uk). Brixton tube/rail. **Box office** *By phone* 24hrs daily. **Tickets** £10-£40. **Credit** MC, V.

It's more than a little ragged around the edges, and if it's not full, the echo can be overwhelming. Still, this 4,700-capacity south London venue is one of the best in town, thanks to its excellent sightlines, decent sound and preponderance of well-staffed bars. Acts run the gamut from Zero 7 to ZZ Top.

Carling Academy Islington

N1 Centre, 16 Parkfield Street, Islington, N1 0PS (information 7288 4400/box office 0870 771 2000/www.islington-academy.co.uk). Angel tube. **Box office** *In person* 10am-4pm Mon-Sat. *By phone* 24hrs daily. **Tickets** £3-£20. **Credit** MC, V.

Ex-Eurythmic Dave Stewart's relaunch of the venerable Marquee club in this gleaming Islington shopping mall lasted mere months. However, a new group has taken it over, supplementing an eclectic gig roster (the Fall, Martina Topley Bird, Hanson) with unpretentious, late-opening club nights.

Carling Apollo Hammersmith

Queen Caroline Street, Hammersmith, W6 9QH (information 8748 8660/box office 0870 606 3400/www.cclive.co.uk). Hammersmith tube. **Box office** *By phone* 24hrs daily. **Tickets** £10-£40. **Credit** AmEx, MC, V.

Now owned by global entertainment giant Clear Channel, the longtime Hammersmith Odeon and former Labatts Apollo was relaunched in October 2003 as an all-standing, 5,000-capacity venue. AC/DC headlined its re-opening night; the likes of the Darkness and Goldfrapp followed.

Earl's Court Exhibition Centre

Warwick Road, Earl's Court, SW5 9TA (7385 1200/ box office 7370 8078/www.eco.co.uk). Earl's Court tube. **Box office** *In person* 9am-6pm Mon-Fri. *By phone* 24hrs daily. **Tickets** £17-£50. **Credit** MC, V. **Map** p396 A11.

Among the acts who played here at the tail end of 2003 were Radiohead, Stereophonics and Justin Timberlake, which probably gives away that this is an immense aircraft hangar of a venue (its capacity of 20,000 makes it London's largest). It is cursed by horrible acoustics and expensive concessions.

Electric Ballroom

Camden High Street, Camden, NW1 8QP (7485 9006/www.electricballroom.co.uk). Camden Town tube. **Box office** 9am-5pm Mon-Thur; 10.30am-1am Fri, Sat; 10.30am-5pm Sun. **Tickets** £7-£10. **No credit cards**.

An absolute Camden archetype: a little down 'n' dirty, yet popular for its live shows and weekly clubs, which include the long-running goth/metal/ industrial night Full Tilt. Go soon, as it's under threat from London Underground, which wants to expand Camden Town station next door into a complex containing flats, offices and shops.

Forum

9-17 Highgate Road, Kentish Town, NW5 1JY (information 7284 1001/box office 7344 0044/ www.meanfiddler.com). Kentish Town tube/rail/N2 bus. **Box office** *In person* from the Astoria or the Jazz Café. *By phone* 24hrs daily. **Tickets** £5-£15. **Credit** AmEx, MC, V (phone bookings only).

Seemingly forgotten about by the indie acts that once graced its stage, the Forum's now sadly underused. A pity, really: its grey location aside, this once-grand theatre, blessed with fine sound and friendly staff, is arguably the best of the Mean Fiddler venues, and certainly a thousand times more inviting than the far more popular Astoria (*see p306*).

Ocean

270 Mare Street, Hackney, E8 1HE (switchboard 8986 5336/box office 8533 0111/24hr bookings 0845 070 1571/www.ocean.org.uk). Hackney Central or Hackney Downs rail. **Box office** noon-6pm Mon-Fri; later on performance nights. **Tickets** £3-£30. **Credit** MC, V.

This dazzling, high-tech complex opened with a fair amount of fanfare in early 2001, but hasn't really found its feet yet. Its three good-looking and well-maintained halls draw a wide mix of shows that can include anything from Dionne Warwick to Lloyd Cole to Howard Marks, so much so that Ocean's had trouble creating an identity for itself. In a way, it's a victim of its own success.

Shepherd's Bush Empire

Shepherd's Bush Green, W12 8TT (8354 3300/ box office 0870 771 2000/www.shepherds-bush-empire.co.uk). Shepherd's Bush tube. **Box office** *In person* noon-5pm Mon-Sat. *By phone* 24hrs daily. **Tickets** £10-£40. **Credit** MC, V.

This 2,000-capacity hall, a former BBC theatre, is still London's best mid-sized venue. The sound is usually splendid (unless you're in the low-ceilinged alcove behind the stalls bar, where it's dreadfully muffled), the atmosphere is cosy, and the staff are among London's friendliest. For the best views, get tickets for one of the (non-smoking) balconies: sightlines from the all-standing stalls are not great.

Union Chapel

Compton Terrace, Islington, N1 2UN (7226 1686/ box office 0870 120 1349/www.union chapel.org.uk). Highbury & Islington tube/rail/N19, N65, N92 bus. **Box office** 24hrs daily. **Tickets** £3-£25. **Credit** MC, V.

This Islington landmark, a former *Time Out* Live Venue of the Year, leads an intriguing double existence as both church and concert venue. It's quite simply a gorgeous space, in the ruins of a historic old sanctuary. Still, it has its drawbacks, and you're best off sticking to concerts from small ensembles: the hall's muddying echo has ruined a few shows.

Wembley Arena

Empire Way, Wembley, Middx, HA9 0DW (0870 739 0739/www.wembleyticket.com). Wembley Park tube/Wembley Central tube/rail. **Box office** *In person* 10.30am-4.30pm Mon-Sat. *By phone* 24hrs daily. **Tickets** £5-£100. **Credit**, MC, V.

Competition is stiff, but this might well be the worst music venue in London. Sure, few halls this size (it holds over 10,000) are appealing places, but this joyless aircraft hangar has zero atmosphere and is a less than impressive place to see bands.

Club venues

Borderline

Orange Yard, Manette Street, Soho, W1D 4JB (7734 2095/www.borderline.co.uk). Tottenham Court Road tube. **Box office** 10am-6pm Mon-Sat. **Open** *Gigs* 8-11pm Mon-Sat. *Club* 11.30pm-3am Mon-Sat. **Admission** *Gigs* £6-£16. *Club* £3-£8. **Credit** MC, V. **Map** p399 K6.

This is a fine little basement space with great sound and, crucially, an enthusiastic promoter whose policy of mixing the best in imported Americana, roots and alt-country acts with homegrown indie hopefuls has yielded dividends for a venue that was on the skids only a few years ago. A couple more bar staff wouldn't go amiss, but otherwise, this is a terrific place to either see a band or dance the night away.

Garage

20-22 Highbury Corner, Islington, N5 1RD (information 8963 0940/box office 0870 150 0044/www.meanfiddler.com). Highbury & Islington tube/rail. **Box office** 24hrs daily. **Open** *Gigs* 8pm-midnight Mon-Thur, some Sun; 8pm-3am Fri, Sat. **Admission** £5-£15. **Credit** MC, V.

The Garage is home to indie-leaning acts too big to play the Barfly (*see p310*) but not famous enough for the Astoria (*see p306*). But, frankly, the sooner they go one way or the other, the better. The sound

Revenge of the (music) nerds

Everybody knows one. Their CDs, all 2,000 of them, are neatly alphabetised; they spend their weekends making taped compilations (or, more likely, CDR compilations) for friends, relatives and, most often, unrequited loves; they know the jukebox in their local so well that they can programme it without flicking the discs to find their favourites; they can tell you the link between Todd Rundgren and David Bowie, even if you didn't especially want to know.

Ordinarily, these bespectacled (and they're always bespectacled), beer-bellied thirty- and fortysomethings, clad invariably in jeans and a rather weathered T-shirt boasting the legend 'Motörhead – No Sleep Til Hammersmith – UK Tour 1981' or somesuch, are treated with kid gloves by outsiders, regarded as amiable eccentrics. But increasingly in London, they're becoming treasured friends, people to keep on your good side, pals to have on handy speed-dial on your mobile phone. Why? Because the increase in trivia quizzes that's swept London's pubs in recent years has spawned a bastard child: the pop quiz.

The format's simple. Show up at a pub with a few friends, pop some money in a pot by way of an entry fee (never more than a couple of pounds), settle down with a pint or nine and answer a bunch of music questions. Some will be just simple trivia; some (of the guess-the-intro variety) will be on tape; a few might even entail recognising obscure album covers. It helps if one of your mates is the type of music nut detailed above. But if not, it's still a terrifically entertaining way to waste a midweek evening.

London's best two music quizzes are both held on Tuesday nights. At Stoke Newington's punningly named **Stoke Tup** (136 Stoke Newington Church Street, 7249 1318), a contagiously cheery woman named Mel presides weekly over an excellent quiz that circumnavigates the decades with ease; you're as likely to get a question about Bob Dylan as Britney Spears. At roughly the same time, the **Boogaloo** in Highgate (312 Archway Road, 8340 2928) fills with callow music journalists, grizzled locals and a few visiting hipsters, all ears as bluff northerner Martin asks the questions; rock-oriented, generally, but with enough twists to please even a Chubby Checker fan.

Two other music quizzes merit mention. The slightly joyless Monday-night affair at Islington's **Rosemary Branch** (2 Shepperton Road, 7704 2730) is one for the true obsessive. Meanwhile, although the one at the **Old Dairy** in Finsbury Park (1-3 Crouch Hill, 7263 3337) every Thursday night can be just as competitive, it's also, simultaneously, rather more approachable for those with a life outside their headphones.

Prizes vary. The top three teams at the Rosemary Branch and the Stoke Tup get drinks, for example, while the leading trio of teams at the Boogaloo get to choose from a new-release music book, a just-out CD and a bottle of (surprisingly decent) champagne. But all that's secondary: you're playing for bragging rights. Among true music obsessives, you see, it's not the taking part that counts: it's the winning.

(Oh, and the link between David Bowie and Todd Rundgren? Brothers Tony and Hunt Sales, sons of TV comic Soupy Sales, played bass and drums respectively on several early Rundgren albums, and later went on to become the rhythm section for Bowie's ill-fated band Tin Machine. Well, you asked...)

at this low-ceilinged venue is usually below average, and it can get unbearably hot in here if it's more than about two-thirds full. Smaller sister venue Upstairs at the Garage (guess where it is) is a little better.

ICA

The Mall, St James's, SW1Y 5AH (box office 7930 3647/www.ica.org.uk). Piccadilly Circus tube or Charing Cross tube/rail. **Box office** noon-9.30pm daily. **Tickets** £2-£25. **Credit** AmEx, MC, V. **Map** p401 K8.

The Institute of Contemporary Arts hosts everything from visual art installations to discussions about masturbation, but merits mention here for its musical programme, expanded in recent years to take in regular club nights and live shows from deeply hip alternative and arty acts. Nice bar too.

Lock 17

Middle Yard, Camden Lock, Chalk Farm Road, Camden, NW1 8LA (box office 7428 5929/ Ticketmaster 7344 4040/www.dingwalls.com). Camden Town or Chalk Farm tube. **Box office** *In person* tickets from Rhythm Records, 281 Camden High Street (7267 0123). *By phone* 24hrs daily. **Open** *Gigs* 7.30pm-midnight, nights vary. **Admission** £5-£15. **Credit** AmEx, MC, V.

At weekends, the chairs and tables come out and the venue that was known until very recently as Dingwalls morphs into the popular Jongleurs comedy club (*see p275*). Midweek, though, this is still a regular gig venue, and was, under its previous name, borderline famous. The bands it attracts are new and interesting, but this is a frustrating place: the multi-level layout is fine for sit-down comedy shows, but messy for all-standing music events.

100 Club

100 Oxford Street, Fitzrovia, W1D 1LL (7636 0933/ www.the100club.co.uk). Oxford Circus or Tottenham Court Road tube. **Open** *Gigs* 7.30pm-midnight Mon-Thur; noon-3pm, 8pm-1am Fri; 7.30pm-1am Sat; 7.30-11.30pm Sun. **Tickets** £7-£15. **Credit** AmEx, MC, V. **Map** p399 K6.

When it was first established 60 years ago, this was a haunt for Glenn Miller. In the '50s it became a leading trad-jazz joint, in the '60s a blues and R&B hangout, and in the '70s it was the home of punk. These days, a mix of indie, unsigned wannabes and old-school jazz can be heard in the awkward-shaped room. Extra points for the real ale at the bar.

Mean Fiddler

165 Charing Cross Road, Soho, WC2H 0EN (information 7434 9592/box office 7344 0044/ www.meanfiddler.com). Tottenham Court Road tube. **Box office** *In person* 10am-6pm Mon-Sat. *By phone* 24hrs daily. **Tickets** £10-£25. **Credit** AmEx, MC, V. **Map** p399 K6.

An underused little brother to the adjacent Astoria (*see p306*), the Fiddler stages fewer gigs than its sibling, despite the presence of a superior sound system and better sightlines. If the band's rubbish, head to the glassed-off bar to the left of the balcony.

Metro

19-23 Oxford Street, Soho, W1R 1RF (www.blowupmetro.com). Tottenham Court Road tube. **Open** 8-11pm daily. **Admission** from £5. **Map** p399 K6.

This basement space has fast cemented a reputation as *the* place to play for many of the country's fast-rising indie acts, despite (or, perhaps, because of; these alt-rock kids can be contrary buggers) the mushy sound and frankly horrible room layout. Things can get enjoyably messy here; expect your shirt to be drenched with both sweat and beer by the time you leave. And expect to be happy.

Spitz

Old Spitalfields Market, 109 Commercial Street, Spitalfields, E1 6BG (7392 9032/box office 0970 120 1149/www.spitz.co.uk). Liverpool Street tube/ rail. **Open** 11am-12am Mon-Sat; 10am-10.30pm Sun. **Box office** 24hrs daily. **Tickets** £4-£12. **Credit** MC, V. **Map** p403 R5.

On the edge of Spitalfields and opposite the imposing Christ Church, the Spitz tries to be all things to all people: gallery, restaurant, café and (upstairs) live music venue. Expect anything from experimental electronica to gutsy country.

Underworld

174 Camden High Street, Camden, NW1 0NE (7482 1932). Camden Town tube. **Open** *Gigs* 7pm-10.30am, nights vary. **Admission** £5-£20. **No credit cards**.

This is a maddening underground space, a maze of corridors and pillars and bars and, eventually, a decent live room deep below Camden Town. Avoid, if at all possible, the upstairs World's End bar, rammed nightly with people too unimaginative to meet anywhere other than the nearest pub to the tube station, which is what this is.

University of London Union (ULU)

Malet Street, Bloomsbury, WC1E 7HY (box 7664 2000/www.ulu.lon.ac.uk). Goodge Street tube. **Box office** 8.30am-11pm Mon-Fri; 9am-11pm Sat, Sun. **Open** *Gigs* 8-11pm, nights vary. **Admission** £8-£15. **Credit** MC, V. **Map** p399 K4.

British students are not known for their sophisticated tastes in music, and the acts who fill this cosy but anonymous hall will invariably have been featured heavily in the *NME* not long before their show. Still, the beer's cheap, and this is your chance to decide whether the *NME* is right about anything.

Pub & bar venues

In addition to the venues listed below, both the Hank Dogs' Wednesday-night **Easycome** acoustic club at the Ivy House (Stuart Road, Nunhead, www.the-ivyhouse.co.uk) and Alan Tyler's country-rockin' shindig **Come Down and Meet the Folks**, held every Sunday at the Fiddlers Elbow (1 Malden Road, Hampstead, www.comedownandmeetthefolks.co.uk) are worth investigating.

Arts Café at Toynbee Hall

28 Commercial Street, Spitalfields, E1 6LS (7247 5681). Aldgate East tube. **Open** 10am-8pm Mon-Fri, 7pm-12am Sat. *Gigs* 8.30-11.30pm, nights vary. **Admission** £3.50-£7. **Credit** MC, V.

A nice spot and a fairly recent addition to the London circuit. The music is generally good – expect acts from the more non-conformist end of the alternative rock field – and the pizza's even better.

Barfly

49 Chalk Farm Road, Camden, NW1 8AN (7691 4244/box office 0870 907 0999/www.barflyclub.com). Chalk Farm tube. **Open** 7.30-11pm Mon-Thur; 7.30pm-2am Fri, Sat; 7.30-10.30pm Sun. *Gigs* 8.15pm daily. **Admission** £4-£8. **Credit** *Box office only* AmEx, MC, V.

The Barfly club sure knows how to churn 'em out: around 20 indie acts – three a night – play here weekly. A few go on to bigger things, the rest vanish. Your best bets for catching one of the former is at Xposure, hosted by alt-rock station Xfm. Friday nights see DJ duo the Queens of Noize spinning all kinds of trashy nonsense.

Betsey Trotwood

56 Farringdon Road, Clerkenwell, EC1 (7253 4285). Farringdon tube. **Open** 8am-11pm Mon-Fri; 11am-11pm Sat; noon-10.30pm Sun. *Gigs* 9pm Mon-Sat. **Admission** £4-£5. **Credit** MC, V.

For several years the chaps from the Water Rats (*see p311*) have promoted nights of indie-kid bliss in the 70-capacity upstairs room at this boozer, an ideal place for spotting lo-fi alt-rock microcelebs. But there's trouble in the air, as a variety of problems have brought about serious rumours that it may be threatened with closure. The owners say they don't know what the future holds for this beloved joint, so phone before you go.

Boston Arms

178 Junction Road, Tufnell Park, N19 5QQ (7272 8153/www.dirtywaterclub.com). Tufnell Park tube. **Open** 11am-midnight Mon-Wed, Sun; 11am-1am Thur-Sat. *Gigs* 10pm, day varies. *Club* 9pm every other Fri. **Admission** £4-£6. **No credit cards.**

This place briefly became the trendiest venue in Britain when the White Stripes rolled into town in 2001 and claimed it as their home from home. On Fridays, the Dirty Water Club turns it into a swinging-'60s retro-bash: expect DJs playing R&B, classic beats and mod grooves, plus bands of the trashy garage punk variety.

Buffalo Bar

259 Upper Street, Islington, N1 1RU (7359 6191/www.thebuffalobar.com). Highbury & Islington tube/rail. **Open** 8.30am-2am Mon-Sat; 7pm-12am Sun. **Admission** free-£5. **Credit** MC, V.

This small Highbury Corner hangout stages all manner of events, and while the focus tends towards the DJs, there are regular shows here. Among the highlights are the good Tuesday night shindigs hosted by Artrocker (www.artrocker.com).

Bull & Gate

389 Kentish Town Road, NW5 2TJ (7485 5358). Kentish Town tube/rail. **Open** 11am-midnight Mon-Sat; noon-10.30pm Sun. *Gigs* 8.30pm daily. **Admission** £4-£5. **No credit cards.**

Renovations smartened up what used to be a real dive of a venue a few years back, but the bills are the same as ever: guitar-toting hopefuls in search of a big break. In the pantheon of pub venues, this one sits below the Barfly but above the Dublin Castle.

Dublin Castle

94 Parkway, Camden, NW1 7AN (7485 1773/www.dublincastle.co.uk). Camden Town tube. **Open** noon-1am Mon-Sat; noon-midnight Sun. *Gigs* 8.45pm Mon-Sat; 8.30pm Sun. **Admission** £4.50-£6. **No credit cards.**

Though the refurbishment a couple of years ago improved it, some think the Dublin Castle is still better used as a pub than as a music venue. But many disagree – Oasis members drink here from time to time; acts are of the struggling indie variety.

Hope & Anchor

207 Upper Street, Islington, N1 1RL (7354 1312). Highbury & Islington tube/rail. **Open** noon-1am Mon-Sat; noon-12am Sun. *Gigs* 8pm daily. **Admission** £4-£6. **Credit** MC, V. **Map** p402 O1.

This minuscule cellar was a rock and punk legend a quarter-century ago. These days, the pub upstairs is considerably smarter and the acts are less noteworthy. Again, it's mostly indie up-and-comers.

12 Bar Club: where the musicians go to hear bands. See p312.

Notting Hill Arts Club

21 Notting Hill Gate, Notting Hill, W11 3JQ (7460 4459/www.nottinghillartsclub.com). Notting Hill Gate tube. **Open** 6pm-1am Mon-Wed; 6pm-2am Thur, Fri; 4pm-2am Sat; 4pm-12.30am Sun. *Gigs* times vary. **Admission** free-£8. **Credit** MC, V.

This painfully hip basement in the heart of Notting Hill has all the charm of root canal work, its decor artfully downmarket and its staff all too easily distracted. Still, Rota on Saturday afternoons often throws up some decent live acts, as does Alan McGee's riotously entertaining Wednesday-night Death Disco shindig.

Verge

147 Kentish Town Road, Camden, NW1 8PB (7284 1178). Camden Town or Kentish Town tube/rail. **Box office** noon-6pm daily. **Open** 8pm-midnight Mon-Wed, Sun; 8pm-2am Thur-Sat. **Admission** £3-£15. **Credit** AmEx, MC, V.

Its location isn't the only thing about the Verge that's just ever so slightly removed from Camden. The line-ups here tend to be of the alt-rock variety, but with a little more variety than most similar venues ten or so minutes down the road.

Water Rats

328 Gray's Inn Road, King's Cross, WC1X 8BZ (7837 7269/www.plumpromotions.co.uk). King's Cross tube/rail. **Open** *Gigs* 8.30-11pm Mon-Sat. **Admission** £4-£6. **No credit cards**. **Map** p399 M3.

Bob Dylan played his first UK gig in the quietly impressive back room of this King's Cross boozer four decades ago. These days, the line-ups tend to be a little noisier: alt-rock and metal types, sometimes on the edge of big things or secretly showcasing new material.

Windmill

22 Blenheim Gardens, Brixton, SW2 5BZ (8671 0700/www.windmillbrixton.com). Brixton tube/rail. **Open** *Gigs* 7-11pm Mon-Sat; 7-10.30pm Sun. **Admission** free-£3. **No credit cards**.

A typically shambling Brixton boozer with an atypically decent selection of live music. Tim Perry's country-infused Twisted AM Lounge, held here irregularly on Sundays, anchors the programme, but there are also gigs on some Fridays and Saturdays.

Roots venues

Cecil Sharp House

2 Regent's Park Road, Camden, NW1 7AY (7485 2206/www.efdss.org). Camden Town tube. **Open** *Gigs* 7pm, nights vary. **Admission** £3-£8. **Credit** MC, V.

This is the centre of the English Folk Dance and Song Society. Sharp's Folk Club on Tuesdays is fun and totally untouched by the modern era, and is supplemented by regular barn dances, *ceilidhs* and folk dance classes. Swaddling Songs, a night of warped folk music produced by the best in town, appears sporadically throughout the year.

Hammersmith & Fulham Irish Centre

Blacks Road, Hammersmith, W6 9DT (8563 8232/www.lbhf.gov.uk/irishcentre). Hammersmith tube. **Open** *Gigs* 8.15pm, nights vary. **Admission** £4-£10. **No credit cards**.

You'll find all kinds of Irish music events, from free *ceilidhs* to biggish-name Irish acts such as the Popes, on offer at this small, friendly *craic* dealer.

12 Bar Club

22-3 Denmark Place, St Giles's, WC2H 8NL (information 7916 6989/box office 7209 2248/ www.12barclub.com). Tottenham Court Road tube. **Open** 8pm-1am Mon-Thur; 8pm-3am Fri; 5.30pm-12.30am Sun. **Admission** £5-£10. **Credit** MC, V. **Map** p399 K6.

A hidden gem, literally: this cupboard is tucked away around the back of Denmark Street. It's tiny: you can't get more than three people on stage without it being a ridiculous crush. Still, the line-ups, often singer-songwriters, are usually worthwhile, the atmosphere's pleasant, and a recent expansion has opened the bar area up nicely.

Jazz venues

Bull's Head

373 Lonsdale Road, Barnes, SW13 9PY (8876 5241/www.thebullshead.com). Barnes Bridge rail. **Open** 11am-11pm Mon-Sat; noon-10.30pm Sun. *Gigs* 8.30pm Mon-Sat; 2-4.30pm, 8-10.30pm Sun. **Admission** £3-£10. **Credit** AmEx, DC, MC, V.

This delightful riverside pub (and Thai bistro) is something of a jazz landmark, staging gigs by musicians from both here and the States. In true jazz tradition, it also has a well-stocked bar; check out, in particular, the selection of malt whiskies.

Jazz Café

5 Parkway, Camden, NW1 7PG (information 7916 6060/box office 0870 150 0044/www.jazzcafe.co.uk). Camden Town tube. **Open** 7pm-1am Mon-Thur; 7pm-2am Fri, Sat; 7pm-1am Sun. *Gigs* 9pm daily. **Admission** £8-£25. **Credit** MC, V.

The name doesn't tell the whole story: jazz is a small piece in the jigsaw of events here, which also takes in funk, hip hop, soul, R&B, singer-songwriters and more besides. Pray that the expense-accounters who pack the balcony don't talk through the entire set.

Pizza Express Jazz Club

10 Dean Street, Soho, W1C 5RL (restaurant 7437 9595/Jazz Club 7439 8722/www.pizzaexpress.co.uk). Tottenham Court Road tube. **Open** *Restaurant* 11.30am-midnight daily. *Jazz Club* 7.45pm-midnight daily. *Gigs* 9pm daily. **Admission** £15-£20. **Credit** AmEx, DC, MC, V. **Map** p399 K6.

The food takes second billing in the basement of this eaterie: this is all about the (non-challenging, largely contemporary) jazz. Audiences are surprisingly respectful: there's no talking through the sets here. Other Pizza Express branches offer live jazz, albeit more as background noise than anything else.

Pizza on the Park

11 Knightsbridge, Knightsbridge, SW1X 7LY (7235 5273). Hyde Park Corner tube. **Open** 8.30am-midnight Mon-Fri; 9.30am-midnight Sat, Sun. *Gigs* 9.15pm, 10.45pm daily. **Admission** £10-£20. **Credit** AmEx, DC, MC, V. **Map** p400 G8.

Pizza on the Park used to be owned by the same company as Pizza Express, and takes a similar tack with the jazz programming in its basement: music here is professional, if totally mainstream.

Ronnie Scott's

47 Frith Street, Soho, W1D 4HT (7439 0747/www.ronniescotts.co.uk). Leicester Square or Tottenham Court Road tube. **Open** 8.30pm-3am Mon-Sat. *Gigs* 9.30pm Mon-Sat. **Admission** (non-members) £15 Mon-Thur; £25 Fri, Sat. **Credit** AmEx, DC, MC, V. **Map** p399 K6.

Scott died in 1996 after running one of the world's most famous jazz clubs for almost four decades. This place has struggled a little since then, but it's still there, and it remains a Soho fixture. Old-timers and critics say that the roster of acts, who play two sets a night for runs of at least a week, is not as interesting (or as jazzy) as it was, and it seems as if the crowds are even brasher and chattier than ever. Still, after hours, when the tourists have headed home and only the diehards remain, Ronnie Scott's is as atmospheric as it gets. Call ahead to book a table.

606 Club

90 Lots Road, Chelsea, SW10 0QD (7352 5953/ www.606club.co.uk). Earl's Court or Fulham Broadway tube/11, 211 bus. **Open** 7.30pm-1.30am Mon-Wed; 8pm-1.30am Thur; 8pm-2am Fri, Sat; 8pm-midnight Sun. *Gigs* 8pm-1am Mon-Wed; 9.30pm-1.30am Thur; 10pm-2am Fri, Sat; 9.30pm-midnight Sun. **Admission** *Music charge* (non-members) £6 Mon-Thur; £8 Fri, Sat; £7 Sun. **Credit** MC, V. **Map** p396 C13.

A restaurant, late-night club and popular musicians' hangout, this Chelsea joint has the laudable policy of placing an emphasis on booking British-based jazz musicians. So this is mostly home-grown talent, and it brings in the crowds. There's no entry fee: the musicians are funded from a music charge that is added to your bill at the end of the night. Alcohol is only served with meals.

Vortex

139-41 Stoke Newington Church Street, Stoke Newington, N16 0UH (7254 6516/www.vortexjazz.co.uk). Stoke Newington rail/67, 73, 76, 106, 243 bus. **Open** 10am-5pm, 8pm-midnight daily. *Gigs* 9.15pm daily. **Admission** free-£10. **Credit** MC, V.

The future of this Stoke Newington staple is a little uncertain, as in March 2004 its lease on the endearingly shambling Church Street building where it has long operated expires. As of late 2003, a move to new premises a mile or so away in Dalston looked quite likely; certainly we hope that the club will continue in some form elsewhere, for it'd be a shame for British jazz to lose one of its devoted supporters. Check online for the latest developments.

Nightlife

You want it, London's got it.

The capital's nightlife remains unrivalled. Its diversity alone ensures that the city retains its position as the creative nucleus for what is now really a global club scene. While other clubbing destinations are characterised by their close affiliation with particular types of music (house 'n' trance in Ibiza, techno in Berlin), in London, every genre is celebrated. So you get the big five – hip hop, house, techno, drum 'n' bass, and breaks – as well as critical recent dance movements such as UK garage and electroclash.

At the moment, there's a real sense of excitement about London's nightlife. The city has settled into a 21st-century groove, with clubs and musical hybrids all multiplying and dividing at a fantastic rate. Nothing is discarded and everything is gained: older scenes such as hardcore and trance still have a loyal following, and newer mutations like UK bass are constantly gaining ground. In recent years, live music has become a feature at many club nights, creating even more variety.

The choice is overwhelming, but if it's based on the music you love, the decision is actually easy. Trickier to navigate are London's club venues, the 'super-clubs' and the smaller club-bars, which differ in size and price only. At leading venues of both types, the music is almost always excellent, the queues are almost always long and the drinks are always expensive. Consequently, in the areas where clubs and bars are concentrated – Brixton, the West End, and the East End (including Shoreditch, Hoxton and Clerkenwell) – Friday and Saturday nights can be madly crowded and it can be a bit difficult to find the clubs.

While that's half the fun, it's also worth remembering that London's nightlife is just as vibrant, and often cheaper, during the week. So if the crowds get you down, try out classic London clubs such as THIS on Mondays at **Bar Rumba**.

Of course, the best parties are often the most clandestine, so it pays to be resourceful and investigate further than magazine club listings. Pick up flyers in shops, keep your eye out for street posters, and if you have a favourite DJ or record label, check up on their UK activities online. That's not to say listings guides can't be useful – the next few pages provide you with a starting point by presenting an overview of London's best clubs and bars.

Clubs

Aquarium

256 Old Street, Hoxton, EC1V 9DD (7251 6136/ www.clubaquarium.co.uk). Old Street tube/rail. **Open** 10pm-3am Thur, Sun; 10pm-4am Fri; 10pm-5am Sat. **Admission** £8-£16. **Map** p403 R3.

A nightclub with a swimming pool, a large T-shaped Roman pool, in fact, with a mirrored wall and a six-person jacuzzi and a window looking on to the dancefloor. The music, mainly house, garage and the requisite club classics, has been given a boost by the arrival of the hugely popular and funky '70s night Carwash on Saturdays.

Bar Rumba

36 Shaftesbury Avenue, Soho, W1V 7DD (7287 6933/www.barrumba.co.uk). Piccadilly Circus tube. **Open** 9pm-3.30am Mon. 6pm-3am Tue-Wed; 6pm-3.30am Thur-Fri; 9pm-5am Sat; 8pm-2am Sun. **Admission** £3-£12; free before 9pm Tue, 10pm Weds, 8pm Thur, 10pm Fri **Map** p401 K7.

Some of the best dancing in town goes on in this long-established basement club. Gilles Peterson's long-running jazzy, funky Monday-nighter THIS (That's How It Is) has a large and loyal following, Movement (Thursdays) is a storming drum 'n' bass blowout, and there are excellent one-nighters all through the week.

Camden Palace

1A Camden High Street, Camden, NW1 0JH (09062 100200/www.camdenpalace.com). Camden Town or Mornington Crescent tube. **Open** 10pm-2.30am Tue; 10pm-6am Fri, Sat. **Admission** £3-£25.

This former music hall was transformed into a massive, multi-level extravaganza in the early '80s. The tiered bars and plush seating are looking a little

The best Clubs

For a big night out
Fabric. *See p316.*

For an ace soundsystem
Plastic People. *See p318.*

For that super-club throng
Ministry of Sound. *See p317.*

For club-bar intimacy
Herbal. *See p317.*

europe's most famous funk clu

every sat at the aquarium, 256 old st. ec

the best of everything funk

0870 246 1966 www.carwash.co.u

disco vibes_disco glamour_disco chic_disco everythin

weary these days, but indie-rock night Feet First on Tuesdays and Friday's hard house gig, Peach, show there's life in the old dog yet.

Canvas

Kings Cross Goods Yard, off York Way, N1 0UZ (7833 8301). Kings Cross tube/rail. **Open** 10pm-6am Fri, Sat. **Admission** £10-£20.

Formerly Bagley's Studios, the renamed and revamped new Canvas venue continues to uphold its reputation as a rave mecca. It's housed in a massive warehouse space taking in three dancefloors and two bars, so club promoters pull out all the stops to pull in big crowds.

Cargo

Kingsland Viaduct, 83 Rivington Street, Shoreditch, EC2A 3AY (7739 3440/www.cargo-london.com). Old Street tube/rail. **Open** noon-1am Mon-Thur; noon-3am Fri; 6pm-3am Sat; 1pm-midnight Sun. **Admission** free-£8. **Map** p403 R4.

Set in the heart of super-cool Shoreditch, Cargo is a stylish urban-industrial under-the-arches kind of place, serving up good food, decent drink and fresh, often innovative music. A mixture of DJ sets and live bands mean variety's the name of the game. Be prepared to queue if there are big names on the bill, but it'll almost certainly be worth it.

The Cross

Arches, 27-31 King's Cross Goods Yard, off York Way, King's Cross, N1 0UZ (7837 0828/www.the-cross.co.uk). King's Cross tube/rail. **Open** 11pm-5am Fri; 10pm-6am Sat; 11pm-5am every other Sun. **Admission** £12-£15. **Map** p399 L2.

A hip brick-and-arches venue, but this one has a garden area – all lush plants and comfy sofas – that becomes another dancefloor in summer. Well known for glam house nights Renaissance, Type, Serious, Drama and Prologue (on rotation Saturdays) as well as Fiction on Fridays and Vertigo on Sundays, the Cross can also get funky. The friendly, sussed crowd whip up a great atmosphere: just get there early to avoid queuing for hours.

Deluxe Gallery

2-4 Hoxton Square, 1st Floor, Hoxton, N1 6NU (7729 8503/www.deluxe-arts.org.uk). Old Street tube/rail. **Open** 11am-6pm Mon-Fri; noon-5pm Sat. **Admission** Free. There is sometimes a varied charge for music events.

24-hour party people

London's not good on 24-hour culture. Traditionally, a night on the town around here amounts to no more than an evening at the pub. Draconian drink licensing laws and public transport schedules still conspire to send many Londoners back home to bed by midnight, or at least spilling out on to the streets in a beer-fuelled frenzy after the dreaded last call for drinks at 11pm.

Still, over the last 15 years, the rise of club culture across the UK has done much to alleviate such restrictions. After raves were forced indoors by the Criminal Justice Act of 1994, perhaps the only consolation was that throughout the subsequent decade, an all-night mentality – à la party capitals such as Barcelona – became the norm. Closing times for London's biggest venues can now extend to 7am, though 5am or 6am is generally the standard. And the growth of pre-club-bars, plus after-hours parties, means that, come the weekend, there is plenty of dancing beyond dawn. For the devotees of house or garage, south London club **Ministry of Sound** (*see p317*) is still the first port of call. In the west and east, the **End** (*see p316*), **Turnmills** (*see p318*) and **Fabric** (*see p316*) all offer excellent all night variations on the house 'n' techno theme, with equal space given to drum 'n' bass and breaks. No self-respecting hard house club closes until morning, with many events concentrated around Brixton: be cool in the **Fridge** (*see p316*), and chill after hours at the Fridge Bar.

In the back of King's Cross station, pumping house, techno and electro clubs at the **Cross** (*see p315*), the **Key** (*see p317*) and **Canvas** (*see p315*) all draw crowds.

The gay club scene also continues to be a huge influence on how long, how hard and how fast London clubbers party. The pioneering after-hours club Trade appears at **Turnmills** for public holidays and summer events, while promoter Laurence Malice keeps the flame alive with after-hours clubs at **EGG** (*see p316*).

Throughout Sunday afternoon and evening London's club-bars reopen for business, with the added attraction of food. The **Social** bars (*see p321*) in central and north London feature delicious menus alongside the post-party vibes, while out east, **Cargo** (*see p315*), **93 Feet East** (*see p317*) and the **Vibe Bar** (*see p321*) all present more soul- and funk-oriented clubs, all having the advantage of outdoor beer gardens. Of course, come Sunday night, all London's club venues are open, with many diehards winding up the weekend at 'polysexual' hard house night DTPM at **Fabric** (*see p316*).

Hmmm, usually people are dancing at **EGG**...

Much more than a small white art gallery, the Deluxe hosts a variety of multimedia events at which the irony quotient is often high. Phone for information on upcoming musical evenings.

EGG

200 York Way, King's Cross, N7 9AX (7609 8364/ www.egglondon.net). King's Cross tube/rail. **Open** 6pm-6am Fri; 10pm Sat-1pm Sun; phone for weekday openings. **Admission** £6-£15.

Relatively new venue EGG has quickly made its mark, attracting cutting-edge crowds by championing live music within edgy house, techno and electro as well as house nights. The Mediterranean-style three-floored interior is both labyrinthine and low-ceilinged with an intimate atmosphere. The upstairs bar in red ostrich leather is particularly elegant, while the main dancefloor downstairs aims at, and achieves, a warehouse rave feel. EGG also boasts a large terrace and covered courtyard.

The End

18 West Central Street, Holborn, WC1A 1JJ (7419 9199/www.the-end.co.uk). Holborn or Tottenham Court Road tube. **Open** 10pm-3am Mon, Wed; 10pm-4am Thur; 10pm-5am Fri; 10pm-7am Sat; phone for details Sun. **Admission** £4-£15. **Map** p399 L6.

This place covers all the bases, with a minimalist design, a quality sound system, and a monthly rotation of funky techno, drum 'n' bass, garage and deep house parties. Crowds of eager clubbers show their appreciation every weekend, and it's also the home of Trash's glam, electronica, punk, pop and disco mix-mash on Mondays.

Fabric

77A Charterhouse Street, Farringdon, EC1M 3HN (7336 8898/advance tickets for Fri 7344 4444/ www.fabriclondon.com). Farringdon tube/rail. **Open** 9.30pm-5am Fri; 10pm-7am Sat. **Admission** £12-£15. **Map** p402 O5.

Now one of London's biggest and best-loved clubs, this place was once a meat cellar. It has a diverse selection of music and a cool but unpretentious crowd. The music policy here is eclectic, revolving around underground DJ talent, live acts and the most inspiring new beats, all cranked through the scary Bodysonic dancefloor.

The Fortress

34-8 Provost Street, Old Street, N1 (020 7251 6200/ www.fortressstudios.co.uk). Old Street tube/rail. **Open** 10.30pm-6am Fri, Sat. **Admission** £5-£10. **Map** p403 Q3.

Operating as a recording studio by day, the no-nonsense stone-walled Fortress is favoured by underground collectives for storming house, techno, electro and breakbeat events. These do sometimes appear in club listings, but more often on posters around town, consequently pulling in a dressed-down, musically discerning breed of clubber. Keep an eye out for the signs, or check the website.

The Fridge

1 Town Hall Parade, Brixton Hill, Brixton, SW2 1RJ (7326 5100/www.fridge.co.uk). Brixton tube/rail. **Open** 10pm-6am Fri, Sat. **Admission** £8-£20.

Brixton's biggest venue has been delivering the goods for years, and it still does today. Flocks of techno heads and dreadlocked ravers descend on this former theatre for nights such as Frantic and Logic, as well as gay night Love Muscle, then later the party continues on even later at the buzzy, groovy Fridge bar next door.

Ghetto

5-6 Falconberg Court, (behind the Astoria), Soho, W1 (www.ghetto-london.co.uk). Tottenham Court Road tube. **Open** 10.30pm-3am Mon-Thur; 10.30pm-4am Fri; 10.30pm-5am Sat; 10pm-3am Sun. **Admission** free-£7. **Map** p399 K6.

Done out in raving red, this fabulously louche basement venue has really come into its own. It hosts two of London's hippest electroclash fests, the Cock on Fridays and Nag Nag Nag on Wednesdays. Both attract a gay/straight crowd of club characters and disco dollies, who work up a sweat on a dancefloor with minimal air-conditioning.

...like this.

Herbal

10-14 Kingsland Road, Shoreditch, E2 8DA (7613 4462/www.herbaluk.com). Old Street tube/rail. **Open** 9pm-2am Wed, Thur; 9pm-3am Fri, Sat; 9pm-2am Sun. **Admission** free-£6. **Map** p403 R3.
This well-designed club-bar maintains a warm and cosy vibe, although it gets sweaty. Bang in the middle of Coolsville, the crowd is laid-back, friendly and up for fun. The music is funky and urban (the monthly All Over My Face is fantastic).

The Key

King's Cross Freight Depot, King's Cross, N1 (7837 1027/www.thekeylondon.com). King's Cross tube/rail. **Open** 10.30pm-4.30am Fri, Sat. **Admission** £10.
Set into King's Cross railway arches (you'll hear it when you're near it, but look at the website for a map to locate it), this cavernous new venue has a flashing dancefloor. The monthly Friday night Human Zoo has helped put the venue on the map, joining the dots between house, electro and disco in an innovative manner, and inspiring the sophisticated yet enthusiastic crowd.

Madame Jo Jo's

8-10 Brewer Street, Soho, W1 F0SP (7734 3040/ www.madamejojos.com). Leicester Square or Piccadilly Circus tube. **Open** 10.30pm-3am Wed, Fri; 9.30pm-3am Thur; 10pm-3am Sat. **Admission** £5-£8. **Map** p401 K6.
A great venue, enhanced by a touch of Soho cabaret sleaze. There are some promising midweek funk and hip hop nights, but the big draw is Keb Darge's Deep Funk, where blindingly funky chickens move furiously to obscure '60s and '70s cuts.

Ministry of Sound

103 Gaunt Street, Walworth, South London, SE1 (7378 6528/ www.ministryofsound.com). Elephant & Castle tube/rail. **Open** 10pm-3am Wed (student night); 10.30pm-5am Fri; 11pm-8am Sat. **Admission** £12-£15. **Map** p404 O10.
This is London's best-known club, so it's sneered at by cutting-edge clubbers, but MoS still draws huge crowds every single night that it's open. It also attracts big-name guest DJs from the US and UK to spin house, garage and R&B anthems.

93 Feet East

150 Brick Lane, Spitalfields, E1 6QN (7247 3293/ www.93feeteast.co.uk). Aldgate East/Liverpool Street tube. **Open** 11am-11pm Mon-Thur; 11am-1am Fri, Sat; noon-10.30pm Sun. **Admission** £5-£10; free before 11pm weekdays. **Map** p403 S5.
A large three-room venue with a solid reputation for its variety and music. A stylish downstairs bar, kitschy upstairs bar and main dancefloor conspire to create winning nights (London Xpress, Bashy). On Mondays the three-piece band 90 Free Mondays graces the building with its presence.

Neighbourhood

12 Acklam Road, W10 5QZ (7524 7979/ www.neighbourhoodclub.net). Ladbroke Grove/ Westbourne Park tube. **Open** 8pm-2am Thur-Sat; 5pm-12am Sun; check website for weeknight times and events. **Admission** £5-10.
The brand-new 500-capacity Neighbourhood was built on the site of the once-sterling west London venue Subterania. Run by Ben Watt (Everything But the Girl) and Alan Grant, its varied repertoire includes live music, one-off weeknight events and fantastic high-quality house music on weekends.

Notting Hill Arts Club

21 Notting Hill Gate, Notting Hill, W11 3JQ (7460 4459/www.nottinghillartsclub.com). Notting Hill Gate tube. **Open** 6pm-1am Mon-Wed; 6pm-2am Thur, Fri; 4pm-2am Sat; 4pm-1am Sun. **Admission** £8; free (every night before 8pm exc Sun). **Map** p394 A7.
Artists, DJs and musicians swap ideas in this cool westside success story, where the music and visual arts are all about cultural diversity and innovation. Everyone takes to the dancefloor for clubs such as Death Disco on Wednesdays and Sundaysonic.

Pacha London

Terminus Place, Victoria, SW1V 1JR (7833 3139/www.pachalondon.com). Victoria tube/rail. **Open** 10pm-6am Fri, Sat. **Admission** £15-£20. **Map** p400 H10.
This lavish outpost of the global club giant that has dominated Ibiza for years was made for lording it: chandeliers, oak panels and a stained-glass ceiling ensure a chic clubbing experience. Glammed-up clubbers dress in keeping with the sumptuous decor, shaking their booty to house beats.

Plan B

418 Brixton Road, Brixton, SW9 (7733 0926/ www.plan-brixton.co.uk). Brixton tube/rail. **Open** 5pm-late Tue; 5pm-2am Wed, Thur; 5pm-4am Fri, Sat; 5pm-1am Sun. **Admission** free before 9pm; £3 after 9pm; £5 after 10pm Fri, Sat.
A new addition to Brixton, this gleaming, spacious club-bar is modern rather than trendy in design. Similarly, it attracts a good-natured local crowd to its weekly hip hop, soul, funk and breaks nights. On Saturdays, the ace soundsystem pumps it out.

Plastic People

147-9 Curtain Road, Shoreditch, EC2 (7739 6471/ www.plasticpeople.co.uk). Old Street tube/rail. **Open** 10pm-2am Mon-Thur; 10pm-3.30am Fri, Sat; 7pm-midnight Sun. **Admission** £3-£7. **Map** p403 R4.

This tiny downstairs club is also a good place to come for after-hours drinks without breaking the bank, and it's a music lover's paradise. Sounds range from Afro-jazz and hip hop, to Latin and deep house: watch the little dancefloor get rammed with a chilled but funky crowd. Imaginative visuals add to the atmosphere. The sound system is bliss.

Scala

275 Pentonville Road, King's Cross, N1 9NL (7833 2022/www.scala-london.co.uk). King's Cross tube/rail. **Open** 10pm-5am Fri, Sat. **Admission** £6-£14. **Map** p399 L3.

Operating as both a club and live venue, the Scala's main room might be cavernous, but this doesn't mean the atmosphere's hollow. It pulls in a relaxed, (usually) trainer-friendly clientele who rock out to a variety of beats: as well as Friday gay night Popstarz, there's Saturday's UK garage stalwart Cookies and Cream.

Shoreditch Electricity Showrooms

39a Hoxton Square, Hoxton, N1 (7739 6934). Old Street tube/rail. **Open** from 7pmTue, Fri-Sun. **Admission** phone for details.

Encapsulating the best and worst of trendy Shoreditch, this longstanding club-bar is all chic minimalism, but prices are high. Food is served in the upstairs bar, while the sleek downstairs space plays host to a variety of clubs, including the hip electro night Nerd every second Sunday. On the third Sunday of the month, Pacman brings in a lively gay crowd. Raison d'Etre, on Tuesdays offers live music and dancing till midnight.

Studio 33

100 Tinworth Street, off Albert Embankment, Vauxhall, SE11 5EQ (7820 1702). Vauxhall tube/ rail. **Open** 10pm-6am Fri, Sat. **Admission** £14-£20.

A new and improved version of former hard house-haven the Chunnel club, Studio 33 has undergone a £1 million refurbishment, resulting in a slick new venue with mezzanine floors, a walk-across bridge and lounge, plus two dancefloors. Friday clubs include Ratpack (old skool), Valve (drum 'n' bass), and Bedlam (funky house/hard trance) as well as monthly electro Saturday nighter Dopamine.

333

333 Old Street, Hoxton, EC1V 9LE (7739 5949/ www.333mother.com). Old Street tube/rail. **Open** *Bar* 8pm-3am Mon-Wed, Fri; 8pm-4am Thur, 8pm-1am Sat. *Club* 10pm-5am Fri, Sat. **Admission** *Club* £5-£10. **Map** p403 Q4.

A landmark on fashionable Old Street, this pivotal East End venue houses a no-frills three-storey interior. The lively punters (a whole lot of 'em, too: beware the queues) are there for the music, which is always excellent and varied. The basement usually bounces to techno, drum 'n' bass or crazy mash-ups, while the main room heaves to house and electro. The top-floor bar, Mother, is plusher: a great hang-out that runs good nights of its own.

Telegraph

228 Brixton Hill, Brixton, SW2 1HE (8678 0777). Brixton tube/rail. **Open** 5.30pm-2.30am Mon-Thur; 5.30-4am Fri; noon-6am Sat; noon-12.30am Sun. **Admission** £5-£10.

Situated at the top of Brixton Hill, further up than some may care to venture, this spacious old Brixton pub isn't out to impress, and tends to keep it in the family with a series of clubs from local promoters and DJs. However, these merit attention, since they often feature big names who enjoy keepin' it real. Faithful crowds make the trek for quality house, breaks and hip hop. If you wish, line your stomach before drinking with one of the Thai or continental dishes from the mini-restaurant.

Turnmills

63B Clerkenwell Road, Clerkenwell, EC1M 5PT (7250 3409/www.turnmills.com). Farringdon tube/rail. **Open** 6.30pm-midnight Tue; 10.30pm-7.30am Fri; 10pm-7am Sat; 10pm-5am Sun. **Admission** £5-£15. **Map** p402 N4.

Turnmills' nooks and crannies are a hedonist's playground, the whole venue a legend in its own lifetime. While it offers the full musical spectrum, the long-running house and trance night, Gallery, on Friday night is particularly well known. However, newer Saturday-night residencies are just as impressive. Anexo, a sister venue, opened next door in 2002.

The Whoopee Club

www.thewhoopeeclub.com

Started by a veteran of east London's strip pub circuit, the capital's first and so far only burlesque night is an absolute riot, equal parts sexy, arty, camp and hysterical. Frilly-knickered girls can can with unbridled enthusiasm; strippers disrobe down to pasties (not Cornish ones but nipple tassle ones) and a G-string as a saxophone squeals; the audience, male and female, whoop and holler as a man peels off his City pinstripes to reveal an outlandish basque and suspenders. DJs bookend the on-stage entertainment. During 2003 the Whoopee occupied a monthly slot in west London, but check its website for dates and venues, and dress up to blend in.

DJ bars

Since the late 1990s, it seems like DJ bars have been springing up all over London. They've revolutionised the city's drinking culture, and have proved to be a firm favourite with older clubbers who have tired of dancing all night but still want to go out and listen to good music. Conversely, they have provided a platform for the next generation of DJs to hone their skills and gain a following. The bigger names also relish the opportunity to play a more eclectic

Unsurprisingly, she's very popular at **The Whoopee Club**. *See p317.*

selection in an intimate setting, which makes many of these venues an excellent value for money, enabling crowds to witness high-profile DJs for under a fiver. However, DJ bars have become a victim of their own success, as cash-hungry investors have ripped up old pubs all over London, repeating the successful formula and building identikit bars – all featuring exposed brick and piping, with decks in the corner almost as an afterthought. Seek out some of the venues listed here, though – all part of the first wave of DJ bars – and quality is assured.

AKA

18 West Central Street, Holborn, WC1A 1JJ (7836 0110/www.akalondon.com). Holborn or Tottenham Court Road tube. **Open** 6pm-3am Mon-Fri; 7pm-7am Sat; 8pm-3am Sun. **Admission** £3 after 11pm Tue, Wed; £5 after 11pm Thur; £7 after 10pm Fri; £10 after 9pm Sat. **Map** p399 L6.

Joined – physically as well as musically – to the End next door (*see p316*), this popular hangout attracts top international DJs, who entertain punters loosened up by good food and cocktails. The venue is incorporated into the End's club nights on Fridays and Saturdays; be prepared to queue at weekends.

Barfly

49 Chalk Farm Road, Camden, NW1 8AR (7691 4244/barflyclub.com). Camden Town/Chalk Farm tube. **Open** 7.30pm-1am Mon-Thur; 7.30pm-3am Fri, Sat; 7.30-11pm Sun. **Admission** varies.

Part of the Barfly chain, this spit 'n' sawdust venue has a spacious ground-floor bar and upstairs stage area. It has done its time as a workaday live venue, but its profile has been raised by the revival of rock and live music, as it is now home to fashionable rock club Queens of Noize on Fridays.

Bug Bar

The Crypt, St Matthew's Church, Brixton Hill, Brixton, SW2 1JF (7738 3366/www.bugbrixton.co.uk). Brixton tube/rail. **Open** 7pm-2am Wed; 8pm-2am Thur, Sun; 8pm-3am Fri, Sat. **Admission** free before 9pm; £4 after 9pm; £6 after 11pm.

The nicely refurbished Bug Bar is always alive and kicking. Live music, top-quality DJs and competitively priced drinks ensure Bug maintains its kudos.

Cherry Jam

58 Porchester Road, Bayswater, W2 (7727 9950/www.cherryjam.net). Royal Oak tube. **Open** 6pm-2am Mon-Sat; 6pm-midnight Sun. **Admission** £5-£8 after 8pm, depending on nights; phone for details. **Map** p394 C5.

Part-owned by Notting Hill Arts Club aficionados Alan Grant and Everything But the Girl's Ben Watt, there's a rich calendar of exhibitions, live music and DJ nights to elevate and entertain the west London clientele in an atmospheric and intimate setting.

Dogstar

389 Coldharbour Lane, Brixton, SW9 8lQ (7733 7515/www.thedogstar.com). Brixton tube/rail. **Open** noon-2.30am Mon-Thur; noon-4.30am Fri, Sat; noon-2.30am Sun. **Admission** £3 after 10pm Fri, Sat; free at other times.

A Brixton institution, Dogstar is set in a large old street-corner pub, and it exudes urban authenticity. The atmosphere can be intense, and it is absolutely never less than vibrant. It's something of a training ground for the DJ stars of tomorrow, so it's worth visiting. Music varies from night to night, but it always feels like the weekend. This is where the DJs go when they want to hang out.

Elbow Room

89-91 Chapel Market, Angel, N1 9EX (7278 3244/www.theelbowroom.co.uk). Angel tube. **Open** 5pm-2am Mon; noon-2am Tue-Thur; noon-3am Fri, Sat; noon-midnight Sun. **Admission** £2 9-10pm, £5 after 10pm Fri, Sat; free most other times. **Credit** MC, V.

The biggest London location of this decidedly upscale DJ bar/club/pool hall, Elbow Room follows a well-established, slick, good-time formula that wins it many friends round here.

Electro-a-go-go

There's a new eclecticism in London clubbing these days. Due partly to the continued '80s pop revival and the current resurgence of rock music, it also owes much to the staying power of electroclash, the dance music genre that has outlived its own hype to become an integral part of London's nightlife. Combining synth-pop with '90s techno, plus a strong visual aesthetic, the scene has united music fans, trend-seekers, gay, fetish and fashion contingents in an unprecedented manner.

Electroclash club nights are among the most flamboyant and theatrical in the capital, with an anything goes atmosphere that's due in part to raucous music and camp live shows, but mostly to crowds wearing eyeliner, fishnets and knowing smiles.

Famed for a proliferation of celebrity visitors, **Nag Nag Nag** (Wednesdays at the Ghetto, *see p316*) is the epitome of electroclash cool, though prepare for long queues and style-conscious crowds. More rough and ready is the The **Cock** (Fridays at the Ghetto, *see p316*), a gay-ish night that draws a mixed, dance-crazy crowd.

Computer Blue (monthly at Deluxe Gallery, *see p315*) and **Nerd** (monthly at Shoreditch Electricity Showrooms, *see p318*) are both sizzling grassroots events that did much to popularise the genre in London.

Electroclash is now established enough to make the move into the capital's bigger venues, and so it has appeared at places like Hoxton's **333** clubs (*see p318*), which feature several of the movement's current stars, including the Nag Nag Nag DJs.

EGG, one of London's newest and most innovative venues (*see p316*), gives a platform to collectives from around the UK and the rest of Europe on Saturdays – check *Time Out* magazine for its ever-changing highlights. The venue is also visited by DJs from the pioneering electroclash record label International Deejay Gigolos.

There is some overlap between electroclash and the punk-funk and indie club scenes. Because of that, the importance of **Trash** (Mondays at the End, *see p316*) cannot be overstated – with its open-ended musical policy and its open-minded attitude, this influential club has made clubbers and pop music the stars of the show again, as they were meant to be. Similarly idiosyncratic nights include **And Did We Mention Our Disco** (Fridays, Plastic People, *see p318*) and **Warm Leatherette** (monthly at Herbal, *see p317*), while **Death Disco** (Thursdays at Notting Hill Arts Club, *see p317*) and **Queens of Noize** (Fridays at Barfly, *see p319*) are two of London's leading indie-rock nights. It's a rare feat for a club to be cutting edge without being intimidating, but all these clubs somehow manage it. And by their very success, they are breathing new life into the scene, lending it both character and a welcome dose of humour.

Other locations: 103 Westbourne Grove, Notting Hill, W2 4UW (7221 5211); 97-113 Curtain Road, Shoreditch, EC2A 3BF (7613 1316).

Fridge Bar

1 Town Hall Parade, Brixton Hill, Brixton, SW2 1RJ (7326 5100/www.fridge.co.uk). Brixton tube/rail. **Open** 6pm-2am Mon-Thur; 6pm-4am Fri; 5.30pm-11am, 8pm-4am Sat; 5.30-11am, 9pm-3am Sun. **Admission** free Mon-Thur; £5-£8 Fri-Sun.

The name is apt, as this place can be a chilled, spacious hangout with mellow global beats, or it can change completely into a packed-out, feverish party atmosphere: the Fridge Bar does it all. Although it hosts after-parties on behalf of the club next door, it also makes the most of its dark basement dancefloor to throw decent parties all by itself.

ICA Bar

ICA, The Mall, St James's, SW1Y 5AH (7930 3647/ www.ica.org.uk). Charing Cross tube/rail, Piccadilly Circus tube **Open** noon-10.30pm Mon; noon-1am Tue-Sat; noon-11pm Sun.

A relaxed white and silver space set within the classy Institute of Contemporary Arts, the ICA bar has long been particularly popular with the clubbing community, thanks to a range of interesting multi-media events that often fuse music and film. It also offers periodic electronic music festivals, and holds a famous monthly mid week club, Blacktronica. This is one of the nicest places in town to go clubbing. The atmosphere is hard to beat.

Ion

161-5 Ladbroke Grove, Ladbroke Grove, W10 6HJ (8960 1702/www.meanfiddler.com). Ladbroke Grove tube. **Open** 5pm-midnight Mon-Fri; noon-midnight Sat; 5pm-midnight Sun. **Admission** free; £5 after 7.30pm Fri-Sun.

The red and brown velvet sofas in this lounge bar make it a particularly good place to relax. The music is varied and soulful, and the vibe is pure west London cool. Be prepared for a goldfish-in-a-bowl sensation if you're self-conscious, though, as there's a big glass window in the front.

Market Place

11 Market Place, Marylebone, W1W 8AH (7079 2020). Oxford Circus tube. **Open** 11am-midnight Mon-Wed; 11am-1am Thur-Sat; 1-11pm Sun. **Admission** £3 after 9pm Fri, 8pm Sat; £7 after 11pm Fri, Sat (redeemable against food and drink). Free during rest of week. **Map** p398 J6.

Another new recruit, the wooden chalet-style basement of Market Place oozes warmth and cosiness, while the global cuisine and dynamic music line-ups make it an essential stop off. Just off Oxford Circus, it tends to attract a post-work crowd in the week, but weekends have more of a party spirit.

Medicine Bar

181 Upper Street, Islington, N1 1RX (7704 9536). Highbury & Islington tube/rail. **Open** 5pm-midnight Mon-Thur; 5pm-2am Fri; noon-2am Sat; noon-10.30pm Sun. **Map** p402 O1.

Stylish but comfortable, this funky and popular Islington hangout fills with pre-clubbers as the after-work drinkers fade away. With its newly added upper floor, it's a great place to hear classic soul, disco and funk. Membership may be required on busy weekend nights.

Other location: 89 Great Eastern Street, Shoreditch (7739 5173).

Redstar

319 Camberwell Road, Camberwell, SE5 (7326 0055/www.redstarbar.co.uk). Oval tube then 36, 185 bus. **Open** 5pm-1am Mon-Thur; 5pm-4am Fri; noon-4am Sat; noon-midnight Sun. **Admission** free before 11pm; £4 after 11pm Fri, Sat

With consistently great DJs, an easygoing loungey ambience, decent prices and views over Camberwell Green, it's not surprising this place is so popular, especially with students from the local art college.

Salmon & Compasses

58 Penton Street, Islington, N1 9PZ (7837 3891). Angel tube. **Open** 5pm-midnight Mon-Wed; 5pm-3am Thur-Sat; 2pm-midnight Sun. **Admission** free; £3 after 9pm Fri, Sat. **Map** p402 N2.

Islington's no-nonsense DJ bar packs in an up-for-it crowd on weekends with a rotating series of theme nights. Early in the week, it's chilled.

The Social

5 Little Portland Street, Marylebone, W1 (7636 4992/www.thesocial.com). Oxford Circus tube. **Open** noon-11pm Mon-Sat. **Admission** free; £3 acoustic nights. **Map** p398 J5.

Established by Heavenly Records in 1999, the Social is popular with music industry workers, minor alt-rock celebs and other sassy trendies, but a fantastic sound system and great music roster mean it pulls in anyone who's up for a quality time.

Other location: 33 Linton Street, Islington, N1 7DU (7354 5809).

Vibe Bar

Old Truman Brewery, 91-5 Brick Lane, Shoreditch, E1 6QL (7426 0491/www.vibe-bar.co.uk). Liverpool Street tube/rail/Aldgate East tube. **Open** 11am-11.30pm Mon-Thur; 11am-1am Fri, Sat; 11am-11.30pm Sun. **Admission** £3 after 8pm Fri, Sat. **Map** p403 S5.

The first arrival along Brick Lane, this well-loved bar attracts a lively crowd who live it up in the summertime in the massive fairy-lit courtyard to diverse tunes: you'll be tempted to pop in if you're passing. Conveniently near to 93 Feet East (*see p317*), the Vibe is packed at weekends, but it has interesting music throughout the week.

Pretty, shiny lights at **Studio 33**. *See p318.*

Casinos

Until 1999 British casinos were forbidden to advertise. Even now, advertisements have to be 'informative' rather than 'promotional'. However, the law allows visitors to apply for membership of a casino in advance, rather than having to turn up in person. Legally speaking, all casinos have to be notified of your intention to play at least 24 hours in advance, and you must either be a member yourself, or be the guest of a member in order to enter.

While British law forbids us to list casinos in this guide, a flip through the *Yellow Pages* or a chat to the concierge of your hotel will help you find a gaming establishment near you. Most casinos are open from mid-afternoon through to around 4am every night, and the vast majority are in central London (not least in and around the traditional rich gents' playground that is Mayfair). Check with the casino directly if you're worried about a dress code. However, as a rule of thumb, while casual attire – though not jeans or trainers – may be acceptable for the afternoons, in the evenings gentlemen almost always have to don a jacket and tie.

Sport & Fitness

It's time to get moving.

Check the weekly Sport section of *Time Out* magazine for a comprehensive guide to the main action. For a more in-depth approach to keeping fit in the capital, choose the *Time Out Sport, Health and Fitness Guide* (£8.99).

Major stadia

Crystal Palace National Sports Centre

Ledrington Road, Crystal Palace, SE19 2BB (8778 0131/www.crystalpalace.co.uk). Crystal Palace rail.
This Grade II-listed building is shamefully shabby, but good enough for the Grand Prix athletics every summer, and activities and competitions year round.

Wembley Arena & Conference Centre

Elvin House, Stadium Way, Wembley, Middx HA9 0DW (8902 0902/www.wembley.co.uk). Wembley Park tube/Wembley Stadium rail.
Show jumping, boxing, snooker and basketball tournaments take place infrequently in an area much diminished by the closure of its famous stadium.

Spectator sports

Basketball

If basketball ever catches on here, London's home-grown slam-dunkers may actually become household names. The **Towers** (*see below*) are in the British Basketball League. For more information – including a list of indoor and outdoor courts – contact the English Basketball Association (0870 7744 225/ www.england basketball.co.uk).

Kinder London Towers

Crystal Palace National Sports Centre, Ledrington Road, Crystal Palace, SE19 2BB (8776 7755/ www.london-towers.co.uk). Crystal Palace rail.
Admission £7-£8; £5-£6 concessions.

Cricket

Cricket games can go on a bit, so if you're pushed for time, catch a one-day match in the C&G Trophy or Norwich Union League rather than a County Championship match. **Lord's** (home to Middlesex) and the **Oval** (Surrey's home ground) also host Test matches and one-day internationals, for which you should book ahead. The season runs April to September.

AMP Oval

Kennington Oval, Kennington, SE11 5SS (7582 6660/7764/www.surreycricket.com). Oval tube.
Tickets £5-£50; free under-17s when accompanied by an adult.

Lord's

St John's Wood Road, St John's Wood, NW8 8QN (MCC 7289 1611/tickets 7432 1066/www.lords.org.uk). St John's Wood tube. **Tickets** £10-£50; half-price or free for concessions.

Football

London claims the title as the birthplace of the game that half the world calls soccer and the other half knows as football. The modern version of the game was formulated in a pub (quel surprise) in 1863, and over the subsequent hundred or so years it gradually became the national game. Today, frankly it's a bit of an obsession, albeit one that divides the country: a minority will have nothing to do with football, but the majority spend winter Saturdays in a kind of agony until the final whistle blows.

Sadly, though, here in the heart of the land of football, it's hard for a casual spectator to see a good game. Tickets for teams in the top league, which is known as the Premiership, are all but impossible to come by, so that means that it's hard to see games with teams such as Manchester United, Arsenal and Chelsea. But there are also London clubs in all three divisions of the Nationwide League, for which tickets are cheaper and easier to obtain.

For more information, try www.the-fa.org. The prices quoted are for adult non-members; ring for concessionary and advance rates.

Arsenal

Arsenal Stadium, Avenell Road, Highbury, N5 1BU (7704 4040/www.arsenal.com). Arsenal tube.
Tickets £26-£48. **Premiership**.

Brentford

Griffin Park, Braemar Road, Brentford, Middx (8847 2511/www.brentfordfc.co.uk). South Ealing tube/Brentford rail. **Tickets** £14 standing; £18 seated. **Division 2**.

Charlton Athletic

The Valley, Floyd Road, Charlton, SE7 8BL (8333 4010/www.cafc.co.uk). Charlton rail. **Open** *Box office* 8am-6pm Mon-Fri; 10am-noon Sat. **Tickets** £25-£35. **Premiership**.

Chelsea

Stamford Bridge, Fulham Road, Chelsea, SW6 1HS (7386 7799/www.chelseafc.co.uk). Fulham Broadway tube. **Tickets** £20-£67. **Premiership**.

Crystal Palace

Selhurst Park, Whitehorse Lane, Selhurst, SE25 6PU (8771 8841/www.cpfc.co.uk). Selhurst rail. **Tickets** £19-£25. **Division 1**.

Queens Park Rangers

Rangers Stadium, South Africa Road, Shepherd's Bush, W12 (8740 2575/www.qpr.co.uk). White City tube. **Tickets** £14-£20. **Division 2**.

Fulham

Rangers Stadium, South Africa Road, W12 7PA (0870 442 1234/www.fulhamfc.co.uk). White City tube. **Tickets** £26-£43. **Premiership**.

Leyton Orient

Matchroom Stadium, Brisbane Road, E10. Leyton tube. **Tickets** £12-£16. Division 3.

Millwall

TheDen,ZampaRoad,Bermondsey,SE16 3LN (7231 1199/www.millwallfc.co.uk). South Bermondsey rail. **Tickets** £16-£22. **Division 1**.

Tottenham Hotspur

White Hart Lane Stadium, 748 High Road, Tottenham, N17 0AP (0870 420 5000). White Hart Lane rail. **Tickets** £25-£65. **Premiership**.

West Ham United

Boleyn Ground, Green Street, West Ham, E13 (0870 112 2700). Upton Park tube. **Tickets** £26-£46. **Division 1**.

Greyhound racing

A night at the dogs might not sound like much, but it is the perfect opportunity for anyone wanting to get to the heart of what really goes on in the suburbs. It's also far less shady than you might think (and twice as much fun as you can probably imagine), it's an experience that allows you to drink cheap beer, shout yourself hoarse and even make a few pounds (for a very small stake) in the process.

Sadly, 2003 was a bad, indeed the last, year for the dogs at Catford, in south-east London. The famous track, which had put this otherwise unremarkable part of town on the map for 71 years, ceased trading in November after a long financial struggle. For more information, visit www.thedogs.co.uk.

Walthamstow Stadium

Chingford Road, Walthamstow, E4 8SJ (8531 4255/ www.wsgreyhound.co.uk). Walthamstow Central tube/rail then 97, 215 bus. **Races** 2pm Mon; 11.30am Fri; 7.30pm Tue, Thur, Sat. **Admission** £1-£6; free lunchtimes Mon, Fri.

The lido's lovely

If outdoor swimming is your thing, go to the 'Lidos in London' link on the website for the **Serpentine** (*see p136 and below*), for a comprehensive list of pools.

Brockwell Lido

Dulwich Road, Herne Hill, SE24 0PA (7274 3088/ www.thelido.co.uk). Herne Hill rail. **Open** *June-Sept* 6.45am-7pm Mon-Fri; noon-6pm Sat, Sun. **Admission** £5; £3 children.

Finchley Lido

Great North Leisure Park, High Road, Finchley, N12 0AE (8343 9830). East Finchley or Finchley Central tube. **Open** 6.45-8.30am, 9am-6.30pm, (ladies only) 7-9.30pm Mon; 6.45-8.30am, 9am-9.30pm Tue, Thur, Fri; 6.45-8.30am, 9am-8pm Wed; 8am-4.30pm Sat, Sun. **Admission** £2.90; £1.70 5-16s.

Hampstead Heath Ponds

Hampstead Heath, NW5 1QR (7485 4491/ www.cityoflondon.gov.uk/openspaces). Hampstead tube/Gospel Oak or Hampstead Heath rail/C2, C11, 214 bus. **Open** *May-Sept* 7am-7pm daily. **Admission** free.

Parliament Hill Lido

Hampstead Heath, Gordon House Road, NW5 1QR (7485 3873/www.cityoflondon.gov.uk/open-spaces). Gospel Oak rail/C11 bus. **Open** *May-Sept* 7-9am, 10am-6pm daily. *Oct-Apr* 7-10am daily. **Admission** £1.80-£3.60; free 7-9.30am.

Pools on the Park

Old Deer Park, Twickenham Road, Richmond, Surrey TW9 2SF (8940 0561). Richmond tube/rail. **Open** *Apr-Sept* 6.30am-8pm Mon-Fri; 7am-6pm Sat, Sun. **Admission** £3.50; £2.60 children.

Serpentine Lido

Hyde Park, W2 2UH (7706 3422/www.serpentine lido.com). Knightsbridge or South Kensington tube. **Open** *Mid June-Sept* 10am-5.30pm daily. **Admission** £3; 60p children.

Tooting Bec Lido

Tooting Bec Road, Tooting Bec Common, SW16 1RU (8871 7198). Tooting Bec tube/ Streatham rail. **Open** *Late May-Aug* 6am-8pm daily. *Sept* 6am-5pm daily. *Oct-May* closed except for club members. **Admission** £2.50-£3.65; £2.50 children.

Wimbledon Stadium

Plough Lane, Wimbledon, SW17 0BL (8946 8000/ www.wimbledondogs.co.uk). Tooting Broadway tube/ Wimbledon tube/rail/Haydons Road rail. **Races** 7.30pm Tue, Fri, Sat. **Admission** £5.50.

Horse racing

The racing year is divided into the flat racing season, which runs from April to September, and the National Hunt season over jumps, going through the winter from October to April. For more information about the sport of kings, visit www.discover-racing.com.

The courses nearest London skirt some pretty county towns, so take time to explore the surrounding area once you've lost your shirt.

Ascot

High Street, Ascot, Berks SL5 7JX (01344 622211/ www.ascot.co.uk). Ascot rail. **Open** *Box office* 9am-5pm Mon-Fri. **Admission** £7-£52.

Ascot is best known for the pomp of the Royal Meeting in June, although that event (in particular Ladies Day, with its unspeakable hats) is regarded with derision by many hardcore race-goers.

Epsom

Epsom Downs, Epsom, Surrey KT18 5LQ (01372 726311/www.epsomderby.co.uk). Epsom Downs or Tattenham Corner rail. **Open** *Box office* 9am-5pm Mon-Fri. **Admission** £5-£35.

The annual Derby, held here in June, is one of the great events in Britain's social and sporting calendar. Around 150,000 people descend on the park for the race. Ten other meetings are held each year.

Kempton Park

Staines Road East, Sunbury-on-Thames, Middx TW16 5AQ (01932 782292/www.kempton.co.uk). Kempton Park rail. **Open** *Box office* 9am-5pm Mon-Fri. **Admission** £13-£20.

Not a glamorous course, but the year-round meetings are well attended, especially in summer.

Sandown Park

Portsmouth Road, Esher, Surrey KT10 9AJ (01372 463072/www.sandown.co.uk). Esher rail. **Open** *Box office* 9am-8pm Mon-Fri. **Admission** £5-£30.

Most famous for hosting the Whitbread Gold Cup in April and the Coral Eclipse Stakes in July, both races push horses to the limit with an infamous hill finish.

Windsor

Maidenhead Road, Windsor, Berks SL4 5JJ (01753 498400). Windsor & Eton Riverside rail. **Open** *Box office* 9.3am-5.3pm Mon-Fri. **Admission** £5-£18.

A pleasant Thames-side location in the shadow of Windsor Castle makes this a lovely spot for first-timers and families, especially during the three-day festival in May or on one of its summer Monday evening meetings. Views of the course may not be the best around (except for those who dine in the Castle restaurant overlook the finishing post).

Motor sport

Wimbledon Stadium is the place to come for pedal-to-the-metal entertainment: Wednesday is Speedway motorbike racing; every other Sunday bangers, hot rods and stock cars come together for family-oriented mayhem.

Wimbledon Stadium

Plough Lane, Wimbledon, SW17 0BL (stadium 8946 8000/stock car information 01420 588020/www.wimbledonstadium.co.uk). Tooting Broadway tube/Wimbledon tube/rail/Earlsfield/ Haydons Road rail. **Races** 6pm every other Sun. **Admission** £11; £5 children, concessions.

Rugby union

The immense popularity of the ruffians' sport is never so apparent as during the annual **Six Nations Championship** (January to March). Tickets for these games – which take place at Twickenham (Rugby Road, Twickenham, Middx, 8892 2000; *see also p179*), the home of **English Rugby Union**, with a capacity of over 60,000 – are virtually impossible to get hold of, but those for other matches are readily available. The **Zurich Premiership** and the three-division **National League** play from August to May; most games are played on Saturday and Sunday afternoons.

Listed below are the Premiership clubs: for a more comprehensive list visit www.rfu.com.

London Wasps

Twyford Avenue Sports Ground, Twyford Avenue, Acton, W3 9QA (www.wasps.co.uk). Ealing Common tube. **Admission** £6-£16.

NEC Harlequins

Stoop Memorial Ground, Langhorn Drive, Twickenham, Middx TW2 7SX (8410 6000/ www.quins.co.uk). Twickenham rail. **Open** *Box office* 9am-5pm Mon-Fri. **Admission** £12-£25.

Saracens

Vicarage Road Stadium, Watford, Herts WD18 0EP (01923 496222/www.saracens.com). Watford High Street tube. **Open** *Box office* 9am-6pm Mon-Fri. **Admission** £12-£25.

Tennis

Despite having originated in the Middle East, the starchy politeness of tennis seems typically English. Which makes it even more of a shame that we're generally so bad at it. Regardless, the eyes of the world will once again fall on our one hope, which is usually Tim Henman, at **Wimbledon**'s Lawn Tennis Club from 21 June to 4 July 2004. Getting to see the main action requires forethought, as seats on Centre and Number One courts must be applied for by

Into **Hampstead Heath Ponds**. *See p323.*

ballot the previous year, although enthusiasts who queue on the day may gain entry to the outer courts, where freedom to wander about means you're never far from the action. Wimbledon is preceded by the Stella Artois tournament, where stars from the mens' circuit can be seen warming up for the main event: the 2004 tournament will be held 7-13 June at **Queen's Club** (*see below*).

All England Lawn Tennis Club

PO Box 98, Church Road, Wimbledon, SW19 5AE (8944 1066/information 8946 2244/www.wimbledon.org). Southfields tube.

Queen's Club

Palliser Road, West Kensington, W14 9EQ (7385 3421/www.queensclub.co.uk). Barons Court tube.

Participation sports

Athletics

The following facilities are open for casual use.

Crystal Palace National Sports Centre, *Ledrington Road, Crystal Palace, SE19 2BB (8778 0131/www.crystalpalace.co.uk). Crystal Palace rail.* **Cost** £85/day.

Millennium Arena, *Battersea Park, East Carriage Drive, Battersea, SW11 4NJ (8871 7537). Battersea Park rail.* **Cost** £2/day.

Regent's Park Track, *Regent's Park, Outer Circle, Camden, NW1 4NR (7486 7905). Camden Town tube then 274 bus.* **Cost** free.

Cycling

Speed merchants can pedal round the following bike circuits. For bike hire, *see p361.*

Herne Hill Velodrome

Burbage Road, Herne Hill, SE24 9HE (7737 4647/www.hernehillvelodrome.org.uk). Herne Hill or North Dulwich rail. **Open** *Summer* 10am-6pm Mon-Fri; 9am-12.30pm Sat. *Winter* 10am-4pm Mon-Fri; 9am-1pm Sat. **Cost** *With bike hire* £8. *With own bike* £5.50.

The oldest cycle circuit in the world is scarily fast.

Lee Valley Cycle Circuit

Quartermile Lane, Stratford, E10 5PD (8534 6085/www.leevalleypark.com). Leyton tube. **Open** Summer 8am-8pm daily. Winter 8am-4pm daily. **Cost** With bike hire £4.80; £3.75 under-16s. With own bike £2.50; £1.35 under-16s.

BMX, road-racing, mountain biking, time trials and cyclo-cross are all on the menu.

Golf

It's not as stuffy as it was and you don't have to be a member to tee up at any of the public courses below – but book in advance. For a fuller list of courses, see www.thelondongolfer.com.

Dulwich & Sydenham Hill

Grange Lane, College Road, Dulwich, SE21 7LH (8693 8491/www.dulwichgolf.co.uk). West Dulwich rail. **Open** 8am-dusk daily. **Green fee** £30 Mon-Fri.

North Middlesex

Manor House, Friern Barnet Lane, Arnos Grove, N20 0NL (8445 3060/www.northmiddlesexgc.co.uk). Arnos Grove or Totteridge & Whetstone tube. **Open** 8am-4pm Mon-Fri; 1pm-dusk Sat, Sun. **Green fee** £15-£25 Mon-Fri; £25-£30 Sat, Sun.

Richmond Park

Roehampton Gate, Priory Lane, Richmond, SW15 5JR (8876 3205/www.richmondparkgolf.co.uk). Richmond tube/rail. **Open** 7am-dusk Mon-Fri; dawn-dusk Sat, Sun. **Green fee** £6-£18 Mon-Fri; £6-£21 Sat, Sun.

Ice skating

Broadgate is the only outdoor rink in the list on page 326, but beautiful **Somerset House** has an outdoor rink over the Christmas period (*see p96*), as does **Marble Arch** (*see p109*). Most indoor arenas offer skating classes, ice hockey coaching and discos.

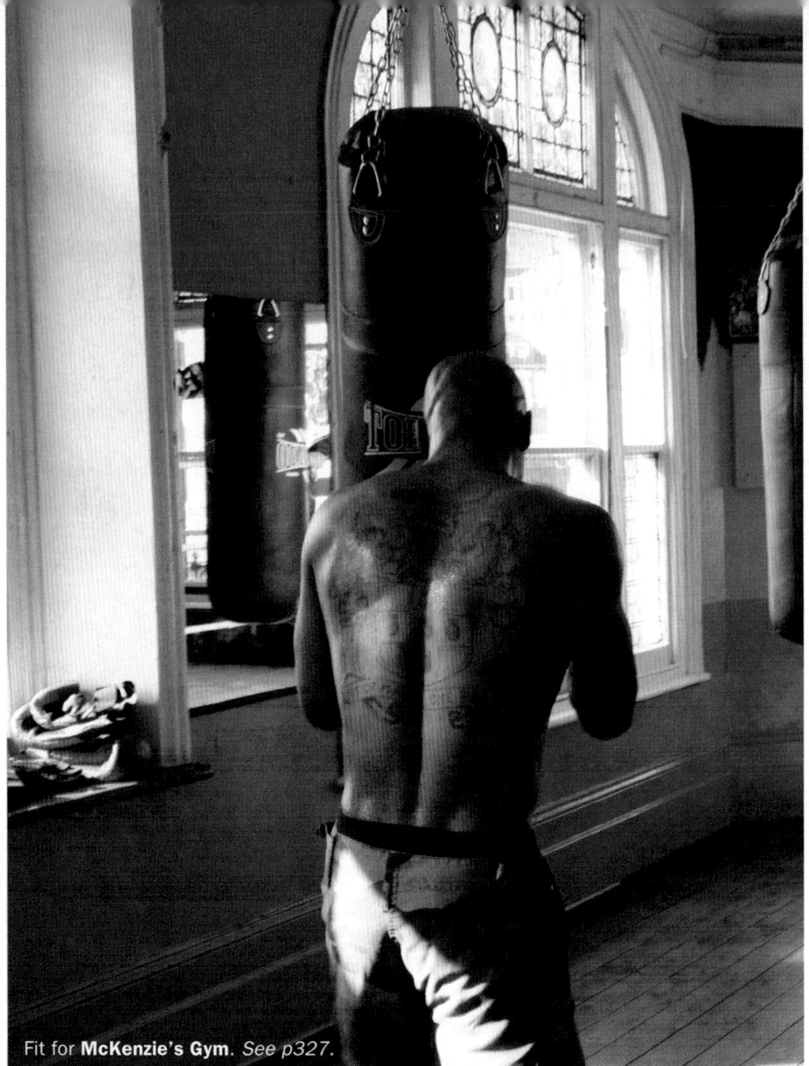

Fit for **McKenzie's Gym**. *See p327.*

Alexandra Palace Ice Rink

Alexandra Palace Way, N22 7AY (8365 4386). Wood Green tube/W3 bus. **Open** 11am-1.30pm, 2-5.30pm Mon-Thur; 11am-1.30pm, 2-5.30pm, 8.30-11pm Fri; 10.30am-12.30pm, 2-4.30pm, 8.30-11pm Sat, Sun. **Admission** £4.20-£5.50; £3.50-£4.50 children.

Broadgate Ice Rink

Broadgate Circle, EC2A 2QS (7505 4068/ www.broadgateestates.co.uk). Liverpool Street tube/rail. **Open** *Nov-mid Apr* noon-2.30pm, 3.30 6pm Mon-Thur; noon-2.30pm, 3.30-6pm, 7-10pm Fri; 11am-1pm, 2-4pm, 5-8.30pm Sat; 11am-1pm, 2-4pm, 5-7pm Sun. **Admission** (incl skate hire) £7; £4 children. **Map** p403 Q5.

Lee Valley Ice Centre

Lea Bridge Road, Lea Bridge, E10 7QL (8533 3154/ www.leevalleypark.org.uk). Walthamstow Central tube/rail, 48, 55, 56 bus. **Open** noon-4pm Mon, Tue; 11am-2pm Wed; noon-4pm, 8.30-10.30pm Thur; noon-4pm, 7.30-10pm Fri; noon-4pm, 8.30-11pm Sat; 12.30-4pm, 8.30-10.30pm Sun. **Admission** £6; £5 children; £3.50 Thur, Sun evenings.

Leisurebox

First Bowl, 17 Queensway, Bayswater, W2 4QP (7229 0172/www.queensbowling.com). Queensway tube. **Open** 10am-1.45pm, 2-4.45pm, 5-6.45pm, 8-10.45pm Mon-Thur; 10am-1.45pm, 3-4.45pm, 5-6.45pm, 7.30-10.45pm Fri, Sat. 10am-1.45pm, 2-4.45pm, 5-6.45pm, 8-10pm Sun. **Admission** (£5.50-£6.50. **Map** p394 C6.

Pack a punch

It wasn't always like this, you know. Sure, some things never change: the hard slap of flesh being pounded, the searing blindness of blood in the eyes. But there were dark days when boxing wasn't something you did after shutting down your laptop and slipping off your silk tie. There was a time when it wasn't for losing weight, or building leadership qualities. An Olympic sport by 686 BC, boxers were wrapping their fists in leather straps for increased damage 200 years later. The Romans added copper and iron studs, and fights were to the death.

By comparison, boxing as it developed in the UK from the late 17th century was always a more sociable event, if brutal and largely unregulated. The bouts were fought bare-knuckled, and resolved by knockouts only. It wasn't until 1743, when Jack Brownton introduced the first Code of Rules, that fists alone were used, with below the belt boxing made illegal.

Boxers have always fought for fame, but while Lennox Lewis and Audley Harrison now slug it out under the big screens at Wembley Arena, the original prizefighters faced off in pubs.

These days, the relatively new phenomenon of 'white collar boxing' caters for the hordes of City boys who need to work off some steam, and is practised at the **Peacock Gymnasium** in the East End (7476 8427), while those seeking a more punishing regime should go to the **Repton Amateur Boxing Club** (7739 3595), a converted bathhouse that demands nothing short of total devotion from its disciples.

A happier middle ground exists at popular **McKenzie's Gym**, above the Half Moon pub in Herne Hill (7737 2338), where ex-light-welterweight British champ Clinton McKenzie assesses individual abilities and then works them accordingly both in and out of the ring. **Enzo Giordano** in Archway (07956 293768/www.boxercise-net.co.uk) offers a similarly wide-ranging outfit, while the excellent facilities at All Stars Gym in Westbourne Park (8960 7724/www.allstars-gym.com) have attracted professionals including Lewis, although if you fancy your chances against the pros, you'll need to get a medical certificate first. Get your head examined while you're at it.

Streatham Ice Arena

386 Streatham High Road, Streatham, SW16 6HT (8769 7771/www.streathamicearena.co.uk). Streatham Common rail. **Open** 10.30am-4pm Mon, Sun; 10.30am-4pm, 8-10.30pm Tue, Thur; 10.30am-4pm, 4.30-6.30pm, 8-10.30pm Wed; 10am-4pm, 6-8pm, 8.30-11.30pm Fri, Sat. **Admission** (incl skate hire) £6.20-£7.

Riding

There are a number of stables in and around the city; for a list of those approved by the British Horse Society, see www.bhs.org.uk. Those listed below offer outdoor classes for all ages.

Hyde Park & Kensington Stables

63 Bathurst Mews, Paddington, W2 2SB (7723 2813/www.hydeparkstables.com). Lancaster Gate tube. **Open** *Summer* 7.15am-4pm daily. *Winter* 7.15am-3pm daily. **Fees** *Lessons* £40-£60/hr. **Map** p395 D6.

Wimbledon Village Stables

24 High Street, Wimbledon, SW19 5DX (8946 8579/www.wimbledonvillagestables.co.uk). Wimbledon tube/rail. **Open** 10am-5pm Tue-Sun. **Fees** £30-£38/hr.

Sport & leisure centres

Outdoor aerobic exercise can be taken at one of the many city parks with jogging trails. Sport centres have iron pumping, swimming and exercise classes. Here are some good central ones; check the Yellow Pages for more.

Eqvvs Personal Training

43A Cheval Place, Knightsbridge, SW7 1EW (7838 1138/www.eqvvs.com). Knightsbridge tube. **Open** 6am-9pm Mon-Fri; 8am-4pm Sat. **Map** p397 E9

The swankily refurbished Eqvvs attracts rich people with one-on-one fitness tuition; prices are high.

Jubilee Hall Leisure Centre

30 The Piazza, Covent Garden, WC2E 8BE (7836 4835/www.jubileehallclubs.co.uk). Covent Garden tube. **Open** 7am-10pm Mon-Fri; 9am-9pm Sat; 10am-5pm Sun. Last entry 45mins before closing. **Map** p401 L7.

For cardiovascular workouts in calm surroundings.

Queen Mother Sports Centre

223 Vauxhall Bridge Road, Victoria, SW1V 1EL (7630 5522/www.courtneys.co.uk). Victoria tube/rail. **Open** 6.30am-10pm Mon-Fri; 8am-8pm Sat, Sun. **Map** p400 J10.

Busy venue with pool, sweating and lifting facilities.

Seymour Leisure Centre

Seymour Place, Marylebone, W1H 5TJ (7723 8019/ www.courtneys.co.uk). Marble Arch tube. **Open** 6.30am-10pm Mon-Fri; 7am-8pm Sat; 8am-8pm Sun. **Map** p395 F5.
Unglamorous but central, with pool and weights.

Westway Sports Centre

1 Crowthorne Road, Ladbroke Grove, W10 6RP (8969 0992/www.westway.org). Latimer Road tube. **Open** 8am-10pm Mon-Fri; 8am-8pm Sat; 10am-10pm Sun.
A smart, diverse activity centre, with all-weather pitches, tennis courts and the largest indoor climbing facility in the country.

Street sports

PlayStation Skate Park and **Stockwell Skate Park** (*see p272*) are the city's most popular skateboarding venues, although many prefer the unofficial spaces, such as under the Royal Festival Hall (*see p73*) and the expanse beside the *Cutty Sark* in Greenwich (*see p167*). Skaters collect at the **Sprite Urban Games**, held on Clapham Common (*see p173*) every July, and **Board-X** at Alexandra Palace (*see p152*) in November (both www.board-x.com).

Inline skaters and BMXers tend to use the same skateparks (BMXers may be required to wear helmets). Rollerbladers should keep one eye on www.londonskaters.com for a diary of inline events across the city.

Swimming

To find your nearest pool check the Yellow Pages. Listed below are three of the best (*see also p327* **Sport & leisure centres**). For pools particularly suited to children, *see p272*.

Highbury Pool

Highbury Crescent, Highbury, N5 1RR (7704 2312/ www.aquaterra.org). Highbury & Islington tube/rail. **Open** 6.30am-9.30pm Mon-Fri; 7.30am-7.70pm Sat; 7.30am-9.30pm Sun. Women only 7.30-10pm Tue. **Admission** £2.90; £1.30 5-16s; free under-4s.

Ironmonger Row Baths

Ironmonger Row, Finsbury, EC1V 3QN (7253 4011/ www.aquaterra.org). Old Street tube/rail. **Open** 6.30am-9pm Mon; 6.30am-8pm Tue-Thur; 6.30am-7pm Fri; 9am-5.30pm Sat; noon-5pm Sun. **Admission** £2.90; £1.30 4-16s; free under-3s. **Map** p402 P4.

Oasis Sports Centre

32 Endell Street, Covent Garden, WC2H 9AG (7831 1804). Holborn tube. **Open** *Indoor pool* 6.30am-6.30pm Mon, Wed; 6.30-7.15pm Tue, Thur, Fri; 9.30am-5.30pm Sat, Sun. *Outdoor pool* 7am-9pm Mon-Fri; 9.30am-5.30pm Sat, Sun. **Admission** £3.10; £1.20 5-16s; free under-5s. **Map** p399 L6.

Tennis

Many parks in the city have courts that cost little or nothing to use. For lessons, try the **Regent's Park Golf & Tennis School** (7724 0643). For grass courts, phone the Lawn Tennis Association's Information Department (7381 7000). The Islington Tennis Centre has indoor as well as outdoor courts, as does the **Westway Sports Centre** (*see above*).

Islington Tennis Centre

Market Road, Barnsbury, N7 9PL (7700 1370/ www.aquaterra.org). Caledonian Road tube. **Open** 7am-11pm Mon-Thur; 7am-10pm Fri; 8am-10pm Sat, Sun. **Fees** *Outdoor* £7.40/hr. *Indoor* £16.50/hr.

Ten-pin bowling

A useful first stop when looking for lanes is the **British Ten-pin Bowling Association** (8478 1745). Prices in the many bowling venues around the city shouldn't exceed £5 per person per game, and always include the hire of some historically awful special shoes. *See also p326* **Leisurebox**.

Rowans Bowl

10 Stroud Green Road, Finsbury Park, N4 2DF (8800 1950/www.rowans.co.uk). Finsbury Park tube/rail. **Open** 10.30am-12.30am Mon-Thur, Sun; 10.30am-2.30am Fri, Sat. **Cost** *Per game* £2-£3.25. **Lanes** 24.

Streatham MegaBowl

142 Streatham Hill, Streatham, SW2 4RU (8678 6007/www.megabowl.co.uk). Streatham Hill rail. **Open** noon-midnight Mon; noon-1am Tue-Fri; 10am-1am Sat; 10am-midnight Sun. **Cost** *Per game* £4.75/£3.75 children. **Lanes** 36.

Watersports

Of the companies listed, Globe is good for beginner rowers (accomplished oarsmen should contact the Thames Rowing Club in Putney: 8788 0798/www.thamesrc.demon.co.uk). Docklands deals in jet ski and wet bike hire.

Docklands Watersports Club

Tereza Joanne, Gate 14, King George V Dock, Woolwich Manor Way, Woolwich, E16 2NJ (7511 7000/www.tereza-joanne.com). Gallions Reach DLR/North Woolwich rail. **Open** *Summer* 11am-dusk Wed-Sun. *Winter* 11am-dusk Thur-Sun.

Globe Rowing Club

Trafalgar Rowing Centre, Crane Street, SE10 (8858 2106/www.globe.cwc.net). Cutty Sark DLR/Maze Hill rail. **Open** 6-9pm Mon, Wed; 8am-noon Sat, Sun.

Theatre

Watch as the winds of change whip up a dramatic storm.

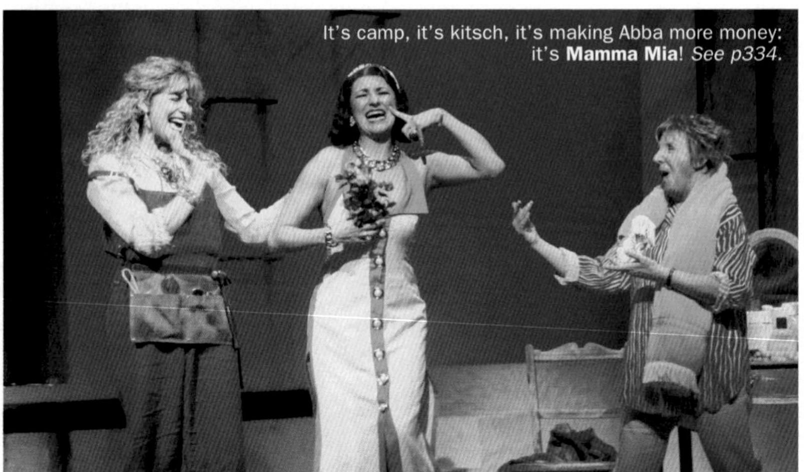

It's camp, it's kitsch, it's making Abba more money: it's **Mamma Mia**! *See p334.*

A tribe of new artistic directors arrived at the city's most respected theatres in 2003. Perhaps the most significant newcomer was Nicholas Hytner, whose first season at the venerable **Royal National Theatre** (*see p330*) made waves and drew new audiences. The changes will continue in 2004, now that the **Royal Shakespeare Company** (*see p333*) has given up its home at the **Barbican**, and is desperate to find itself a new London base.

The most exciting news of the last year hasn't yet panned out: a year ago the famous **Old Vic** theatre (Waterloo Road, 7369 1722) promised that actor Kevin Spacey was to take over directorship, but since then not a peep has been heard of this starry alliance.

Still, there is real change afoot in the **West End**, the traditional theatrical heartland of London where the main artery is Shaftesbury Avenue. A new plan by Cameron Mackintosh to tidy up his theatres and build a new one has begun. The first stage in Mackintosh's project is the refurbishment of the **Duke of York** theatre, and it's underway.

Artistically in the West End, the trends of recent times continue. The use of stars from television and film as guaranteed income continues to spread, with varying results. There's been a great run of Ibsen thanks to Ralph Fiennes, Patrick Stewart and Natasha Richardson returning to the stage. But there have also been a number of sub-standard turns from celebs of lower ranking.

As always, the good stuff is out there. If you're keen to see a 'big' musical, go for the names you know; the worst you're going to get then is a slightly tired rendition of an otherwise great show. Don't, having missed out on tickets to *Phantom* or *Les Mis,* opt for some two-month-old supposed blockbuster without researching first. *Time Out* magazine is the most thorough resource for finding a good show, offering a brief review of every West End show running.

The best Theatres

For cutting edge
Soho Theatre. *See p336.*

For new ideas
BAC. *See p335.*

For the longest runner in town
St Martin's. *See p334.*

For class acts
The Almeida. *See p335.*

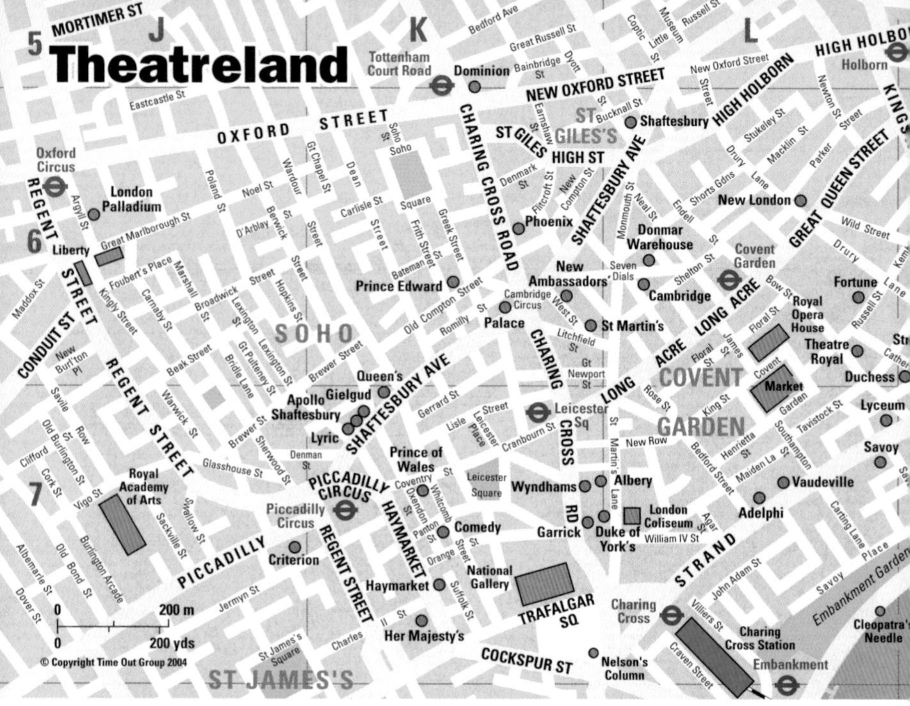

WHERE TO GO AND WHAT TO SEE

The **West End** is a cultural term, rather than a geographic one. Some of its leading theatres lie well outside the traditional boundaries of London's theatreland. The most reliable of West End venues, with an exciting repertory of new plays and classics rather than fixed, long-running programmes, are the building-based companies such as the South Bank's **Shakespeare's Globe** and its **Royal National Theatre**.

Off-West End (the next rung down in terms of size and income) is where you'll find the best mix of quality and originality. These theatres are usually heavily subsidised; top writers, directors and actors are lured by the prospect of artistic liberty. Still, even these have a pecking order: wealthier theatres such as the **Young Vic** (*see p336*) and the **Almeida** (*see p334*) lead the pack, with the likes of the **Gate** (*see p336*) and the **King's Head** (*see p336*) often dependent on hopefuls willing to work for nothing.

The Fringe, meanwhile, is made up of the myriad smaller theatres scattered all around town, and is a theatrical underclass where standards are variable. Try the **New End Theatre** (27 New End, Hampstead, NW3, 7794 0022) for fare that is rarely very adventurous but that always seems well funded, or, for a taste of theatre on the edge, try the creative **Arcola** (27 Arcola Street, E8, 7503 1646). Although it was only recently dragged into existence in London's East End, it's already made a name for itself.

Tickets & information

The first rule to observe when buying tickets for London performances is to book ahead. The second rule is to go direct to the theatre's box office. Booking agencies such as **Ticketmaster** (7344 4444, www.ticketmaster.co.uk) and **First Call** (7420 0000, www.firstcalltickets.com) sell tickets to many shows, but you'll get hit with booking fees that could top 20 per cent.

In a late bid to fill their venues, many West End theatres offer reduced-price tickets for shows that have not sold out. These seats, available only on the night, are known as 'standby' tickets, and usually sell for about half what a top-priced ticket would cost. Always call to check both availability and conditions: some standby deals are limited to those with student ID, and it varies as to when tickets go on sale.

Alternatively, try **tkts**, a non-profit-making organisation run from the Clock Tower building in Leicester Square by the Society of London Theatres that sells tickets for West End shows on a first-come, first-served basis on the day of the performance. Each ticket is subject to a fee of £2.50 and a maximum of four are allowed per customer, but it's worth fighting your way through it all, as tickets for many shows can be snapped up for as much as 50 per cent off face value. Be aware that the other gaudy booths advertising cheap seats around Leicester Square are unofficial and can be expensive.

tkts

Leicester Square, WC2 (www.officiallondon theatre.co.uk). Leicester Square tube. **Open** 10am-7pm Mon-Sat; noon-3pm Sun. **Credit** AmEx, DC, MC, V. **Map** p401 K7.

West End

Repertory companies

Open Air Theatre

Regent's Park, NW1 4NR (7486 2431/www.openair theatre.org). Baker Street tube. **Repertory season** June-Sept; phone for details. **Tickets** £9.50-£26. Standby £9 (approx). **Credit** AmEx, DC, MC, V. **Map** p398 G3.

It's all in the name: the Open Air Theatre sits outside in London's loveliest park, bare to the elements. The productions here tend to be mainstream, but the quality is far higher than you might expect from a venue with such massive tourist appeal.

Royal Court

Sloane Square, Chelsea, SW1W 8AS (7565 5000/ www.royalcourttheatre.com). Sloane Square tube. **Box office** 10am-6pm Mon-Sat. **Tickets** 10p-£27.50; all tickets £7.50 Mon. **Credit** AmEx, MC, V. **Map** p400 G11.

The Royal Court is the undisputed centre of new writing in Britain, and has been since it first opened its doors in 1956: among the first productions here was John Osborne's *Look Back in Anger*. Now back in its long-time Sloane Square home after a £25m refurbishment, it boasts two performing spaces – the imaginatively titled Upstairs (a small studio theatre) and Downstairs (a proscenium arch main stage) – plus a snazzy restaurant and bar.

Royal National Theatre

South Bank, SE1 9PX (information 7452 3400/box office 7452 3000/www.nationaltheatre.org.uk). Embankment or Southwark tube/Waterloo tube/rail. **Box office** 10am-8pm Mon-Sat. **Tickets** Olivier & Lyttelton £10-£34. Cottesloe £10-£25. Standby £17. **Credit** AmEx, DC, MC, V. **Map** p401 M8.

Much of Nicholas Hytner's effort in his first year as artistic director seems to have been devoted to bringing both prices and the average age of the audience down. A season of plays in the National's largest theatre, the Olivier, where more than half the

Jerry Springer – The Opera: talk to the hand. *See p334.*

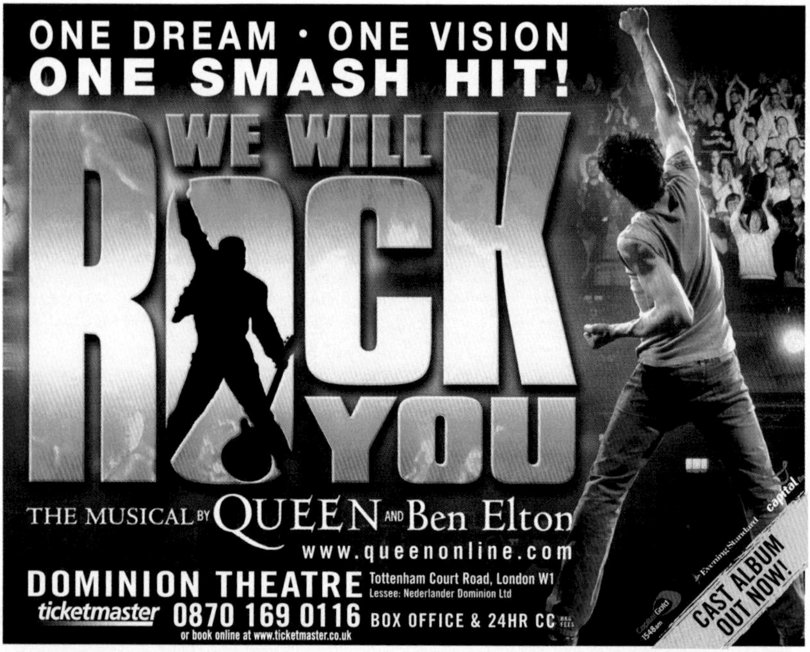

ONE DREAM · ONE VISION
ONE SMASH HIT!

WE WILL ROCK YOU

THE MUSICAL BY QUEEN AND Ben Elton
www.queenonline.com

DOMINION THEATRE Tottenham Court Road, London W1
Lessee: Nederlander Dominion Ltd

ticketmaster 0870 169 0116 BOX OFFICE & 24HR CC
or book online at www.ticketmaster.co.uk

CAST ALBUM OUT NOW!

The Best Shows
The Best Seats
The Best Prices

The only **OFFICIAL** Half Price and Discount Theatre Ticket Booth
Find us at the Clocktower Building Leicester Square
Mon - Sat 10.00 - 7.00 Sun 12.00 - 3.00
www.OfficialLondonTheatre.co.uk

tkts is the new name for the Half Price Ticket Booth. **tkts** is a trademark owned by and used under licence from Theatre Development Fund Inc. There is no other relationship or affiliation between The Society of London Theatre and Theatre Development Fund Inc, a New York not-for-profit corporation. Computerised ticketing services provided by First Call.

Culture alfresco: the **Open Air Theatre** in Regent's Park. *See p331.*

tickets were offered for a tenner, has been judged a great success. Artistically, plays such as *Jerry Springer – The Opera* and *Henry V* (playing as Britain went to war) have forged the perception that the National is relevant again. But with the same kind of friendly pricing uncertain in 2004, one can only hope that the good times will last. The National's annual free festival, called 'Watch This Space', brings the theatricals outdoors.

Royal Shakespeare Company

www.rsc.org.uk

In 2002, the controversial decision to give up the RSC's residence at the Barbican led to the resignation of artistic director Adrian Noble. Now, under Michael Boyd, the search is on for a new permanent residence. In the meantime, the company is still bringing shows to London, it's just difficult to say for sure where you'll be able to see them.

Shakespeare's Globe

21 New Globe Walk, SE1 9DT (74019919/www.shakespeares-globe.org). Mansion House tube/Blackfriars tube/rail. **Box office** *Off season* 10am-5pm Mon-Fri. *Theatre* 10am-8pm daily. **Tickets** £5-£29. **Credit** AmEx, MC, V. **Map** p404 O7.

This place is certainly partly a tourist attraction, but only partly; under its adventurous artistic director Mark Rylance, the reconstructed Globe has nailed itself a deserved reputation as a serious theatre as well as a daytime role as a presenter of neatly packaged Britlit history to coach parties of Americans and Germans (*see p78*). The season runs only from April to October (it's open-air, of course) and is no friend of artistic nuance, but it does offer interesting insights into how Will dealt with mob dynamics. That said, it's unlikely he had to contend with planes flying overhead every few minutes.

Long-runners & musicals

Most theatres have evening shows Monday to Saturday (starting 7.30-8pm) and matinées on one weekday (usually Wednesday) and Saturday. Check *Time Out* magazine for details.

Blood Brothers

Phoenix Theatre, Charing Cross Road, St Giles's, WC2 0JP (7369 1733/www.theambassadors.com). Tottenham Court Road tube. **Box office** *In person* 10am-7.45pm Mon-Sat. *By phone* 9am-9pm daily. *Ticketmaster* 24hrs daily. **Tickets** £15-£40. Standby £15. **Credit** AmEx, MC, V. **Map** p399 K6.

Scouse sentiment and toe-tapping songs in Willy Russell's likeable, long-running melodrama about two brothers separated at birth and exiled to opposite ends of the social ladder.

Bombay Dreams

Apollo Victoria, Wilton Road, Pimlico, SW1V 1LG (0870 4000 650/www.clearchannel.co.uk). Victoria tube/rail. **Box office** *In person* 9am-8pm Mon-Sat; 11.15am-3.15pm Sun. *Ticketmaster* 24hrs daily. **Tickets** £8-£42.50. **Credit** AmEx, MC, V. **Map** p400 H10.

Meera Syal's cheery rags-to-Bollywood-riches script misses, but AR Rahman's wonderfully sensual score and some thrilling choreography hit it big.

Chicago

Adelphi Theatre, Strand, Covent Garden, WC2E 7NA (Ticketmaster 08704 030303). Charing Cross tube/rail. **Box office** *In person* 10am-8pm Mon-Sat. *By phone* 24hrs daily. **Tickets** £15-£40. **Credit** AmEx, MC, V. **Map** p401 L7.

Not the most spectacular musical in the West End, but with a vibrant on-stage band and a range of razzle-dazzle numbers, it's the most vital.

Things get a little crazy during Watch this Space at the **Royal National Theatre.** *See p331.*

Chitty Chitty Bang Bang

London Palladium, Argyll Street, W1A 3AB (0870 890 1108/www.chittythemusical.co.uk). Oxford Circus tube. **Box office** *In person* 10am-7.30pm Mon-Sat. *Ticketmaster* 24hrs daily. **Tickets** £15-£40. **Credit** AmEx, MC, V. **Map** p398 J6.

The car's great, the cast's great, the kids will have a nice time… but there's precious little here for adults.

Jerry Springer – The Opera

Cambridge Theatre, Covent Garden, WC2H 9HU (7494 5399/0870 890 1102 Way Ahead Ticket Service/www.jerryspringertheopera.com). Covent Garden tube. **Box office** *In person* 10am-8pm Mon-Sat. *Ticketmaster* 24hrs daily. **Tickets** £12.50-£50. **Credit** AmEx, MC, V. **Map** p399 L6.

Not strictly a long-runner yet, but this transfer from the National is practically guaranteed to run for some time in 2004. Irreverent and very rude, it was *the* theatrical hit of 2003.

Les Misérables

Palace Theatre, Shaftesbury Avenue, Soho, W1V 8AY (0870 160 2878/www.lesmis.com). Leicester Square tube. **Box office** 10am-8pm Mon-Sat. *Ticketmaster* 24hrs daily. **Tickets** £10-£42.50. Standby £17.50. **Credit** AmEx, MC, V. **Map** p399 K6.

Boubil and Schonberg's 15-year-old money-spinner continues to idealise the struggles of the poor in Victor Hugo's revolutionary Paris.

The Lion King

Lyceum Theatre, Wellington Street, Covent Garden, WC2E 7DA (0870 243 9000). Covent Garden tube/Charing Cross tube/rail. **Box office** 10am-6pm Mon-Sat. *Ticketmaster* 24hrs daily. **Tickets** £10-£45. **Credit** AmEx, MC, V. **Map** p401 L7.

This Disney extravaganza about a young lion cub struggling to grow up has been widely acclaimed, particularly by those who have small children.

Mamma Mia!

Prince Edward Theatre, Old Compton Street, Soho, W1 6HS (7447 5400/www.mamma-mia.com). Leicester Square or Tottenham Court Road tube. **Box office** *In person* 10am-7pm Mon-Sat. *By phone* 24hrs daily. **Tickets** £22.50-£40. **Credit** AmEx, MC, V. **Map** p399 K6.

This feel-good musical links Swedish supergroup Abba's greatest hits into a continuous but utterly spurious story. It's endlessly popular.

The Mousetrap

St Martin's Theatre, West Street, Covent Garden, WC2H 9NZ (0870 162 8787). Leicester Square tube. **Box office** 10am-8pm Mon-Sat. **Tickets** £11.50-£31.50. **Credit** AmEx, MC, V. **Map** p399 K6.

Agatha Christie's long-running mystery is still going strong (*see p335* **Trapped in time**) and shows no sign of giving up.

Phantom of the Opera

Her Majesty's Theatre, Haymarket, St James's, SW1Y 4QR (0870 160 2878/www.thephantomoftheopera.com). Piccadilly Circus tube. **Box office** *In person* 10am-8pm Mon-Sat. *By phone* 24hrs daily. **Tickets** £20-£42.50. **Credit** AmEx, MC, V. **Map** p401 K7.

Lloyd Webber's best musical, a must-see for its '80s spectacle and a score packed with great songs.

We Will Rock You

Dominion Theatre, Tottenham Court Road, Fitzrovia, W1P 0AG (7413 1713/www.london-dominion.co.uk). Tottenham Court Road tube. **Box office** *In person* 9am-7.45pm Mon-Sat. *Ticketmaster* 24hrs. **Tickets** £12.50-£50. **Credit** AmEx, MC, V. **Map** p399 K5.

All your favourite Queen hits, unconvincingly rendered and stitched together by a deeply feeble Ben Elton plot. Freddie would've hated it.

The Woman in Black

Fortune Theatre, Russell Street, WC2B 5HH (7369 1737/www.thewomaninblack.com). Covent Garden tube. **Box office** 10am-8pm Mon-Sat. **Tickets** £10-£32.50. Standby £10. **Credit** AmEx, MC, V. **Map** p399 L6.

This is a persistently popular West End spine-chiller written by Susan Hill.

Off-West End

Almeida

Almeida Street, Almeida Street, Islington, N1 1TA (7359 4404/www.almeida.co.uk). Angel tube. **Box office** *In person* 10am-7pm Mon-Sat. *By phone* 24hrs daily. **Tickets** £6-£27.50. **Credit** AmEx, MC, V. **Map** p399 L2.

Former artistic directors Jonathan Kent and Ian Mcdiarmid have already earned the Almeida a reputation for presenting classy plays with famous actors. Its first season under Michael Attenborough started well; a rash of British and world premières is planned for 2004.

BAC (Battersea Arts Centre)

Lavender Hill, Battersea, SW11 5TN (7223 2223/www.bac.org.uk). Clapham Common tube/Clapham Junction rail/77, 77A, 345 bus. **Box office** *In person* 10.30am-6pm Mon-Sat; 4-6pm Sun. **Tickets** £5.50-£12.75; 'pay what you can' Tue. **Credit** MC, V.

The BAC has three theatres (a main house and two studios) that together carry much of the capital's best fringe work. Their laudable Scratch programme shows work at various stages of its development. Head honcho Tom Morris has just been poached by the National, so 2004 may see changes as his (as yet unnamed successor) makes his/her mark.

Trapped in time

1952 saw Queen Elizabeth II ascend the British throne, and the first performance in the West End of Agatha Christie's *The Mousetrap.* It is possible that the Queen wishes she had had as easy a ride through the last half-century as this long-running show. For, while the Royal Family has undergone scandal after scandal, changing with the times, the whodunnit has had a relatively smooth time.

For more than 21,000 performances, the show's action has unfolded the same, night after night. In fact, its last major upheaval was in 1975, when it was transferred to St Martin's Theatre from the Ambassadors.

Agatha Christie originally wrote the play as a 30-minute radio drama to celebrate the 80th birthday of Queen Mary. Five years later an extended version hit the West End featuring Richard Attenborough and his wife Sheila Sims in the main roles. The original investors must have known they were on to a winner. It has, in fact, repaid them 1,000 times over. Not everyone was so lucky of course: the poor guys who bought the film rights unfortunately agreed not to start shooting until the theatre production closed.

The show is well accustomed to breaking records. It became the longest-running show ever in 1958 and now seems unlikely to be beaten. Along the way, it has picked up the record for the most performances by the same actor in the same part (David Raven as Major Metcalfe – 4,575 performances) and for the world's most enduring understudy (Nancy Seabrooke sat in the wings doing her crochet for 15 years).

Unofficially too, it holds the record for the world's best-kept secret. Each audience since the show started has been asked not to reveal the play's ending, and, even with a lifetime audience equal to approximately twice the population of Ireland, the identity of the murderer is still not common knowledge.

But is this show all 'never mind the quality, feel the history'? In a way, perhaps. There can be little doubt that it seems hopelessly old-fashioned alongside other West End plays. The concept seems laughably clichéd: several upper class types stuck in a country house when a murder occurs. Still, bear in mind that this play set the standard for whodunnits; it is the best play written by the best writer in the genre.

The Bush

Shepherd's Bush Green, Shepherd's Bush, W12 8QD (7610 4224/www.bushtheatre.co.uk). Goldhawk Road or Shepherd's Bush tube. **Box office** *In person* 5-8pm Mon-Sat. *By phone* 10am-7pm Mon-Sat. **Tickets** £8-£13.50. **Credit** AmEx, MC, V.

Imagine the Royal Court without the glamour or the money, and you have the Bush. This under-funded pub theatre is an important venue for new writing.

Donmar Warehouse

41 Earlham Street, Covent Garden, WC2H 9LX (7369 1732/www.donmar-warehouse.com). Covent Garden tube. **Box office** *In person* 10am-7.30pm Mon-Sat. *By phone* 9am-9pm Mon-Sat; 10am-6pm Sun. *Ticketmaster* 24hrs daily. **Tickets** £15-£26. **Credit** AmEx, MC, V. **Map** p399 L6.

Oscar-winner Sam Mendes left the post of artistic director at the Donmar at the end of 2002, and Michael Grandage, who succeeded him, has had a hard act to follow. His programming has been bold. Reactions, predictably, have been moderate to good rather than ecstatic.

Drill Hall

16 Chenies Street, Fitzrovia, WC1E 7EX (7307 5060/www.drillhall.co.uk). Goodge Street tube. **Box office** *In person* 10am-9.30pm Mon-Sat; 10-6pm Sun. **Tickets** £5-£15. **Credit** AmEx, MC, V. **Map** p399 K5.

London's biggest gay and lesbian theatre is not generally separatist, though Mondays are women-only from 6pm and Thursdays are non-smoking days.

The Gate

Above Prince Albert Pub, 11 Pembridge Road, Notting Hill, W11 3HQ (7229 0706/www.gatetheatre.co.uk). Notting Hill Gate tube. **Box office** 10am-6pm Mon-Fri. **Tickets** £6-£12; 'pay what you can' Mon. **Credit** MC, V. **Map** p394 A7.

Another west London pub theatre, the Gate presses on with its programme of script-driven entertainment in a plain, usually setless black box space.

Hampstead Theatre

Eton Avenue, Swiss Cottage, NW3 3EU (7722 9301/www.hampstead-theatre.co.uk). Swiss Cottage tube. **Box office** 9am-8pm Mon-Sat. **Tickets** £12.50-£19.50. **Credit** MC, V.

In 2003 the Hampstead moved into new buildings, and bade goodbye to its longtime artistic director. It produces contemporary, script-based drama.

King's Head

115 Upper Street, Islington, N1 1QN (7226 1916/www.kingsheadtheatre.org). Angel tube/Highbury & Islington tube/rail. **Box office** 10am-8pm Mon-Sat; noon-4pm Sun. **Tickets** £14-£18. **Credit** MC, V. **Map** p402 O1.

This is the oldest pub theatre in the city, and it still shuffles on, despite Islington Council shamefully cutting back its funding. The programme here is a real mishmash, from straight drama to musical revue, with quality similarly varied. As a plus, the pub out front is excellent.

Lyric Hammersmith

King Street, Hammersmith, W6 0QL (08700 500511/www.lyric.co.uk). Hammersmith tube. **Box office** 10am-8pm Mon-Sat. **Tickets** £9-£24. **Credit** AmEx, DC, MC, V.

From the outside, the Lyric looks purely modern, yet its main stage is gloriously old-fashioned, with plush seats and a proscenium arch. This stage and the smaller studio space specialise in work that, while alternative in nature, is by no means inaccessible.

Orange Tree

1 Clarence Street, Richmond, Surrey TW9 2SA (8940 3633/www.orangetreetheatre.co.uk). Richmond tube/rail. **Box office** 10am-7pm Mon-Sat. **Tickets** £6-£16. **Credit** MC, V.

It's very definitely a locals' theatre, the Orange Tree, and is something of a haul to get to from central London. Still, the usually impressive performances make the trek worthwhile, as does the uniqueness of the space: this is London's only theatre set up permanently in the round.

Soho Theatre

21 Dean Street, Soho, W1D 3NE (7478 0100/www.sohotheatre.com). Tottenham Court Road tube. **Box office** 10am-8pm Mon-Sat. **Tickets** £5-£15. **Credit** AmEx, MC, V. **Map** p399 K6.

One of the real success stories of London theatre in the last few years, the once homeless Soho Theatre opened in these swanky premises in early 2000 and has since served up an enticing mix of new plays and foreign imports.

Theatre Royal Stratford East

Gerry Raffles Square, Stratford, E15 1BN (8534 0310/www.stratfordeast.com). Stratford DLR/tube/rail. **Box office** 10am-7pm Mon-Sat. **Tickets** £8-£20. **Credit** MC, V.

Catering particularly for the black community, Theatre Royal Stratford East has scored several minor hits by focusing on populist programming, very often musicals. Financial problems, however, mean that 2004 may be a lean year.

Tricycle

269 Kilburn High Road, Kilburn, NW6 7JR (7328 1000/www.tricycle.co.uk). Kilburn tube. **Box office** 10am-9pm Mon-Sat; 2-9pm Sun. **Tickets** £7.50-£20. **Credit** MC, V.

Tilting its programme squarely at its local population, the Tricycle specialises in high-quality black and Irish shows. The centre also incorporates an art gallery and cinema, plus an agreeable bar.

Young Vic

66 The Cut, Waterloo, SE1 8LZ (7928 6363/www.youngvic.org). Southwark tube/Waterloo tube/rail. **Box office** 10am-8pm Mon-Sat. **Tickets** £12.50-£25. **Credit** MC, V. **Map** p404 N8.

Like the Old Vic, only younger? Well, not far off. The Young Vic stages a variety of theatrical entertainments in its two spaces, from home and abroad in runs both long and short.

Trips Out of Town

Features

Trips Out of Town

Sally forth to shires and shores.

Map p389

A useful first stop for the visitor planning a trip away from London is the **Britain & London Visitor Centre** (*see below*). We've also listed the local tourist information centres in the **Town & city breaks** listed below; these can provide further information about the area. For the main entries, we've included details of opening times, admission and transport, but be aware that these can change without notice: always phone to check that a sight is open if you're planning a visit around it. Major sights are open all through the year, but many minor attractions close from November to March.

Britain & London Visitor Centre

1 Regent Street (south of Piccadilly Circus), SW1Y 4XT (no phone/www.visitbritain.com). Piccadilly Circus tube. **Open** *Oct-May* 9.30am-6.30pm Mon; 9am-6.30pm Tue-Fri; 10am-4pm Sat, Sun. *June-Sept* 9.30am-6.30pm Mon; 9am-6.30pm Tue-Fri; 9am-5pm Sat; 10am-4pm Sun. **Credit** AmEx, MC, V. **Map** p401 K7.
Come in person to pick up free leaflets and advice on destinations in the UK and Ireland. You can also book rail, road or air travel, reserve tours, theatre tickets and hotels. There's a bureau de change too.

Getting there

By train

For information on train times and ticket prices, call **08457 484950**. Ask about the cheapest ticket for the journey you are planning, and be aware that for long journeys, the earlier you book, the cheaper the ticket. If you need extra help, there are **rail travel centres** in London's main-line stations, as well as in Heathrow and Gatwick airports. These can give you guidance for things like timetables and booking. The journey times we give are the fastest available.

The website www.virgintrains.co.uk gives online timetable information for any British train company; buy tickets online for any train operator in the UK via www.thetrainline.com.

London main-line rail stations

Charing Cross *Strand, Covent Garden, WC2.* **Map** p401 L7.
For trains to and from south-east England (including Dover, Folkestone and Ramsgate).
Euston *Euston Road, Euston, NW1.* **Map** p399 K3.
For trains to and from north and north-west England and Scotland, and a north London suburban line.
King's Cross *Euston Road, King's Cross, N1.* **Map** p399 L2.
For trains to and from north and north-east England and Scotland; lines to north London and Herts.
Liverpool Street *Liverpool Street, the City, EC2.* **Map** p403 R5.
For trains to and from the east coast and Stansted airport; also for trains to East Anglia and suburban services to north and east London.
London Bridge *London Bridge Street, SE1.* Map p405 Q8.
For trains to and from south-east England and Kent; also suburban services to south London.
Paddington *Praed Street, Paddington, W2.* **Map** p395 D5.
For trains to and from south-west and west England, south Wales and the Midlands.
Victoria *Terminus Place, Victoria, SW1.* **Map** p400 H10.
For fast trains to and from the Channel ports (Dover, Folkestone, Newhaven); also for trains to and from Gatwick, plus services to south London.
Waterloo *York Road, Waterloo, SE1.* **Map** p401 M8.
For fast trains to and from the south and south-west of England (Portsmouth, Southampton, Dorset, Devon), the Eurostar to Paris and Brussels, and suburban services to south London.

By coach

National Express (0870 580 8080) coaches travel throughout the country and depart from Victoria Coach Station on Buckingham Palace Road, five minutes' walk from Victoria rail and tube stations. **Green Line Travel** (0870 608 7261) runs coaches as well.

The best Days out

By the sea
Broadstairs. *See p353.*

With your mates
Brighton. *See p342.*

From the hurly-burly
Blackwater Valley Path. *See p342.*

To feast your eyes
Sissinghurst Castle Garden. *See p352.*

To soothe your tortured soul
Winchester Cathedral. *See p349.*

The old West Pier has truly gone west, in sunny, trendy **Brighton**. *See p342.*

Victoria Coach Station
164 Buckingham Palace Road, Victoria, SW1W 9TP (7730 3466). Victoria tube/rail. **Map** p400 H11.
Britain's most comprehensive coach company **National Express** and **Eurolines** (01582 404511), which travels to the Continent, are based at Victoria Coach Station. There are many other companies operating to and from London (some departing from Marble Arch).

By car

If you're in a group of three or four, it may be cheaper to hire a car (*see p361*), especially if you plan to take in several sights within an area. The road directions given in the listings below should be used in conjunction with a map. (We've used a little shorthand, though, so for example, 'J13 off M11' means 'exit the M11 motorway at Junction 13'.)

Bicycle tours

Capital Sport (01296 631671, www.capital-sport.co.uk) offers gentle cycling tours along the River Thames from London. Leisurely itineraries include plenty of time to explore royal palaces, parks and historic attractions.

Or you could try **Country Lanes** (01425 655022, www.countrylanes.co.uk), which has representatives who meet you off the train from London and lead you on cycling tours of the New Forest in Hampshire and the Cotswolds.

Bath

An ancient spa town surrounded like Rome by seven hills, Bath's ability to restore and revive officially dates from Roman times but, according to Celtic legend, as far back as 863 BC a swineherd bathed his leprous pigs in the naturally hot waters and they were cured. From there, Bath's reputation for healing extended beyond livestock, until the 18th century, when a housing boom signalled the rise of Georgian Bath. The visionary architect John Wood the Elder (1704-54), and his son were responsible for the extraordinary unity of the architecture, which is elegant English Palladianism.

Bath's heyday lasted almost a century, until Jane Austen's time (she lived here from 1800 to 1805), after which it declined until after World War II when the current revival began. The city is as beautiful as ever now, although it can be stiflingly crowded in the summer when it often seems as if all of its three million annual visitors descend all at once.

Most head first for the beautiful, steam-enshrouded **Roman Baths Museum**. Once a temple to Sulis Minerva, this is the city's most famous attraction. The hot water bubbles up at a rate of 250,000 gallons (over a million litres) a day, filling the pool, surrounded by classical statues. You can taste the sulphuric water in the adjoining **Pump Room**, if you're so inclined. Someday soon you may be able to dive into the water at the **Thermae Bath Spa** on Hot Bath Street (01225 335678, www.thermaebath spa.com, open daily). Its opening is behind schedule, and it has been beset by problems, but when construction is completed it will once again open the famous healing waters to the public.

Adjacent to the Roman baths are the noble towers of **Bath Abbey** (Abbey Churchyard, 01225 422462). It was built on the site of the

► For more great getaways, pick up a copy of *Time Out Weekend Breaks from London* (£12.99).

Get online for great deals.

Wherever you're going, we've got a deal for you. Simply book online at www.hertz.co.uk for low, inclusive rates and the personal service you would expect from the world's # 1 car rental company.

Isn't it time you turned to Hertz?

www.hertz.co.uk

Hertz rents Fords and other fine cars.

Saxon church where Edgar, first king of a united England, was crowned back in 973. If the crypt is open you can trace the building's history through the centuries in its stones and artefacts.

Bath has close to 20 museums, including the **Building of Bath Museum** and the **Museum of East Asian Art**, which contains a fine collection of Chinese jade carvings. Opposite, in the Assembly Rooms (the social focus of high society in Georgian times), there's the renowned **Museum of Costume**, where the oldest posh togs displayed date back to the 1660s. On Bridge Street, the **Victoria Art Gallery** (01225 477233) houses a collection of British and European art from the 15th century to the present. The **American Museum in Britain** contains reconstructed US domestic interiors from the 17th, 18th and 19th centuries.

The grandest street in Bath is the much-photographed **Royal Crescent**, a curl of 30 grand white houses designed by John Wood the Younger between 1767 and 1775. The house at **No.1** is furnished in period style with a restored Georgian garden (closed Dec-mid Feb). Nearby is the **Circus**, designed by the elder John Wood and completed by his son in 1767.

The **River Avon**, spanned by the Italianate shop-lined **Pulteney Bridge**, adds to the city's appeal. There are walks beside the river and the Kennet and Avon Canal; in summer boats can be hired from the Victorian **Bath Boating Station** (Forester Road, 01225 312900).

American Museum in Britain

Claverton Manor, BA2 7BD (01225 460503/www.americanmuseum.org). **Open** *Late Mar-Oct, Mid Nov-mid Dec* noon-5pm Tue-Sun. Closed early Nov, mid Dec-late Mar. **Admission** £6.50; £5 concessions; free under-5s. **Credit** AmEx, MC, V.

Building of Bath Museum

The Countess of Huntingdon's Chapel, The Vineyards, BA1 5NA (01225 333895/www.bath-preservation-trust.org.uk). **Open** *Mid Feb-Nov* 10.30am-5pm Tue-Sun. Closed Dec-mid Feb. **Admission** £4; £3 concessions; £1.50 6-16s; free under-6s. **Credit** AmEx, MC, V.

Museum of Costume

The Assembly Rooms, Bennett Street, BA1 2QH (01225 477789/www.museumofcostume.co.uk). **Open** 10am-5pm daily. Last entry 4.30pm. **Admission** £5.50; £3.75-£4.50 concessions; free under-6s. **Credit** MC, V.

No.1 Royal Crescent

1 Royal Crescent, BA1 2LR (01225 428126/www.bath-preservation-trust.org.uk). **Open** *Mid Feb-Oct* 10.30am-5pm Tue-Sun. *Nov* 10.30am-4pm Tue-Sun. *1st 2wks Dec* 10.30am-4pm Sat, Sun. Last entry 30mins before closing. Closed mid Dec-mid Feb. **Admission** £4; £3.50 concessions; free under-5s; family £10. **No credit cards**.

Roman Baths

Abbey Churchyard, BA1 1LZ (01225 477785/www.romanbaths.co.uk). **Open** *Nov-Feb* 9.30am-5.30pm daily. *Mar-June, Sept, Oct* 9am-6pm daily. *July, Aug* 9am-10pm daily. Last entry 1hr before closing. **Admission** £8.50; £4.80-£7.50 concessions; free under-6s. **Credit** MC, V.

Where to eat & drink

Bath has a formidable gourmet reputation. Three of the best restaurants are **Fishworks** (6 Green Street, 01225 448707, main courses £9-£14.90), the classy Modern British **Moody Goose** (7A Kingsmead Square, 01225 466688, main courses £16-£19.50) and **The Olive Tree** (Queensbury Hotel, Russell Street, 01225 447928; main courses £12.50-£18.95).

At **Sally Lunn's Refreshment House & Museum** (4 North Parade Passage, 01225 461634, main courses £8-£9) you can sample the buns made fashionable in the 1680s.

Popular pubs include the **Bell Inn** in Walcot Street, the **Old Green Tree** on Green Street, and the 300-year-old **Crystal Palace** on Abbey Green with its walled garden.

Where to stay

Harington's Hotel (8-10 Queen Street, 01225 461728, doubles £88-£128) is the best-value central hotel. **Holly Lodge** (8 Upper Oldfield Park, 01225 424042, doubles £79-£97) is a classy B&B perched high above the city. The **Queensberry Hotel** (Russell Street, 01225 447928, doubles £100-£285) provides Regency elegance in the centre of town. **Royal Crescent Hotel** (16 Royal Crescent, 01225 823333, doubles £207-£377) is the place to come if money is no object.

Getting there

By train

Trains to Bath Spa leave hourly from Paddington most days (1hr 25mins).

By coach

National Express from Victoria (3hrs 20mins).

By car

Take Junction 18 off the M4, then follow the A46 to Bath. Use park & rides to get into the centre.

Tourist information

Tourist Information Centre

Abbey Chambers, Abbey Churchyard, BA1 1LY (0906 711 2000/www.visitbath.co.uk). **Open** *May-Sept* 9.30am-6pm Mon-Sat; 10am-4pm Sun. *Oct-Apr* 9.30am-5pm Mon-Sat; 10am-4pm Sun.

Take to the hills

Ken Livingstone's Congestion Charge may be doing a great job of coaxing Londoners out of their cars, but, if the figures are to be believed, taking a walk has long been one of the nation's favourite pastimes. On average, seven million people venture out into the countryside each weekend in England alone. It makes sense: putting one foot in front of the other is cheap, requires no training and the whole family can get involved.

'There's a physical benefit to walking,' says Paul Bell of the Ramblers' Association, 'but for me it's not as important as the mental benefit of being able to get away from it all. The sights and sounds of the city just disappear.'

Greater London has a number of natural and designated walks. The longest ones are the **London LOOP**, an almost round 150-mile (241 kilometre) journey from Erith to Rainham in 24 stages. Along the way it offers some sweeping views of the city from the woods and waterways. The more central **Capital RING** travels for 72 miles (115 kilometres) around the city on a circular trip that starts in Woolwich, with public transport never more than a few minutes away if it all gets too much. *Walking in London* guides are available for £1 from the Ramblers' Association.

You could conceivably walk all the way from London through Hertfordshire, thanks to various footpaths heading shireward out of town. One such is the **Lee Valley Walk**, a 50-mile path along the River Lee, which stretches from Islington in north London as far as Luton in Bedfordshire, through the open countryside of Hertfordshire. Visit www.leevalley-online.co.uk for all the details

Brighton

Pretty Victorian Brighton seems to trip down the hill upon which it is built, and dash toward the sea on a perpetual holiday. It's creamy gold and white architecture has long been a draw for coachloads of tourists and day-trippers from London, just over an hour away by train.

The presence of universities and language schools make this one of the youngest and most multicultural cities outside London. With more than 60 per cent of the population under the age of 45, the 'vegetarian capital of Europe' also has a large and thriving gay and lesbian scene.

Brighton began life as Bristmestune, a small fishing village, and so it remained until 1783, when Prince George (later George IV) rented a farmhouse here. While taking in the sea air, he became the centre of a kind of hip court in waiting, and he kept the architect John Nash busy converting a modest abode into a faux-oriental pleasure palace. That building is now the elaborate-to-the-point-of-gaudy **Royal Pavilion**, where guided tours are full of quirky facts. Next door, the **Brighton Museum & Art Gallery** (Royal Pavilion Gardens, 01273 290900) has entertaining displays and a good permanent art collection.

of walks, watery activities and recommended pubs along the way, as there are plenty to make the trip even more pleasant.

If the idea of gracefully traversing the capital just doesn't appeal as much as the concept of transcending it completely, you're in luck: London's surrounding counties offer some of the best outdoor hiking in the country, with a seemingly endless choice of routes mapped out in pamphlets and brochures, most of them available free from the relevant county councils. Surrey (0845 6009009/www.surrey cc.gov.uk) is a good place to start. Much of the landscape between Leatherhead and Dorking is a patchwork quilt of hills and dales, and forms the setting of the **Mole Gap Trail**, which runs for six miles (ten kilometres) between the two towns, initially following the River Mole (look out for the beautiful Shell Bridge near Thorncroft Manor), and later skirting the grounds of Norbury Park House, passing through Westhumble and bisecting the vineyards of the Denbies Wine Estate.

For all the ramblers, puffed-out school kids and Home Counties day-trippers who hit the North Downs, **Box Hill**'s pulling power lies in its proximity to London and the spectacular views it avails over the truly lovely Kent Weald and the curves of the South Downs. Those who make the 564-feet (172-metre) summit will find an information centre (01306 888793), shop, café and an 1890s fort.

Less busy, perhaps, is the Blackwater Valley (01252 331353), a charming area of outstanding countryside between the borders of Berkshire, Hampshire and Surrey. The 23-mile (37-kilometre) **Blackwater Valley Path**, which starts near Aldershot and ends in the village of Swallowfield, takes in parkland and nature reserves along the way.

Buckinghamshire is a similarly majestic hiker's paradise, from its picture perfect village pubs (many of them frequented by Ferrari-driving footballers' wives, but offering a lovely break from the beaten track all the same) to its wide open spaces of almost unbroken natural beauty. Not all of the walks here are odysseys: the four-mile (three-kilometre) **Great Missenden** walk combines a sharp climb with gentle, undulating countryside and ancient woods. More challenging are the long-distance routes, including the **North Bucks Way**, which passes through charming villages on its 35-mile (56-kilometre) meander through the Vale of Aylesbury. There's also **Swan's Way**, which, at 65 miles (104 kilometres), crosses virtually the entire county.

Even more hardcore are the **South East National Trails** (www.nationaltrail.co.uk), which include the 151-mile (246-kilometre) **North Downs Way** immortalised in Chaucer's *Canterbury Tales*, the 85-mile (136-kilometre) **Ridgeway** (along an ancient chalk ridge first used as a transport route by prehistoric man) and the **Thames Path**, which follows the river from its source in Gloucestershire all the way back to London – practically a snip at just 184 miles (294 kilometres).

For some of these you'll need proper walking and hiking gear: buy them at **Blacks'** (7404 5681) or **Snow & Rock** (7420 1444). For more walks around town check out the *Time Out Book of London Walks* (£11.99).

National Trails Office

Holton, Oxon OX33 1QQ (01865 810224/ www.nationaltrail.co.uk).

Ramblers' Association

7339 8500/www.ramblers.org.uk.

Only two of Brighton's three Victorian piers are (barely) still standing. Lacy, delicate **Brighton Pier** is a clutter of hotdog stands, karaoke, candyfloss and fairground rides, filled with customers in the summertime. Sadly, though, the **West Pier** is now a spooky, twisted ruin. It had been closed since 1975, while the city dithered over what to do about it. As they did nothing, time did its work, weakening the pier's foundations. Finally, in 2003 a violent storm and fire damage delivered the coup de grace. At the moment the pier's future is undecided, but the West Pier Trust hope that reconstruction will go ahead.

With seven miles of coastline, Brighton has all the seaside resort trappings, hence the free **Brighton Fishing Museum** (201 King's Road Arches, on the lower prom between the piers, 01273 723064) and the **Sea-Life Centre**, the world's oldest functioning aquarium.

Perhaps reflecting its singular character, the town has a huge number of independent shops, boutiques and art stores. The best shopping for clothes, records and gift shops is found in and around **North Laine** and in the charming network of narrow cobbled streets known as the **Lanes**, which contain dozens of jewellers, clothiers and antiques shops.

After dark, Brighton offers opportunities for party overkill. Pick up club flyers on Gardner Street and Kensington Gardens on Saturday afternoons, or check listings mags such as *The Latest* or *The Brighton Source*.

The Royal Pavilion

Brighton, BN1 1EE (01273 292820/www.royal pavilion.org.uk). **Open** *Apr-Sept* 9.30am-5.45pm daily. *Oct-Mar* 10am-5.15pm daily. Last admission 45mins before closing. **Admission** £5.80; £3.40-£4 concessions. Joint ticket with Preston Manor £8.20. **Guided tours** (£1.25 extra) 11.30am, 2.30pm daily. **Credit** AmEx, MC, V.

Sea-Life Centre

Marine Parade, BN2 1TB (01273 604234/www. sealife.co.uk). **Open** *Mar-Oct* 10am-6pm daily. Last entry 5pm. *Nov-Feb* 10am-5pm. Last entry 4pm. **Admission** £7.95; £4.95-£6.95 concessions; free under-2s. **Credit** AmEx, DC, MC, V.

Where to eat & drink

A drab concrete box exterior and simple café-like interior are at odds with the quality of pan-Asian cuisine on offer at **Black Chapati** (12 Circus Parade, New England Road, 01273 699011, main courses £11.90-£15.50), one of Brighton's best restaurants. There's a menu of beautifully presented, authentic French fare at **La Fourchette** (105 Western Road, 01273 722556, main courses £14.50).

One of the country's most celebrated vegetarian restaurants is here: **Terre à Terre** (71 East Street, 01273 729051, main courses £10.90-£11.95) is known for its innovative menu. Great food and considerate staff make **Seven Dials** (1 Buckingham Place, 01273 885555, main courses £14.50) an excellent choice for dinner.

This city's laidback attitude makes it ideal for coffeeshop culture, and its great coffee shops include **Nia Café Bar** (87-8 Trafalgar Street, 01273 671371) and **Alfresco** (Milkmaid Pavilion, King's Road Arches, 01273 206523).

Of the traditional pubs, the **Cricketers** (15 Black Lion Street), the **Druid's Head** (9 Brighton Place) and the **Battle of Trafalgar** (34 Guildford Road) all have the most charm.

Classic Brighton boozer the **Prince Albert** (48 Trafalgar Street) has theme nights. **St James** (16 Madeira Place) is a pre-club bar with DJs. **Sidewinder** (65 Upper St James Street) and the **Hampton** (57 Upper North Street) and **Riki-Tik** (18A Bond Street) are also cool.

Of the gay bars, the most fun is to be had at the **Amsterdam Hotel** (11-12 Marine Parade). **Doctor Brighton's** (16 King's Road) on the seafront features DJs playing house and techno. The **Candy Bar** (33 St James Street) is a women-only lesbian hangout.

Where to stay

Given Brighton's popularity, it's perhaps unsurprising that hotel prices here can be high. Best in town is one of the newest: **Hotel du Vin** (2-6 Ship Street, 01273 718588, www.hotelduvin.com; doubles £119-£295). **Blanch House** (17 Atlingworth Street, 01273 603504, www.blanchhouse.co.uk, doubles £125-£220), unassuming from the outside, is also chic. **Nineteen** (19 Broad Street, 01273 675529, www.hotelnineteen.co.uk, doubles £95-£160) has just seven rooms in a stylish townhouse. **Hotel Pelirocco** (10 Regency Square, 01273 327055,www.hotelpelirocco.co.uk, doubles £85-£125) is funky, with themed decor in the bedrooms. **Hotel Twenty One** (21 Charlotte Street, 01273 686450, doubles £60-£95) is a well-run B&B a few minutes' walk from the Palace Pier and town centre. **Oriental Hotel** (9 Oriental Place, 01273 205050, doubles £60-£100) is laid-back and centrally located. For a clean, cheap, central but bland chain try **Brighton Premier Lodge** (144 North Street, 0870 700 1334, doubles £52).

Getting there

By train

From Victoria (50mins) or King's Cross (1hr 10mins).

By coach

National Express (1hr 50mins).

By car

Take the M23, then the A23 to Brighton.

Tourist information

Tourist Information Centre

10 Bartholomew Square (0906 711 2255/ www.visitbrighton.com). **Open** *July, Aug* 9am-5.30pm Mon-Fri; 10am-6pm Sat; 10am-4pm Sun. *Jan-June, Sept, Oct* 9am-5pm Mon-Fri; 10am-5pm Sat; 10am-4pm Sun. *Nov, Dec* 9am-5pm Mon-Fri; 10am-5pm Sat.

Cambridge

Gorgeous, intimidating Cambridge has the feel of an enclosed city. With its narrow streets and tall old buildings blocking out the sun in the town centre, it has a way of conveying disapproval to visitors. But it's worth persevering as behind the façade is a pretty little town of green parks and streams where time seems to have stopped in the 18th century.

Cambridge first became an academic centre when a fracas at Oxford – apparently involving a dead woman, an arrow and a scholar holding a bow – led to some of the learned monks bidding a hasty farewell to Oxford and a hearty how do you do to Cambridge.

Once the dust settled, the monks needed somewhere to peddle their knowledge. The first college, **Peterhouse**, was established in 1284. The original hall survives, though most of the present buildings are 19th century. Up the road is **Corpus Christi College**, founded in 1352. Its Old Court dates from that time and is linked by a gallery to its original chapel, the 11th-century **St Bene't's Church** (Bene't Street, 01223 353903), the oldest surviving building in Cambridge.

Down Silver Street is 15th-century **Queens' College**; most of its original buildings remain, including the timbered president's lodge. The inner courts are wonderfully picturesque.

Further up on King's Parade, grand **King's College** was founded by Henry VI in 1441 and is renowned for its **chapel** (01223 331155), built between 1446 and 1515. It has a breathtaking interior with the original stained glass. Attend a service in term-time to hear its choirboys.

Further north, pretty **Trinity College** was founded in 1336 by Edward III and then refounded by Henry VIII in 1546. A fine crowd of Tudor buildings surrounds the Great Court where, legend has it, Lord Byron was known to bathe naked in the fountain with his pet bear. Wittgenstein studied and taught here, and the library (designed by Wren) is open to visitors at certain times (noon-2pm Mon-Fri all year, 10.30am-12.30pm Sat term-time, 01223 338400).

Further on, at the corner of Bridge and St John's Streets, is the 12th-century **Round Church** (Church of the Holy Sepulchre, Bridge Street, 01223 311602), the oldest of only four remaining round churches in the country.

Behind the main colleges, the beautiful meadows bordering the willow-shaded River Cam are known as the **Backs**. This is idyllic for summer strolling, or 'punting' (pushing flat boats with long poles). Punts can be hired; **Scudamore's Boatyard** (01223 359750) is the largest operator. If you get handy at the surprisingly difficult skill of punting, you could boat down to the **Orchard Tea Rooms** (Mill Way, Grantchester, 01223 845 788) where Rupert Brooke lodged when he was a student. There's a small museum dedicated to Brooke in the car park outside.

Among Cambridge's relatively few non-collegiate attractions, the **Fitzwilliam Museum** on Trumpington Street (01223 332900), has an outstanding collection of antiquities and Old Masters; **Kettle's Yard** (Castle Street, 01223 352124) has fine displays of 20th-century art; and the **Botanic Gardens** (01223 336265) on Bateman Street offer a relaxing place to watch the grass grow.

Where to eat & drink

At **Venue on the Roof** (Cambridge Arts Theatre, 4th floor, 6 St Edward's Passage, 01223 367333, main courses £12.95-£17.95) the artistically presented dishes draw on international influences; it's classy with fair prices to boot. **Midsummer House** (Midsummer Common, 01223 369299, £45 three courses, fixed price menus only), is where chef patron Daniel Clifford creates posh and inventive French dishes in a bid to earn a second Michelin star.

Overlooking the Cam, with a little balcony to make the best of its location, the **Galleria Restaurant** (33 Bridge Street, 01223 362054, main courses £6.75-£15) is clean and bright, with simple meals such as noodles with vegetables or mushroom tagliatelle. For a healthy, inexpensive meal try **Dojo Noodle Bar** in Miller's Yard (Mill Lane, 01223 363471, main courses £4.80-£6.20).

Cambridge has many creaky old inns in which to enjoy the decent local ales. The **Eagle** on Bene't Street (01223 505020) is the most famous, but there are many, including the **Pickerel Inn** (30 Magdalene Street, 01223 355068), **Fort St George** by the river on Midsummer Common (01223 354327), the **Mill** (14 Mill Lane, 01223 357026) and the **Anchor** (Silver Street, 01223 353554) on the river.

A stroll along the Cam from Midsummer Common will take you to the picturesque **Green Dragon** (5 Water Street, 01223 505035). with its beer garden by the river.

Where to stay

Because of the university, there are plenty of guesthouses in town, and the **Meadowcroft Hotel** (16 Trumpington Road, 01223 346120, doubles £100-£120) is one of the best. Also lovely is the **Cambridge Garden House Moat House** (Granta Place, Mill Lane, 01223 259988, www.moathousehotels.com, doubles £200-£254) on the banks of the Cam. A mile out of town, the new **Hotel Felix** has a great restaurant, landscaped gardens and stylishly elegant rooms (Whitehouse Lane, Huntingdon Road, 01223 277977, www.hotelfelix.co.uk, doubles £155-£260). For budget travellers, the simple modern cells of the **Sleeperz Hotel** betray Scandinavian and Japanese influences (Station Road, 01223 304050, doubles £55).

Getting there

By train

From King's Cross (50mins) or Liverpool Street (1hr 15mins).

By coach

By National Express (1hr 50mins).

By car

Take Junction 11 or Junction 12 off the M11.

Tourist information

Tourist Information Centre

Old Library, Wheeler Street (0906 586 2526/ www.tourismcambridge.com). **Open** *Apr-Oct* 10am-6.30pm Mon-Fri; 10am-5pm Sat; 11am-4pm Sun. *Nov-Mar* 10am-5.30pm Mon-Fri; 10am-5pm Sat.

Canterbury

The soaring towers of the cathedral, and the swirl of medieval streets around it, never let you forget where you are when you're wandering through this lovely, historic town. The home of the Church of England since St Augustine was based here in 597, the ancient city of Canterbury is rich in atmosphere.

Its busy tourist trade and large university provide a colourful counterweight to the brooding mass of history present in its old buildings and, of course, the glorious **Canterbury Cathedral**. Be warned this is one of the most egregious of England's charging cathedrals – you have to pay even to get into the walled-off cathedral close. But it is, quite simply, worth it. It has superb stained glass, stone vaulting and a vast Norman crypt. A plaque near the altar marks what is believed to be the exact spot where Archbishop Thomas à Becket was murdered. **Trinity Chapel** contains the site of the original shrine, plus the tombs of Henry IV and the Black Prince.

The pilgrimage to Becket's tomb was the focus of Chaucer's *Canterbury Tales*. At the exhibition named after the book, visitors are given a device that they point at tableaux inspired by Chaucer's tales of a knight, a miller and others, to hear the stories.

Eastbridge Hospital (High Street, 01227 471688), founded to provide shelter for pilgrims, retains the smell of ages past. The **Roman Museum** has the remains of a townhouse and mosaic floor among its treasures.

The city centre nestling up to the cathedral is a pleasure to explore – the tiny shops and restaurants hold their own beside the chains.

Canterbury Cathedral

The Precincts, CT1 2EH (01227 762862/ www.canterbury-cathedral.org). **Open** *Easter-Sept* 9am-5pm Mon-Sat; 12.30-2.30pm, 4.30-5.30pm Sun. *Oct-Easter* 9am-4.30pm Mon-Sat; 12.30-2.30pm, 4.30-5.30pm Sun. During evensong certain parts of cathedral are closed. **Admission** £4; £3 concessions; free under-5s. **Credit** MC, V.

Canterbury Tales

St Margaret's Street, CT1 2TG (01227 454888/ 01227 479227/www.canterburytales.org.uk). **Open** *Mid Feb-June, Sept, Oct* 10am-5pm daily. *July, Aug* 9.30am-5pm daily. *Nov-mid Feb* 10am-4.30pm daily. **Admission** £6.75; £5.25-£5.75 concessions; free under-4s. **Credit** MC, V.

Roman Museum

Butchery Lane, CT1 2JR (01227 785575/www. canterbury-museums.co.uk). **Open** *Nov-May* 10am-5pm Mon-Sat. *June-Oct* 10am-5pm Mon-Sat; 1.30-5pm Sun. Last entry 1hr before closing. **Admission** £2.70; £1.70 concessions; free under-5s. **No credit cards.**

Where to eat & drink

The Goods Shed, (Station Road West, 01227 459153, main courses £8-£16) is just perfect for a leisurely lunch. **Café des Amis du Mexique** (No.95, 01227 464390, main courses £6.95-£14.95) is upbeat and popular, while **Lloyds** (No.89, 01227 768222, main courses £11-£18) offers international cuisine. Further afield on St Dunstan's Street, stop for a drink in the peaceful **Unicorn** with its kitsch garden (01227 463187), or at the ancient and sedate **Thomas Becket** (01227 464384) in Best Lane.

Where to stay

Prices are good at the **Acacia Lodge & Tanglewood**, a B&B formed from 1880s farm cottages and run by a former town guide (39-40 London Road, 01227 769955, doubles £45-£52). Similarly affordable is the **Coach House**, a pretty B&B (34 Watling Steet, 01227 784324, doubles £45-£50). At the other end of the scale, the **Falstaff** is a lovely historic hotel (8-10 St Dunstan's Street, 01227 462138, doubles £110).

Getting there

By train

From Victoria Station to Canterbury East (1hr 20mins), or from Charing Cross to Canterbury West (1hr 30mins).

By coach

National Express from Victoria (1hr 50mins).

By car

Take the A2 then the M2 then the A2 again.

Tourist information

Tourist Information Centre

12-13 Sun Street, The Buttermarket, CT1 2HX (01227 378100/www.canterbury.co.uk). **Open** *Jan-Mar, Nov, Dec* 9.30am-5pm Mon-Sat, 10am-4pm Sun. *Apr-Oct* 9.30am-5.30pm Mon-Sat; 10am-4pm Sun.

Oxford

With its soaring spires, domed library and narrow old streets, Oxford has a noble, ancient beauty that is not undone by the packs of French schoolchildren roaming its streets and giggling at its robed students glumly trudging off to take their formal exams.

The myriad colleges that make up **Oxford University** have defined this town since the middle of the 12th century. Nearly everything else in town – the galleries and museums, the good restaurants, the expansive green parks – stems from the schools.

This wasn't always the way. Oxford arose as a Saxon burg built to defend Wessex from the dastardly Danes – the 11th-century **St Michael's Tower** in Cornmarket Street is the only surviving building of this period. The dissolution of the monasteries under Henry VIII meant that much of Oxford's land and money passed from the Church to the colleges, setting the town's course.

Most of Oxford's many colleges are open to the public and the chapel at **Christ Church College** also serves as Oxford's cathedral. **Magdalen College** (pronounced 'maudlin') has a lovely meadow and deer park. Nearby **Merton College**, founded in 1264, has a medieval library and garden.

Other centres of academia include the grand **Bodleian**, the university's huge, reference-only library in a spectacular building, with the oldest part dating back to 1488. It contains every book published in the United Kingdom and Ireland.

The **University Botanic Gardens** (Rose Lane, 01865 286690) are the oldest in Great Britain and have occupied this spot by the River Cherwell for more than 375 years.

Oxford's non-university sights include **Carfax Tower** (01865 792653), the only surviving part of the 14th-century church of St Martin, with its two 'quarter-boy' clocks (they chime every quarter-hour). Climb the 99 steps to the top for fanatastic views.

A wealth of museums range from the quirky (and free) **Pitt Rivers** (Parks Road; 01865 270927), with its voodoo dolls, shrunken heads and other ethnological delights, to the all-embracing (also free) **Ashmolean** (Beaumont Street, 01865 278000), the country's oldest museum housing the university's collection of art and antiquities. There's also the recently revamped **Modern Art Oxford** (30 Pembroke Street, 01865 722733), which has established an international reputation for pioneering exhibitions of contemporary work.

Central Oxford, with its sweet **Covered Market** (opened in 1774) linking Market Street to the High, its car-unfriendly streets and bicycling youth, is a wonderful place to wander. It can get uncomfortably clogged with tourists, but there are always the neighbourhoods of Jericho, Summertown and Cowley to explore. Beyond Jericho, wild horses roam on the vast expanse of lovely **Port Meadow**.

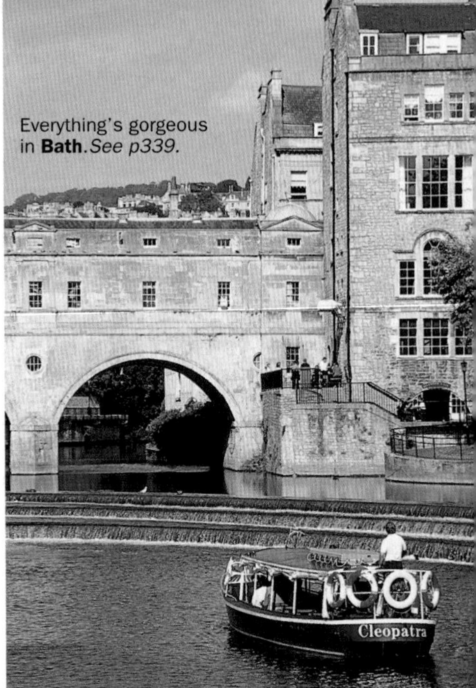

Everything's gorgeous in **Bath**. *See p339.*

Bodleian Library

Broad Street, OX1 3BG (01865 277000/www.bodley.ox.ac.uk). **Open** 9am-4.45pm Mon-Fri; 9am-1pm Sat. **Guided tours** (01865 277224) *Mid Mar-Oct* 10.30am, 11.30am, 2pm, 3pm Mon-Fri; 10.30am, 11.30am Sat. *Nov-mid Mar* 2pm, 3pm Mon-Fri; 10.30am, 11.30am Sat. **Admission** *Guided tour £4. Audio tour £2. Ages 14 & over only.* **No credit cards**.

Where to eat & drink

Swish, metropolitan brasserie **Le Petit Blanc** (71-2 Walton Street, 01865 510999, main courses £9.25-£17.25) is excellent value for great grub. Children get their own menu. The **Branca Bar Italian Brasserie** (111 Walton Street, 01865 556111, main courses £7.95-£16.95) is perfect for those seeking a zippy atmosphere with their pasta. At the fabulously quaint **Gee's** (61A Banbury Road, 01865 553540, main courses £10.95-£24.50), food is predominantly British, taken from the finest local produce. **Cherwell Boathouse Restaurant** (Bardwell Road, 01865 552746, main courses £10-£12) is a riverside favourite.

Oxford has loads of pubs, but few are cheap or quiet – the 16th-century **King's Arms** in Holywell Street (01865 242369) is studenty with good beer; the **Turf Tavern** (01865 243235) between Hertford and New Colleges is Oxford's oldest inn.The **Perch** (01865 728891) on Binsey Lane has a garden with children's play area.

Where to stay

Burlington House is an outstanding small hotel with B&B prices, but a little way out of town (374 Banbury Road, 01865 513513, doubles £75-£85). The **Old Parsonage** (1 Banbury Road, 01865 310210, doubles £135-£195), home to Oscar Wilde when he was an undergraduate, is classy and ancient, and the **Old Bank Hotel** is sleek, modernist and arty (92-4 High Street, 01865 799599, doubles £160-£320). Next to the station, the **Royal Oxford Hotel** has worked hard to lose that clinical Travelodge look, and its rates are reasonable for the city centre (Park End Street, 01865 248432, doubles £129).

Getting there

By train

There are regular trains from Paddington (1hr); your rail ticket qualifies you for a free ride into the centre on an electric bus (every 10mins).

By coach

There are frequent, cheap, fast services from several London departure points; details from **National Express** (1hr 40mins), **Stagecoach** (01865 772250) and **Oxford Bus Company** (01865 785410).

By car

Take Junction 8 off the M40, and then the A40 into town. Park at the edge and use the park & rides.

Tourist information

Oxford Information Centre

15-16 Broad Street, OX1 3AS (01865 726871/ www.visitoxford.org). **Open** *Easter-Oct* 9.30am-5pm Mon-Sat; 10am-3.30pm Sun. *Nov-Easter* 9.30am-5pm Mon-Sat.

Stratford-upon-Avon

This chocolate-box of a town is England's second biggest tourist draw (after London), and for good reason. It's charming, historic and filled with interesting little sights, but is best visited in the off-season, as it gets so crowded in the summertime that it's hard to enjoy its beauty. Don't be put off by the aggressive marketing of 'Shakespeare Country' – half-timbered architecture overkill, over zealous cobbling and teashops everywhere. It can all be forgiven if you're one of Will's fans.

There's never a shortage of his works to see, and the **Royal Shakespeare Theatre** is the place to see them. If you can't get a ticket, take a backstage tour and visit the **RSC Collection** museum of props and costumes.

Stratford has been a **market** town since 1169 and, in a way, that's still what it does best. See it on a Friday, when locals flock in from outlying villages to the colourful stalls at the top of Wood Street.

In the town centre, with its medieval grid pattern, many fine old buildings survive, among them **Harvard House** (High Street, 01789 204507, open June-Oct), which dates from 1596. It was home to Katharine Rogers, mother of John Harvard, founder of Harvard University, and now houses a pewter collection.

In the town centre are **Shakespeare's Birthplace** (01789 204016) on Henley Street; **Hall's Croft** (01789 292107) on Old Town, named after Dr John Hall, who married the Bard's daughter Susanna; and **Nash's House** (01789 292325) on Chapel Street, which once belonged to the first husband of Shakespeare's granddaughter, Elizabeth. In the garden of the latter are the foundations of **New Place**, the writer's last home, demolished in 1759. Shakespeare was educated at **Stratford Grammar School**, on Church Street, and buried in **Holy Trinity church**.

A mile and a half (2.5 kilometres) away at **Shottery**, and accessible from Stratford by public footpath, is **Anne Hathaway's Cottage** (01789 292100), where Shakespeare's wife lived before she married him. The girlhood home of his mother, **Mary Arden's House** (01789 293455), is at **Wilmcote**, a pleasant four-mile (6.5-kilometre) stroll along the Stratford Canal. Both may also be reached by bus; there are also trains to Wilmcote.

Stratford's charms are enhanced by the **River Avon** and the **Stratford Canal** and the walks alongside. Spend some time on the water by hiring a boat at **Stratford Marina**. The long-established **Avon Boating** (01789 267073) has punts and rowing boats for hire.

Royal Shakespeare Company

Waterside, CV37 6BB (box office 0870 609110/ tours 01789 403405/www.rsc.org.uk). **Backstage tours** times vary; phone to check. **Tickets** *Tour* £4; £3 concessions. *Performances* prices vary. **Credit** MC, V.

Where to eat & drink

The **Opposition** (13 Sheep Street, 01789 269980, main courses £9.25-£15.95) is a great bistro, **Russon's** (8 Church Street, 01789

268822, main courses £9.50-£15.75) specialises in imaginative fish dishes, and **Callands** (13-14 Meer Street, 01789 269304, main courses £18.50) offers eclectic modern cooking.

Drink with thesps at the **Dirty Duck** (aka the **Black Swan**, Waterside, 01789 297312).

Where to stay

Caterham House Hotel (58-9 Rother Street, 01789 267309, doubles £80-£85) is close to the Royal Shakespeare Theatre and popular with both audience and actors. **The Falcon Hotel** (Chapel Street, 0870 609 6122, doubles £80-£140) is well olde worlde: at least 20 of the 84 en suite rooms are in a 16th-century inn. Another good choice, **Victoria Spa Lodge** (Bishopton Lane, 01789 267985, doubles £65) has the feel of a grand country house; Princess Victoria stayed here in 1837.

Tourist information

Tourist Information Centre

Bridgefoot, CV37 6GW (01789 293127/ www.shakespeare-country.co.uk). **Open** *Apr-Sept* 9.30am-5.30pm Mon-Sat; 10.30am-4.30pm Sun. *Oct-Mar* 9.30am-5pm Mon-Sat.

Getting there

By train

Regular service from Paddington (2hrs 10mins).

By coach

National Express (2hrs 45mins).

By car

Take Junction 15 off the M40, then A46 into town.

Winchester

Lovely, regal Winchester, the ancient capital of Wessex is often overlooked by international travellers, and more's the pity. It dates back to 450 BC, when an Iron Age settlement was established on St Catherine's Hill, just to the east. The Romans moved it to create the city of Venta Belgarum west of the River Itchen in around AD 70. The first cathedral was begun after the arrival of the Saxons, in 648.

The town is on the long list of possible locations for King Arthur's Camelot. In homage, a round table is hung in the **Great Hall** (Great Hall Castle Avenue, 01962 846476), the last remaining part of what was for 500 years one of England's principal royal palaces.

Winchester's medieval core is still very much the heart of town, with winding lanes of typically English charm – neat, compact and easy to wander. The **cathedral**, a majestic Norman edifice begun in 1079, dominates it all. Inside, there are too many treasures to detail, among them 12th-century wall paintings and the grave of Jane Austen. The Triforium gives you a spectacular view of the transepts. In the 17th-century library the centrepiece is the Winchester Bible, a gorgeous illuminated manuscript begun in 1160.

Winchester College was founded in 1382. The oldest continuously running public school in England, it remains prominent in the life of the town. On College Street, the now ruined **Wolvesey Castle** (01962 854766) was the main residence of the Bishops of Winchester in the 12th century.

South of town the **Hospital of St Cross** (St Cross Road, 01962 851375), founded in 1136 as an almshouse, is the oldest still-functioning house of charity in the country.

Seven miles south, **Marwell Zoological Park** has some 1,000 animals living in 100 acres of parkland, with picnic areas, World of Lemurs and Penguin World.

Winchester is located at a junction of many long-distance footpaths across the **South Downs** and coastward. The tourist office has maps and guidance.

Marwell Zoological Park

Colden Common, Winchester, SO21 1JH (07626 943163/01962 777407/www.marwell.org.uk). **Open** *Apr-Oct* 10am-6pm daily. Last entry 4.30pm. *Nov-Mar* 10am-4pm daily. Last entry 2.30pm. **Admission** £11; £7.50-£9 concessions. **Credit** MC, V.

Winchester Cathedral & Close

The Close, SO23 9LS (01962 857200/ www.winchester-cathedral.org.uk). **Open** *Cathedral* 8.30am-6pm Mon-Sat; 8.30am-5pm Sun. *Triforium & library* 2-4.30pm Mon; 11am-4.30pm Tue-Fri; 10.30am-4.30pm Sat. *Visitors' centre* 9.30am-5.30pm daily. **Admission** *Cathedral* free; recommended donation £3.50. *Triforium & library* £1; 50p concessions. **Credit** AmEx, MC, V.

Where to eat & drink

The kooky **Wykeham Arms** (75 Kingsgate Street, 01962 853834, main courses £10.75-£15.35) dates to 1755 and is more institution than pub. It's particularly popular with the upper echelons of Winchester society, so there'll be no dancing on the tables. There's a posh dining room and an inn (doubles £90-£120). **Chesil Rectory** (1 Chesil Street, 01962 851555) dates to the 15th century. Each new six-course menu (£45) designed by chef Philip Storey spends three months in development. A stylishly modern set-up at **Loch Fyne** (18 Jewry Street, 01962 872930, main courses £10-£15) includes a menu dominated by fish with a Scottish heritage.

Of the many pubs, the tiny **Eclipse Inn** (25 The Square, 01962 865676, main courses £5.40-£6.50), once the rectory of St Lawrence's church, has reliable pub nosh, but the **Old Vine**, also on the Square (01962 854616, £4.50-£7), is bigger and has a wider choice. Near the river, the **Mash Tun** on Eastgate Street (01962 861440) is a student favourite.

Where to stay

First choice for nostalgia junkies would be the **Wykeham Arms** (*see p349*), but **Hotel du Vin & Bistro** offers sober luxury and the bistro bit is a lovely place for a meal (14 Southgate Street, 01962 841414, www.hotelduvin.com, doubles £105-£285, main courses £14). A top end B&B, **Enmill Barn** is in a huge converted barn just two miles outside Winchester (Pitt, 01962 856740, doubles £60).

Getting there

By train

Regular service from Waterloo (1hr).

By coach

National Express (2hrs).

By car

Take Junction 9 off the M3, then park & ride.

Tourist information

Tourist Information Centre

The Guildhall, The Broadway, SO23 9LJ (01962 840500/www.winchester.gov.uk). **Open** *May-Sept* 9.30am-5.30pm Mon-Sat; 11am-4pm Sun. *Oct-Apr* 10am-5pm Mon-Sat.

Castles & country houses

Althorp – the burial place of Diana, Princess of Wales – is in Northamptonshire, a 90-minute drive from London (contact 0870 167 9000, www.althorp.com for details). The house is only open during July, August and September. It is a very good idea to book ahead.

Arundel Castle

Arundel, West Sussex, BN18 9AB (01903 882173/www.arundelcastle.org). **Getting there** *By train* from Victoria (1hr 30mins). *By car* A24 then A280 and A27. **Open** *Apr-Oct* noon-5pm Mon-Fri, Sun (last entry 4pm). **Admission** £9; £7 concessions; £5.50 5-16s; £24.50 family. **Credit** MC, V.

The original castle, built in the 11th century, was damaged during the Civil War, then remodelled in the 18th and 19th centuries. Inside is a collection of 16th-century furniture, and paintings by Van Dyck, Gainsborough and Reynolds, among others. Don't miss the 14th-century Fitzalan Chapel, a Roman Catholic chapel inside an Anglican church so that the dukes and their families could worship according to Catholic rites. Home to a clutch of tombs of Dukes of Norfolk past, it shows no signs of the time when Oliver Cromwell used it as a stable.

Audley End

Saffron Walden, Essex, CB11 4JF (01799 522399/www.english-heritage.org.uk). **Getting there** *By train* Liverpool Street to Audley End (1hr) then 1-mile (1.5km) walk or 2min taxi ride. *By car* J8 off M11 then B1383. **Open** *Apr-Sept* 11am-5pm Wed-Sun; tours by appointment. **Admission** £8; £6 concessions; £4 5-16s; £20 family. **Credit** MC, V.

This unmissable Jacobean mansion was the largest house in the country when it was built for Thomas Howard, first Earl of Suffolk, in 1614. It was later owned by Charles II, but was given back to the Howards in the 18th century. The latter demolished

It's all so very quaint at **Windsor**. *See p351.*

two-thirds of it in order to make the place more manageable. Many of the rooms, brimming with the accumulated wealth of its aristocratic owners, have been restored to Robert Adam's 1760s designs. Capability Brown landscaped the gardens.

Hatfield House

Hatfield, Hertfordshire AL9 5NQ (01707 287010/ www.hatfield-house.co.uk). **Getting there** *By train* from King's Cross to Hatfield (25mins). *By car* J4 off A1(M). **Open** Easter-Sept only. *House* noon-4pm daily. *Tours* noon-4pm Mon-Fri. *West Gardens* 11am-5.30pm daily. *East Gardens* 11am-5.30pm Fri. **Admission** *House, park & gardens* £7.50; £4 5-15s. *Park & gardens* £4.50; £3.50 5-15s. *Park only* £2; £1 5-15s. **Credit** MC, V.

Built by Robert Cecil, Earl of Salisbury, in 1611, this superb Jacobean mansion oozes history. In the grounds stands the remaining wing of the Royal Palace of Hatfield, the childhood home of Queen Elizabeth I: she held her first Council of State here in 1558. The gardens include herb terraces, orchards and fountains restored to their former glory by the present-day marchioness, as well as a woodland timber playground for children. Special events such as craft fairs run throughout the year.

Hever Castle

Hever, nr Edenbridge, Kent, TN8 7NG (01732 865224/www.hevercastle.co.uk). **Getting there** *By train* Victoria to Edenbridge (1hr), then 5min taxi journey, or Victoria to Hever (1hr), then 1-mile walk. *By car* J5 off M25 then B2042 and B269, or J6 off M25 then A22, A25 and B269. **Open** *Mar-Oct* 11am-6pm daily. *Nov* 11am-dusk daily. **Admission** *House & gardens* £8.40; £7.10 concessions; £4.60 5-14s; free under-5s; £21.40 family. *Garden only* £6.70; £5.70 concessions; £4.70 5-14s; £17.80 family. **Credit** MC, V.

The childhood home of Anne Boleyn, and scene of Henry VIII's wooing of her, Hever is a 13th-century castle and 15th-century manor house. The buildings, gardens and lake were restored in the early 20th century by American millionaire Waldorf Astor (of posh hotel fame), who also built the 'Tudor' village behind it. Among other excellent exhibits, the castle contains precious paintings, a gruesome (and appropriate) exhibition of instruments of execution and two rare Book of Hours – illuminated manuscripts inscribed by Anne Boleyn. The grounds are glorious with a yew maze, secret grottoes and classic statuary. The water maze is inundated with dripping children in sunny weather. Check the website for seasonal events.

Leeds Castle

Broomfield, nr Maidstone, Kent, ME17 1PL (01622 765400/www.leeds-castle.com). **Getting there** *By train* Victoria to Bearsted (1hr), then 10min bus transfer. *By car* J8 off M20. **Open** *Mar-Oct* 10am-7pm daily (last entry 5pm). *Nov-Feb* 10am-5pm daily (last entry 3pm). **Admission** *Castle & park (peak season)* £12; £10.50 concessions; £8.50 4-15s; £35 family. **Credit** MC, V.

The castle of queens (many a king gave it to the wife), Leeds Castle was built by Normans shortly after 1066, and fortified by various royal householders, including Henrys V and VIII. The last private owner was Lady Baillie, an Anglo-American heiress, who bequeathed the place to the Leeds Castle Foundation in 1974.

The old castle takes in the 12th-century cellar and the 13th-century chapel, the gloriette or keep, the bedrooms of various queens and the heraldry room. The New Castle, rebuilt in 1822, has conference rooms and halls. A Dog Collar Museum is in the gatehouse. Outside, the woodland is fabulous in spring and the gardens include glasshouses, vineyards and an aviary. Black swans glide in the moat. The yew maze has at its centre a shell and stone grotto. The Culpeper Garden, the castle's kitchen garden, is fragrant with herbs, including the national collection of bergamot.

Windsor Castle

High Street, Windsor, Berkshire, SL4 1NJ (01753 831118/www.royal.gov.uk). **Getting there** *By train* Paddington to Slough then change for Windsor Central (45mins); Waterloo to Eton & Windsor Riverside (1hr). *By car* J6 off M4. **Open** *Mar-Sept* 9.45am-5.15pm (4pm last entry) daily. *Oct-Feb* 9.45am-4.15pm (3pm last entry) daily. *Changing of the Guard* (weather permitting) Apr-June 11am daily; July-Mar every other day, call ahead. **Admission** £11.50; £9.50 concessions; £6 4-15s; £29 family. **Credit** AmEx, MC, V.

One of the Queen's official residences, Windsor was the scene of many a red face back in June 2003, when comedian Aaron Barshak gatecrashed Prince William's 21st birthday party. Usually, however, the many visitors to this, the oldest occupied castle in the world, are well behaved. The 15th-century St George's Chapel is the burial place of ten monarchs, including Henry VIII and Queen Elizabeth the Queen Mother, who died in 2002. The chapel is closed to visitors on Sunday, although worshippers are welcome. Queues are longest for the Queen Mary's Dolls' House, designed by Edward Lutyens. The miniature home has flushing loos, real wine in tiny casks and electric lights. State apartments include the Waterloo Chamber, built to celebrate the victory over the French in 1815. The Long Walk crosses Windsor Great Park, a 5,000-acre hunting ground dating back to the 13th century.

Blenheim Palace

Woodstock, Oxfordshire, OX20 1PX (01993 811325/ www.blenheimpalace.com). **Getting there** *By train* Paddington to Oxford (1hr) then 30-40min bus ride. *By car* J9 off M40 then A34 and A44. **Open** *Palace & gardens* mid Mar-Oct 10.30am-4.45pm (last entry) daily. *Park* 9am-4.45pm daily. **Admission** *Palace, park & gardens* £10; £8 concessions; £5 5-15s. *Park only* £7.50 per car (incl occupants); £2.50 pedestrians; £1 5-15s. **Credit** AmEx, MC, V.

After defeating the French at the Battle of Blenheim in 1704, John Churchill, first Duke of Marlborough, was so handsomely rewarded that he could afford

Haughty culture

In the moneyed shires that cosy up to Greater London, grand country houses and their lush acreage have provided the perfect canvas for a number of the more creative and well-to-do gardeners. Vita Sackville-West, passionate plantswoman and creator of **Sissinghurst Castle Garden**, was one of them. Her garden is still in the grounds of the 16th-century mansion, and its borders and sheltered 'rooms' are so varied that year-round interest, fragrance and colour are all but guaranteed.

Kent, known as the Garden of England, has all the best plots. **Groombridge Place Gardens** started life as a pig pasture before it was sold to Norman barons who built a moated castle here. The present manor house (a private residence) was built in the 17th century, after the castle was destroyed. The house and land changed hands several times before being opened to the public in 1994. The listed walled gardens are stunning. Peacocks strut among floral bowers, a secret garden affords space for contemplation and the well-bred formality of the knot garden is a testament to generations of hard work. Groombridge also markets itself as a family day out; diversions for non-horticulturalists include the Enchanted Forest, Dinosaur Valley and the Dark Walk Adventure Trail.

Gardener to the stars in the 18th century, Lancelot 'Capability' Brown (the name comes from his enthusiasm for the 'capabilities' of the natural landscape) planted gardens across England, perhaps most successfully at **Stowe**, in Buckinghamshire. Its 325 acres were first laid out in 1680, but since then the landscaping has been complemented by monuments designed by almost every big-name architect of the time, among them James Gibbs and John Vanbrugh. The effect is beautiful and quintessentially English, although little of the house can be seen because it's occupied by Stowe School.

Anyone with Capability Brown tendencies would do well to join the **Royal Horticultural Society**, the British gardening charity with a history dating back 200 years. It's the world's leading horticultural organisation, with an education and research programme and a mission to support gardeners of all, erm, capabilities. The flagship garden of the RHS, **Wisley** in Surrey, is 240 acres of borders, glasshouses, vegetable gardens beautiful flowers and orchards.

As enchanting as any English country garden, **Derek Jarman's garden** is far removed from the wealth and privilege that nourished the roots of many a grander plot. Spread out in the shingle with the uncompromising bulk of Dungeness Nuclear Power Station at its back, this is the garden the filmmaker created while terminally ill. Jarman used plants that could tolerate the flinty land and salt air, and planted sculptural chunks of driftwood. His cottage and garden are private property, but discreet visitors are permitted to admire the planting. For more information on the Dungeness area, contact the Tourist Information Centre at **Rye** (*see p354*).

Groombridge Place Gardens

Groombridge Place, Groombridge, nr Tunbridge Wells, Kent, TN3 9QG (01892 861444/recording 01892 863999/ www.groombridge.co.uk). **Getting there** *By train* Tunbridge Wells then taxi. *By car* A264 off A21. **Open** *Easter-early Nov* 9am-6pm (dusk if earlier) daily. **Admission** £8.30; £7 concessions; £6.80 3-12s; free under-3s; £27.50 family. **Credit** MC, V.

RHS Gardens, Wisley

nr Woking, Surrey, GU23 6QB (01483 224234/www.rhs.org.uk). **Getting there** *By train* West Byfleet or Woking rail then taxi or bus. Wisley Bus runs from Woking to Wisley May-Sept (call 01483 224234 for times). *By car* J10 off M25. **Open** *Mar-Oct* 10am-6pm Mon-Fri; 9am-6pm Sat-Sun. *Nov-Feb* 10am-4pm Mon-Fri; 9am-6pm Sat, Sun. Last entry 1hr before closing. **Tours** by arrangement; phone for details. **Admission** £6; £2 6-16s; free under-6s. **Credit** MC, V.

Sissinghurst Castle Garden

Sissinghurst, Cranbrook, Kent, TN17 2AB (01580 712850/www.national trust.org.uk). **Getting there** *By train* Charing Cross to Staplehurst (53mins) then 10min taxi ride. *By car* J5 off M25 then A21 and A262. **Open** *late Mar-Oct* 11am-6.30pm (last entry 5pm) Mon, Tue, Fri; 10am-6.30pm (last entry 5pm) Sat, Sun. **Admission** £6.50; £3 5-15s. **Credit** AmEx, MC, V.

Stowe

Buckinghamshire, MK18 5EH (gardens 01280 822850/house 01280 818282). **Getting there** *By train* Euston to Milton Keynes (40mins) then bus to Buckingham (30mins) then 5min taxi ride. *By car* J10 off M40 then A43 and A422, or J14 off M1 then A5 and A422. **Open** *Mar-Oct* 10am-5.30pm (last entry 4pm) Wed-Sun. *Nov-Dec* 10am-4pm (last entry 3pm) Wed-Sun. **Admission** *Gardens* £5; £2.50 5-15s; £15 family. *House* £2 or £3 with guided tour; £1.50 5-15s. **Credit** MC, V.

to build this fabulous palace. Designed by Sir John Vanbrugh and set in huge grounds landscaped by Capability Brown, it's the only non-royal residence in the country grand enough to be given the title 'palace'. The grounds include a butterfly house, miniature railway, lake for boating and fishing, and the world's biggest symbolic hedge maze.

Waddesdon Manor

Waddesdon, nr Aylesbury, Buckinghamshire, HP18 0JH (01296 653226/www.waddesdon.org.uk). **Getting there** *By train* Marylebone to Aylesbury (53mins) then bus. *By car* J9 off M40 then A41. **Open** *House* Apr-Oct 11am-4pm Wed-Sun. *Grounds* Mar-Dec 10am-5pm Wed-Sun. **Admission** *House & grounds* £11; £8 5-16s; free under-5s. *Grounds only* £4; £2 5-16s; free under-5s. **Credit** AmEx, MC, V.

Ferdinand de Rothschild's French Renaissance-style château was constructed in the 1870s and houses one of the world's best collections of 18th-century French decorative art, sadly depleted after a burglary in June 2003. The wine cellars are famous worldwide, and wine tastings and events take place regularly. The garden has specimen trees, seasonal bedding and a rococo-style aviary.

Seaside towns

See also p342 **Brighton**.

Broadstairs & Margate

The **Isle of Thanet**, with its 24-mile (39-kilometre) coastal path, sandy coves and bucket-and-spade seaside towns, is like the land that time forgot. It's still 1954 here, and probably always will be.

Broadstairs is where Charles Dickens spent several years; the town enjoys an annual Dickens Festival– (19-27 June 2004; phone 01843 861827 for details). The **Dickens House Museum** closes from mid October to Easter (2 Victoria Parade, 01843 861232).

Elsewhere, the popularity of Broadstairs derives from its seven beaches, the largest of which, **Viking Bay**, combines a crescent shoreline with a picturesque harbour and shops, amusements and ice-cream stalls. Several beaches are more secluded – hence their popularity with 18th-century smugglers.

The town's many small and winding streets are lined with fishermen's cottages converted into pubs, cafés and gift shops. The oldest working lighthouse in England overlooks the North Foreland, and is best seen from Joss Bay.

Margate was Britain's first ever seaside resort. Back in the 1730s, visitors witnessed the newfangled deckchair, the unheard-of employment of donkeys as ride givers and the first bathing machine, which allowed for naked sea-dipping with modesty intact. It remains the quintessential family beach resort for one very good reason: the **Main Sands Bay**, with kids' amenities, from donkeys to swings and slides. It still packs them in every summer.

Don't miss the subterranean **Shell Grotto** (01843 220008) dug into the chalk and covered with strange markings of unknown age or origin. Even if you want to miss it, all of the brochures and signs about town won't let you.

Other spots of interest include the **Margate Caves** (01843 220139), once a hangout for smugglers and unsavoury types.

BASICS

Broadstairs: Getting there *By train* Broadstairs rail. *By car* J5 off M2. **Tourist information** 6B High Street, Broadstairs, Kent CT10 1LH (01843 583334/www.tourism.thanet.gov.uk). **Open** *Easter-Sept* 9.15am-4.45pm Mon-Fri; 10am-4.45pm Sat; 10am-4pm Sun. *Oct-Easter* 9.15am-4.45pm Mon-Fri; 10am-4.45pm Sat.

Margate: Getting there *By train* Margate rail. *By car* M2 then A2. **Tourist information** 12-13 The Parade, Margate, Kent CT9 1EY (01843 220241/ 583334/www.tourism.thanet.gov.uk). **Open** as for Broadstairs.

Hastings & Battle

Hastings is an odd combination of fading resort, still-active fishing port and bohemian outpost (fittingly, the **Hastings Museum and Art Gallery** is on Bohemia Road). The barely there ruins of William the Conqueror's Norman **castle** sit atop a cliff above the seaside town's rock shops and crazy golf course. It houses the **1066 Story** (01424 781112), but the **Smugglers' Adventure** (01424 422964) in St Clement's Caves is more grisly and more exciting. Smuggling was one of Hastings' major industries until the early 19th century, although tourism keeps the locals busy now.

Five miles (8 kilometres) inland, **Battle** is where William and Harold slugged it out for the English crown. To thank God for his victory, William built **Battle Abbey** (01424 773792) on the spot where Harold was killed. The abbey is now reduced to evocative ruins, but an audio-visual display fills in the details. The town is rather touristy, but the 14th-century **Almonry** on the High Street is worth a look if only for the 300-year-old Guy Fawkes effigy in the hallway. The **Battle Museum of Local History** (01424 775 9555) opened in 2003; it costs £1 for adults and is closed November to March.

BASICS

Getting there *By train* Charing Cross to Hastings (1hr 50mins). *By car* M25 then A21. **Tourist information** Queens Square, Priory Meadow, Hastings, TN34 1TL (01424 781111/www.hastings.gov.uk). **Open** 8.30am-6.15pm Mon-Fri; 8.30am-5pm Sat; 9.30am-4.30pm Sun.

Rye

Rye was one of the original Cinque Ports, but its river silted up, the sea retreated and the town found itself two miles inland. Nowadays its narrow cobbled streets and skew-whiff little houses draw hordes of snap-happy visitors (it's best to visit out of season). Novelist Henry James lived here at **Lamb House** (01892 890651). **Rye Castle** (01797 226728) and **Rye Art Gallery** (01797 222433) are worth a peek.

A few miles east of Rye, **Dungeness** is gloriously desolate. The promontory on which it sits is the world's biggest accumulation of shingle, built up over 1,000 years. Investigate the area's ecology at the Dungeness **RSPB Nature Reserve** (01797 320588), enjoy the views from the **Old Lighthouse** (01797 321300) or watch the miniature railway, built in 1927 by racing driver Captain Howey, puff across the bleak landscape. Eat the best fish and chips at the **Britannia** (01797 321959), which can also provide a bed for the night.

BASICS

Getting there *By train* Charing Cross to Ashford then change for Rye (1hr 40mins). *By car* J10 off M20 then A2070 and A259. **Tourist information** The Heritage Centre, Strand Quay, TN31 7AY (01797 226696/www.rye.org.uk/heritage). **Open** 9.30am-5pm Mon-Sat; 10am-5pm Sun.

Whitstable

This rickety old fishing town in Kent is quite fashionable; many an ex-Londoner has been lured to live by its pebbly shoreline. The small harbour provides plenty to see and enjoy, especially at the end of July, when the **Oyster Festival** brings a party atmosphere. The best places for oysters are the well-run **Whitstable Oyster Fishery Company** (01227 276856), an upmarket choice offering unfussy dishes, or the more basic **Wheeler's** (01227 273311), the town's oldest oyster bar. **Crab & Winkle** (01227 779377) on Whitstable Harbour has seafood, fish and chips and great breakfasts. You can learn more about the oysters than how to eat them at the **Whitstable Museum & Gallery** (01227 276998). Want to stay? Book one of the restored 1860s **Fishermen's Huts** (01227 280280, doubles £100-£150). **Copeland House** (01227 266207, doubles from £65) has simple rooms and fine sea views.

BASICS

Getting there *By train* Victoria to Whitstable (1hr 15mins). *By car* J7 off M2 then A99. **Tourist information** 7 Oxford Street, Whitstable (01227 275482). **Open** *July, Aug* 10am-5pm Mon-Sat. *Sept-June* 10am-4pm Mon-Sat.

Directory

Features

Directory

Getting Around

Arriving & leaving

For London's domestic rail and coach stations, *see p338*.

By air

Gatwick Airport
0870 0002468/www.baa.co.uk/gatwick. About 30 miles (50km) south of central London, off the M23.
Of the three rail services that link Gatwick to London, the quickest is the **Gatwick Express** (0845 850 1530/www.gatwickexpress.co.uk) to Victoria Station, which takes about 30 minutes and runs 5.20am to 1.35am daily: the second train is at 5.50am, then there are trains every 15 minutes until 12.50am. Tickets cost £11 for a single, £11.70 for a day return (after 9.30am) and £21.50 for a period return (valid for 30 days). Under-15s get half-price tickets; under-5s travel free.

Connex (08457 484950/www.connex.co.uk) also runs a rail service between Gatwick and Victoria, with trains around every 15 minutes (or half hourly 1-4am). It takes up to eight minutes longer than the Gatwick Express but tickets are cheaper: £8.20 for a single, £8.30 for a day return (after 9.30am) and £16.40 for a period return (valid for one month). Under-15s get half-price tickets, and under-5s go for free.
If you're staying in Bloomsbury or catching a train at King's Cross, take the **Thameslink** service (08457484950/www.thameslink.co.uk) through Blackfriars, City Thameslink, Farringdon and King's Cross; journey times vary. Tickets to King's Cross cost £9.80 single (after 9.30am), £15.40 for a day return and £20 for a 30-day period return.

If you want your hand held from airport to hotel and have £20 to spare, try **Hotelink** (01293 552251/fax 01293 531131/www.hotelink.co.uk).

A taxi will cost about £100.

Heathrow Airport
0870 000 0123/www.baa.co.uk/heathrow. About 15 miles (24km) west of central London, off the M4.
The **Heathrow Express** (0845 600 1515/www.heathrowexpress.co.uk), which runs to Paddington every 15 minutes between 5.10am and 12.30am daily, takes 15-20 minutes. The train can be boarded at either of the airport's two tube stations. Tickets cost £13 each way or £25 return; under-16s go half-price. Many airlines have check-in desks at Paddington.

A longer but considerably cheaper journey is by tube on the **Piccadilly line**. Tickets for the 50- to 60-minute ride into central London cost £4 one way (£1.60 under-16s). Trains run every few minutes from about 5am-11.45pm daily except Sunday, when they run 6am-11pm.

National Express (08705 808080/www.nationalexpress.com) runs daily coach services to London Victoria between 5.30am and 9.30pm daily, leaving Heathrow Central bus terminal every 30 minutes. For a 40-minute journey to London, you'll pay £10 for a single (£5 under-15s) or £15 (£7.50 under-15s) for a return. As at Gatwick, **Hotelink** (*see above*) offers a hand-holding service for £14 per person each way.

A taxi into town will cost roughly £100 and take ages.

London City Airport
7646 0000/www.londoncityairport.com. About 9 miles (14km) east of central London, Docklands.
Silvertown & City Airport rail station, on the Silverlink line, offers a service that runs around every 20 minutes to Stratford for the tube.

Most people head to London on the blue **Shuttlebus** (7646 0088), whose 25-minute ride to Liverpool Street Station goes via Canary Wharf. It leaves every ten minutes (6.50am-9.20pm during the week; 6.50am-11pm on Saturdays; and 11am-9.20pm on Sundays). Tickets to Liverpool Street Station cost £6 one-way, or £3 to Canary Wharf.
A taxi costs around £20.

Luton Airport
01582 405100/www.london-luton.com. About 30 miles (50km) north of central London, J10 off the M1.
Luton Airport Parkway Station is close to the airport, but not in it: there's still a short shuttle-bus ride. The **Thameslink** service (*see above*) calls at many stations (King's Cross among them) and has a journey time of 30-40 minutes. Trains leave every 15 minutes or so, and cost £10 single and £18.50 return, or £10.20 for a cheap day return (available after 9.30am Monday to Friday).

The journey from Luton to Victoria takes 60-90 minutes by coach. **Green Line** (0870 608 7261/www.greenline.co.uk) runs a 24-hour service with a frequency of around 30 minutes at peak times. An adult single costs £8, £4 for under-15s, while returns cost £11.50 and £5.75.

A taxi costs upwards of £50.

Stansted Airport
0870 0000303/www.baa.co.uk/stansted. About 35 miles (60km) north-east of central London, J8 off the M11.
The quickest way to get to London from Stansted is on the Stansted Express train (08457 484950) to Liverpool Street Station; the journey time is 40-45 minutes. Trains leave every 15-30 minutes depending on the time of day, and tickets cost £13 for a single and £23 for a period return; under-15s travel half-price.

The **Airbus A6** (08705 808080) coach service from Stansted to Victoria takes at least an hour and 40 minutes and runs 24 hours. Coaches run roughly every 30 minutes, more frequently during peak times. An adult single costs £8-£10 (£4-£5 for under-15s), a return is £15 (£7.50 for under-15s).
A taxi costs about £80.

By rail

Eurostar
Waterloo International Terminal, SE1 (08705 186186/www.eurostar.com). Waterloo tube/rail. **Map** p401 M8.
Eurostar trains arrive into the central Waterloo Station.

Public transport

Information

Details on public transport in London can be found online at www.thetube.com and/or www.tfl.gov.uk, or on 7222 1234. The TfL website has a journey planner to help you find the quickest route.

Travel Information Centres

TfL's Travel Information Centres provide maps and information about the tube, buses and Docklands Light Railway (DLR; *see below*). You can find them in the stations listed below. Call 7222 5600 for more information.

Heathrow Airport *Terminals 1, 2 & 3 Underground station* 6.30am-7pm Mon-Sat; 7.15am-7pm Sun. *Terminal 4 Arrivals Hall* 6.15am-5pm Mon-Fri; 7.15am-4pm Sat, Sun.
Liverpool Street 7.15am-9pm Mon- Sat; 8.15am-8pm Sun.
Victoria 8am-7pm Mon-Sat; 8.45am-7pm Sun.

Travelcards

Bus and tube fares are based on a zone system. There are six zones stretching 12 miles (20 kilometres) out from the centre of London. For most visitors, the Travelcard (*see below*) is the cheapest way of getting around. Beware of on-the-spot £10 penalty fares for anyone caught without a ticket. Travelcards can be bought at stations, Travel Information Centres or newsagents that display the relevant sign.

One-Day LT Cards

One-Day LT Cards will only be of interest if you intend to travel before 9.30am on weekdays using zones 1-6 and make several journeys during the day. They're valid for travel throughout Greater London on tube, Tramlink and Docklands Light Railway services, but not on National Rail or on the Bakerloo line between Kenton and Harrow & Wealdstone. They are also valid for travel across the London bus network, but not on special bus services or excursions. A One-Day LT card costs £8 and £3.50 for children (5-15s), and is valid from midnight on the date of validity and for any journey that starts before 4.30am the following day.

Day Travelcards

Day Travelcards (peak) can be used from 00.01 Mondays to Fridays (except public holidays). They cost from £5.10 (£2.50 for children) for Zones 1 and 2, with prices rising to £10.70 (£5.30 children) for an all-zones card. If you need a zones 1-5 or 1-6 card and are not using National Rail services, it is cheaper to buy an LT Card. All tickets are valid for journeys before 4.30am the next day. Most people are happy with the off-peak day Travelcard, which allows you to start travelling from 9.30am. This costs from £4.30 for zones 1 and 2, rising to £5.60 for zones 1-6.

Family Travelcards

Anyone travelling with children can take advantage of this Travelcard. It offers unlimited travel for up to two adults and up to four children. During the week each adult pays £2.80, and each child 80p, in zones 1 and 2, rising to £3.90 per adult and 80p per child for zones 1-6. Each child in the Family Travelcard group travels free in all zones on weekends and bank holidays.

Weekend Travelcards

If you plan to spend a weekend charging around town you'd do well to buy a Weekend Travelcard, which offers unlimited travel for Saturday and Sunday for £6.40 (zones 1 & 2), rising to £8.40 for zones 1-6.

Oyster card

The Oyster card is a travel smart card, currently available to adult 7-day, Annual and Monthly Travelcard and Annual Bus Pass customers on the internet at www.oystercard.com, by telephone on 0870 849 9999 or at Tube station ticket offices. Oyster cards speed up passage through the ticket gates as they need only touch a special yellow card reader. Oyster cards can also be used on London buses, Docklands Light Railway, Tramlink and National Rail.

Children

On all buses, tubes and local trains, under-14s are classified as children; under-5s travel free. Children travelling with adult (7-day or longer) travelcard holders can have a travelcard for just £1. Children aged 5-10 or 11-15 who make regular journeys on public transport can travel at a reduced rate, or free (on London Buses and Tramlink) if they possess a child photocard, available from local travel ticket outlets or Travel Information Centres. Proof of ID and a photograph are required

Photocards

Photocards are required for adult 7-day Travelcards taking in zones 3-6 (zones 1 and 2 only travelcards do not require a photocard). Photocards can be obtained from any tube station, local travel ticket outlet or Travel Information Centre. Proof of ID and a photograph are required.

London Underground

Delays are common. Escalators are often out of action. Some lines close at weekends for engineering. It's hot and crowded in rush hour (8-9.30am and 4.30-7pm Mon-Fri). Still, the underground rail system, or tube, is still the quickest way to get around.

Using the system

Tube tickets can be purchased from a ticket office or from self-service machines. You can buy most tickets, including carnets and One-Day LT Cards, from self-service machines. Ticket offices in some stations close early (around 7.30pm), but it's best to keep change with you at all times: using a ticket machine is quicker than queuing at a ticket office.

To enter the tube, insert your ticket in the automatic checking gates with the black magnetic strip facing down, then pull it out of the top to open the gates. Exiting the system at your destination is done in much the same way, though if you have a single journey ticket, it will be retained by the gate as you leave. Oyster card (*see above*) holders touch their card on the yellow reader on top of the ticket gate.

There are 12 Underground lines, colour-coded on the tube map for ease of use. There's a full map of the London Underground on the back page of this book.

Underground timetable

Tube trains run daily from around 5.30am (except Sunday, when they start an hour or two later, depending on the line). The only exception is Christmas Day, when there is no service. Generally, you won't have to wait more than ten minutes for a train, and during peak times the service should run every two or three minutes. Times of last trains vary, though they're usually around 11.30pm-1am daily except Sunday, when they finish 30 minutes to an hour earlier. The only all-night public transport is by night bus (*see p359*).

Fares

The single Underground fare for adults within zone 1 is £2. For zones 1 and 2 it's £2.20. An all-zones single fare is £3.80.

The single Underground fare for children in zone 1 is 60p, or 80p for zones 1 and 2, rising to £1.50 for an all-zone ticket.

Carnet

If you're planning on making a lot of short-hop journeys within zone 1 over a period of several days, it makes sense to buy a carnet of ten tickets for £15 (£5 for children). Note that if you exit a station outside of zone 1 and are caught with only a carnet ticket, you'll be liable to a £10 penalty fare.

CAR HIRE

The simplest, smartest way around London

Hire a Smart car from **£8.99** a day

Why lease when you can **contract hire**?

Have your Smart ***delivered*** and ***collected***

Recommend a friend and receive a ***10% discount***

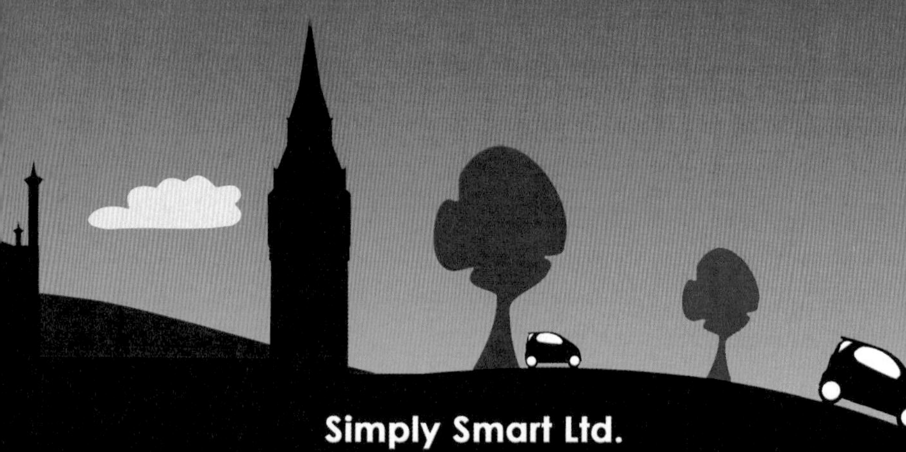

Simply Smart Ltd.

Tel: 020 7371 1444 Fax: 020 7371 4111

245 Warwick Rd, Kensington, London W14 8PX

Web: www.simply-smart.co.uk Email: sales@simply-smart.co.uk

Docklands Light Railway (DLR)

7363 9700/www.dlr.co.uk.
The DLR is administered as part of the tube system. Its driverless trains run on a raised track from Bank (Central or Waterloo & City lines) or Tower Gateway, close to Tower Hill tube (Circle and District lines), to Stratford, Beckton and down the Isle of Dogs to Island Gardens, then south of the river to Greenwich, Deptford and Lewisham. Trains run 5.30am-12.30am Monday to Saturday and 7.00am-11.30pm Sunday.

Fares

Docklands Shuttle South (Lewisham to Canary Wharf) tickets cost £2; Docklands Shuttle East (valid between Beckton/Stratford and Island Gardens via Westferry) tickets are £2.60; City Flyer South (valid between Bank and Lewisham) tickets are £3.60; and City Flyer East (valid between Beckton/Stratford and Bank) tickets are £4. Child tickets cost from 80p to £2.

The DLR also offers one-day 'Rail & River Rover' tickets that combine unlimited DLR travel with a riverboat trip between Greenwich, Tower and Westminster piers (boats run 10am-6pm; call City Cruises on 7740 0400 for exact round-trip times). Starting at Tower Gateway, trains leave on the hour (from 10am), with a DLR guide giving passengers the lowdown on the area as the train glides along. Tickets cost £8.80 for adults, £4.50 for kids and £23 for a family pass (two adults and up to three kids); under-5s travel free. Note that family tickets may only be purchased in person from the piers.

Buses

Improvements in the London bus network, the provision of more lanes and the introduction of the Congestion Charge (*see p360*) have made the bus a far more reliable, if still comparatively slow, option. Many buses in London now require you to pay before you board, either at dedicated machines at the bus stop, or at Travel Information Centres.

Fares

Single bus fares are £1 (40p children). A one-day bus pass for unlimited bus travel is £2.50 (£1 children). Children aged 5-10 in possession of a valid photocard travel free on buses.

Savers

Bus Saver tickets are the equivalent of the tube's carnet: a book of six tickets costs £4.20 (£2.10 children). Savers can be bought at newsagents displaying the relevant sign and at London Underground ticket offices.

Night buses

Night buses are the only form of public transport that runs all night, operating from 11pm to 6am about once an hour on most routes (more often on Fridays and Saturdays). Many pass through central London and the majority stop around Trafalgar Square, so head there if you're unsure which bus to get. Night buses have the letter 'N' before their number, and are free to holders of One-Day Travelcards, Weekend Travelcards, Family Travelcards and One-Day LT Cards. You'll find free maps and timetables at Travel Information Centres (*see p357*). Fares for night buses are the same as for day buses.

Green Line buses

Green Line buses (0870 608 7261/ www.greenline.co.uk) serve the suburbs and towns within a 40-mile (64km) radius of London. Their main departure point is Eccleston Bridge, SW1 (Colonnades Coach Station, behind Victoria).

Routes 205 & 705

Bus routes 205 and 705 (7222 1234) connect all the main London rail termini (except Charing Cross) on circular trips. These express services are convenient for the disabled, the elderly, people laden with luggage or those with small children. Bus 205 runs from Whitechapel station to Euston Square station via Aldgate, Aldgate East, Liverpool Street, Moorgate, Old Street, Angel, King's Cross, St Pancras and Euston. Starting at around 5am (6am on Sunday) to just after midnight every day, they run around every 10-15 minutes; check the timetable. Route 705 starts at Paddington around 7.50am (8.15am from Liverpool Street) and runs around every 30 minutes until 7.50pm (8.15pm from Liverpool Street), stopping at Victoria, Waterloo, London Bridge and Fenchurch Street.

Rail services

Independently run commuter services leave from the city's main rail stations (*see p338*). Travelcards are valid on these services within the right zones. Perhaps the most useful is **Silverlink** (0845 601 4867/ www.silverlink-trains.com; or National Rail Enquiries on 08457 484950), which runs from Richmond in the south-west to North Woolwich in the east, via London City Airport. Trains run about every 20 minutes daily except Sunday, when they run every half-hour.

Tramlink

Trams run between Beckenham, Croydon, Addington and Wimbledon in South London. Travelcards and bus passes taking in zones 3-6 can be used on trams; otherwise, cash single fares cost from 90p (40p children). A weekly Tram Pass costs £8 (zone 4) or £11 (zones 3 and 4).

Water transport

The times of London's assortment of river services vary, but most operate every 20 minutes to one hour between 10.30am and 5pm. Services may be more frequent and run later in summer. Journey times are longer than by tube, but it's a nicer way to travel. Call the operators listed below for schedules and fares, or see www.tfl.gov.uk. Travelcard holders can expect one-third off scheduled Riverboat fares.

Thames Clippers (www.thamesclippers.com) runs a fast, reliable, commuter boat service. Piers to board the Clippers from are: Savoy (near Embankment tube), Blackfriars, Bankside (for the Globe), London Bridge and St Katharine's (Tower Bridge).

The names in bold below are the names of piers.

Embankment–Tower (30mins)–**Greenwich** (30mins); Catamaran Cruises 7987 1185.

Greenland Dock–Canary Wharf (8mins)–**St Katharine's** (7mins)–**London Bridge City** (4mins)–**Bankside** (3mins)–**Blackfriars** (3mins)–**Savoy** (4mins); Collins River Enterprises 7977 6892.

Savoy–Cadogan (15-20mins)–**Chelsea** (2mins); Riverside Launches 07831 574774.

Westminster–(Thames) Barrier Gardens (1hr 30mins); Thames Cruises 7930 3373/www.thamescruises.com.
Westminster–Festival (5mins)–**London Bridge City** (20mins)–**St Katharine's** (5mins); Crown River 7936 2033/www.crownriver.com.
Westminster–Greenwich (1hr); Westminster Passenger Services 7930 4097/www.westminsterpier.co.uk.
Westminster–Kew (1hr 30mins)–**Richmond** (30mins)–**Hampton Court** (1hr 30mins); Westminster Passenger Service Association 7930 2062.
Westminster–Tower (25-30mins); City Cruises 7740 0400/www.citycruises.com.

Taxis

Black cabs

Licensed London taxis are known as black cabs – even though they now come in a variety of colours – and are a quintessential feature of London life. Drivers of black cabs must pass a test called the Knowledge to prove they know every street in central London and the shortest route to it.

If a taxi's yellow 'For Hire' sign is switched on, it can be hailed. If a taxi stops, the cabbie must take you to your destination, provided it's within seven miles. Expect to pay slightly higher rates after 8pm on weekdays and all weekend.

You can book black cabs in advance. Both **Radio Taxis** (7272 0272; credit cards only) and **Dial-a-Cab** (7253 5000) run 24-hour services for black cabs (there'll be a booking fee in addition to the regular fare). Enquiries or complaints about black cabs should be made to the Public Carriage Office. Note the badge number of the offending cab, which should be displayed in the rear of the cab as well as on its back bumper. For lost property, *see p368*.

Public Carriage Office
200 Baker Street, Marylebone, NW1 5RZ (7918 2000). Baker Street tube. **Open** *By phone* 9am-4pm Mon-Fri. *In person* 9am-2pm Mon-Fri.

Minicabs

Minicabs (saloon cars) are generally cheaper than black cabs, but be sure to use only licensed firms and avoid minicab drivers who tout for business on the street (common at Victoria Station, in Soho and outside many nightclubs). They'll be unlicensed and uninsured, almost certainly won't know how to get around, and charge extortionate fares.

There are, happily, plenty of trustworthy and licensed local minicab firms. Among Londonwide firms are **Lady Cabs** (7254 3501), which employs only women drivers (great for women travelling alone), and **Addison Lee** (7387 8888). Whoever you use, ask the price when you book and confirm it with the driver when the car arrives.

Driving

Congestion Charge

Every driver driving in central London – an area defined as within King's Cross (N), Old Street roundabout (NE), Aldgate (E), Old Kent Road (SE), Elephant & Castle (S), Vauxhall (SW), Hyde Park Corner (W) and Edgware Road tube (NW) – between 7am and 6.30pm Monday to Friday has to pay a £5 fee. Expect a fine of £80 if you fail to do so (reduced to £40 if you pay within 14 days). Passes can be bought from newsagents, garages and the like; the scheme is enforced by countless CCTV cameras. For more info call 0845 900 1234 or go to www.cclondon.com. See also the **Central London by Area** map, *pp392-3*.

Breakdown services

If you're a member of a motoring organisation in another country, check to see if it has a reciprocal agreement with a British organisation. Both the AA and the RAC offer schemes that cover Europe in addition to the UK.

AA (Automobile Association)
Information 08705 500600/breakdown 0800 887766/members 0800 444999/www.theaa.co.uk. **Open** 24hrs daily. **Membership** £43-£192/yr. **Credit** MC, V.

ETA (Environmental Transport Association) *68 High Street, Weybridge, Surrey KT13 8RS (01932 828882/www.eta.co.uk).* **Open** *Office* 8am-6pm Mon-Fri; 9am-4pm Sat. *Breakdown service* 24hrs daily. **Membership** £25/yr. **Credit** MC, V.

RAC (Royal Automobile Club)
RAC House, 1 Forest Road, Feltham, Middx TW13 7RR (breakdown 0800 828282/office & membership 08705 722722/www.rac.co.uk). **Open** *Office* 8am-8pm Mon-Fri; 8.30am-5pm Sat. *Breakdown service* 24hrs daily. **Membership** £39-£148. **Credit** AmEx, DC, MC, V.

Parking

Central London is scattered with parking meters, but finding a free one could take ages, and when you do it'll cost you up to £1 for every 15 minutes to park there, and you'll be limited to two hours on the meter. Parking on a single or double yellow line, a a red line or in residents' parking areas during the day is illegal, and you may end up being fined, clamped or towed.

However, in the evening (from 6pm or 7pm in much of central London) and at various times at weekends, parking on single yellow lines is legal and free. If you find a clear spot on a single yellow line during the evening, check a nearby sign before you leave your car: this sign should tell you at which times parking is legal; times vary from street to street. Meters also become free after a certain time in the evening and at various times on weekends: check before paying, as it could save you several quid. Parking on double yellow lines and red routes is, by and large, illegal at all times.

NCP 24-hour car parks (7499 7050/www.ncp.co.uk) in and around central London are numerous but expensive. Prices vary with location, but expect to pay £6-£10 for two hours. Among its central car parks are those at Arlington House, Arlington Street, St James's, W1; Upper Ground, Southwark, SE1; and 2 Lexington Street, Soho, W1.

A word of warning: almost all NCPs in central London are underground, and a few – such as the car park on Adeline Place behind Tottenham Court Road – are frequented by drug users looking for a quiet place in which to indulge. Take care.

Clamping

The immobilising of illegally parked vehicles by attaching a clamp to one wheel is commonplace in London. There will be a label attached to the car telling you which payment centre to phone or visit. You'll have to stump up an £80 clamp release fee and show a valid licence (there's a 50% discount on the fine if you pay within two weeks). If you can't show a valid licence, you'll have to pay a release fee of £120 for motorcycles and cars, £600 for any other vehicle.

Staff at the payment centre will promise to de-clamp your car some time within the next four hours, but they won't tell you exactly when. You are also warned that if you don't remove your car immediately, they might clamp it again. This means you may have to spend quite some time waiting by your car.

If you feel you've been clamped unfairly you can look for the appeals procedure and contact number on the back of your ticket for redress. If your appeal is turned down and you still wish to take matters further, call the Clamping and Vehicle Section (7747 4700), an independent governing body.

Vehicle removal

If your car has mysteriously disappeared, chances are that, if it was legally parked, it's been nicked; if not, it's probably been hoisted on to the back of a truck and taken to a car pound, and you're facing a stiff penalty: a fee of £160 is levied for removal, plus £15 per day from the first midnight after removal. To add insult to injury, you'll probably get a parking ticket of £40-£80 when you collect the car (there's a 50% discount if you pay within 14 days). To find out where your car has been taken and how to retrieve it, call the Trace Service hotline (7747 4747).

Vehicle hire

To hire a car, you must have at least one year's driving experience with a full current driving licence; in addition, many car hire firms refuse to hire vehicles out to people under the age of 23. If you're an overseas visitor, your current driving licence is valid in Britain for a year.

Prices vary wildly; always ring several competitors for a quote (see the Yellow Pages or www.yell.com). As well as the companies listed below Easycar's online-only service, at www.easycar.com, offers competitive rates, just so long as you don't mind driving a branded car around town.

Alamo *0870 400 4508/www.alamo.com.* **Open** 8am-7pm Mon-Fri; 8am-6pm Sat; 9am-4pm Sun. **Credit** AmEx, MC, V.
Avis *08705 900500/www.avis.co.uk.* **Open** 24hrs daily. **Credit** AmEx, DC, MC, V.
Budget *0800 181181/www.gobudget.com.* **Open** 8am-8pm daily. **Credit** AmEx, DC, MC, V.
Enterprise *01252 353620/www.enterprise.com.* **Open** 8am-6pm Mon-Fri; 8am-noon Sat. **Credit** AmEx, MC, V.
Europcar *0870 607 5000/www.europcar.co.uk.* **Open** 24hrs daily. **Credit** AmEx, DC, MC, V.
Hertz *0870 599 6699/www.hertz.co.uk.* **Open** 24hrs daily. **Credit** AmEx, MC, V.

Motorbike hire

HGB Motorcycles *69-71 Park Way, Ruislip Manor, Middx, HA4 8NS (01895 676451/www.hgbmotorcycles.co.uk). Ruislip Manor tube.* **Open** 9am-6pm Mon-Fri; 9am-4pm Sat. **Credit** MC, V.
Map p399 M3.
It costs £75 a day or £385 a week to hire an ST1100 Pan European. All rental prices include 250 miles (402km) a day, with excess mileage at 10p a mile, AA cover, insurance and VAT. Bikes can only be hired with a credit card and a deposit (£350-£850, depending on bike size). There's no crash helmet hire.

Cycling

The traffic being what it is, London is an unfriendly town for cyclists, but the London Cycle Network (7974 2016/www.londoncyclenetwork.org) or the London Cycling Campaign (*see below*) help make it better. A safety helmet, a filter-mask and a determined attitude are advisable.

London Cycling Campaign

Unit 228, 30 Great Guildford Street, South Bank, SE1 0HS (7928 7220/www.lcc.org.uk). **Open** *Phone enquiries* 10am-5pm Mon-Fri.
Individual membership (£27.50 a year) allows discounts at selected bike shops, advice and information on bike maintenance, insurance deals, route maps and a subscription to *London Cyclist* magazine.

Cycle hire

London Bicycle Tour Company

1A Gabriel's Wharf, 56 Upper Ground, South Bank, SE1 9PP (7928 6838/www.londonbicycle.com). Southwark tube, Blackfriars or Waterloo tube/rail. **Open** *Easter-Oct* 10am-6pm daily. *Nov-Easter* by appointment. **Hire** £2.50/hr; £12/1st day; £6/day thereafter. **Deposit** £100 (unless paying by credit card). **Credit** AmEx, DC, MC, V.
Map p404 N7.
Bike hire, rickshaw hire (which costs £12/hour, self-drive) and daily bicycle tours. *See also p68.*

Walking

The best way to see London is on foot. However, this sprawling city is extremely complicated in terms of its street layout – so much so, in fact, that even locals carry *A-Z* map books around with them most, if not all, of the time. This means that you should be prepared to get lost on at least a semi-regular basis.

We've included a selection of street maps covering central London in the back of this book (starting on *p394*), but we recommend that you also buy a separate map of the city: both the standard Geographers' *A–Z* and Collins' *London Street Atlas* versions come in a variety of sizes and are very easy to use.

Resources A-Z

Addresses

London addresses invariably come with a postcode attached. This helps indicate where the street is found, but also helps differentiate between streets with the same name in different parts of London.

A London postcode written in its most basic form takes a point of the compass – N, E, SE, SW, W and NW, plus EC (East Central) and WC (West Central) – and then a number; for example, N1, WC2, SE23. Those numbered 1 denote the area nearest the centre, then the numbers are, roughly, ordered alphabetically by area, so E1 is Whitechapel, then E2 is Bethnal Green, E3 is Bow, etc.

Age restrictions

You must be 17 or older to drive in the United Kingdom, and 18 to buy cigarettes or be served alcohol (to be safe, carry photo ID if you're under 22 years of age, or look as if you might be). For both hetero- and homosexuals, the age of consent in Britain is 16.

Business

Conventions & conferences

London Tourist Board & Convention Bureaux

7932 2020/www.londontown.com.
The LTB runs a venue enquiry service for conventions and exhibitions. Call or email for an information pack that lists the facilities offered by various venues.

Queen Elizabeth II Conference Centre

Broad Sanctuary, Westminster, SW1P 3EE (7222 5000/www.qeiicc.co.uk). St James's Park tube. **Open** 8am-6pm Mon-Fri. *Conference facilities* 24hrs daily. **Map** p401 K9.
This purpose-built centre has some of the best conference facilities in the capital. Rooms have capacities ranging from 40 to 1,100, all with wireless LAN technology installed.

Couriers & shippers

DHL and FedEx offer local and international courier services; Excess Baggage is the UK's largest shipper of luggage.

DHL *St Alphage House, 2 Fore Street, EC2Y 5DA (08701 100 300/www.dhl.co.uk). Moorgate tube.* **Open** 9am-6pm Mon-Fri. **Credit** AmEx, DC, MC, V. **Map** p401 L7.
Excess Baggage *168 Earl's Court Road, Earl's Court, SW5 9QQ (7373 1977/www.excess-baggage.com). Earl's Court tube.* **Open** 8am-6pm Mon-Fri; 9am-2pm Sat. **Credit** AmEx, MC, V. **Map** p396 B10.
FedEx *0800 123800/www.fedex.com.* **Open** 7.30am-7.30pm Mon-Fri. **Credit** AmEx, DC, MC, V.

Office hire & business centres

ABC rents office equipment, while British Monomarks offers communications services.

ABC Business Machines *59 Chiltern Street, Marylebone, W1U 6NF (7486 5634/www.abcbusiness.co.uk). Baker Street tube.* **Open** 9am-5.30pm Mon-Fri; 9.30am-12.30pm Sat. **Credit** MC, V. **Map** p398 G5.
British Monomarks *Monomarks House, 27 Old Gloucester Street, WC1N 3XX (7419 5000/www.britishmonomarks.co.uk). Holborn tube.* **Open** *Mail forwarding* 9.30am-5.30pm Mon-Fri. *Telephone answering* 9am-6pm Mon-Fri. **Credit** AmEx, MC, V. **Map** p399 L5.

Customs

The following guidelines exist for EU citizens on tobacco and alcohol they have bought tax paid that are for their own consumption. See www.hmce.gov.uk for more details.

- 3,200 cigarettes or 400 cigarillos or 200 cigars or 3 kilograms (6.6 pounds) of tobacco;
- 90 litres wine plus either 10 litres of spirits or liqueurs (more than 22% alcohol by volume) or 20 litres of fortified wine (under 22% abv), sparkling wine or other liqueurs.

Disabled

Many of the capital's sights make provision for wheelchair users, but transport can be a problem. For information on provision for the disabled on the tube, check out the *Access to the Underground* booklet, available free from ticket offices, or call the Travel and Information line 7222 1234).

Artsline

54 Chalton Street, Somers Town, NW1 1HS (tel/textphone 7388 2227/www.artsline.org.uk). Euston tube/rail. **Open** 9.30am-5.30pm Mon-Fri. **Map** p399 K3.
Information on disabled access to entertainment events in London is available from Artsline.

Can Be Done

11 Woodcock Hill, Harrow, HA1 2RZ (8907 2400/www.canbedone.co.uk). Kenton tube/rail. **Open** 9am-5.30pm Mon-Fri. **Map** p396 A9.
Disabled-adapted holidays and tours in London and around the UK are offered here.

DAIL (Disability Arts in London)

Diorama Arts Centre, 34 Osnaburgh Street, Fitzrovia, NW1 3ND (7916 6351/www.ldaf.net). Great Portland Street tube. **Enquiries** 11am-4pm Mon-Fri. **Map** p398 H4.
DAIL produces a monthly magazine with reviews and articles on the arts and the disabled (£10 per year, £30 for overseas subscribers). DAIL is part of **LDAF** (London Disability Arts Forum; 7916 5484), which organises events for disabled people in London.

Greater London Action on Disability

336 Brixton Road, Brixton, SW9 7AA (7346 5800/textphone 7326 4554/www.glad.org.uk). Brixton tube/rail. **Open** *Phone enquiries* 9am-5pm Mon-Fri.
A valuable source of information for disabled visitors and residents.

Holiday Care Service

0845 124 9971/www.holidaycare.org.uk. **Open** *Helpline* 9am-5pm Mon, Tue; 9am-1pm Wed-Fri.
An advisory service specialising in disabled holiday accommodation.

London Sports Forum for Disabled People

Ground floor, Leroy House, 436 Essex Road, Islington, N1 3QP (7354 8666/textphone 7354 9554/ www.londonsportsforum.org.uk). **Open** *Helpline* 9am-5pm Mon-Fri. LSF holds a database of contacts for a broad range of sports, and works with local authorities and individual sports centres to develop facilities for people of all ages with disabilities.

Royal Association for Disability & Rehabilitation

12 City Forum, 250 City Road, Islington, EC1V 2PU (7250 3222/ textphone 7250 4119/www. radar.org.uk). Old Street tube/rail. **Open** 9am-4pm Mon-Fri. **Map** p402 P3. A central organisation for disabled voluntary groups gives advice on almost any aspect of life and publishes the monthly newsletter *Bulletin*.

Wheelchair Travel & Access Mini Buses

1 Johnston Green, Guildford, Surrey GU2 9XS (01483 233640/ www.wheelchair-travel.co.uk). **Open** 9am-5.30pm Mon-Fri; 9am-noon Sat. Hires out converted vehicles, including adapted minibuses (with or without driver), plus cars with hand controls and 'Chairman' cars.

Electricity

The United Kingdom uses the standard European 220-240V, 50-cycle AC voltage. British plugs use three pins rather than the standard two, so travellers with appliances from mainland Europe should bring an adaptor, as should anyone using US appliances, which run off a 110-120V, 60-cycle.

Embassies & consulates

See also the Yellow Pages.

American Embassy *24 Grosvenor Square, Mayfair, W1A 1AE (7499 9000/www.usembassy.org.uk). Bond Street or Marble Arch tube.* **Open** 8.30am-5.30pm Mon-Fri. **Map** p400 G7.

Australian High Commission *Australia House, Strand, Holborn, WC2B 4LA (7379 4334/ www.australia.org.uk). Holborn or Temple tube.* **Open** 9.30am-3.30pm Mon-Fri. **Map** p401 M6.

Canadian High Commission *38 Grosvenor Street, Mayfair, W1K 4AA (7258 6600/www.canada. org.uk). Bond Street or Oxford Circus tube.* **Open** 8-4pm Mon-Fri. **Map** p400 H7.

Irish Embassy *17 Grosvenor Place, Belgravia, SW1X 7HR (7235 2171/passports & visas 7225 7700). Hyde Park Corner tube.* **Open** 9.30am-1pm, 2.30-5.30pm Mon-Fri. **Map** p400 G9.

New Zealand High Commission *New Zealand House, 80 Haymarket, St James's, SW1Y 4YQ (7930 8422/www.nzembassy.com). Piccadilly Circus tube.* **Open** 9am-5pm Mon-Fri. **Map** p401 K7.

South African High Commission *South Africa House, Trafalgar Square, St James's, WC2N 5DP (7451 7299/www.southafrica house.com). Charing Cross tube/rail.* **Open** 8.45am-12.45pm Mon-Fri. **Enquiries** 8.30am-5pm Mon-Fri. **Map** p401 K7.

Emergencies

In the event of a serious accident, fire or incident, call **999** – free from any phone, including payphones – and specify whether you require ambulance, fire service or police. For addresses of Accident & Emergency departments in central London hospitals, *see below*; for helplines, *see p366*; and for city police stations, *see p369*.

Gay & lesbian

For help and information, try either of these phone services.

London Friend *7837 3337.* **Open** 7.30-10pm daily.

London Lesbian & Gay Switchboard *7837 7324/www.queery.org.uk.* **Open** 24hrs daily.

Health

Free emergency medical treatment under the National Health Service (NHS) is available to the following:

- European Union nationals, plus those of Iceland, Norway and Liechtenstein. They are also entitled to specific treatment for a non-emergency condition on production of form E112 or E128.
- Nationals (on production of a passport) of Bulgaria, the Czech and Slovak Republics, Gibraltar, Hungary, Malta, New Zealand, Russia, former Soviet Union states (not Latvia, Lithuania and Estonia) and the former Yugoslavia.
- Residents, irrespective of nationality, of Anguilla, Australia, Barbados, British Virgin Islands, Channel Islands, Falkland Islands, Iceland, Isle of Man, Montserrat, Poland, Romania, St Helena, Sweden, Turks & Caicos Islands.
- Anyone who has been in the UK for the previous 12 months.
- Anyone who has come to the UK to take up permanent residence.
- Students and trainees whose courses require more than 12 weeks in employment during the first year. Others living in the UK for more than six months may also not have to pay.
- Refugees and others who have sought refuge in the UK.
- Anyone formally detained by the immigration authorities.
- People with HIV/AIDS at a special clinic for the treatment of sexually transmitted diseases. The treatment covered is limited to a diagnostic test and counselling associated with that test.

There are no NHS charges for the following services:

- Treatment in Accident & Emergency departments.
- Certain district nursing, midwifery or health visiting.
- Emergency ambulance transport to a hospital.
- Diagnosis and treatment of certain communicable diseases, including STDs.
- Family planning services.
- Compulsory psychiatric treatment.

Accident & emergency

Below are listed most of the central London hospitals that have 24-hour Accident and Emergency departments.

Charing Cross Hospital *Fulham Palace Road, Hammersmith, W6 8RF (8846 1234). Barons Court or Hammersmith tube.*

Chelsea & Westminster Hospital *369 Fulham Road, Chelsea, SW10 9NH (8746 8000). South Kensington tube.* **Map** p396 C12.

Guy's Hospital *St Thomas Street (entrance Snowsfields), Bankside, SE1 9RT (7955 5000). London Bridge tube/rail.* **Map** p404 P8.

Homerton Hosptial *Homerton Row, Homerton, E9 6SR (8510 5555). Homerton rail.*

Book online today at avis.co.uk

Renting with Avis couldn't be more convenient with locations at all major airports, stations and across central London.

AVIS
We try harder.

Avis recommends Vauxhall cars

Discover the history of the Knights Hospitallers

St. John's Gate

Come and celebrate our 500th anniversary
1504 - 2004

Open: Mon - Fri 10am - 5pm Sat 10am - 4pm
Tours: Tues-Fri & Sat 11am & 2.30pm

Museum of the Order of St. John
St. John's Lane, Clerkenwell EC1M 4DA
☎: 020 7324 4070
CHARITY NUMBER 1077265

LOKMA

OCAKBAŞI RESTAURANT · BBQ

628 Finchley Road
Golders Green
NW11 7RR

Tel: 020 8731 6866
Fax: 020 8731 7595

OPEN 7 DAYS A WEEK
11.30 AM - 12 MIDNIGHT

PRIVATE PARTIES
WELCOME UP TO 50 PEOPLE!

'A main course of lamb yoghurtlu beyti was nice and spicy, coming with a thick tomato-rich sauce'

'... the food was enjoyable and Lokma has the makings of a good local eaterie'

Time Out Eating & Drinking Guide 2004

Royal Free Hospital *Pond Street, Hampstead, NW3 2QG (7794 0500). Belsize Park tube/Hampstead Heath rail.*
Royal London Hospital *Whitechapel Road, Whitechapel, E1 1BB (7377 7000). Whitechapel tube.*
St Mary's Hospital *Praed Street, Paddington, W2 1NY (7886 6666). Paddington tube/rail.* **Map** p395 D5.
St Thomas's Hospital *Lambeth Palace Road, Lambeth, SE1 7EH (7928 9292). Westminster tube/Waterloo tube/rail.* **Map** p401 M9.
University College Hospital *Grafton Way, Fitzrovia, WC1E 3BG (7387 9300). Euston Square or Warren Street tube.* **Map** p398 J4.
Whittington Hospital *Highgate Hill, Archway, N19 5NF (7272 3070). Archway tube.*

Complementary medicine

British Homeopathic Association

0870 444 3950/ www.trust homeopathy.org. **Open** *Phone enquiries* 9am-5pm Mon-Fri.
The BHA will indicate your nearest homeopathic chemist and/or doctor.

Contraception & abortion

Family planning advice, contraceptive supplies and abortions are free to British citizens on the National Health Service. This also applies to EU residents and foreign nationals living in Britain. If you decide to go private, contact one of the organisations listed below. Phone the Contraception Helpline on 0845 310 1334 for your local **Family Planning Association**. The 'morning after' pill (£20), effective up to 72 hours after intercourse, is available over the counter.

British Pregnancy Advisory Service

08457 304030/www.bpas.org.
Callers are referred to their nearest clinic for treatment. Contraceptives are available, as is pregnancy testing.

Brook Advisory Centre

Headquarters: 421 Highgate Studios, 53-79 Highgate Road, Kentish Town, NW5 1TL (7284 6040/ helpline 0800 018 5023/ www.brook.org.uk). **Open** *Helpline* 9am-5pm Mon-Fri. **Map** p399 K2.
Advice and referrals on sexual health, contraception and abortion, plus free pregnancy tests for under-25s. Call for your nearest clinic.

Marie Stopes House

Family Planning Clinic/Well Woman Centre *108 Whitfield Street, Fitzrovia, W1P 6BE (family planning clinic 7388 0662/ terminations 0845 300 8090/ www.mariestopes.org.uk). Warren Street tube.* **Open** *Clinic* 9am-5pm Mon-Fri. *Termination helpline* 7am-10pm Mon-Fri. **Map** p398 J5.
For contraceptive advice, emergency contraception, pregnancy testing, unplanned pregnancy counselling, an abortion service, cervical and health screening or gynaecological services.

Travel advice

For up-to-date information on travel to a specific country – including the latest news on safety and security, health issues, local laws and customs – contact your home country government's department of foreign affairs. Most have websites packed with useful advice for would-be travellers.

Australia
www.dfat.gov.au/travel

Canada
www.voyage.gc.ca

New Zealand
www.mft.govt.nz/travel

Republic of Ireland
www.irlgov.ie/iveagh

UK
www.fco.gov.uk/travel

USA
http://travel.state.gov

Dentists

Dental care is free for resident students, under-18s and people on benefits. All other patients must pay. NHS charges start from around £14 for a check-up. To find an NHS dentist, get in touch with the local Health Authority or a Citizens' Advice Bureau (*see p366*), or the following:

Dental Emergency Care Service

Guy's Hospital, St Thomas Street, Bankside, SE1 9RT (7955 2186). **Open** 9am-3pm Mon-Fri (try to arrive before 1.30pm).
The DECS refers callers to a surgery open for treatment (private or NHS).

Doctors

If you're a British citizen or working in the United Kingdom, you can go to any general practitioner (GP). If you're not visiting your usual GP, you'll be asked for details of the doctor with whom you are registered, in order that your records can be updated. People ordinarily resident in the UK, including overseas students, are also permitted to register with an NHS doctor.

Great Chapel Street Medical Centre

13 Great Chapel Street, Soho, W1F 8FL (7437 9360). Leicester Square, Oxford Circus or Tottenham Court Road tube. **Open** *Drop in appointments* 11am-12.30pm, 2-4pm Mon, Tue, Thur; 2-4pm Wed, Fri. **Map** p399 K6.
A walk-in NHS surgery for anyone without a doctor. Phone first, as it operates different clinics each day.

Hospitals

For a list of hospitals with A&E departments, *see p363*; for other hospitals, see the Yellow Pages.

Pharmacies

Most keep shop hours (9am-6pm; closed Sun). For late-night pharmacies, *see p252*.

Prescriptions

In the UK, most drugs are only available on prescription. A pharmacist will dispense medicines on receipt of a prescription from a GP. NHS prescriptions cost £6.30, but under-16s and over-60s are exempt, and contraception is free for all. If you're not eligible to see an NHS doctor, you'll be charged cost price for medicines prescribed by a private doctor. Pharmacists, who must be qualified, can advise on the appropriate treatment for minor ailments.

STDs, HIV & AIDS

NHS Genito-Urinary Clinics (such as the Centre for Sexual Health; *see below*) are affiliated to major hospitals. They provide free, confidential treatment of STDs and other problems, such as thrush and cystitis; offer counselling about HIV and other STDs; and can conduct blood tests to determine HIV status.

The 24-hour **Sexual Healthline** (0800 567123/ textphone 0800521361/ www.playingsafely.co.uk) is free and confidential. For other helplines, *see below*; for abortion and contraception services, *see p365*.

Ambrose King Centre

Royal London Hospital, Whitechapel Road, Whitechapel, E1 1BB (7377 7306). Whitechapel tube. **Open** 9.30am-4pm Mon, Tue; noon-4pm Wed, Thur; 9.30am-noon Fri.
The centre provides a specific gay health clinic, East One, Thursday 6.30-8.30pm, by appointment only – call 7377 7313.

Centre for Sexual Health

Genito-Urinary Clinic, Jefferiss Wing, St Mary's Hospital, Praed Street, Paddington, W2 1NY (7886 1697). Paddington tube/rail. **Open** *Walk-in clinic* 8.45am-6.15pm Mon, Tue, Thur; 11.45am-6.15pm Wed; 8.45am-1.15pm Fri. **Map** p395 D5.
A free and confidential walk-in clinic. New patients must arrive at least 30mins before closing.

Mortimer Market Centre for Sexual Health

Mortimer Market Centre, Mortimer Market, off Capper Street, Bloomsbury, WC1E 6JD (appointments 7530 5050). Goodge Street or Warren Street tube. **Open** 9am-6pm Mon, Tue, Thur; 1-7pm Wed; 9am-2.45pm Fri. **Map** p398 J4.
A clinic for gay and bisexual men and women under 26. There are walk-in clinics for women (Mon 3.45-6pm) and men (Thur 7-9pm), but make an appointment if you can.

Terrence Higgins Trust Lighthouse

52-4 Gray's Inn Road, Holborn, WC1X 8JU (office 78310330/ helpline 0845 122 1200/www.tht.org.uk). Chancery Lane tube. **Open** *Office* 9.30am-5.30pm Mon-Fri. *Helpline* 10am-10pm Mon-Fri; noon-6pm Sat, Sun.
This charity advises and counsels those with HIV/AIDS, their relatives, lovers and friends. It also offers free leaflets about AIDS and safer sex.

Helplines

See also above **STDs, HIV & AIDS**.

Citizens' Advice Bureaux

The council-run CABs offer free legal, financial and personal advice. Check the phone book for your nearest.

NHS Direct

0845 4647/www.nhsdirect.nhs.uk. **Open** 24hrs daily.
NHS Direct is a first-stop service for medical advice on all subjects.

National Missing Persons Helpline

0500 700 700/ www.missingpersons.org. **Open** 24hrs daily.
The volunteer-run NMPH publicises information on anyone reported missing, helping to find missing persons through a network of contacts. It can artificially age photographs and its 'Message Home' freephone service (0800 700 740) allows runaways to reassure friends or family of their wellbeing without revealing their whereabouts.

Rape & Sexual Abuse Support Centre

8683 3300. **Open** noon-2.30pm, 7-9.30pm Mon-Fri; 2.30-5pm Sat, Sun.
Provides support and information for victims and families.

Rights of Women

7251 6577. **Open** *Helpline* 2-4pm, 7-9pm Tue-Thur; noon-2pm Fri.
Legal advice for women.

Samaritans

08457 909090/www.samaritans.org.uk. **Open** 24hrs daily.
The Samaritans listen to anyone with emotional problems. It's a popular service, so persevere when phoning.

Victim Support

National Office, Cranmer House, 39 Brixton Road, Brixton, SW9 6DZ (0845 303 0900/www.victimsupport.com). **Open** *Support line* 9am-9pm Mon-Fri; 9am-7pm Sat, Sun.
Victims of crime are put in touch with a volunteer who provides emotional and practical support, including information and advice on legal procedures. Interpreters can be arranged where necessary.

Insurance

Insuring personal belongings is highly advisable. It's difficult to arrange once you've arrived in London, so do so before you leave.

Medical insurance is often included in travel insurance packages. Unless your country has a reciprocal medical treatment arrangement with Britain (*see p363*), it's very important to check that you do have adequate health cover.

Internet

Many hotels in London now have modem points in each room; those that don't sometimes offer surfing facilities elsewhere. There are also a huge number of cybercafés around town, of which the biggest are in the **easyEverything** chain.

There are now a great many ISPs that do not charge a subscription fee, only billing for calls. If you do want to get set up online over here, check one of the UK's many internet publications for details on current deals when you arrive; the best one for this is *Internet* magazine.

For the best London websites, *see p376*.

Internet access

Café Internet *22-4 Buckingham Palace Road, Belgravia, SW1 (7233 5786). Victoria tube/rail.* **Open** 8am-10pm Mon-Fri; 10am-8pm Sat; noon-8pm Sun. **Net access** £2/hr; after 8pm £1/hr. **Terminals** 22. **Map** p400 H10.
Cybergate *3 Leigh Street, Bloomsbury, WC1H 9EW (7387 3210/www.c-gate.com). Russell Square tube.* **Open** 9am-9pm Mon-Sat; noon-8pm Sun. **Net access** £1/30mins. **Terminals** 24. **Map** p399 L3.
easyInternetcafé *160-66 Kensington High Street, W8 7RG (www.easyeverything.com). High Street Kensington tube.* **Open** 7.30am-11.30pm daily. **Net access** from 50p. **Terminals** 394. **Map** p396 B9.
Other locations: throughout the city.

Left luggage

Airports

Call the following numbers for details on left luggage.

Gatwick Airport *South Terminal 01293 502014/North Terminal 01293 502013.*
Heathrow Airport *Terminal 1 8745 5301/Terminals 2-3 8745 4599/Terminal 4 8897 6874.*
London City Airport *7646 0162.*
Stansted Airport *01279 663213.*

Rail & bus stations

The threat of terrorism has meant that London stations tend to have left-luggage desks rather than lockers; to find out whether a train station offers this facility, call 08457 484950.

Legal help

Those in difficulties can visit a Citizens' Advice Bureau (*see p366*) or contact the groups below. Try the Legal Services Commission (7759 0000/www.legalservices.gov.uk) for info.

Community Legal Services Directory

0845 608 1122/www.justask.org.uk. **Open** 9am-5.30pm daily.
This free telephone service guides those with legal problems to government agencies and law firms that may be able to help.

Joint Council for the Welfare of Immigrants

115 Old Street, Hoxton, EC1V 9RT (7251 8706). Old Street tube/rail. **Open** *Phone enquiries* 2-5pm Tue, Thur.
JCWI's telephone-only legal advice line offers guidance and referrals.

Law Centres Federation

Duchess House, 18-19 Warren Street, Fitzrovia, W1T 5LR (7387 8570/www.lawcentres.org.uk). Warren Street tube/rail. **Open** *Phone enquiries* 10am-6pm Mon-Fri.
Free legal help for people who can't afford a lawyer. Local centres only offer advice to those living or working in their immediate area; this central office connects you with the nearest.

Release

388 Old Street, Hoxton, EC1V 9LT (77299904). Old Street tube/rail. **Open** 10am-5pm Mon-Fri.
Legal advice and counselling for those with drug problems.

Libraries

Unless you're a London resident, you won't be able to join a lending library. Only the exhibition areas of the British Library are open to non-members: the other libraries listed can be used for reference.

Barbican Library *Barbican Centre, Silk Street, EC2 (7638 0569/www.cityoflondon.gov.uk/libraries). Barbican tube/Moorgate tube/rail.* **Open** 9.30am-5.30pm Mon, Wed, Thur; 9.30am-7.30pm Tue; 9.30am-2pm Fri; 9.30am-4pm Sat. **Map** p402 P5.
British Library *96 Euston Road, Somers Town, NW1 2DB (7412 7000/www.bl.uk). King's Cross tube/rail.* **Open** 9.30am-6pm Mon, Wed-Fri; 9.30am-8pm Tue; 9.30am-5pm Sat; 11am-5pm Sun. **Map** p399 K3.
Holborn Library *32-8 Theobald's Road, Bloomsbury, WC1X 8PA (7974 6345). Chancery Lane tube.* **Open** 10am-7pm Mon, Thur; 10am-6pm Tue, Fri; 10am-5pm Sat. **Map** p399 M5.
Kensington Central Library *12 Philimore Walk, Kensington, W8 7RX (7937 2542). High Street Kensington tube.* **Open** 9.30am-8pm Mon, Tue, Thur; 9.30am-5pm Wed, Fri, Sat. **Map** p396 A9.
Marylebone Library *109-17 Marylebone Road, NW1 (7641 1041/www.westminster.gov.uk/libraries). Baker Street tube/Marylebone tube/rail.* **Open** 9.30am-8pm Mon, Tue, Thur, Fri 9.30am-8pm; 10am-8pm Wed; 9.30am-5pm Sat; 1.30-5pm Sun. **Map** p395 F4/5.
Victoria Library *160 Buckingham Palace Road, Belgravia, SW1W 9UD (7641 4287). Victoria tube/rail.* **Open** 9.30am-7pm Mon, Tue, Thur, 10am-7pm Wed; 9.30am-8pm Fri; 9.30am-5pm Sat. *Music library* 11am-7pm Mon-Fri; 10am-5pm Sat. **Map** p400 H10.
Westminster Reference Library *35 St Martin's Street, Westminster, WC2H 7HP (7641 4636). Leicester Square tube.* **Open** 10am-8pm Mon-Fri; 10am-5pm Sat. **Map** p401 K7.

Lost property

Always inform the police if you lose anything, if only to validate insurance claims. *See p369* or the Yellow Pages for your nearest police station. Only dial 999 if violence has occurred. Report lost passports both to the police and to your embassy (*see p363*).

Airports

For property lost on the plane, contact the relevant airline or handling agents; for items lost in a particular airport, contact the following:

Gatwick Airport *01293 503162.*
Heathrow Airport *8745 7727.*
London City Airport *7646 0000.*
Luton Airport *01582 395219.*
Stansted Airport *01279 663293.*

Public transport

If you've lost property in an overground station or on a train, call 08700 005151; an operator will connect you to the appropriate station. For any property lost on the underground or on a bus, *see below*.

Transport For London

Lost Property Office, 200 Baker Street, Marylebone, NW1 5RZ (7918 2000/fax 7918 1028). Baker Street tube. **Open** 9am-2pm Mon-Fri. **Map** p398 G4.
Allow three working days from the time of loss. If you lose something on a bus, call 7222 1234 and ask for the phone numbers of the depots at either end of the route. If you lose something on a tube, pick up a lost property form from any station.

Taxis

Taxi Lost Property

200 Baker Street, Marylebone, NW1 5RZ (7918 2000). Baker Street tube. **Open** 9am-2pm Mon-Fri. *Phone enquiries* 9am-4pm Mon-Fri. **Map** p398 G4.
This office deals only with property found in registered black cabs. For items lost in a minicab, contact the office from which you hired the cab.

Media

Magazines

Loaded, *FHM* and *Maxim* are big men's titles, while women haven taken to handbag-sized *Glamour*, alongside *Vogue*, *Marie Claire* and *Elle*. Celebrity magazines like *Heat* do well, and style mags like *i-D* and *Dazed and Confused* have found a profitable niche.

The *Spectator*, the *New Statesman*, *Prospect* and the *Economist* are about as good as it gets at the serious end of the market, while the satirical fortnightly *Private Eye* adds a little levity. It helps if you buy the *Big Issue*, sold on the streets by homeless people.

Newspapers

For newspapers, at the serious end of the scale is the broadsheet. The right-wing *Daily Telegraph* and *The Times* (which is best for sport) are balanced by the *Independent* (which now also comes in handy tabloid size) and the *Guardian* (best for arts). All have bulging Sunday equivalents bar the *Guardian*, which has a sister Sunday paper, the *Observer*. The pink *Financial Times* (daily except Sunday) is the best for business facts and figures. In the middle of the market, the leader is the right-wing *Daily Mail* (and *Mail on Sunday*); its rival, the *Daily Express* (and *Sunday Express*), tries to compete.

The most popular kind of newspaper is still the tabloid, with the *Sun* (and Sunday's *News of the World*) the undisputed leader. The *Daily Star* and *Mirror* are the main lowbrow contenders. The *People*, the *Sunday Mirror* and a new Sunday *Star* provide weekend sleaze.

London's main daily paper is the dull, right-wing *Evening Standard*, which comes out in several editions during the day (Mon-Fri). The free morning paper *Metro* is picked up and discarded at tube stations.

Radio

BBC Radio 1 *98.8 FM.* Youth-oriented pop, indie, metal and dance.
BBC Radio 2 *89.1 FM.* Still bland during the day, but good after dark.
BBC Radio 3 *91.3 FM.* Classical music dominates, but there's also discussion, world music and other arts (try Andy Kershaw, 10.15-11.30pm Fri, or Late Junction, 10.15pm-midnight Mon-Thur).
BBC Radio 4 *93.5 FM, 198 LW.* The BBC's main speech station. Today (6-9am Mon-Fri) bristles with self-importance.
BBC Radio 5 Live *693, 909 AM.* Rolling news and sport. Avoid the phone-ins, but Up All Night (1-5am nightly) is terrific.
BBC London *94.9 FM.* A shadow of its former (GLR) self, but Robert Elms (noon-3pm Mon-Fri) is ok.
BBC World Service *648 AM.* A distillation of the best of all the other BBC stations; transmitted worldwide.
Capital FM *95.8 FM.* London's best-known station .
Classic FM *100.9 FM.* Easy-listening classical.
Heart FM *106.2 FM.* Capital for grown-ups.
Jazz FM *102.2 FM.* Smooth jazz (aka elevator music) now dominates.
LBC *1152 AM.* Phone-ins and features. The cabbies' favourite.
Liberty *963 & 972 AM.* Cheesy hits from the '70s and '80s.

Television

The next generation of TV in the UK is here, in the form of Sky Digital, ONdigital and various other digital cable TV companies, so the non-network sector is now crammed with stations on a variety of formats (satellite and cable, as well as digital). We've listed the pick of the channels.

Network channels

BBC1 The Corporation's mass-market station. There's a smattering of soaps and game shows, and the odd quality programme. Daytime programming isn't great. As with all BBC radio and TV stations, there are no commercials.
BBC2 In general, BBC2 offers a reasonably intelligent cultural cross-section and plenty of documentaries.
ITV1 Carlton provides weekday monotonous, mass-appeal shows, with oft-repeated successes for ITV. LWT (London Weekend Television) takes over at the weekend with more of the same. ITV2 is on digital.
Channel 4 C4's output includes a variety of extremely successful US imports (*Friends, ER, The Sopranos* and so on), but it still comes up with some gems, particularly films.
Five Plenty of sex, US TV movies, a lot of rubbish comedy US sport and the occasional good documentary.

Satellite, digital & cable channels

BBC3 *EastEnders* reruns and other light fare.
BBC4 Highbrow stuff, including earnest documentaries and dramas.
BBC News 24 The Beeb's rolling news network.
Bravo B-movies and cult TV.
CNN News and current affairs.
Discovery Channel Science and nature documentaries.
FilmFour Channel 4's movie outlet.
History Channel Self-explanatory.
MTV Rock/pop channel that borrows from its US counterpart.
Performance Dance, theatre and opera, plus interviews with the stars.
Sky News Rolling news.
Sky One Sky's version of ITV.
Sky Sports Sports. There are also Sky Sports 2 and Sky Sports 3.

Money

Britain's currency is the pound sterling (£). One pound equals 100 pence (p). Coins are copper (1p, 2p), silver (round: 5p, 10p; seven-sided: 20p, 50p), yellowy-gold (£1) or silver in the centre with a yellowy-gold edge (£2). Paper notes are blue (£5), orange (£10), purple (£20) or red (£50). You can exchange foreign currency at banks, bureaux de change and post offices, where there's no commission charge. If you want to open a bank or building society account, you'll need a passport and probably a reference from your home bank.

Western Union

0800 833833/www.westernunion.com. The old standby for bailing cash-challenged travellers out of trouble. Beware: it's pricey.

ATMs

Other than inside and outside banks themselves, cash machines can be found in some supermarkets, in certain shops, and in larger tube and rail stations. The vast majority accept withdrawals on major credit cards, and most also allow withdrawals using the Maestro/Cirrus debit system.

Banks

Minimum banking hours are 9.30am to 3.30pm Monday to Friday, but most branches close at 4.30pm (some stay open until 5pm). Exchange and commission rates on currency vary hugely, so it pays to shop around. Commission is sometimes charged for cashing travellers' cheques in foreign currencies, but not for sterling travellers' cheques, provided you cash the cheques at a bank affiliated to the issuing bank (get a list when you buy your cheques); it's also charged if you change cash into another currency. You always need ID, such as a passport, to exchange travellers' cheques.

Bureaux de change

You'll be charged for cashing travellers' cheques or buying and selling foreign currency at a bureau de change. Commission rates, which should be clearly displayed, vary. **Chequepoint**, **Lenlyn**, **Travelex** and **Thomas Cook** have branches all over town. Major rail and tube stations in central London have bureaux, and there are many in tourist areas and on the city's best-known shopping streets. Most are open 8am-10pm, but Chequepoint opens 24 hours daily.

Chequepoint *548-50 Oxford Street, Marylebone, W1N 9HJ (0800 699799). Marble Arch tube.* **Open** 24hrs daily. **Map** p398 G6.
Other locations: throughout the city.

Garden Bureau
30A Jubilee Market Hall, Covent Garden, WC2 8BE (7240 9921). Covent Garden tube. **Open** 9.30am-6pm daily.
This independent bureau has decent rates and was recently voted the best in London in a *Times* survey.

Credit cards

Many places now accept credit cards. Visa and Mastercard are the most widely accepted, American Express and Diners Club less so.

Report **lost/stolen credit cards** immediately to both the police and the 24-hour services below, and inform your bank by phone and in writing.

American Express *01273 696933.*
Diners Club *01252 513500.*
JCB *7499 3000.*
MasterCard/Eurocard *0800 964767.*
Switch *08706 000459.*
Visa/Connect *0800 895082.*

Tax

With the exception of food, books, newspapers, children's clothing and a few other choice items, UK purchases are subject to VAT – Value Added Tax, aka sales tax – of 17.5 per cent. Unlike in the US, this is included in prices quoted in shops (a price tag of £10 does *not* mean you pay £11.75). In hotels, always check that the room rate quoted includes tax.

Opening hours

The following are general guidelines: actual hours can vary in all cases. Times for specific establishments appear in the main listings, and opening hours on public holidays can be erratic.

Banks 9am-4.30pm (some close at 3.30pm) Mon-Fri.
Bars 11am-11pm Mon-Sat; noon-10.30pm Sun.
Businesses 9am-5pm Mon-Fri.
Post offices 9am-5.30pm Mon-Fri; 9am-noon Sat.
Shops 10am-6pm Mon-Sat.

Police stations

The police are a good source of information about the locality and are used to helping visitors. If you've been robbed, assaulted or involved in an infringement of the law, go to your nearest police station. (We've listed a handful in central London; look under 'Police' in the phone book or call Directory Enquiries on 118 118/500/888 for more). If you have a complaint, ensure that you take the offending police officer's identifying number (it should be displayed on his or her epaulette). You can then register a complaint with the **Police Complaints Authority** (10 Great George Street, SW1P 3AE, 7273 6450), contact any police station or visit a solicitor or Law Centre.

Belgravia Police Station *202-206 Buckingham Palace Road, Pimlico, SW1W 9SX (7730 1212). Victoria tube/rail.* **Map** p400 H10.
Charing Cross Police Station *Agar Street, Covent Garden, WC2N 4JP (7240 1212). Charing Cross tube/rail.* **Map** p401 L7.
Chelsea Police Station *2 Lucan Place, Chelsea, SW3 3PB (7589 1212). Sloane Square tube.* **Map** p397 E10.
Islington Police Station *2 Tolpuddle Street, Islington, N1 0YY (7704 1212). Angel tube.* **Map** p402 N2.
Kensington Police Station *72-4 Earl's Court Road, Kensington, W8 6EQ (7376 1212). High Street Kensington tube.* **Map** p396 B11.
King's Cross Police Station *76 King's Cross Road, King's Cross, WC1X 9QG (7713 1212). King's Cross tube/rail.* **Map** p399 M3.
Marylebone Police Station *1-9 Seymour Street, Marylebone, W1H 7BA (7486 1212). Baker Street tube/Marylebone tube/rail.* **Map** p395 F6.
Paddington Green Police Station *2-4 Harrow Road, Paddington, W2 1XJ (7402 1212). Edgware Road tube.* **Map** p396 E5.
West End Central Police Station *27 Savile Row, Mayfair, W1X 2DU (7437 1212). Piccadilly Circus tube.* **Map** p400 J7.

Postal services

You can buy stamps at all post offices and many newsagents. Current prices are 28p for first-class letters and 20p for second-class letters and 38p for letters to EU countries. Postcards cost 38p to send within Europe and 42p to countries outside Europe. Rates for other letters and parcels vary with weight and destination.

Post offices

Post offices are usually open 9am-5.30pm Monday-Friday and 9am-noon Saturday, with the exception of **Trafalgar Square Post Office** (24-8 William IV Street, WC2N 4DL; 08457 223344, Charing Cross tube/rail), which is open 8.30am-6.30pm Monday-Friday and 9am-5.30pm Saturday. The busiest time of day is usually 1-2pm. Listed below are the other main central London offices. For general post office enquiries, call the central information line on 08457 223344 or consult www.postoffice.co.uk.

43-4 Albemarle Street *Mayfair, W1S 4DS (08456 223344). Green Park tube.* **Map** p400 J7.
111 Baker Street *Marylebone, W1M 1FE (08456 223344). Baker Street tube.* **Map** p398 G5.
54 Great Portland Street, *Fitzrovia, W1N 5AH (08456 223344). Great Portland Street tube.* **Map** p398 H4.
1-5 Poland Street *Soho, W1F 8AA (08456 223344). Oxford Circus tube.* **Map** p398 J6.

Poste restante

If you want to receive mail while you are away, you can have it sent to Trafalgar Square Post Office, where it will be kept at the enquiry desk for a month. Your name and 'Poste Restante' must be clearly marked on the letter, followed by the address given above. You'll need ID to collect it.

Religion

Anglican

St Paul's Cathedral *For listings details, see p89.* **Services** 7.30am, 8am, 12.30pm, 5pm Mon-Fri; 8am, 8.30am, 12.30pm, 5pm Sat; 8am, 10.15am, 11.30am, 3.15pm, 6pm Sun. **Map** p404 O6.
Times may vary; phone to check.
Westminster Abbey *For listings details, see p134.* **Services** 7.30am, 8am, 12.30pm, 5pm Mon-Fri; 8am, 9am, 12.30pm, 3pm Sat; 8am, 10am, 11.15am, 3pm, 5.45pm Sun. **Map** p401 K9.

Baptist

Bloomsbury Central Baptist Church *235 Shaftesbury Avenue, Covent Garden, WC2H 8EP (7240 0544/www.bloomsbury.org.uk). Tottenham Court Road tube.* **Open** 10am-4pm Mon-Fri; 10am-8.30pm Sun. *Friendship Centre* noon-2.30pm Tue; 10.30am-8.30pm Sun. **Services & meetings** phone ahead. **Map** p399 L6.

Buddhist

Buddhapadipa Thai Temple *14 Calonne Road, Wimbledon, SW19 5HJ (8946 1357/www.buddhapadipa.org). Wimbledon tube/rail then 93 bus.* **Open** *Temple* 1-6pm Sat, Sun. *Meditation retreat* 7-9pm Tue, Thur; 4-6pm Sat, Sun.

Catholic

London Oratory *For listings, see p139.* **Services** 7am, 8am (Latin mass), 10am, 12.30am, 6pm Mon-Fri; 7am, 8.30am, 10am, 6pm Sat; 7am, 8.30am, 10am (tridentine), 11am (sung Latin), 12.30pm, 3.30pm, 4.30pm, 7pm Sun. **Map** p397 E10.
Westminster Cathedral *For listings, see p135.* **Services** 7am, 8am, 9am, 10.30am, 12.30pm, 5pm Mon-Fri; 8am, 9am, 12.30pm, 6pm Sat; 7am, 8am, 9am, 10.30am, noon, 5.30pm, 7pm Sun. **Map** p400 J10.

Hindu

Swaminarayan Hindu Mission *105-19 Brentfield Road, Church End, NW10 8JP (8961 5031/www.swaminarayan.org). Neasden tube/Harlesden tube/rail.* **Open** 9am-6.30pm daily. **Services** 7.15am, 11.45am, 7pm daily. *See also p188.*

Islamic

London Central Mosque *146 Park Road, St John's Wood, NW8 7RG (7724 3363). Baker Street tube/74 bus.* **Open** dawn-dusk daily. **Services** 5.30am, 1pm, 4pm, 7pm, 8.30pm daily.
East London Mosque *82-92 Whitechapel Road, E1 1JQ (7247 1357/www.eastlondonmosque.co.uk). Aldgate East or Whitechapel tube.* **Open** 10am-10pm daily. **Services** *Friday prayer* 1.30pm (1.15pm in winter). **Map** p405 S6.

Jewish

Liberal Jewish Synagogue *28 St John's Wood Road, St John's Wood, NW8 7HA (7286 5181/www.ljs.org). St John's Wood tube.* **Open** 9am-5pm Mon-Thur; 9am-1pm Fri. **Services** 6.45pm Fri; 11am Sat.
West Central Liberal Synagogue *21 Maple Street, Fitzrovia, W1T 4BE (7636 7627/www.wcls.org.uk). Warren Street tube.* **Services** 3pm Sat. **Map** p398 J4.

Methodist

Methodist Central Hall *Westminster Central Hall, Storey's Gate, Westminster, SW1H 9NH (7222 8010/www.wch.co.uk). St James's Park tube.* **Open** *Chapel* 9am-6pm daily. **Services** 12.45pm Wed; 11am, 6.30pm Sun. **Map** p401 K9.

Quaker

Religious Society of Friends (Quakers) *Friends House, 173-7 Euston Road, Bloomsbury, NW1 2BJ (7663 1000/www.quaker.org.uk). Euston tube/rail.* **Open** 8.30am-9.30pm Mon-Fri; 8.30am-4.30pm Sat. **Meetings** 11am Sun. **Map** p399 K3.

Sikh

Sri Guru Singh Sabha Southall *Havelock Road, Southall, Mddx UB2 4NP (8574 8901/www.sgsss.org).* **Open** 3am-9pm daily. *See also p188.*

Safety & security

Use common sense and follow these basic rules.

- **Keep** wallets and purses out of sight, and handbags securely closed.
- **Don't** leave briefcases, bags or coats unattended.
- **Don't** leave bags or coats beside, under or on the back of a chair.
- **Don't** put bags on the floor near the door of a public toilet.
- **Don't** take short cuts through dark alleys and car parks.
- **Don't** keep your passport, money, credit cards, etc, together.
- **Don't** carry a wallet in your back pocket.

Smoking

Smoking is permitted in almost all pubs and bars – though an increasing number have non-smoking areas – and in most restaurants, but specify when

Directory

you book that you'd like a table in the smoking section. Smoking is forbidden in shops and on public transport.

Study

Being a student in London is as expensive as it is exciting; *Time Out*'s *Student Guide*, available from September each year, provides the lowdown on London and how to survive it. In this guide, entry prices for students are usually designated 'concessions'. You'll have to show ID (an NUS or ISIC card) to get these rates. Students, whether EU citizens or not, wanting or needing to find work in the UK as a way of boosting their funds should turn to p375.

Language classes

The places listed below offer various courses; call for details.

Aspect Covent Garden Language Centre *3-4 Southampton Place, Covent Garden, WC1A 2DA (7404 3080/www.aspectworld.com). Holborn tube.* **Map** p399 L5.

Central School of English *1 Tottenham Court Road, Bloomsbury, W1T 1BB (7580 2863/www.centralschool.co.uk). Tottenham Court Road tube.* **Map** p397 K5.

Frances King School of English *77 Gloucester Road, South Kensington SW7 4SS (070 0011 2233/www.francesking.co.uk). Gloucester Road tube.* **Map** p395 F9.

London Study Centre *Munster House, 676 Fulham Road, Fulham, SW6 5SA (7731 3549/ www.londonstudycentre.com). Parsons Green tube.*

Sels College *64-5 Long Acre, Covent Garden, WC2E 9SX (7240 2581/www.sels.co.uk). Covent Garden tube.* **Map** p399 L6.

Shane English School *59 South Molton Street, Mayfair, W1K 5SN (7499 8533/www.sgvenglish.com). Bond Street tube.* **Map** p398 H6.

Students' unions

Many unions only let in students with relevant ID, so always carry your NUS or ISIC card. We've listed those with the best student bars, all of which offer a good night out.

Imperial College *Beit Quad, Prince Consort Road, South Kensington, SW7 2BB (7589 5111). South Kensington tube.* **Open** noon-2pm, 5-11pm Mon-Fri; noon-11pm Sat; noon-10.30pm Sun (times vary out of term-time). **Map** p397 D9.

International Students House *229 Great Portland Street, Marylebone, W1W 5PN (7631 8300). Great Portland Street tube.* **Open** noon-2pm, 5-11pm Mon, Tue; noon-2pm, 5pm-midnight Wed; noon-2pm, 5pm-1am Thur; noon-2pm, 5pm-3am Fri; noon-midnight Sat; noon-10.30pm Sun. **Map** p398 H4.

King's College *Macadam Building, Surrey Street, Covent Garden, WC2R 2NS (7836 7132). Temple tube.* **Open** *Waterfront* noon-11pm Mon-Fri; 7-11pm Sat. *Tutu's* 9pm-3am Fri; 10.30pm-3am Sat. **Map** p401 M7.

London Metropolitan University *166-220 Holloway Road, Holloway, N7 8DB (7607 2789). Holloway Road tube.* **Open** *Rocket* 11am-11pm Mon, Tue, Thur; 11am-2am Wed; 11am-6am Fri, Sat (event dependent).

University of London Union (ULU) *Malet Street, Bloomsbury, WC1E 7HY (7664 2000). Goodge Street tube.* **Open** 11am-11pm Mon-Thur; 11am-1am Fri, Sat; noon-10.30pm Sun. **Map** p399 K4.

Universities

Brunel University *Cleveland Road, Uxbridge, Middx UB8 3PH (01895 274000/students' union 01895 462200). Uxbridge tube.*

City University *Northampton Square, Clerkenwell, EC1V 0HB (7040 5060/students' union 7040 5600). Angel tube.* **Map** p402 O3.

London Metropolitan University *166-220 Holloway Road, Holloway, N7 8DB (7607 2789/students' union 7133 2769). Holloway Road tube.*

South Bank University *Borough Road, Borough, SE1 0AA (7928 8989/students' union 7815 6060). Elephant & Castle tube/rail.* **Map** p404 O9.

University of Greenwich *Old Royal Naval College, Park Row, Greenwich, SE10 9LS (8331 8000/students' union 8331 8256). Greenwich DLR.*

University of Middlesex *Trent Park, Bramley Road, Cockfosters, N14 4YZ (8411 5000/students' union 8411 6450). Cockfosters or Oakwood tube.*

University of Westminster *309 Regent Street, Mayfair, W1B 2UW (7911 5000/students' union 7915 5454). Oxford Circus tube.* **Map** p398 H4.

University of London

The University consists of 34 colleges, spread across the city; only the seven largest are listed below. All London universities (with the exception of Imperial College) are affiliated to the National Union of Students (NUS; 7272 8900/www.nusonline.co.uk).

Goldsmiths' College *Lewisham Way, SE14 6NW (7919 7171/ students' union 8692 1406). New Cross/New Cross Gate tube/rail.*

Imperial College *Exhibition Road, SW7 2AZ (7589 5111/students' union 7594 8060). South Kensington tube.* **Map** p397 D9.

King's College *Strand, WC2R 2NS (7836 5454/students' union 7836 7132). Temple tube.* **Map** p401 M7.

Kingston University *Penrhyn Road, Kingston, Surrey KT1 2EE (8547 2000/students' union 8547 8868). Kingston rail.*

London School of Economics (LSE) *Houghton Street, WC2A 2AE (7405 7686/students' union 7955 7158). Holborn tube.* **Map** p399 M6.

Queen Mary University of London *327 Mile End Road, Stepney, E1 4NS (7882 5555/ students' union 7882 5390). Mile End or Stepney Green tube.*

University College London (UCL) *Gower Street, Bloomsbury, WC1E 6BT (7679 2000/students' union 7387 3611). Euston Square, Goodge Street or Warren Street tube.* **Map** p399 K4.

Useful organisations

More useful organisations for students in this country, including BUNAC and the Council on International Educational Exchange, can be found on *p374*.

National Bureau for Students with Disabilities *Chapter House, 18-20 Crucifix Lane, SE1 3JW (0800 328 5050/textphone 0800 068 2422/ www.skill.org.uk).* **Open** *Phone enquiries* 1.30-4.30pm Mon-Thur.

Telephones

London's dialling code is 020. If you want to call a London number from within London, you omit the code (020) and dial the last eight digits. We've therefore listed London numbers without their 020 code throughout this book. If you're calling from outside the UK, dial the international access code from the country from which you're calling, then the UK code 44, then the full London number, omitting the first 0 from the code. For example, to make a call to 020 7813 3000 from the US, dial 011 44 20 7813 3000. To dial abroad from the UK, first dial 00, then the relevant country code from the list below. For more international dialling codes, check this useful website: www.kropla.com/dialcode.htm

Australia 61; **Austria** 43; **Belgium** 32; **Brazil** 55; **Canada** 1; **Czech Republic** 420; **Denmark** 45; **France** 33; **Germany** 49; **Greece** 30; **Hong Kong** 852; **Iceland** 354; **India** 91; **Ireland** 353; **Israel** 972; **Italy** 39; **Japan** 81; **Netherlands** 31; **New Zealand** 64; **Norway** 47; **Portugal** 351; **South Africa** 27; **Spain** 34; **Sweden** 46; **Switzerland** 41; **USA** 1.

Public phones

Public payphones take coins, credit cards or prepaid phonecards (sometimes all three). The minimum cost is 20p: this buys a 110-second local call (11p per minute). But be careful: some payphones, such as the counter-top ones found in many pubs, require more.

Operator services

Operator

Call **100** for the operator if you have difficulty in dialling; for an early-morning alarm call; to make a credit card call; for information about the cost of a call; and for help with international person-to-person calls. Dial **155** if you need to reverse the charges (call collect) or if you can't dial direct, but be warned that this service is very expensive.

Directory enquiries

Following a high-profile campaign in 2003, the service is now provided by various six-digit 118 numbers. They're pretty pricey to call: dial 0800 953 0720 for a rundown of options and prices. The best known is 118 118, which charges 49p per call, then 9p per minute thereafter. 118 888 charges 20p per call, then 20p per minute thereafter. 118 180 charges 25p per call, then 30p per minute thereafter.

Talking Pages

This 24-hour free service lists the numbers of thousands of businesses in the UK. Dial **0800 600900** and say what type of business you require, and in what area of London.

Telephone directories

There are three telephone directories for London (two for private numbers, one for companies), which are available at post offices and libraries. Hotels have them too. These hefty tomes are issued free to all residents, as is the invaluable Yellow Pages directory (also accessible online at www.yell.com), which lists businesses and services.

Mobile phones

Mobile phones in the UK work on either the 900 or 1800 GSM system. As this is used through much of Europe, it's worth checking whether your service provider has a reciprocal arrangement with a UK-based service provider. The situation is complex for US travellers. If your service provider in the US uses the GSM system, your phone probably runs on the 1900 band, so you'll need a tri-band handset.

The simplest option may be to buy a 'pay as you go' phone (about £40-£200); there's no monthly fee, you top up talk time using a card. Check before you buy a phone whether it can make and receive international calls.

Alternatively you can rent a mobile phone from the AmEx office at Heathrow Airport.

Telegrams

To send telegrams abroad, call 0800 190190. This is also the number to call to send an international telemessage: phone in your message and it will be delivered by post the next day (at a cost of £1.18 a word, including the recipient's name and address).

Time

London operates on Greenwich Mean Time, which is five hours ahead of the US's Eastern Standard time. In spring (28 March 2004) the UK puts its clocks forward by one hour to British Summer Time (BST). In autumn (31 October 2004) the clocks go back to GMT.

Tipping

In Britain it's accepted that you tip in taxis, minicabs, restaurants (some waiting staff rely heavily on tips), hotels, hairdressers and some bars (not pubs). Ten per cent is normal, with some restaurants adding as much as 15 per cent. Always check if service has been included in your bill: some restaurants include service, then leave the space for a gratuity on your credit card slip blank.

Toilets

Public toilets are few and far between in London, and pubs and restaurants reserve their toilets for customers only. However, all main-line rail stations and a very few tube stations – Piccadilly Circus, for one – have public toilets (you may be charged a small fee). It's also usually possible to sneak into a large department store such as John Lewis.

Tourist information

Visit London (7932 2000/www.visitlondon.com) is the city's official tourist information company. There are also tourist offices in Greenwich and next to St Paul's (**Map** p404 O6).

Britain & London Visitor Centre
1 Lower Regent Street, Piccadilly Circus, SW1Y 4XT (7808 3864/www.visitbritain.com). Piccadilly Circus tube. **Open** *Oct-May*

9.30am-6.30pm Mon; 9am-6.30pm Tue-Fri; 10am-4pm Sat, Sun. *June-Sept* 9.30am-6.30pm Mon; 9am-6.30pm Tue-Fri; 9am-5pm Sat; 10am-4pm Sun. **Map** p401 K7.

London Information Centre *Leicester Square, W1 (7437 4370/www.londontown.com). Leicester Square tube.* **Open** 8am-midnight Mon-Fri; 10am-6pm Sat, Sun.

London Visitor Centre *Arrivals Hall, Waterloo International Terminal, SE1 7LT.* **Open** 8.30am-10.30pm Mon-Sat; 9.30am-10.30pm Sun. **Map** p405 M9.

Visas & immigration

Citizens of EU countries don't require a visa to visit the United Kingdom; citizens of other countries, including the USA, Canada and New Zealand, require a valid passport for a visit of up to six months in duration. The immigration department of the Home Office (*see below*) deals with queries on immigration, visas and work permits from Commonwealth countries.

To apply for a UK visa or to check your visa status **before you travel**, contact the British embassy, consulate or high commission in your own country. The visa allows you entry for a maximum of six months. For information about work permits, *see p377*.

Home Office *Immigration & Nationality Bureau, Lunar House, 40 Wellesley Road, Croydon, Surrey CR9 1AT (0870 606 7766/application forms 0870 241 0645/www.homeoffice.gov.uk).* **Open** *Phone enquiries* 9am-4.45pm Mon-Thur; 9am-4.30pm Fri.

Weights & measures

The United Kingdom is slowly but surely moving towards full metrication. Distances are still measured in miles but all goods are now officially sold in metric quantities, with no legal requirement for the imperial equivalent to be given.

The following are some useful conversions.

1 centimetre (cm) = 0.39 inches (in)
1 inch (in) = 2.54 centimetres (cm)
1 yard (yd) = 0.91 metres (m)
1 metre (m) = 1.094 yards (yd)
1 mile = 1.6 kilometres (km)
1 kilometre (km) = 0.62 miles
1 ounce (oz) = 28.35 grammes (g)
1 gramme (g) = 0.035 ounces (oz)
1 pound (lb) = 0.45 kilogrammes (kg)
1 kilogramme (kg) = 2.2 pounds (lb)
1 pint (US) = 0.8 pints (UK)
1 pint (UK) = 0.55 litres (l)
1 litre (l) = 1.75 pints (UK)

When to go

Climate

The British climate is famously unpredictable, but Weathercall on 09003 444 900 (60p per min) can offer some guidance. *See also p374* **Weather report**. The best websites for weather news and features include www.metoffice.com; www.weather.com and www.bbc.co.uk/london/weather which both offer good detailed long-term international forecasts and are easily searchable.

Spring extends approximately from March to May, though winter often seems to stretch beyond February. March winds and April showers may be a month early or a month late, but May is often very pleasant.

Summer (June, July and August) can be unpredictable, with searing heat one day followed by sultry greyness and violent thunderstorms the next. High temperatures, humidity and pollution can create problems for those with hayfever or breathing difficulties. Temperatures down in the tube can reach dangerous levels, particularly during rush hour.

Autumn starts in September, although the weather can still have a mild, summery feel. Real autumn comes with October, when the leaves start to fall. When the November cold, grey and wet sets in, you'll be reminded that London is situated on a fairly northerly lattitude.

Winter can have some delightful crisp, cold days, but don't bank on them. The usual scenario is for a disappointingly grey, wet Christmas, followed by a cold snap in January and February, when we may even see a sprinkling of snow, and public transport chaos ensues.

Public holidays

On public holidays (widely known as bank holidays), many shops remain open, but public transport services generally run to a Sunday timetable. The exception is Christmas Day, when almost everything shuts.

New Year's Day Thur 1 Jan 2004; Sat 1 Jan 2005.
Good Friday Fri 9 Apr 2004; Fri 25 Mar 2005.
Easter Monday Mon 12 Apr 2004; Mon 28 Mar 2005.
May Day Holiday Mon 3 May 2004; Mon 1 May 2005.
Spring Bank Holiday Mon 31 May 2004; Mon 29 May 2005.
Summer Bank Holiday Mon 30 Aug 2004; Mon 28 Aug 2005.
Christmas Day Sat 25 Dec 2004; Sun 25 Dec 2005.
Boxing Day Sun 26 Dec 2004; Tue 26 Dec 2005.

Women

London is home to dozens of women's groups and networks, from day centres to rights campaigners; www.gn.apc.org or www.wrc.org.uk provide information and many links.

Visiting women are unlikely to be harassed. Bar the very occasional sexually motivated attack, London's streets are no more dangerous to women than to men, if you follow the usual precautions (*see p370*).

The Women's Library

25 Old Castle Street, Whitechapel, E1 7NT (7320 2222/www.thewomenslibrary.ac.uk). Aldgate or Aldgate East tube. **Open** *Reading room* 9.30am-5pm Tue, Wed, Fri; 9.30am-8pm Thur; 10am-4pm Sat.

Europe's largest women's studies archive has made a £4m move to larger premises (on the same road). Check for details of current exhibitions.

Working in London

Finding temporary work in London can be a full-time job in itself. Those with a reasonable level of English who are EU citizens or have work permits should be able to find work in catering, labouring, bars/pubs or shops. Graduates with an English or foreign-language degree could try teaching. Ideas can be found in *Summer Jobs in Britain*, published by Vacation Work, 9 Park End Street, Oxford OX1 1HJ (£9.99 plus £1.50 postage & packing).

Good sources of job information are the *Evening Standard*, local/national newspapers and newsagents' windows. Vacancies for temporary and unskilled work are often displayed on Jobcentre noticeboards; your nearest Jobcentre can be found under 'Employment Agencies' in the *Yellow Pages*. If you have good typing (over 40 wpm) or word processing skills and know how to dress the part, you could sign on with some of the temp agencies. Many of them have specialist areas beyond the obvious admin/secretarial roles, such as translation.

Work permits

With few exceptions, citizens of non-European Economic Area (EEA) countries have to have a work permit before they can legally work in the United Kingdom. Employers who are unable to fill particular vacancies with a resident or EEA national must apply for a permit to the Department for Education and Employment (DfEE; *see below*). Permits are issued only for high-level jobs.

Au Pair Scheme

Citizens aged 17-27-from the following non-EEA countries are permitted to become au pairs: Andorra, Bosnia-Herzegovina, Croatia, Cyprus, Czech Republic, Faroe Islands, Greenland, Hungary, Macedonia, Malta, Monaco, San Marino, Slovak Republic, Slovenia, Switzerland and Turkey.

Sandwich students

Approval for course-compulsory sandwich placements at recognised UK colleges must be obtained for potential students by their college from the DfEE's **Overseas Labour Service** (*see below* **Department for Education & Employment**).

Students

Visiting students from the US, Canada, Australia or Jamaica can get a blue BUNAC, which lets them work in the UK for up to six months. Contact the Work in Britain Department of the **Council on International Educational Exchange** or call **BUNAC**. Students should obtain an application form OSS1 (BUNAC) from BUNAC, which is submitted to the nearest Jobcentre to obtain permission to work.

Working holidaymakers

Citizens of Commonwealth countries aged 17-27 may apply to come to the UK as a working holidaymaker, by contacting their nearest British Diplomatic Post in advance. They are then allowed to take part-time work without a DfEE permit.

Useful addresses

BUNAC

16 Bowling Green Lane, Clerkenwell, EC1R 0QH (7251 3472/www.bunac.org.uk). Farringdon tube/rail. **Open** 9.30am-5.30pm Mon-Thur; 9.30am-5pm Fri. **Map** p402 N4.

Council on International Educational Exchange

3rd Floor, 7 Custom House Street, Portland, Maine, ME 04101 USA (00 1 207 553 7600/www.ciee.org). **Open** 9am-5pm Mon-Fri.
The Council on International Educational Exchange aids young people to study, work and travel abroad. It's divided into international study programmes and exchanges.

Department for Education & Employment

Work Permits UK helpline 0114 259 4074/www.workpermits.gov.uk. **Open** *Phone enquiries* 9am-5pm Mon-Fri.
Employers seeking work permit application forms should phone 08705 210224 or visit the website.

Home Office

Immigration & Nationality Directorate, Lunar House, 40 Wellesley Road, Croydon, Surrey CR9 2BY (0870 606 7766/www.ind.homeoffice.gov.uk). **Open** *Phone enquiries* 9am-4.45pm Mon-Thur; 9am-4.30pm Fri.
The Home Office is able to provide advice on whether or not a work permit is required.

Overseas Visitors Records Office

180 Borough High Street, Borough, SE1 (7230 1208). Borough tube/Elephant & Castle or London Bridge tube/rail. **Open** 9am-4.30pm Mon-Fri. **Map** p404 P9.
In a former incarnation this was the Aliens Registration Office run by the Metropolitan Police. These days, though, it's known as the vastly less scary Overseas Visitors Records Office, and it charges £34 to register a person if they already have a work permit.

Weather report

Average daytime temperatures, rainfall and hours of sunshine in London

	Temp (˚C/˚F)	**Rainfall** (mm/in)	**Sunshine** (hrs/dy)
Jan	6/43	54/2.1	1.5
Feb	7/44	40/1.6	2.3
Mar	10/50	37/1.5	3.6
Apr	13/55	37/1.5	5.3
May	17/63	46/1.8	6.4
June	20/68	45/1.8	7.1
July	22/72	57/2.2	6.4
Aug	21/70	59/2.3	6.1
Sept	19/66	49/1.9	4.7
Oct	14/57	57/2.2	3.2
Nov	10/50	64/2.5	1.8
Dec	7/44	48/1.9	1.3

Further Reference

Books

Fiction

Peter Ackroyd *Hawksmoor; The House of Doctor Dee; Great Fire of London* Intricate studies of arcane London.
Monica Ali *Brick Lane* Arranged marriage in Tower Hamlets.
Debi Alper *Nirvana Bites* Peckham-based writer's debut.
Martin Amis *London Fields* Darts and drinking way out east.
Iain Banks *Dead Air* Shock jock's post 9/11 experiences.
Paul Bryers *The Used Women's Book Club* Murder most torrid in contemporary Spitalfields.
Jonathan Coe *The Dwarves of Death* Mystery, music, mirth, malevolence.
Norman Collins *London Belongs to Me* A witty saga of '30s Kennington.
Wilkie Collins *The Woman in White* Spooky goings-on.
Joseph Conrad *The Secret Agent* Anarchism in seedy Soho.
Charles Dickens *Oliver Twist; David Copperfield; Bleak House; Our Mutual Friend* Four of the master's most London-centric novels.
Sir Arthur Conan Doyle *The Complete Sherlock Holmes* Reassuring sleuthing shenanigans.
Maureen Duffy *Capital* The bones beneath our feet and the stories they tell.
Christopher Fowler *Soho Black* Walking dead in Soho.
Anthony Frewin *London Blues* One-time Kubrick assistant explores '60s porn movie industry.
Neil Gaiman *Neverwhere* A new world above and below the streets by *Sandman* creator.
Graham Greene *The End of the Affair* Adultery and Catholicism.
Tobias Hill *Underground* Women. tube trains and secret tunnels.
Alan Hollinghurst *The Swimming Pool Library* Gay life around Russell Square.
Maria Lexton (vol 1)/Nicholas Royle (vol 2) (eds) *Time Out Book of London Short Stories Volumes 1 & 2* Writers pay homage to their city.
Colin MacInnes *City of Spades; Absolute Beginners* Coffee 'n' jazz, Soho 'n' Notting Hill.
Derek Marlowe *A Dandy in Aspic* A capital-set Cold War classic.
Andrew Martin *The Necropolis Railway* Death on the graveyard line.
Michael Moorcock *Mother London* A love letter to London.
George Orwell *Keep the Aspidistra Flying* Saga of a struggling writer.
Derek Raymond *I Was Dora Suarez* The blackest London noir.
Jean Rhys *After Leaving Mr Mackenzie; Good Morning, Midnight* Sad women haunt the squares of Bloomsbury.
Nicholas Royle *The Matter of the Heart; The Director's Cut* Abandoned buildings and secrets from the past.
Edward Rutherfurd *London* A city's history given a novel voice.
Will Self *Grey Area* Short stories.
Iain Sinclair *Downriver; Radon Daughters; White Chappell, Scarlet Tracings* The Thames's *Heart of Darkness*; William Hope Hodgson; Ripper murders and book dealers.
Jane Stevenson *London Bridges* Greek monks and murder.
Barbara Vine *King Solomon's Carpet; Grasshopper* From the Underground to a rooftop love story.
Evelyn Waugh *Vile Bodies* Shameful antics in 1920s Mayfair.
Angus Wilson *The Old Men at the Zoo* London faces down oblivion.
Virginia Woolf *Mrs Dalloway* A kind of London *Ulysses*.

Non-fiction

Peter Ackroyd *London: The Biography* Wilfully obscurantist city history.
Marc Atkins & Iain Sinclair *Liquid City* Sinclair haunts photographed.
Nicholas Barton *The Lost Rivers of London* Fascinating studies of old watercourses and their legacy.
Anthony Burgess *A Dead Man in Deptford* The life and murder of Elizabethan playwright Christopher Marlowe.
Margaret Cox *Life and Death in Spitalfields 1700-1850* The removal and analysis of bodies from Christ Church Spitalfields.
Daniel Farson *Soho in the Fifties* An affectionate portrait.
Geoffrey Fletcher *The London Nobody Knows* Old bits of London revealed by an opinionated expert.
Stephen Halliday *The Great Stink of London* The sewage crisis in London in 1858.
Derek Hanson *The Dreadful Judgement* The embers of the Great Fire re-raked.
Sarah Hartley *Mrs P's Journey* Biography of Phyllis Pearsall, the woman who created the *A–Z*.
Stephen Inwood *A History of London* A recent, readable history.
Ian Jack (ed) *Granta, London: the Lives of the City* Fiction, reportage and travel writing.
Edward Jones & Christopher Woodward *A Guide to the Architecture of London* What it says. A brilliant work.
Jack London *The People of the Abyss* Extreme poverty in the East End.
Nick Merriman (ed) *The Peopling of London* 2,000 years of settlement.
Tim Moore *Do Not Pass Go* A hysterically funny Monopoly addict's London.
Gilda O'Neill *Pull No More Bines; My East End* A social histories of east London.
George Orwell *Down and Out in Paris and London* Waitering and starving.
Samuel Pepys *Diaries* Fires, plagues, bordellos and more.
Liza Picard *Dr Johnson's London; Restoration London*. London past, engagingly revisited.
Patricia Pierce *Old London Bridge* The story of the world's longest inhabited bridge.
Roy Porter *London: A Social History* An all-encompassing history.
Jonathan Raban *Soft City* The city as state of mind; a classic.
Iain Sinclair *Lights Out for the Territory; London Orbital.* Time-warp visionary crosses London; and circles it on the M25.
Derek Sumeray *Discovering London Plaques* A monumental piece of research.
Judith Summers *Soho: A History of London's Most Colourful Neighbourhood.* So-Ho! Great local history.
Adrian Tinniswood *His Invention So Fertile* Illuminating biography of Christopher Wren.
Richard Trench *London Under London* The subterranean city.
Ben Weinreb & Christopher Hibbert (eds) *The London Encyclopaedia* Fascinating, thorough, indispensable.
Andrew White (ed) *Time Out Book of London Walks Volumes 1 & 2.*

Writers, cartoonists, comedians and historians take a walk through town.
Jerry White *London in the 20th Century: A City and Its People.*
The city transforms itself.

Films

Alfie *dir. Lewis Gilbert* (1966)
What's it all about, Michael?
Beautiful Thing *dir. Hettie MacDonald* (1996)
A tender, amusing coming-of-age flick.
A Clockwork Orange *dir. Stanley Kubrick* (1971)
Kubrick's vision still shocks.
Blow-Up *dir. Michelangelo Antonioni* (1966)
Swingin' London captured in unintentionally hysterical fashion.
Croupier *dir. Mike Hodges* (1997)
Gambling and drinking dominate.
Death Line *dir. Gary Sherman* (1972)
Cannibalism on the tube. Yikes.
Jubilee *dir. Derek Jarman* (1978)
A horribly dated but still interesting romp through the punk era.
The Krays *dir. Peter Medak* (1990)
The Kemps as East End gangsters.
Life is Sweet; **Naked**; **Secrets & Lies**; **Career Girls**; **All or Nothing** *dir. Mike Leigh* (1990; 1993; 1996; 1997; 2002)
An affectionate look at Metroland; a character study; familial tensions; old friends meet; family falls apart.
Lock, Stock & Two Smoking Barrels; **Snatch** *dir. Guy Ritchie* (1998; 2000)
Mr Madonna's pair of East End faux-gangster flicks.
London; **Robinson in Space** *dir. Patrick Keiller* (1994; 1997)
Fiction meets documentary.
The Long Good Friday *dir. John MacKenzie* (1989)
Bob Hoskins stars in the classic London gangster flick.
Mona Lisa; **The Crying Game** *dir. Neil Jordan* (1986; 1992)
Prostitution, terrorism, transvestism.
Mrs Dalloway *dir. Marleen Goris* (1997)
Vanessa Redgrave stars in this adaptation of the Woolf novel.
Nil by Mouth *dir. Gary Oldman* (1997)
A violenttale of working-class life.
Notting Hill *dir. Roger Michell* (1999)
Hugh Grant and Julia Roberts get it on in west London.
The Optimist of Nine Elms *dir. Anthony Simmons (1973)*
Peter Sellers rises above the drab in a hard-edged South London drama.
Peeping Tom *dir. Michael Powell* (1960)
Powell's creepy murder flick.
Performance *dir. Nicolas Roeg, Donald Cammell* (1970)
The cult movie to end all cult movies made west London cool for life.
28 Days *dir. Danny Boyle* (2002)
Post-apocalyptic London.
Wonderland *dir. Michael Winterbottom* (1999)
Love, loss and deprivation.

Music

Albums

Blur *Modern Life is Rubbish* (1993); *Park Life* (1994)
Modern classics by the Essex exiles.
The Clash *London Calling* (1979)
Epoch-making punk classic.
Ian Dury & the Blockheads *New Boots & Panties* (1977)
The late Dury's seminal work.
Handel *Water Music; Music For the Royal Fireworks* (1717; 1749)
The glory days of the 18th century.
The Jam *This is the Modern World* (1977)
Paul Weller at his splenetic finest.
Madness *Rise & Fall* (1982)
The nutty boys wax lyrical.
Morrissey *Vauxhall & I* (1994)
His finest solo album.
Anthony Newley *The Very Best of…* (1997)
Cockney scallywag's retrospective.
The Rolling Stones *December's Children (and Everybody's)* (1965)
Moodily cool evocation of the city.
The Sex Pistols *Never Mind the Bollocks* (1977)
The best ever punk album.
So Solid Crew *They Don't Know* (2001)
Mainstream urban garage.
Simon Warner *Waiting Rooms* (1997)
Bedsit decadence; a lost gem.

Songs

assorted *A Foggy Day (in London Town); A Nightingale Sang in Berkeley Square; Let's All Go Down the Strand; London Bridge is Falling Down; Maybe It's Because I'm a Londoner*
David Bowie *London Boys*
Elvis Costello & the Attractions *(I Don't Want to Go to) Chelsea*
Noël Coward *London Pride*
Ray Davies *London Song*
Nick Drake *Mayfair*
Eddy Grant *Electric Avenue*
The Kinks *Denmark Street; Muswell Hillbillies; Waterloo Sunset*
Pet Shop Boys *King's Cross; West End Girls; London*
The Pogues *A Rainy Night in Soho; Misty Morning, Albert Bridge*
Gerry Rafferty *Baker Street*
Roxy Music *Do the Strand*
St Etienne *London Belongs to Me*
Simple Minds *Chelsea Girl*
Squeeze *Up the Junction*
Sugar Minott *Riot Inna Brixton*
XTC *Towers of London*

Poems

Anthology *London Lines*(Methuen).
The places and faces of London in poetry and song.
Anthology *Fifty Fifty* (South Bank Centre)
The Poetry Library's 50th birthday anthology.
Anthology *Poems on the Underground* 10th Edition (Cassell & Co)
Commuters' lines.
TS Eliot *The Waste Land* (Faber)
Eliot's long view.
Spike Milligan *Hidden Words* (Michael Joseph)
Collected poems.
The Earl of Rochester *Rochester The Complete Works* publisher: Penguin Books Ltd.
The royal porno poet.
Benjamin Zephaniah *Too Black Too Strong.* (Bloodaxe)
The oral poet's 2001 anthology.

Websites

BBC London *www.bbc.co.uk/london*
Online news, travel, weather, entertainment and sport.
Classic Cafés *www.classiccafes.co.uk*
London's '50s and '60s caffs.
Greater London Authority *www.london.gov.uk*
See what the Mayor and co are up to.
London Active Map *www.uktravel.com*
Click on a tube station and find out which attractions are nearby.
LondonTown *www.londontown.com*
The official tourist board website is stuffed full of information and offers.
London Underground Online *www.thetube.com*
A website devoted to the capital's beleaguered Underground network.
Meteorological Office *www.met-office.gov.uk*
Find out what the Met Office says before you head out. Not always accurate, but the best you'll get.
Place Names *www.krysstal.com/londname.html*
Neighbourhood names explained.
Pubs.com *www.pubs.com*
London's traditional boozers.
The River Thames Guide *www.riverthames.co.uk*
Places along the riverbank.
Street Map *www.streetmap.co.uk*
Grid references and postcodes.
This is London *www.thisislondon.co.uk*
The *Evening Standard* online.
Time Out *www.timeout.com*
An essential source, of course.
Transport for London *www.londontransport.co.uk*
The official website for buses, DLR, river services with travel info.
Yellow Pages Online *www.yell.com*
The business directory.

Index

Note: page numbers in **bold** indicate section(s) giving key information on a topic; *italics* indicate illustrations.

Hotels

Pubs & Bars

Restaurants & Cafés

Advertisers' Index

Please refer to the relevant sections for contact details

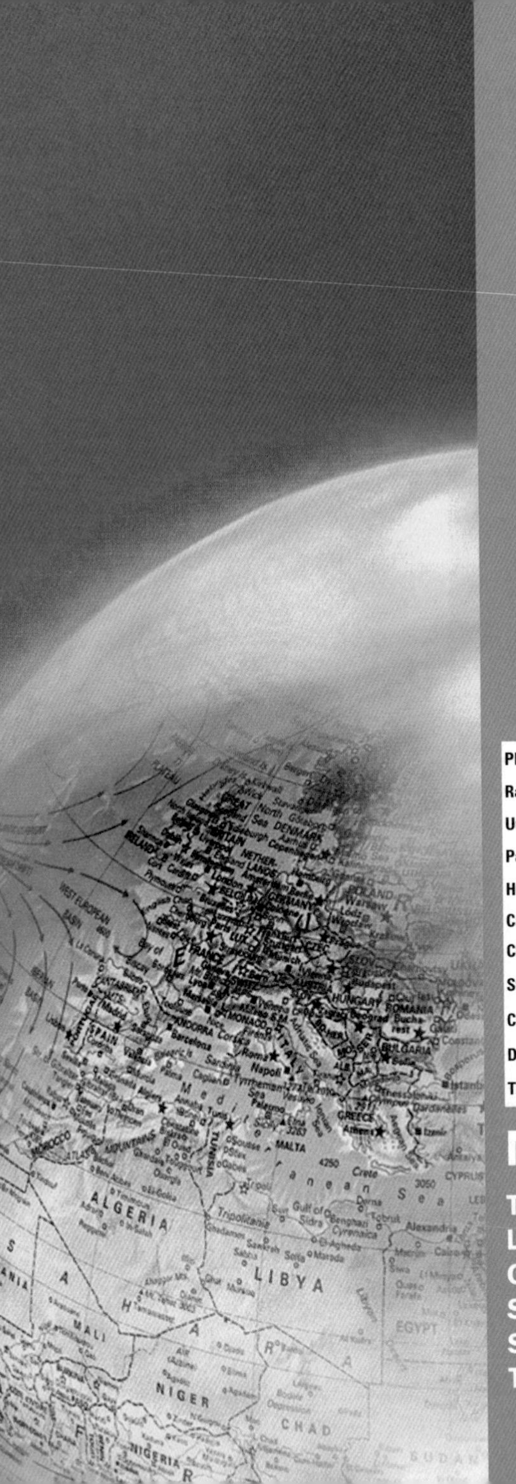

Legend	
Places of interest or entertainment	
Railway stations	
Underground stations	
Parks	
Hospitals	
Casualty units	
Churches	
Synagogues	
Congestion Zone	
Districts	MAYFAIR
Theatre	

Maps

Come on board the Cutty Sark, the last of the clippers.

In her 50th year in dry berth in Greenwich

Open Daily 10am-4.30pm
(Closed 24-26 December)

Special Group Rates

☎ 020 8858 3445
www.cuttysark.org.uk

THAI FOOD BROUGHT TO YOU BY MANTANAH

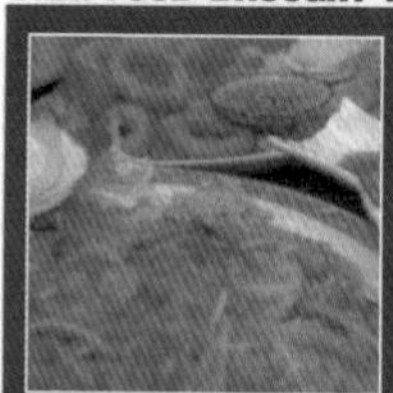

Fresh ingredients from Thailand.
All dishes are cooked only to order, and if you fancy something that's not featured on the menu, then tell the friendly staff and they will endeavour to recreate it for you.

Open: Tues - Sat: 6.30pm - 11pm
Sunday: 6.30pm - 10.30pm

All major credit cards and debit cards accepted. Parties catered for, children welcome. Booking is advisable.

10% discount on take aways over £15.00
Credit Cards accepted on orders over £10.00

2 Orton Buildings, Portland Road, South Norwood, London SE25 4UD

Tel: 020 8771 1148

www.mantanah.co.uk Email: thaifood@mantanah.co.uk

金寶城酒樓

146 - 150 STATION RD
HARROW
MIDDLESEX
HA1 2RH
TEL: 020-8863 2333
020-8424 8899

Trips Out of Town

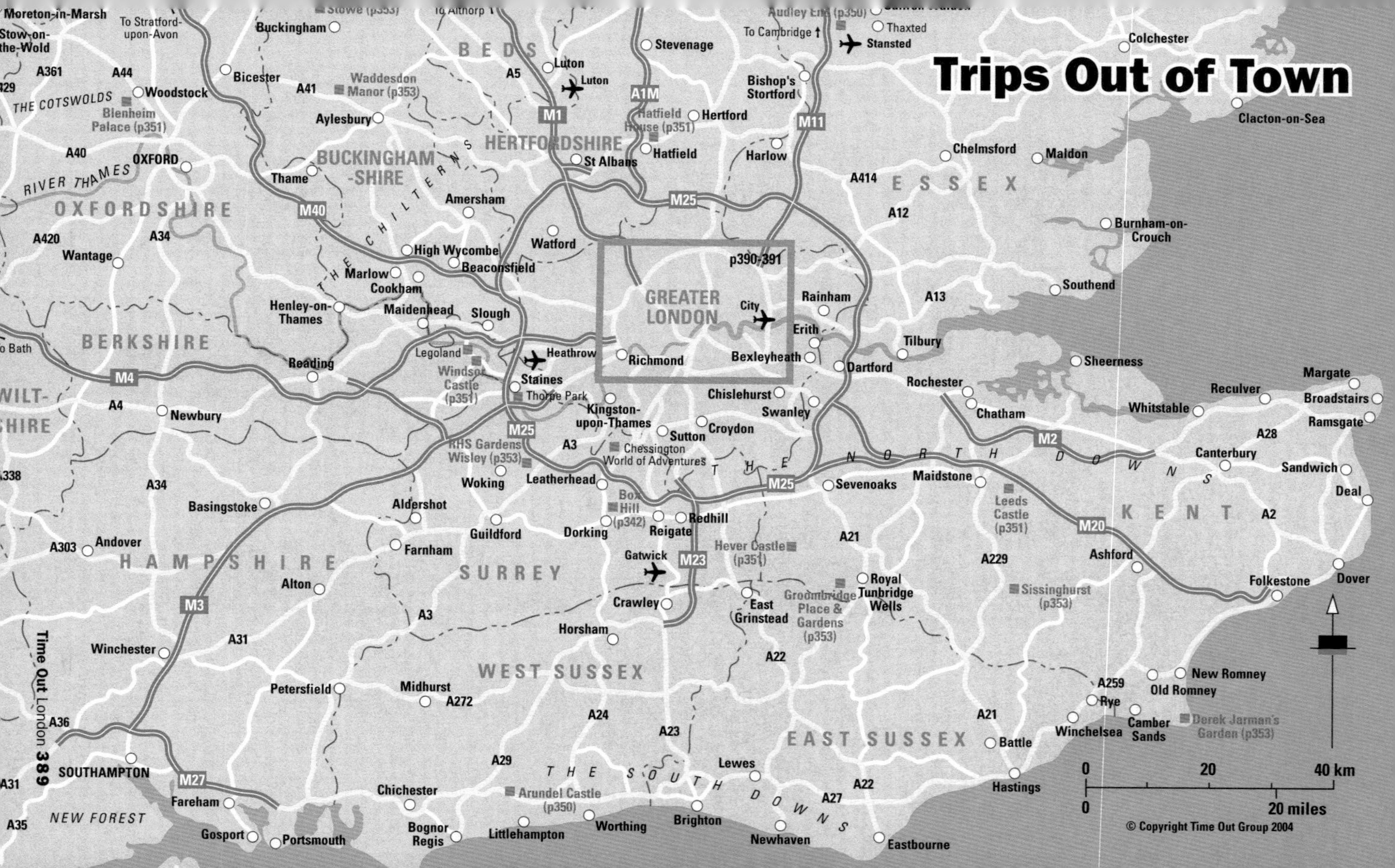

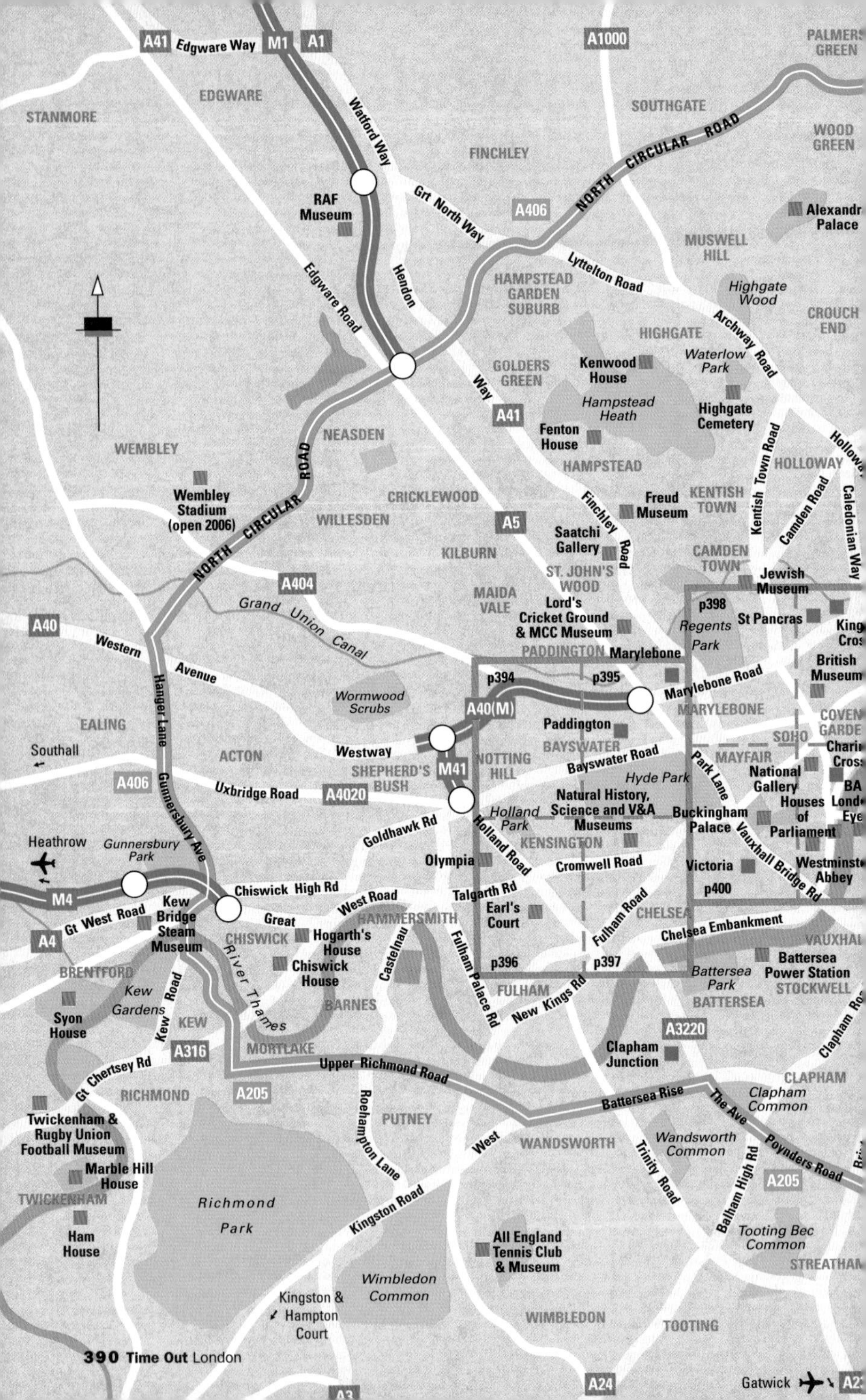

A41 Edgware Way M1 A1
A1000
PALMERS GREEN
EDGWARE
STANMORE
SOUTHGATE
Watford Way
FINCHLEY
WOOD GREEN
NORTH CIRCULAR ROAD
RAF Museum
Grt North Way
A406
Alexandra Palace
MUSWELL HILL
Edgware Road
Hendon
Lyttelton Road
HAMPSTEAD GARDEN SUBURB
Highgate Wood
CROUCH END
Archway Road
HIGHGATE
GOLDERS GREEN
Kenwood House
Waterlow Park
Way
A41
Hampstead Heath
Highgate Cemetery
WEMBLEY
NEASDEN
Fenton House
Kentish Town Road
Holloway
HAMPSTEAD
HOLLOWAY
NORTH CIRCULAR ROAD
Wembley Stadium (open 2006)
CRICKLEWOOD
Freud Museum
KENTISH TOWN
Camden Road
Caledonian Way
WILLESDEN
Finchley Road
A5
Saatchi Gallery
KILBURN
CAMDEN TOWN
ST. JOHN'S WOOD
Jewish Museum
A404
MAIDA VALE
Lord's Cricket Ground & MCC Museum
p398
St Pancras
Kings Cross
Grand Union Canal
Regents Park
A40
Western Avenue
PADDINGTON
Marylebone
British Museum
Hanger Lane
p394
p395
Marylebone Road
Wormwood Scrubs
A40(M)
MARYLEBONE
EALING
Paddington
COVENT GARDEN
SOHO
BAYSWATER
Charing Cross
Westway
Bayswater Road
Southall
ACTON
NOTTING HILL
MAYFAIR
Park Lane
National Gallery
SHEPHERD'S BUSH
M41
Hyde Park
A406
Uxbridge Road
A4020
Natural History, Science and V&A Museums
Houses of Parliament
Gunnersbury Ave
Holland Park
Buckingham Palace
Goldhawk Rd
Holland Road
KENSINGTON
Heathrow
Gunnersbury Park
Vauxhall Bridge Rd
Olympia
Cromwell Road
Victoria
Westminster Abbey
M4
Chiswick High Rd
Talgarth Rd
p400
Kew Bridge Steam Museum
West Road
Earl's Court
Gt West Road
Great
HAMMERSMITH
Fulham Road
CHELSEA
A4
CHISWICK
Hogarth's House
Chelsea Embankment
VAUXHALL
River Thames
Castelnau
Fulham Palace Rd
p396
p397
Battersea Power Station
BRENTFORD
Chiswick House
Battersea Park
Kew Gardens
Kew Road
BARNES
FULHAM
STOCKWELL
BATTERSEA
Syon House
KEW
New Kings Rd
A3220
Clapham Road
A316
MORTLAKE
Clapham Junction
Gt Chertsey Rd
Upper Richmond Road
CLAPHAM
RICHMOND
A205
Battersea Rise
Clapham Common
The Ave
Roehampton Lane
PUTNEY
Twickenham & Rugby Union Football Museum
West
WANDSWORTH
Poynders Road
Wandsworth Common
Trinity Road
Balham High Rd
Marble Hill House
A205
TWICKENHAM
Richmond Park
Kingston Road
Ham House
All England Tennis Club & Museum
Tooting Bec Common
STREATHAM
Wimbledon Common
Kingston & Hampton Court
WIMBLEDON
TOOTING
A24
Gatwick
A3

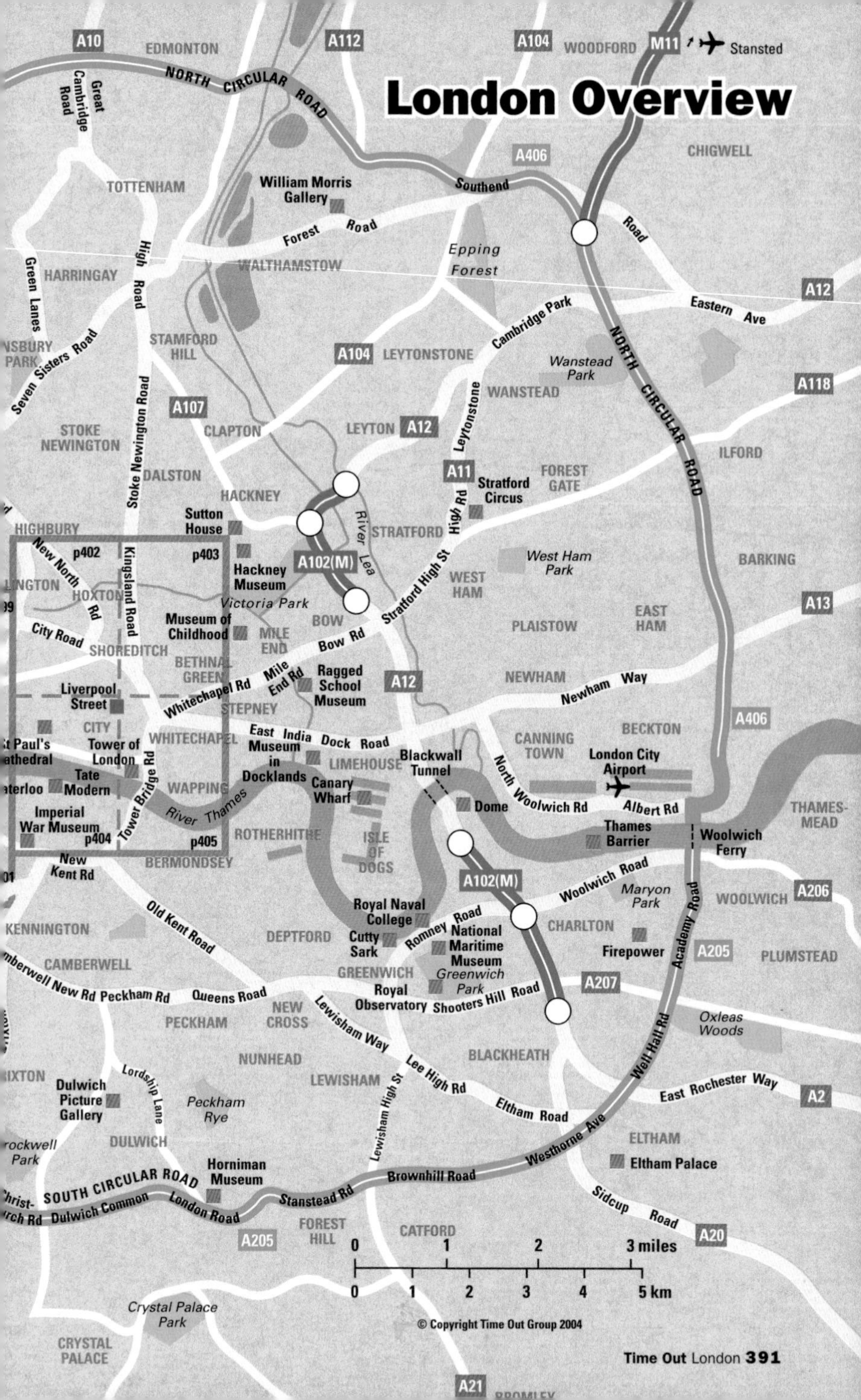

© Copyright Time Out Group 2004

Central London
by Area
Kilburn High Road
PRIMROSE HILL
CAMDEN
SOMERS TOWN
ST JOHN'S WOOD
MAIDA VALE
Little Venice
PADDINGTON
Paddington
Marylebone
MARYLEBONE
FITZROVIA
SOHO
BAYSWATER
Marble Arch
MAYFAIR
ST JAMES'S
WESTMINSTER
KENSINGTON
KNIGHTSBRIDGE
Harrods
Victoria & Albert
Science Museum
Natural History
Wellington Arch
BELGRAVIA
Victoria
Euston
London Zoo
REGENT'S PARK
Queen Mary's Gardens
HYDE PARK
KENSINGTON GARDENS
The Round Pond
The Long Water
The Serpentine
GREEN PARK
ST JAMES'S PARK
BUCKINGHAM PALACE GARDENS
BROMPTON
EARL'S COURT
SOUTH KENSINGTON
CHELSEA
Chelsea Physic Garden
PIMLICO
WEST BROMPTON
Brompton Cemetery
FULHAM
BATTERSEA
NINE ELMS
RIVER THAMES
Grand Union Canal
Grand Union (Regents) Canal
WESTWAY
A40(M)
ADELAIDE ROAD
PRINCE ALBERT ROAD
MARYLEBONE ROAD
EUSTON ROAD
EDGWARE ROAD
HARROW ROAD
OXFORD STREET
BAYSWATER ROAD
PARK LANE
PICCADILLY
KENSINGTON ROAD
KNIGHTSBRIDGE
CROMWELL ROAD
BROMPTON ROAD
KING'S ROAD
FULHAM ROAD
CHELSEA EMBANKMENT
GROSVENOR ROAD
VAUXHALL BRIDGE ROAD

© Copyright Time Out Group 2004

A
B
C
4
5
6
7
8
Chippenham Mews
Marylands Rd
Sutherland Ave
HARROW ROAD A404
Amberley Road
Regent's Canal
Formosa St
Warwick
Bristol Gdns
CLIFTON GDNS
Warwick Avenue
Clifton Villas
Ave
Blomfield Road
Warwick Place
Delamere Terrace
Elkstone Road
Woodchester Square
Senior Street
Lord Hills Road
Chichester Road
Blomfield Villas
Little Venice
Warwick Crescent
Alfred Rd
Cirencester St
Bourne Terrace
Warwick Estate
Westbourne Park
GREAT WESTERN ROAD
Tavistock Cres
Tavistock Road
Aldridge Rd Villas
Leamington Rd Villas
WESTWAY A40 (M)
Westbourne Park Villas
St Lukes Rd
Lancaster Road
WESTBOURNE PARK ROAD
Shrewsbury Rd
Royal Oak
Westbourne Park Road
Gloucester Terrace
Westbourne Terrace
Dartmouth Close
CHEPSTOW ROAD
Talbot Road
Kildare Terrace
Durham Terrace
Alexander St
Porchester Centre
PORCHESTER ROAD
Porchester Sq
Porchester Terr North
Orsett Terrace
BISHOPS BRIDGE ROAD
Powis Terr
Powis Gdns
Talbot Road
Courtnell St
Moorhouse Road
Sutherland Pl
Northumberland Place
Bridstow Place
Hereford Road
Westbourne Gdns
Hatherley Gr
Queensway
Pickering Mews
Powis Sq
Colville Terrace
Ledbury Road
Artesian Road
Newton Road
WESTBOURNE GROVE
Inverness Terrace
Hallfield Estate
Cleveland
BAYSWATER
Colville Road
Lonsdale Road
Westbourne Grove
Cleveland Square
Leinster Pl
Leinster Gardens
Cleveland Square
Queen's Gardens
Craven Hill Gdns
CRAVEN HILL
PEMBRIDGE VILLAS
Pembridge Place
Chepstow Place
Leinster Sq
Prince's Square
Garway Road
Gardens Square
Kensington
Redan Place
Whiteleys
Porchester Gardens
Salem Rd
QUEENSWAY
Queensborough Terrace
Porchester Terrace
Denbigh Rd
Denbigh Terr
Chepstow Villas
Chepstow Cres
Portobello Road
Pembridge Cres
Pemb'ge Mews
Dawson Place
Greek Cathedral
Ilchester Gdns
Moscow Road
Bayswater
Poplar Place
Inverness Terrace
LEINSTER TERR
Kensington Park Road
Kensington Park Gdns
Pembridge Square
Chapel Side
St Petersburgh Mews
St Petersburgh Place
Bark Place
Caroline Pl
Orme Lane
Orme Ct
Palace Court
Ossington St
Victoria Gdn Mews
Clanricarde Gdns
Linden Gardens
Pembridge Gdns
PEMBRIDGE RD
Queensway
Lancaster Ga
Ladbroke Square
NOTTING HILL
Ladbroke Road
Ladbroke Terr
BAYSWATER ROAD
Diana, Princess of Wales Memorial Playground
Notting Hill Gate
Bulmer Place
NOTTING HILL GATE
Ladbroke Walk
PALACE GARDENS TERRACE
Palace Garden Mews
Kensington Mall
KENSINGTON
Uxbridge Street
Hillgate Street
Jameson St
Hillgate Place
Kensington Place
Campden
Hillsleigh Rd
Campden Hill Gardens
Hill Sq
Edge St
Campden Hill Road
Aubrey Road
Aubrey Walk
Peel Street
Campden Street
Bedford Gardens
KENSINGTON CHURCH STREET
Brunswick Gdns
Kensington Palace Gardens
The Broad Walk
Round Pond
Kensington Palace
Sheffield Terrace
Tor Gdns
Gloucester Walk
Vicarage Gate
Palace Avenue
Holland Walk
Holland Park
Campden Grove
Gordon Place
Dukes La
York House Place
Pitt Street
KENSINGTON
Youth Hostel
Holland House
Sheldrake Place
Phillimore
Duchess of Bedford's Walk
Town Hall
Holland Street
Hornton Street
Drayton Mews
Campden Hill
Old Court Place
See p396
KENSINGTON ROAD
Open Air Theatre
Argyll
WC

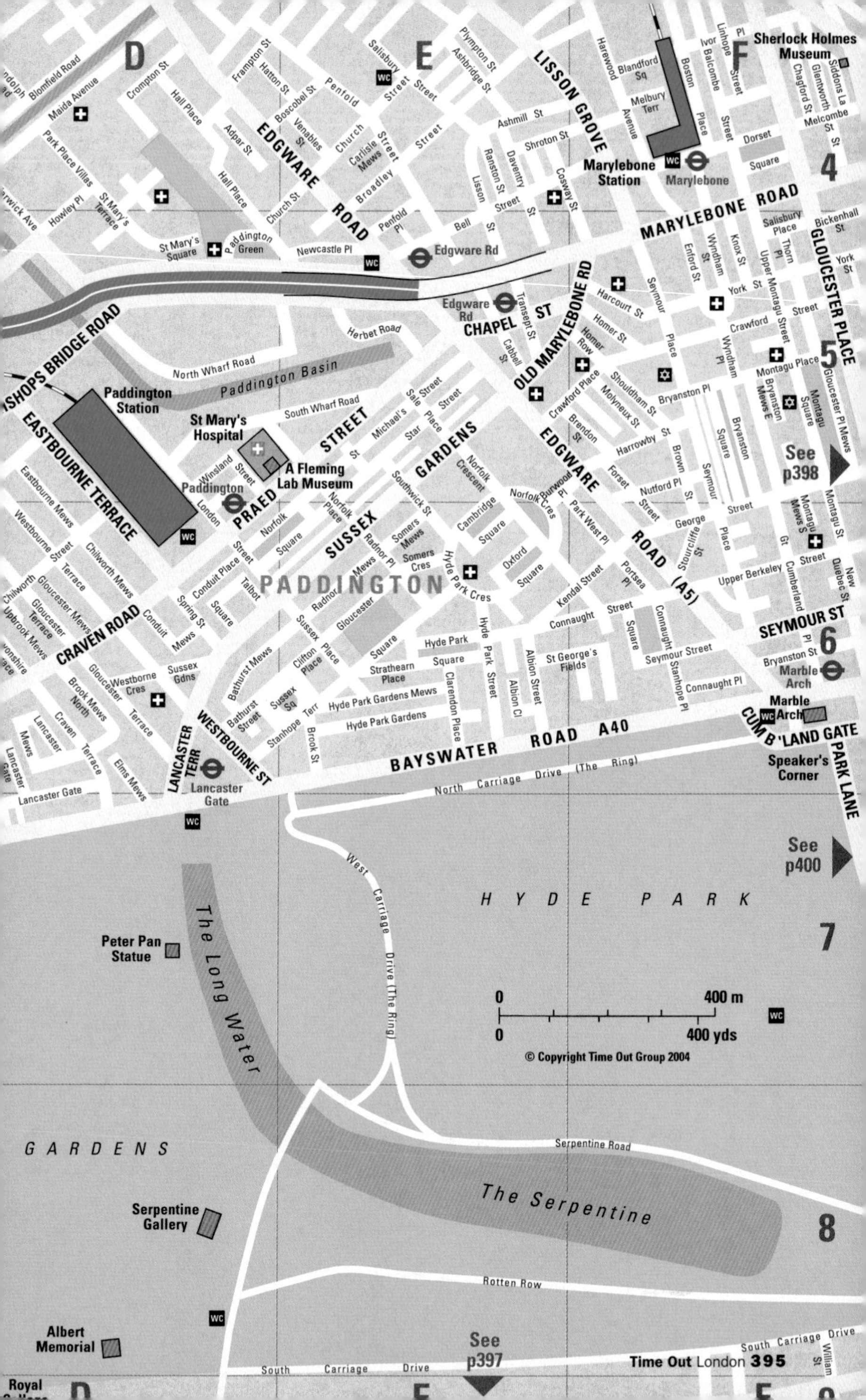
D
E
F
4
5
6
7
8
Blomfield Road
Maida Avenue
Crompton St
Hall Place
Frampton St
Hatton St
Boscobel St
Venables St
Salisbury Street
Penfold Street
Church Street
Carlisle Mews
Broadley Street
Plympton St
Ashbridge St
LISSON GROVE
Harewood Avenue
Blandford Sq
Melbury Terr
Boston Place
Ivor Place
Balcombe Street
Linhope St
Sherlock Holmes Museum
Chagford St
Glentworth St
Siddons La
Melcombe St
Dorset Square
Marylebone Station
Marylebone
Ashmill St
Shroton St
Ranston St
Lisson Street
Daventry St
Cosway St
Adpar St
EDGWARE ROAD
Park Place Villas
St Mary's Terrace
Howley Pl
Warwick Ave
St Mary's Square
Paddington Green
Church St
Penfold Pl
Bell St
Newcastle Pl
Edgware Rd
MARYLEBONE ROAD
Salisbury Place
Bickenhall St
GLOUCESTER PLACE
York St
Enford St
Wyndham St
Knox St
Thorn Pl
Upper Montagu Street
Seymour Place
Harcourt St
Homer St
Homer Row
Crawford Street
Wyndham Pl
Montagu Place
Bryanston Mews E
Montagu Square
Gloucester Pl Mews
Edgware Rd
CHAPEL ST
Transept St
Cabbell St
OLD MARYLEBONE RD
BISHOPS BRIDGE ROAD
Herbert Road
North Wharf Road
Paddington Basin
Paddington Station
EASTBOURNE TERRACE
South Wharf Road
St Mary's Hospital
A Fleming Lab Museum
Winsland Street
Paddington
London St
PRAED STREET
St Michael's St
Sale Place
Star St
SUSSEX GARDENS
Norfolk Crescent
Southwick St
Crawford Place
Shouldham St
Molyneux St
Bryanston Pl
Bryanston Square
Brendon St
Harrowby St
Brown St
Seymour Pl
See p398
Montagu Mews S
Montagu St
Forset St
Nutford Pl
Burwood Pl
Norfolk Cres
Park West Pl
George Street
Stourcliffe St
Quebec St
New Quebec St
Eastbourne Mews
Westbourne Street
Chilworth Mews
Norfolk Place
Norfolk Square
Somers Mews
Somers Cres
Cambridge Square
Oxford Square
ROAD (A5)
Upper Berkeley Street
Cumberland Gt
Chilworth St
Gloucester Mews
Gloucester Terrace
Upbrook Mews
Devonshire Terrace
Conduit Place
Talbot Square
Radnor Pl
Radnor Mews
PADDINGTON
Hyde Park Cres
Kendal Street
Portsea Pl
SEYMOUR ST
CRAVEN ROAD
Conduit Mews
Spring St
Gloucester Square
Sussex Place
Clifton Place
Hyde Park Square
Hyde Park Street
Connaught Street
Connaught Square
Albion Street
Albion Cl
St George's Fields
Seymour Street
Stanhope Pl
Connaught Pl
Bryanston St
Marble Arch
Brook Mews North
Westbourne Cres
Sussex Gdns
Bathurst Mews
Bathurst Street
Sussex Sq
Strathearn Place
Hyde Park Gardens Mews
Hyde Park Gardens
Clarendon Place
Stanhope Terr
Brook St
Craven Terrace
Lancaster Mews
Lancaster Gate
Elms Mews
LANCASTER TERR
WESTBOURNE ST
BAYSWATER ROAD A40
CUMB'LAND GATE
PARK LANE
Speaker's Corner
North Carriage Drive (The Ring)
Lancaster Gate
WC
See p400
West Carriage Drive (The Ring)
HYDE PARK
Peter Pan Statue
The Long Water
0
400 m
0
400 yds
© Copyright Time Out Group 2004
GARDENS
Serpentine Road
The Serpentine
Serpentine Gallery
Rotten Row
Albert Memorial
South Carriage Drive
William St
Royal
See p397

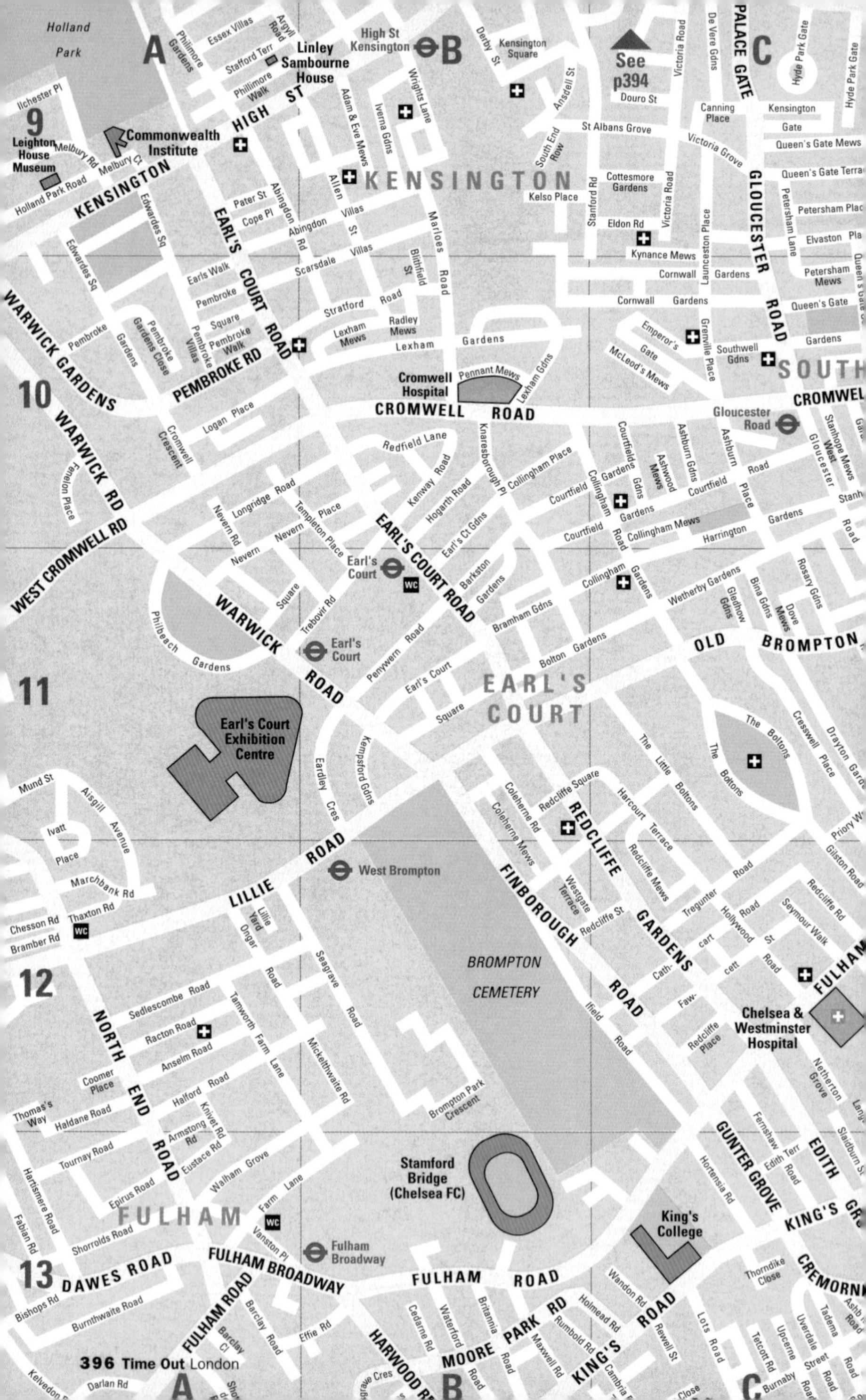

See p394

© Copyright Time Out Group 2004

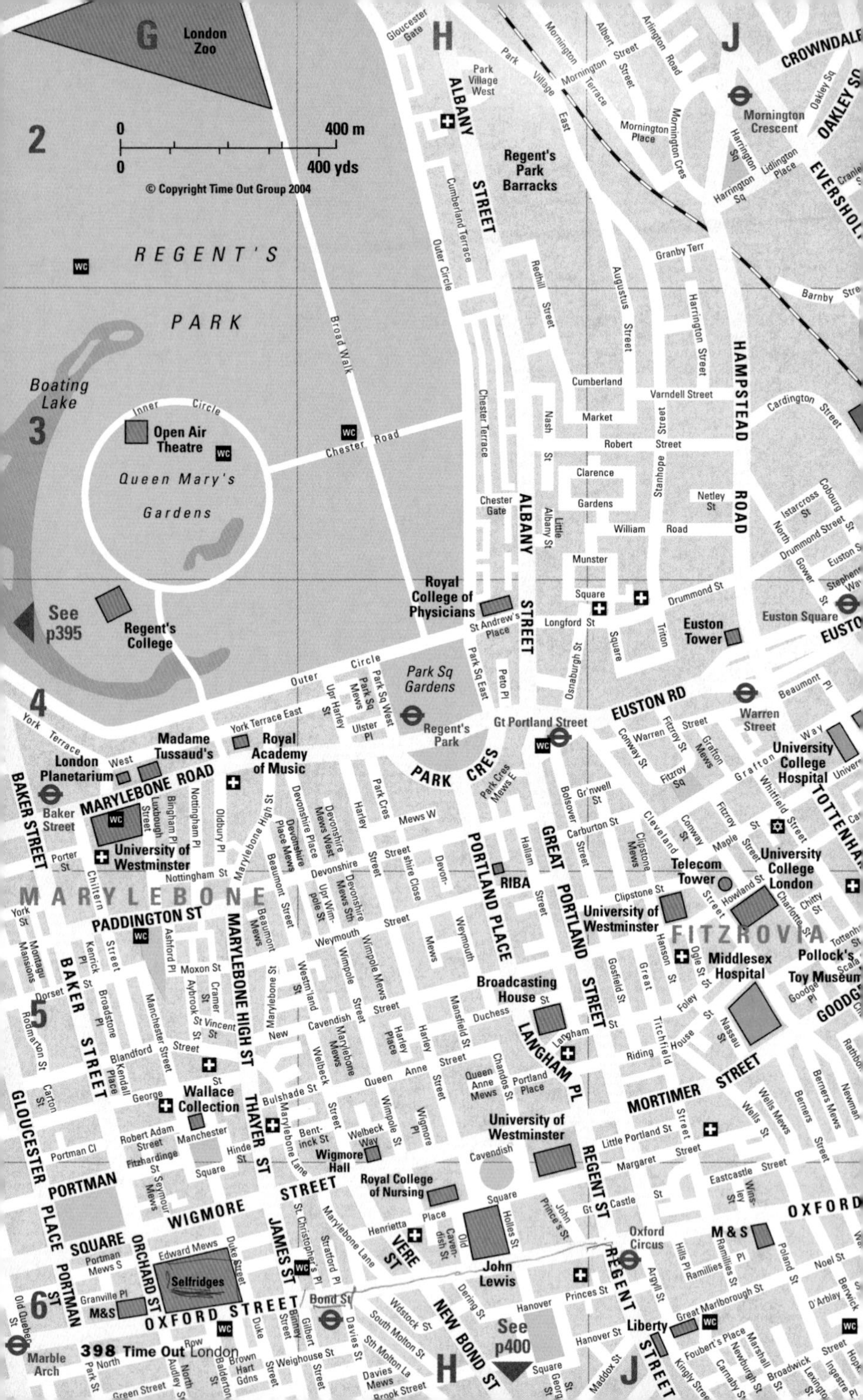
G
H
J
London Zoo
2
3
4
5
6
0
400 m
400 yds
© Copyright Time Out Group 2004
REGENT'S
PARK
Boating Lake
Inner Circle
Open Air Theatre
Queen Mary's Gardens
Broad Walk
Chester Road
Outer Circle
See p395
Regent's College
York Terrace
York Terrace East
York Terrace West
Madame Tussaud's
London Planetarium
Royal Academy of Music
MARYLEBONE ROAD
BAKER STREET
Baker Street
University of Westminster
MARYLEBONE
PADDINGTON ST
MARYLEBONE HIGH ST
Wallace Collection
THAYER ST
GLOUCESTER PLACE
PORTMAN SQUARE
ORCHARD ST
Selfridges
OXFORD STREET
Marble Arch
WIGMORE STREET
Wigmore Hall
Royal College of Nursing
JAMES ST
VERE ST
John Lewis
NEW BOND ST
Bond St
See p400
Gloucester Gate
Park Village West
ALBANY STREET
Cumberland Terrace
Regent's Park Barracks
Mornington Crescent
CROWNDALE
OAKLEY SQ
EVERSHOLT
HAMPSTEAD ROAD
Chester Terrace
Chester Gate
Royal College of Physicians
St Andrew's Place
Park Sq Gardens
Regent's Park
PARK CRES
Gt Portland Street
EUSTON RD
Euston Tower
Euston Square
Warren Street
University College Hospital
TOTTENHAM
PORTLAND PLACE
RIBA
GREAT PORTLAND STREET
Telecom Tower
University College London
FITZROVIA
University of Westminster
Middlesex Hospital
Pollock's Toy Museum
Broadcasting House
LANGHAM PL
MORTIMER STREET
Cavendish Square
REGENT ST
Oxford Circus
OXFORD
M & S
Liberty
REGENT STREET
Great Marlborough St
Hanover Square
Princes St

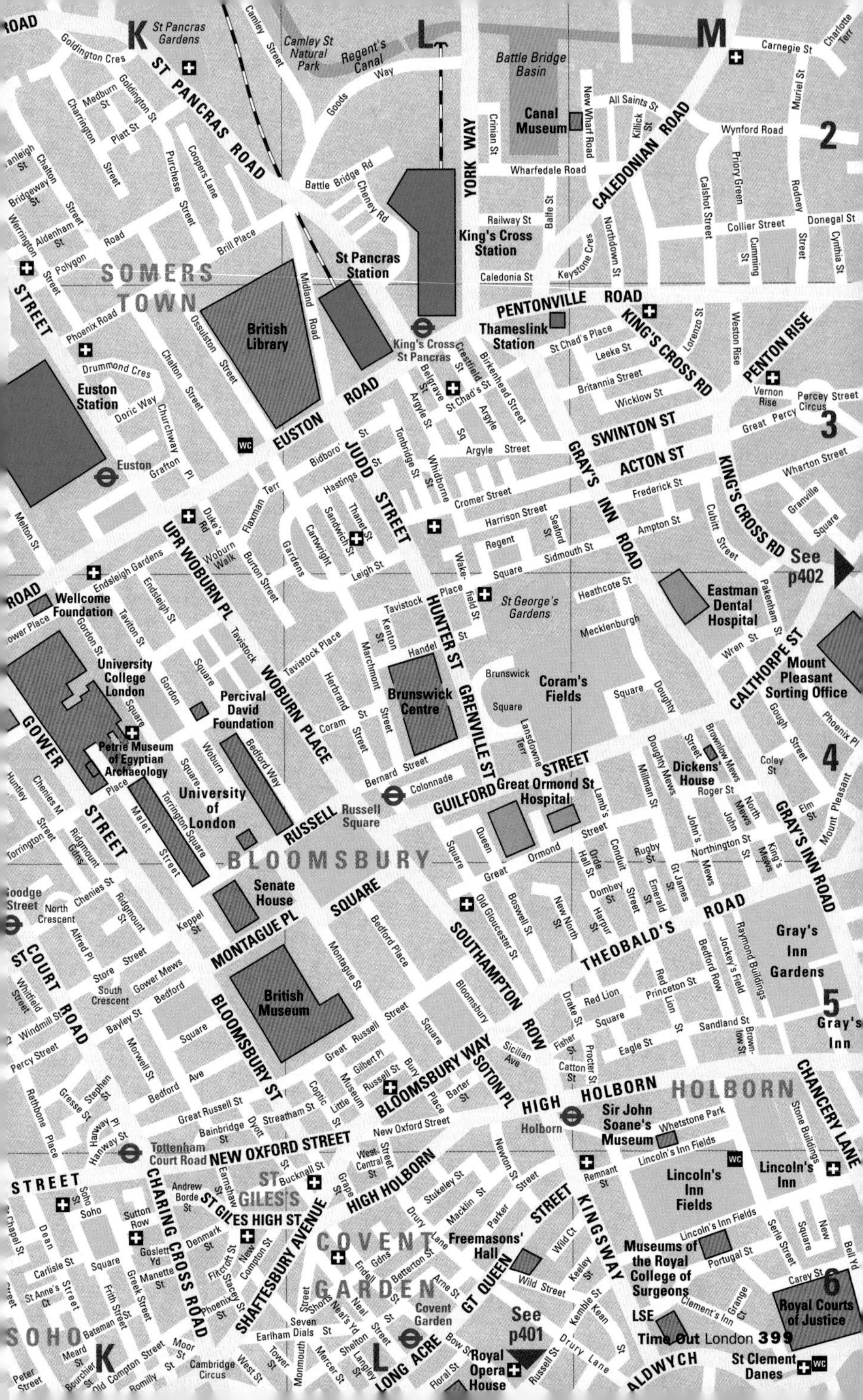
K
L
M
2
3
4
5
6
ROAD
St Pancras Gardens
Goldington Cres
ST PANCRAS ROAD
Camley Street
Camley St Natural Park
Regent's Canal
Goods Way
Battle Bridge Basin
Canal Museum
Carnegie St
Charlotte Terr
Muriel St
Medburn St
Goldington St
Charrington St
Platt St
Crinian St
New Wharf Road
All Saints St
Killick St
CALEDONIAN ROAD
Wynford Road
YORK WAY
Wharfedale Road
Purchese Street
Coopers Lane
Battle Bridge Rd
Cheney Rd
Leigh St
Chalton St
Bridgeway St
Werrington St
Aldenham St
Street
Road
Brill Place
Polygon
Railway St
Baife St
Northdown St
Calshot Street
Priory Green
Rodney Street
Collier Street
Donegal St
Cumming St
Cynthia St
SOMERS TOWN
British Library
Midland Road
St Pancras Station
King's Cross Station
Keystone Cres
Caledonia St
STREET
Ossulston Street
PENTONVILLE ROAD
Phoenix Road
Thameslink Station
KING'S CROSS RD
Lorenzo St
Weston Rise
PENTON RISE
Drummond Cres
Euston Station
King's Cross St Pancras
Crestfield St
Belgrave St
St Chad's Place
Leeke St
Britannia Street
Wicklow St
Vernon Rise
Percey Street
Percy Circus
Doric Way
Chalton Street
Churchway
EUSTON ROAD
Argyle St
St Chad's St
Birkenhead Street
Argyle Sq
Great Percy St
SWINTON ST
WC
Euston
Grafton Pl
Bidborough St
JUDD STREET
Tonbridge St
Whidborne St
Argyle Street
GRAY'S INN ROAD
ACTON ST
Wharton Street
Hastings St
Cromer Street
Frederick St
Duke's Rd
Flaxman Terr
Thanet St
Sandwich St
Cartwright Gardens
Harrison Street
Seaford St
Ampton St
KING'S CROSS RD
Granville Square
Melton St
UPR WOBURN PL
Woburn Walk
Burton Street
Leigh St
Regent Square
Sidmouth St
Cubitt Street
See p402
Endsleigh Gardens
Wake-field St
Tavistock Place
HUNTER ST
Heathcote St
ROAD
Wellcome Foundation
Endsleigh St
Taviton St
Gower Place
Gordon St
St George's Gardens
Eastman Dental Hospital
Pakenham St
Kenton St
Tavistock Square
Mecklenburgh Square
Wren St
Tavistock Place
Marchmont St
Handel St
CALTHORPE ST
Mount Pleasant Sorting Office
University College London
Gordon Square
WOBURN PLACE
Herbrand St
Brunswick Centre
Brunswick Square
Coram's Fields
Doughty St
GRENVILLE ST
Percival David Foundation
Coram St
Lansdowne Terr
Gough Street
Phoenix Pl
GOWER STREET
Petrie Museum of Egyptian Archaeology
Woburn Square
Bedford Way
Bernard Street
Colonnade
GUILFORD STREET
Great Ormond St Hospital
Doughty Mews
Millman St
Brownlow Mews
Dickens' House
Coley St
Huntley St
Chenies M
Torrington Square
University of London
RUSSELL SQUARE
Russell Square
Lamb's Conduit
Roger St
North Mews
John St
GRAY'S INN ROAD
Elm St
Mount Pleasant
Torrington Pl
Ridgmount Gdns
Malet Street
Queen Square
Great Ormond Street
John's Mews
Rugby St
Northington St
King's Mews
BLOOMSBURY
Orde Hall St
Gt James St
Goodge Street
North Crescent
Chenies St
Ridgmount St
Senate House
Old Gloucester St
Boswell St
New North St
Dombey St
Harpur St
Emerald St
Keppel St
SQUARE
MONTAGUE PL
SOUTHAMPTON ROW
THEOBALD'S ROAD
Raymond Buildings
Gray's Inn Gardens
COURT ROAD
Alfred Pl
Store Street
Gower Mews
South Crescent
Bedford Square
British Museum
Montague St
Bedford Place
Bloomsbury Square
Red Lion Street
Princeton St
Bedford Row
Jockey's Field
Whitfield Street
Windmill St
Bayley St
Morwell St
BLOOMSBURY ST
Great Russell Street
Drake St
Red Lion Square
Fisher St
Sandland St
Brownlow St
Gray's Inn
Percy Street
Bedford Ave
Gilbert Pl
Museum St
Bury Place
BLOOMSBURY WAY
Sicilian Ave
SOTON PL
Eagle St
Procter St
Catton St
CHANCERY LANE
Rathbone Place
Gresse St
Stephen St
Great Russell St
Coptic St
Little Russell St
Barter St
HIGH HOLBORN
HOLBORN
Hanway Pl
Hanway St
Bainbridge St
Dyott St
Streatham St
New Oxford Street
Holborn
Sir John Soane's Museum
Whetstone Park
Stone Buildings
Tottenham Court Road
NEW OXFORD STREET
West Central St
Newton St
Lincoln's Inn Fields
WC
Lincoln's Inn
STREET
CHARING CROSS ROAD
Earnsham St
Bucknall St
Grape St
HIGH HOLBORN
Remnant St
Lincoln's Inn Fields
Soho Sq
Andrew Borde St
ST GILES'S
Stukeley St
Drury Lane
Macklin St
Parker St
GT QUEEN STREET
KINGSWAY
Soho
Sutton Row
ST GILES HIGH ST
SHAFTESBURY AVENUE
Freemasons' Hall
Wild Ct
Lincoln's Inn Fields
Serle Street
New Square
Chapel St
Dean Street
Goslett Yd
Denmark St
Flitcroft St
New Compton St
COVENT GARDEN
Endell St
Betterton St
Museums of the Royal College of Surgeons
Portugal St
Bell Yd
Carlisle St
Square
Manette St
Greek Street
Stacey St
Arne St
Wild Street
Keeley St
Carey St
St Anne's Ct
Frith Street
Phoenix St
Shorts Gdns
Neal St
Covent Garden
Kemble St
Kean St
Clement's Inn
Grange Ct
Royal Courts of Justice
SOHO
Bateman St
Seven Dials
Earlham St
Neal's Yd
Shelton St
Langley St
See p401
LSE
Time Out London 399
Meard St
Moor St
Monmouth St
Mercer St
Tower St
Bow St
Drury Lane
Peter Street
Bourchier St
Old Compton Street
Romilly St
Cambridge Circus
West St
LONG ACRE
Floral St
Royal Opera House
Russell St
ALDWYCH
St Clement Danes

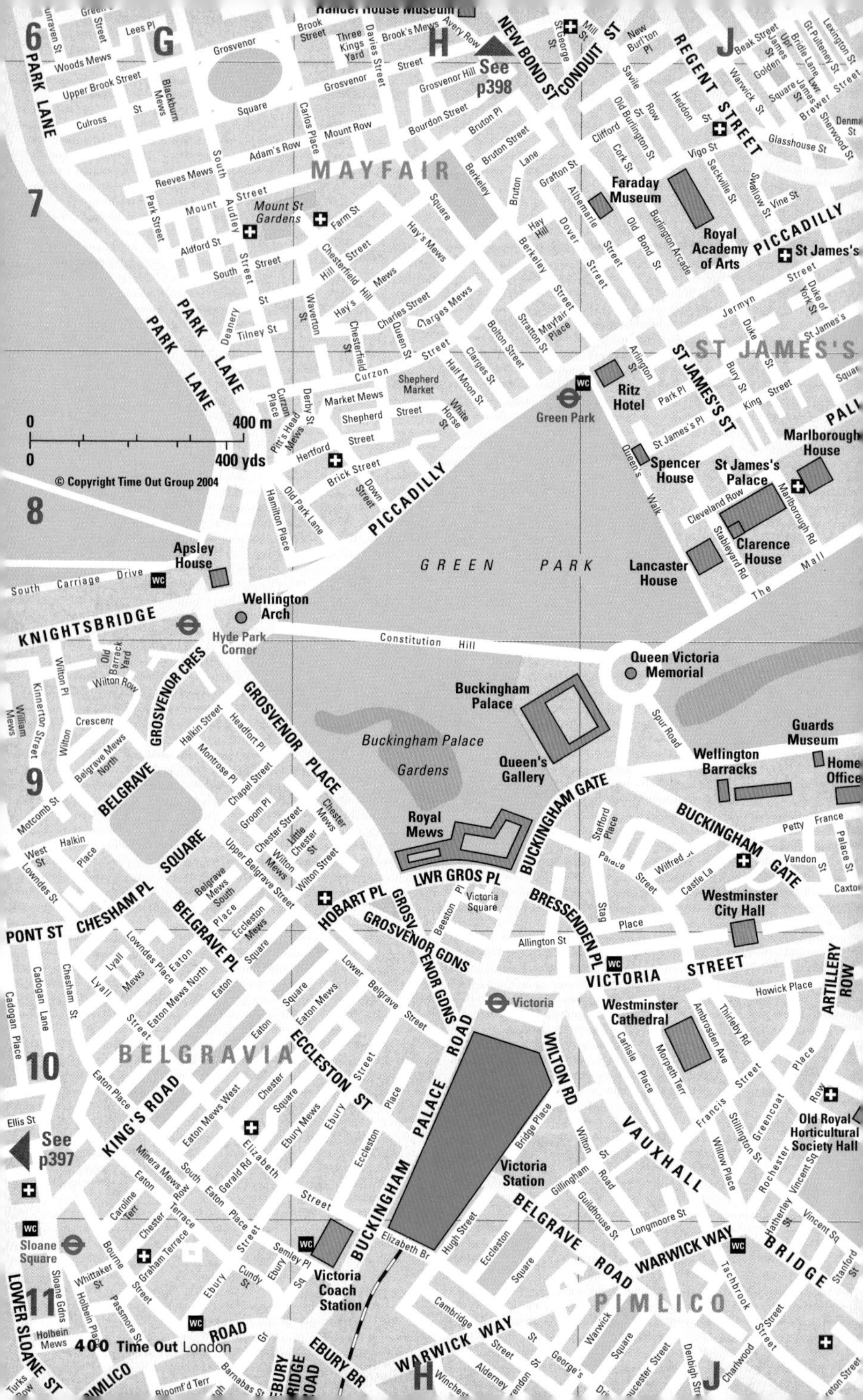

Handel House Museum
6
7
8
9
10
11
G
H
J
See p398
See p397
MAYFAIR
ST JAMES'S
BELGRAVIA
PIMLICO
GREEN PARK
PARK LANE
Park Lane
Lees Pl
Green St
Unraven St
Woods Mews
Upper Brook Street
Culross St
Blackburn Mews
Grosvenor Square
Brook Street
Three Kings Yard
Davies Street
Brook's Mews
Avery Row
Grosvenor Street
Grosvenor Hill
Carlos Place
Mount Row
Bourdon Street
Adam's Row
Reeves Mews
South Audley Street
Mount Street
Park Street
Mount St Gardens
Farm St
Aldford St
South Street
Hay's Mews
Chesterfield Hill
Chesterfield Street
Hill Street
Hay's Mews
Charles Street
Waverton St
Deanery St
Tilney St
Queen St
Clarges Mews
Curzon Street
Curzon Place
Derby St
Shepherd Market
Market Mews
Shepherd Street
Pitt's Head Mews
Hertford Street
Brick Street
Down Street
Old Park Lane
Hamilton Place
Half Moon St
Clarges St
White Horse St
Bolton Street
Stratton Street
Mayfair Place
Berkeley Street
Berkeley Square
Bruton Pl
Bruton Street
Bruton Lane
Hay Hill
Dover Street
Grafton St
Albemarle Street
Old Bond St
NEW BOND ST
St George St
Mill St
CONDUIT ST
New Burl'ton Pl
Savile Row
Old Burlington St
Clifford St
Cork St
Burlington Arcade
Faraday Museum
Royal Academy of Arts
REGENT STREET
Heddon St
Vigo St
Sackville St
Swallow St
Vine St
Beak Street
Warwick St
Golden Square
Upr James St
Lwr James St
Bridle Lane
Gt Pulteney St
Lexington St
Brewer Street
Sherwood St
Denman St
Glasshouse St
PICCADILLY
St James's
Jermyn Street
Duke of York St
Duke St
St James's Square
Arlington St
Bury St
King Street
Park Pl
ST JAMES'S ST
St James's Pl
Ritz Hotel
Green Park
PALL MALL
Marlborough House
Spencer House
Queen's Walk
St James's Palace
Cleveland Row
Marlborough Rd
Stableyard Rd
Clarence House
Lancaster House
The Mall
400 m
400 yds
© Copyright Time Out Group 2004
Apsley House
South Carriage Drive
Wellington Arch
KNIGHTSBRIDGE
Hyde Park Corner
Constitution Hill
Queen Victoria Memorial
Buckingham Palace
Buckingham Palace Gardens
Queen's Gallery
Spur Road
Guards Museum
Wellington Barracks
Home Office
Royal Mews
BUCKINGHAM GATE
Petty France
Palace St
Stafford Place
Palace Street
Wilfred St
Castle La
Vandon St
Caxton St
Westminster City Hall
Stag Place
Allington St
BRESSENDEN PL
VICTORIA STREET
ARTILLERY ROW
Howick Place
Victoria
Westminster Cathedral
Ambrosden Ave
Thirleby Rd
Carlisle Place
Morpeth Terr
Francis Street
Stillington St
Greencoat Place
Rochester Row
Old Royal Horticultural Society Hall
Willow Place
Vincent Sq
Hatherley St
Old Barrack Yard
Wilton Pl
Wilton Row
Wilton Crescent
Kinnerton Street
William Mews
GROSVENOR CRES
Halkin Street
Headfort Pl
Montrose Pl
Chapel Street
Belgrave Mews North
BELGRAVE SQUARE
GROSVENOR PLACE
Chester Mews
Groom Pl
Chester Street
Little Chester St
Wilton Mews
Wilton Street
Motcomb St
West Halkin St
Halkin Place
Lowndes St
Upper Belgrave Street
Belgrave Mews South
Eccleston Mews
HOBART PL
LWR GROS PL
Victoria Square
Beeston Pl
GROSVENOR GDNS
GROSV ENOR GDNS
PONT ST
CHESHAM PL
BELGRAVE PL
Lowndes Place
Eaton Square
Eaton Mews North
Lyall Mews
Lyall Street
Chesham St
Cadogan Lane
Cadogan Place
Lower Belgrave Street
Eaton Mews
ECCLESTON ST
Eaton Place
Eccleston Street
Eccleston Place
Chester Square
Ebury Mews
Ebury Street
BUCKINGHAM PALACE ROAD
WILTON RD
Bridge Place
Victoria Station
Wilton Road
Gillingham St
Guildhouse St
VAUXHALL BRIDGE ROAD
Longmoore St
BELGRAVE ROAD
WARWICK WAY
Tachbrook Street
Stanford St
KING'S ROAD
Ellis St
Eaton Mews West
Elizabeth Street
Gerald Rd
South Eaton Place
Minera Mews
Eaton Row
Eaton Terrace
Caroline Terr
Chester Row
Graham Terrace
Bourne Street
Sloane Square
Whittaker St
Holbein Place
Sloane Gdns
Holbein Mews
Passmore St
Cundy St
Ebury Sq
Semley Pl
Elizabeth Br
Hugh Street
Eccleston Square
Victoria Coach Station
Cambridge Street
Alderney Street
Warwick Square
St George's
Denbigh Street
Charlwood
LOWER SLOANE ST
ROAD
PIMLICO ROAD
Bloomf'd Terr
EBURY BRIDGE ROAD
EBURY BR
WARWICK WAY

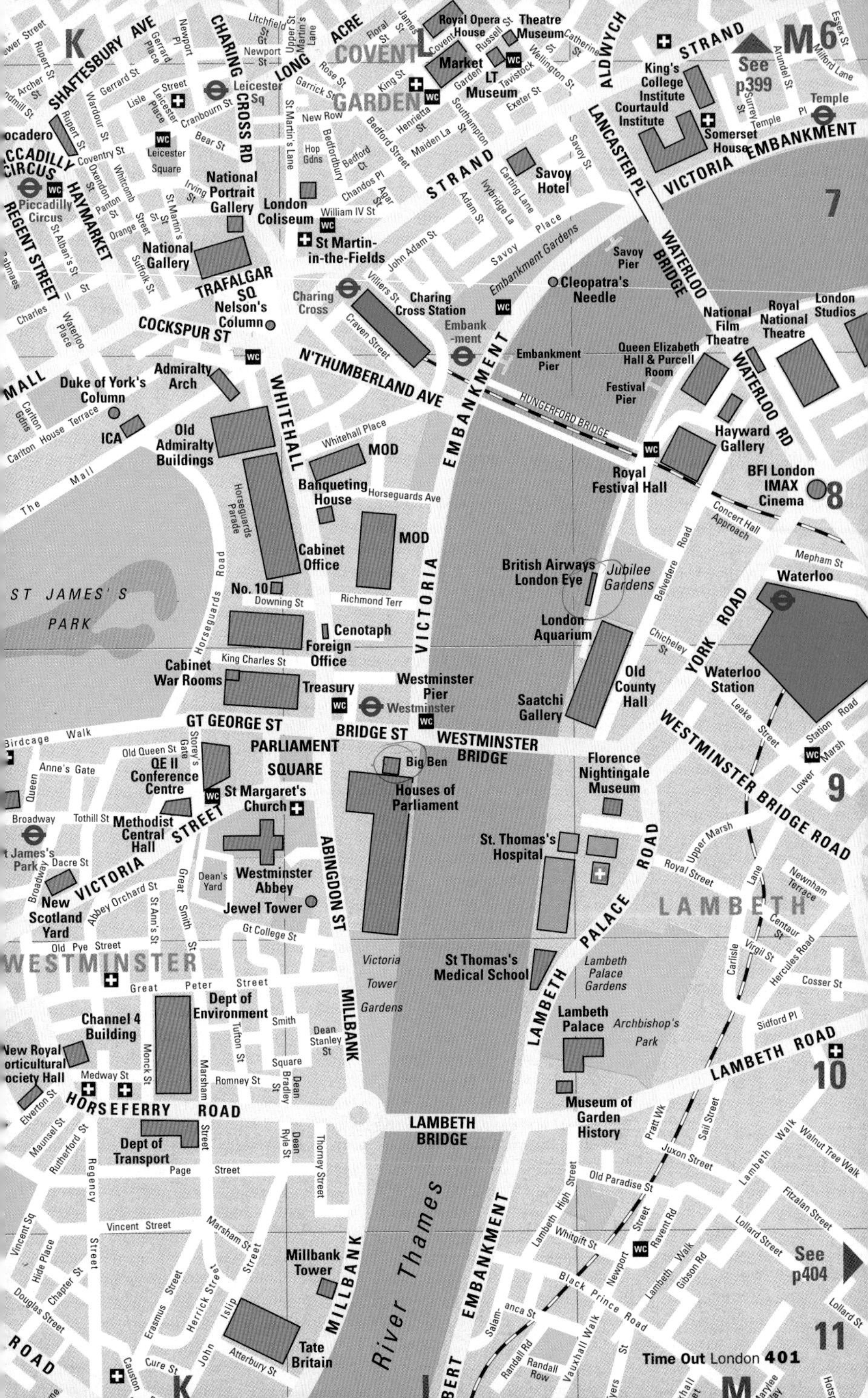

K
L
M
6
7
8
9
10
11
See p399
See p404
SHAFTESBURY AVE
CHARING CROSS RD
LONG ACRE
COVENT GARDEN
Royal Opera House
Theatre Museum
Market
LT Museum
ALDWYCH
STRAND
King's College Institute
Courtauld Institute
Somerset House
Temple
VICTORIA EMBANKMENT
Leicester Sq
Leicester Square
Piccadilly Circus
PICCADILLY CIRCUS
HAYMARKET
REGENT STREET
National Portrait Gallery
London Coliseum
St Martin-in-the-Fields
National Gallery
TRAFALGAR SQ
Nelson's Column
COCKSPUR ST
Charing Cross
Charing Cross Station
Savoy Hotel
Savoy Pier
Cleopatra's Needle
Embankment
Embankment Pier
WATERLOO BRIDGE
National Film Theatre
Royal National Theatre
London Studios
Queen Elizabeth Hall & Purcell Room
Festival Pier
HUNGERFORD BRIDGE
Hayward Gallery
Royal Festival Hall
BFI London IMAX Cinema
WATERLOO RD
N'THUMBERLAND AVE
WHITEHALL
Admiralty Arch
Duke of York's Column
ICA
Old Admiralty Buildings
The Mall
MOD
Banqueting House
Horseguards Parade
Horseguards Road
Cabinet Office
No. 10
Downing St
Richmond Terr
Cenotaph
Foreign Office
Cabinet War Rooms
King Charles St
Treasury
ST JAMES'S PARK
VICTORIA EMBANKMENT
British Airways London Eye
Jubilee Gardens
London Aquarium
Old County Hall
Saatchi Gallery
Waterloo
Waterloo Station
YORK ROAD
Westminster Pier
Westminster
GT GEORGE ST
BRIDGE ST
WESTMINSTER BRIDGE
PARLIAMENT SQUARE
Big Ben
Houses of Parliament
QE II Conference Centre
St Margaret's Church
Methodist Central Hall
VICTORIA STREET
Westminster Abbey
Jewel Tower
New Scotland Yard
St James's Park
Broadway
ABINGDON ST
Florence Nightingale Museum
St. Thomas's Hospital
WESTMINSTER BRIDGE ROAD
LAMBETH
LAMBETH PALACE ROAD
WESTMINSTER
Victoria Tower Gardens
St Thomas's Medical School
Lambeth Palace Gardens
Lambeth Palace
Archbishop's Park
Dept of Environment
Channel 4 Building
New Royal Horticultural Society Hall
HORSEFERRY ROAD
MILLBANK
LAMBETH BRIDGE
LAMBETH ROAD
Museum of Garden History
Dept of Transport
River Thames
Millbank Tower
Tate Britain
ALBERT EMBANKMENT
Black Prince Road
Vauxhall Walk
Lambeth Walk

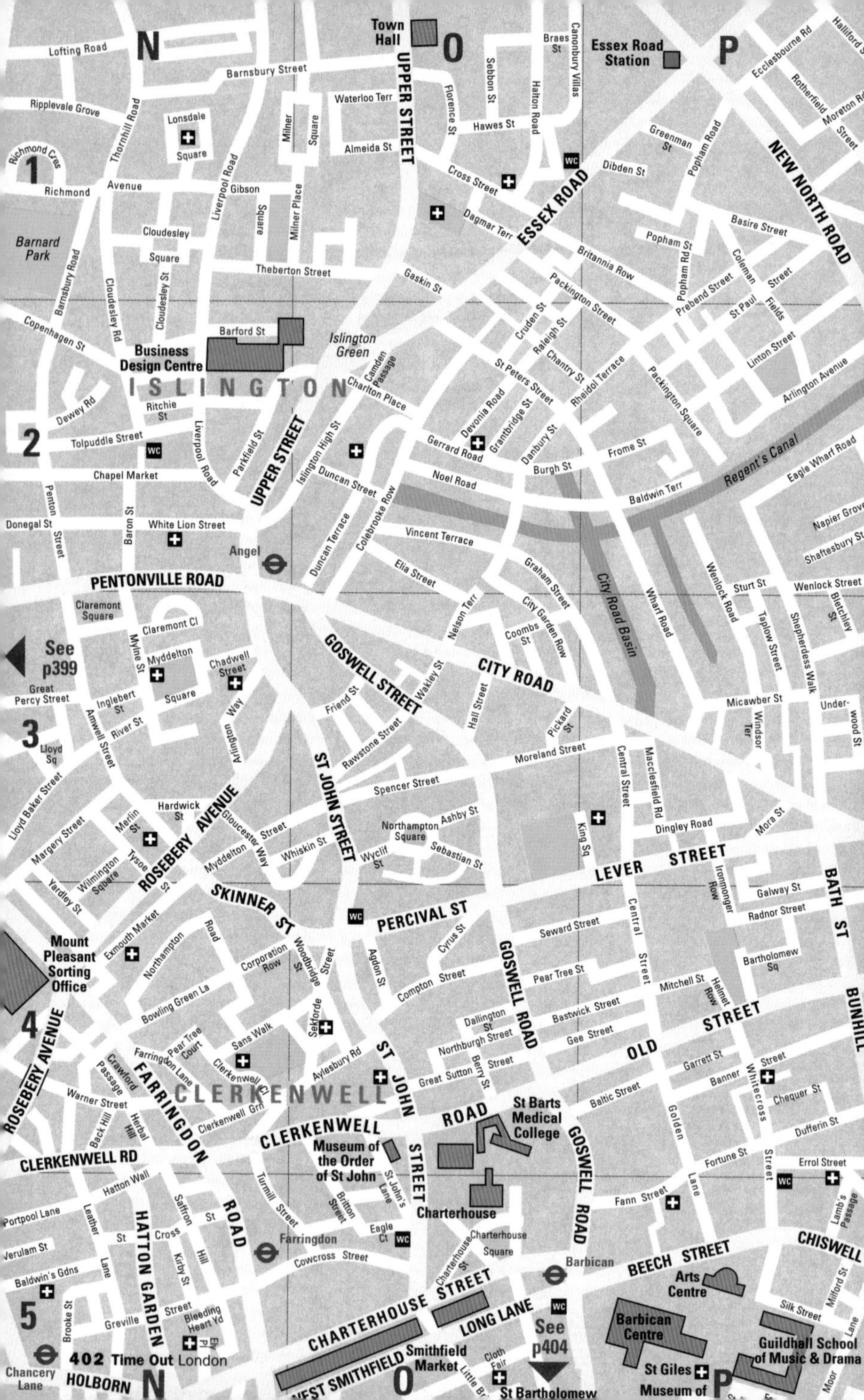

N
O
P
1
2
3
4
5
Town Hall
Essex Road Station
Lofting Road
Barnsbury Street
Ripplevale Grove
Richmond Cres
Richmond
Avenue
Thornhill Road
Lonsdale Square
Liverpool Road
Gibson Square
Milner Square
Milner Place
Waterloo Terr
Almeida St
UPPER STREET
Florence St
Sebbon St
Halton Road
Braes St
Canonbury Villas
Hawes St
Cross Street
Dagmar Terr
ESSEX ROAD
Dibden St
Greenman St
Popham Road
Ecclesbourne Rd
Rotherfield Street
Moreton Rd
Halliford St
NEW NORTH ROAD
Basire Street
Popham St
Britannia Row
Barnard Park
Barnsbury Road
Cloudesley Square
Cloudesley Rd
Cloudesley St
Theberton Street
Gaskin St
Packington Street
Popham Rd
Prebend Street
Coleman Fields
Street
St Paul St
Linton Street
Arlington Avenue
Copenhagen St
Barford St
Business Design Centre
Islington Green
ISLINGTON
Camden Passage
Charlton Place
Cruden St
Raleigh St
Chantry St
St Peters Street
Rheidol Terrace
Packington Square
Dewey Rd
Ritchie St
Tolpuddle Street
Liverpool Road
Parkfield St
Islington High St
Devonia Road
Grantbridge St
Danbury St
Gerrard Road
Frome St
Burgh St
Regent's Canal
Eagle Wharf Road
Chapel Market
Duncan Street
Noel Road
Baldwin Terr
Colebrooke Row
Penton Street
Donegal St
Baron St
White Lion Street
Duncan Terrace
Vincent Terrace
Napier Grove
Shaftesbury St
Angel
Elia Street
Graham Street
City Road Basin
Wharf Road
Wenlock Road
Sturt St
Wenlock Street
PENTONVILLE ROAD
Claremont Square
Claremont Cl
City Garden Row
Nelson Terr
Coombs St
Taplow Street
Shepherdess Walk
Bletchley St
See p399
Mylne St
Myddelton Square
Chadwell Street
GOSWELL STREET
Wakley St
CITY ROAD
Great Percy Street
Inglebert St
River St
Amwell Street
Arlington Way
Friend St
Hall Street
Pickard St
Micawber St
Windsor Ter
Underwood St
Lloyd Sq
Rawstone Street
Moreland Street
Central Street
Macclesfield Rd
Lloyd Baker Street
ROSEBERY AVENUE
Hardwick St
Gloucester Way
ST JOHN STREET
Spencer Street
Northampton Square
Ashby St
King Sq
Dingley Road
Mora St
Margery Street
Merlin St
Myddelton Street
Whiskin St
Wyclif St
Sebastian St
LEVER STREET
Ironmonger Row
BATH ST
Wilmington Square
Tysoe St
Yardley St
SKINNER ST
PERCIVAL ST
Galway St
Radnor Street
Seward Street
Mount Pleasant Sorting Office
Exmouth Market
Northampton Road
Corporation Row
Woodbridge Street
Agdon St
Cyrus St
GOSWELL ROAD
Central Street
Bartholomew Sq
Pear Tree St
Bowling Green La
Compton Street
Mitchell St
Helmet Row
BUNHILL
Sekforde St
Dallington St
Bastwick Street
OLD STREET
Pear Tree Court
Sans Walk
Northburgh Street
Gee Street
Farringdon Lane
Crawford Passage
Clerkenwell Cl
Aylesbury Rd
ST JOHN
Great Sutton Street
Berry St
Garrett St
Banner Street
Whitecross Street
CLERKENWELL
FARRINGDON
Warner Street
Chequer St
Clerkenwell Grn
St Barts Medical College
Baltic Street
Back Hill
Herbal Hill
CLERKENWELL
ROAD
Golden Lane
Dufferin St
CLERKENWELL RD
Museum of the Order of St John
STREET
Fortune St
Errol Street
Hatton Wall
Turnmill Street
St John's Lane
Britton Street
Charterhouse
Fann Street
Lamb's Passage
Portpool Lane
Leather Lane
HATTON GARDEN
Saffron St
Cross St
ROAD
Eagle Ct
Charterhouse Square
CHISWELL
Verulam St
Hill
Kirby St
Farringdon
Cowcross Street
Charterhouse St
Barbican
BEECH STREET
Arts Centre
Milford St
Baldwin's Gdns
Lane
CHARTERHOUSE STREET
Silk Street
Brooke St
Greville Street
Bleeding Heart Yd
LONG LANE
See p404
Barbican Centre
Guildhall School of Music & Drama
Ely Pl
Smithfield Market
Chancery Lane
WEST SMITHFIELD
Cloth Fair
St Giles
HOLBORN
Little Br
St Bartholomew
Museum of
Moor

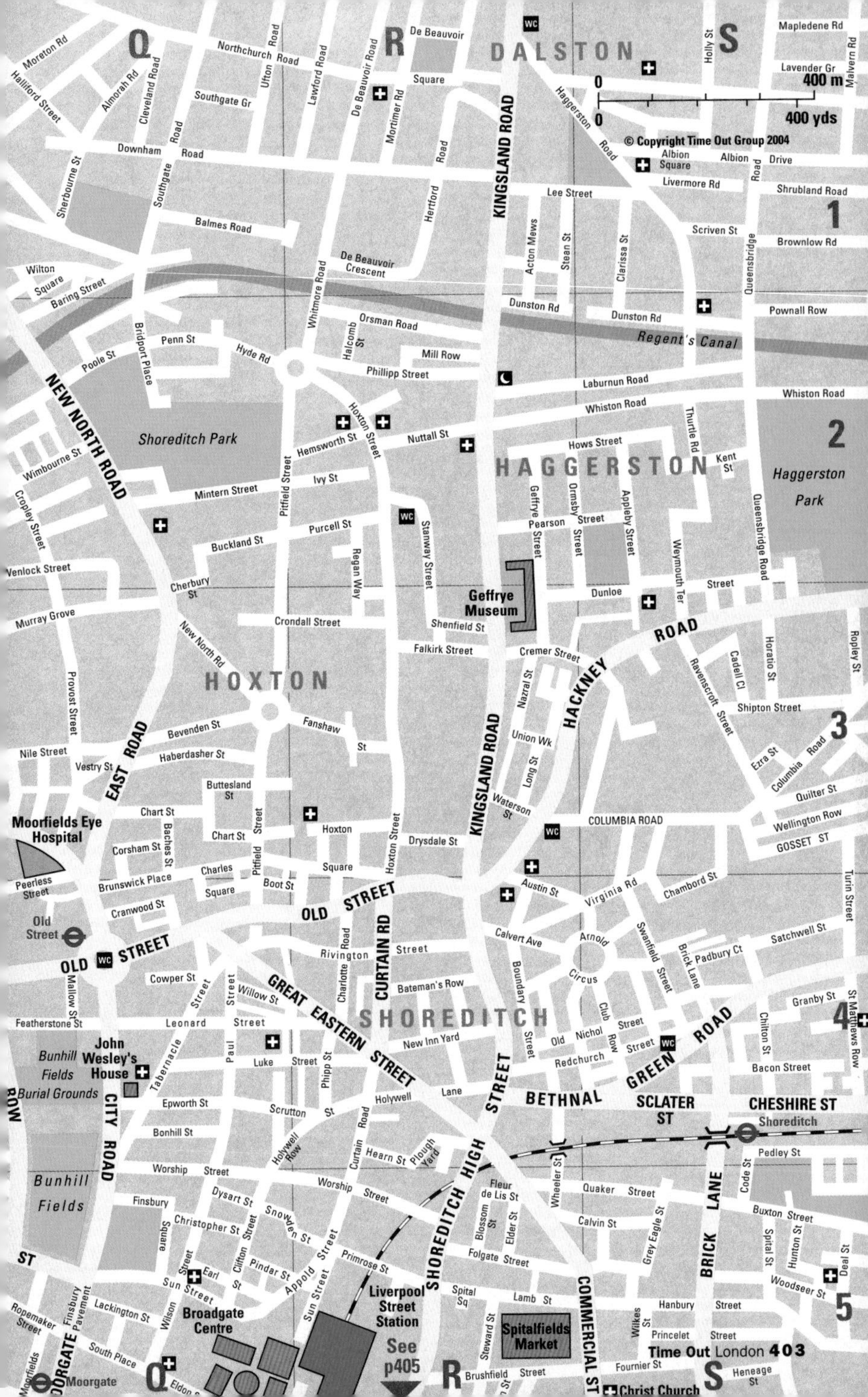
Q
R
S
DALSTON
HAGGERSTON
HOXTON
SHOREDITCH
1
2
3
4
5
0
400 m
0
400 yds
© Copyright Time Out Group 2004
Moreton Rd
Halliford Street
Almorah Rd
Cleveland Road
Northchurch Road
Ufton Road
Lawford Road
De Beauvoir Road
De Beauvoir Square
Mortimer Rd
Southgate Gr
Downham Road
Southgate Road
Sherbourne St
Balmes Road
Hertford Road
De Beauvoir Crescent
Whitmore Road
Kingsland Road
Haggerston Road
Holly St
Mapledene Rd
Lavender Gr
Malvern Rd
Albion Square
Albion Drive
Livermore Rd
Lee Street
Queensbridge Road
Shrubland Road
Scriven St
Brownlow Rd
Acton Mews
Stean St
Clarissa St
Wilton Square
Baring Street
Dunston Rd
Pownall Row
Regent's Canal
Orsman Road
Halcomb St
Mill Row
Bridport Place
Penn St
Hyde Rd
Poole St
Phillipp Street
Laburnun Road
Whiston Road
New North Road
Shoreditch Park
Hoxton Street
Hemsworth St
Nuttall St
Hows Street
Thurtle Rd
Kent St
Haggerston Park
Wimbourne St
Cropley Street
Mintern Street
Ivy St
Pitfield Street
Geffrye Street
Ormsby Street
Appleby Street
Pearson Street
Buckland St
Purcell St
Regan Way
Stanway Street
Weymouth Ter
Venlock Street
Cherbury St
Geffrye Museum
Dunloe Street
Murray Grove
Crondall Street
Shenfield St
Falkirk Street
Cremer Street
Hackney Road
Ropley St
Horatio St
Cadell Cl
Ravenscroft Street
Provost Street
Fanshaw St
Bevenden St
Nazral St
Union Wk
Shipton Street
Nile Street
Haberdasher St
Vestry St
East Road
Long St
Ezra St
Columbia Road
Quilter St
Buttesland St
Waterson St
Wellington Row
Moorfields Eye Hospital
Chart St
Baches St
Hoxton Square
Drysdale St
COLUMBIA ROAD
GOSSET ST
Corsham St
Charles Square
Brunswick Place
Peerless Street
Boot St
Austin St
Virginia Rd
Chambord St
Turin Street
Cranwood St
Old Street
Old Street
Curtain Rd
Calvert Ave
Arnold Circus
Swanfield Street
Brick Lane
Padbury Ct
Satchwell St
Rivington Street
Charlotte Road
Boundary Street
Cowper St
Mallow St
Bateman's Row
Willow St
Great Eastern Street
Club Row
Granby St
St Matthews Row
Featherstone St
Leonard Street
Paul Street
Tabernacle Street
Old Nichol Street
Redchurch Street
Bethnal Green Road
Chilton St
John Wesley's House
Bunhill Fields Burial Grounds
New Inn Yard
Luke Street
Phipp St
Bacon Street
City Road
Epworth St
Holywell Lane
Shoreditch High Street
Bethnal Green
Sclater St
Cheshire St
Scrutton St
Shoreditch
Bonhill St
Holywell Row
Hearn St
Plough Yard
Wheeler St
Pedley St
Code St
Worship Street
Finsbury Square
Dysart St
Fleur de Lis St
Quaker Street
Grey Eagle St
Buxton Street
Christopher St
Blossom St
Elder St
Calvin St
Bunhill Fields
Snowden St
Folgate Street
Spital St
Hunton St
Deal St
Earl St
Clifton Street
Pindar St
Primrose St
Appold Street
Sun Street
Liverpool Street Station
Spital Sq
Lamb St
Commercial St
Woodseer St
Hanbury Street
Lackington St
Finsbury Pavement
Wilson Street
Broadgate Centre
Steward St
Spitalfields Market
Wilkes St
Princelet Street
Ropemaker Street
South Place
See p405
Brushfield Street
Fournier St
Heneage St
Moorgate
Eldon St
Christ Church
Moorfields

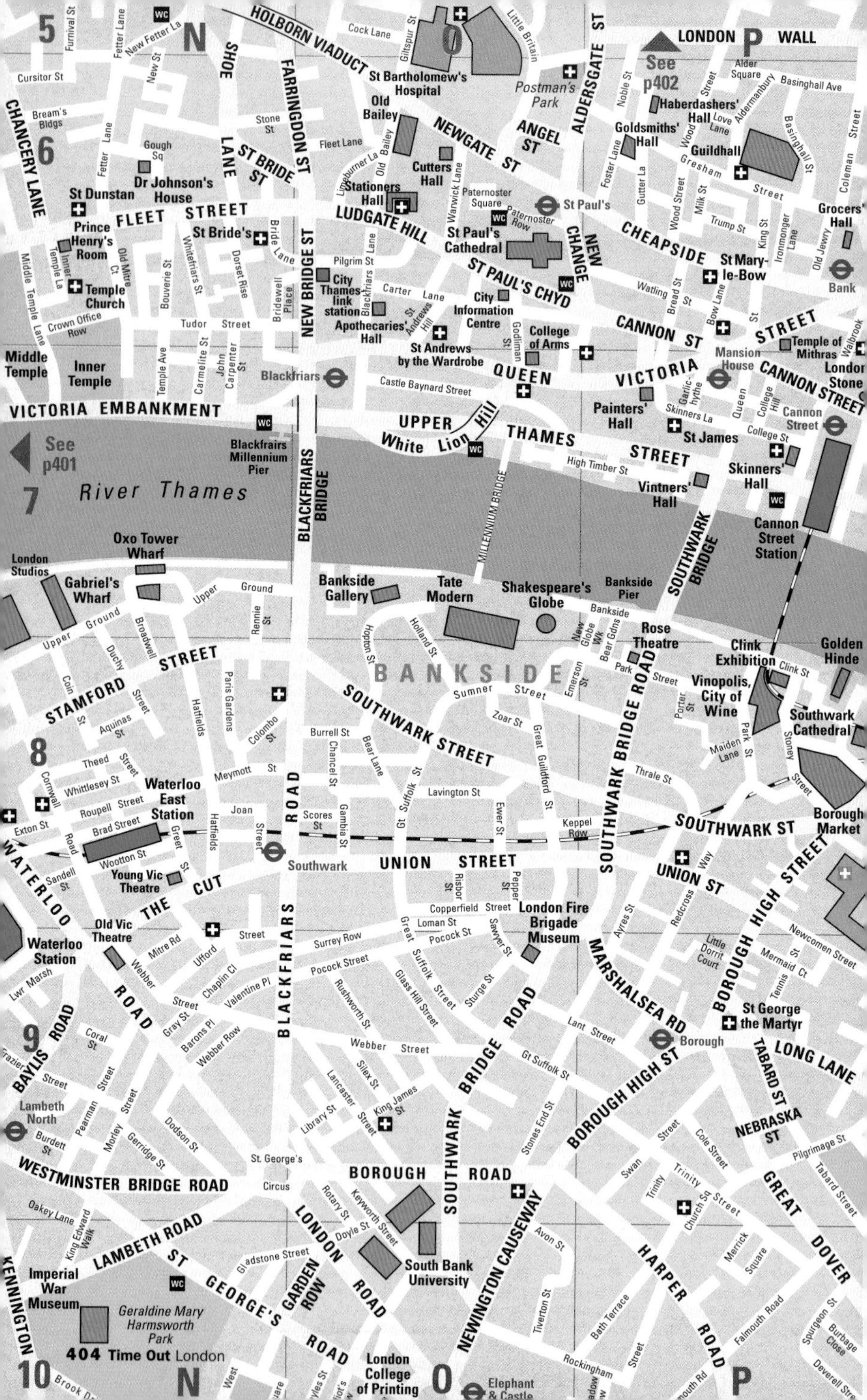

5
N
O
P
6
7
8
9
10
HOLBORN VIADUCT
LONDON WALL
See p402
See p401
Furnival St
Fetter Lane
New Fetter La
New St
SHOE LANE
FARRINGDON ST
Cock Lane
Giltspur St
Little Britain
ALDERSGATE ST
Alder Square
Basinghall Ave
Cursitor St
St Bartholomew's Hospital
Postman's Park
Noble St
Haberdashers' Hall
Love Lane
Aldermanbury
Basinghall St
CHANCERY LANE
Bream's Bldgs
Stone St
Old Bailey
NEWGATE ST
ANGEL ST
Goldsmiths' Hall
Wood Street
Guildhall
Coleman St
Fetter Lane
Gough Sq
ST BRIDE ST
Fleet Lane
Limeburner La
Cutters Hall
Warwick Lane
Foster Lane
Gutter La
Gresham Street
Dr Johnson's House
Stationers Hall
Paternoster Square
St Paul's
Milk St
Grocers' Hall
St Dunstan
FLEET STREET
LUDGATE HILL
Paternoster Row
Wood Street
Trump St
Prince Henry's Room
St Bride's
Bride Lane
St Paul's Cathedral
NEW CHANGE
CHEAPSIDE
King St
Ironmonger Lane
Old Jewry
Inner Temple La
Old Mitre Ct
Whitefriars St
Dorset Rise
Pilgrim St
Blackfriars Lane
ST PAUL'S CHYD
St Mary-le-Bow
Bank
Middle Temple Lane
Temple Church
Bouverie St
Bridewell Place
NEW BRIDGE ST
City Thames-link station
Carter Lane
City Information Centre
Watling St
Bread St
Bow Lane
Crown Office Row
Tudor Street
Apothecaries' Hall
St Andrews Hill
Godliman St
College of Arms
CANNON ST
STREET
Walbrook
Middle Temple
Inner Temple
Temple Ave
Carmelite St
John Carpenter St
Blackfriars
St Andrews by the Wardrobe
QUEEN
VICTORIA
Mansion House
Temple of Mithras
London Stone
Castle Baynard Street
Garlick-hythe
Queen St
College Hill
CANNON STREET
VICTORIA EMBANKMENT
UPPER THAMES
White Lion Hill
Painters' Hall
Skinners La
Cannon Street
College St
St James
THAMES STREET
High Timber St
Blackfriars Millennium Pier
River Thames
BLACKFRIARS BRIDGE
MILLENNIUM BRIDGE
Vintners' Hall
Skinners' Hall
Cannon Street Station
SOUTHWARK BRIDGE
Oxo Tower Wharf
London Studios
Gabriel's Wharf
Upper Ground
Rennie St
Bankside Gallery
Tate Modern
Shakespeare's Globe
Bankside Pier
Bankside
Upper Ground
Broadwell
Duchy
Hopton St
Holland St
New Globe Wk
Bear Gdns
Rose Theatre
Clink Exhibition
Clink St
Golden Hinde
STREET
BANKSIDE
Park Street
Emerson St
Vinopolis, City of Wine
Porter St
Coin St
Paris Gardens
Hatfields
Sumner Street
SOUTHWARK BRIDGE ROAD
Southwark Cathedral
STAMFORD ST
Aquinas St
Colombo St
SOUTHWARK STREET
Zoar St
Great Guildford St
Park St
Maiden Lane
Stoney Street
Burrell St
Chancel St
Bear Lane
Theed Street
Cornwall Road
Whittlesey St
Meymott St
Gt Suffolk St
Lavington St
Thrale St
Waterloo East Station
Roupell Street
Joan Street
Scores St
Gambia St
Ewer St
Keppel Row
SOUTHWARK ST
Borough Market
Exton St
Brad Street
Hatfields
ROAD
Greet St
Wootton St
Southwark
UNION STREET
UNION ST
Way
WATERLOO
Sandell St
Young Vic Theatre
THE CUT
Risbor St
Pepper St
BOROUGH HIGH STREET
Copperfield Street
London Fire Brigade Museum
Redcross
Ayres St
Old Vic Theatre
Loman St
Pocock St
Sawyer St
Newcomen Street
Waterloo Station
Street
Mitre Rd
Ufford
Surrey Row
Great Suffolk Street
Little Dorrit Court
Mermaid Ct
Lwr Marsh
Webber
Chaplin Cl
Valentine Pl
Pocock Street
Glass Hill Street
Sturge St
MARSHALSEA RD
Tennis St
ROAD
Street
Rushworth St
ROAD
BOROUGH
St George the Martyr
BAYLIS ROAD
Gray St
Barons Pl
Webber Row
BLACKFRIARS
Lant Street
Borough
Coral St
Webber Street
Gt Suffolk St
TABARD ST
LONG LANE
Frazier Street
Street
Silex St
SOUTHWARK BRIDGE
BOROUGH HIGH ST
Lambeth North
Street
Lancaster Street
Library St
King James St
Stones End St
NEBRASKA ST
Burdett St
Pearman
Morley
Gerridge St
Dodson St
Street
Cole Street
Pilgrimage St
St. George's Circus
Swan
WESTMINSTER BRIDGE ROAD
BOROUGH ROAD
SOUTHWARK
Trinity
Trinity Street
GREAT DOVER
Tabard Street
Oakey Lane
King Edward Walk
LAMBETH ROAD
LONDON ROAD
Rotary St
Keyworth Street
Doyle St
NEWINGTON CAUSEWAY
Church Sq
Avon St
Merrick Square
HARPER ROAD
Imperial War Museum
ST GEORGE'S ROAD
Gladstone Street
GARDEN ROW
South Bank University
KENNINGTON
Geraldine Mary Harmsworth Park
Tiverton St
Bath Terrace
Street
Falmouth Road
Spurgeon St
Burbage Close
Rockingham
Elephant & Castle
London College of Printing
West
Brook Dr
Deverell Street

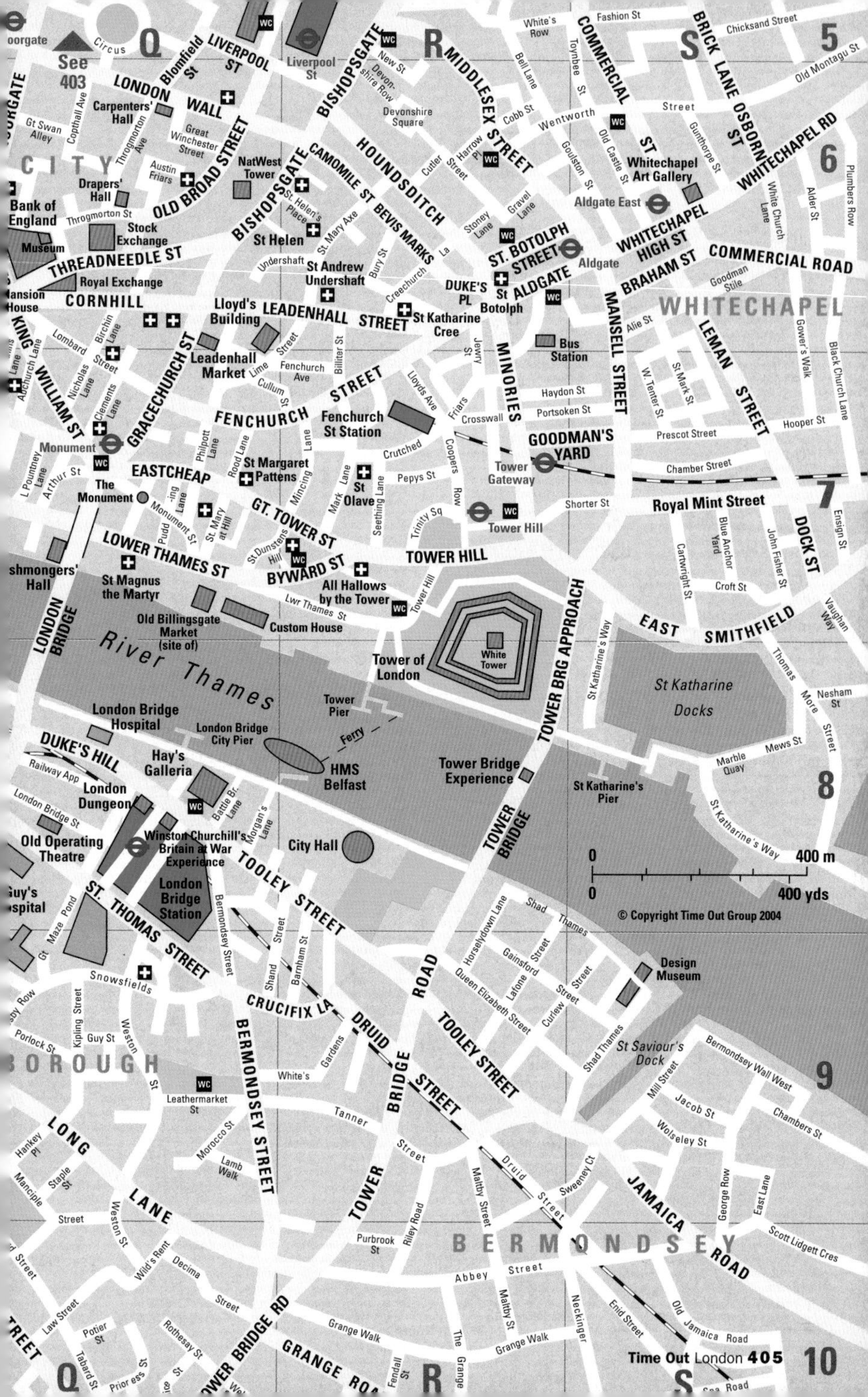

Q
R
S
5
6
7
8
9
10
See 403
Circus
Liverpool St
LIVERPOOL ST
Blomfield St
LONDON WALL
Carpenters' Hall
Copthall Ave
Gt Swan Alley
Throgmorton Ave
Great Winchester Street
CITY
Austin Friars
NatWest Tower
OLD BROAD STREET
Drapers' Hall
Bank of England
Throgmorton St
Stock Exchange
Museum
THREADNEEDLE ST
Royal Exchange
Mansion House
CORNHILL
KING WILLIAM ST
Lombard Street
Birchin Lane
Abchurch Lane
Nicholas Lane
Clements Lane
GRACECHURCH ST
Leadenhall Market
Lime Street
Cullum St
Fenchurch Ave
Billiter St
FENCHURCH STREET
Monument
Arthur St
L Pountney Lane
The Monument
EASTCHEAP
Philpott Lane
Rood Lane
St Margaret Pattens
Mincing Lane
Pudding Lane
Monument St
St Mary at Hill
GT. TOWER ST
LOWER THAMES ST
St Dunstens Hill
BYWARD ST
St Magnus the Martyr
Fishmongers' Hall
All Hallows by the Tower
Lwr Thames St
Old Billingsgate Market (site of)
Custom House
LONDON BRIDGE
River Thames
BISHOPSGATE
New St
Devonshire Row
Devonshire Square
CAMOMILE ST
HOUNDSDITCH
BEVIS MARKS
St Helen's Place
St Mary Axe
St Helen
Undershaft
St Andrew Undershaft
Bury St
Creechurch La
Lloyd's Building
LEADENHALL STREET
St Katharine Cree
Jewry St
Lloyds Ave
Fenchurch St Station
Crutched Friars
Pepys St
Mark Lane
St Olave
Seething Lane
Coopers Row
Trinity Sq
Tower Hill
TOWER HILL
Tower of London
White Tower
Tower Pier
Ferry
HMS Belfast
London Bridge City Pier
London Bridge Hospital
DUKE'S HILL
Railway App
Hay's Galleria
London Dungeon
London Bridge St
Battle Br. Lane
Old Operating Theatre
Winston Churchill's Britain at War Experience
Morgan's Lane
City Hall
Guy's Hospital
London Bridge Station
ST. THOMAS STREET
TOOLEY STREET
Maze Pond
Bermondsey Street
Shand Street
Barnham St
Snowsfields
CRUCIFIX LA
Kipling Street
Guy St
Weston St
Porlock St
BOROUGH
White's Grounds
Leathermarket St
Tanner Street
Morocco St
Lamb Walk
BERMONDSEY STREET
LONG LANE
Hankey Pl
Staple St
Manciple Street
Weston St
Wild's Rent
Decima Street
Law Street
Potier St
Rothesay St
Tabard St
TOWER BRIDGE RD
GRANGE ROAD
Grange Walk
Fendall St
The Grange
MIDDLESEX STREET
Bell Lane
White's Row
Fashion St
Toynbee St
COMMERCIAL ST
Wentworth Street
Cobb St
Harrow Pl
Cutler Street
Goulston St
Old Castle St
Stoney Lane
Gravel Lane
ST. BOTOLPH STREET
Aldgate
ALDGATE
DUKE'S PL
St Botolph
MINORIES
Bus Station
Haydon St
Portsoken St
Crosswall
GOODMAN'S YARD
Tower Gateway
Shorter St
MANSELL STREET
TOWER BRG APPROACH
Tower Bridge Experience
TOWER BRIDGE
TOWER BRIDGE ROAD
DRUID STREET
Druid Street
Maltby Street
Riley Road
Purbrook St
BERMONDSEY
Abbey Street
Neckinger
Enid Street
BRICK LANE
Chicksand Street
OSBORN ST
Old Montagu St
Gunthorpe St
Whitechapel Art Gallery
WHITECHAPEL RD
Aldgate East
WHITECHAPEL HIGH ST
BRAHAM ST
COMMERCIAL ROAD
Goodman Stile
WHITECHAPEL
White Church Lane
Alder St
Plumbers Row
Alie St
LEMAN STREET
W. Tenter St
St Mark St
Gower's Walk
Black Church Lane
Prescot Street
Hooper St
Chamber Street
Royal Mint Street
Cartwright St
Blue Anchor Yard
John Fisher St
DOCK ST
Ensign St
Craft St
EAST SMITHFIELD
Vaughan Way
St Katharine's Way
St Katharine Docks
Thomas More Street
Nesham St
Marble Quay
Mews St
St Katharine's Pier
St Katharine's Way
0
400 m
400 yds
© Copyright Time Out Group 2004
Shad Thames
Horselydown Lane
Gainsford Street
Lafone Street
Queen Elizabeth Street
Curlew Street
Design Museum
St Saviour's Dock
Shad Thames
TOOLEY STREET
Mill Street
Bermondsey Wall West
Jacob St
Chambers St
Wolseley St
Sweeney Ct
JAMAICA ROAD
George Row
East Lane
Scott Lidgett Cres
Old Jamaica Road

Street Index

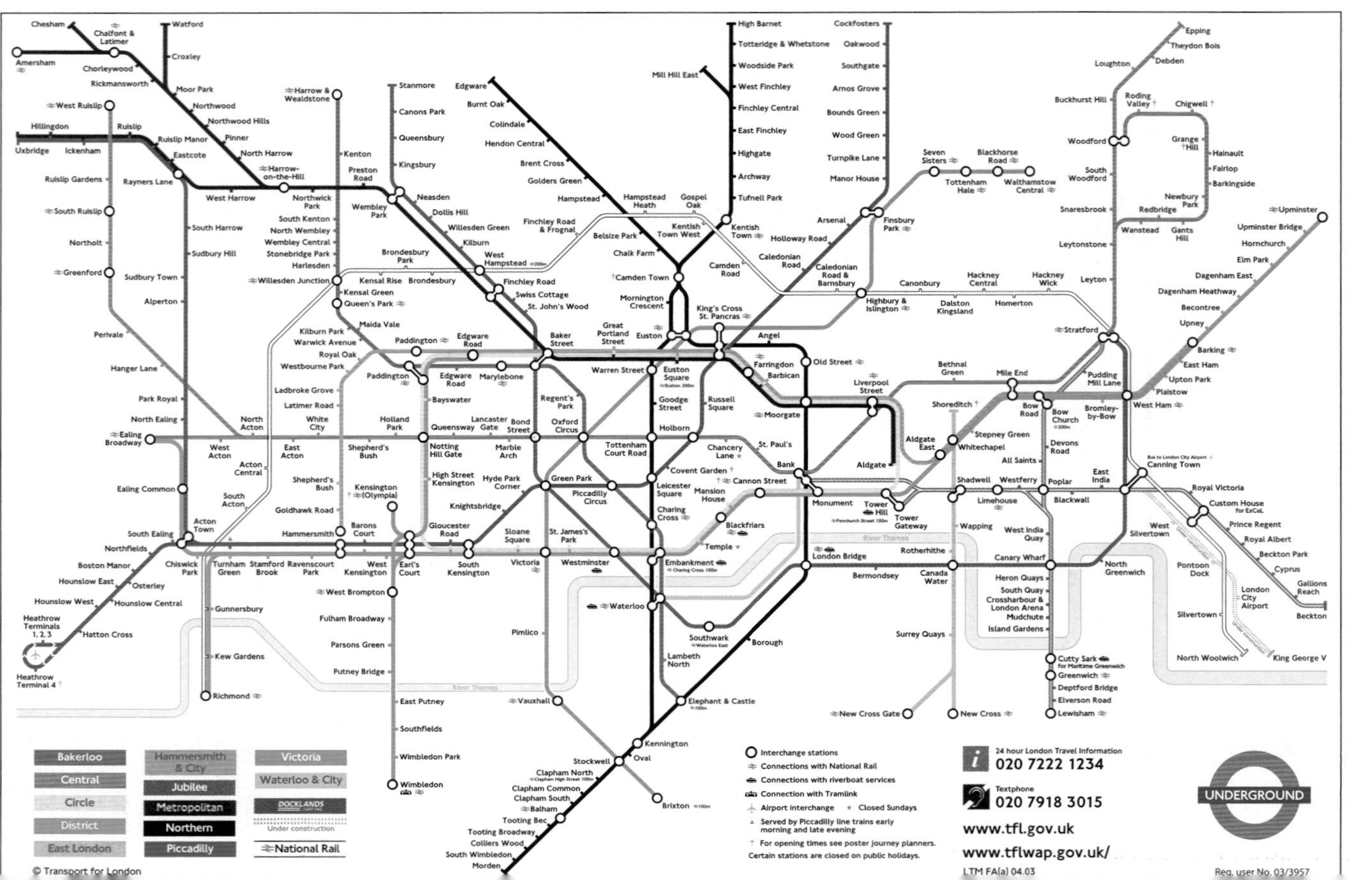
Chesham
Amersham
Chalfont & Latimer
Chorleywood
Rickmansworth
Watford
Croxley
Moor Park
Northwood
Northwood Hills
Pinner
North Harrow
Harrow-on-the-Hill
West Harrow
West Ruislip
Hillingdon
Uxbridge
Ickenham
Ruislip
Ruislip Manor
Eastcote
Rayners Lane
Ruislip Gardens
South Ruislip
Northolt
Greenford
Perivale
Hanger Lane
Park Royal
North Ealing
Ealing Broadway
Ealing Common
South Ealing
Northfields
Boston Manor
Osterley
Hounslow East
Hounslow Central
Hounslow West
Hatton Cross
Heathrow Terminals 1, 2, 3
Heathrow Terminal 4
South Harrow
Sudbury Hill
Sudbury Town
Alperton
Harrow & Wealdstone
Kenton
South Kenton
North Wembley
Wembley Central
Stonebridge Park
Harlesden
Willesden Junction
Kensal Green
Queen's Park
Northwick Park
Preston Road
Wembley Park
Stanmore
Canons Park
Queensbury
Kingsbury
Neasden
Dollis Hill
Willesden Green
Kilburn
West Hampstead
Finchley Road
Swiss Cottage
St. John's Wood
Edgware
Burnt Oak
Colindale
Hendon Central
Brent Cross
Golders Green
Hampstead
Hampstead Heath
Finchley Road & Frognal
Belsize Park
Chalk Farm
Gospel Oak
Kentish Town West
Brondesbury Park
Kensal Rise
Brondesbury
Kilburn Park
Maida Vale
Warwick Avenue
Royal Oak
Westbourne Park
Paddington
Edgware Road
Marylebone
Baker Street
Bayswater
Ladbroke Grove
Latimer Road
White City
North Acton
West Acton
East Acton
Acton Central
South Acton
Acton Town
Chiswick Park
Turnham Green
Stamford Brook
Ravenscourt Park
Gunnersbury
Kew Gardens
Richmond
Shepherd's Bush
Goldhawk Road
Hammersmith
Holland Park
Kensington (Olympia)
Barons Court
West Kensington
Earl's Court
West Brompton
Fulham Broadway
Parsons Green
Putney Bridge
East Putney
Southfields
Wimbledon Park
Wimbledon
Queensway
Notting Hill Gate
High Street Kensington
Gloucester Road
South Kensington
Lancaster Gate
Marble Arch
Bond Street
Hyde Park Corner
Knightsbridge
Sloane Square
Victoria
Pimlico
Vauxhall
Regent's Park
Oxford Circus
Green Park
Piccadilly Circus
St. James's Park
Westminster
Great Portland Street
Warren Street
Euston
Euston Square
Goodge Street
Tottenham Court Road
Leicester Square
Charing Cross
Embankment
Waterloo
Mill Hill East
High Barnet
Totteridge & Whetstone
Woodside Park
West Finchley
Finchley Central
East Finchley
Highgate
Archway
Tufnell Park
Kentish Town
Camden Town
Camden Road
Mornington Crescent
King's Cross St. Pancras
Cockfosters
Oakwood
Southgate
Arnos Grove
Bounds Green
Wood Green
Turnpike Lane
Manor House
Arsenal
Holloway Road
Caledonian Road
Caledonian Road & Barnsbury
Finsbury Park
Seven Sisters
Tottenham Hale
Blackhorse Road
Walthamstow Central
Highbury & Islington
Canonbury
Dalston Kingsland
Hackney Central
Homerton
Hackney Wick
Angel
Farringdon
Barbican
Old Street
Moorgate
Russell Square
Holborn
Chancery Lane
St. Paul's
Covent Garden
Bank
Cannon Street
Mansion House
Blackfriars
Temple
Monument
Tower Hill
Tower Gateway
Liverpool Street
Aldgate
Aldgate East
Whitechapel
Shoreditch
Bethnal Green
Mile End
Stepney Green
London Bridge
Southwark
Lambeth North
Elephant & Castle
Borough
Kennington
Oval
Stockwell
Brixton
Clapham North
Clapham Common
Clapham South
Balham
Tooting Bec
Tooting Broadway
Colliers Wood
South Wimbledon
Morden
Bermondsey
Canada Water
Rotherhithe
Surrey Quays
New Cross Gate
New Cross
Wapping
Shadwell
Limehouse
Westferry
All Saints
Poplar
West India Quay
Canary Wharf
Heron Quays
South Quay
Crossharbour & London Arena
Mudchute
Island Gardens
Cutty Sark for Maritime Greenwich
Greenwich
Deptford Bridge
Elverson Road
Lewisham
Bow Road
Bow Church
Devons Road
Bromley-by-Bow
Pudding Mill Lane
Blackwall
East India
North Greenwich
Stratford
West Ham
Plaistow
Upton Park
East Ham
Barking
Upney
Becontree
Dagenham Heathway
Dagenham East
Elm Park
Hornchurch
Upminster Bridge
Upminster
Leyton
Leytonstone
Snaresbrook
South Woodford
Woodford
Buckhurst Hill
Loughton
Debden
Theydon Bois
Epping
Roding Valley
Chigwell
Grange Hill
Hainault
Fairlop
Barkingside
Newbury Park
Redbridge
Wanstead
Gants Hill
Bus to London City Airport
Canning Town
Royal Victoria
Custom House for ExCeL
Prince Regent
Royal Albert
Beckton Park
Cyprus
Gallions Reach
Beckton
West Silvertown
Pontoon Dock
London City Airport
Silvertown
North Woolwich
King George V
River Thames
Bakerloo
Central
Circle
District
East London
Hammersmith & City
Jubilee
Metropolitan
Northern
Piccadilly
Victoria
Waterloo & City
DOCKLANDS
Under construction
National Rail
© Transport for London
Interchange stations
Connections with National Rail
Connections with riverboat services
Connection with Tramlink
Airport interchange
Closed Sundays
Served by Piccadilly line trains early morning and late evening
For opening times see poster journey planners.
Certain stations are closed on public holidays.
24 hour London Travel Information
020 7222 1234
Textphone
020 7918 3015
www.tfl.gov.uk
www.tflwap.gov.uk/
LTM FA(a) 04.03
UNDERGROUND
Reg. user No. 03/3957